T0006343

AMERICAN MUSEUM
OF NATURAL HISTORY

BIRDS
OF NORTH
AMERICA
EASTERN REGION

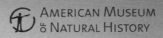

AMERICAN MUSEUM
of NATURAL HISTORY

BIRDS
OF NORTH
AMERICA
EASTERN REGION

Editor-in-Chief
François Vuilleumier

Content previously published in
Birds of North America

DK | Penguin Random House

AMERICAN MUSEUM OF NATURAL HISTORY

Editor-in-chief
François Vuilleumier, Ph.D.
Consultant
Paul Sweet
Project Coordinators
Alex Navissi, Caitlin Roxby,
Molly Leff
Global Business Development
Joanna Hostert

DEDICATION
We dedicate this book to the memory of John Bull, John Farrand, and Stuart Keith, top birders, field guide authors, AMNH colleagues, first-rate ornithologists, and friends.

DORLING KINDERSLEY

Senior Art Editors
Caroline Hill, Ina Stradins
Senior Editor
Angeles Gavira Guerrero
US Senior Editors
Shannon Beatty, Jill Hamilton
Project Editor
Nathan Joyce
Designers
Sonia Barbate, Helen McTeer
Editors
Jamie Ambrose, Lori Baird,
Tamlyn Calitz, Marcus Hardy,
Lizzie Munsey, Patrick Newman,
Siobhan O'Connor, David
Summers, Cressida Tuson,
Miezan van Zyl, Rebecca Warren
Design Assistant
Becky Tennant
Editorial Assistant
Jaime Tenreiro
Creative Technical Support
Adam Brackenbury,
John Goldsmid
Production Editors
Joanna Byrne, Maria Elia
Production Controllers
Erika Pepe, Rita Sinha
Jacket Designer
Mark Cavanagh
Illustrators
John Cox, Andrew Mackay
Picture Editor
Neil Fletcher
Picture Researchers
Laura Barwick, Will Jones
Managing Art Editor
Michelle Baxter
Managing Editor
Sarah Larter
Publishing Manager
Liz Wheeler
Art Directors
Phil Ormerod, Bryn Walls
Publisher
Jonathan Metcalf

DK INDIA

Editors
Megha Gupta, Rukmini Kumar,
Garima Sharma, Dipali Singh
Project Designer
Mahua Mandal
Senior Designer
Mini Dhawan
Editorial Manager
Glenda Fernandes
DTP Designers
Shanker Prasad, Arjinder Singh,
Jaypal Singh, Bimlesh Tiwary,
Anita Yadav, Tanveer Abbas Zaidi
Senior DTP Designer
Harish Aggarwal
DTP Manager
Balwant Singh
Picture Researcher
Sakshi Saluja

FOR SECOND EDITION

DK LONDON

US Editor
Jill Hamilton
Managing Editor
Angeles Gavira Guerrero
Managing Art Editor
Michael Duffy
Jacket Design Development Manager Sophia MTT
Production Editor
Kavita Varma
Senior Production Controller
Meskerem Berhane
Associate Publishing Director
Liz Wheeler
Publishing Director
Jonathan Metcalf
Art Director
Karen Self

DK INDIA

Project Editor
Tina Jindal
Project Art Editor
Meenal Goel
Editor
Kanika Praharaj
Assistant Editor
Chhavi Nagpal
Assistant Art Editors
Aarushi Dhawan, Arshti Narang
Senior Managing Editor
Rohan Sinha
Managing Art Editor
Sudakshina Basu
DTP Designers
Rakesh Kumar, Tanveer
Abbas Zaidi
Pre-production Manager
Balwant Singh
Production Manager
Pankaj Sharma
Senior Jacket Designer
Suhita Dharamjit

Content first published in
Birds of North America 2009.

This American edition, 2021
First American Edition, 2011
Published in the United States by DK Publishing
1450 Broadway, Suite 801, New York, NY 10018

DK books are available at special discounts when purchased in bulk for sales promotions, premiums, fund-raising, or educational use. For details, contact: DK Publishing Special Markets,
1450 Broadway, Suite 801, New York, NY 10018
SpecialSales@dk.com

Printed and bound in China

For the curious
www.dk.com

MIX
Paper from
responsible sources
FSC™ C018179

This book was made with Forest Stewardship Council ™ certified paper – one small step in DK's commitment to a sustainable future. For more information go to www.dk.com/our-green-pledge

CONTRIBUTORS

David Bird, Ph.D.; Nicholas L. Block; Peter Capainolo; Matthew Cormons; Malcolm Coulter, Ph.D.; Joseph DiCostanzo; Shawneen Finnegan; Neil Fletcher; Ted Floyd; Jeff Groth, Ph.D.; Paul Hess; Brian Hiller; Rob Hume; Thomas Brodie Johnson; Kevin T. Karlson; Stephen Kress, Ph.D.; William Moskoff, Ph.D.; Bill Pranty; Michael L. P. Retter; Noah Strycker; Paul Sweet; Rodger Titman, Ph.D.; Elissa Wolfson

Map Editor
Paul Lehman

Project Coordinator
Joseph DiCostanzo

AMERICAN BITTERN
A typically solitary bird, the American Bittern has a cryptic coloration and a still, vertical posture that help camouflage it in reed beds.

CONTENTS

AMERICAN MUSEUM OF NATURAL HISTORY

The American Museum of Natural History, founded in 1869 and currently celebrating its 150th anniversary, is one of the world's preeminent scientific, educational, and cultural institutions. The Museum encompasses 45 permanent exhibition halls, including the Rose Center for Earth and Space and the Hayden Planetarium, as well as galleries for temporary exhibitions. The Museum's scientists draw on a world-class research collection of more than 34 million artifacts and specimens, some of which are billions of years old, and on one of the largest natural history libraries in the world. Through its Richard Gilder Graduate School, the Museum grants the Ph.D. degree in Comparative Biology and the Master of Arts in Teaching (MAT) degree, the only such free-standing, degree-granting programs at any museum in the United States. In addition to its campus, the Museum's exhibitions and Space Shows can be seen in venues on six continents, and its website, digital videos, and apps for mobile devices extend its collections, exhibitions, and educational programs to millions more around the world. Visit amnh.org for more information.

AMERICAN MUSEUM OF NATURAL HISTORY

DK BIRD SOUNDS APP

The songs and calls of more than 200 species of birds are featured on the new DK Bird Sounds app. Bird calls are usually short and simple, and are used to pass on information, such as an alarm call that warns of a predator or a contact call that helps birds stay in touch with each other. Songs are longer and made up of a complex set of notes, and are used by males to defend a territory or attract a mate. A bird may have several sounds in its repertoire, but each type is usually constant and unique to a species. As bird sounds carry a long way, you will often hear a bird before you can see it, and this app will help you identify it.

EDITOR-IN-CHIEF

Lifelong studies of birds made François Vuilleumier (1938–2017) uniquely qualified to be Editor-in-Chief of *Birds of North America*. After obtaining a Ph.D. at Harvard University, he started a long association with the American Museum of Natural History in New York City. He served as the Chairman of the Department of Ornithology from 1987 to 1992 and was Curator when he retired in 2005. His research took him all over the world, especially South America. Author of about 250 papers and one book, Dr. Vuilleumier taught ornithology at the College of the Atlantic, Bar Harbor, Maine. He watched birds from the Canadian High Arctic and south to Mexico. His life list was about 4,000 species, and he was familiar in the field with all but a handful of the species treated in this book.

CONSULTANT

Paul Sweet was born in Bristol, England, and has been interested in natural history for as long as he can remember. After completing a degree in zoology at the University of Liverpool, he worked at the Raffles Museum in Singapore. In 1991 he moved to the American Museum of Natural History, where he is now the Collection Manager of the Ornithology Department, the largest bird collection in the world.

To download the app, go to:

www.dk.com/bird-sounds-na

The birds featured on the app have this symbol next to their common name in this book.

PREFACE

THRUSHES
Back in the early 1900s, the great wildlife artist Louis Agassiz Fuertes already painted birds in the style of modern field guides, as shown in this plate from Chapman's *Handbook of the Birds of Eastern North America.*

W ITH ITS EASTERN AND WESTERN volumes, *Birds of North America* attempts to fill a gap in the North American bird book market. No other work offers, for every North American bird species, the same combination of stunning iconography, including beautiful photographs and precise distribution maps; scientifically accurate and readable accounts of salient characteristics; data on identification, behavior, habitat, voice, social structure, nest construction, breeding season, food, and conservation status; diagrams of flight patterns; statistics of size, wingspan, weight, clutch size, number of broods per year, and lifespan; and geographic information about breeding, wintering, and migration. Furthermore, no other bird book introduces, in such an up-to-date and lavishly illustrated manner, general material about birds: their evolution, classification, anatomy, flight, migration, navigation, courtship, mating, nests, and eggs. Scientific jargon has been avoided, but a glossary identifies concepts that benefit from an explanation. With its user-friendly format, these eastern and western guides to *Birds of North America* should permit readers either to enjoy studying one species account at a time, or browse to make cross comparisons.

Many field guides exist, as well as treatises on groups like gulls, hummingbirds, or sparrows; other books are dictionary-like, or focus on species of conservation concern. However, no bird book today can be called a "handbook," a concise reference work that can be conveniently carried around. I hope that these books will be useful in this role to all persons interested in birds, whether young or older, enthusiastic birder or beginner.

Historically, *Birds of North America* can be viewed as a successor to Frank M. Chapman's epochal *Handbook of the Birds of Eastern North America,* published in 1895. During his 54 years at the American Museum of Natural History in New York City, Chapman, dean of American ornithologists, blazed a trail that contributed substantially to what American ornithology, bird conservation, and birding have become. The facts that the new book has the imprint of the American Museum of Natural History, and that I, as its Editor-in-Chief, have worked there for 31 years as Curator of Ornithology and as Chairman of its Department of Ornithology, are not coincidental.

In his Handbook, Chapman treated all birds found in Eastern North America. The description of each species was followed by data on distribution, nest, and eggs, and a readable, often even brilliant text about habitat, behavior, and voice. The illustrations included plates by two pioneer American wildlife artists, Louis Agassiz Fuertes and Francis Lee Jaques, whose style inspired all those who followed them. Some of these

EASTERN AND WESTERN REGIONS

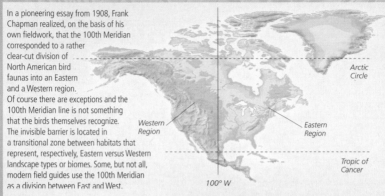

In a pioneering essay from 1908, Frank Chapman realized, on the basis of his own fieldwork, that the 100th Meridian corresponded to a rather clear-cut division of North American bird faunas into an Eastern and a Western region. Of course there are exceptions and the 100th Meridian line is not something that the birds themselves recognize. The invisible barrier is located in a transitional zone between habitats that represent, respectively, Eastern versus Western landscape types or biomes. Some, but not all, modern field guides use the 100th Meridian as a division between East and West.

Arctic Circle

Western Region

Eastern Region

Tropic of Cancer

100° W

plates were, already then, executed in field guide fashion. Anybody who examines Chapman's *Handbook* today is struck by how modern it is. "Museum man" and "birder," Chapman was also a gifted educator and a good writer: a rare combination. Museum research gave him the taxonomic background, and fieldwork throughout North America sharpened his birding skills. As Editor-in-Chief of *Birds of North America*, working in the department Chapman created, enjoying the same extraordinary collection and library resources, and traveling as widely as he did, I have endeavored to make this new book a work of which he would have been proud. Don't leave home without it—and bring along binoculars and a pencil to jot down notes.

François Vuilleumier

François Vuilleumier
American Museum of Natural History,
New York City
February 2011

CATCHING THE LIGHT
The only hummingbird species breeding in the Eastern region is the Ruby-throated Hummingbird. With the right lighting, this male displays his brilliantly colored throat patch.

HOW THIS BOOK WORKS

This guide covers about 550 Eastern North American bird species. The species are arranged into three sections: the first profiles common species, each being given full-page treatment; the second covers rarer birds in quarter-page entries; the third section consists of a list of rare visitors.

▽ INTRODUCTION

The species are organized conventionally by order, family, and genus. Related birds appear together, preceded by a group introduction. The book follows the most up-to-date avian classification system, based on the latest scientific research.

MAPS

In this book, North America is defined as the area from the southern tip of Florida and the US–Mexico border northward to the Canadian High Arctic. Each species profile includes a map showing its range, with different colors reflecting seasonal movements.

KEY

Resident all year

Breeding distribution

Nonbreeding distribution

During migration

GROUP NAME

The common name of the group each species belongs to is at the top of each page.

COMMON NAME

IN FLIGHT

Illustrations show the bird in flight, from above and/or below —differences of season, age, or sex are not always visible.

DESCRIPTION

Conveys the main features and essential character of the species including:

VOICE

A description of the species' calls and songs, given phonetically where possible.

NESTING

The type of nest and its usual location; the number of eggs in a clutch; the number of broods in a year; the breeding season.

FEEDING

How, where, and what the species feeds on.

SIMILAR SPECIES

Similar-looking species are identified and key differences pointed out.

LENGTH, WINGSPAN, AND WEIGHT

Length is tip of tail to tip of bill; measurements and weights are averages or ranges.

SOCIAL

The social unit the species is usually found in.

LIFESPAN

The length of life, in years, obtained from either zoo birds or from banding and recovery records of wild birds. The actual average or maximum life expectancy of many bird species is still unknown.

STATUS

The conservation status of the species; (p) means the data available is only provisional. "Localized" means the species may be widespread but restricted to smaller areas of suitable habitat and climatic conditions.

SYMBOLS

♂ Male	☘ Spring
♀ Female	✿ Summer
☾ Juvenile	🍂 Autumn
◗ Immature	❄ Winter

▽ COMMON SPECIES

The main section of the book features the 395 most commonly seen bird species in Eastern North America. Each entry is clear and detailed, following the same format.

Order **Passeriformes**	Family **Icteridae**

Baltimore Oriole ◗

black and orange tail · white-edged black wings

orange-yellow shoulder patch

MALE (1ST FALL)

MALE

IN FLIGHT

orange rump

black tail with orange outer tail feathers

yellow-olive rump · olive upperparts

two wing bars · pale orange underparts

FEMALE

The Baltimore Oriole's brilliant colors are familiar to many persons in the East because this bird is tolerant of human presence. This species originally favored the American elm for nesting, but Dutch elm disease decimated these trees. The oriole since adapted to using sycamores, cottonwoods, and other trees, helped expand its range to areas densely occupied by humans. The Baltimore Oriole is Maryland's State Bird, somewhat ironically for its nesting sites. Its ability to use suburban gardens and parks has helped expand its range to areas densely occupied by humans.
VOICE Loud, clear, melodious song comprising one or two several short notes in series, often of varying lengths.
NESTING Round-bottomed basket usually woven of grass, toward the end of branches; 4–5 eggs; 1 brood; May–July.
FEEDING Hops or flits among leaves and branches picking and spiders; fond of caterpillars; also eats fruit and sips nectar.

SIMILAR SPECIES		
ORCHARD ORIOLE see p.388 — darker overall	BULLOCK'S ORIOLE see p.468 — incomplete black hood · chestnut-colored belly	black eyeline · orange cheeks · huge white patch

Length **8–10in (20–26cm)**	Wingspan **10–12in (26–?)**
Social **Solitary/Pairs**	Lifespan **Up to 11 years**

DATE SEEN	WHERE

MAPS

See panel, left. The occurrence caption describes the bird's preferred habitats and range within North America.

RARE SPECIES

| Family Passerellidae | Species Peucaea botterii |

Botteri's Sparrow
Of the nine or ten subspecies of Botteri's Sparrow, a species of the Mexican grasslands, two occur in the US: *P. b. texana* is found in coastal southern Texas, and *P. b. arizonae* in the Southwest. Botteri's Sparrow is usually difficult to spot, as its flees stealthily from disturbance, and quickly hides itself out of sight.
OCCURRENCE Breeds in grasslands of southeastern Arizona and southwestern New Mexico, and in coastal prairies of southern Texas. Winters in Mexico.
VOICE Call a *chip* or double *tsip*; song starts with stuttering, mechanical *chips* and ends in an accelerating trill.

ADULT

Length 18–20in (46–51cm)   Wingspan 27–28in (68–90cm)

| Family Passerellidae | Species Peucaea cassinii |

Cassin's Sparrow
Cassin's Sparrow, named for the famous Philadelphia ornithologist John Cassin, is drab-looking, even for an American sparrow. Its plain appearance is made up for by its rather spectacular flight displays, during which it emits a whistled song. This sparrow is found in grassland interspersed with shrubs, and shows variations in numbers in different years and locations.
OCCURRENCE Grasslands with shrubs, like mesquite and cactus, from western Nebraska to central Mexico; US populations mostly winter in Mexico.
VOICE Calls high *seeps* and *tsips*, often in series; song *see-ze-di-i-i-i-i-i zee-zeee* zee-ZWEAAY, emphatic in a questioning note.

ADULT

Length 6in (15cm)   Wingspan 8in (21cm)

| Family Passerellidae | Species Arremonops rufivirgatus |

Olive Sparrow
The rather drab, shy Olive Sparrow spends most of its time hopping around in the undergrowth of dense woodlands and thorn scrub. This resident of the Lower Rio Grande Valley can be heard more than it is seen, although some individuals appear at birdfeeders.
OCCURRENCE From southern Texas and northwestern Mexico south locally to northwestern Costa Rica, mostly in thorn scrub.
VOICE Dry *chip* call, also a drawn-out *sweeee*, song a series of accelerating *chips*.

ADULT

Length 8½in (16cm)   Wingspan 8in (20cm)

| Family Passerellidae | Species Amphispiza bilineata |

Black-throated Sparrow
Because of a certain resemblance in their song, the Black-throated Sparrow has been called the "Song Sparrow of the desert." This resident is easy to identify as it possesses a bold white "eyebrow" in all plumages. The Black-throated Sparrow is common within its western range, in a variety of arid habitats containing cactus and mesquite.
OCCURRENCE Found in desert scrub of the Great Basin east to Texas, south to Baja California and central Mexico. Breeds locally in eastern Washington state. Casual visitor to the Pacific Coast and the East.
VOICE Weak and call, song consists of few short, clear notes, followed by higher trill; *tsuk tsuk-tsuk tseeeee*; also *ti-ti-tsuk chweeeeeeeee.

ADULT

Length 5½in (14cm)   Wingspan 7½in (19.5cm)

466

◁ RARE SPECIES
Over 100 less common birds are presented on pages 443–470. Arranged in the same group order used in the main section, these entries consist of one photograph of the species accompanied by a description of the bird. Information on geographical distribution, occurrence, and voice is also given.

VAGRANTS AND ACCIDENTALS

THE LIST THAT FOLLOWS includes species that occur rarely in eastern North America (defined in this book as Canada and the continental United States east of the 100th Meridian). These species can reach North America from Eurasia, Central and even Oceania and Antarctica. The US and Canada can receive birds that drift off course, during migration, from eastern Asia across the Pacific Ocean, or from Europe across the Atlantic.

The occurrence of these "vagrant" species is classified by the American Birding Association, depending on their relative frequency, and this terminology is followed in the "status" column for each species. **Rare** species are reported every year in small numbers. **Casual** visitors have been recorded at least a dozen times. **Accidental** species have been recorded no more than five times.

Because of biological, climatological, or other factors, the status of "vagrant" species is constantly changing. There are ever greater numbers of competent birdwatchers who permit the regular, even annual, detection of species that were once considered rare or accidental.

ORIOLES AND BLACKBIRDS

Species *Icterus galbula*

black head

black back

straight blue-gray bill

black upper breast

orange underparts

MALE

FLIGHT: strong with rapid wingbeats; full downstrokes during flight create great power.

PERFECT FOR FORAGING
The Baltimore Oriole forages alone in dense foliage of trees and bushes or on the ground.

OCCURRENCE
Forest edges and tall, open mixed hardwoods, especially close to rivers; regularly uses forested parks, suburban and urban areas with abundant tall trees. Small numbers winter in southeastern US and Florida, but most birds move to Central and South America.

| Weight 1⅛–1¼oz (30–35g) |
| Status **Secure** |

NOTES

389

CLASSIFICATION
The top band of each entry provides the scientific names of order, family, and species (see glossary, pp. 473–474, for full definitions of these terms).

COLOR BAND
The information bands at the top and bottom of each entry are color coded for each family.

PHOTOGRAPHS
These illustrate the species in different views and plumage variations. Significant differences relating to age, sex, and season (breeding/nonbreeding) are shown and the images labeled accordingly; if there is no variation, the images have no label. Unless stated otherwise, the bird shown is an adult.

FLIGHT PATTERNS
This feature illustrates and briefly describes the way the species flies. See panel below.

VAGRANTS ▷
Very rare and accidental visitors are listed at the back of the book with a brief indication of the species' status.

HABITAT/ BEHAVIOR
Photographs reveal the species in its habitat or show interesting behavior.

FLIGHT PATTERNS

Simple line diagrams are used to illustrate eight basic flight patterns.

wing beats

Woodpecker-like: bursts of wing beats between deeply undulating glides.

Finch-like: light, bouncy action with flurries of wing beats between deep, undulating glides.

Grouse-like: bursts of wing beats between short, straight glides.

Accipiter-like: straight, with several quick, deep beats between short glides.

Gull-like: continually flapping, with slow, steady wing beats; also glides.

Duck-like: continually flapping, with fast wing beats.

Buteo-like: deep, slow wing beats between soaring glides.

Swallow-like: swooping, with bursts of wing beats between glides.

EVOLUTION

O RNITHOLOGISTS AGREE THAT BIRDS evolved from dinosaurs about 150 million years ago, but there is still debate about the dinosaur group from which they descended. Around 10,000 species of birds exist today, living in many different kinds of habitats across the world, from desert to Arctic tundra. To reconstruct how avian evolution occurred, from *Archaeopteryx* on up to the present, scientists use many clues, especially fossil birds, and now DNA.

MISSING LINK?
Archaeopteryx, shown here, is a 145-million-year-old fossil. It had dinosaur-like teeth, but bird-like feathers.

SPECIATION

What are species and how do they evolve? Species are biological entities. When two species of a genus overlap they rarely interbreed and produce hybrids. The Northern Flicker has an eastern (yellow-shafted) and a western (red-shafted) form; after the discovery that these two forms interbreed in the Great Plains, the flickers, which were formerly "split" into two species, are now considered one. In other cases, a previously single species, such as the Sage Grouse, has been divided. Such examples illustrate how species evolve, first by geographic separation, followed in time by overlap. This process can take from tens of thousands to millions of years.

BIRD GENEALOGY

The diagram below is called a phylogeny, and shows how selected groups of birds are related to each other. The timescale at the top of the diagram is derived from both fossil and DNA evidence, which allows ornithologists to estimate when different lineages of birds diverged. The names of groups shown in bold are those living in North America.

MILLIONS OF YEARS AGO

| 70 | 60 | 50 | 40 | 30 | 20 | 10 | 0 |

Ratites, Tinamous

Megapodes, **Cracids**, **New World Quails**, **Grouse**, **Turkeys**, and Relatives

Screamers, **Ducks**, **Geese**

Nightjars and Relatives

Swifts and Hummingbirds

Cuckoos, Bustards, Turacos

Pigeons, Sandgrouse

Rails, Cranes, and Relatives

Flamingos, Grebes

Shorebirds, Gulls, Terns, Auks, and Relatives

Tropicbirds, Loons, Penguins, Tubenoses, Storks, Frigatebirds, Gannets, Cormorants, Ibises, Herons, and Pelicans

Hoatzins

New World Vultures, Ospreys, Hawks, Kites, and Relatives

Owls

Mousebirds, Trogons, Rollers, Hoopoes, Hornbills, Bee-eaters, Todies, Motmots, Kingfishers, Jacamars, Puffbirds, Honeyguides, Woodpeckers, Barbets, Toucans

Seriemas, Falcons, Caracaras, and Parrots

Songbirds

Neornithes

BLENDING IN

This magnificent species is diurnal, unlike most other owls, which are nocturnal. The Snowy Owl breeds in the Arctic tundra and if the ground is covered with snow, it blends in perfectly.

CONVERGENCE

The evolutionary process during which birds of two distantly related groups develop similarities is called convergence. Carrion-eating birds of prey are one example. Old World vultures belong to the hawk family (Accipitridae), while New World vultures are more closely related to storks. However, both groups are characterized by hooked bills, bare heads, and weak talons. Convergence can involve anatomy and behavior, as in the vultures, or other traits, including habitat preference.

PARALLEL EVOLUTION

The African longclaws (family Motacillidae) and North American meadowlarks (family Icteridae) show convergence in plumage color and pattern. Both groups live in grassland.

CAPE LONGCLAW

EASTERN MEADOWLARK

EXTINCTION

During the last 150 years, North America has lost the Passenger Pigeon, the Great Auk, the Carolina Parakeet, the Labrador Duck, and the Eskimo Curlew. Relentless hunting and habitat destruction are the main factors that have led to extinction. Some species that seemed doomed have had a reprieve. Thanks to a breeding and release program, the majestic California Condor soars once again over the Grand Canyon.

OVERHUNTING
The Passenger Pigeon was eradicated as a result of over-hunting.

CLASSIFYING BIRDS

All past and present animal life is named and categorized into groups. Classifications reflect the genealogical relationships among groups, based on traits such as color, bones, or DNA. Birds make up the class "Aves," which includes "orders"; each "order" is made up of one or more "families." "Genus" is a subdivision of "family," and contains one or more "species." A species is a unique group of similar organisms that interbreed and produce fertile offspring. Some species have distinct populations, which are known as subspecies.

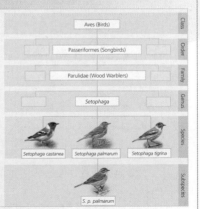

Aves (Birds)	Class
Passeriformes (Songbirds)	Order
Parulidae (Wood Warblers)	Family
Setophaga	Genus
Setophaga castanea · Setophaga palmarum · Setophaga tigrina	Species
S. p. palmarum	Subspecies

ANATOMY AND FLIGHT

I N SPITE OF THEIR EXTERNAL DIVERSITY, birds are remarkably similar internally. To allow flight, birds have a skeleton that is both rigid and light. Rigidity is achieved by the fusion of some bones, especially the lower vertebrae, while lightness is maintained by having hollow limb bones. These are connected to air sacs, which, in turn, are connected to the bird's lungs.

"hand"
"forearm"
bill
neck vertebrae
furcula
keeled sternum
fused tail vertebrae
secondaries
tail feathers
uppertail coverts
rump
tertials
scapulars
primaries
axillaries
breast
bill
belly
undertail coverts
toes

SKELETON
Avian skeletal features include the furcula (wishbone), the keeled sternum (breastbone), and the fused tail vertebrae.

FLIGHT ADAPTATIONS

For birds to be able to fly, they need light and rigid bones, a lightweight skull, and hollow wing and leg bones. In addition, pouch-like air sacs are connected to hollow bones, which reduce a bird's weight. The air sacs also function as a cooling system, which birds need because they have a high metabolic rate. The breast muscles, which are crucial for flight, attach to the keeled sternum (breastbone). Wing and tail feathers help support birds when airborne. Feathers wear out, and are regularly replaced during molt.

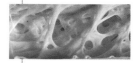

BIRD BONE STRUCTURE
Most bird bones, except those of penguins and other flightless birds, are hollow, which reduces their weight. A honeycomb of internal struts makes the bones remarkably strong.

LEGS, FEET, AND TOES

When you look at a bird's leg, you do not see its thigh, which is inside the body cavity, but the leg from the knee down. When we talk about a bird's feet we really mean its toes. The shin is a fused tibia and fibula. This fused bone plus the heel are known as the "tarso-metatarsus." The four examples below illustrate some toe arrangements.

UNDERPARTS
Underwing coverts have a regular pattern of overlapping rows. Short feathers cover the head, breast, belly, and flanks. In most birds, the toes are unfeathered.

enables grip on ground

enables strong grip on branches

WALKING
Ground-foraging birds usually have a long hind claw.

CLIMBING
Most climbers have two toes forward and two backward.

webbing provides thrust in water

used to grasp prey

SWIMMING
Waterbirds have webbing between their toes.

HUNTING
Birds of prey have powerful toes and strong, sharp claws.

primary
coverts

secondary
coverts

coverts

neck

nape

crown

chin

throat

mantle

alula
(bastard wing)

UPPERPARTS
The wing feathers from
the "hand" of the bird
are the primaries, and those
on the "forearm" are the
secondaries. Each set has
its accompanying row of
coverts. The tertials are
adjacent to the secondaries.

FEATHERS

All birds, by definition, have feathers.
These remarkable structures, which
are modified scales, serve two main
functions: insulation and flight.
Special muscles allow birds to raise
their feathers or to flatten them
against the body. In cold weather,
fluffed-out feathers keep an
insulating layer of air between the
skin and the outside. This insulating
capacity is why humans often find
wearing "down" jackets so effective
against the cold. The first feathers
that chicks have after hatching
are down feathers. The rigidity
of the flight feathers helps create
a supporting surface that birds use
to generate thrust and lift.

TYPES OF FEATHERS
Birds have three main kinds
of feathers: down, contour,
and flight feathers. The rigid
axis of all feathers is called
the "rachis."

DOWN
FEATHER

CONTOUR
FEATHER

FLIGHT
FEATHER

WING FUNCTIONS

Flapping, soaring, gliding, and hovering are among the ways birds use their
wings. They also exhibit colors or patterns as part of territorial and courtship
displays. Several birds, such as herons, open their wings like an umbrella
when foraging in water for fish. An important aspect of wings is their
relationship to a bird's weight. The ratio of a bird's wing area to weight is
called wing loading, which may be affected also by wing shape. An eagle has
a large wing area to weight ratio, which means it has lower wing loading,
whereas a swallow has a small wing
area to weight ratio, and therefore
high wing loading. This means that
the slow, soaring eagle is capable of
much more energy-efficient flight
than the fast, agile swallow.

LONG AND BROAD
The broad, long, rectangular wings of an
eagle allow it to soar. The outstretched
alulae (bastard wings) give it extra lift.

POINTED
Broad at their base and tapering toward
a point, and bent at the wrist, a swallow's
wings enable fast flight and sharp turns.

SHORT AND ROUND
Short, broad, and round wings permit warblers
to move easily in dense vegetation.

WING AERODYNAMICS

The supporting surface of a bird's wing enables it to takeoff and
stay aloft. Propulsion and lift are linked in birds—which use
their wings for both—unlike in airplanes in which these two
functions are separate. Large and heavy birds, like swans, flap
their wings energetically to create propulsion, and need
a long, watery runway before they can fly off. The California
Condor can takeoff from a cliff with little or no wing flapping,
but Black and Turkey Vultures hop up from carrion then flap
vigorously and finally use air flowing across their wings to
soar. This diagram shows how airflow affects lift.

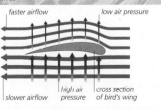

faster airflow   low air pressure

slower airflow   high air   cross section
                    pressure   of bird's wing

MIGRATION

U NTIL RECENTLY, THE MECHANICS, or the "how" of migration, was poorly understood. Today, however, ornithologists know that birds use a variety of cues including visual and magnetic, whether they migrate by day or by night. Birds do not leave northern breeding areas because of the winter cold, but because day-length is getting shorter and food scarcer.

NIGHT MIGRANTS
During migration, ornithologists can point a telescope on the moon and count the birds that cross its surface.

REFUELING
Red Knots stop on their journey from Tierra del Fuego to the Arctic to eat horseshoe crab eggs.

INSTINCTIVE MOVE

Even though many birds use visual cues and landmarks during their migration, for example, birds of prey flying along the Appalachians, "instinctive" behavior must control much of how and where they move. Instinct is a loose term that is hard to define, but ornithologists generally understand it as a genetically programmed activity. They assume that natural selection has molded a behavior as complex as migration by acting on birds' DNA; this hypothesis is reasonable, but hard to prove. Nevertheless, it would seem to be the only explanation why many juvenile shorebirds leave their breeding grounds after their parents, and yet find their way to their final destination.

NAVIGATION

One of the most puzzling aspects of migration is understanding how birds make their way from their summer breeding grounds to their winter destination. Ornithologists have devised experiments to determine the different components. Some of these components are innate, others learned. For example, if visual landmarks are hidden by fog, a faint sun can give birds a directional clue; if heavy clouds hide the sun, then the birds' magnetic compass may be used to ascertain their direction.

FINDING THE WAY
Birds coordinate information their brains receive from the sun, moon, stars, landmarks, and magnetite, or iron oxide, and use it as a compass.

OVERLAND FLIERS
Sandhill Cranes migrate over hills and mountains, from their Arctic tundra breeding grounds to the marshes of the Platte River in the midwestern US.

GLOBETROTTERS

Some bird species in North America are year-round residents, although a few individuals of these species move away from where they hatched at some time in the year. However, a large number of North American species are migratory. A few species breed in Alaska, but winter on remote southwest Pacific islands. Others breed in the Canadian Arctic Archipelago, fly over land and the Pacific Ocean, and spend the winter at sea off the coast of Peru. Many songbirds fly from the Gulf Coast to northern South America. The most amazing globetrotters, such as the Red Knot, fly all the way to Tierra del Fuego, making only a few stops along the way after their short breeding season in the Arctic tundra. The return journeys of some of these travelers are not over the same route—instead, their entire trip is elliptical in shape.

EPIC JOURNEY
The Arctic Tern is a notorious long-distance migrant, breeding in Arctic and subartic regions, and wintering in the pack ice of Antarctica before returning north, a round-trip distance of at least 25,000 miles (40,000km).

KEY

→ Trans-Pacific route
→ Coastal Pacific route
→ Arctic to Pacific route
→ Trans-Gulf route
→ Atlantic to Caribbean route
→ Argentina to Arctic route
→ Arctic-Atlantic Neotropical route

NEOTROPICAL MIGRANT
Many wood warblers, such as this Blackpoll Warbler, breed in boreal forests, before migrating to their wintering grounds in the Caribbean, or Central or South America.

MIGRATION ROUTES
The map above shows the range of migration routes that some North American species take to and from their breeding grounds.

V-FORMATION
Geese and other large waterbirds fly in a V-formation. The leader falls back and is replaced by another individual, saving energy for all the birds.

PARTIAL MIGRANT

The American Robin is a good example of a partial migrant, a species in which the birds of some populations are resident, whereas others migrate out of their breeding range. Most Canadian populations of the American Robin fly south, US populations are largely resident, and quite a few birds from either population spend the winter in the Southwest, Florida, or Mexico.

KEY ■ Breeding distribution
■ Resident all year
■ Nonbreeding distribution

COURTSHIP AND MATING

Whether monogamous or not, males and females need to mate for their species to perpetuate itself. With most species, the male plays the dominant role of advertising a territory to potential mates using vocal or visual displays. Females then select a male, and if the two respond positively to each other, a period of courtship follows ending in mating. The next steps are nest building, egg laying, and rearing the young.

DANCING CRANES
During courtship, Sandhill Cranes perform spectacular dances, the two birds of a pair leaping into the air with wings opened and legs splayed.

DISPLAYS

Mutual attraction between the sexes starts with some sort of display, usually performed by the male. These displays can take a number of forms, from flashing dazzling breeding plumage, conducting elaborate dancing rituals, performing complex songs, offering food or nesting material, or actually building a nest. Some birds, such as grebes, have fascinatingly intricate ceremonies, in which both male and female simultaneously perform the same water-dance. Because they are usually very ritualized, displays help ornithologists understand relationships among birds.

WELCOME HOME
Northern Gannets greet their mates throughout the breeding season by rubbing bills together and opening their wings.

LADIES' CHOICE
On a lek (communal display area), male Sage-Grouse inflate chest pouches while females flock around them and select a mate. Sage-Grouse are found in the West.

COURTSHIP FEEDING

In some species, males offer food to their mate to maintain the pair-bond. For example, male terns routinely bring small fish to their mates in a nesting colony, spreading their wings and tail until the females accept the fish.

MAINTAINING RELATIONS
A male Northern Cardinal offers food to the female, which is a way of reinforcing their pair bond.

BREEDING

After mating, a nest is made, often by the female, where she lays from one to a dozen eggs. Not all birds make nests, however. Nightjars, for example, lay their eggs directly on the ground. In many species, incubation doesn't start until the female has laid all the eggs. Incubation, again usually done by the female, varies from 12 days to about 45 days. Songbirds breeding from the temperate zone northward to the Arctic show a range in clutch size, with more eggs produced in the North than in the South. The breeding process can fail at any stage, for example, a predator can eat the eggs or the chicks. Some birds will nest again, but others give up breeding for the season.

MATING TERNS
Mating is usually brief, and typically takes place on a perch or on the ground, but some species, like swifts, mate in the air. This male Black Tern balances himself by opening his wings.

MUTUAL PREENING
Many species of albatrosses, like these Black-footed Albatrosses from the Pacific, preen each other, with one bird softly nibbling the feathers on the other's head.

POLYGAMY
This Winter Wren collects nesting material for one of the several nests he will build.

MONOGAMOUS BONDS
Some birds, such as Snow Geese, remain paired for life after establishing a bond.

SINGLE FATHER
A male Red-necked Phalarope incubates eggs in the Arctic tundra. Phalaropes are well known for their reversal of breeding roles. The female, who is the larger and more colorful of the two sexes, aggressively competes for males, and after mating with several of them, plays no role in nest building, incubation, or caring for chicks, but tends to her territory instead. Although the chicks can feed by themselves immediately after hatching, they remain with a male before growing feathers and living on their own.

NESTS AND EGGS

M OST BIRD SPECIES BUILD THEIR OWN NEST, which is a necessary container for their eggs. Exceptions include some species of cuckoos and cowbirds, that lay their eggs in other species' nests. Nest-building is often done by the female alone, but in some species the male may help or even build it himself. Eggs are incubated either by females only, or by males and females, depending on the species. Eggs, consisting of 60 percent water, contain a fatty yolk for nourishment of the embryo as well as sugars and proteins. Eggshells are hard enough to sustain the weight of incubating parents, yet soft enough for a chick to break its way out. Hatching is an energy-draining process, and can last for several hours.

NEST TYPES

In addition to the four types shown below, nests range from a simple scrape in the ground with a few added pebbles to an elaborate woven basket-like structure. Plant matter forms basic nest material. This includes twigs, grass stems, bark, lichens, mosses, plant down, and rootlets. Some birds add mud to their nest for strength. Others incorporate animal hair or feathers to improve its softness and insulation. Female eider ducks line their nest with down feathers plucked from their belly. Some birds include bits of plastic or threads in their nests. Several species of flycatchers add shed snakeskins to their nests. Many birds make their nest or lay their eggs deep inside the empty burrows of other animals. Burrowing Owls nest in prairie dog burrows, where they coexist with the rodents.

UNTIDY NEST
Huge stick nests, built on top of dead trees, are the hallmark of Ospreys. They also readily use custom-made nesting platforms erected by humans specifically for them.

EGG CUP
A clutch of three Blue Robin's eggs rest in a cup lined with grass stems and strengthened with mud. Robins build their nests either in shrubs or trees.

NATURAL CAVITY
This Northern Saw-whet Owl is nesting at the bottom of a cavity, in a tree that has probably been excavated by a woodpecker.

NEST BOX
Cavity-nesting bluebirds have been affected by habitat loss, and compete with other birds for nest sites, which may include manmade structures.

COMPLEX WEAVE
New World orioles weave intricate nests from dried grass stems and other plant material, and hang them from the tip of branches, often high up in trees.

EGG SHAPES

There are six basic egg shapes among birds, as illustrated to the right. The most common egg shapes are longitudinal or elliptical. Murres lay pear-shaped eggs, an adaptation for nesting on the narrow ledges of sea cliffs; if an egg rolls, it does so in a tight circle and remains on the ledge. Spherical eggs with irregular red blotches are characteristic of birds of prey. Pigeons and doves lay white oval eggs, usually two per clutch. The eggs of many songbirds, including sparrows and buntings, are conical and have a variety of dark markings on a pale background.

COLOR AND SHAPE
Birds' eggs vary widely in terms of shape, colors, and markings. The American Robin's egg on the left is a beautiful blue.

PEAR SHAPED   **LONGITUDINAL**   **ELLIPTICAL**

NEAT ARRANGEMENT
Many shorebirds, such as plovers and sandpipers, lay four conical eggs with the narrow ends pointed in toward each other.

OVAL   **CONICAL**

SPHERICAL

HATCHING CONDITION

After a period of incubation, which varies from species to species, chicks break the eggshell, some of them using an egg tooth, a special bill feature that falls off after hatching. After a long and exhausting struggle, the chick eventually tumbles out of the shell fragments. The transition from the watery medium inside the egg to the air outside is a tremendous physiological switch. Once free of their shell, the hatchlings recover from the exertion and either beg food from their parents or feed on their own.

FOOD DELIVERY
Tern chicks, although able to move around, cannot catch the fish they need to survive, and must rely on their parents to provide food until they can fly.

PARENTAL CARE
Birds of prey, such as these Snowy Owl owlets, need their parents to care for them longer than some other bird species, and do not leave the nest until their feathers are sufficiently developed for their first flight.

FAST FEEDER
Coots, gallinules, and rails hatch with a complete covering of down, and can feed by themselves immediately after birth.

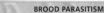

BROOD PARASITISM

Neither cowbirds in the New World nor cuckoos in the Old World make a nest. Female cowbirds deposit up to 20 eggs in the nests of several other species. If the foster parents accept the foreign egg, they will feed the chick of the parasite until it fledges. In the picture below, a tiny wood warbler feeds its adopted chick, a huge cowbird hatchling that has overgrown the nest. Whereas some host species readily incubate the foreign egg, others reject it or abandon the nest.

IDENTIFICATION

Some species are easy to identify, but in many other cases, species identification is tricky. In North America, a notoriously difficult group in terms of identification is the wood warblers, especially in the fall, when most species have similar greenish or yellowish plumage.

GEOGRAPHIC RANGE
Each bird species in North America lives in a particular area that is called its geographic range. Some species have a restricted range; for example, Kirtland's Warbler occurs only in Michigan. Other species, such as the Red-tailed Hawk, range from coast to coast and from northern Canada to Mexico. Species with a broad range usually breed in a variety of vegetation types, while species with narrow ranges often have a specialized habitat; Kirtland's Warblers' is jack pine woodland.

bright blue wings

white belly

chestnut flanks

BLUEBIRD VARIATIONS
Species of the genus *Sialia*, such as the Mountain Bluebird above, and the Eastern Bluebird left, are easy to identify.

SIZE AND WEIGHT
From hummingbird to Tundra Swan and from extra-light ($\frac{1}{16}$oz) to heavy (15lb), such is the range of sizes and weights found among the bird species of North America. Size can be measured in several ways, for example the length of a bird from bill-tip to tail-tip, or its wingspan. Size can also be estimated for a given bird in relationship with another that is familiar. For example, the less familiar Bicknell's Thrush can be compared with the well-known American Robin.

SIZE MATTERS
Smaller shorebirds, with shorter legs and bills, forage in shallow water, but larger ones have longer legs and bills and can feed in deeper water.

SEMIPALMATED PLOVER   LESSER YELLOWLEGS   HUDSONIAN GODWIT   LONG-BILLED CURLEW

GENERAL SHAPE
Just as birds come in all sizes, their body shapes vary, but size and shape are not necessarily correlated. In the dense reed beds in which it lives, the American Bittern's long and thin body blends in with stems. The round-bodied Sedge Wren hops in shrubby vegetation or near the ground where slimness is not an advantage. In dense forest canopy, the slender and long-tailed Yellow-billed Cuckoo can maneuver easily. Mourning Doves inhabit rather open habitats and their plumpness is irrelevant when it comes to their living space. The relative shape and length of the wings and tail are often, but not always, an component on how a particular bird species behaves.

tall, narrow body

short tail

AMERICAN BITTERN

YELLOW-BILLED CUCKOO

long tail

slender shape

small head

tiny tail

thickset body

long, pointed tail

round body

MOURNING DOVE

SEDGE WREN

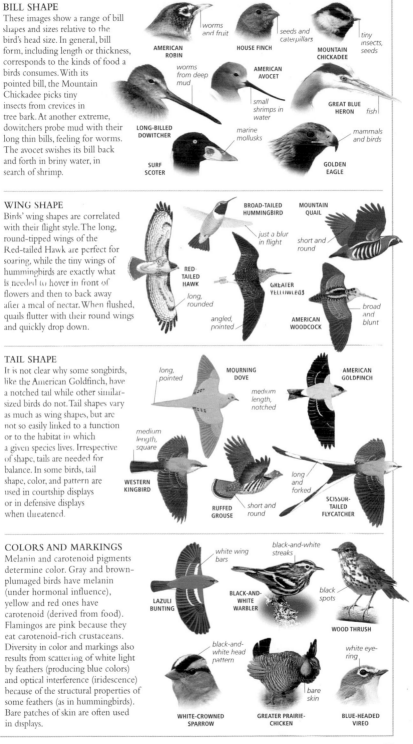

BILL SHAPE

These images show a range of bill shapes and sizes relative to the bird's head size. In general, bill form, including length or thickness, corresponds to the kinds of food a birds consumes. With its pointed bill, the Mountain Chickadee picks tiny insects from crevices in tree bark. At another extreme, dowitchers probe mud with their long thin bills, feeling for worms. The avocet swishes its bill back and forth in briny water, in search of shrimp.

AMERICAN ROBIN — worms and fruit
HOUSE FINCH — seeds and caterpillars
MOUNTAIN CHICKADEE — tiny insects, seeds
LONG-BILLED DOWITCHER — worms from deep mud
AMERICAN AVOCET — small shrimps in water
GREAT BLUE HERON — fish
SURF SCOTER — marine mollusks
GOLDEN EAGLE — mammals and birds

WING SHAPE

Birds' wing shapes are correlated with their flight style. The long, round-tipped wings of the Red-tailed Hawk are perfect for soaring, while the tiny wings of hummingbirds are exactly what is needed to hover in front of flowers and then to back away after a meal of nectar. When flushed, quails flutter with their round wings and quickly drop down.

RED-TAILED HAWK — long, rounded
BROAD-TAILED HUMMINGBIRD — just a blur in flight
MOUNTAIN QUAIL — short and round
GREATER YELLOWLEGS — angled, pointed
AMERICAN WOODCOCK — broad and blunt

TAIL SHAPE

It is not clear why some songbirds, like the American Goldfinch, have a notched tail while other similar-sized birds do not. Tail shapes vary as much as wing shapes, but are not so easily linked to a function or to the habitat in which a given species lives. Irrespective of shape, tails are needed for balance. In some birds, tail shape, color, and pattern are used in courtship displays or in defensive displays when threatened.

MOURNING DOVE — long, pointed
AMERICAN GOLDFINCH — medium length, notched
WESTERN KINGBIRD — medium length, square
RUFFED GROUSE — short and round
SCISSOR-TAILED FLYCATCHER — long and forked

COLORS AND MARKINGS

Melanin and carotenoid pigments determine color. Gray and brown-plumaged birds have melanin (under hormonal influence), yellow and red ones have carotenoid (derived from food). Flamingos are pink because they eat carotenoid-rich crustaceans. Diversity in color and markings also results from scattering of white light by feathers (producing blue colors) and optical interference (iridescence) because of the structural properties of some feathers (as in hummingbirds). Bare patches of skin are often used in displays.

LAZULI BUNTING — white wing bars
BLACK-AND-WHITE WARBLER — black-and-white streaks
WOOD THRUSH — black spots
WHITE-CROWNED SPARROW — black-and-white head pattern
GREATER PRAIRIE-CHICKEN — bare skin
BLUE-HEADED VIREO — white eye-ring

SPECIES GUIDE

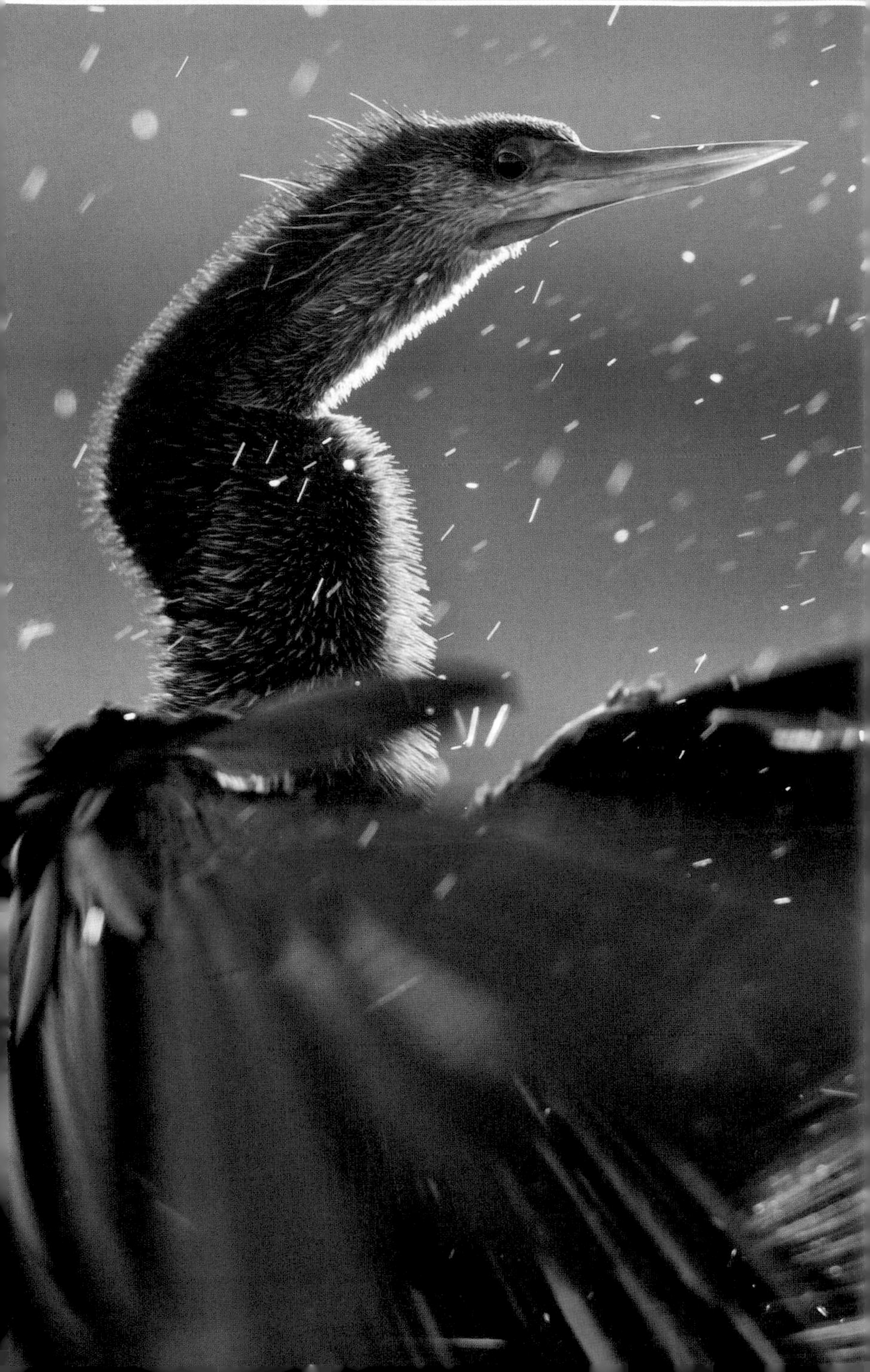

DUCKS, GEESE, AND SWANS

RECENT GENETIC studies indicate that waterfowl are most closely related to members of the order Galliformes. Most species of waterfowl molt all their flight feathers at once after breeding, making them flightless for several weeks until they grow new ones.

GEESE
Ornithologists group geese and swans together into the subfamily Anserinae. Geese are generally intermediate between swans and ducks in body size and neck length. They are more terrestrial than either swans or ducks, often being seen grazing on dry land. Like swans, geese pair for life. They are highly social, and most species are migratory, flying south for the winter in large flocks.

SWANS
Swans are essentially large, long-necked geese. Their heavier weight makes them ungainly on land, and they tend to be more aquatic than their smaller relatives. On water, however, they are extremely graceful. When feeding, a swan stretches its long neck to reach water plants at the bottom, submerging up to half its body as it does so. The Trumpeter Swan of the Northwest is North America's largest native waterfowl, growing up to 5ft (1.5m) long, and weighing up to 25lb (12kg).

INSTANT TAKEOFF
Puddle ducks like the Mallard can shoot straight out of the water and into the air.

DUCKS
Classified into several subfamilies, ducks are more varied than swans or geese, with many more species. They are loosely grouped by their feeding habits. Dabblers, or puddle ducks, such as the Mallard, teals, and wigeons, eat plants and invertebrates. They feed by upending "on the surface of shallow water. By contrast diving ducks, a group that includes scaups, scoters, eiders, mergansers, and the Ruddy Duck, dive deep underwater for their food.

GAGGLING GEESE
Gregarious Snow Geese form large, noisy flocks during migration and on winter feeding grounds.

Order **Anseriformes**	Family **Anatidae**	Species ***Dendrocygna bicolor***

Fulvous Whistling-Duck

ADULT
dark wings
white rump
tawny head and underparts
IN FLIGHT
gray toes extend beyond tail
white flank plumes
barred back
faint crest
tawny buff head and neck
gray bill
ADULT
tawny buff underparts

Although often thought of as dabbling ducks, whistling-ducks act more like swans, as they form long-term pairs, but without an elaborate courtship display, and the male helps to raise the brood. The Fulvous Whistling-Duck is a widespread species in tropical regions, but in the US it is closely associated with rice fields, where numbers of these noisy birds have steadily recovered from the use of pesticides in the 1960s.

VOICE High-pitched squeaky *pi-teeeew*; often calls in flight.
NESTING Simple bowl-shaped nest made of plant matter; among dense floating plants, or on ground; 6–20 eggs; 1 brood; April–September.
FEEDING Filter feeds on rice, seeds of water plants, insects, worms, snails, and clams by swimming, wading, or dabbling along or below the surface.

FLIGHT: fairly shallow wingbeats; legs extend beyond tail.

BOTTOMS UP!
When feeding in water, the bird often upends to feed on snails and submerged rice seeds.

SHORT NECKED
The Fulvous Whistling-Duck is shorter-necked than its black-bellied relative, and can be confused with other ducks when its long legs are hidden.

SIMILAR SPECIES

BLACK-BELLIED WHISTLING-DUCK see p.444
all-black tail
bold white wing stripe

NORTHERN PINTAIL ♀ see p.41
longer neck
no white on flanks
brown-and-black mottled plumage

OCCURRENCE
Permanent resident in southern Texas and Florida; range expands in summer to coastal Texas and Louisiana. In the US, often found in rice fields together with the Black-bellied Whistling-Duck. Casual vagrant as far north as British Columbia and Nova Scotia.

Length **16½–20in (42–51cm)**	Wingspan **33–37in (85–93cm)**	Weight **19–34oz (550–975g)**
Social **Flocks**	Lifespan **Up to 7 years**	Status **Localized**

DATE SEEN	WHERE	NOTES

| Order **Anseriformes** | Family **Anatidae** | Species *Anser caerulescens* |

Snow Goose 🔊

dark flight feathers

ADULT (BLUE)

gray wing patch

ADULT (WHITE)

IN FLIGHT

gray bill

gray uppperts

pale underparts

gray legs and toes

IMMATURE (BLUE FORM)

blackish brown back

pale wing feathers

long neck

dark belly

ADULT (BLUE FORM)

elongated, white head

black patch on long bill

white upperparts

gray-brown all over

grayish legs

IMMATURE (WHITE FORM)

FLIGHT: direct, strong flight with moderate wingbeats in either V-shaped or bunched flocks.

pink legs

ADULT (WHITE FORM)

The abundant Snow Goose has two subspecies. The "greater" (*A. c. atlantica*) is slightly larger and is found breeding farther east. The smaller "lesser" (*A. c. caerulescens*) breeds farther west. Snow Geese have two color forms—white and "blue" (actually dark grayish brown with a white head), and there are also intermediate birds.
VOICE Basic call a nasal *whouk*, *kowk*, or *kow-luk*, also higher-pitched *heenk*; feeding call a series of *hu-hu-hur*.
NESTING Scrapes on hummock, lined with plant material and down; 2–6 eggs; 1 brood; May–July.
FEEDING Grazes on aquatic and terrestrial vegetation, including stems, seeds, leaves, tubers, and roots; also grain and young leaves in agricultural fields in winter.

TOUCHING DOWN
Snow Geese are well known for migrating in flocks that number in the tens of thousands.

SIMILAR SPECIES

GREATER WHITE-FRONTED GOOSE
see p.27
dark head and neck
barred underparts

ROSS'S GOOSE
see p.26
white forehead
shorter bill
much smaller overall

OCCURRENCE
Breeding colonies in High Arctic from Wrangel Island in the West to Greenland in the East; a population of "lesser" Snow Geese breeds near Hudson Bay. Winters along interior valleys westward to coastal lowlands and central plateau of Mexico; Atlantic populations winter in coastal marshes.

| Length **27–33in (69–83cm)** | Wingspan **4¼–5½ft (1.3–1.7m)** | Weight **3¾–6½lb (1.7–3kg)** |
| Social **Flocks** | Lifespan **Up to 27 years** | Status **Secure** |

DATE SEEN	WHERE	NOTES
....	....	....
....	....	....
....	....	....
....	....	....
....	....	....

Order **Anseriformes**	Family **Anatidae**	Species *Anser rossii*

Ross's Goose

ADULT (WHITE)
black wing tips

IN FLIGHT

light gray crown
dusky line through eye
gray wash on upperparts

IMMATURE (WHITE FORM)

round head
short, triangular bill
short, deeply furrowed neck

clean white upperparts

mostly dark brown upperparts
white rump and tail

ADULT (BLUE FORM)

ADULT (WHITE FORM)

reddish pink legs

FLIGHT: strong and direct, with rapid wingbeats.

This diminutive white goose is not much bigger than a Mallard, and half the weight of a Snow Goose; like its larger relative, it also has a "blue" form. About 95 percent of Ross's Geese once nested at a single sanctuary in Arctic Canada, but breeding pairs have spread eastward along Hudson Bay and in several island locations. Hunting reduced numbers to just 6,000 in the early 1950s, but since then numbers have increased to around 2 million individuals.

VOICE Call a *keek keek keeek*, higher-pitched than Snow Goose; also a harsh, low *kork* or *kowk*; quiet when feeding.
NESTING Plant materials placed on ground, usually in colonies with Lesser Snow Geese; 3–5 eggs; 1 brood; June–August.
FEEDING Grazes on grasses, sedges, and small grains.

TRAVELING IN FAMILIES
Groups migrate thousands of miles together, for example from northern Canada to central California.

SIMILAR SPECIES

SNOW GOOSE white form; see p.25
larger bill
longer neck
pink legs

SNOW GOOSE blue form; see p.25
longer neck
black patch on bill

OCCURRENCE
Breeding grounds are amid tundra in scattered, High Arctic locations. Main wintering areas in California. On the wintering grounds, it feeds in agricultural fields, and also grasslands. Roosts overnight in several types of wetlands.

Length **22½–25in (57–64cm)**	Wingspan **3¼ft (1.1m)**	Weight **1¾–4½lb (0.85–2kg)**
Social **Flocks**	Lifespan **Up to 21 years**	Status **Secure**

DATE SEEN	WHERE	NOTES

| Order **Anseriformes** | Family **Anatidae** | Species *Anser albifrons* |

Greater White-fronted Goose

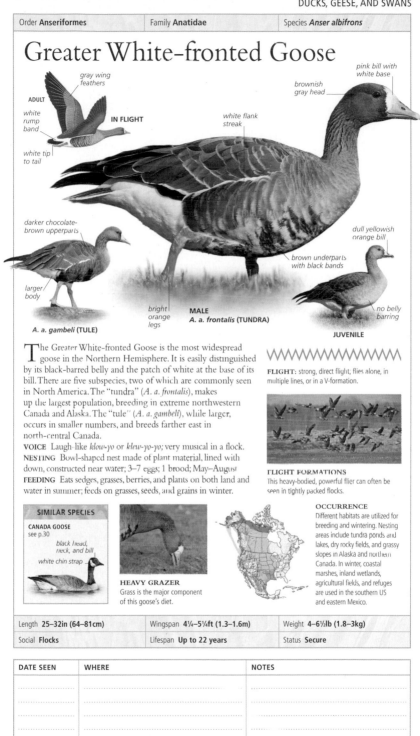

gray wing feathers

ADULT

white rump band

IN FLIGHT

white tip to tail

pink bill with white base

brownish gray head

white flank streak

darker chocolate-brown upperparts

dull yellowish orange bill

brown underparts with black bands

larger body

bright orange legs

MALE
***A. a. frontalis* (TUNDRA)**

no belly barring

***A. a. gambeli* (TULE)**

JUVENILE

The Greater White-fronted Goose is the most widespread goose in the Northern Hemisphere. It is easily distinguished by its black-barred belly and the patch of white at the base of its bill. There are five subspecies, two of which are commonly seen in North America. The "tundra" (*A. a. frontalis*), makes up the largest population, breeding in extreme northwestern Canada and Alaska. The "tule" (*A. a. gambeli*), while larger, occurs in smaller numbers, and breeds farther east in north-central Canada.

VOICE Laugh-like *klow-yo* or *klew-yo-yo*; very musical in a flock.
NESTING Bowl-shaped nest made of plant material, lined with down, constructed near water; 3–7 eggs; 1 brood; May–August.
FEEDING Eats sedges, grasses, berries, and plants on both land and water in summer; feeds on grasses, seeds, and grains in winter.

FLIGHT: strong, direct flight; flies alone, in multiple lines, or in a V-formation.

FLIGHT FORMATIONS
This heavy-bodied, powerful flier can often be seen in tightly packed flocks.

SIMILAR SPECIES

CANADA GOOSE
see p.30
black head, neck, and bill
white chin strap

HEAVY GRAZER
Grass is the major component of this goose's diet.

OCCURRENCE
Different habitats are utilized for breeding and wintering. Nesting areas include tundra ponds and lakes, dry rocky fields, and grassy slopes in Alaska and northern Canada. In winter, coastal marshes, inland wetlands, agricultural fields, and refuges are used in the southern US and eastern Mexico.

| Length **25–32in (64–81cm)** | Wingspan **4¼–5¼ft (1.3–1.6m)** | Weight **4–6½lb (1.8–3kg)** |
| Social **Flocks** | Lifespan **Up to 22 years** | Status **Secure** |

DATE SEEN	WHERE	NOTES

| Order **Anseriformes** | Family **Anatidae** | Species *Branta bernicla* |

Brant 🔊

pale bars across wings

ADULT (WESTERN)

ADULT (EASTERN)

white rump

black neck and head

IN FLIGHT

weakly barred flanks

small, white "necklace" not crossing throat

dark gray-brown upperparts

grayish white flank patch

broad white necklace crosses throat

black chest

bold, barred flanks

black neck stops abruptly at breast

pale belly

ADULT *B. b. nigricans* (WESTERN)

B. b. hrota (EASTERN)

A small-billed, dark, stocky sea goose, the Brant winters on both the East and West Coasts of North America. There are two subspecies in the US (three overall)—the pale-bellied "Atlantic" Brant (*B. b. hrota*), found in the East, and the darker "black" Brant (*B. b. nigricans*), in the West. In addition, there is an intermediate gray-bellied form that winters in the Puget Sound region along the Washington State Coast. Unlike other North American geese, the Brant feeds mainly on eelgrass in winter.

VOICE Nasal *cruk*, harsh-sounding in tone; rolling series of *cut cut cut cronk*, with an upward inflection at end.

NESTING Scrape lined with grass, plant matter, and down on islands or gravel spits; 3–5 eggs; 1 brood; May–July.

FEEDING Eats grass and sedges when nesting; eelgrass in winter; also green algae, saltmarsh plants, and mollusks.

FLIGHT: rapid and strong; low, irregular flight formations.

GRASSY MEAL
In winter, Brants forage almost exclusively on eelgrass between the high and low tide marks.

SIMILAR SPECIES

SNOW GOOSE (BLUE FORM) 🔊
see p.25

pale wing feathers

CACKLING GOOSE
see p.29

broad, white chin strap

browner coloration

darker underparts

OCCURRENCE
Breeds in colonies in northern Canada and Alaska, and winters along both Pacific and Atlantic Coasts. The western breeding population of the Brant ("black") winters from the Aleutian Islands to northern Mexico, while the pale-bellied form ("Atlantic") is restricted in range to the East Coast.

| Length **22–26in (56–66cm)** | Wingspan **3½–4ft (1.1–1.2m)** | Weight **2½–4lb (1–1.8kg)** |
| Social **Flocks** | Lifespan **Up to 25 years** | Status **Secure** |

DATE SEEN	WHERE	NOTES

| Order **Anseriformes** | Family **Anatidae** | Species *Branta hutchinsii* |

Cackling Goose

plain grayish brown wings

ADULT

small, black head

white U-shaped patch on rump   **IN FLIGHT**

broad, white neck ring

black line separates white chin strap

darker breast

ADULT
B. h. leucopareia

dark brown breast

ADULT
B. h. minima

small stubby bill

white chin strap

no black under chin

pale breast

black tail

ADULT
B. h. hutchinsii

The Cackling Goose has recently been split from the Canada Goose; it can be distinguished from the latter by its short stubby bill, steep forehead, and short neck. There are four subspecies of Cackling Goose, which vary in breast color, ranging from dark in *C. h. minima,* fairly dark in *C. h. leucopareia,* and pale in *C. h. hutchinsii.* The Cackling Goose is much smaller than all subspecies of Canada Goose, except the "lesser" Canada Goose, which has a longer neck and a less sloped forehead.
VOICE Male call a *honk* or *bark;* females have higher pitched *hrink;* also high-pitched yelps.
NESTING Scrape lined with available plant matter and down; 2–8 eggs; 1 brood; May–August.
FEEDING Consumes plants in summer; in winter, grazes on grass livestock and dairy pastures; also in agricultural fields.

FLIGHT: strong with rapid wingbeats; flies in bunched V-formations.

LITTLE GEESE
Cackling Geese are tiny when seen together with the larger Canada Goose.

SIMILAR SPECIES

CANADA GOOSE
see p.30

more sloped forehead

larger overall (except one subspecies)

BRANT
see p.28

black neck

barred flanks

pale belly

OCCURRENCE
At the northernmost fringe of the Canada Goose's range, in the tundra, it breeds on rocky tundra slopes from the Aleutians east to Baffin Island and Hudson Bay. Winters from British Columbia to California, also central US, Texas, and New Mexico in pastures and agricultural fields.

| Length **21½–30in (55–75cm)** | Wingspan **4¼–5ft (1.3–1.5m)** | Weight **2–6½lb (0.9–3kg)** |
| Social **Flocks** | Lifespan **Unknown** | Status **Secure** |

DATE SEEN	WHERE	NOTES

29

Order **Anseriformes**	Family **Anatidae**	Species *Branta canadensis*

Canada Goose 🔊

plain grayish brown wings with darker flight feathers

ADULT

IN FLIGHT

white U-shaped patch on rump

grayish brown upperparts and sides

white undertail feathers

ADULT

very long neck

black head

broad white chin strap

paler upper breast

smaller, white chin strap

ADULT

dark brown overall

ADULT

The Canada Goose is the most common, widespread, and familiar goose in North America. Given its vast range, it is not surprising that the Canada Goose should have much geographic variation. Twelve subspecies have been recognized. With the exception of the Cackling Goose, which has recently been separated, it is difficult to confuse it, with its distinctive white chin strap, black head and neck, and grayish brown body, with any other species of goose. It is a monogamous species, and once pairs are formed, they stay together for life.

VOICE Male call a *honk* or *bark*; females have higher pitched *hrink*.
NESTING Scrape lined with available plant matter and down, near water; 1–2 broods; 2–12 eggs; May–August.
FEEDING Grazes on grasses, sedges, leaves, seeds, agricultural crops and berries; also insects.

FLIGHT: strong and direct with fairly slow, deep wingbeats; often flies in V-formation.

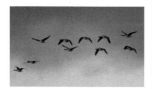

TRICK OF THE LIGHT
A low sun can play tricks—these birds are actually pale grayish underneath.

SIMILAR SPECIES

GREATER WHITE-FRONTED GOOSE see p.27

white on base of pink bill

bright orange legs

CACKLING GOOSE see p.29

steep forehead

smaller overall

OCCURRENCE
Variety of inland breeding habitats near water, including grassy urban areas, marshes, prairie, parkland, coastal temperate forest, northern coniferous forest, and Arctic tundra. Winters in agricultural fields, mudflats, saltwater marshes, lakes, and rivers.

Length 2¼–3½ft (0.7–1.1m)	Wingspan 4¼–5½ft (1.3–1.7m)	Weight 6½–9¾lb (3–4.4kg)
Social **Flocks**	Lifespan **Up to 25 years**	Status **Secure**

DATE SEEN	WHERE	NOTES

| Order **Anseriformes** | Family **Anatidae** | Species *Cygnus olor* |

Mute Swan

ADULT

extended neck

IN FLIGHT

long, pointed tail extends past toes

black-based dusky bill

blotchy brown body

JUVENILE

white overall

often arches wings over back

large, heavy body

long, S-shaped neck

small knob on bill

FEMALE

swollen knob during breeding

MALE

conspicuous black knob at base of orange bill

ADULT

One of the heaviest birds in North America, the Mute Swan was introduced from Europe because of its graceful appearance on water, if not on land, and easy domestication. However, this is an extremely territorial and aggressive bird. When threatened, it points its bill downward, arches its wings, hisses, and then attacks. Displacement of native waterfowl species and overgrazing by this species have led to efforts to reduce its numbers in North America.

VOICE Not mute; hisses, grunts, snorts, and snores; during courtship, trumpets, although more quietly than other swans.

NESTING Platform nest of plant materials, built on ground near water; 4–8 eggs; 1–2 broods; March–October.

FEEDING Dabbles, dips, and upends, mainly for underwater plants, but occasionally for small creatures too.

FLIGHT: strong, steady wingbeats; creating a distinctive whirring and throbbing sound.

FORMATION FLYING
Groups of Mute Swans will sometimes fly in a line, and at other times, as here, they will arrange themselves in a "V" formation.

SIMILAR SPECIES

TRUMPETER SWAN ☾
see p.444

larger head

gray plumage

TUNDRA SWAN ☾
much smaller; see p.32

pink at base of bill

straighter, black bill

straighter neck

OCCURRENCE
Bulk of population is found along the Atlantic Coast from Maine to North Carolina; smaller populations around the Great Lakes and southern British Columbia. Breeds and lives year-round on sluggish rivers, ponds, or lakes, preferring still water with emergent vegetation.

| Length **4–5ft (1.2–1.5m)** | Wingspan **6½–7½ft (2–2.3m)** | Weight **12–32lb (5.5–14.5kg)** |
| Social **Pairs/Family groups** | Lifespan **Up to 21 years** | Status **Localized** |

DATE SEEN	WHERE	NOTES

Order **Anseriformes**	Family **Anatidae**	Species ***Cygnus columbianus***

Tundra Swan

ADULT

small head and bill

dark legs | **IN FLIGHT** | fairly thick neck

dull grayish body

dirty pink bill

JUVENILE

eye stands out from face at close range

yellow facial skin next to eye

large yellow bill patch

BEWICK'S SWAN

all-white plumage

ADULT

Nesting in the Arctic tundra, this well-named species is North America's most widespread and smallest swan. Two populations exist, with one wintering in the West, and the other along the East Coast. The Tundra Swan can be confused with the Trumpeter Swan, but their different calls immediately distinguish the two species. When they are silent, weight and bill structure are the best way to tell them apart. In Eurasia, this species is known as Bewick's Swan and possesses a larger yellow patch at the base of its bill.
VOICE Clear, high-pitched yodeling *whoo-hooo* calls mixed with garbles, yelping, and barking sounds.
NESTING Mound-shaped nest made of plant matter near water; 3–6 eggs; 1 brood; May–September.
FEEDING Eats aquatic vegetation, insects, mollusks; also grain.

FLIGHT: flight pattern like that of other swans but with slightly faster wingbeats.

WINTER FLOCKS
Its size, white plumage, and flocking habits make the Tundra Swan a conspicuous species.

SIMILAR SPECIES

MUTE SWAN ♺
see p.31

pointed tail | *heavier bodied*

TRUMPETER SWAN
see p.444

more curved neck | *straighter edge from eye to bill* | *all-black bill*

OCCURRENCE
Nests around lakes and pools in northern tundra from the Aleutians to the Yukon, and east to northwest Québec. Winters in southern British Columbia, western US, and mid-Atlantic states, mostly New Jersey to South Carolina. Winter habitat includes shallow coastal bays, ponds, and lakes.

Length **4–5ft (1.2–1.5m)**	Wingspan **6¼–7¼ft (1.9–2.2m)**	Weight **12–18lb (5.5–8kg)**
Social **Flocks**	Lifespan **Up to 21 years**	Status **Secure**

DATE SEEN	WHERE	NOTES

| Order **Anseriformes** | Family **Anatidae** | Species *Aix sponsa* |

Wood Duck

blue wing patch
long wings
MALE
head held high
IN FLIGHT

bold, tear-shaped eye-ring
smaller crest
brownish breast
white-edged feathers
helmet-like head profile
FEMALE

subdued facial pattern
brown eye
grayish bill
IMMATURE

red eye
complex, white facial markings
black tip of bill
white-flecked maroon breast appears black at a distance
white, vertical breast stripe

burgundy flanks
long, dark tail
MALE

The male Wood Duck is perhaps the most striking of all North American ducks. With its bright plumage, red eye and bill, and its long sleek crest that gives its head a helmet-shaped profile, the male is unmistakable. It is related to the Mandarin Duck of Asia. The Wood Duck is very dependent on mature swampy forestland. It is typically found on swamps, shallow lakes, ponds, and park settings that are surrounded by trees. Although it adapts to human activity, it is quite shy. When swimming, the Wood Duck can be seen jerking its head front to back. Of all waterfowl, this is the only species that regularly raises two broods each season.
VOICE Male gives a wheezy up-slurred whistle *zweeet*; female's call a double-note, rising *oh-eek oh-eek*.
NESTING Nests in natural tree cavities or nest boxes in close proximity to water; 10–13 eggs; 2 broods, April–August.
FEEDING Forages for seeds, tree fruit, and small acorns; also spiders, insects, and crustaceans.

FLIGHT: rapid flight with deep wingbeats; flies with head up; leaps straight off the water.

PLAIN BELLY
Wings raised, a male reveals one of the only plain areas of its plumage—its pale belly and underwing.

SIMILAR SPECIES

BUFFLEHEAD ♀ see p.55
white on cheek
shorter neck
shorter tail

HOODED MERGANSER ♀ narrower wings; see p.58
long, tan crest
no eye-ring

OCCURRENCE
Usually found throughout the year, along rivers, streams, and creeks, in swamps, and marshy areas. Has a preference for permanent bodies of water. If good aquatic feeding areas are unavailable, the Wood Duck feeds in open areas, including agricultural fields.

| Length **18½–21½in (47–54cm)** | Wingspan **26–29in (66–73cm)** | Weight **16–30oz (450–850g)** |
| Social **Small flocks** | Lifespan **Up to 18 years** | Status **Secure** |

DATE SEEN	WHERE	NOTES

| Order **Anseriformes** | Family **Anatidae** | Species *Spatula discors* |

Blue-winged Teal 🔊

powdery blue forewing with green patch

MALE (BREEDING)

white facial crescent

white underwing stripe

IN FLIGHT

broken, contrasting, white eye-ring

grayish brown overall

pale eyebrow, dark cape, and eye-line

FEMALE

pale spot at base of bill

white facial crescent

dark grayish head

black bill

MALE (FALL)

black spots on rich, buff-brown breast and flanks

white facial crescent

long blackish bill

rich tan flanks

warmer brown overall

MALE (BREEDING)

conspicuous white patch

This small dabbling duck is a common and widespread North American breeding species. With a bold white crescent between bill and eye on its otherwise slate-gray head and neck, the male Blue-winged Teal is quite distinctive. The Blue-winged and Cinnamon Teals, together with the Northern Shoveler, constitute the three "blue-winged" ducks; this is a feature that is conspicuous when the birds are flying. The Cinnamon and the Blue-winged Teals are almost identical genetically and interbreed to form hybrids. The Blue-winged Teal winters mostly south of the US and migrates back north in spring.
VOICE Male a high-pitched, raspy *peew* or low-pitched *paay* during courtship; female a loud single *quack*.
NESTING Bowl-shaped depression lined with grasses, close to water's edge, in meadows; 6–14 eggs; 1 brood; April–September.
FEEDING Eats seeds of a variety of plants; feeds heavily on insect larvae, crustaceans, and snails, when breeding.

FLIGHT: fast, twisting flight; flies in compact, small groups.

OUTSTRETCHED WING
Wing stretch behavior shows the white feathers between the blue forewing and green speculum.

SIMILAR SPECIES

CINNAMON TEAL ♀
see p.471
plain face

warmer brown

GREEN-WINGED TEAL ♀
see p.42
different wing pattern

streaked rump

smaller, more compact body

smaller bill

OCCURRENCE
Nests across North America, with highest numbers in the prairie and parkland regions of the midcontinent. Prefers shallow ponds or marshes during nesting; freshwater to brackish water and (less so) saltwater marshes during migration. In winter, prefers saline environments, including mangroves.

| Length **14½–16in (37–41cm)** | Wingspan **23½–25in (60–64cm)** | Weight **11–18oz (300–500g)** |
| Social **Flocks** | Lifespan **Up to 17 years** | Status **Secure** |

DATE SEEN	WHERE	NOTES

Order **Anseriformes**	Family **Anatidae**	Species *Spatula clypeata*

Northern Shoveler 🔊

dark, narrow eye-line

brown overall

dusky olive-gray to orange bill

FEMALE

grayish blue wing patch

pale blue wing patch

IN FLIGHT

whitish tail

long bill

FEMALE

heavy fronted

MALE

dark green head

pale-edged, brown flank feathers

yellow eye

large, dark spatula-shaped bill

MALE

white breast

chestnut belly and flanks

black-and-white rump

The Northern Shoveler is a common, medium-sized, dabbling duck found in North America and Eurasia. It is monogamous—pairs remain together longer than any other dabbler species. Its distinctive long bill is highly specialized; it is wider at the tip and contains thin, comb-like structures (called "lamellae") along the sides, used to filter food items from the water. Shovelers often form tight feeding groups, swimming close together as they sieve the water for prey.

VOICE Male call a nasal, muffled *thuk thuk…thuk thuk*; also a loud, nasal *paaaay*; female call a variety of *quacks*, singly or in a series of 4–5 descending notes.

NESTING Scrape lined with plant matter and down, in short plants, near water; 6–19 eggs; 1 brood; May–August.

FEEDING Forages for seeds; filters small crustaceans and mollusks out of the water.

FLIGHT: strong direct flight; male's wings make a rattling noise when taking off.

UPSIDE DOWN FEEDER
This male upends to feed below the water's surface, revealing his orange legs.

FILTER FEEDING
Their bills open, these ducks sieve small invertebrates from the water.

OCCURRENCE
Widespread across North America, south of the tundra. Breeds in a variety of wetlands, in edges of shallow pools with nearby tall and short grasslands. Occurs in fresh- and saltmarshes, ponds, and other shallow bodies of water in winter; does not feed on land.

SIMILAR SPECIES

MALLARD ♀
larger; see p.38

darker blue wing patch

slimmer bill

CINNAMON TEAL ♀
see p.471

plainer plumage

plainer face

longer tail

Length **17½–20in (44–51cm)**	Wingspan **27–33in (69–84cm)**	Weight **14–29oz (400–825g)**
Social **Flocks**	Lifespan **Up to 18 years**	Status **Secure**

DATE SEEN	WHERE	NOTES

| Order **Anseriformes** | Family **Anatidae** | Species *Mareca strepera* |

Gadwall 🔊

conspicuous white patch

mostly white underwings

MALE (WINTER)

white belly **IN FLIGHT**

silvery gray area

rusty sides

MALE (ECLIPSE)

brown, scalloped back

dark eyestripe

white wing patch

FEMALE

dark grayish overall

brown, rounded head

black uppertail

black bill

MALE (WINTER)

orange-yellow legs

finely patterned gray flanks and breast

Although the Gadwall's appearance is somewhat somber, many birders consider this duck one of North America's most elegant species because of the subtlety of its plumage. Despite being common and widespread, Gadwalls are often overlooked because of their retiring behavior and relatively quiet vocalizations. This dabbling duck is slightly smaller and more delicate than the Mallard, yet female Gadwalls are often mistaken for female Mallards. Gadwalls associate with other species, especially in winter.

VOICE Low, raspy *meep* or *reb* given in quick succession; female *quack* similar to that of female Mallard, but higher-pitched and more nasal; high-pitched *peep*, or *pe-peep*; both sexes give *tickety-tickety-tickety* chatter while feeding.

NESTING Bowl nest made of plant material in a scrape; 8–12 eggs; 1 brood; April–August.

FEEDING Dabbles on the surface or below for seeds, aquatic vegetation, and invertebrates, including mollusks and insects.

FLIGHT: direct flight with fast wingbeats; leaps straight off the water.

BROOD ON THE MOVE
Females lead their ducklings from their nest to a brood-rearing habitat that provides cover and ample food for the ducklings to forage.

SIMILAR SPECIES

MALLARD ♀ see p.38
darker eye-line
whitish tail

MOTTLED DUCK ♀ see p.40
thicker, longer bill
olive to yellow bill
buffier face

OCCURRENCE
From the western prairie pothole country of Canada and the northern US, the Gadwall's range has expanded as it has adapted to manmade bodies of water, such as reservoirs and ponds. In winter, mostly found on lakes, marshes, and along rivers.

| Length **18–22½in (46–57cm)** | Wingspan **33in (84cm)** | Weight **18–45oz (500–1,250g)** |
| Social **Winter flocks** | Lifespan **Up to 19 years** | Status **Secure** |

DATE SEEN	WHERE	NOTES

| Order **Anseriformes** | Family **Anatidae** | Species *Mareca americana* |

American Wigeon 🔊

MALE (BREEDING)

white underwing patch

rufous-edged wing feathers

dark smudge around eye

gray head

narrow, black line along bill

IN FLIGHT

long, pointed tail

gray head contrasts with pinkish brown breast and flanks

FEMALE

warm brown breast and flanks

cream forehead and crown

green band from eye to nape

MALE (BREEDING)

black rump

pinkish brown flanks

black-tipped bill

Often found in mixed flocks with other ducks, the American Wigeon is a common and widespread, medium-sized dabbling duck. This bird is an opportunist that loiters around other diving ducks and coots, feeding on the vegetation they dislodge. It is more social during migration and in the nonbreeding season than when breeding.

VOICE Slow and fast whistles; male's most common call a slow, high-pitched, wheezy, three-syllable *whew-whew-whew*, with middle note loudest; also, a faster *whee* whistle.

NESTING Depression lined with plant material and down, usually in tall grass away from water; 5–10 eggs; 1 brood; May–August.

FEEDING Grazes on grass, clover, algae, and, in agricultural fields; feeds on many seeds, insects, mollusks, and crustaceans during the breeding season.

FLIGHT: rapid, fairly deep wingbeats; leaps almost vertically off the water.

COMING IN FOR LANDING
This male's cream-colored forehead is clearly visible, as is the sharp contrast between the white belly, and the pinkish breast and flanks.

FLAPPING WINGS
This bird has a white patch on its underwing, while the Eurasian Wigeon has a gray patch.

OCCURRENCE
The northernmost breeder of the dabbling ducks, occurs from Alaska to the Maritimes. Prefers pothole and grassland habitats; found almost anywhere near water in winter. Winters south to northern South America and the Caribbean, in freshwater and coastal bay habitats.

SIMILAR SPECIES

GADWALL ♀
see p.36

white patch

dark line through eye

GREEN-WINGED TEAL ♂
see p.42

longer bill

green patch on wing

black-and-orange bill

| Length **17½–23in (45–58cm)** | Wingspan **33in (84cm)** | Weight **1⅛–3lb (0.5–1.3kg)** |
| Social **Flocks** | Lifespan **Up to 21 years** | Status **Secure** |

DATE SEEN	WHERE	NOTES

Order **Anseriformes**	Family **Anatidae**	Species *Anas platyrhynchos*

Mallard ◀))

olive-yellow bill

grayer head

broad-based wings

orange bill with blackish patch

dark eye-line and cap

MALE (SUMMER) rusty underparts

short, round, pale tail

MALE (WINTER)

yellowish brown back

heavy body

mottled brown belly

metallic green head

FEMALE

FEMALE

blue wing patch

warm gray body

bright yellow bill

narrow, white neck collar

brown underparts

IN FLIGHT

whitish outer tail feathers

short, black curls above white tail

chestnut-brown breast

MALE (WINTER)

The Mallard is perhaps the most familiar of all ducks, and occurs in the wild all across the Northern Hemisphere. It is the ancestor of most domestic ducks, and hybrids between the wild and domestic forms are frequently seen in city lakes and ponds, often with patches of white on the breast. Mating is generally a violent affair, but outside the breeding season the wild species is strongly migratory and gregarious, sometimes forming large flocks that may join with other species.
VOICE Male's call a quiet raspy *raab*; during courtship a high-pitched whistle; female call a *quack* or repeated in series.
NESTING Scrape lined with plant matter, usually near water, often on floating vegetation; 6–15 eggs; 1 brood; February–September.
FEEDING Feeds omnivorously on insects, crustaceans, mollusks, and earthworms when breeding; otherwise largely vegetarian; takes seeds, acorns, agricultural crops, aquatic vegetation, and bread.

FLIGHT: fast, shallow, and regular; often flies in groups.

STICKING TOGETHER
The mother leads her ducklings to water soon after they hatch. She looks after them until they can fend for themselves.

SIMILAR SPECIES

GADWALL ♀ see p.36

steeper forehead

slimmer body

white wing patch

orange strip on bill

AMERICAN BLACK DUCK ♀ see p.39

dark tail

dark olive bill

darker/brown overall

OCCURRENCE
Occurs throughout the region, choosing shallow water in natural wetlands, such as marshes, prairie potholes, ponds, and ditches; can also be found in manmade habitats such as city parks and reservoirs, preferring more open habitats in winter.

Length **19½–26in (50–65cm)**	Wingspan **32–37in (82–95cm)**	Weight **1⅞–3lb (0.9–1.4kg)**
Social **Flocks**	Lifespan **Up to 29 years**	Status **Secure**

DATE SEEN	WHERE	NOTES

| Order **Anseriformes** | Family **Anatidae** | Species *Anas rubripes* |

American Black Duck

rich violet patch

white underwing

MALE

dark **IN FLIGHT**
dark tail

heavily streaked head and neck

olive bill

cinnamon-edged flank feathers

FEMALE

pale head

dark cap

narrow, dark eye-line

greenish yellow bill

dark body

MALE

The American Black Duck, a large dabbling duck, is closely related to the Mallard. In the past, the two species were separated by different habitat preferences—the American Black Duck preferring forested locations, and the Mallard favoring more open habitats. Over the years, these habitats became less distinct as the East was deforested and trees were planted in the Midwest. As a result, there are now many hybrids between the two species. It has also been argued that the introduction of Mallards to various areas in the East has further increased interbreeding. The American Black Duck breeds throughout a wide area in the northern part of its range. When breeding, males can be seen chasing away other males to maintain their territories.

VOICE Male's call a reedy *raeb*, given once or twice; female *quack* sounds very similar to Mallard.

NESTING Scrape lined with plant material and down, usually on ground or close to water; 4–10 eggs; 1 brood, March–September.

FEEDING An omnivore, the American Black Duck eats plant leaves and stems, roots, seeds, grains, fruit, aquatic plants, fish, and amphibians.

FLIGHT: fast, shallow, and regular; often flies in groups.

DARK PLUMAGE
This species is the darkest of all the Mallard-type ducks that occur in North America.

OCCURRENCE
Nests in eastern Canada and adjacent areas of the US in a variety of habitats including northerly and mixed hardwood forest, wooded uplands, bogs, salt- and freshwater marshes, and on islands. Resident in the central part of its range, but large numbers winter in saltwater marshes.

SIMILAR SPECIES

MALLARD ♀
see p.38

orange bill

whitish tail

paler body

MOTTLED DUCK ♀
see p.40

mottled brown upperparts

unstreaked face

| Length **21½–23in (54–59cm)** | Wingspan **35–37in (88–95cm)** | Weight **1½–3½lb (0.7–1.6kg)** |
| Social **Flocks** | Lifespan **Up to 26 years** | Status **Secure** |

DATE SEEN	WHERE	NOTES

| Order **Anseriformes** | Family **Anatidae** | Species *Anas fulvigula* |

Mottled Duck

iridescent blue-green
wing patch

bright white
underwing

MALE

IN FLIGHT

dark
eye-line

dull green to
orange-yellow bill

paler breast
than male

duller orange
legs than male

FEMALE

unstreaked
face and
throat

paler edges to dark
body feathers

dark body

pale buffy
head and
neck

no
white
on tail

olive-
yellow bill

MALE

orange legs

A long with the American Black Duck, the Mottled Duck belongs to the so-called "Mallard complex," in which all three species are closely related and interbreed easily, especially with feral or semi-domesticated Mallards. There is concern that the fertile hybrid ducks produced may dilute the purity of the Mottled Duck population, and so eventually displace it. The Mottled Duck is a little smaller and darker than the similar female Mallard, and lacks a white edge to the blue wing patch.
VOICE Males give a variety of raspy *raab* calls; females *quack*.
NESTING Bowl-shaped depression constructed in dense grass; 8–12 eggs; 1 brood; January–September.
FEEDING Dabbles for aquatic vegetation, crustaceans, mollusks, insects, rice, seeds, and some small fish.

FLIGHT: direct with regular wingbeats; flies at relatively low levels.

COLOR CONTRAST
The male Mottled Duck has a yellower bill than the smaller, orange-billed female.

STANDING MALE
This male has a cleaner, buffier face and brighter orange legs than the female Mottled Duck.

SIMILAR SPECIES

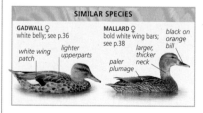

GADWALL ♀
white belly; see p.36

white wing
patch

lighter
upperparts

MALLARD ♀
bold white wing bars; see p.38

black on
orange
bill

larger,
thicker
neck

paler
plumage

OCCURRENCE
Prefers shallow freshwater wetlands, breeding on coastal marshes. This nonmigratory species has distinct populations in the Gulf of Mexico between Alabama and Tamaulipas, and in central and southern Florida, though both populations may stray slightly outside this range in winter.

Length **17½–24in (44–61cm)**	Wingspan **33–34in (83–87cm)**	Weight **21–46oz (0.6–1.4kg)**
Social **Flocks**	Lifespan **Up to 13 years**	Status **Declining**

DATE SEEN	WHERE	NOTES

Order **Anseriformes**	Family **Anatidae**	Species *Anas acuta*

Northern Pintail 🔊

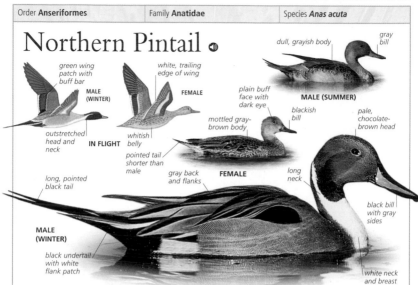

MALE (WINTER)

green wing patch with buff bar

MALE (WINTER)

white, trailing edge of wing

FEMALE

outstretched head and neck **IN FLIGHT**

whitish belly

pointed tail shorter than male

dull, grayish body

gray bill

plain buff face with dark eye

MALE (SUMMER)

blackish bill

pale, chocolate-brown head

mottled gray-brown body

gray back and flanks **FEMALE**

long neck

long, pointed black tail

black bill with gray sides

MALE (WINTER)

black undertail with white flank patch

white neck and breast

An elegant, long-necked dabbler, the Northern Pintail has extremely distinctive marking and a very long tail—in fact, the longest tail to be found on any freshwater duck. One of the earliest breeders in the year, these ducks begin nesting soon after the ice thaws. Northern Pintails were once one of the most abundant prairie breeding ducks. However, in recent decades, droughts, combined with the reduction of habitat on both their wintering and breeding grounds, have resulted in a significant decline in their population.

VOICE Male call a high-pitched rolling *prrreep prrreep;* lower-pitched wheezy *wheeeee*, which gets louder then drops off; female call a quiet, harsh *quack* or *kuk* singularly or as short series; also a loud *gaak*, often repeated.

NESTING Scrape lined with plant materials and down, usually in short grass, brush, or even in the open; 3–12 eggs; 1 brood; April–August.

FEEDING Feeds on grains, rice, seeds, aquatic weeds, insect larvae, crustaceans, and snails.

FLIGHT: fast, direct flight; can be very acrobatic in the air.

FEEDING TIME
Even when tipping up to feed, these pintails can be identified by their long, black, pointed tails.

SIMILAR SPECIES

GADWALL ♀
see p.36
shorter tail
orange-sided bill
white wing patch

AMERICAN WIGEON ♀
see p.37
shorter tail
darker gray head
chestnut breast and flanks

OCCURRENCE
Widely distributed in North America; breeding in open country in shallow wetlands or meadows in mountainous forest regions. Found in tidal wetlands and saltwater habitats in migration and winter; dry harvested and flooded agricultural fields in autumn and winter.

Length **20–30in (51–76cm)**	Wingspan **35in (89cm)**	Weight **18–44oz (500–1,250g)**
Social **Flocks**	Lifespan **Up to 21 years**	Status **Declining**

DATE SEEN	WHERE	NOTES

| Order **Anseriformes** | Family **Anatidae** | Species *Anas crecca* |

Green-winged Teal 🔊

MALE
green-and-black patch on hindwing

short neck

IN FLIGHT gray flanks

horizontal, white line on sides

lacks white vertical bar

rufous head

dark green ear patch

small, narrow, black bill

A. c. crecca
(EURASIAN: RARE)

black-spotted breast

steeper forehead

darker face

white vertical bar

FEMALE

finely detailed pattern

shoulder feathers with narrow pale edges

weaker face pattern

yellowish buff undertail feathers

MALE

JUVENILE

The Green-winged Teal, the smallest North American dabbling duck, is slightly smaller than the Blue-winged and Cinnamon Teals, and lacks their blue wing patch. Its population is increasing, apparently because it breeds in more pristine habitats, and farther north, than the prairie ducks. The species has three subspecies, *A. c. crecca* (Eurasia), *A. c. carolinensis* (North America), and *A. c. nimia* (Aleutian Islands). *Carolinensis* males have a conspicuous vertical white bar, whereas Eurasian *crecca* males do not.
VOICE Male call a high-pitched, slightly rolling *crick crick*, similar to cricket; female call a quiet *quack*.
NESTING Shallow scrape on ground lined with nearby vegetation, often placed in dense vegetation near water; 6–9 eggs; 1 brood; April–September.
FEEDING Eats seeds, aquatic insects, crustaceans, and mollusks year-round; also feeds in grain fields in winter.

FLIGHT: fast flight; often flying in twisting, tight groups reminiscent of shorebird flocks.

SINGLE PARENT
The female duck is deserted by her partner during incubation, so she must provide all parental care.

SIMILAR SPECIES

BLUE-WINGED TEAL ♀
larger overall; see p.34
different wing pattern

whitish spot at base of bill

CINNAMON TEAL ♀
larger overall; see p.471
rich brown overall

longer bill

yellowish legs

OCCURRENCE
Breeds from the central US northward to Canada and Alaska; around ponds in forests and deciduous woodlands. Prefers shallow vegetated wetlands. In winter and migration, inland marshes, sloughs, agricultural fields, and coastal marshes. Winters south of the Caribbean and in southern Mexico.

| Length **12–15½in (31–39cm)** | Wingspan **20½–23in (52–59cm)** | Weight **7–16oz (200–450g)** |
| Social **Flocks** | Lifespan **Up to 20 years** | Status **Secure** |

DATE SEEN	WHERE	NOTES

| Order **Anseriformes** | Family **Anatidae** | Species *Aythya valisineria* |

Canvasback

light gray forewing

black rump and tail

MALE

belly appears white

long neck, held horizontally in flight

IN FLIGHT

dark with mottled gray patches

distinct white eye-ring

dingy brown underparts

IMMATURE

dingy brownish gray upperparts and sides

extended tear drop

FEMALE

brown breast

rich chestnut head and neck

high, peaked black crown

bright red eye

white to pale gray back and flanks

black at both ends

black breast

MALE

A large, elegant, long-billed diving duck, the Canvasback is a bird of prairie pothole country. Its specialized diet of aquatic plants has resulted in a smaller population than other ducks. With legs set toward the rear, it is an accomplished swimmer and diver, and is rarely seen on land. Weather conditions and brood parasitism by Redheads determine how successful the Canvasback's nesting is from year to year.
VOICE Mostly silent except during courtship when males make soft *cooing* noises; females emit a grating *krrrrr krrrrrr krrrrrr*; females give loud *quack* when taking off; during winter, both sexes make soft wheezing series of *rrrr rrrr rrrr* sounds.
NESTING Platform over water built of woven vegetation; occasionally on shore; 8–11 eggs; 1 brood; April–September.
FEEDING Mainly eats aquatic tubers, buds, root stalks, and shoots, particularly those of wild celery; also eats snails when preferred plants are unavailable.

FLIGHT: direct strong flight; one of the fastest ducks; forms V-shaped flocks.

DEEP WATER
Canvasbacks prefer deeper-bodied waters that support the aquatic vegetation they eat.

SIMILAR SPECIES

REDHEAD ♂
see p.44

yellow eye

shorter gray, black-tipped bill

LESSER SCAUP ♂
see p.47

darker gray on back

smaller overall

yellow eye

OCCURRENCE
Found in potholes, marshes, and ponds in prairie parkland, tundra; northerly forests preferred where their favorite foods grow. Winters in large numbers in large bays and lakes, and deltas, with smaller numbers scattered across North America and Mexico.

| Length **19–22in (48–56cm)** | Wingspan **31–35in (79–89cm)** | Weight **1¾–3½lb (0.8–1.6kg)** |
| Social **Flocks** | Lifespan **Up to 22 years** | Status **Secure** |

DATE SEEN	WHERE	NOTES

Order **Anseriformes**	Family **Anatidae**	Species *Aythya americana*

Redhead

MALE

dark-gray forewing

brick-red head

black breast

IN FLIGHT

dark crown

tawny brown overall

gray bill with black tip

FEMALE

yellow eye

MALE (ECLIPSE)

white band

brick-red upper neck and head

yellow eye

long blue bill with black tip

medium-gray mantle and sides

black rump

black lower neck

MALE

The Redhead, a medium-sized diving duck belonging to the Pochard group, is native only to North America. Only when seen up close is it apparent that the male's seemingly gray upperparts and flanks are actually white, with dense, black, wavy markings. The Redhead often feeds at night and forages mostly around dusk and dawn, drifting during the day. It parasitizes other duck nests more than any other duck species, particularly those of the Canvasback and even other Redheads.
VOICE Male courtship call a wheezy rising then falling *whee ough*, also *meow*; female call a low, raspy *kurr kurr kurr*.
NESTING Weaves solid nest over water in dense vegetation such as cattails, lined with down; 7–14 eggs; 1 brood; May–September.
FEEDING Omnivorous; feeds on aquatic plants, seeds, tubers, algae, insects, spiders, fish eggs, snails, and insect larvae; diet is variable depending on location.

FLIGHT: direct flight; runs on water prior to takeoff.

MALE DISPLAY
This male is performing a spectacular courtship display called a head throw, while remaining otherwise completely still on the water.

EASY IDENTIFICATION
The long blue bill with a whitish band and black tip is clearly visible in males.

OCCURRENCE
Breeds in shallow wetlands across the Great Basin and Prairie Pothole region, very densely in certain marsh habitats. The bulk of the population winters in coastal lagoons along the Atlantic Coast and the Gulf of Mexico.

SIMILAR SPECIES		

CANVASBACK ♀
see p.43

wedge-shaped black bill

grayish back

RING-NECKED DUCK ♀
see p.45

peaked head shape

dark-brown back

Length **17–21in (43–53cm)**	Wingspan **30–31in (75–79cm)**	Weight **1⅜–3¼lbs (0.6–1.5kg)**
Social **Flocks**	Lifespan **Up to 21 years**	Status **Secure**

DATE SEEN	WHERE	NOTES

| Order **Anseriformes** | Family **Anatidae** | Species *Aythya collaris* |

Ring-necked Duck

dark forewing

MALE

IN FLIGHT bold white underwing

bold white eye-ring

dark brown back

white band on bill

yellow eye

FEMALE

thin chestnut ring (hard to see)

rounded gray sides

MALE

tall, peaked head

gray bill with white and black tip

black neck and breast

A resident of freshwater ponds and lakes, the Ring-necked Duck is a fairly common medium-sized diving duck. A more descriptive and suitable name might have been Ring-billed Duck as the bold white band on the bill tip is easy to see whereas the thin chestnut ring around the neck can be very difficult to observe. The tall, pointed head is quite distinctive, peaking at the rear of the crown. When it sits on the water, this bird typically holds its head high.

VOICE Male normally silent; female makes low *kerp kerp* call.

NESTING Floating nest built in dense aquatic vegetation, often in marshes; 6–14 eggs; 1 brood; May–August.

FEEDING Feeds in water at all times, either by diving, tipping up, or dabbling for aquatic plant tubers and seeds; also eats aquatic invertebrates such as clams and snails.

FLIGHT: strong flier with deep, rapid wingbeats; flight somewhat erratic.

UNIQUE BILL
A white outline around the base of the bill and the white band on the bill are unique markings.

FLAPPING WINGS
Bold white wing linings are apparent when the Ring-necked Duck flaps its wings.

SIMILAR SPECIES

LESSER SCAUP ♂
see p.47
wavy-patterned gray mantle
rounded head

TUFTED DUCK ♂
see p.471
crested tufts
white sides

OCCURRENCE
Breeds across Canada, south of the Arctic zone, in shallow freshwater marshes and bogs; sporadically in the western US. Winters in freshwater and brackish habitats such as swamps, lakes, estuaries, reservoirs, and flooded fields. Migrants are found in the Midwest near stands of wild rice.

| Length **15–18in (38–46cm)** | Wingspan **24–25in (62–63cm)** | Weight **1⅛–2lbs (500–900g)** |
| Social **Flocks** | Lifespan **Up to 20 years** | Status **Secure** |

DATE SEEN	WHERE	NOTES

Order **Anseriformes**	Family **Anatidae**	Species *Aythya marila*

Greater Scaup

gray forewing

MALE (NONBREEDING)

broad, white wing stripe

IN FLIGHT

little or no white around bill

bold white patches at base of bill

medium to dark brown overall

gray-brown sides **JUVENILE**

smooth, round, black head with purple-green gloss

FEMALE (NONBREEDING)

blue-gray bill, wider at tip

reduced white around bill

gray-frosted shoulder feathers and sides

wavy-patterned gray back

FEMALE (BREEDING)

dark brown overall

blackish brown head

gray-and-brown back

MALE (BREEDING)

almost all white sides

MALE (ECLIPSE)

A great swimmer and diver, the Greater Scaup is the only diving duck (genus *Aythya*) that breeds both in North America and Eurasia. Due to its more restricted coastal breeding and wintering habitat preference, it is far less numerous in North America than its close relative, the Lesser Scaup. The Greater Scaup forms large, often sexually segregated flocks outside the breeding season. If both scaup species are present together, they will also segregate within the flocks according to species. Correct identification is difficult.
VOICE During courtship, male call a soft, fast, wheezy *week week wheeu*; female gives a series of growled monotone *arrrr* notes.
NESTING Simple depression lined with grasses and down, nest sites need to have dense cover of vegetation from previous year; 6–10 eggs; 1 brood; May–September.
FEEDING Dives for aquatic plants, seeds, insects, crustaceans, snails, shrimp, and bivalves.

FLIGHT: strong, fast, and agile; flocks shift and twist during prolonged flight.

FOND OF FLOCKING
Greater Scaups flock together on the water. Males have distinct black-and-white markings.

SIMILAR SPECIES

CANVASBACK ♂
see p.43

chestnut brown head

black tail

LESSER SCAUP ♂
see p.47

slimmer head

grayer flanks

OCCURRENCE
Majority breed in western coastal Alaska on tundra wetlands; also in lower densities in northwest and eastern Canada. Almost all birds winter offshore, along the Atlantic and Pacific Coasts, or on the Great Lakes because of increased food availability. Small groups found inland and midcontinent, on unfrozen water bodies.

Length **15–22in (38–56cm)**	Wingspan **28–31in (72–79cm)**	Weight **1¼ 3lb (0.6–1.4kg)**
Social **Flocks**	Lifespan **Up to 22 years**	Status **Declining**

DATE SEEN	WHERE	NOTES

| Order **Anseriformes** | Family **Anatidae** | Species **Aythya affinis** |

Lesser Scaup 🔊

MALE
whitish underwings
black head
IN FLIGHT whitish belly

pale brown flanks
brown rear end

MALE (1ST WINTER)

rich brown head and neck
white patch around base of gray bill

brown back
brown flank feathers with gray fringes FEMALE

purple-green gloss on head

narrow head with bump at the rear

narrow, thin, blue-gray bill

dark wavy pattern on upperparts

black rear end

MALE
pale flanks

black breast and neck

The Lesser Scaup, far more numerous than its somewhat larger relative (their size and weight ranges overlap), is also the most abundant diving duck in North America. The two species are very similar in appearance and are best identified by shape. Identification must be done cautiously as head shape changes with position. For example, the crown feathers are flattened just before diving in both species; thus, scaups are best identified when they are not moving.
VOICE Males mostly silent except during courtship when they make a wheezy *wheeow wheeow wheeow* sound; females give repetitive series of grating *garrrf garrrf garrrf* notes.
NESTING Nest built in tall vegetation or under shrubs, sometimes far from water, also on islands and mats of floating vegetation; 8–11 eggs; 1 brood; May–September.
FEEDING Feeds mainly on leeches, crustaceans, mollusks, aquatic insects, and aquatic plants and seeds.

FLIGHT: rapid, direct flight; can jump off water more easily than other diving ducks.

PREENING SCAUP
Ducks are meticulous preeners, and the Lesser Scaup is no exception.

SIMILAR SPECIES

RING-NECKED DUCK ♀
see p.45
prominent white eye-ring
solid dark back

GREATER SCAUP ♀
see p.46
more tawny brown upperparts
more white around bill

OCCURRENCE
Breeds inland from Alaska to eastern Canada in open northern forests and forested tundra. Winters in the Caribbean, southern US, and south to northern South America. Majority winter along coasts; others winter inland on lakes and reservoirs.

| Length **15½–17½in (39–45cm)** | Wingspan **27–31in (68–78cm)** | Weight **1–2¾lb (0.45–1.2kg)** |
| Social **Flocks** | Lifespan **Up to 18 years** | Status **Secure** |

DATE SEEN	WHERE	NOTES

| Order **Anseriformes** | Family **Anatidae** | Species *Somateria spectabilis* |

King Eider

MALE (BREEDING)

white underwing

IN FLIGHT

short neck

long-billed profile

brown-black upperparts

scalloped breast

V-shaped markings on sides

FEMALE

white patch on face

MALE MOLTING (2ND WINTER)

white breast

orange to reddish frontal shield, outlined in black

pale blue crown and nape

green cheek

reddish orange bill

long feathers form triangular "sails"

rose blush on breast

MALE (BREEDING)

white flank patch

black underparts

The scientific name of the King Eider, *spectabilis*, means "worth seeing," and its gaudy marking and coloring around the head and bill make it hard to mistake. Females resemble the somewhat larger and paler Common Eider. The female King Eider has a more rounded head, more compact body, and a longer bill than the male. King Eiders may dive down to 180ft (55m) when foraging.

VOICE Courting males give a repeated series of low, rolled dove-like *arrrrooooo* calls, each rising, then falling, followed by softer *cooos*; females give grunts and croaks.

NESTING Slight depression in tundra lined with nearby vegetation and down; 4–7 eggs; 1 brood; June–September.

FEEDING Dives for mollusks; other food items include crustaceans, starfish, and when breeding, insects and plants.

FLIGHT: direct and rapid flight; migrates in long lines, abreast in a broad front, or in clusters.

GROUP FLIGHT
Migratory King Eiders move in large groups to their northern breeding habitats.

SIMILAR SPECIES

COMMON EIDER ♀ larger overall; see p.49

longer, more wedge-shaped bill

flatter head

BLACK SCOTER ♀ smaller overall; see p.53

pale cheek and dark cap

longer, cocked tail

OCCURRENCE
Nests along coasts and farther inland than Spectacled or Steller's Eiders in the High Arctic, in a variety of habitats; around low marshes, lakes, and islands; prefers well-drained areas. During winter, found mostly along the southern edge of the ice pack, in coastal waters up to 66ft (20m) deep.

| Length **18½–25in (47–64cm)** | Wingspan **37in (94cm)** | Weight **2¾–4¾lb (1.2–2.1kg)** |
| Social **Flocks** | Lifespan **Up to 15 years** | Status **Secure** |

DATE SEEN	WHERE	NOTES

| Order **Anseriformes** | Family **Anatidae** | Species *Somateria mollissima* |

Common Eider

black cap

dark brown overall

MALE (SUMMER)

FEMALE
brown overall

olive-green wash on nape

greenish olive bill

white flecking

MALE (WINTER)
whitish underwing

IN FLIGHT

MALE (2ND WINTER)

black rump and tail

white breast, with rose tinge

long, sloping forehead

mottled, black-and-brown upperparts

MALE (WINTER)

FEMALE

The largest duck in North America, the Common Eider is also the most numerous, widespread, and variable of the eiders. Four of its seven subspecies occur in North America, and vary in the markings and color of their heads and bills. Male Common Eiders also have considerable seasonal plumage changes, and do not acquire their adult plumage until the third year.
VOICE Repeated hoarse, grating notes *korr-korr-korr*; male's owl-like *ah-WOO-ooo*; female's low, guttural notes *krrrr-krrrr-krrrr*.
NESTING Depression on ground lined with down and plant matter, often near water; 2–7 eggs; 1 brood; June–September.
FEEDING Forages in open water and areas of shallow water; dives in synchronized flocks for mollusks and crustaceans, but consumes its larger prey above the surface.

FLIGHT: strong flight with relatively slow wing-beats; flies in undulating lines, low over the water.

BROODING FEMALE
Females line their nests with down and cover the eggs with it when leaving the nest.

SIMILAR SPECIES

KING EIDER ♀
smaller overall;
see p.48
flatter crown
thicker neck
shorter, more concave bill

SURF SCOTER ♀
see p.51
shorter, wedge-shaped bill
dark brown overall

OCCURRENCE
Arctic breeder, in both New and Old Worlds, on coastal islands, peninsulas, seldom along freshwater lakes and deltas. One population is sedentary in the Hudson and James Bays region; others winter in the Bering Sea, Hudson Bay, northern British Columbia, Gulf of St. Lawrence, and along the Atlantic Coast.

| Length **19½–28in (50–71cm)** | Wingspan **31–42in (80–108cm)** | Weight **2¾–5¾lb (1.2–2.6kg)** |
| Social **Flocks/Colonies** | Lifespan **Up to 21 years** | Status **Secure** |

DATE SEEN	WHERE	NOTES

49

Order **Anseriformes**	Family **Anatidae**	Species *Histrionicus histrionicus*

Harlequin Duck

MALE — dark wings above and below

pointed tail **IN FLIGHT** short neck

dark sooty brown overall — broad face with whitish patches

scaly, pale brown lower breast and belly

FEMALE

slate-blue with bright rusty sides — two white bands perpendicular to breast and neck — two white facial spots — rust crown stripes — very round head — steep forehead — small dark bill

white bands down either side of back

white crescent

MALE

This small, hardy duck is a superbly skillful swimmer, diving to forage on the bottom of turbulent streams for its favorite insect prey. Despite the male's unmistakable plumage at close range, it looks very dark from a distance. With head and long tail held high, in winter it can be found among crashing waves, alongside larger and bigger-billed Surf and White-winged Scoters, who feed in the same habitat.

VOICE Male a high-pitched squeak earning it the nickname "sea mice"; female's call a raspy *ekekekekek*.

NESTING Nests near water under vegetation or base of tree; also tree cavities; 3–9 eggs; 1 brood; April–September.

FEEDING Dives for insects and their larvae, and fish roe when breeding; in winter, eats mollusks, crustaceans, crabs, snails, fish roe, and barnacles.

FLIGHT: rapid and regular wingbeats; usually flies low over water, in pairs or small groups.

MALE GROUPS
After the breeding season, many males may gather and forage together.

PAIR IN FLIGHT
Note the crisp white markings on the slate-blue male in flight.

OCCURRENCE
Breeds near rushing coastal and mountain streams. During winter, found in small groups or mixed in with other sea ducks close to the shore, particularly along shallow rocky shorelines, jetties, rocky beaches, and headlands. Eastern populations have a restricted range. Also breeds in Iceland.

SIMILAR SPECIES

SURF SCOTER ♀ see p.51 — large, triangular bill — flatter head — elongated body

BUFFLEHEAD ♀ see p.55 — larger head — oblong patch on cheek

Length **13–21½in (33–54cm)**	Wingspan **22–26in (56–66cm)**	Weight **18–26oz (500–750g)**
Social **Small flocks**	Lifespan **Unknown**	Status **Secure**

DATE SEEN	WHERE	NOTES

Order **Anseriformes**	Family **Anatidae**	Species *Melanitta perspicillata*

Surf Scoter

MALE
black wings overall
IN FLIGHT
compact body

whitish facial patches
dark brown overall
FEMALE

all-dark bill

black forehead
small white patch on nape
IMMATURE MALE (2ND WINTER)

white eye
white forehead
large, black spot on bill

velvety black feathers
white nape
long tail feathers
swollen, orange bill with white base
MALE

S urf Scoters, one of three species of scoters living in North America, migrate up and down both coasts, often with other species. They take their name from the way they dive for mollusks on the sea floor, in shallow coastal waters, through heavy surf. Groups often dive and resurface in unison. Black and Surf Scoters can be difficult to tell apart as both have all-black wings. The underside of the Surf Scoter's wings are uniform black, whereas the Black Scoter has gray flight feathers, which contrast with the black underwing feathers.

VOICE Normally silent; courting male's variety of calls includes liquid gurgled *puk-puk*, bubbled whistles, and low croaks; female call a harsh *crahh*, reminiscent of a crow.

NESTING Ground nest lined with down and vegetation on brushy tundra, often under low branches of a conifer tree; 5–10 eggs; 1 brood; May–September.

FEEDING Dives for mollusks and other aquatic invertebrates.

FLIGHT: strong wingbeats; flies in bunched up groups; male's wings hum or whistle in flight.

DISTINGUISHING FEATURES
The white forehead and bright orange bill, in addition to the red orange legs and toes, identify male Surf Scoters.

SIMILAR SPECIES

GREATER SCAUP ♀
see p.46
no white patches on cheek
thinner bill

WHITE-WINGED SCOTER ♀
see p.52
long, sloping forehead
longer bill

OCCURRENCE
Nests on lake islands in forested regions of interior Alaska and northern Canada. Nonbreeders in summer and adults in winter are strictly coastal, with numbers decreasing from north to south along the Pacific Coast. In the East, most overwinter in the mid-Atlantic Coast region.

Length **19–23½in (48–60cm)**	Wingspan **30in (77cm)**	Weight **1¾–2¾lb (0.8–1.2kg)**
Social **Flocks/Pairs**	Lifespan **Unknown**	Status **Declining**

DATE SEEN	WHERE	NOTES

Order **Anseriformes**	Family **Anatidae**	Species *Melanitta deglandi*

White-winged Scoter

white wing patch

ADULT

appears all-black in flight

IN FLIGHT

long, sloping head

blackish bill

two distinct pale patches on face

IMMATURE FEMALE

black knob at base of bill

dark brown overall

feathers extend onto the bill

FEMALE

upturned white "comma" around white eye

all black with brownish sides

pinkish red to yellow-orange bill

MALE

The White-winged Scoter is the largest of the three scoters. When visible, the white wing patch makes identification easy. Females are quite similar to immature male and female Surf Scoters and can be identified by head shape, extent of bill feathering, and shape of white areas on the face. When diving, this scoter leaps forward and up, arching its neck, and opens its wings when entering the water. Underwater, White-winged Scoters open their wings to propel and stabilize themselves.

VOICE Mostly silent; courting males emit a whistling note; female call a growly *karr*.

NESTING Depression lined with twigs and down in dense thickets, often far from water; 8–9 eggs; 1 brood; June–September.

FEEDING Dives for mollusks and crustaceans; sometimes eats fish and aquatic plants.

FLIGHT: direct with rapid wingbeats; flies low over the water in small groups.

WHITE FLASH IN FLIGHT
Scoters often migrate or feed in mixed flocks. The white wing patches are striking in flight.

SIMILAR SPECIES

SURF SCOTER ♂
see p.51

white forehead

white nape

BLACK SCOTER ♂
see p.53

yellow-orange knob

black overall

OCCURRENCE
Majority breed in dense colonies in interior Alaska and western Canada on large freshwater or brackish lakes or ponds, sometimes on saltwater lakes. Winters along both coasts, large bays, inlets, and estuaries. Rarely winters inland, except on the Great Lakes.

Length **19–23in (48–58cm)**	Wingspan **31in (80cm)**	Weight **2¾–4¾lb (0.9–1.9kg)**
Social **Flocks/Colonies**	Lifespan **Up to 18 years**	Status **Vulnerable**

DATE SEEN	WHERE	NOTES

Order **Anseriformes**	Family **Anatidae**	Species *Melanitta americana*

Black Scoter

pale, silvery gray flight feathers

black lining on underwings

ADULT

IN FLIGHT

dark cap

pale brownish gray cheeks

black bill with small yellow patch

smaller bill

dark brown overall

FEMALE

dark brown eye

entirely black, heavily built body

conspicuous yellow-orange knob on black bill

MALE

Black Scoters, the most vocal of the scoters, are medium-sized sea ducks that winter along both coasts of North America. Riding high on the waves, they form dense flocks, often segregated by gender. While swimming, the Black Scoter sometimes flaps its wings and while doing so drops its neck low down, unlike the other two scoters. This scoter breeds in two widely separated subarctic breeding areas and is one of the least studied ducks in North America. The Common Scoter was once thought to be the Black Scoter's Eurasian subspecies, but it has now been split into a separate species.

VOICE Male call a high-whistled *peeew*; female a low raspy *kraaa*.
NESTING Depression lined with grass and down, often in tall grass on tundra; 5–10 eggs; 1 brood; May–September.
FEEDING Dives in saltwater for mollusks, crustaceans, and plant matter; feeds on aquatic insects and freshwater mussels.

FLIGHT: strong wingbeats; male's wings make whistling sound during takeoff.

YELLOW BILL
Male Black Scoters are distinctive with their black plumage and yellow bill-knob.

SIMILAR SPECIES

SURF SCOTER ♀
see p.51

flatter crown

two whitish patches

larger bill

WHITE-WINGED SCOTER ♀
see p.52

more sloping head

longer bill

OCCURRENCE
Breeding habitat is somewhat varied, but is generally close to fairly shallow, small lakes. Winters along both coasts. Populations wintering farther north prefer water over cobbles, gravel, or offshore ledges, whereas in southern locations, sandier habitats are chosen.

Length **17–21in (43–53cm)**	Wingspan **31–35in (79–90cm)**	Weight **1¾–2¾lb (0.8–1.2kg)**
Social **Flocks**	Lifespan **Unknown**	Status **Declining**

DATE SEEN	WHERE	NOTES

Order **Anseriformes**	Family **Anatidae**	Species *Clangula hyemalis*

Long-tailed Duck

MALE (WINTER)

smudgy face pattern

JUVENILE (WINTER)
gray face

blackish head, neck, and breast

MALE (SUMMER)

white head

white eye-ring

large, brown spot on side of head

pinkish band on bill

black breastband

white shoulder feathers

all-dark wings

FEMALE (WINTER)
dark back
brown breastband

FEMALE (SUMMER)
mostly dark brown back, flanks, head, and breast
small, dark bill

MALE (WINTER)
IN FLIGHT
chunky body

FEMALE (WINTER)
short tail
whitish underparts

long dark tail

The Long-tailed Duck is a small, pudgy sea duck with a wide range of plumages depending on the season and the sex of the bird. The male has two extremely long tail feathers, which are often held up in the air like a pennant. The male's loud calls are quite musical, and, when heard from a flock, have a chorus-like quality, hence the name *Clangula*, which is Latin for "loud." This species can dive for a prolonged period of time, and can reach depths of 200ft (60m), making it one of the deepest diving ducks. Its three-part molt is more complex than that of other ducks.

VOICE Male call a *ang-ang-eeeooo* with yodeling quality; female barking *urk* or *uk* alarm call.

NESTING Shallow depression in ground lined with plant matter; 6–9 eggs; 1 brood; May–September.

FEEDING Dives to bottom of freshwater or saltwater habitats for mollusks, crustaceans, insects, fish, and roe.

FLIGHT: flies low over the water, somewhat erratically, with fast, fluttering wingbeats.

UNMISTAKABLE MALE
In winter, dark wings, a white body with black breast-band, and a long tail make this male unmistakable.

SIMILAR SPECIES

BUFFLEHEAD ♀
see p.55
white wing patch
white cheek patch

BLACK GUILLEMOT ❄
see p.155
pale rump
white wing patches

OCCURRENCE
Breeds in Arctic and subarctic, nesting in small groups on islands and peninsulas on lakes, less commonly on tundra and freshwater ponds on islands. Winters mostly along rocky coasts and headlands, protected bays, or on large freshwater lakes.

Length **14–23in (35–58cm)**	Wingspan **28in (72cm)**	Weight **18–39oz (500–1,100g)**
Social **Flocks**	Lifespan **Up to 22 years**	Status **Declining**

DATE SEEN	WHERE	NOTES

Order **Anseriformes**	Family **Anatidae**	Species *Bucephala albeola*

Bufflehead 🔊

black-and-white outer wings

MALE

gray underwings with white patch

pinkish orange legs

IN FLIGHT

oval, white cheek patch

dark brown head

dark, unmarked back

all-dark wings

grayish brown sides

FEMALE

front part of head and neck has iridescent green-and-purple gloss

large, triangular, white patch on head

angled forehead

black back

small, narrow, gray bill

white breast and flanks

MALE

The smallest diving duck in North America, the Bufflehead is a close relative of the Common and Barrow's Goldeneyes. Males make a bold statement with their striking head pattern. In flight, males resemble the larger Common Goldeneye, yet the large white area on their head makes them easy to distinguish. The Common Goldeneye's wings create a whirring sound in flight whereas the Bufflehead's do not. The northern limit of the Bufflehead's breeding range corresponds to that of the Northern Flicker, as the ducks usually nest in abandoned Flicker cavities.

VOICE Male a low growl or squeal; chattering during breeding; female mostly silent except during courtship or calling to chicks.

NESTING Cavity nester, no nesting material added, near water; 7–9 eggs; 1 brood; April–September.

FEEDING Dives for aquatic invertebrates: usually insects in freshwater, mollusks and crustaceans in saltwater; also eats seeds.

FLIGHT: very rapid wingbeats; no flight sound, unlike Goldeneyes.

IMMEDIATE TAKEOFF
Unlike other diving ducks, the small, compact Bufflehead can takeoff almost vertically.

SIMILAR SPECIES

HOODED MERGANSER ♂
see p.58

smaller, with white cheek patch

RUDDY DUCK ♂ ❋
see p.61

dark cap

longer bill

larger size

OCCURRENCE
Breeds in forest from Alaska to eastern Canada, in woodlands near small lakes and permanent ponds, where young are raised. Winters largely along the Pacific and Atlantic Coasts with lower densities scattered across the continent, south to northern Mexico, and in Bermuda.

Length **12½–15½in (32–39cm)**	Wingspan **21½–24in (54–61cm)**	Weight **10–18oz (275–500g)**
Social **Flocks**	Lifespan **Up to 15 years**	Status **Secure**

DATE SEEN	WHERE	NOTES
....	....	....
....	....	....
....	....	....
....	....	....
....	....	....

Order **Anseriformes**	Family **Anatidae**	Species *Bucephala clangula*

Common Goldeneye

white patches on
flanks and wings

white wing patch
with two bars

FEMALE

warm brown
head

bright
yellow eye

**IMMATURE MALE
(1ST WINTER)**

white
collar

mostly white
inner wing

FEMALE

**MALE
(WINTER)**

iridescent
green
head

large,
round
white spot

dusky
underwing

extensive white
shoulder feathers

IN FLIGHT

**MALE
(WINTER)**

Common Goldeneyes closely resemble Barrow's Goldeneyes. Found in North America and Eurasia, this is a medium-sized, compact diving duck. It is aggressive and very competitive with members of its own species, as well as other cavity-nesting ducks. It regularly lays eggs in the nests of other species—a behavior that is almost parasitic. Before diving, the Common Goldeneye flattens its feathers in preparation for underwater foraging. The female's head shape changes according to her posture.
VOICE Courting males make a faint *peent* call; females a harsh *gack* or repeated *cuk* calls.
NESTING Cavity nester in holes made by other birds, including Pileated Woodpeckers, in broken branches or hollow trees; also commonly uses nest boxes; 4–13 eggs; 1 brood; April–September.
FEEDING Dives during breeding season for insects; in winter, mollusks and crustaceans; sometimes eats fish and plant matter.

FLIGHT: rapid with fast wingbeats; male's wings make a tinkling sound in flight.

MALE TAKING OFF
Quite a long takeoff, involving energetically running on the water, leaves a trail of spray.

SIMILAR SPECIES

BUFFLEHEAD ♀
see p.55

smaller
overall

white oval
patch
behind eye

BARROW'S GOLDENEYE ♂
see p.57

smaller bill

large crescent
on face

OCCURRENCE
Breeds along wetlands, lakes, and rivers with clear water in northern forests, where large trees provide appropriate nest cavities. Winters across continent, with highest densities located from north New England to the mid-Atlantic on coastal bays and in the West from coastal southeast Alaska to British Columbia.

Length **15½–20in (40–51cm)**	Wingspan **30–33in (77–83cm)**	Weight **19–44oz (550–1,300g)**
Social **Flocks**	Lifespan **Up to 15 years**	Status **Secure**

DATE SEEN	WHERE	NOTES

| Order **Anseriformes** | Family **Anatidae** | Species *Bucephala islandica* |

Barrow's Goldeneye

white wing
patch

MALE
dark
underwings

IN FLIGHT

narrow, white
wing patch

**FEMALE
(BREEDING)**

darker brown
head

steep forehead

small, yellow
bill

black head with
purple gloss

sloping
crown

grayish brown
wing feathers

white
neck

**IMMATURE MALE
(1ST WINTER)**

white
"piano key"
markings
on sides

bold, white
facial
crescent

MALE

Barrow's Goldeneye is a slightly larger, darker version of the Common Goldeneye. Although the female can be identified by her different head structure, her bill color varies seasonally and geographically. Eastern Barrow's have blacker bills with less yellow, and western populations have entirely yellow bills, which darken in summer. During the breeding season, the majority of Barrow's Goldeneyes are found in mountainous regions of northwestern North America.

VOICE Males normally silent; courting males grunt *ka-KAA*; females *cuc* call, slightly higher pitched than Common Goldeneye.
NESTING Tree cavity in holes formed by Pileated Woodpeckers, often broken limbs or hollow trees; also uses nest boxes; 6–12 eggs; 1 brood; April–September.
FEEDING Dives in summer for insects, some fish, and roe; in winter, mainly mollusks and crustaceans; some plant matter.

FLIGHT: rapid flight with fast, deep wingbeats; flies near water surface on short flights.

COURTING DISPLAY
A male thrusts his head back and gives a guttural call. His legs then kick back, driving him forward.

SIMILAR SPECIES

GREATER SCAUP ♀
browner overall;
see p.46

longer
neck

white
patch

COMMON GOLDENEYE ♀
see p.56

warmer
brown head

more
triangular
head

OCCURRENCE
Winters along the Pacific Coast between southeast Alaska and Washington, with small populations in eastern Canada. Smaller numbers found inland from the lower Colorado River to Yellowstone National Park. Eastern population is localized in winter with the highest count in St. Lawrence estuary.

| Length **17–19in (43–48cm)** | Wingspan **28–30in (71–76cm)** | Weight **17–46oz (475–1,300g)** |
| Social **Flocks** | Lifespan **Up to 18 years** | Status **Secure** |

DATE SEEN	WHERE	NOTES

Order **Anseriformes**	Family **Anatidae**	Species *Lophodytes cucullatus*

Hooded Merganser

triangular wings

black-and-white inner wing patch

MALE (BREEDING)

long tail **IN FLIGHT**

reddish-tinged crest (folded)

brownish buff eye

yellow-based, thin, black bill

brownish gray flanks **FEMALE**

striking yellow eye

small, gray-brown crest (raised)

MALE (ECLIPSE)

longish tail, often raised

crested black-and-white head (crest not raised)

yellow eye

thin, black, serrated bill

black back

white breast

MALE (BREEDING)

warm brown flanks

bold vertical bars

This dapper, miniature fish-eater is the smallest of the three mergansers. Both male and female Hooded Mergansers have crests that they can raise or flatten. When the male raises his crest, the thin horizontal white stripe turns into a gorgeous white fan, surrounded by black. Although easily identified when swimming, the Hooded Merganser and the Wood Duck can be confused when seen in flight since they both are fairly small with bushy heads and long tails.

VOICE Normally silent; during courtship, males produce a low, growly, descending *pah-hwaaaaa*, reminiscent of a frog; females give a soft *rrrep*.

NESTING Cavity nester; nest lined with down feathers in a tree or box close to or over water; 6–15 eggs; 1 brood; February–June.

FEEDING Dives for fish, aquatic insects, and crayfish, preferably in clear and shallow freshwaters, but also in brackish waters.

FLIGHT: low, fast, and direct; shallow wingbeats; quiet whirring noise produced by wings.

FANHEAD SPECTACULAR
The male's magnificent black-and-white fan of a crest is like a beacon in the late afternoon light.

SIMILAR SPECIES

WOOD DUCK ♀ see p.33

blue wing patch

bold, white eye-ring

RED-BREASTED MERGANSER ♀ see p.60

steel gray-and-white plumage

rustier head with ragged crest

OCCURRENCE
Prefers forested small ponds, marshes, or slow-moving streams during the breeding season. During winter, occurs in shallow water in both fresh- and saltwater bays, estuaries, rivers, streams, ponds, freshwater marshes, and flooded sloughs.

Length **15½–19½in (40–49cm)**	Wingspan **23½–26in (60–66cm)**	Weight **16–31oz (450–875g)**
Social **Small flocks**	Lifespan **Unknown**	Status **Secure**

DATE SEEN	WHERE	NOTES

Order **Anseriformes**	Family **Anatidae**	Species *Mergus merganser*

Common Merganser

dark outer wing

gray-and-white inner wing

reddish brown head

FEMALE

bright, rusty brown head

silver-gray upperparts

black-tipped red bill

FEMALE

small white spot above eye

short, ragged crest

JUVENILE

thin, black bar

gray rump and tail

MALE (NONBREEDING)

black head

IN FLIGHT

all-white or tinged pink underparts

iridescent blackish green head

long nape feathers

black center

black eye

reddish orange hooked bill

serrated sides on bill

white breast and underparts

MALE (BREEDING)

The largest of the three merganser species in North America, the Common Merganser is called a Goosander in the UK. This large fish-eater is common and widespread, particularly in the northern portion of its range. It is often found in big flocks on lakes or smaller groups along rivers. It spends most of its time on the water, using its serrated bill to catch fish underwater.
VOICE Mostly silent, except when alarmed or during courtship; females give a low-pitched harsh *karr* or *gruk*, the latter also given in series; during courtship, males emit a high-pitched, bell-like note and other twangy notes; alarm call a hoarse *grrr* or *wak*.
NESTING Cavity nester sometimes high in trees; uses nest boxes, nests on ground; 6–17 eggs; 1 brood; April–September.
FEEDING Eats mostly fish (especially fond of trout and salmon, but also carp and catfish), aquatic invertebrates, frogs, small mammals, birds, and plants.

FLIGHT: fast with shallow wingbeats; often flying low over the water.

FEEDING ON THE MOVE
This female Common Merganser is trying to swallow, head-first, a rather large fish.

OCCURRENCE
Breeds in northern forests from Alaska to Newfoundland; winters south to north-central Mexico. It winters farther north than most other waterfowl as long as water remains open. Prefers fresh- to saltwater locations.

SIMILAR SPECIES

COMMON GOLDENEYE ♂
see p.56

white patch

black-and-white pattern

RED-BREASTED MERGANSER ♀
see p.60

smaller, more lightly built

thinner bill

Length **21½–28in (54–71cm)**	Wingspan **34in (86cm)**	Weight **1¾–4¾lb (0.8–2.1kg)**
Social **Flocks**	Lifespan **Up to 13 years**	Status **Secure**

DATE SEEN	WHERE	NOTES

| Order **Anseriformes** | Family **Anatidae** | Species **Mergus serrator** |

Red-breasted Merganser

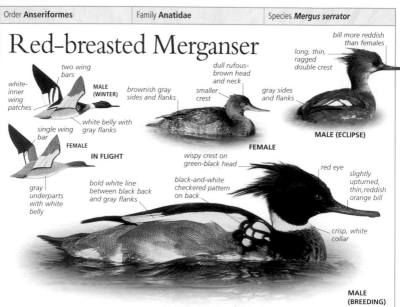

bill more reddish than females

long, thin, ragged double crest

MALE (ECLIPSE)

dull rufous-brown head and neck

smaller crest

gray sides and flanks

FEMALE

two wing bars

white-inner wing patches

MALE (WINTER)

brownish gray sides and flanks

white belly with gray flanks

single wing bar

FEMALE

IN FLIGHT

gray underparts with white belly

bold white line between black back and gray flanks

wispy crest on green-black head

black-and-white checkered pattern on back

red eye

slightly upturned, thin, reddish orange bill

crisp, white collar

MALE (BREEDING)

The Red-breasted Merganser, like the other saw-billed mergansers, is an elegant fish-eating duck. Both sexes are easily recognized by their long, sparse, somewhat ragged-looking double crest. Red-breasted Mergansers are smaller than Common Mergansers, but much larger than the Hooded. The Red-breasted Merganser, unlike the other two mergansers, nests on the ground, in loose colonies, often among gulls and terns, and is protected by its neighbors.

VOICE During courtship males make a raucous *yeow-yeow* call; females emit a raspy *krrr-krrr*.

NESTING Shallow depression on ground lined with down and plant material, near water; 5–11 eggs; 1 brood; May–July.

FEEDING Dives for small fish such as herring and minnows; also salmon eggs; at times flocks coordinate and drive fish together.

FLIGHT: fast flying duck with very rapid, regular, and shallow flapping.

KEEPING CLOSE
Red-breasted Mergansers are gregarious at all times of year, often feeding in loose flocks.

SIMILAR SPECIES

HOODED MERGANSER ♀
see p.58

fuller, cinnamon-tinged crest

darker back

smaller overall

COMMON MERGANSER ♀
see p.59

smaller bill

full crest

larger and more robust

rusty-red head

white breast and chin

OCCURRENCE
Most northern range of all the mergansers, nests across Arctic and subarctic regions, tundra and northerly forests, along coasts, inland lakes, river banks, marsh edges, and coastal islands. Winters farther south than other mergansers, mostly in protected bays, estuaries, or on the Great Lakes.

| Length **20–25in (51–64cm)** | Wingspan **26–29in (66–74cm)** | Weight **1¾–2¾lb (0.8–1.3kg)** |
| Social **Flocks/Colonies** | Lifespan **Up to 9 years** | Status **Secure** |

DATE SEEN	WHERE	NOTES

| Order **Anseriformes** | Family **Anatidae** | Species *Oxyura jamaicensis* |

Ruddy Duck 🔊

broad, short wings with whitish wing linings

pale belly

MALE (BREEDING) IN FLIGHT

dull gray-brown two-tone body

duller head

blackish bill

MALE (NONBREEDING)

arched dark line on cheek

dark bill

brownish upperparts

paler flanks

FEMALE

black cap and nape

large head

rich cinnamon body and neck

long tail, often erect

bright blue bill, slightly knobby at base

large, white cheek patches

MALE (BREEDING)

Small and stiff-tailed, the Ruddy Duck is comical in both its appearance and behavior. Both sexes often hold their tail in a cocked position, especially when sleeping. During courtship displays, the male points its long tail skyward while rapidly thumping its electric blue bill against its chest, ending the performance with an odd, bubbling sound. In another display, males make a popping sound by slapping their toes on the water's surface. Large toes, on legs set far back on its body, make the Ruddy Duck an excellent swimmer and diver; however, on land it is perhaps one of the most awkward of diving ducks. Females are known to push themselves along instead of walking.

VOICE Females give a nasal *raanh* and high-pitched *eeek*; males vocally silent, but make popping noises with toes.

NESTING Platform, bowl-shaped nest built over water in thick emergent vegetation, rarely on land; 6–10 eggs; 1 brood; May–September.

FEEDING Dives for aquatic insects, larvae, crustaceans, and other invertebrates, particularly when breeding; during winter, also eats plants.

FLIGHT: rapid and direct, with fast wingbeats; not very agile in flight, which seems labored.

HEAVY HEAD
A female "sitting" on the water streamlines her body before she dives, making her look large-headed.

SIMILAR SPECIES

MASKED DUCK ♂ see p.444

black tip to bill

black face

ruddy-colored back with black streaks

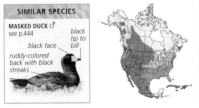

OCCURRENCE
Breeds in the prairie pothole region in wetland habitats; marshes, ponds, reservoirs, and other open shallow water with emergent vegetation and open areas. Majority winter on freshwater habitats from ponds to large lakes; smaller numbers found on brackish coastal marshes, bays, and estuaries.

Length **14–17in (35–43cm)**	Wingspan **22–24in (56–62cm)**	Weight **11–30oz (300–850g)**
Social **Flocks**	Lifespan **Up to 13 years**	Status **Secure**

DATE SEEN	WHERE	NOTES

Order **Anseriformes**	Family **Anatidae**	Species *Alopochen aegyptiaca*

Egyptian Goose

white forewing

long neck

black-and-white underwing

IN FLIGHT

dark brown face patch

stubby pink bill

large white wing patch

pale breast and underside

brown with white patches

gray bill

JUVENILE

ADULT

long pink legs

FLIGHT: low, quick, powerful with regular deep wingbeats; may flutter up to a high perch such as the branch of a tree.

Originally from Africa, Egyptian Geese have become naturalized in North America following "escapes" from ornamental wildfowl collections. Many were imported in the late 19th century but breeding in the wild was not known until 1967 (California) and the 1980s (Florida). They have not spread very widely yet, but have become common in parts of Texas, where they are often seen on golf courses and near city-park lakes. While increasing numbers in the UK are a cause of concern, in North America, there is no evidence that they are a threat to native wildlife. Nevertheless, numbers are controlled in some districts.

VOICE Staccato, guttural quacking notes; noisy if disturbed near nest.

NESTING Nests in tree hole up to 65ft (20m) high; 6–10 eggs; 1 brood; May–June.

FEEDING Eats roots, shoots, seeds, and other vegetable matter from shallow water and margins of freshwater.

PUZZLING NEWCOMERS
Unexpectedly large, pale birds swimming in a lake or grazing on grassy spaces nearby can be mistaken for other species. The pale head and dark mask indicate Egyptian Geese.

OCCURRENCE
Found in wet grasslands and marshy areas with old trees, and in nearby areas of short grass; most common in southern Florida, southeastern Texas, and around Los Angeles, California.

Length **25–29in (63–73cm)**	Wingspan **3½–4¼ft (1.1–1.3cm)**	Weight **3½–5½lb (1.5–2.3kg)**
Social **Small flocks**	Lifespan **10–20 years**	Status **Secure**

DATE SEEN	WHERE	NOTES

QUAILS, GROUSE, TURKEYS, AND RELATIVES

THIS DIVERSE AND ADAPTABLE group of birds thrives in habitats ranging from hot desert to frozen tundra. Galliforms spend most of their time on the ground, springing loudly into the air when alarmed.

NEW WORLD QUAILS
Among the most terrestrial of all galliforms, quails are renowned for their great sociability, often forming large family groups, or "coveys," of up to 100 birds. The Northern Bobwhite is the only quail species found in the East, and ranges over a variety of habitats. Each of the five species found in western North America lives in a specific habitat or at a particular elevation.

DRESSED TO THRILL
With its striking plumage, Gambel's Quail is one of the best-known desert birds in southwestern North America.

GROUSE
The most diverse and widespread birds in the order Galliforms in North America, the 12 different species of grouse can be divided into three groups based on their preferred habitats. Forest grouse include the Ruffed Grouse in the East, the Spruce Grouse in the North, and the Sooty Grouse and Dusky Grouse in the West.

Prairie grouse, including the Sharp-tailed Grouse, are found throughout the middle of the continent. All three tundra and mountaintop grouse or ptarmigans are found in the extreme North and the Rockies. Grouse often possess patterns that match their surroundings, providing camouflage from both animal and human predators.

GRASSLAND GROUSE
The aptly named Sharp-tailed Grouse is locally common in western prairies. It searches for grasshoppers in the summer.

PHEASANTS AND PARTRIDGES
These Eurasian galliforms were introduced into North America in the 19th and 20th centuries to provide additional targets for recreational hunters. While some introductions failed, species such as the colorful Ring-necked Pheasant adapted well and now thrive in established populations.

SNOW BIRD
The Rock Ptarmigan's white winter plumage camouflages it against the snow, helping hide it from predators.

Order **Galliformes**	Family **Odontophoridae**	Species **Colinus virginianus**

Northern Bobwhite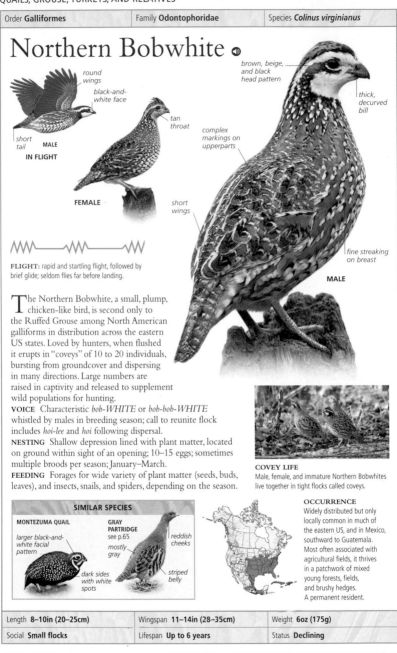

round wings

black-and-white face

brown, beige, and black head pattern

thick, decurved bill

tan throat

complex markings on upperparts

short tail **MALE**
IN FLIGHT

FEMALE

short wings

fine streaking on breast

MALE

FLIGHT: rapid and startling flight, followed by brief glide; seldom flies far before landing.

The Northern Bobwhite, a small, plump, chicken-like bird, is second only to the Ruffed Grouse among North American galliforms in distribution across the eastern US states. Loved by hunters, when flushed it erupts in "coveys" of 10 to 20 individuals, bursting from groundcover and dispersing in many directions. Large numbers are raised in captivity and released to supplement wild populations for hunting.

VOICE Characteristic *bob-WHITE* or *bob-bob-WHITE* whistled by males in breeding season; call to reunite flock includes *hoi-lee* and *hoi* following dispersal.

NESTING Shallow depression lined with plant matter, located on ground within sight of an opening; 10–15 eggs; sometimes multiple broods per season; January–March.

FEEDING Forages for wide variety of plant matter (seeds, buds, leaves), and insects, snails, and spiders, depending on the season.

COVEY LIFE
Male, female, and immature Northern Bobwhites live together in tight flocks called coveys.

SIMILAR SPECIES

MONTEZUMA QUAIL

larger black-and-white facial pattern

dark sides with white spots

GRAY PARTRIDGE
see p.65

mostly gray

reddish cheeks

striped belly

OCCURRENCE
Widely distributed but only locally common in much of the eastern US, and in Mexico, southward to Guatemala. Most often associated with agricultural fields, it thrives in a patchwork of mixed young forests, fields, and brushy hedges. A permanent resident.

Length **8–10in (20–25cm)**	Wingspan **11–14in (28–35cm)**	Weight **6oz (175g)**
Social **Small flocks**	Lifespan **Up to 6 years**	Status **Declining**

DATE SEEN	WHERE	NOTES

| Order **Galliformes** | Family **Phasianidae** | Species ***Perdix perdix*** |

Gray Partridge

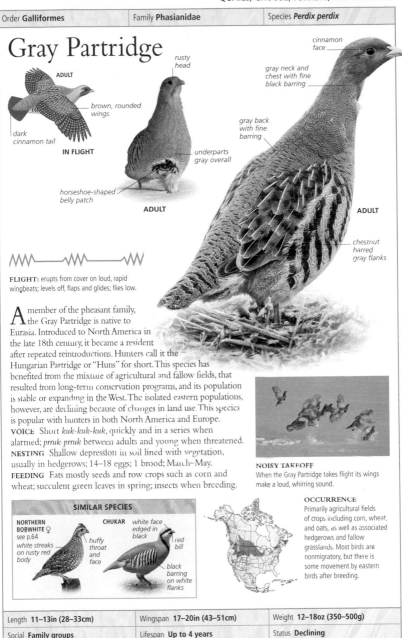

rusty head

cinnamon face

gray neck and chest with fine black barring

ADULT

brown, rounded wings

gray back with fine barring

dark cinnamon tail

IN FLIGHT

underparts gray overall

horseshoe-shaped belly patch

ADULT

ADULT

chestnut barred gray flanks

FLIGHT: erupts from cover on loud, rapid wingbeats; levels off, flaps and glides; flies low.

A member of the pheasant family, the Gray Partridge is native to Eurasia. Introduced to North America in the late 18th century, it became a resident after repeated reintroductions. Hunters call it the Hungarian Partridge or "Huns" for short. This species has benefited from the mixture of agricultural and fallow fields, that resulted from long-term conservation programs, and its population is stable or expanding in the West. The isolated eastern populations, however, are declining because of changes in land use. This species is popular with hunters in both North America and Europe.
VOICE Short *kuk-kuk-kuk*, quickly and in a series when alarmed; *prruk-prruk* between adults and young when threatened.
NESTING Shallow depression in soil lined with vegetation, usually in hedgerows; 14–18 eggs; 1 brood; March–May.
FEEDING Eats mostly seeds and row crops such as corn and wheat; succulent green leaves in spring; insects when breeding.

NOISY TAKEOFF
When the Gray Partridge takes flight its wings make a loud, whirring sound.

SIMILAR SPECIES

NORTHERN BOBWHITE ♀ see p.64
white streaks on rusty red body

CHUKAR white face edged in black
buffy throat and face
red bill
black barring on white flanks

OCCURRENCE
Primarily agricultural fields of crops including corn, wheat, and oats, as well as associated hedgerows and fallow grasslands. Most birds are nonmigratory, but there is some movement by eastern birds after breeding.

| Length **11–13in (28–33cm)** | Wingspan **17–20in (43–51cm)** | Weight **12–18oz (350–500g)** |
| Social **Family groups** | Lifespan **Up to 4 years** | Status **Declining** |

DATE SEEN	WHERE	NOTES

Order **Galliformes**	Family **Phasianidae**	Species **Phasianus colchicus**

Ring-necked Pheasant 🔊

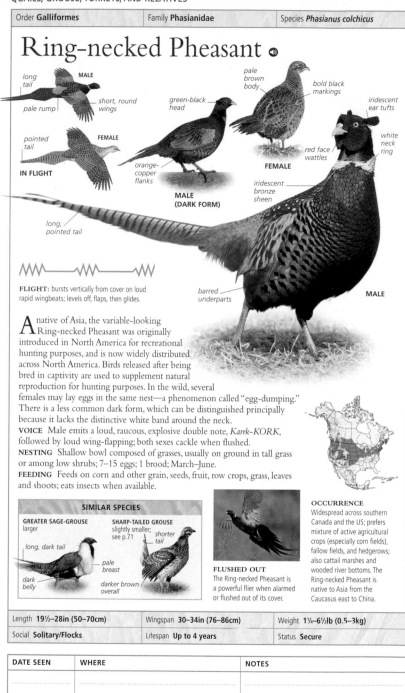

MALE
long tail
short, round wings
pale rump

FEMALE
pointed tail

IN FLIGHT

orange-copper flanks

green-black head

pale brown body
bold black markings

iridescent ear tufts

red face wattles

white neck ring

FEMALE

MALE (DARK FORM)

iridescent bronze sheen

long, pointed tail

FLIGHT: bursts vertically from cover on loud rapid wingbeats; levels off, flaps, then glides.

barred underparts

MALE

A native of Asia, the variable-looking Ring-necked Pheasant was originally introduced in North America for recreational hunting purposes, and is now widely distributed across North America. Birds released after being bred in captivity are used to supplement natural reproduction for hunting purposes. In the wild, several females may lay eggs in the same nest—a phenomenon called "egg-dumping." There is a less common dark form, which can be distinguished principally because it lacks the distinctive white band around the neck.

VOICE Male emits a loud, raucous, explosive double note, *Karrk-KORK*, followed by loud wing-flapping; both sexes cackle when flushed.

NESTING Shallow bowl composed of grasses, usually on ground in tall grass or among low shrubs; 7–15 eggs; 1 brood; March–June.

FEEDING Feeds on corn and other grain, seeds, fruit, row crops, grass, leaves and shoots; eats insects when available.

SIMILAR SPECIES

GREATER SAGE-GROUSE larger
long, dark tail
dark belly

SHARP-TAILED GROUSE slightly smaller; see p.71
shorter tail
pale breast
darker brown overall

FLUSHED OUT
The Ring-necked Pheasant is a powerful flier when alarmed or flushed out of its cover.

OCCURRENCE
Widespread across southern Canada and the US; prefers mixture of active agricultural crops (especially corn fields), fallow fields, and hedgerows; also cattail marshes and wooded river bottoms. The Ring-necked Pheasant is native to Asia from the Caucasus east to China.

Length **19½–28in (50–70cm)**	Wingspan **30–34in (76–86cm)**	Weight **1¼–6½lb (0.5–3kg)**
Social **Solitary/Flocks**	Lifespan **Up to 4 years**	Status **Secure**

DATE SEEN	WHERE	NOTES

| Order **Galliformes** | Family **Phasianidae** | Species ***Bonasa umbellus*** |

Ruffed Grouse 🔊

ADULT (RUFOUS FORM)

IN FLIGHT

brown-barred underparts

rusty tail with black band

spotted gray upperparts

heavy white spotting on brown upperparts

dark patch on neck

raised crest

gray-barred underparts

ADULT (GRAY FORM)

feathered legs

ADULT (RUFOUS FORM)

The Ruffed Grouse is perhaps the most widespread galliform in North America. There are two color forms, rufous and gray, both allowing the birds to remain camouflaged and undetected on the forest floor, until they eventually burst into the air in an explosion of whirring wings. The male is well known for his extraordinary wing beating or "drumming" display, which he performs year-round, but most frequently in the spring.

VOICE Hissing notes, and soft *purrt, purrt, purrt* when alarmed, by both sexes; males "drumming" display when heard from distance resembles small engine starting, *thump...thump thump...thump thump...thuthuthuth*.

NESTING Shallow, leaf-lined bowl set against a tree trunk, rock or fallen log in forest; 6–14 eggs; 1 brood; March–June.

FEEDING Forages on ground for leaves, buds, and fruit; occasionally insects.

FLIGHT: an explosive takeoff, usually at close range, glides for a short distance before landing.

OCCURRENCE
Found in young, mixed forests throughout the northern US and much of Canada except tundra. Southern edge of range extends along higher elevations of the Appalachians and middle levels of the Rocky Mountains, if suitable habitat is available.

SIMILAR SPECIES

SPRUCE GROUSE ♀
smaller overall; see p.68

rusty orange tip

shorter tail

DUSKY GROUSE
larger and darker overall

heavier barring on chest

less barring

WARM RED
The rufous form of the Ruffed Grouse is more common in wetter parts of the continent.

| Length **17–20in (43–51cm)** | Wingspan **20–23in (51–58cm)** | Weight **20–22oz (575–625g)** |
| Social **Solitary/Small flocks** | Lifespan **Up to 10 years** | Status **Secure** |

DATE SEEN	WHERE	NOTES

Order **Galliformes**	Family **Phasianidae**	Species **Falcipennis canadensis**

Spruce Grouse

MALE
(FRANKLIN'S)

ADULT

IN FLIGHT

white spots
on black tail

paler
overall

FEMALE
F. c. canadensis
(TAIGA)

heavy barring
on underparts

bright red comb
above eye

black
throat

black
breast

gray
upperparts

heavily
barred
underparts

triangular white
spots on underparts

MALE
F. c. canadensis
(TAIGA)

FEMALE
F. c. franklinii
(FRANKLIN'S)

Perhaps because of the remoteness of their habitat and lack of human contact, Spruce Grouse are not afraid of humans. This lack of wariness when approached has earned them the name "fool hens." Their specialized diet of pine needles causes the intestinal tract to expand in order to accommodate a large volume of food to compensate for its low nutritional value. There are two groups of Spruce Grouse, the Taiga and the Franklin's, both of which have red and gray forms: "taiga" is the eastern one.

VOICE Mostly silent; males clap their wings during courtship display; females often utter long cackle at dawn and dusk.

NESTING Lined with moss, leaves, feathers; often at base of tree; naturally low area in forest floor 4–6 eggs; 1 brood; May–July.

FEEDING Feeds mostly on pine but also spruce needles; will eat insects, leaves, fruit, and seeds when available.

FLIGHT: generally avoids flying; when disturbed, bursts into flight on whirring wings.

RUFOUS BAND
The male "taiga" form displays the thin rufous band on the tip of his tail.

SIMILAR SPECIES

RUFFED GROUSE
see p.67

spotted gray
upperparts

gray-barred
underparts

DUSKY GROUSE

longer,
charcoal-
gray tail

much
larger

grayer
overall

OCCURRENCE
Present year-round in forests dominated by conifers, including jack, lodgepole, spruce, red spruce, black spruce, balsam fir, subalpine fir, hemlock, and cedar. Found from western Alaska to the Atlantic Coast.

Length **14–17in (36–43cm)**	Wingspan **21–23in (53–58cm)**	Weight **16oz (450g)**
Social **Solitary**	Lifespan **Up to 10 years**	Status **Secure**

DATE SEEN	WHERE	NOTES

Order **Galliformes**	Family **Phasianidae**	Species *Lagopus lagopus*

Willow Ptarmigan

white between eye and black bill

red comb

reddish brown body

black tail

ADULT (WINTER)

all-white body

IN FLIGHT

black bill

black bill

MALE (SUMMER)

lacks red comb

rich reddish brown body

yellow-brown body

ADULT (WINTER)

dark, scaly bars

white belly

FEMALE (SUMMER)

MALE (SUMMER)

feathered legs

FLIGHT: strong, rapid wingbeats before gliding; prefers to walk.

The most common and widespread of the three ptarmigan species, the Willow Ptarmigan is the state bird of Alaska. The Willow Ptarmigan is an unusual Galliform species, as male and female remain bonded throughout the chick-rearing process, in which the male is an active participant. The "Red Grouse" of British moors is a subspecies (*L. l. scoticus*) of the Willow Ptarmigan.

VOICE Variety of purrs, clucks, hissing, meowing noises; *Kow-Kow-Kow* call given before flushing, possibly alerting others.

NESTING Shallow bowl scraped in soil, lined with plant matter, protected by overhead cover; 8–10 eggs; 1 brood; March–May.

FEEDING Mostly eats buds, stems, and seeds, but also flowers, insects, and leaves when available.

PERFECT BLEND IN
Its reddish brown upperparts camouflage this summer ptarmigan in the shrubby areas it inhabits.

SIMILAR SPECIES

WHITE-TAILED PTARMIGAN ✿

browner plumage

smaller overall

ROCK PTARMIGAN ✿
see p.70

grayer plumage

darker

OCCURRENCE
Prefers tundra, in Arctic, subarctic and subalpine regions. Thrives in willow thickets along low, moist river corridors; also in the low woodlands of the subarctic tundra.

Length **14–17½in (35–44cm)**	Wingspan **22–24in (56–61cm)**	Weight **15–28oz (425–800g)**
Social **Winter flocks**	Lifespan **Up to 9 years**	Status **Secure**

DATE SEEN	WHERE	NOTES

| Order **Galliformes** | Family **Phasianidae** | Species *Lagopus muta* |

Rock Ptarmigan

brown-and-black barring

black tail

MALE (WINTER)

mostly gray upperparts

white wings

small, round head

red comb

all-white wings

small bill

mottled belly

gray wing patch

IN FLIGHT

FEMALE (SUMMER)

MALE (SUMMER)

"salt-and-pepper" barring on gray upperparts

small, delicate bill

black line between eye and bill

white plumage

FEMALE (WINTER)

MALE (WINTER)

white belly

MALE (SUMMER)

feathered toes

FLIGHT: bursts into flight with rapid wingbeats, followed by gliding and shallow flapping.

The Rock Ptarmigan is the most northern of the three ptarmigan species found in North America. Although some birds make a short migration to more southern wintering grounds, many remain on their breeding grounds year-round. This species is well known for its distinctive seasonal variation in plumage, which helps to camouflage it against its surroundings. Ptarmigan are a common food of the Inuit, who inhabit the same Arctic habitat.
VOICE Quiet; male call a raspy *krrrh*, also growls and clucks.
NESTING Small scrape or natural depression, lined with plant matter, often away from cover; 8–10 eggs; 1 brood; April–June.
FEEDING Feeds on buds, seeds, flowers, and leaves, especially birch and willow; eats insects in summer.

IN BETWEEN PLUMAGE
Various transitional plumage patterns can be seen on the Rock Ptarmigan in spring and fall.

SIMILAR SPECIES

WHITE-TAILED PTARMIGAN ✿ all-white tail in winter;

smaller overall

WILLOW PTARMIGAN ✿ see p.69

larger overall

lighter brown upperparts

OCCURRENCE
Local in dry, rocky tundra and shrubby ridge tops; will use edges of open meadows and dense evergreen stands along fairly high-elevation rivers and streams during winter. Occurs throughout the Northern Hemisphere in Arctic tundra from Iceland to Kamchatka in the Russian Far East.

| Length **12½–15½in (32–40cm)** | Wingspan **19½–23½in (50–60cm)** | Weight **16–23oz (450–650g)** |
| Social **Winter flocks** | Lifespan **Up to 8 years** | Status **Secure** |

DATE SEEN	WHERE	NOTES

| Order **Galliformes** | Family **Phasianidae** | Species *Tympanuchus phasianellus* |

Sharp-tailed Grouse

tan eyebrow

naked pink skin

long central tail feather

heavily mottled brown, white, and black upperparts

ADULT

mottled wings

IN FLIGHT

pale, wedge-shaped tail, with protruding central feathers

white undertail feathers

MALE

brown wings with white dots

white underside, with dark brown arrowheads along flanks

FLIGHT: flushes from hiding with rapid wingbeats, then switches to glide-flap-glide.

The most widespread of the three species in its genus, the Sharp-tailed Grouse is able to adapt to the greatest variety of habitats. It is not migratory, but undertakes seasonal movements between grassland summer habitats and woodland winter habitats. These birds are popular with hunters and are legal quarry in most of their range. Elements of this grouse's spectacular courtship display have been incorporated into the culture and dance of Native American people, including foot stomping and tail feather rattling.
VOICE Male calls a variety of unusual clucks, cooing, barks, and gobbles during courtship; females cluck with different intonations.
NESTING Shallow depression lined with plant matter close at hand as well as feathers from female, usually near overhead cover; 10–12 eggs; 1 brood; March–May.
FEEDING Forages primarily for seeds, leaves, buds, and fruit; also takes insects and flowers when available.

PRAIRIE DANCER
The courtship dance of the Sharp-tailed Grouse heralds the arrival of spring to the grasslands.

SIMILAR SPECIES

GREATER PRAIRIE-CHICKEN see p.72
shorter, square tail
longer tail
more heavily barred
naked orange skin

RING-NECKED PHEASANT ♀ see p.66
light brown
scalloped pattern on underparts

OCCURRENCE
Has a northern and western distribution in North America, from Alaska (isolated population) southward to northern prairie states. Prefers a mixture of fallow and active agricultural fields combined with brushy forest edges and woodlots along river beds.

| Length **15–19in (38–48cm)** | Wingspan **23–26in (58–66cm)** | Weight **26–34oz (750–950g)** |
| Social **Flocks** | Lifespan **Up to 7 years** | Status **Declining (p)** |

DATE SEEN	WHERE		NOTES

Order **Galliformes**	Family **Phasianidae**	Species *Tympanuchus cupido*

Greater Prairie-Chicken

rounded wings

MALE

IN FLIGHT

display feathers against neck

barred overall

MALE

no display feathers

FEMALE

square tail

two sets of feathers raised during display

orange skin over eye

beard-like feathers

bright orange skin of "air sac"

MALE (DISPLAYING)

FLIGHT: bursts from cover with loud, rapid wingbeats when approached.

Once common in prairie and woodland across central and eastern North America, populations of the Greater Prairie-Chicken have been greatly reduced as their habitats gave way to agriculture. The Atlantic Coast population (Heath Hen) became extinct in 1932. During the breeding season, males defend communal territories called "leks" and perform spectacular displays, inflating the air sacs on their necks, and "booming."
VOICE During courtship, males emit "booming" sounds like a three-part low hoot; also cackling calls.
NESTING Depression in soil lined with vegetation and feathers, in thick grass or other cover; 10–12 eggs; 1 brood; April–July.
FEEDING Eats berries, leaves, seeds, and grain; also insects.

BOOMING MALES
At a "lek" in the early morning, a male sends out a booming call and displays to attract a female.

SIMILAR SPECIES

SHARP-TAILED GROUSE
see p.71
pink skin
pointed tail
slightly larger
V-shaped markings on underparts

LESSER PRAIRIE-CHICKEN
pronged feathers
smaller overall
reddish orange skin

OCCURRENCE
Separate populations occur in the Dakotas, Minnesota, Colorado, Nebraska, Kansas, Illinois, Oklahoma, Texas, and Missouri. Breeds in openings mixed with oak-forested river corridors, especially where these interact with areas of native tallgrass prairie; resident year-round.

Length **15½–17½in (40–45cm)**	Wingspan **26–29in (66–74cm)**	Weight **30–36oz (850–1,000g)**
Social **Flocks**	Lifespan **Up to 4 years**	Status **Vulnerable**

DATE SEEN	WHERE	NOTES

| Order **Galliformes** | Family **Phasianidae** | Species *Meleagris gallopavo* |

Wild Turkey 🔊

MALE (EAST)

tail fanned in display

unfeathered blue-and-red head

black-and-white barred wings

IN FLIGHT

rusty tail with black band

humped back

no feathers on head

IMMATURE

long legs

dark body, with bronze iridescence

MALE (WEST)

dark overall

iridescent bronze-and-purplish body

hair-like "beard" on breast

FEMALE

Once proposed by Benjamin Franklin as the national emblem of the US, the Wild Turkey—the largest galliform in North America—was eliminated from most of its original range by the early 1900s because of over-hunting and habitat destruction. Since then, habitat restoration and the subsequent reintroduction of Wild Turkeys has been very successful.

VOICE Well-known gobble, given by males especially during courtship; female makes various yelps, clucks, and purrs, based on mood and threat level.

NESTING Scrape on ground lined with grass, placed against or under protective cover; 10–15 eggs; 1 brood; March–June.

FEEDING Omnivorous, it scratches in leaf litter on forest floor for acorns and other food, mostly vegetation; also takes plants and insects from agricultural fields.

FLIGHT: after running, leaps into the air with loud, rapid wingbeats, then glides.

COLLECTIVE DISPLAY
Once the population expands into new areas, numerous males will be seen displaying together.

SIMILAR SPECIES

GREATER SAGE-GROUSE

dark head

pointed tail

white breast

TURKEY VULTURE
see p.219

small red head

dark overall

OCCURRENCE
Found in mixed mature woodlands, fields with agricultural crops; also in various grasslands, close to swamps, but adaptable and increasingly common in suburban and urban habitats. Quite widespread, but patchily distributed across North America.

| Length **2¾–4ft (0.9–1.2m)** | Wingspan **4–5ft (1.2–1.5m)** | Weight **10–24lb (4.5–11kg)** |
| Social **Flocks** | Lifespan **Up to 9 years** | Status **Secure** |

DATE SEEN	WHERE	NOTES

GREBES

GREBES RESEMBLE LOONS and share many of their aquatic habits, but anatomical and molecular features show that they are actually unrelated; and they are placed in a different order—the Podicipediformes. Their bodies are streamlined, offering little resistance when diving and swimming. Grebes' toes have broad lobes that splay when the bird thrusts forward through the water. Underwater their primary means of propulsion is the sideways motion of their lobed toes. The legs are placed far back on the body, which greatly aids the bird when swimming above or below the surface. Grebes have short tails, and their trailing legs and toes serve as rudders when they fly. The position of the legs makes it impossible, however, for grebes to stand upright for long or easily walk on land. Thus, even when breeding they are tied to water; and their nests are usually partially floating platforms, built on beds of water plants. They dive to catch fish with a short, forward-arching spring. Unusual among birds, they swallow feathers, supposedly to trap fish bones and protect their stomachs, then periodically disgorge them. Like loons, grebes can control their buoyancy by exhaling air and compressing their plumage so that they sink quietly below the surface. They are strong fliers and are migratory.

A FINE DISPLAY
This Horned Grebe reveals the colorful plumes on its head, as part of its elaborate courtship display.

PIGEONS AND DOVES

THE LARGER SPECIES within the family Columbidae are known as pigeons, and the smaller ones as doves, although there is no actual scientific basis for the distinction. They are all fairly heavy, plump birds with relatively small heads and short necks. They also possess slender bills with their nostrils positioned in a fleshy mound at the base. Among other things, members of this family have strong wing muscles, making them powerful and agile fliers. When alarmed, they burst into flight, with their wings emitting a distinctive clapping or swishing sound. Pigeons and doves produce a nutritious "crop-milk," which they secrete to feed their young. Despite human activity having severely affected members of this family in the past (the leading cause of the Passenger Pigeon's extinction early in the 1900s is thought to be over-hunting), the introduced Rock Pigeon has adapted and proliferated worldwide, as has the recently introduced Eurasian Collared-Dove, albeit on a smaller scale. The introduced Spotted Dove has not shown a similar tendency for explosive expansion, however, and remains limited to southern California and the islands of Hawaii. Among the species native to North America, only the elegant Mourning Dove is as widespread as the various species of introduced birds.

DOVE IN THE SUN
The Mourning Dove sunbathes each side of its body in turn, its wings and tail outspread.

| Order **Podicipediformes** | Family **Podicipedidae** | Species *Podilymbus podiceps* |

Pied-billed Grebe 🔊

outstretched neck

ADULT (BREEDING)

lighter flight feathers

IN FLIGHT

yellowish bill

whitish throat

ADULT (NONBREEDING)

brown eye

whitish, hooked bill with a black ring

brownish gray body

reddish brown neck and breast

ADULT (BREEDING)

black throat patch

white undertail

The widest ranging of the North American grebes, the Pied-billed Grebe is tolerant of highly populated areas and is often seen breeding on lakes and ponds across North America. It is a powerful swimmer and can remain submerged for 16–30 seconds when it dives. In contrast to some of the elaborate displays from other grebe species, its courtship ritual is more vocal than visual and a pair usually duet-call in the mating season. Migration, conducted at night, is delayed until its breeding area ices up and food becomes scarce. The Pied-billed Grebe is capable of sustained flights of more than 2,000 miles (3,200km).

VOICE Various grunts and wails; in spring, call a cuckoo like repeated gobble *kup-kup-Kaow-Kaow-kaow*, gradually speeding up.

NESTING Floating nest of partially decayed plants and clipped leaves, attached to emergent vegetation in marshes and quiet waters; 4–7 eggs; 2 broods; April–October.

FEEDING Dives to catch a variety of crustaceans, fish, amphibians, insects, and other invertebrates; also picks prey from emergent vegetation, or catches them mid-air.

FLIGHT: strong, direct flight with rapid wingbeats, but rarely seen.

BACK OFF
When alarmed, a Pied-billed Grebe may flap its wings in a defensive display.

SIMILAR SPECIES

LEAST GREBE ☼
see p.445

smaller bill

yellow eye

darker body

OCCURRENCE
Breeds on a variety of water bodies, including coastal brackish ponds, seasonal ponds, marshes, and even sewage ponds. Winters in the breeding area if food and open water are available, otherwise chooses still waters resembling its breeding habitat.

| Length **12–15in (31–38cm)** | Wingspan **18–24in (46–62cm)** | Weight **13–17oz (375–475g)** |
| Social **Family groups** | Lifespan **At least 3 years** | Status **Vulnerable** |

DATE SEEN	WHERE	NOTES

| Order **Podicipediformes** | Family **Podicipedidae** | Species **Podiceps auritus** |

Horned Grebe

flattish top of head

white cheek

white sides to neck

ADULT (WINTER)

black crown

red eye

gold streak from eye to nape

short, dark bill with whitish tip

rufous neck

black throat

ADULT (SPRING MOLT)

ADULT (SUMMER)

neck and head in line with body

ADULT (SUMMER)

IN FLIGHT

The timing of the Horned Grebe's migration depends largely on the weather—this species may not leave until its breeding grounds get iced over, nor does it arrive before the ice melts. Its breeding behavior is well documented since it is approachable on nesting grounds and has an elaborate breeding ritual. This grebe's so-called "horns" are in fact yellowish feather patches located behind its eyes, which it can raise at will.
VOICE At least 10 calls, but descending *aaanrrh* call most common in winter, ends in trill; muted conversational calls when birds are in groups.
NESTING Floating, soggy nest, hidden in vegetation, in small ponds and lake inlets; 3–9 eggs; 1 brood; May–July.
FEEDING Dives in open water or forages among plants, mainly for small crustaceans and insects, but also leeches, mollusks, amphibians, fish, and some vegetation.

FLIGHT: strong, rapid wingbeats; runs on water to become airborne; rarely takes off from land.

HITCHING A RIDE
In common with other grebes, Horned Grebe chicks often ride on the back of a swimming parent.

SIMILAR SPECIES

RED-NECKED GREBE ❋
see p.77

brownish cap

darker eye

EARED GREBE ❋
see p.78

upturned bill

dark cheek

OCCURRENCE
Breeds in small freshwater, even slightly brackish, ponds and marshes, including manmade ponds. Prefers areas with open water and patches of sedges, cattails, and other wetland vegetation. Winters on saltwater close to shore; also on large bodies of freshwater. Also breeds in Eurasia.

| Length **12–15in (30–38cm)** | Wingspan **18–24in (46–62cm)** | Weight **11–20oz (300–575g)** |
| Social **Pairs/Loose flocks/Colonies** | Lifespan **Up to 5 years** | Status **Declining** |

DATE SEEN	WHERE	NOTES

Order **Podicipediformes**	Family **Podicipedidae**	Species ***Podiceps grisegena***

Red-necked Grebe

head and neck in line with body

white-edged inner wing

ADULT (BREEDING)

IN FLIGHT

pale, reddish brown crescent near ear

brownish cap

mostly yellowish bill

broad stripes on cheek and ear

JUVENILE

ADULT (NONBREEDING)

broad head with crest at rear

black cap

grayish white cheeks and throat

gray flanks

chestnut brown neck and chest

base of the bill yellow

ADULT (BREEDING)

The Red-necked Grebe is smaller than Western and Clark's Grebes, but larger than the other North American grebes. It migrates over short to medium distances and spends the winter along both coasts, where large flocks may be seen during the day. It runs along the water's surface to become airborne, although it rarely flies. This grebe doesn't come ashore often; it stands erect, but walks awkwardly, and prefers to sink to its breast and shuffle along.
VOICE Nasal, gull-like call on breeding grounds, evolves into bray, ends with whinny; also honks, rattles, hisses, purrs, and ticks.
NESTING Compact, buoyant mound of decayed and fresh vegetation in sheltered, shallow marshes and lakes, or artificial wetlands; 4–5 eggs; 1 brood; May–July.
FEEDING An opportunistic hunter, eats fish, crustaceans, aquatic insects, worms, mollusks, salamanders, and tadpoles.

FLIGHT: fast, direct, wingbeats, with head and outstretched neck mostly level with line of body.

COURTSHIP DISPLAY
This courting pair face each other, with outstretched necks and raised neck feathers.

SIMILAR SPECIES

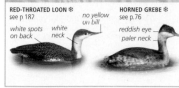

RED-THROATED LOON ❊
see p.182

white spots on back

white neck

no yellow on bill

HORNED GREBE ❊
see p.76

reddish eye
paler neck

OCCURRENCE
Breeds from northern prairies and forests, almost to the tree line in the northwest; limited to suitable interior bodies of water such as large marshes and small lakes. Winters primarily in estuaries, inlets, bays, and offshore shallows along Atlantic and Pacific Coasts; can also be found on the Great Lakes.

Length **16½–22in (42–56cm)**	Wingspan **24–35in (61–88cm)**	Weight **1¾–3½lb (0.8–1.6kg)**
Social **Pairs/Loose flocks**	Lifespan **Up to 6 years**	Status **Vulnerable**

DATE SEEN	WHERE	NOTES

| Order **Podicipediformes** | Family **Podicipedidae** | Species ***Podiceps nigricollis*** |

Eared Grebe

darker flanks

white patch on wing

ADULT (SUMMER)

browner plumage

outstretched neck

JUVENILE

dusky cheek

upturned bill

dusky white flanks

grayish neck

IN FLIGHT

large, wispy gold patch behind red eye

dark back

black neck

ADULT (WINTER)

black crest

red eye

thin, upturned bill

rufous breast and sides

ADULT (SUMMER)

The most abundant grebe in North America, the Eared Grebe is quite remarkable in terms of physiology. After breeding, it undergoes a complex and drastic reorganization of body-fat stores, along with changes in muscle, heart, and digestive organ mass to prepare it for fall migration. All of this increases the bird's energy reserves and body mass, but renders it flightless. It may have the longest periods of flightlessness of any flying bird—up to 10 months.

VOICE Various trills during courtship, including squeaky, rising *poo-eep*; sharp *chirp* when alarmed; usually silent at other times.

NESTING Sodden nest of decayed bottom plants anchored in thinly spaced reeds or submerged vegetation in shallow water of marshes, ponds, and lakes; 1 brood; 1–8 eggs; May–July.

FEEDING Forages underwater for small crustaceans and aquatic insects; also small fish and mollusks; consumes worms in winter.

FLIGHT: flies with neck outstretched, held at a low angle; rarely flies except during migration.

SALTY WATER
The Eared Grebe prefers salty water at all times except when breeding.

SIMILAR SPECIES

RED-NECKED GREBE ❄
see p.77

browner cap

thicker bill

HORNED GREBE ❄
see p.76

more distinct white cheek

white tip on bill

OCCURRENCE
Breeds in marshes, shallow lakes, and ponds. After breeding, many birds seek saline waters, such as Mono Lake, or lakes in Utah where their favorite foods thrive—brine shrimp and alkali flies. Winters in coastal bays of Pacific Coast and is a vagrant on Atlantic Coast. Also breeds in Eurasia.

| Length **12–14in (30–35cm)** | Wingspan **22½–24in (57–62cm)** | Weight **7–26oz (200–725g)** |
| Social **Flocks** | Lifespan **Up to 12 years** | Status **Secure** |

DATE SEEN	WHERE	NOTES

| Order **Columbiformes** | Family **Columbidae** | Species *Columba livia* |

Rock Pigeon 🔊

black wing bars

white underwings

white rump

ADULT

IN FLIGHT

no wing bars

variably colored body

ADULT (FERAL)

dark-tipped tail

iridescence on neck

gray back

two black wing bars

short bill

ADULT (ANCESTRAL FORM)

The Rock Pigeon was introduced to the Atlantic Coast of North America by 17th century colonists. Now feral, this species is found all over the continent, especially around farms, cities, and towns. This medium-sized pigeon comes in a wide variety of plumage colors and patterns, including bluish gray, checkered, rusty red, and nearly all-white. Its wings usually have two dark bars on them—unique among North American pigeons. The variability of the Rock Pigeon influenced Charles Darwin as he developed his theory of natural selection.
VOICE Soft, gurgling *coo, roo-c'too-coo*, for courtship and threat.
NESTING Twig nest on flat, sheltered surface, such as caves, rocky outcrops, and buildings; 2 eggs; several broods; year-round.
FEEDING Eats seeds, fruit, and rarely insects; human foods such as popcorn, bread, peanuts; various farm crops in rural areas.

FLIGHT: strong, direct; can reach speeds up to around 60mph (95kph).

CITY PIGEONS
Most Rock Pigeons in North America descend from domesticated forms and exhibit many colors.

SIMILAR SPECIES

WHITE-CROWNED PIGEON
mangroves; see p.446

white crown

dark gray overall

BAND-TAILED PIGEON
western

yellow bill with dark tip

white band on nape

OCCURRENCE
Across southern Canada and North America; nests in human structures of all sorts; resident. Original habitat in the Old World was (and still is) sea cliffs and inland canyons; found wild in some places, such as dry regions of North Africa, but feral in much of the world.

| Length **11–14in (28–36cm)** | Wingspan **20–26in (51–67cm)** | Weight **9–14oz (250–400g)** |
| Social **Solitary/Flocks** | Lifespan **Up to 6 years** | Status **Secure** |

DATE SEEN	WHERE		NOTES

Order **Columbiformes**	Family **Columbidae**	Species *Streptopelia decaocto*

Eurasian Collared-Dove

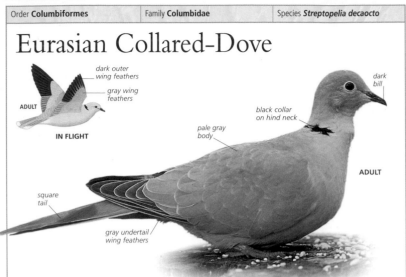

ADULT

dark outer wing feathers

gray wing feathers

IN FLIGHT

dark bill

black collar on hind neck

pale gray body

ADULT

square tail

gray undertail wing feathers

A stocky bird, the Eurasian Collared-Dove is easily recognized by the black collar on the back of its neck and its square tail. First released at New Providence, Bahamas, in the mid-1970s, this species is spreading rapidly across the continental mainland, thanks to multiple local releases, the planting of trees in urban and suburban habitats, the popularity of bird feeders making food readily available, and the bird's extraordinarily high reproductive rate. This species soon becomes very confiding and tolerant of humans, regularly nesting and feeding in urban areas. One consequence of this is that it often falls prey to domestic cats, but this has little effect on the expanding population. Based on sightings from locations all over North America—and on the evidence from Europe, throughout which it has spread since only the 1940s—it is highly likely that the Eurasian Collared-Dove will soon become a common species in North America.

VOICE Repeated four-note *coo-hoo-HOO-cook* that is quick and low-pitched; also harsh, nasal *krreeew* in flight.

NESTING Platform of twigs, stems, and grasses in trees or on buildings; 2 eggs; multiple broods; March–November.

FEEDING Eats seed and grain, plant stems and leaves, berries, and some invertebrates; feeds on the ground for seed, but also visits elevated feeders.

〰〰〰〰〰〰〰〰〰〰〰

FLIGHT: strong, stiff flight reminiscent of hawks; occasional swoops and dives.

COLLARED COLONIZER
The Eurasian Collared-Dove has spread throughout Europe in just a few decades, and now looks set to do the same in North America.

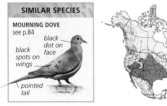

SIMILAR SPECIES

MOURNING DOVE
see p.84

black dot on face

black spots on wings

pointed tail

OCCURRENCE
Can be seen almost anywhere in North America south of the northern forest zone, but occurs mainly in suburban and urban areas (though not large cities) and agricultural areas with seeds and grain for food and deciduous trees for nesting and roosting. May roost in manmade structures such as barns.

Length **11½–12in (29–30cm)**	Wingspan **14in (35cm)**	Weight **5–6oz (150–175g)**
Social **Large flocks**	Lifespan **Up to 13 years**	Status **Localized**

DATE SEEN	WHERE	NOTES

| Order **Columbiformes** | Family **Columbidae** | Species *Columbina inca* |

Inca Dove

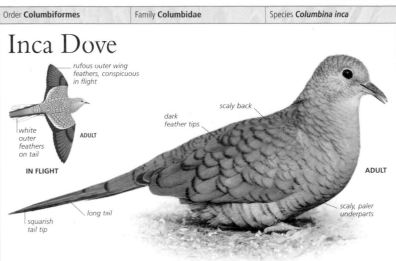

rufous outer wing feathers, conspicuous in flight

scaly back

dark feather tips

white outer feathers on tail

ADULT

IN FLIGHT

ADULT

long tail

squarish tail tip

scaly, paler underparts

FLIGHT: fast, direct flights of short duration, with a noisy takeoff.

This small, brownish gray dove has expanded its range from Central America and Mexico into the southern US in the last 100 years or so, and now breeds in all of the southwestern states from California east to the Mississippi River. Resembling a baby Mourning Dove because of its slender shape and long tail, the Inca Dove can be distinguished by its "scaly" pattern. Although it is a secretive species, hiding in low, dense vegetation, it is tame and frequently occurs in human settlements. When encountered, the Inca Dove often flushes almost from underfoot, flashing the reddish coloration of its wings.

VOICE Repeated 2-note chant, *pol-pah*, which can sound like the words "no hope;" sometimes low, trilling *coo*.

NESTING Compact platform of twigs and leaves in a variety of trees and shrubs; 2 eggs; several broods; March–November.

FEEDING Pecks at grains, seeds, and weeds on the ground, among vegetation; also fruit.

WING-UP DISPLAY
The wing-up posture is used by territorial male Inca Doves in aggressive displays.

A "TALL" TAIL
An Inca Dove's tail makes up a third of the bird's total length.

SIMILAR SPECIES

RUDDY GROUND DOVE
see p.472

smaller overall

shorter tail

OCCURRENCE
Breeds and winters all year in areas of human habitation: cities, towns, farms containing shrubs and small trees for nesting. Forages on lawns and barnyards and occasionally near rivers and streams but appears to favor drier areas in the south of its range.

| Length **7–9in (18–23cm)** | Wingspan **11in (28cm)** | Weight **1¹⁄₁₆–2oz (30–60g)** |
| Social **Solitary/Large flocks** | Lifespan **Up to 7 years** | Status **Localized** |

DATE SEEN	WHERE	NOTES

Order **Columbiformes**	Family **Columbidae**	Species ***Columbina passerina***

Common Ground Dove

rufous outer wing feathers

MALE

short tail

IN FLIGHT

pinkish or red base to bill

scaly, gray breast

FEMALE

black spots on wings

scaly looking head

scaly breast with pink tinge

square tail

MALE

The Common Ground Dove, the smallest of all North American doves, is only slightly larger than a sparrow. Both of these qualities are reflected in its scientific name—*Columbina*—meaning "little dove," and *passerina* being the Latin for sparrow. It is also different from other doves in that it retains its pair-bond throughout the year and tends not to form flocks. Birds in a pair usually remain within a few yards of each other. Besides its diminutive size, the Common Ground Dove is recognizable by prominent black spots on its wings, scaly underparts (seen while perched), the reddish appearance of its wings, and its square, blackish tail while in flight. It is found coast to coast along the most southerly regions of the continent, but vagrants can appear almost anywhere.

VOICE Simple, repeated, ascending double-note *wah-up* given every 2–3 seconds.

NESTING Depression on ground lined with grasses and palm fibers, or frail nest in trees; 2 eggs; several broods; April–August.

FEEDING Pecks on the ground at grass and weed seeds, grains, small berries, insects, and snails; also takes seeds from feeders; prefers drier, scrubby ground.

FLIGHT: direct, quick, sometimes jerky flight with stiff, rapid wingbeats; usually short duration.

EASILY OVERLOOKED
Ground Doves blend in with the ground and can be overlooked as they quietly feed.

SIMILAR SPECIES

RUDDY GROUND DOVE
see p.472

plain gray head

dark bill

OCCURRENCE
Mostly prefers dry, sandy areas with short, open vegetation, although it can be found in a variety of habitats, such as open pine woodlands, woodland edges, citrus groves, mesquite and riverside thickets, farm fields, suburban areas, and cultivated land, including orchards.

Length **6–7in (15–18cm)**	Wingspan **11in (28cm)**	Weight **1¹⁄₁₆–1⁷⁄₁₆oz (30–40g)**
Social **Pairs**	Lifespan **Up to 7 years**	Status **Declining**

DATE SEEN	WHERE	NOTES

Order **Columbiformes**	Family **Columbidae**	Species *Zenaida asiatica*

White-winged Dove 🔊

ADULT

white band in wing

IN FLIGHT

white-edged tail

dark flight feathers

brownish upperparts

rounded gray tail

ADULT

reddish purple crown and nape

iridescent greenish gold on sides of neck

bare blue skin around orange-red eyes

longish blue-black bill

black mark below ear feathers

large white wing patches

dark gray flight feathers

red legs and toes

FLIGHT: swift, direct flight with quick, regular wingbeats; maximum height about 200ft (60m).

As one of the larger gray-colored dove species in North America, the White-winged Dove is best identified in flight by the conspicuous white bands on its wings. When perched, the bright blue skin around its orange eyes and its longish, square tail with a white tip can be seen. This species has been expanding its population northward in recent decades, though not as rapidly as the Eurasian Collared-Dove. Increased farmland habitat and ornamental trees, both favorite roosting places, are the most likely cause. In common with many other doves, the nest is a somewhat flimsy structure, and eggs or nestlings frequently fall to their end if the nest is disturbed, or when there are high winds.

VOICE Distinctive, drawn-out cooing: *who-cooks-for-you*; also makes five-note variation from the nest: *la-coo-kla-coo-kla*.

NESTING Frail platform of twigs, moss, and grasses, on a sturdy branch in dense-canopied trees; 2 eggs; 2 broods; March–September.

FEEDING Forages for seeds, wild nuts, and fruit on the ground and in elevated locations; prefers corn, sorghum, wheat, and sunflower.

DESERT DWELLER
The White-winged Dove is much more at home in semiarid and desert areas than the Mourning Dove.

SIMILAR SPECIES

MOURNING DOVE see p.84
smaller, rounder head

no white wing patch

longer tail

OCCURRENCE
Breeds and winters in dense, thorny woodlands dominated by mesquite and Texas ebony; deserts with cactus, palo verde, and other scrub plants; riverside woodlands, orchards, and residential areas. Formerly only abundant in the US in the Rio Grande Valley, it has now expanded north to Oklahoma.

Length **11½in (29cm)**	Wingspan **19in (48cm)**	Weight **5oz (150g)**
Social **Solitary/Flocks**	Lifespan **Up to 21 years**	Status **Localized**

DATE SEEN	WHERE	NOTES

| Order **Columbiformes** | Family **Columbidae** | Species *Zenaida macroura* |

Mourning Dove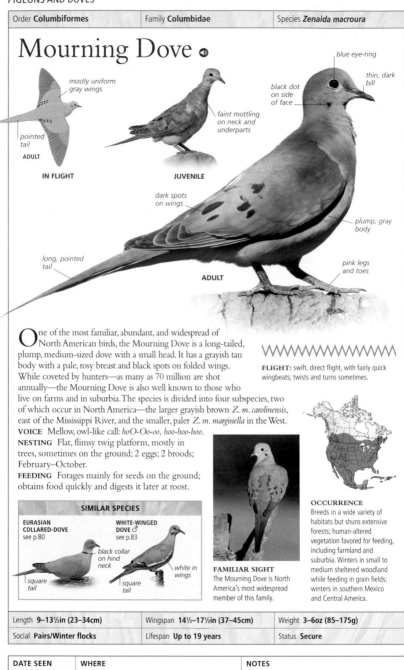

mostly uniform gray wings

pointed tail

ADULT

IN FLIGHT

faint mottling on neck and underparts

JUVENILE

blue eye-ring

thin, dark bill

black dot on side of face

dark spots on wings

plump, gray body

long, pointed tail

ADULT

pink legs and toes

One of the most familiar, abundant, and widespread of North American birds, the Mourning Dove is a long-tailed, plump, medium-sized dove with a small head. It has a grayish tan body with a pale, rosy breast and black spots on folded wings. While coveted by hunters—as many as 70 million are shot annually—the Mourning Dove is also well known to those who live on farms and in suburbia. The species is divided into four subspecies, two of which occur in North America—the larger grayish brown *Z. m. carolinensis*, east of the Mississippi River, and the smaller, paler *Z. m. marginella* in the West.

VOICE Mellow, owl-like call: *hoO-Oo-oo, hoo-hoo-hoo*.

NESTING Flat, flimsy twig platform, mostly in trees, sometimes on the ground; 2 eggs; 2 broods; February–October.

FEEDING Forages mainly for seeds on the ground; obtains food quickly and digests it later at roost.

FLIGHT: swift, direct flight, with fairly quick wingbeats; twists and turns sometimes.

SIMILAR SPECIES

EURASIAN COLLARED-DOVE see p.80

black collar on hind neck

square tail

WHITE-WINGED DOVE ♂ see p.83

white in wings

square tail

FAMILIAR SIGHT
The Mourning Dove is North America's most widespread member of this family.

OCCURRENCE
Breeds in a wide variety of habitats but shuns extensive forests; human-altered vegetation favored for feeding, including farmland and suburbia. Winters in small to medium sheltered woodland while feeding in grain fields; winters in southern Mexico and Central America.

| Length **9–13½in (23–34cm)** | Wingspan **14½–17½in (37–45cm)** | Weight **3–6oz (85–175g)** |
| Social **Pairs/Winter flocks** | Lifespan **Up to 19 years** | Status **Secure** |

DATE SEEN	WHERE	NOTES

CUCKOOS

THE FAMILY CUCULIDAE includes typical cuckoos, anis, and roadrunners. Cuckoos favor forested areas, anis prefer more open bush country, and roadrunners are found in dry, bushy semidesert or desert regions. Cuckoos are mainly insectivorous, specializing in caterpillars from the ground or gleaned from foliage. Anis have a more varied diet. They are sociable, blackish, heavy-billed birds, found only in Florida and along the Gulf Coast but more widespread in Central America. Roadrunners are ground-feeders, rarely flying but able to run fast in pursuit of prey, which ranges from insects through small lizards to snakes (famously including rattlesnakes) and small rodents.

PERCHED TO KILL
After catching a lizard, the Greater Roadrunner bashes it repeatedly against a rock before gulping it down.

NIGHTJARS

THE NIGHTJARS ARE active mostly around dusk and dawn, and so are not well known to many people, although their remarkable songs and calls may be more familiar. Common Nighthawks are easily seen and may even be spotted over suburban areas, but most nightjars are elusive species. Some inhabit scrub and bushy slopes and plains, while others are found in woodlands. They are medium-sized birds with long wings and wide tails. They have tiny legs and minute bills, but very wide mouths: they catch flying insects such as moths in the air, directly into the open gape. Their mouths are surrounded by bristles that help guide insects in when the birds are foraging.

ELEGANT HUNTER
This male Lesser Nighthawk soars through the air, hunting for insects, which it catches on the wing. Lesser Nighthawks are rare in the East.

PART OF THE LITTER
Not many bird species match the leaf litter of the forest floor as well as nightjars, as this Chuck-will's-widow shows.

Order **Cuculiformes**	Family **Cuculidae**	Species *Geococcyx californianus*

Greater Roadrunner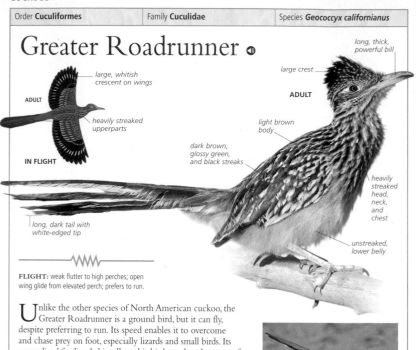

long, thick, powerful bill

large crest

ADULT

large, whitish crescent on wings

ADULT

light brown body

heavily streaked upperparts

IN FLIGHT

dark brown, glossy green, and black streaks

heavily streaked head, neck, and chest

long, dark tail with white-edged tip

unstreaked, lower belly

FLIGHT: weak flutter to high perches; open wing glide from elevated perch; prefers to run.

Unlike the other species of North American cuckoo, the Greater Roadrunner is a ground bird, but it can fly, despite preferring to run. Its speed enables it to overcome and chase prey on foot, especially lizards and small birds. Its generalized feeding habits allow this bird to take advantage of whatever food resources it comes across. This may be one of the main reasons roadrunners are expanding their range.

VOICE Cooing *coo-coo-coo-cooo-cooooo* series of 4–5 descending notes.

NESTING Shallow, loosely organized cup of twigs and branches, lined with grass, animal hair, and feathers; 3–5 eggs; 2 broods; April–September.

FEEDING Eats a wide variety of insects, small reptiles such as lizards, birds, and mammals; also eggs and carrion.

DRINKING
Roadrunners obtain much of their moisture from the food they eat, but will take full advantage of water whenever it's available.

LOFTY ABODE
This species nests off the ground, and can occasionally be seen occupying elevated perches.

SIMILAR SPECIES

PLAIN CHACHALACA see p.444

darker, solid color

unstreaked upperparts

larger overall

RING-NECKED PHEASANT ♀ see p.66

no crest

lighter brown overall

plump body

OCCURRENCE
Widespread across southwestern US, from California to Louisiana, and north to Utah, Colorado, Kansas, and Arkansas; lives at low elevations in open brushy areas mixed with thorn scrub such as mesquite; also pinyon-juniper shrubbery, and deserts and chaparral. Resident.

Length **21in (53cm)**	Wingspan **23in (58cm)**	Weight **11oz (300g)**
Social **Solitary/Pairs**	Lifespan **Up to 6 years**	Status **Secure**

DATE SEEN	WHERE	NOTES

| Order **Cuculiformes** | Family **Cuculidae** | Species *Coccyzus americanus* |

Yellow-billed Cuckoo

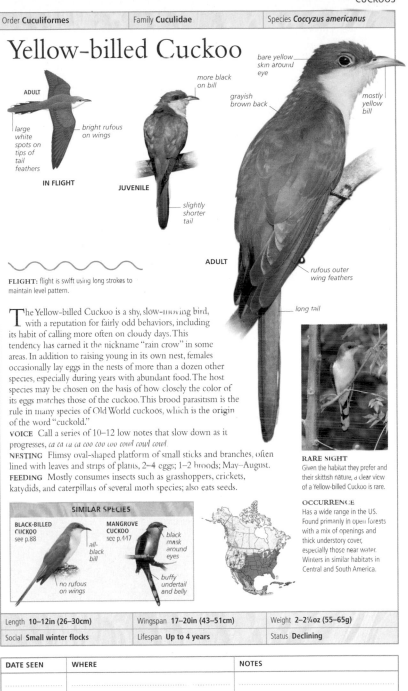

ADULT

IN FLIGHT
- large white spots on tips of tail feathers
- bright rufous on wings

JUVENILE
- more black on bill
- slightly shorter tail

ADULT
- bare yellow skin around eye
- grayish brown back
- mostly yellow bill
- rufous outer wing feathers
- long tail

FLIGHT: flight is swift using long strokes to maintain level pattern.

The Yellow-billed Cuckoo is a shy, slow-moving bird, with a reputation for fairly odd behaviors, including its habit of calling more often on cloudy days. This tendency has earned it the nickname "rain crow" in some areas. In addition to raising young in its own nest, females occasionally lay eggs in the nests of more than a dozen other species, especially during years with abundant food. The host species may be chosen on the basis of how closely the color of its eggs matches those of the cuckoo. This brood parasitism is the rule in many species of Old World cuckoos, which is the origin of the word "cuckold."

VOICE Call a series of 10–12 low notes that slow down as it progresses, *ca ca ca ca coo coo coo cowl cowl cowl*.

NESTING Flimsy oval-shaped platform of small sticks and branches, often lined with leaves and strips of plants, 2–4 eggs; 1–2 broods; May–August.

FEEDING Mostly consumes insects such as grasshoppers, crickets, katydids, and caterpillars of several moth species; also eats seeds.

RARE SIGHT
Given the habitat they prefer and their skittish nature, a clear view of a Yellow-billed Cuckoo is rare.

OCCURRENCE
Has a wide range in the US. Found primarily in open forests with a mix of openings and thick understory cover, especially those near water. Winters in similar habitats in Central and South America.

SIMILAR SPECIES

BLACK-BILLED CUCKOO see p.88
- all-black bill
- no rufous on wings

MANGROVE CUCKOO see p.447
- black mask around eyes
- buffy undertail and belly

| Length **10–12in (26–30cm)** | Wingspan **17–20in (43–51cm)** | Weight **2–2¼oz (55–65g)** |
| Social **Small winter flocks** | Lifespan **Up to 4 years** | Status **Declining** |

DATE SEEN	WHERE	NOTES

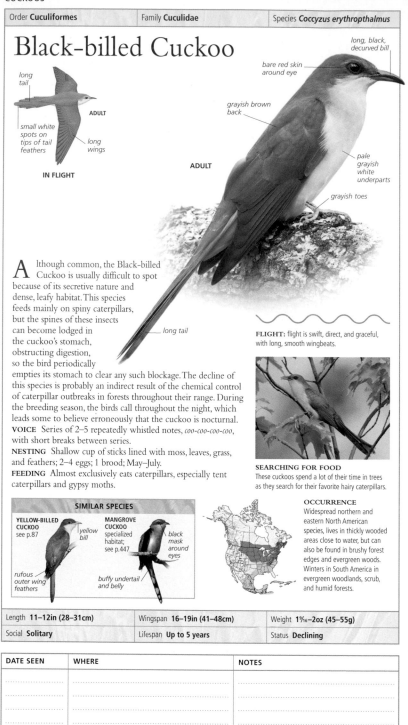

| Order **Cuculiformes** | Family **Cuculidae** | Species *Coccyzus erythropthalmus* |

Black-billed Cuckoo

long, black, decurved bill

bare red skin around eye

grayish brown back

long tail

ADULT

small white spots on tips of tail feathers

long wings

IN FLIGHT

ADULT

pale grayish white underparts

grayish toes

long tail

Although common, the Black-billed Cuckoo is usually difficult to spot because of its secretive nature and dense, leafy habitat. This species feeds mainly on spiny caterpillars, but the spines of these insects can become lodged in the cuckoo's stomach, obstructing digestion, so the bird periodically empties its stomach to clear any such blockage. The decline of this species is probably an indirect result of the chemical control of caterpillar outbreaks in forests throughout their range. During the breeding season, the birds call throughout the night, which leads some to believe erroneously that the cuckoo is nocturnal.
VOICE Series of 2–5 repeatedly whistled notes, *coo-coo-coo-coo*, with short breaks between series.
NESTING Shallow cup of sticks lined with moss, leaves, grass, and feathers; 2–4 eggs; 1 brood; May–July.
FEEDING Almost exclusively eats caterpillars, especially tent caterpillars and gypsy moths.

FLIGHT: flight is swift, direct, and graceful, with long, smooth wingbeats.

SEARCHING FOR FOOD
These cuckoos spend a lot of their time in trees as they search for their favorite hairy caterpillars.

SIMILAR SPECIES

YELLOW-BILLED CUCKOO see p.87
yellow bill
rufous outer wing feathers

MANGROVE CUCKOO specialized habitat; see p.447
black mask around eyes
buffy undertail and belly

OCCURRENCE
Widespread northern and eastern North American species, lives in thickly wooded areas close to water, but can also be found in brushy forest edges and evergreen woods. Winters in South America in evergreen woodlands, scrub, and humid forests.

| Length **11–12in (28–31cm)** | Wingspan **16–19in (41–48cm)** | Weight **1⁹⁄₁₆–2oz (45–55g)** |
| Social **Solitary** | Lifespan **Up to 5 years** | Status **Declining** |

DATE SEEN	WHERE	NOTES

| Order **Caprimulgiformes** | Family **Caprimulgidae** | Species ***Chordeiles minor*** |

Common Nighthawk 🔊

- pointed wings

MALE
- white bars on outer wing feathers
- narrow wings
- long wings

IN FLIGHT

- white throat
- white wing patch **MALE**
- very small bill
- large, dark eye
- delicate, gray-black pattern overall

FEMALE
- barring on gray underparts

FLIGHT: erratic flight with deep wingbeats interrupted by banking glides.

Common Nighthawks are easy to spot as they swoop over parking lots, city streets, and athletics fields during the warm summer months. They are more active at dawn and dusk than at night, pursuing insect prey up to 250ft (76m) in the air. The species once took the name Booming Nighthawk, a reference to the remarkable flight display of the male birds, during which they dive rapidly toward the ground, causing their feathers to vibrate and produce a characteristic "booming" sound.
VOICE Nasal *peeent*; also soft clucking noises from both sexes.
NESTING Nests on ground on rocks, wood, leaves, or sand, also on gravel-covered rooftops in urban areas; 2 eggs; 1 brood; May–July.
FEEDING Catches airborne insects, especially moths, mayflies, and beetles, also ants; predominantly active at dusk and dawn.

A RARE SIGHT
Common Nighthawks are seen in flight more often than other caprimulgids, but it is a rare treat to see one resting on a perch.

SIMILAR SPECIES

LESSER NIGHTHAWK
more buffy barring on underside of wings; see p.447

COMMON PAURAQUE
longer, rounded tail with white patches; see p.447
- browner plumage
- larger overall

OCCURRENCE
Wide variety of open habitats such as cleared forests, fields, grassland, beaches, and sand dunes; also common in urban areas, including cities. The most common and widespread North American nighthawk, this species also occurs in Central and South America.

| Length **9–10in (23–26cm)** | Wingspan **22–24in (56–61cm)** | Weight **2⅞oz (80g)** |
| Social **Solitary/Flocks** | Lifespan **Up to 9 years** | Status **Declining** |

DATE SEEN	WHERE	NOTES

| Order **Caprimulgiformes** | Family **Caprimulgidae** | Species ***Antrostomus carolinensis*** |

Chuck-will's-widow

ADULT

pale cinnamon underparts

IN FLIGHT

some white on tail

long, rounded tail

long, grayish eyebrow

very small bill

tawny buff-brown upperparts

reddish brown throat

whitish collar

ADULT

tan feathers on wings

The largest North American nightjar, the Chuck-will's-widow is also one of the least known. This species is very tolerant of human development and nests in suburban and urban areas. Unlike other nightjars it often feeds by hawking—flying continuously and capturing its prey in the air. It is also known to forage on the ground under streetlights and has occasionally been observed chasing down and swallowing bats and small birds, such as warblers, whole. Chuck-will's-widow is crepuscular, meaning that it hunts mostly at dawn and dusk. It is also active whenever there is a full moon, possibly because levels of light are similar to its preferred foraging times.

VOICE Whistled *chuck-will's-wid-ow*, begins softly, then increases in volume with emphasis on the two middle syllables.

NESTING Eggs laid directly on ground litter, including evergreen needles and fallen leaves; 2 eggs; 1 brood; May–June.

FEEDING Primarily catches flying insects, especially moths and beetles; usually hunts at dusk and dawn.

FLIGHT: alternation of slow flapping flight with erratic glides.

DAYTIME SLEEPER
Well-camouflaged on the forest floor, this species of nightjar sleeps during the day.

SIMILAR SPECIES	
COMMON POORWILL see p.448	**EASTERN WHIP-POOR-WILL** see p.91
grayer overall	darker with more gray than brown
more white on tail	

OCCURRENCE
Breeds in forests composed of a mixture of deciduous and evergreen trees, and in open fields. A truly North American species, it is found mainly in the eastern US. Winters in Florida, Mexico, and in northern Central America.

Length **11–12½in (28–32cm)**	Wingspan **25–28in (63–70cm)**	Weight **3½oz (100g)**
Social **Solitary**	Lifespan **Up to 14 years**	Status **Secure**

DATE SEEN	WHERE	NOTES

| Order **Caprimulgiformes** | Family **Caprimulgidae** | Species *Antrostomus vociferus* |

Eastern Whip-poor-will

rounded wings

MALE

IN FLIGHT

buffy corners to tail

buffy throat stripe

FEMALE

black-and-gray bands across back

huge eyes

tawny patch on cheeks

flat, wide bill with long bristles

whitish throat stripe

MALE

cinnamon barring on dark wings

white corners to tail

As with many of the nightjars, the Eastern Whip-poor-will is heard more often than seen. Its camouflage makes it extremely difficult to spot on the forest floor and it usually flies away only when an intruder is very close—sometimes only a few feet. This species apparently has an unusual breeding pattern—while the male feeds the first brood until fledging, the female lays eggs for a second brood. Both eggs from one brood may hatch simultaneously near a full moon, when there is most light at night, allowing the parents more time to forage for their young.
VOICE Loud, 3-syllable whistle *WHIP-perrr-WIIL.*
NESTING Lays eggs on leaf litter on forest floor, often near overhead plant cover; 2 eggs; 2 broods; April–July
FEEDING Flies upward quickly from perch to capture passing moths and other insects, such as mosquitoes.

FLIGHT: slow, erratic flight, with alternating bouts of flapping and gliding.

WAITING IN AMBUSH
This species waits in ambush for its prey from a perch on the forest floor, or on a rock.

OCCURRENCE
Mixed mature forests with open understory, especially oak and pine forests on dry upland sites. Breeds from southeastern US north to southern Canada.

SIMILAR SPECIES

COMMON POORWILL
see p.448

smaller, grayer overall

square tail

CHUCK-WILL'S-WIDOW
see p.90

cinnamon-brown chin

larger overall

| Length **9–10in (23–26cm)** | Wingspan **17–20in (43–51cm)** | Weight **1⁹⁄₁₆–2¼oz (45–65g)** |
| Social **Solitary** | Lifespan **Up to 15 years** | Status **Secure** |

DATE SEEN	WHERE	NOTES

SWIFTS

SWIFTS SPEND VIRTUALLY ALL their daylight hours as well as many night hours plying the skies. The most aerial birds in North America—if not the world—swifts eat, drink, court, mate, and even sleep on the wing. Swifts are some of the fastest and most acrobatic flyers of the bird world. Several species have been clocked at more than 100mph (160kph). They feed on insects caught in aerial pursuits. The family name, based on the Greek *apous*, which means "without feet," originates from the ancient belief that swifts had no feet and lived their entire lives in the air.

CHIMNEY SWIFT
Widespread in the East, the Chimney Swift has readily adapted to human structures.

HUMMINGBIRDS

FOUND ONLY IN THE Americas, hummingbirds are sometimes referred to as the crown jewels of the bird world. The first sight of a glittering hummingbird can be a life-changing experience. The amount of iridescence in their plumage varies from almost none to what seems like every feather. Most North American male hummingbirds have a colorful throat patch

AGGRESSIVE MALES
This male Ruby-throated Hummingbird defends his territory from a perch.

called a gorget, but females tend to lack this gorgeous attribute. Because iridescent colors are structural and not pigment-based, a gorget can often appear blackish until seen at the correct angle toward the light. Hummingbirds are the only birds that can fly backward, an adaptation that allows them to move easily between flowers. Flying sideways, up, down, and hovering are also within hummingbirds' abilities, and all are achieved by their unique figure-eight, rapid wing strokes and reduced wing bone structure. Their long, thin bills allow them access to nectar in tubular flowers. The only common hummingbird in the East is the Ruby-throated Hummingbird.

NECTAR FEEDERS
All North American hummingbirds, such as this Black-chinned, subsist on nectar from wildflowers. This species is rare in the East.

| Order **Apodiformes** | Family **Apodidae** | Species *Chaetura pelagica* |

Chimney Swift 🔊

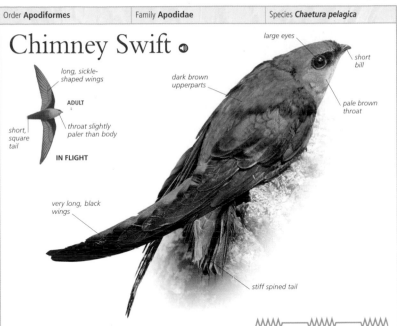

large eyes

short bill

long, sickle-shaped wings

dark brown upperparts

ADULT

pale brown throat

throat slightly paler than body

short, square tail

IN FLIGHT

very long, black wings

stiff spined tail

FLIGHT: fast, acrobatic, and erratic; very rapid, vibrating wingbeats; soars with tail fanned.

Nicknamed "spine-tailed," the Chimney Swift is a familiar summer sight and sound, racing through the skies east of the Rockies, its rolling twitters often heard. These birds do almost everything on the wing—feeding, drinking, and even bathing. Chimney Swifts have adapted to nest in human structures, including chimneys, although they once nested in tree holes. It remains a common bird, although local populations have declined; and it has expanded its range west and south.
VOICE High, rapid chips and twittering; notes from individuals in a flock run together into a rapid, descending chatter.
NESTING Shallow cup of twigs and saliva attached to inside of chimney or other artificial structure, rarely hollow tree; 4–5 eggs; 1 brood; April–August.
FEEDING Pursues a large variety of small aerial insects.

HIGH FLYER
Swifts feed at heights on sunny days, and only feed near the ground when it is cold and cloudy.

SIMILAR SPECIES

BLACK SWIFT

broader wings

larger overall

VAUX'S SWIFT

paler rump

shorter wings and tail

paler throat

OCCURRENCE
Widespread in eastern North America, over many habitats: urban and suburban areas, small towns; in sparsely populated areas nests in hollow trees and caves; regular in summer in southern California, present late March to early November. Winters in Amazonian South America.

| Length **5in (13cm)** | Wingspan **14in (36cm)** | Weight **⅝–1¹⁄₁₆oz (17–30g)** |
| Social **Flocks** | Lifespan **Up to 15 years** | Status **Declining** |

DATE SEEN	WHERE	NOTES

| Order **Apodiformes** | Family **Trochilidae** | Species *Archilochus colubris* |

Ruby-throated Hummingbird 🔊

MALE

IN FLIGHT (MALE)

dark, forked tail

pale-tipped crown feathers

bronzy-green upperparts

greenish speckling on throat

IMMATURE MALE

green crown

black face

straight, black bill

orange-red throat

white chest

greenish sides and flanks

grayish white underparts

MALE

white chin and throat

FEMALE

white underparts with buff wash on sides and flanks

rounded tail

glittering green upperparts

The only hummingbird to breed east of the Mississippi River, the Ruby-throated Hummingbird is a welcome addition to gardens throughout its range. It is easily identified in most of its range, though more difficult to distinguish in areas where other species are found, particularly during migration. Males perform a deep diving display for females. Before migration, these birds add about 1/16oz (2g) of fat to their weight to provide enough fuel for their nonstop 800-mile (1,300km) flight across the Gulf of Mexico.
VOICE Call a soft, thick *chic*, sometimes doubled; twittered notes in interactions; chase call a fast, slightly buzzy *tsi-tsi-tsi-tsi-tsi-tsi-tsi-tsi*; soft, rattling song very rarely heard.
NESTING Tiny cup of plant down, with bud scales and lichen on the exterior, bound with spider's silk, usually in deciduous trees; 2 eggs; 1–2 broods; April–September.
FEEDING Drinks nectar from many species of flowers; feeds on small insects and spiders, caught aerially or gleaned from foliage.

FLIGHT: swift, forward flight with very fast wingbeats; hovers at flowers and darts after insects.

CATCHING THE LIGHT
Although the throat patch often appears all black, the right lighting sets it afire with color.

SIMILAR SPECIES

BLACK-CHINNED HUMMINGBIRD ♀
see p.448

broader outer feathers

longer bill

ANNA'S HUMMINGBIRD ♀
harder, sharper call notes

thicker neck

grayer underparts

OCCURRENCE
Favors a variety of woodlands and gardens; earliest migrants appear in the South as early as late February; most leave by November; regular in winter in southern Florida; small numbers winter elsewhere on the Gulf Coast; rare in the West. The bulk of the population migrates to Central America for the winter.

| Length **3½in (9cm)** | Wingspan **4¼in (11cm)** | Weight **1/16–7/32oz (2–6g)** |
| Social **Solitary** | Lifespan **Up to 9 years** | Status **Secure** |

DATE SEEN	WHERE	NOTES

| Order **Apodiformes** | Family **Trochilidae** | Species *Selasphorus rufus* |

Rufous Hummingbird 🔊

green to bronze-green crown

white spot near eye

straight, smooth bill

MALE

rufous tail base with dark tips

IN FLIGHT

rufous upperparts

white patch on breast

wrinkled top bill

mostly green back

rich, rufous underparts

buff face coloration

rufous uppertail feathers

IMMATURE

whitish underparts

MALE

FEMALE

One of the most aggressive hummingbirds, the Rufous Hummingbird packs quite a punch, despite its small size; it often chases other hummingbirds away from nectar sources. This bird also breeds farther north than any other North American species of hummingbird and undertakes a lengthy migration. Males are recognizable by their overall fiery orange-rufous color, but females and immature birds are difficult to distinguish from Allen's Hummingbirds.

VOICE Call a hard *chuk*, sometimes in steady series or doubled; also short, buzzy warning call, *tssrr*; chase call a fast, raspy twitter, *tzzerr tichupy tichupy*.

NESTING Tiny cup of plant down, lichen, and other plant matter on exterior, bound with spider's silk, in shrubs or trees; 2 eggs; 1–2 broods; April–July.

FEEDING Drinks nectar from flowers and sap from trees; catches small insects and other arthropods in the air or gleans them off foliage.

FLIGHT: fast flight with extremely rapid wingbeats; hovers at flowers; darts after insects.

SIMILAR SPECIES

BROAD-TAILED HUMMINGBIRD ♀
higher-pitched call

ALLEN'S HUMMINGBIRD ♂

dull pinkish flanks

broad tail

entirely green back

FIERY MALE
With temperaments matching their bold, flame-like color, males aggressively defend territories.

OCCURRENCE
This Western species has become a regular fall visitor in the East. Breeds in old-growth forest clearings, bushy country, and urban gardens; early migrants appear in March; most leave by August; it has become a regular winter inhabitant along the Gulf Coast and southern California.

| Length **3½in (9cm)** | Wingspan **5in (13cm)** | Weight **³⁄₃₂–⁷⁄₃₂oz (3–6g)** |
| Social **Solitary** | Lifespan **Up to 12 years** | Status **Secure** |

DATE SEEN	WHERE	NOTES

RAILS, CRANES, AND RELATIVES

THESE BIRDS OF THE marshes and WETLANDS include many distinctive groups. The Rallidae, or rail family, is a diverse group of small- to medium-sized marsh birds, represented in the US and Canada by four long-billed rails, three short-billed rails, two gallinules, and a coot. The cranes, or Gruidae, include very large to huge birds, superficially similar to storks and the largest of the herons and egrets. However, genetic and anatomical differences place cranes and the limpkin in a different order from storks, and herons and egrets.

RAILS

Rails are mostly secretive, solitary, and inconspicuous in dense marsh vegetation, whereas coots and gallinules are seen on open water. Rails are all somewhat chicken-like birds with stubby tails and short, rounded wings, looking round-bodied from the side but very slender end-on. The rails of the genus *Rallus* have excellent camouflage, and are long-legged, long-toed, long-billed, and narrowbodied—the origin of the saying "as thin as a rail." The short-billed species are similar, but with shorter necks and stout, stubby bills. Both groups walk through wet marsh vegetation, though they can swim well. The gallinules, including the Common Gallinule and the Purple Gallinule, are more colorful than rails. They have long, slender toes. The American Coot has broad lobes along the sides of its toes, making it a more proficient swimmer and diver in deeper water. None has a particularly specialized diet; they eat insects, small crabs, slugs, snails, and plant matter. Breeding pairs of rails keep in close contact in dense vegetation by calling out loudly.

FLAT LANDING
Purple Gallinules can land safely on lily pads because their large toes spread their weight.

CRANES

The two North American species of cranes have long necks, small heads, and short bills. The long plumes on their inner wing feathers form a bustle, cloaking the tail on a standing crane, thereby giving them a different profile than any heron. Cranes fly with their necks straight out, rather than in the tight S-curve that is regularly seen in similar-sized herons. Cranes are long-distance migrants. The Whooping Crane, one of the world's rarest birds, is the tallest bird in North America, standing nearly 5ft (1.5m) high.

CRANE RALLY
Large numbers of Sandhill Cranes gather on feeding grounds in winter, groups arriving in V-formation.

| Order **Gruiformes** | Family **Rallidae** | Species *Coturnicops noveboracensis* |

Yellow Rail

dark brown crown

stubby yellow to olive-gray bill

dark stripe runs from cheek to bill

dangling legs

ADULT

white patch on inner wing feathers

IN FLIGHT

long tan stripes on blackish background

buff or yellow breast

ADULT

short tail

FLIGHT: low, weak, short, and direct with stiff wingbeats; dangling legs.

Although widespread, the diminutive, secretive, nocturnal Yellow Rail is extremely difficult to observe in its dense, damp, grassy habitat, and is detected mainly by its voice. The Yellow Rail, whose Latin name of *noveboracensis* means "of New York," has a small head, almost no neck, a stubby bill, a plump, almost tail-less body, and short legs. The bill of the male turns yellow in the breeding season; for the rest of the year, it is olive-gray like the female's. Although the Yellow Rail tends to dart for cover when disturbed, when it does fly, it reveals a distinctive white patch on its inner wing.

VOICE Two clicking calls followed by three more given by males, usually at night, reminiscent of two pebbles being struck together; also descending cackles, quiet croaking, and soft clucking.

NESTING Small cup of grasses and sedges, on the ground or in a plant tuft above water, concealed by overhanging vegetation; 8–10 eggs; 1 brood; May–June.

FEEDING Plucks seeds, aquatic insects, various small crustaceans, and mollusks (primarily small freshwater snails) from vegetation or ground; forages on the marsh surface or in shallow water, hidden by grass.

CURIOUS LISTENER
Imitating the "tick" calls of the Yellow Rail is often an effective way to lure it out into the open.

OCCURRENCE
Breeds in brackish and freshwater marshes and wet sedge meadows in Canada and the north-central US; there is an isolated breeding population in Oregon. Winters predominantly in coastal marshes along the eastern seaboard.

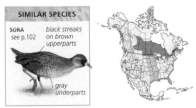

SIMILAR SPECIES

SORA see p.102 — black streaks on brown upperparts; gray underparts

| Length **7¼in (18.5cm)** | Wingspan **11in (28cm)** | Weight **1¾oz (50g)** |
| Social **Pairs** | Lifespan **Unknown** | Status **Endangered** |

DATE SEEN	WHERE	NOTES

| Order **Gruiformes** | Family **Rallidae** | Species *Laterallus jamaicensis* |

Black Rail

ADULT
white spotted back
reddish brown nape

IN FLIGHT
dark overall

slate-gray head
red eye
chestnut-brown nape and upper mantle
blackish upperparts, flecked with white
small, straight bill
dark gray breast and upper belly
darker gray underparts
greenish gray legs
ADULT (SUMMER)

This tiny, mouse-sized rail is so elusive that few people have ever seen it; consequently, much remains unknown about its life history and it is of great interest to birdwatchers. It is usually detected by its territorial call that is given during the breeding season from the cover of marsh grass. The best chance to see a Black Rail is when high tides force it to move to higher ground. Unfortunately, this is when it can fall prey to herons.

VOICE Distinctive, 3-note *kik-kee-do* given by male, mostly at night, during breeding season; makes low growl when agitated.

NESTING Small, deep cup of grasses and sedges placed on the ground, with an overhanging canopy of woven plants; 5–9 eggs; 2 broods; March–July.

FEEDING Forages on the wet marsh surface beneath the cover of grass for snails, insects, spiders, and seeds of marsh plants.

FLIGHT: reluctant flier, short flights with dangling legs; longer flights; fast and direct.

ELUSIVE BIRD
The highly secretive Black Rail is almost never seen by birdwatchers, and is a prize find.

SIMILAR SPECIES

VIRGINIA RAIL
see p.101
longer bill
larger overall

SORA ♀
see p.102
downy back
yellow bill

OCCURRENCE
The Black Rail has a disjointed distribution across the US. It is found among reeds in freshwater, salt, and brackish marshes or wet meadows. It also occurs patchily in the West Indies (its scientific name is *jamaicensis*, after the island Jamaica), Central America, and South America.

Length **6in (15cm)**	Wingspan **9in (23cm)**	Weight **1¹⁄₁₆oz (30g)**
Social **Solitary**	Lifespan **Unknown**	Status **Secure**

DATE SEEN	WHERE	NOTES

| Order **Gruiformes** | Family **Rallidae** | Species *Rallus crepitans* |

Clapper Rail

gray cheeks

drab gray overall

long, down-curved bill

ADULT (GULF COAST)

IN FLIGHT

R. c. saturatus
(GULF COAST)

long, thick legs

long bill

pale underparts

**R. c. crepitans
(ATLANTIC)**

Closely related to the King Rail and Ridgway's Rail, the Clapper Rail is a common and widespread species on the Atlantic and Gulf Coasts. The Clapper Rail can be found in a variety of habitats but it is closely tied to brackish and saltwater marshes dominated by *Spartina* cord grass. However, in southern Florida, this rail is found close to mangrove swamps. The Clapper Rail's distinctive, insistent calls are the best way to recognize its presence, as it is rarely seen.

VOICE Grunting calls; repeated loud *kek* notes.

NESTING Bulky cup of grasses and plant stems lined with finer material; bends growing plants to form a canopy; 4–14 eggs; 1 brood; March–August.

FEEDING Forages by crouching low and stalking through marsh, eating snails, insects, spiders, clams, fish, bird eggs, and seeds.

FLIGHT: low and weak; flies with outstretched neck and dangling legs.

LOUD AND CLEAR
The repeated, insistent *kek* call may be heard more than a mile away.

OCCURRENCE
Found mostly in saltwater and brackish marshes along the Atlantic Seaboard. The Clapper Rail winters south of its breeding range.

SIMILAR SPECIES

KING RAIL
see p.100

smaller overall

black-and-white streaking on flanks

VIRGINIA RAIL
see p.101

gray face

black-and-white barred flanks

| Length **14½in (37cm)** | Wingspan **19in (48cm)** | Weight **10oz (275g)** |
| Social **Solitary** | Lifespan **Up to 7 years** | Status **Localized** |

DATE SEEN	WHERE	NOTES

Order **Gruiformes**	Family **Rallidae**	Species *Rallus elegans*

King Rail

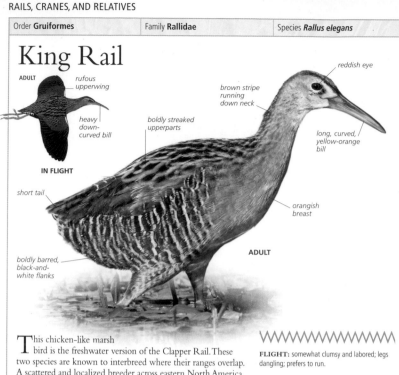

ADULT

rufous upperwing

heavy down-curved bill

IN FLIGHT

reddish eye

brown stripe running down neck

boldly streaked upperparts

long, curved, yellow-orange bill

short tail

orangish breast

ADULT

boldly barred, black-and-white flanks

This chicken-like marsh bird is the freshwater version of the Clapper Rail. These two species are known to interbreed where their ranges overlap. A scattered and localized breeder across eastern North America, the King Rail depends on extensive freshwater marsh habitats with tall, emergent reeds and cattails. Concealed by this vegetation, the King Rail is rarely seen and is most often detected by its distinctive calls.

VOICE Male call similar to Clapper Rail but lower; emits a loud *kik kik kik* during breeding season.

NESTING Cup of vegetation, often hidden by bent stems that form a canopy; 6–12 eggs; 2 broods; February–August.

FEEDING Forages in concealed locations for insects, snails, spiders, and crustaceans such as shrimps, crabs, and barnacles; also fish, frogs, and seeds.

FLIGHT: somewhat clumsy and labored; legs dangling; prefers to run.

LARGEST RAIL
Easily confused with the closely related Clapper Rail, this is the largest North American rail.

SIMILAR SPECIES

CLAPPER RAIL
see p.99

flank barring diffused

grayer overall

VIRGINIA RAIL
see p.101

gray face

red bill

smaller overall

OCCURRENCE
Mostly breeds in freshwater marshes in the eastern US and in extreme southern Ontario. Also found throughout the year along the southern coast of the US, including Florida, and in central Mexico and Cuba.

Length **15in (38cm)**	Wingspan **20in (51cm)**	Weight **13oz (375g)**
Social **Pairs**	Lifespan **Unknown**	Status **Endangered**

DATE SEEN	WHERE	NOTES

Order **Gruiformes**	Family **Rallidae**	Species *Rallus limicola*

Virginia Rail

gray cheeks

rufous upperwing

streaked black and brown upperparts

ADULT (BREEDING)

dark outer wing feathers

IN FLIGHT

white undertail

curved, red bill

reddish brown breast

black-and-white barring on flanks

reddish legs and toes

ADULT (BREEDING)

diffused streaking

dark bill

dark, blotchy breast

ADULT (NONBREEDING)

A smaller version of the King Rail, this freshwater marsh dweller is similar to its other relatives, more often heard than seen. Distributed in a wide range, the Virginia Rail spends most of its time in thick, reedy vegetation, which it pushes using its "rail thin" body and flexible vertebrae. Although it spends most of its life walking, it can swim and even dive to escape danger. The Virginia Rail is a partial migrant that leaves its northern breeding grounds in winter.

VOICE Series of pig-like grunting *oinks* that start loud and sharp, becoming steadily softer; also emits a series of double notes *ka-dik ka-dik.*

NESTING Substantial cup of plant material, concealed by bent-over stems; 5–12 eggs; 1–2 broods; April–July.

FEEDING Actively stalks prey or may wait and dive into water; primarily eats snails, insects, and spiders, but may also eat seeds.

FLIGHT: weak and struggling with outstretched neck and legs trailing behind.

HARD TO SPOT
The secretive Virginia Rail is difficult to spot in its reedy habitat.

SIMILAR SPECIES

CLAPPER RAIL see p.99

weak flank barring

KING RAIL see p.100

less gray face
larger overall

orange face

dark undertail

yellow-orange bill

OCCURRENCE
Breeds in freshwater habitats across North America, though is found throughout the year along the West Coast of the US. In winter, eastern populations move to saltwater and freshwater marshes in the southern US, including Florida, and in northern and central Mexico.

Length **9½in (24cm)**	Wingspan **13in (33cm)**	Weight **3oz (85g)**
Social **Pairs**	Lifespan **Unknown**	Status **Secure**

DATE SEEN	WHERE	NOTES

Order **Gruiformes**	Family **Rallidae**	Species *Porzana carolina*

Sora

white markings on back

ADULT (BREEDING)

long, trailing legs

IN FLIGHT

reduced black on face

ADULT (NONBREEDING)

white barring on flanks

short tail

no black mask

buffy breast

JUVENILE

brown cheek patch

yellow bill

black mask

gray breast

yellowish green legs

ADULT (BREEDING)

Despite being the most widely distributed rail in North America, the Sora is rarely seen. It breeds in freshwater marshes and migrates hundreds of miles south in winter despite its weak and hesitant flight. It swims well, with a characteristic head-bobbing action. The Sora can be spotted walking at the edge of emergent vegetation—its yellow bill and black mask distinguish it from other rails.

VOICE Call a long, high, and loud, descending, horse-like whinny *ko-wee-hee-hee-hee-hee*; has an up-slurred whistle.

NESTING Loosely woven basket of marsh vegetation suspended above water or positioned in clumps of vegetation on the water's surface; 8–11 eggs; 1 brood; May–June.

FEEDING Rakes vegetation with toes or pulls with bill in search of seeds of wetland plants, insects, spiders, and snails.

FLIGHT: appears weak, yet strenuous; wingbeats hurried and constant.

CHICKEN-LIKE WALK
A rare sight, the Sora walks chicken-like through a marsh, its body in a low crouch.

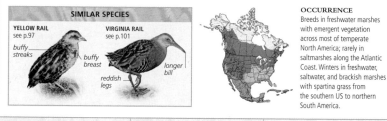

SIMILAR SPECIES

YELLOW RAIL
see p.97

buffy streaks

buffy breast

VIRGINIA RAIL
see p.101

longer bill

reddish legs

OCCURRENCE
Breeds in freshwater marshes with emergent vegetation across most of temperate North America; rarely in saltmarshes along the Atlantic Coast. Winters in freshwater, saltwater, and brackish marshes with spartina grass from the southern US to northern South America.

Length **8½in (22cm)**	Wingspan **14in (36cm)**	Weight **2⅝oz (75g)**
Social **Solitary**	Lifespan **Unknown**	Status **Secure**

DATE SEEN	WHERE	NOTES

| Order **Gruiformes** | Family **Rallidae** | Species *Porphyrio martinicus* |

Purple Gallinule

pale blue frontal shield

yellow-tipped red bill

iridescent green back and rump

blue wings

ADULT (BREEDING)

long, trailing legs

IN FLIGHT

dark blue breast and belly

greenish frontal shield

grayish breast

brownish upperparts

ADULT (BREEDING)

yellow legs with very large toes

IMMATURE

This vibrantly colored rail inhabits freshwater marshes in the southeastern US. The Purple Gallinule is extremely conspicuous because of its purple head and neck, bright red bill, and yellow legs. This species is well known for long distance vagrancy far outside its normal breeding range; it has been found as far away as Labrador, South Georgia, Switzerland, and South Africa.

VOICE Call a chicken-like clucking; also grunts and higher-pitched single notes.

NESTING Bulky cup of plant material built up slightly above the water's surface, usually placed in marsh vegetation; 5–10 eggs; 1 brood; April–August.

FEEDING Omnivorous diet; seeds, leaves, insects, spiders, and worms; will sometimes turn over lily pads to find aquatic insects.

FLIGHT: weak and slow with its heavy legs trailing behind.

EXTREMELY LONG TOES
The Purple Gallinule's long toes enable it to walk across floating vegetation

OCCURRENCE
Breeds in lush wetlands containing emergent vegetation of the southeastern US; mostly freshwater marshes. Winter habitat similar to breeding; non-Florida populations withdraw southward in winter; Florida population nonmigratory.

SIMILAR SPECIES

COMMON GALLINULE see p.104
glossy brown back
greenish yellow legs

AMERICAN COOT see p.105
black head
white bill
black-and-gray plumage

| Length **13in (33cm)** | Wingspan **22in (56cm)** | Weight **8oz (225g)** |
| Social **Pairs** | Lifespan **Unknown** | Status **Localized** |

DATE SEEN	WHERE	NOTES

RAILS, CRANES, AND RELATIVES

| Order **Gruiformes** | Family **Rallidae** | Species **Gallinula galeata** |

Common Gallinule 🔊

small, round wings

ADULT

long trailing legs

IN FLIGHT

glossy brown back

square-topped, red facial shield

shiny slate-gray breast

pale gray-brown body

white patch on side of tail

dull bill

white streaks on flanks

JUVENILE

pale green legs with very long toes

ADULT

FLIGHT: rather weak and labored with legs trailing.

The Common Gallinule is fairly widespread in southern Canada and the eastern US; its distribution is more scattered in the western states. It has similarities in behavior and habitat to both the true rails and the coots. Equally at home on land and water, its long toes allow it to walk easily over floating vegetation and soft mud. When walking or swimming, the Common Gallinule nervously jerks its short tail, revealing its white undertail feathers, and bobs its head.
VOICE A variety of rapid, raucous, cackling phrases and an explosive *krrooo*.
NESTING Bulky platform of aquatic vegetation with growing plants pulled over to conceal it, or close to water; 5–11 eggs, 1–3 broods; May–August, maybe year-round in Florida.
FEEDING Forages mainly on aquatic and terrestrial plants and aquatic vegetation; also eats snails, spiders, and insects.

DUAL HABITAT
A walker and a swimmer, the Gallinule is equally at home on land and in water.

OCCURRENCE
Breeds in freshwater habitats in the eastern US and Canada; more localized in the West. Winters in warmer areas with open water, such as the southern US, and Mexico. Also found in Central and South America.

SIMILAR SPECIES

PURPLE GALLINULE see p.103 — blue frontal shield — bright yellow legs

AMERICAN COOT see p.105 — white bill — darker plumage

| Length **14in (36cm)** | Wingspan **21in (53cm)** | Weight **11oz (325g)** |
| Social **Pairs** | Lifespan **Up to 10 years** | Status **Secure** |

DATE SEEN	WHERE	NOTES

104

| Order **Gruiformes** | Family **Rallidae** | Species *Fulica americana* |

American Coot 🔊

ADULT (BREEDING)

dark gray body

white bill

white-edged feathers

IN FLIGHT

black head

red eye

black ring on bill

ADULT (BREEDING)

dull grayish plumage

JUVENILE

long, greenish yellow legs

lobed toes

This duck-like species is the most abundant and widely distributed of North American rails. Its lobed toes make it well adapted to swimming and diving, but they are somewhat of an impediment on land. Its flight is clumsy; it becomes airborne with difficulty, running along the water surface before taking off. American Coots form large flocks on open water in winter, often associating with ducks—an unusual trait for a member of the rail family.

VOICE Various raucous clucks, grunts, and croaks and an explosive *keek*.

NESTING Bulky cup of plant material placed in aquatic vegetation on or near water; 5–15 eggs; 1–2 broods; April–July.

FEEDING Forages on or by diving under shallow water and on land; primarily herbivorous, but also eats snails, insects, spiders, tadpoles, fish, and even carrion.

FLIGHT: low and labored; runs for quite a long distance to takeoff.

SWIMMING AWAY
The red-headed, baldish looking American Coot chicks leave the nest a day after hatching.

SIMILAR SPECIES

PURPLE GALLINULE
see p.103

COMMON GALLINULE ♀
see p.104

red bill with yellow tip

bright yellow legs

white streaks on flanks

OCCURRENCE
Breeds in open water habitats west of the Appalachians and in Florida. Moves from the northern parts of its range in winter to the southeastern US, where open water persists; also migrates to western and southern Mexico.

| Length **15½in (40cm)** | Wingspan **24in (61cm)** | Weight **16oz (450g)** |
| Social **Flocks** | Lifespan **Up to 22 years** | Status **Secure** |

DATE SEEN	WHERE	NOTES

Order **Gruiformes**	Family **Aramidae**	Species *Aramus guarauna*

Limpkin

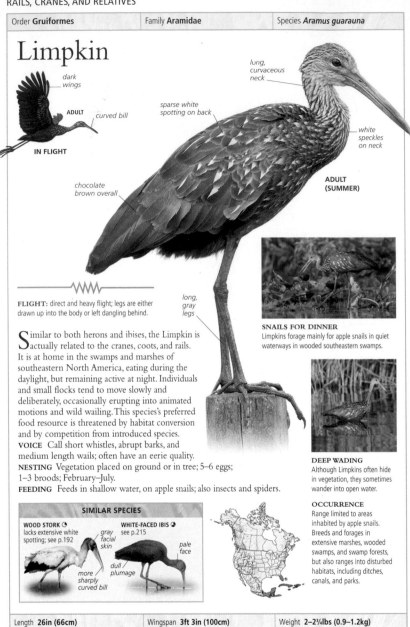

dark wings

ADULT

curved bill

IN FLIGHT

long, curvaceous neck

sparse white spotting on back

white speckles on neck

chocolate brown overall

ADULT (SUMMER)

long, gray legs

—/\/\/\—

FLIGHT: direct and heavy flight; legs are either drawn up into the body or left dangling behind.

Similar to both herons and ibises, the Limpkin is actually related to the cranes, coots, and rails. It is at home in the swamps and marshes of southeastern North America, eating during the daylight, but remaining active at night. Individuals and small flocks tend to move slowly and deliberately, occasionally erupting into animated motions and wild wailing. This species's preferred food resource is threatened by habitat conversion and by competition from introduced species.

VOICE Call short whistles, abrupt barks, and medium length wails; often have an eerie quality.

NESTING Vegetation placed on ground or in tree; 5–6 eggs; 1–3 broods; February–July.

FEEDING Feeds in shallow water, on apple snails; also insects and spiders.

SNAILS FOR DINNER
Limpkins forage mainly for apple snails in quiet waterways in wooded southeastern swamps.

DEEP WADING
Although Limpkins often hide in vegetation, they sometimes wander into open water.

OCCURRENCE
Range limited to areas inhabited by apple snails. Breeds and forages in extensive marshes, wooded swamps, and swamp forests, but also ranges into disturbed habitats, including ditches, canals, and parks.

SIMILAR SPECIES

WOOD STORK ☾
lacks extensive white spotting; see p.192

gray facial skin

more sharply curved bill

WHITE-FACED IBIS ☾
see p.215

pale face

dull plumage

Length **26in (66cm)**	Wingspan **3ft 3in (100cm)**	Weight **2–2¾lbs (0.9–1.2kg)**
Social **Solitary**	Lifespan **Up to 12 years**	Status **Declining**

DATE SEEN	WHERE	NOTES

Order **Gruiformes**	Family **Gruidae**	Species *Antigone canadensis*

Sandhill Crane 🔊

black wing tips

head held straight

ADULT

IN FLIGHT

trailing legs

brownish head

body with pale brown smudges

JUVENILE

red crown

long, black bill

pale cheek

long neck

ADULT

rusty body

shaggy feathers

long, black legs

"IRON-STAINED" PLUMAGE

FLIGHT: alternates slow, steady flapping with periods of gliding; flocks in single-file.

These large, slender, and long-necked birds are famous for their elaborate courtship dances, far-carrying vocalizations, and remarkable migrations. Their bodies are sometimes stained with a rusty color, supposedly because they probe into mud which contains iron; when a bird preens, this is transferred from its bill to its plumage. Sandhill Cranes are broadly grouped into "Lesser" and "Greater" populations that differ in the geographical location of their breeding grounds and migration routes.

VOICE Call loud, wooden, hollow bugling, audible at great distances; noisy in flight and courtship.
NESTING Mound of sticks and grasses placed on ground; 1 egg; 1 brood; April–September.
FEEDING Eats shoots, grain; also aquatic mollusks and insects.

MEMORABLE IMAGE
Its long neck, large wings, and distinctive red crown make it unmistakable.

OCCURRENCE
Breeds in muskeg, tundra, and forest clearings across northwestern North America, east to Québec and the Great Lakes; large wintering and migratory flocks often densely packed, roosting in or near marshes. Winters south to northern Mexico.

SIMILAR SPECIES

GREAT BLUE HERON ◑ see p.203

dark crown

paler legs

WHOOPING CRANE see p.118

red on face

all-white plumage

larger overall

Length **2¾–4ft (0.8–1.2m)**	Wingspan **6–7½ft (1.8–2.3m)**	Weight **7¾–11lb (3.5–5kg)**
Social **Flocks**	Lifespan **Up to 25 years**	Status **Secure**

DATE SEEN	WHERE	NOTES

SHOREBIRDS, GULLS, AUKS, AND RELATIVES

THE DIVERSE SHOREBIRD, gull, and auk families together form the order Charadriiformes. They are small to medium-sized, mostly migratory birds, associated with aquatic habitats. More than 100 species are found in North America.

TYPICAL GULL
Most large gulls, such as this Ring-billed Gull, have white heads and underparts with long wings and a bright sturdy bill.

SHOREBIRDS

The various species popularly known as shorebirds belong to several different families. In North America there are the oystercatchers (Haematopodidae), the avocets and stilts (Recurvirostridae), the plovers (Charadriidae), and the sandpipers and phalaropes (Scolopacidae). They have long legs in proportion to their bodies, and a variety of bills, ranging from short to long, thin, thick, straight, down-curved and up-curved.

GULLS

More than 20 species of North American gulls in the subfamily Larinae share similar stout body shapes, sturdy bills, and webbed toes. Nearly all are scavengers. Closely associated with coastal areas, few gulls venture far out to sea. Some species are seen around fishing ports and harbors, or inland, especially in urban areas and garbage dumps.

TERNS

Terns are specialized long-billed predators that dive for fish. More slender and elegant than gulls, nearly all are immediately recognizable when breeding, because of their black caps and long, pointed bills. The related Black Skimmer also catches fish, but has a different bill.

AUKS

Denizens of the northern oceans, these birds only come to land to breed. Most nest in colonies on sheer cliffs overlooking the ocean, but puffins excavate burrows in the ground, and some murrelets nest away from predators high up in treetops far inland.

COLOR-CHANGE BILL
The bright colors of a breeding Atlantic Puffin's bill fade to more muted tones in winter, after the breeding season.

ON THE MOVE
Dunlins and other sandpipers gather in large, highly coordinated flocks on migration.

| Order **Charadriiformes** | Family **Recurvirostridae** | Species *Himantopus himantopus* |

Black-necked Stilt

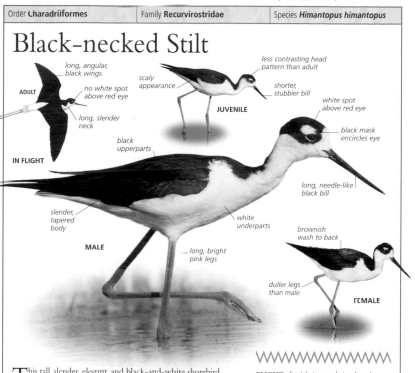

ADULT

long, angular, black wings

no white spot above red eye

long, slender neck

IN FLIGHT

black upperparts

slender, tapered body

scaly appearance

JUVENILE

less contrasting head pattern than adult

shorter, stubbier bill

white spot above red eye

black mask encircles eye

long, needle-like black bill

MALE

white underparts

long, bright pink legs

brownish wash to back

duller legs than male

FEMALE

This tall, slender, elegant, and black-and-white shorebird is a familiar sight at ponds and lagoons in the western and southern US. Even among the shorebirds, it is remarkably long legged, at times almost grotesquely so: in flight, it often crosses its trailing legs as if for extra control and support. Breeding takes place in small colonies, with several pairs sharing the same site. In winter, these tall birds are often seen in small flocks of about 25 individuals. These groups feed quietly in sheltered areas, but they aggressively drive visitors away with their raucous calls, dog-like yips, and noisy communal protests. The increased use of pesticides and loss of wetland habitat could cause a decline in its numbers in the future. The US populations belong to the subspecies *mexicanus*.

VOICE Flight and alarm call a loud, continuous poodle like *yip-yip-yip*, given in a long series when alarmed.

NESTING Simple scrape lined with grass in soft soil, 4 eggs; 1 brood; April–May.

FEEDING Walks slowly in shallow water, picking food off surface; diet includes tadpoles, shrimp, snails, flies, worms, clams, small fish, and frogs.

FLIGHT: direct, but somewhat awkward because of its long, trailing legs; deep wingbeats.

FRIENDLY BUNCH
Black-necked Stilts are gregarious by nature, and often roost together in shallow water.

OCCURRENCE
Breeds around marshes, shallow grassy ponds, lake margins, and manmade waterbodies, such as reservoirs; uses similar habitats during migration and winter, as well as shallow lagoons, flooded fields, and mangrove swamps. Southern birds migrate locally only.

| Length **14–15½in (35–39cm)** | Wingspan **29–32in (73–81cm)** | Weight **4–8oz (125–225g)** |
| Social **Small flocks** | Lifespan **Up to 19 years** | Status **Secure** |

DATE SEEN	WHERE		NOTES

| Order **Charadriiformes** | Family **Recurvirostridae** | Species *Recurvirostra americana* |

American Avocet

striking black-and-white pattern

ADULT (BREEDING)

IN FLIGHT

white eye-ring

dark eye

cinnamon-colored head

long, thin, upturned bill

bold shoulder feathers

cinnamon-colored neck

white underparts

FEMALE

less upturned bill

long, bluish legs

MALE

no cinnamon color on head and neck

white plumage

ADULT (NONBREEDING)

WWWWWWWWWWWW

FLIGHT: fast, direct, and graceful; very long legs extend beyond tail.

With its long, thin, and upturned bill, this graceful, long-legged shorebird is unmistakable when foraging. When it takes off, its striking plumage pattern is clearly visible. It is the only one of the four avocet species in the world that changes plumage when breeding. Breeding birds have a cinnamon head and neck, and bold, patterns on their black-and-white wings and upperparts. The American Avocet forms large flocks during migration and in winter.
VOICE Flight call a variable melodic *kleet*, loud and repetitive, given when alarmed and by foraging birds.

FORAGING FLOCK
These birds walk through shallow water in flocks searching mainly for insects and crustaceans.

NESTING Simple scrape in shallow depression; 4 eggs; 1 brood; May–June.
FEEDING Uses specialized bill to probe, scythe, or jab a variety of aquatic invertebrates, small fish, and seeds; walks steadily in belly-deep water to chase its prey.

TRICKY BALANCE
During mating, the male supports himself with raised wings as the female extends her neck forward.

OCCURRENCE
Breeds in temporary wetlands, in dry to arid regions. During migration and in winter, found in shallow water habitats, including ponds, reservoirs, fresh- and saltwater marshes, tidal mudflats, and lagoons. Each year, a flock of about 10,000 birds winters at Bolivar Flats, Texas. Regular East Coast visitor.

| Length **17–18½in (43–47cm)** | Wingspan **29–32in (74–81cm)** | Weight **10–12oz (275–350g)** |
| Social **Large flocks** | Lifespan **Up to 9 years** | Status **Secure** |

DATE SEEN	WHERE	NOTES

| Order **Charadriiformes** | Family **Haematopodidae** | Species *Haematopus palliatus* |

American Oystercatcher 🔊

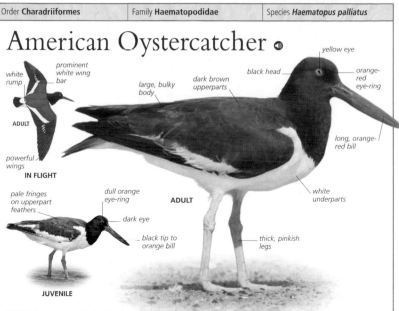

yellow eye

white rump

prominent white wing bar

large, bulky body

dark brown upperparts

black head

orange-red eye-ring

ADULT

long, orange-red bill

powerful wings

IN FLIGHT

pale fringes on upperpart feathers

dull orange eye-ring

ADULT

white underparts

dark eye

black tip to orange bill

thick, pinkish legs

JUVENILE

This large and noisy shorebird is conspicuous on beachfront habitats along the Atlantic and Gulf of Mexico Coastlines. It is the heaviest of all North American shorebirds, and often runs on its thick, powerful legs to escape danger. This species is found in flocks of a few to several hundred birds in winter at its preferred feeding and roosting locations. Up to eight birds can be seen together in synchronized courtship flights, with their heads and necks bowed and wings arched upward.
VOICE Whistled, loud, clear descending *wheeu* call; alarm call sharp *wheep*; flight display call several sharp whistles accelerating into a series of descending piping notes.
NESTING Simple scrape with shell debris on coastal sandy beaches, dunes, and saltmarshes; 2–3 eggs; 1 brood; April–May.
FEEDING Forages on slightly submerged shellfish beds; feeds by probing in subsoil; also by stabbing or hammering open bivalve shells with powerful bill.

FLIGHT: powerful, fast, direct flight with rapid shallow wingbeats.

OPENING UP
This species uses its long, powerful bill to pry open or smash bivalve mollusks on rocks.

SIMILAR SPECIES

BLACK OYSTERCATCHER

all dark plumage

STRONG FLIER
Strong fliers, these birds use their long, powerful wings for swift, short-distance forays.

OCCURRENCE
Exclusive to saltwater coastal habitats; locally common from Massachusetts southward to Gulf Coast; also Caribbean south to Argentina, north from Chile to Baja California, Mexico. Occurs in southern California; recent nesting has been documented in Nova Scotia. Expanding northward on Atlantic Coast.

| Length **15½–17½in (40–44cm)** | Wingspan **29–32in (73–81cm)** | Weight **14–25oz (400–700g)** |
| Social **Flocks** | Lifespan **Up to 17 years** | Status **Secure** |

DATE SEEN	WHERE		NOTES

| Order **Charadriiformes** | Family **Charadriidae** | Species *Pluvialis squatarola* |

Black-bellied Plover 🔊

white-edged, dark-centered feathers

checkered upperparts

white rump

MALE (BREEDING)

black outer wing feathers

white wing stripe

diffused streaks to upper breast

whitish crown

ADULT (NON-BREEDING)

whitish underparts

markedly streaked breast

checkered, black-and-white upperparts

JUVENILE

ADULT (NONBREEDING)

black underwing patch

IN FLIGHT

black cheeks

darker crown

duller plumage than male

black belly

MALE (BREEDING)

FEMALE (MOLTING TO BREEDING PLUMAGE)

FLIGHT: straight and fast; powerful wingbeats.

The Black-bellied Plover is the largest and most common of the three North American *Pluvialis* plovers. Its preference for open feeding habitats, its bulky structure, and very upright stance make it a fairly conspicuous species. The Black-bellied Plover's black underwing patches, visible in flight, are present in both its breeding and nonbreeding plumages and distinguish it from the other *Pluvialis* plovers.

VOICE Typical call a three-syllabled, clear, plaintive, whistled *whEE-er-eee*, with middle note lower; flight song of male during breeding softer, with accent on second syllable.

NESTING Shallow depression lined with mosses and lichens in moist to dry lowland tundra; 1–5 eggs; 1 brood; May–July.

FEEDING Forages mainly along coasts in typical plover style: run, pause, and pluck; eats insects, worms, bivalves, and crustaceans.

CASUAL WADING
The Black-bellied Plover wades in shallow water but does most of its foraging in mudflats.

SIMILAR SPECIES

AMERICAN GOLDEN-PLOVER ❋ see p.113

dark cap

MOUNTAIN PLOVER ❋ see p.449

sandy brown upperparts

dingy, brownish upperparts

white underparts

OCCURRENCE
Breeds in High Arctic habitats from western Russia across the Bering Sea to Alaska, and east to Baffin Island; winters primarily in coastal areas from southern Canada and US, south to southern South America. Found inland during migration. Migrates south all the way to South America.

| Length **10½–12in (27–30cm)** | Wingspan **29–32in (73–81cm)** | Weight **5–9oz (150–250g)** |
| Social **Flocks** | Lifespan **Up to 12 years** | Status **Secure** |

DATE SEEN	WHERE	NOTES

| Order **Charadriiformes** | Family **Charadriidae** | Species *Pluvialis dominica* |

American Golden-Plover

ADULT (BREEDING)
dark tail
black-and-white face

ADULT (NON-BREEDING)
gray underwing
diffused streaks on breast

IN FLIGHT

brownish upperparts
dark cap
small, thin bill
uniformly dusky underparts

ADULT (NONBREEDING)

crisply checkered upperparts
slim, tapered body
neatly mottled breast

JUVENILE

white stripe from forehead to nape
tan-and-black spangled upperparts

black underparts
black legs

ADULT (BREEDING)

WWWWWWWWWWW
FLIGHT: strong, fast, powerful flight on deep wingbeats.

This long-distance migrant is seen in North America only during its lengthy spring and fall journeys to and from its High Arctic breeding grounds and wintering locations in southern South America. An elegant, slender, yet large plover, it prefers inland grassy habitats and plowed fields to coastal mudflats. The American Golden-Plover's annual migration route includes a feeding stop at Labrador, then a 1,550–1,860 miles (2,500–3,000km) flight over the Atlantic Ocean to South America.
VOICE Flight call a whistled 2-note *queE-dle*, or *klee-u*, with second note shorter and lower pitched; male flight song a strong, melodious whistled *kid-eek*, or *kid-EEp*.
NESTING Shallow depression lined with lichens in dry, open tundra, 4 eggs; 1 brood; May–July.
FEEDING Forages in run, pause, and pluck sequence on insects, mollusks, crustaceans, and worms; also berries and seeds.

DISTRACTION TECHNIQUE
This breeding American Golden-Plover is feigning an injury to its wing to draw predators away from its eggs or chicks in its nest.

SIMILAR SPECIES

PACIFIC GOLDEN-PLOVER ✳
see p.471
longer legs

PACIFIC GOLDEN-PLOVER ♀
see p.471
larger bill
checkered gold-and-black upperparts
pale golden wash

OCCURRENCE
Breeds in Arctic tundra habitats. In migration, it occurs in prairies, tilled farmlands, golf courses, pastures, airports; also mudflats, shorelines, and beaches. In spring, seen in Texas and Great Plains; in fall, uncommon in northeast Maritimes and New England; scarce along the Pacific Coast.

| Length **9½–11in (24–28cm)** | Wingspan **23–28in (59–72cm)** | Weight **4–7oz (125–200g)** |
| Social **Solitary/Small flocks** | Lifespan **Unknown** | Status **Secure** |

DATE SEEN	WHERE	NOTES

| Order **Charadriiformes** | Family **Charadriidae** | Species *Charadrius vociferus* |

Killdeer

long wings
white wing bar
ADULT
reddish orange tail and rump
IN FLIGHT

brownish upperparts
rufous wash to back and wings

red eye-ring
black collar encircling neck
brownish crown
small, thin, black bill

MALE

long tail

white underparts

second neck band crosses upper breast

pinkish legs, sometimes with yellowish tinge

FLIGHT: fast, twisting flight with fluid wingbeats.

This loud and vocal shorebird is the most widespread plover in North America, nesting in all southern Canadian provinces and across the US. The Killdeer's piercing call carries for long distances, sometimes causing other birds to fly away in fear of imminent danger. These birds often nest near human habitation, allowing a close observation of their vigilant parental nature with young chicks.
VOICE Flight call a rising, drawn out *deeee*; alarm call a loud, penetrating *dee-ee*, given repetitively; agitated birds also give series of *dee* notes, followed by rising trill.
NESTING Scrape on ground, sometimes in slight depression; 4 eggs; 1 brood (north), 2–3 broods (south); March–July.
FEEDING Forages in typical plover style: run, pause, and pick; eats a variety of invertebrates such as worms, snails, grasshoppers, and beetles; also small vertebrates and seeds.

CLEVER MANEUVER
The Killdeer lures intruders away from its nest with a "broken wing" display.

SIMILAR SPECIES

SEMIPALMATED PLOVER ❋ see p.115
orange-yellow legs
smaller overall

WILSON'S PLOVER see p.117
single dark neckband
single, black collar
pinkish legs
short tail

OCCURRENCE
Widespread across Canada and the US, the Killdeer occurs in a wide variety of habitats. These include shorelines, mudflats, lake and river edges, sparsely grassy fields and pastures, golf courses, roadsides, parking lots, flat rooftops, driveways, and other terrestrial habitats.

| Length **9–10in (23–26cm)** | Wingspan **23–25in (58–63cm)** | Weight **2¼–3⅛ oz (65–90g)** |
| Social **Small flocks** | Lifespan **Up to 10 years** | Status **Declining** |

DATE SEEN	WHERE	NOTES

| Order **Charadriiformes** | Family **Charadriidae** | Species *Charadrius semipalmatus* |

Semipalmated Plover 🔊

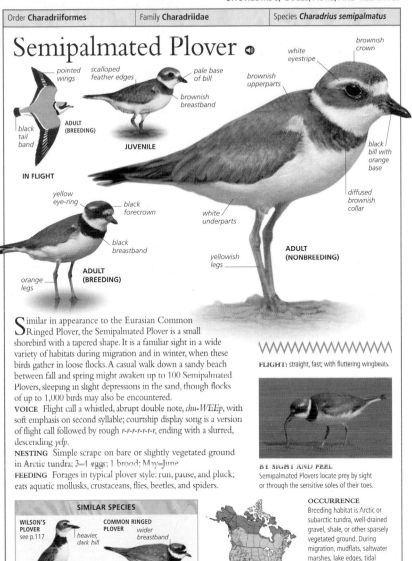

- pointed wings
- scalloped feather edges
- pale base of bill
- brownish breastband
- black tail band
- **ADULT (BREEDING)**
- **JUVENILE**
- **IN FLIGHT**
- brownish crown
- white eyestripe
- brownish upperparts
- black bill with orange base
- diffused brownish collar
- white underparts
- yellow eye-ring
- black forecrown
- white underparts
- black breastband
- yellowish legs
- **ADULT (NONBREEDING)**
- orange legs
- **ADULT (BREEDING)**

Similar in appearance to the Eurasian Common Ringed Plover, the Semipalmated Plover is a small shorebird with a tapered shape. It is a familiar sight in a wide variety of habitats during migration and in winter, when these birds gather in loose flocks. A casual walk down a sandy beach between fall and spring might awaken up to 100 Semipalmated Plovers, sleeping in slight depressions in the sand, though flocks of up to 1,000 birds may also be encountered.

VOICE Flight call a whistled, abrupt double note, *chu-WEEp*, with soft emphasis on second syllable; courtship display song is a version of flight call followed by rough *r-r-r-r-r-r-r*, ending with a slurred, descending *yelp*.

NESTING Simple scrape on bare or slightly vegetated ground in Arctic tundra; 3–4 eggs; 1 brood; May–June.

FEEDING Forages in typical plover style: run, pause, and pluck; eats aquatic mollusks, crustaceans, flies, beetles, and spiders.

FLIGHT: straight, fast; with fluttering wingbeats.

BY SIGHT AND FEEL
Semipalmated Plovers locate prey by sight or through the sensitive soles of their toes.

SIMILAR SPECIES

WILSON'S PLOVER see p.117 — heavier, dark bill, pinkish legs

COMMON RINGED PLOVER — wider breastband

OCCURRENCE
Breeding habitat is Arctic or subarctic tundra, well-drained gravel, shale, or other sparsely vegetated ground. During migration, mudflats, saltwater marshes, lake edges, tidal areas, and flooded fields. During winter, coastal or near coastal habitats.

| Length 6¾–7½in (17–19cm) | Wingspan 17–20½in (43–52cm) | Weight 1¹⁄₁₆–2½oz (30–70g) |
| Social **Solitary/Flocks** | Lifespan **Up to 6 years** | Status **Secure** |

DATE SEEN	WHERE	NOTES

Order **Charadriiformes**	Family **Charadriidae**	Species **Charadrius melodus**

Piping Plover

prominent white wing stripe

stubby bill

dusky tail band

MALE (BREEDING)

IN FLIGHT

less pronounced black markings than male

FEMALE (BREEDING)

breastband sometimes incomplete

black forecrown

pale gray upperparts

black-tipped, orange bill

indistinct, partial breastband

ADULT (NON-BREEDING)

mostly black bill, with slight orange base

thin, white collar throughout year

MALE (BREEDING)

dark breastband

orange legs

FLIGHT: fast, twisting flight; rapid wingbeats.

Small and pale, the Piping Plover is at risk because of eroding coastlines, human disturbance, and predation by foxes, raccoons, and cats. With its pale gray back, it is well camouflaged along beaches or in dunes, but conservation measures, such as fencing off nesting beaches and control of predators, are necessary to restore populations. Two subspecies of the Piping Plover are recognized; one nests on the Atlantic Coast, and the other inland.
VOICE Clear, whistled *peep* call in flight; quiet *peep-lo* during courtship and contact; high-pitched *pipe-pipe-pipe* song.
NESTING Shallow scrape in sand, gravel, dunes, or salt flats; 4 eggs; 1 brood; April–May.
FEEDING Typical run, pause, and pluck plover feeding style; diet includes marine worms, insects, and mollusks.

VULNERABLE NESTS
The fragile nature of their preferred nesting sites has led to this species becoming endangered.

SIMILAR SPECIES

SEMIPALMATED PLOVER ❋
see p.115

dark, brown upperparts

SNOWY PLOVER ❋
see p.118

black bill

narrow, white collar

darker legs

OCCURRENCE
Found along beaches, in saline sandflats, and adjacent mudflats; during winter, found exclusively along the Atlantic and Gulf Coasts, sandflats, and mudflats. Inland subspecies nests on sand or gravel beaches adjacent to large lakes, rivers, and saline lakes.

Length **6½–7in (17–18cm)**	Wingspan **18–18½in (45–47cm)**	Weight **1⅝–2⅜oz (45–65g)**
Social **Small flocks**	Lifespan **Up to 11 years**	Status **Endangered**

DATE SEEN	WHERE	NOTES

| Order **Charadriiformes** | Family **Charadriidae** | Species *Charadrius wilsonia* |

Wilson's Plover

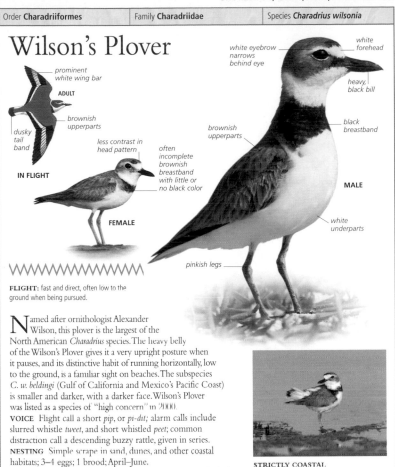

prominent white wing bar

ADULT

brownish upperparts

dusky tail band

IN FLIGHT

less contrast in head pattern

often incomplete brownish breastband with little or no black color

FEMALE

white eyebrow narrows behind eye

white forehead

heavy, black bill

brownish upperparts

black breastband

MALE

white underparts

pinkish legs

FLIGHT: fast and direct, often low to the ground when being pursued.

Named after ornithologist Alexander Wilson, this plover is the largest of the North American *Charadrius* species. The heavy belly of the Wilson's Plover gives it a very upright posture when it pauses, and its distinctive habit of running horizontally, low to the ground, is a familiar sight on beaches. The subspecies *C. w. beldingi* (Gulf of California and Mexico's Pacific Coast) is smaller and darker, with a darker face. Wilson's Plover was listed as a species of "high concern" in 2000.

VOICE Flight call a short *pip*, or *pi-dit;* alarm calls include slurred whistle *tweet*, and short whistled *peet*; common distraction call a descending buzzy rattle, given in series.

NESTING Simple scrape in sand, dunes, and other coastal habitats; 3–4 eggs; 1 brood; April–June.

FEEDING Forages in typical plover style: run, pause, and pluck; mainly eats crustaceans, including fiddler crabs; also insects.

STRICTLY COASTAL.
Wilson's Plover is strongly associated with coastal areas, where it forages at low tide.

SIMILAR SPECIES

SEMIPALMATED PLOVER ❋ see p.115

orange legs

smaller bill

paler plumage

PIPING PLOVER see p.116

smaller overall

orange legs

orange bill

black tip to bill

OCCURRENCE
Found primarily in coastal habitats, including open beaches, vegetated sand dunes, coastal lagoons, saltwater flats, and overwash areas. Located only in North American coastal regions of the southeast Atlantic and Gulf Coasts.

| Length **6½–8in (16–20cm)** | Wingspan **15½–19½in (39–49cm)** | Weight **2–2½oz (55–70g)** |
| Social **Flocks** | Lifespan **Unknown** | Status **Declining** |

DATE SEEN	WHERE	NOTES

| Order **Charadriiformes** | Family **Charadriidae** | Species **Charadrius nivosus** |

Snowy Plover

MALE (BREEDING)

white wing stripe

dusky cheek patch

IN FLIGHT

pale brown back

short tail

MALE (BREEDING)

grayish to pinkish legs

pale cinnamon crown

very pale head markings

very pale upperparts

black forecrown

GULF COAST FEMALE (BREEDING)

short, stubby bill

pale sandy gray back

incomplete, narrow, black breastband at sides of neck and upper breast

GULF COAST MALE (BREEDING)

blocky head

narrow, white collar

ADULT (NONBREEDING)

FLIGHT: individuals fly straight and fast, but flocks wheel and bank in synchrony when alarmed.

The smallest and palest of all North American plovers, the Snowy Plover's cryptic coloration blends in so well with its beach and dune habitat that it often remains unnoticed. This bird often runs faster and covers longer distances than other beach plovers, sprinting along the sand for extended spurts, like sanderlings. Nests are frequently destroyed by weather, disturbance, or predators, but the birds readily construct new nests, even up to six times in the face of regular losses. Nevertheless, habitat destruction has resulted in shrinking populations, and the species is designated as threatened along the Pacific Coast.

VOICE Repeated *tow-heet*; *purrt* and single *churr*; typically silent when not breeding, tinkling *ti* at roosts or before flight.

NESTING Shallow scrape in sand; 2–3 eggs; 2–3 broods; March–June.

FEEDING Feeds in run, pause, and pluck style on terrestrial and aquatic invertebrates, such as snails and clams.

TRULY SNOWY
The Snowy Plover breeds in sandy areas that are as pale as snow.

OCCURRENCE
Breeds on open beach and dune habitats on the Pacific and Gulf Coasts, and inland on brackish lakes in the Great Basin and southern Great Plains region. Coastal birds are only partially migratory, but most inland birds winter at the coast.

SIMILAR SPECIES

SEMIPALMATED PLOVER ♻ see p.115

brown breastband

PIPING PLOVER ♂ see p.116

plumper overall

orange legs

| Length **6–6½in (15–17cm)** | Wingspan **16–18in (41–46cm)** | Weight **1¼–2⅛ oz (35–60g)** |
| Social **Large flocks** | Lifespan **Up to 4 years** | Status **Endangered** |

DATE SEEN	WHERE	NOTES

| Order **Charadriiformes** | Family **Scolopacidae** | Species *Bartramia longicauda* |

Upland Sandpiper

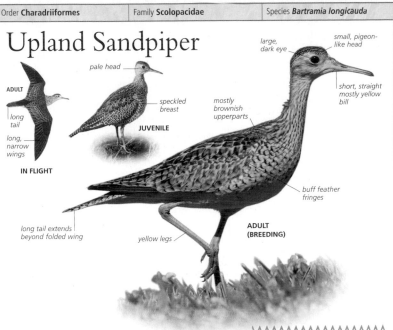

ADULT

long tail

long, narrow wings

IN FLIGHT

pale head

speckled breast

JUVENILE

large, dark eye

small, pigeon-like head

short, straight mostly yellow bill

mostly brownish upperparts

buff feather fringes

long tail extends beyond folded wing

yellow legs

ADULT (BREEDING)

Unlike other sandpipers, this graceful bird spends most of its life away from water in grassy habitats. The Upland Sandpiper's coloration helps it camouflage itself in the grasslands, especially while nesting on the ground. It is well known for landing on fence posts and raising its wings while giving its tremulous, whistling call. The bird is currently listed as endangered in many of its breeding states because of the disappearance of its grassland habitat.

VOICE Flight call a low *qui-pi-pi-pi*; song consists of gurgling notes followed by long, descending "wolf whistle" *whooooleeeeee, wheeelooooo–ooooo*.

NESTING Simple depression in ground among grass clumps; 4 eggs; 1 brood; May.

FEEDING Feeds with head-bobbing motion on adult and larval insects, spiders, worms, centipedes; occasionally seeds.

FLIGHT: strong and swift; rapid, fluttering flight in breeding display.

DRY GROUND WADER
A true grassland species, the Upland Sandpiper is rarely found away from this habitat.

SIMILAR SPECIES

WHIMBREL see p.120

long, curved bill

dull bluish gray legs

LONG-BILLED CURLEW ♂ see p.449

very long, curved bill

much larger overall

OCCURRENCE
Breeds in native tallgrass or mixed-grass prairies. Airports make up large portion of its breeding habitat in the northeast US. During migration and in winter it prefers shortgrass habitats such as grazed pastures, turf farms, cultivated fields.

| Length **11–12½in (28–32cm)** | Wingspan **25–27in (64–68cm)** | Weight **4–7oz (150–200g)** |
| Social **Migrant flocks** | Lifespan **Unknown** | Status **Declining** |

DATE SEEN	WHERE	NOTES

| Order **Charadriiformes** | Family **Scolopacidae** | Species *Numenius phaeopus* |

Whimbrel

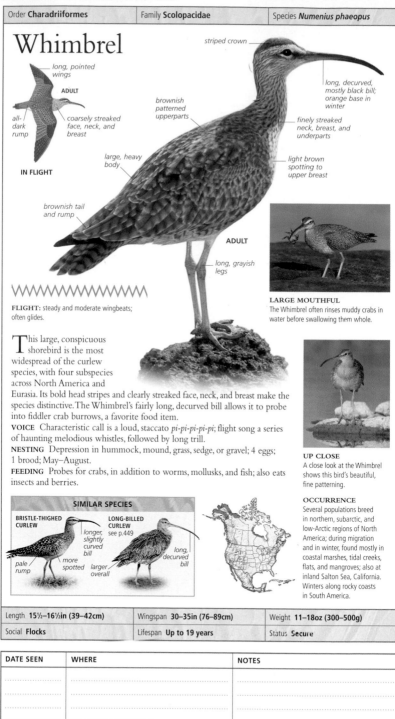

striped crown

long, pointed wings

ADULT

long, decurved, mostly black bill; orange base in winter

brownish patterned upperparts

finely streaked neck, breast, and underparts

all-dark rump

coarsely streaked face, neck, and breast

light brown spotting to upper breast

IN FLIGHT

large, heavy body

brownish tail and rump

ADULT

long, grayish legs

FLIGHT: steady and moderate wingbeats; often glides.

LARGE MOUTHFUL
The Whimbrel often rinses muddy crabs in water before swallowing them whole.

This large, conspicuous shorebird is the most widespread of the curlew species, with four subspecies across North America and Eurasia. Its bold head stripes and clearly streaked face, neck, and breast make the species distinctive. The Whimbrel's fairly long, decurved bill allows it to probe into fiddler crab burrows, a favorite food item.

VOICE Characteristic call is a loud, staccato *pi-pi-pi-pi-pi*; flight song a series of haunting melodious whistles, followed by long trill.

NESTING Depression in hummock, mound, grass, sedge, or gravel; 4 eggs; 1 brood; May–August.

FEEDING Probes for crabs, in addition to worms, mollusks, and fish; also eats insects and berries.

UP CLOSE
A close look at the Whimbrel shows this bird's beautiful, fine patterning.

OCCURRENCE
Several populations breed in northern, subarctic, and low-Arctic regions of North America; during migration and in winter, found mostly in coastal marshes, tidal creeks, flats, and mangroves; also at inland Salton Sea, California. Winters along rocky coasts in South America.

SIMILAR SPECIES

BRISTLE-THIGHED CURLEW

longer, slightly curved bill

pale rump

more spotted

LONG-BILLED CURLEW
see p.449

long, decurved bill

larger overall

| Length **15½–16½in (39–42cm)** | Wingspan **30–35in (76–89cm)** | Weight **11–18oz (300–500g)** |
| Social **Flocks** | Lifespan **Up to 19 years** | Status **Secure** |

DATE SEEN	WHERE	NOTES

| Order **Charadriiformes** | Family **Scolopacidae** | Species *Limosa haemastica* |

Hudsonian Godwit

white wing stripe

ADULT (NONBREEDING)

brownish gray upperparts

pale eyebrow

long, orange-based bill

white rump

off-white underparts

IN FLIGHT

pale, buffy feather fringes

JUVENILE

black-and-white upperparts

brownish streaked head and neck

unpatterned brownish wing feathers

black tail

rich chestnut underparts with black barring

white-feathered chestnut breast

FLIGHT: swift and straight, with fast and powerful wingbeats.

MALE (BREEDING)

FEMALE (BREEDING)

This large, graceful sandpiper, with a long and slightly upturned bill, undertakes a remarkable annual migration from its tundra breeding grounds in Alaska and Canada all the way to extreme southern South America, a distance probably close to 10,000 miles (16,000km) in one direction, with very few stopovers. There are perhaps 50–80,000 breeding pairs. Counts in Tierra del Fuego indicate totals of perhaps 30,000 to 40,000 birds wintering there, all in two areas of tidal mudflats. Between the far North and the far South, North American stops are few, and only in the spring, along a central route mid-continent. Hudsonian Godwits spend six months wintering, two months breeding, and four flying between the two locations.

VOICE Flight call emphatic *peed-wid*; also high *peet* or *kwee*; display song *to-wida to-wida to-wida*, or *to-wit, to-wit, to-wit*.

NESTING Saucer-shaped depression on dry hummock or tussocks under cover; 4 eggs; 1 brood; May–July.

FEEDING Probes in mud for insects, insect grubs, worms, crustaceans and mollusks; also eats plant tubers in fall.

LONG-HAUL BIRD
Hudsonian Godwits only make a few stops on their long flights to and from South America.

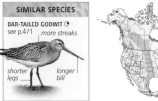

SIMILAR SPECIES

BAR-TAILED GODWIT ♂
see p.471

more streaks

shorter legs

longer bill

OCCURRENCE
Breeds in the High Arctic, in sedge meadows and bogs in scattered tundra; scarce along the Atlantic Coast in fall near coastal freshwater reservoirs; but locally common in flooded rice fields, pastures, and reservoirs in spring. Winters in extreme southern Chile and Argentina.

| Length **14–16in (35–41cm)** | Wingspan **27–31in (68–78cm)** | Weight **7–12oz (200–350g)** |
| Social **Flocks** | Lifespan **Up to 29 years** | Status **Vulnerable** |

DATE SEEN	WHERE	NOTES

Order **Charadriiformes**	Family **Scolopacidae**	Species *Limosa fedoa*

Marbled Godwit

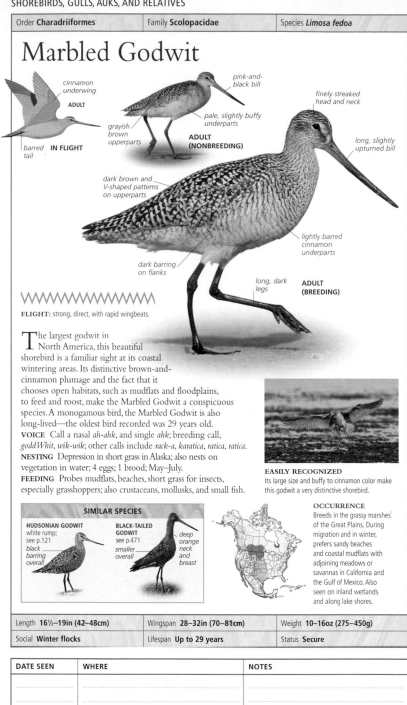

cinnamon underwing

ADULT

barred **IN FLIGHT**
tail

pink-and-black bill

grayish brown upperparts

pale, slightly buffy underparts

ADULT (NONBREEDING)

finely streaked head and neck

long, slightly upturned bill

dark brown and V-shaped patterns on upperparts

lightly barred cinnamon underparts

dark barring on flanks

long, dark legs

ADULT (BREEDING)

FLIGHT: strong, direct, with rapid wingbeats.

The largest godwit in North America, this beautiful shorebird is a familiar sight at its coastal wintering areas. Its distinctive brown-and-cinnamon plumage and the fact that it chooses open habitats, such as mudflats and floodplains, to feed and roost, make the Marbled Godwit a conspicuous species. A monogamous bird, the Marbled Godwit is also long-lived—the oldest bird recorded was 29 years old.

VOICE Call a nasal *ah-ahk*, and single *ahk*; breeding call, *goddWhit*, *wik-wik*; other calls include *rack-a*, *karatica*, *ratica*, *ratica*.

NESTING Depression in short grass in Alaska; also nests on vegetation in water; 4 eggs; 1 brood; May–July.

FEEDING Probes mudflats, beaches, short grass for insects, especially grasshoppers; also crustaceans, mollusks, and small fish.

EASILY RECOGNIZED
Its large size and buffy to cinnamon color make this godwit a very distinctive shorebird.

SIMILAR SPECIES

HUDSONIAN GODWIT
white rump;
see p.121
black barring overall

BLACK-TAILED GODWIT
see p.471
smaller overall

deep orange neck and breast

OCCURRENCE
Breeds in the grassy marshes of the Great Plains. During migration and in winter, prefers sandy beaches and coastal mudflats with adjoining meadows or savannas in California and the Gulf of Mexico. Also seen on inland wetlands and along lake shores.

Length 16½–19in (42–48cm)	Wingspan 28–32in (70–81cm)	Weight 10–16oz (275–450g)
Social **Winter flocks**	Lifespan **Up to 29 years**	Status **Secure**

DATE SEEN	WHERE	NOTES

Order **Charadriiformes**	Family **Scolopacidae**	Species *Arenaria Interpres*

Ruddy Turnstone

bold red patches on back and wings

ADULT (BREEDING)

dark flight feathers

IN FLIGHT

black-and-white head and breast pattern

short, dark, chisel-like bill

brownish head markings

variably streaked, whitish face

brownish upperparts

ADULT (NONBREEDING)

black breast

bright white underparts, at all ages

white-edged, dark feathers

ADULT (BREEDING)

short, orange legs

orange legs

JUVENILE (FALL)

This tame, medium-sized, and stocky sandpiper with a chisel-shaped bill is a common visitor along the shorelines of North and South America. On its High Arctic breeding grounds, it is bold and aggressive and is able to drive off predators as large as the Glaucous Gull and Parasitic Jaeger. The Ruddy Turnstone was given its name because of its reddish back color and because of its habit of flipping and overturning items like mollusk shells and pebbles, or digging in the sand and looking for small crustaceans and other marine invertebrates. Two subspecies live in Arctic North America: *A. i. interpres* in northeastern Canada and *A. i. morinellas* elsewhere in Canada and Alaska.

VOICE Rapid chatter on breeding ground: *TTT-wooo TTT-woooRITititititititit*; flight call a low, rapid *kut-a-kut*.

NESTING Simple scrape lined with lichens and grasses in dry, open areas; 4 eggs; 1 brood; June.
FEEDING Forages along shoreline for crustaceans, insects, including beetles, spiders; also eats plants.

FLIGHT: swift and strong flight, with quick wingbeats.

WINTER GATHERINGS
Ruddy Turnstones often congregate in large winter flocks on rocky shorelines.

SIMILAR SPECIES

BLACK TURNSTONE

darker overall

no rust color in plumage

duller legs

OCCURRENCE
Breeds in High Arctic: wide-open, barren, and grassy habitats and rocky coasts, usually near water. In winter, on sandy or gravel beaches and rocky shorelines, from northern California to South America, and from northern Massachusetts south along Atlantic and Gulf Coasts.

Length **8–10½in (20–27cm)**	Wingspan **20–22½in (51–57cm)**	Weight **3½–7oz (100–200g)**
Social **Flocks**	Lifespan **Up to 7 years**	Status **Secure**

DATE SEEN	WHERE	NOTES

Order **Charadriiformes**	Family **Scolopacidae**	Species **Calidris canutus**

Red Knot

white wing stripe

white eyebrow

ADULT (WINTER)

IN FLIGHT

grayish upperparts

JUVENILE

pale fringes to wing feathers

mostly pale gray upperparts

gray spots on upper breast

yellowish green legs

pale underparts

ADULT (WINTER)

boldly marked black, rust, and white upperparts

dark, straight, and stocky bill

salmon-colored face and breast

white lower belly with dark V-shaped marks

short, dark legs

ADULT (SUMMER)

A substantial, plump sandpiper, the Red Knot is the largest North American shorebird in the genus *Calidris*. There are two North American subspecies—*C. c. rufa* and *C. c. roselaari*. Noted for its extraordinary long-distance migration, *C. c. rufa* flies about 9,300 miles (15,000km) between its High Arctic breeding grounds and wintering area in South America, especially in Tierra del Fuego, at the tip of South America. Recent declines have occurred in this population, attributed to over-harvesting of horseshoe crab eggs—its critical food source. With the population of *C. c. rufa* having declined from more than 100,000 birds in the mid-1980s to below 15,000 today, the Red Knot is now listed as endangered in New Jersey, and faces possible extinction.

VOICE Flight call a soft *kuEEt* or *kuup*; display song *eerie por-meeee por-meeee*, followed by *por-por por por*.

NESTING Simple scrape in grassy or barren tundra, often lined; 4 eggs; 1 brood; June.

FEEDING Probes mud or sand for insects, plant material, small mollusks, crustaceans, especially small snails, worms, and other invertebrates.

FLIGHT: powerful, swift, direct flight with rapid wingbeats.

STAGING AREAS
Red Knots form dense flocks during migration and on their wintering grounds.

SIMILAR SPECIES

BLACK-BELLIED PLOVER see p.112

large, dark eye

longer, dark legs

OCCURRENCE
Breeds in flat, barren tundra in High Arctic islands and peninsulas. Mostly coastal during migration and winter, preferring sandbars, beaches, and tidal flats, where it congregates in huge flocks.

Length **9–10in (23–25cm)**	Wingspan **23–24in (58–61cm)**	Weight **3⅜–8oz (95–225g)**
Social **Large flocks**	Lifespan **Unknown**	Status **Declining**

DATE SEEN	WHERE	NOTES

| Order **Charadriiformes** | Family **Scolopacidae** | Species *Calidris himantopus* |

Stilt Sandpiper

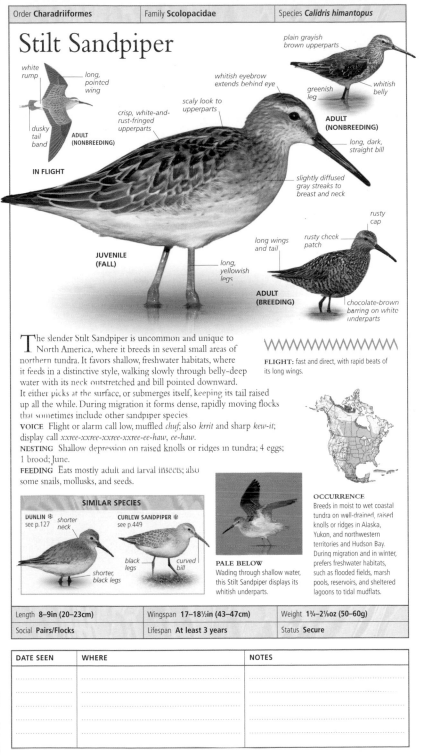

plain grayish
brown upperparts

whitish eyebrow
extends behind eye

greenish
leg

whitish
belly

**ADULT
(NONBREEDING)**

white
rump

long,
pointed
wing

scaly look to
upperparts

crisp, white-and-
rust-fringed
upperparts

dusky
tail
band

**ADULT
(NONBREEDING)**

IN FLIGHT

long, dark,
straight bill

slightly diffused
gray streaks to
breast and neck

rusty
cap

long wings
and tail

rusty cheek
patch

**JUVENILE
(FALL)**

long,
yellowish
legs

**ADULT
(BREEDING)**

chocolate-brown
barring on white
underparts

The slender Stilt Sandpiper is uncommon and unique to
North America, where it breeds in several small areas of
northern tundra. It favors shallow, freshwater habitats, where
it feeds in a distinctive style, walking slowly through belly-deep
water with its neck outstretched and bill pointed downward.
It either picks at the surface, or submerges itself, keeping its tail raised
up all the while. During migration it forms dense, rapidly moving flocks
that sometimes include other sandpiper species.
VOICE Flight or alarm call low, muffled *chuf*; also *krrit* and sharp *kew-it*;
display call *xxree-xxree-xxree-xxree-ee-haw, ee-haw*.
NESTING Shallow depression on raised knolls or ridges in tundra; 4 eggs;
1 brood; June.
FEEDING Eats mostly adult and larval insects; also
some snails, mollusks, and seeds.

FLIGHT: fast and direct, with rapid beats of
its long wings.

SIMILAR SPECIES

DUNLIN ❄
see p.127

shorter
neck

shorter,
black legs

CURLEW SANDPIPER ❄
see p.449

black
legs

curved
bill

PALE BELOW
Wading through shallow water,
this Stilt Sandpiper displays its
whitish underparts.

OCCURRENCE
Breeds in moist to wet coastal
tundra on well-drained, raised
knolls or ridges in Alaska,
Yukon, and northwestern
territories and Hudson Bay.
During migration and in winter,
prefers freshwater habitats,
such as flooded fields, marsh
pools, reservoirs, and sheltered
lagoons to tidal mudflats.

| Length **8–9in (20–23cm)** | Wingspan **17–18½in (43–47cm)** | Weight **1¾–2⅛oz (50–60g)** |
| Social **Pairs/Flocks** | Lifespan **At least 3 years** | Status **Secure** |

DATE SEEN	WHERE	NOTES

| Order **Charadriiformes** | Family **Scolopacidae** | Species **Calidris alba** |

Sanderling

strong white wing stripe

mostly grayish upperparts

black, rust, and white upperparts

ADULT (NONBREEDING)

IN FLIGHT

black-centered back feathers with buff edges

rust and black streaked crown

JUVENILE (FALL)

dark, stocky bill

white face and neck

pearl-gray upperparts

rust wash on breast with black markings

ADULT (BREEDING)

short black legs

clean white underparts

ADULT (NONBREEDING)

The Sanderling is probably the best-known shorebird in the world. It breeds in some of the most remote, High Arctic habitats, from Greenland to Siberia, but occupies just about every temperate and tropical shoreline in the Americas when not breeding. Indeed, its wintering range spans both American coasts, from Canada to Argentina. Feeding in flocks, it is a common sight in winter on sandy beaches. In many places, though, the bird is declining rapidly, with pollution of the sea and shore, and the disturbance caused by people using beaches for various recreational purposes, the main causes.

VOICE Flight call squeaky *pweet*, threat call *sew-sew-sew*; display song harsh, buzzy notes and chattering *cher-cher-cher*.

NESTING Small, shallow depression on dry, stony ground; 4 eggs; 1–3 broods; June–July.

FEEDING Probes along the surf-line in sand for insects, small crustaceans, small mollusks, and worms.

FLIGHT: rapid, free-form; birds in flocks twisting and turning as if they were one.

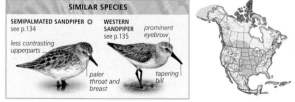

CHASING THE WAVES
The Sanderling scampers after retreating waves to pick up any small creatures stranded by the sea.

SIMILAR SPECIES

SEMIPALMATED SANDPIPER ☼ see p.134

less contrasting upperparts

WESTERN SANDPIPER see p.135

prominent eyebrow

paler throat and breast

tapering bill

OCCURRENCE
Breeds in barren High Arctic coastal tundra of northernmost Canada, including the islands, north to Ellesmere Island. During winter months and on migration, found along all North American coastlines, but especially sandy beaches; inland migrants found along lake and river edges.

| Length **7½–8in (19–20cm)** | Wingspan **16–18in (41–46cm)** | Weight **1⁷⁄₁₆–3½oz (40–100g)** |
| Social **Small flocks** | Lifespan **Up to 10 years** | Status **Declining** |

DATE SEEN	WHERE	NOTES

Order **Charadriiformes**	Family **Scolopacidae**	Species *Calidris alpina*

Dunlin

black-and-cream stripes on back

JUVENILE

black streaks on buff underside

JUVENILE

dull gray-brown head and back

white sided rump

thin white wing bar

IN FLIGHT

long, tapered, black bill

rich chestnut-and-black back

fine dark streaks on whitish breast

large, squarish, black belly patch

ADULT (BREEDING)

dull, gray-streaked breast

ADULT (NONBREEDING)

FLIGHT: swift and direct flight, with rapid wingbeats.

The Dunlin is one of the most abundant and widespread of North America's shorebirds, but of the ten recognized subspecies, only three breed in North America: *C. a. arcticola*, *C. a. pacifica*, and *C. a. hudsonia*. The Dunlin is unmistakable in its striking, red-backed, black-bellied breeding plumage. In winter it sports much drabber colors, but more than makes up for this by gathering in spectacular flocks of many thousands of birds on its favorite coastal mudflats.

VOICE Call accented trill, *drurr-drurr*, that rises slightly, then descends; flight call *jeeezp*; song *wrraah-wrraah*.

NESTING Simple cup lined with grasses, leaves, and lichens in moist to wet tundra; 4 eggs; 1 brood; June–July.

FEEDING Probes for marine, freshwater, terrestrial invertebrates: clams, worms, insect larvae, crustaceans; also plants and small fish.

OLD RED BACK
The Dunlin was once known as the Red-backed Sandpiper because of its distinct breeding plumage.

SIMILAR SPECIES

STILT SANDPIPER ❊
see p.125

longer, thinner neck

yellowish green legs

CURLEW SANDPIPER ❊
see p.449

less streaking on chest

longer legs

OCCURRENCE
Breeds in Arctic and subarctic moist, wet tundra, often near ponds, with drier islands for nest sites. In migration and winter, prefers coastal areas with extensive mudflats and sandy beaches; also feeds in flooded fields and seasonal inland wetlands.

Length **6½–8½in (16–22cm)**	Wingspan **12½–17½in (32–44cm)**	Weight **1⁹⁄₁₆–2¼oz (45–65g)**
Social **Large flocks**	Lifespan **Up to 24 years**	Status **Declining**

DATE SEEN	WHERE	NOTES
....	....	....
....	....	....
....	....	....
....	....	....
....	....	....

Order **Charadriiformes**	Family **Scolopacidae**	Species *Calidris maritima*

Purple Sandpiper

brownish gray upperparts

buff-fringed feathers

heavily streaked head

long bill with drooping tip

dark brownish wash to breast

short, thick neck

ADULT (BREEDING)

thin white wing stripe

ADULT (NONBREEDING)

JUVENILE

grayish wash to head and neck

IN FLIGHT

compact body shape overall

gray inner wing feathers

bill yellow at base, dark at drooping tip

white belly and flanks, with thin streaking

∿∿∿∿∿∿∿∿∿∿∿∿

FLIGHT: reluctant; rapid, low, and direct with full wingbeats.

yellow legs and toes

ADULT (NONBREEDING)

A medium-sized, stocky bird, the Purple Sandpiper shares the most northerly wintering distribution of all North American shorebirds with its close relative, the Rock Sandpiper. The dark plumage and low, squat body of the Purple Sandpiper often disguise its presence on dark tidal rocks, until a crashing wave causes a previously invisible flock to explode into flight.

VOICE Flight call low *kweesh*; when disturbed, *eh-eh-eh*; breeding *kwi-ti-ti-ti-bli-bli-bli* followed by *dooree-dooree-dooree*.

NESTING Simple lined scrape in high-alpine-like or barren low-lying Arctic tundra; 4 eggs; 1 brood; June.

FEEDING Feeds on various invertebrates, including crustaceans, snails, insects, spiders, and worms.

SIMILAR SPECIES

ROCK SANDPIPER *slightly smaller bill*

darker, plainer upperparts

less orange color to base of bill

DUNLIN *see p.127* *plain, pale gray-brown upperparts*

longer black bill

WINTER EXPOSURE The Purple Sandpiper winters mainly on exposed rocky shores along the eastern seaboard.

OCCURRENCE On breeding grounds, found on barren Arctic and alpine tundra habitats in the Canadian Arctic Archipelago. On migration and in winter, predominantly found on rocky, wave-pounded shores on the eastern seaboard.

Length **8–8½in (20–21cm)**	Wingspan **16½–18½in (42–47cm)**	Weight **1¾–3½oz (50–100g)**
Social **Small flocks**	Lifespan **Up to 20 years**	Status **Declining**

DATE SEEN	WHERE	NOTES

| Order **Charadriiformes** | Family **Scolopacidae** | Species *Calidris bairdii* |

Baird's Sandpiper

long, pointed wings

finely streaked head

ADULT

ADULT

IN FLIGHT

wings extend beyond tail

blackish upperparts with silver-edged feathers

dark patch between eye and bill

straight, fine-tipped dark bill

clean, white underparts

scalloped look to upperparts

streaked back

indistinct, pale eye-line

buff, finely streaked upper breast

JUVENILE

blackish legs

FLIGHT: strong and direct, with deep, quick wingbeats.

Baird's Sandpiper is less well known than the other North American *Calidris* sandpipers. It was described in 1861, later than its relatives, by the famous North American ornithologist Elliott Cowes, a former surgeon in the US Army, in honor of Spencer Fullerton Baird. Both men were founding members of the AOU (the American Ornithologists' Union). From its High Arctic, tundra habitat, Baird's Sandpiper moves across North America and the western US, into South America, and all the way to Tierra del Fuego, a remarkable biannual journey of 6,000–9,000 miles (9,700–14,500km).

VOICE Flight call a low, dry *preep*; song on Arctic breeding ground: *brraay, brray, brray,* followed by *hee-aaw, hee-aaw, hee-aaw.*

NESTING Shallow depression in coastal or upland tundra; 4 eggs; 1 brood; June.

FEEDING Picks and probes for insects and larvae; also spiders and pond crustaceans.

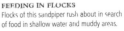

FEEDING IN FLOCKS
Flocks of this sandpiper rush about in search of food in shallow water and muddy areas.

SIMILAR SPECIES

WHITE-RUMPED SANDPIPER
see p.131

prominent, white eyebrow

slightly bulkier body

PECTORAL SANDPIPER
larger; see p.133

yellowish legs

streaked breast-band

OCCURRENCE
Breeds in tundra habitats of High Arctic Alaska and Canada. During migration and winter, inland freshwater habitats: lake and river margins, wet pastures, rice fields; also tidal flats at coastal locations. In winter, common in the high Andes of South America, and sometimes all the way to Tierra del Fuego.

Length 5¾–7¼in (14.5–18.5cm)	Wingspan 16–18½in (41–47cm)	Weight 1¹⁄₁₆–2oz (30–55g)
Social **Flocks**	Lifespan **Unknown**	Status **Secure**

DATE SEEN	WHERE	NOTES

| Order **Charadriiformes** | Family **Scolopacidae** | Species *Calidris minutilla* |

Least Sandpiper

ADULT

dark patch between eye and bill

buff to rust fringed inner wing

JUVENILE

faint tail band

uniform brownish gray upperparts

IN FLIGHT

short tail and wings

small, rounded head

ADULT (BREEDING)

short, yellowish legs

pale, whitish eyebrow

white chin and belly

ADULT (NONBREEDING)

streaked, brownish breast and head

yellow to yellowish green legs

FLIGHT: level flight; fast and direct on quick wingbeats; in mixed flocks.

The little Least Sandpiper is often overlooked because of its muted plumage and preference for feeding unobtrusively near vegetative cover. With its brown or brownish gray plumage, the Least Sandpiper virtually disappears in the landscape when feeding crouched down on wet margins of water bodies. The bird is often found in small to medium flocks, members of which typically are nervous when foraging, and frequently burst into flight, only to alight a short way off.
VOICE Its flight call, *kreeeep*, rises in pitch, often repeated 2-syllable *kree-eep*; display call trilled *b-reeee*, *b-reeee*, *b-reeee*.
NESTING Depression in open, subarctic habitat near water; 4 eggs; 1 brood; May–June.
FEEDING Forages for variety of small terrestrial and aquatic prey, especially sand fleas, mollusks, and flies.

FLOCK IN FLIGHT
The narrow pointed wings of the Least Sandpiper allow it to fly fast and level.

SIMILAR SPECIES

SEMIPALMATED SANDPIPER ☼
see p.134

PECTORAL SANDPIPER
see p.133

larger overall

grayer overall

whiter throat

larger overall

heavier bill

OCCURRENCE
Breeds in wet low-Arctic areas from Alaska and the Yukon to Québec and Newfoundland. During migration and in winter, uses muddy areas such as lake shores, riverbanks, flooded fields, and tidal flats. Winters from southern North America south to Peru and Brazil.

| Length **4¾in (12cm)** | Wingspan **13–14in (33–35cm)** | Weight **⁵⁄₁₆–1oz (9–27g)** |
| Social **Flocks** | Lifespan **Up to 16 years** | Status **Declining** |

DATE SEEN	WHERE	NOTES

| Order **Charadriiformes** | Family **Scolopacidae** | Species *Calidris fuscicollis* |

White-rumped Sandpiper

easily visible white rump

long, tapered wings

ADULT

IN FLIGHT

dark feathers with rust edges

IMMATURE (1ST SUMMER)

dark bill with curved tip

heavily streaked breast

grayish brown upperparts

rust-colored cap and cheek

streaked head

crisp, pale fringed feathers

fine streaks on breast

JUVENILE

The White-rumped Sandpiper undertakes one of the longest migrations of any bird in the Western Hemisphere. From its High Arctic breeding grounds in Alaska and Canada, it migrates in several long jumps to extreme southern South America—about 9,000–12,000 miles (14,500–19,300km), twice a year. Almost the entire population migrates through the central US in spring, with several stopovers, which are critical to the success of its journey. While associating with other shorebird species during migration and winter, it can be overlooked in the crowd. Its insect-like call and white rump aid identification.

VOICE Call a very high-pitched, insect-like *tzeet*; flight song an insect-like, high-pitched, rattling buzz, interspersed with grunts.

NESTING Shallow depression in usually wet but well-vegetated tundra; 4 eggs; 1 brood; June.

FEEDING Picks and probes for insects, spiders, earthworms, and marine worms; also some plant matter.

FLIGHT: fast, strong, and direct flight with deep wingbeats.

WING POWER
Long narrow wings enable this species to migrate to and from the Arctic and Tierra del Fuego.

SIMILAR SPECIES

SEMIPALMATED SANDPIPER see p.134
slightly rufous crown

BAIRD'S SANDPIPER see p.129
no white rump
more distinct streaks on breast

OCCURRENCE
Breeds in wet but well-vegetated tundra, usually near ponds, lakes, or streams. In migration and winter, grassy areas: flooded fields, grassy lake margins, rivers, ponds, grassy margins of tidal mudflats, and roadside ditches. On wintering grounds, often associates with Baird's Sandpiper.

| Length **6–6¾in (15–17cm)** | Wingspan **16–18in (41–46cm)** | Weight **⅞–1¾oz (25–50g)** |
| Social **Flocks** | Lifespan **Unknown** | Status **Secure** |

DATE SEEN	WHERE	NOTES

131

| Order **Charadriiformes** | Family **Scolopacidae** | Species *Calidris subruficollis* |

Buff-breasted Sandpiper

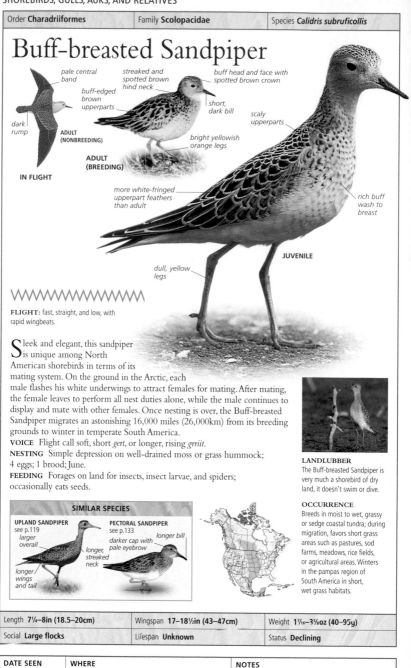

pale central band

streaked and spotted brown hind neck

buff head and face with spotted brown crown

buff-edged brown upperparts

short, dark bill

scaly upperparts

dark rump

ADULT (NONBREEDING)

bright yellowish orange legs

ADULT (BREEDING)

IN FLIGHT

more white-fringed upperpart feathers than adult

rich buff wash to breast

JUVENILE

dull, yellow legs

FLIGHT: fast, straight, and low, with rapid wingbeats.

Sleek and elegant, this sandpiper is unique among North American shorebirds in terms of its mating system. On the ground in the Arctic, each male flashes his white underwings to attract females for mating. After mating, the female leaves to perform all nest duties alone, while the male continues to display and mate with other females. Once nesting is over, the Buff-breasted Sandpiper migrates an astonishing 16,000 miles (26,000km) from its breeding grounds to winter in temperate South America.

VOICE Flight call soft, short *gert*, or longer, rising *grriit*.

NESTING Simple depression on well-drained moss or grass hummock; 4 eggs; 1 brood; June.

FEEDING Forages on land for insects, insect larvae, and spiders; occasionally eats seeds.

LANDLUBBER
The Buff-breasted Sandpiper is very much a shorebird of dry land, it doesn't swim or dive.

OCCURRENCE
Breeds in moist to wet, grassy or sedge coastal tundra; during migration, favors short grass areas such as pastures, sod farms, meadows, rice fields, or agricultural areas. Winters in the pampas region of South America in short, wet grass habitats.

SIMILAR SPECIES

UPLAND SANDPIPER
see p.119
larger overall

longer, streaked neck

longer wings and tail

PECTORAL SANDPIPER
see p.133
darker cap with pale eyebrow

longer bill

| Length **7¼–8in (18.5–20cm)** | Wingspan **17–18½in (43–47cm)** | Weight **1⁷⁄₁₆–3⅜oz (40–95g)** |
| Social **Large flocks** | Lifespan **Unknown** | Status **Declining** |

DATE SEEN	WHERE	NOTES

| Order **Charadriiformes** | Family **Scolopacidae** | Species *Calidris melanotos* |

Pectoral Sandpiper

long, graceful, pointed wings

ADULT

darker flight feathers

IN FLIGHT

rust-edged, dark centered feathers

rust crown and cheeks with black streaks

JUVENILE

brownish upperparts, with buff fringes

streaked crown and face

curved bill with orange base

medium length, stocky bill

ADULT

heavily streaked breast

white belly

yellowish legs

This medium-sized sandpiper is a true champion of long-distance migration. From their breeding grounds in the High Arctic to their wintering grounds on the pampas of southern South America, some birds travel up to 30,000 miles (48,000km) each year. The Pectoral Sandpiper is a promiscuous breeder, with males keeping harems of females in guarded territories. Males mate with as many females as they can attract with a display that includes a deep, booming call, and flights, but take no part in nest duties. Males migrate earlier than females, with both sexes preferring wet, grassy habitats during migration and in winter.

VOICE Flight call low, trilled *chrrk*; display song deep, hollow, hooting: *whoop, whoop, whoop*.

NESTING Shallow depression on ridges in moist to wet sedge tundra; 4 eggs; 1 brood; June.

FEEDING Probes or jabs mud for larvae, and forages for insects and spiders on tundra.

FLIGHT: fast and direct, with rapid, powerful wingbeats; flocks zig-zag when flushed.

SIMILAR SPECIES

UPLAND SANDPIPER see p.119

small head

larger overall

long tail

longer, thinner neck

BUFF-BREASTED SANDPIPER see p.132

plain face

dark bill

LONG JOURNEYS
This species migrates long distances to arrive in southern South America for the winter.

OCCURRENCE
In North America, breeds in northern Alaska, northern Yukon, Northern Territories, and some islands of the Canadian Arctic Archipelago, in wet, grassy tundra, especially near coasts. On migration and in winter favors wet pastures, the grassy margins of ponds and lakes, and saltmarshes.

| Length 7½–9in (19–23cm) | Wingspan 16½–19½in (42–49cm) | Weight 1¾–4oz (50–125g) |
| Social **Migrant flocks** | Lifespan **Up to 4½ years** | Status **Secure** |

DATE SEEN	WHERE	NOTES

Order **Charadriiformes**	Family **Scolopacidae**	Species *Calidris pusilla*

Semipalmated Sandpiper

IN FLIGHT

SUMMER

white eyebrow

pale grayish black legs

pale wing stripe along flight feathers

crisp, pale fringed feathers

short bill with blunt tip

JUVENILE

dark-centered back feathers with buff fringes

slightly paler grayish nape

streaked black and rust crown

short, dark bill

wing tips extend to tail tip

ADULT (SUMMER)

lightly streaked breast

This is the most abundant of the so-called "peep" *Calidris* sandpipers, especially in the eastern US. Flocks of up to 300,000 birds gather on migration staging areas. As a species, though, it can be hard to identify, because of plumage variation between juveniles and breeding adults, and a bill that varies markedly in size and shape from west to east. Semipalmated sandpipers from northeastern breeding grounds may fly nonstop to their South American wintering grounds in the fall.

VOICE Flight call *chrrk* or higher, sharper *chit*; display song monotonous, droning trill, often repeated for minutes at a time.

NESTING Shallow, lined scrape in short grass habitat; 4 eggs; 1 brood; May–June.

FEEDING Probes mud for aquatic and terrestrial invertebrates such as mollusks, worms, and spiders.

FLIGHT: fast and direct on narrow, pointed, wings; flies in large flocks in winter.

SLEEPING TOGETHER
Semipalmated Sandpipers form large feeding or resting flocks on migration and in winter.

SIMILAR SPECIES

SANDERLING
see p.126
more contrasting upperparts

darker breast

WESTERN SANDPIPER ✳
see p.135

puffier head

usually longer legs

usually more pointed bill

LEAST SANDPIPER ✳
see p.130

yellowish legs

smaller overall

OCCURRENCE
Breeds in Arctic and subarctic tundra habitats near water; in Alaska, on outer coastal plain. Migrants occur in shallow fresh- or saltwater and open muddy areas with little vegetation, such as intertidal flats or lake shores. Winters in Central and South America, south to Brazil and Peru.

Length **5¼–6in (13.5–15cm)**	Wingspan **13½–15in (34–38cm)**	Weight **½–1⁷⁄₁₀oz (14–40g)**
Social **Large flocks**	Lifespan **Up to 12 years**	Status **Secure**

DATE SEEN	WHERE	NOTES
....	....	....
....	....	....
....	....	....
....	....	....
....	....	....

| Order **Charadriiformes** | Family **Scolopacidae** | Species *Calidris mauri* |

Western Sandpiper

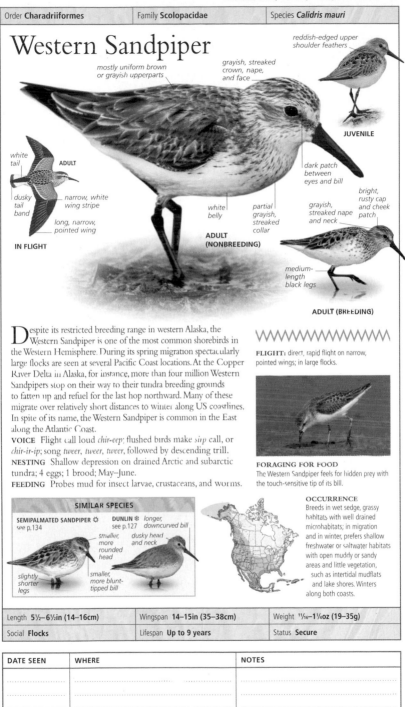

reddish-edged upper shoulder feathers

grayish, streaked crown, nape, and face

mostly uniform brown or grayish upperparts

JUVENILE

white tail

ADULT

dusky tail band

narrow, white wing stripe

long, narrow, pointed wing

IN FLIGHT

dark patch between eyes and bill

bright, rusty cap and cheek patch

white belly

partial grayish, streaked collar

grayish, streaked nape and neck

ADULT (NONBREEDING)

medium-length black legs

ADULT (BREEDING)

Despite its restricted breeding range in western Alaska, the Western Sandpiper is one of the most common shorebirds in the Western Hemisphere. During its spring migration spectacularly large flocks are seen at several Pacific Coast locations. At the Copper River Delta in Alaska, for instance, more than four million Western Sandpipers stop on their way to their tundra breeding grounds to fatten up and refuel for the last hop northward. Many of these migrate over relatively short distances to winter along US coastlines. In spite of its name, the Western Sandpiper is common in the East along the Atlantic Coast.

VOICE Flight call loud *chir-eep*; flushed birds make *sip* call, or *chir-ir-ip*; song *tweer, tweer, tweer*, followed by descending trill.

NESTING Shallow depression on drained Arctic and subarctic tundra; 4 eggs; 1 brood; May–June.

FEEDING Probes mud for insect larvae, crustaceans, and worms.

FLIGHT: direct, rapid flight on narrow, pointed wings; in large flocks.

FORAGING FOR FOOD
The Western Sandpiper feels for hidden prey with the touch-sensitive tip of its bill.

SIMILAR SPECIES

SEMIPALMATED SANDPIPER ☼ see p.134

smaller, more rounded head

slightly shorter legs

DUNLIN ❊ see p.127

longer, downcurved bill

dusky head and neck

smaller, more blunt-tipped bill

OCCURRENCE
Breeds in wet sedge, grassy habitats with well drained microhabitats; in migration and in winter, prefers shallow freshwater or saltwater habitats with open muddy or sandy areas and little vegetation, such as intertidal mudflats and lake shores. Winters along both coasts.

| Length **5½–6½in (14–16cm)** | Wingspan **14–15in (35–38cm)** | Weight **¹¹⁄₁₆–1¼oz (19–35g)** |
| Social **Flocks** | Lifespan **Up to 9 years** | Status **Secure** |

DATE SEEN	WHERE	NOTES

| Order **Charadriiformes** | Family **Scolopacidae** | Species *Limnodromus griseus* |

Short-billed Dowitcher

white slash from rump to mid-back

ADULT (BREEDING)

orange-fringed feathers

flanks less heavily streaked

JUVENILE

orange wash to face, neck, breast, and underparts

long, stout bill

long, pointed wings

IN FLIGHT

dark-centered upperpart feathers

variable spotting on upper breast

ADULT L. g. griseus

slightly larger bill

ADULT L. g. hendersoni

greenish yellow legs

streaked flanks

plain gray upperparts

white belly

WWWWWWWWWW

FLIGHT: swift, powerful with quick wingbeats.

The Short-billed Dowitcher is a common visitor along the Atlantic, Gulf, and Pacific Coasts. Its remote and bug-infested breeding areas in northern bogs have hindered the study of its breeding behavior until recent years. There are three subspecies (*L. g. griseus*, *L. g. hendersoni*, and *L. g. caurinus*,) which differ in plumage, size, and respective breeding areas. Recent knowledge about shape and structure has helped ornithologists distinguish the Short-billed from the Long-billed Dowitcher.

VOICE Flight call low, plaintive *tu-tu-tu*, 3–4 notes; flight song *tu-tu*, *tu-tu*, *toodle-ee*, *tu-tu*, ending with low *anh-anh-anh*.

NESTING Simple depression, typically in sedge hummock; 4 eggs; 1 brood; May–June.

FEEDING Probes in "sewing machine" feeding style with water up to belly for aquatic mollusks, crustaceans, and insects.

ADULT (NONBREEDING)

ORANGE UNDERPARTS
In complete breeding plumage, the Short-billed Dowitcher is orange, even in late afternoon light.

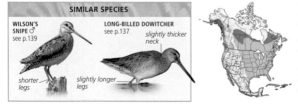

SIMILAR SPECIES

WILSON'S SNIPE ♂
see p.139

shorter legs

LONG-BILLED DOWITCHER
see p.137

slightly thicker neck

slightly longer legs

OCCURRENCE
Breeds mostly in sedge meadows or bogs with interspersed spruce and tamaracks between subarctic tundra and boreal forest. Migrates south to Central and South America, preferring coastal mudflats, saltmarshes, or adjacent freshwater pools.

| Length **9–10in (23–25cm)** | Wingspan **18–20in (46–51cm)** | Weight **2½–5½oz (70–155g)** |
| Social **Pairs/Flocks** | Lifespan **Up to 20 years** | Status **Secure (p)** |

DATE SEEN	WHERE	NOTES

Order **Charadriiformes**	Family **Scolopacidae**	Species *Limnodromus scolopaceus*

Long-billed Dowitcher

lightly streaked head

white belly

black-centered feathers

JUVENILE

bands on tail

ADULT (BREEDING)

dark upperparts with reddish markings

ADULT (BREEDING)

white rump patch

long, pointed wings

IN FLIGHT

brick-red underparts

mostly dusky gray upperparts

short but distinct white eyebrow

long, stout bill

dark patch between eye and bill

variable dark barring on flanks

white belly

ADULT (NONBREEDING)

It was not until 1950 that, after museum and field studies, scientists recognized two separate species of dowitcher in North America. The Long-billed Dowitcher is usually slightly larger, longer-legged, and heavier in the chest and neck than the Short-billed Dowitcher. The breeding ranges of the two species are separate, but their migration and en route stop-over areas overlap. The Long-billed Dowitcher is usually found in freshwater wetlands, and in the fall most of its population occurs west of the Mississippi River.

VOICE Flight and alarm call sharp, whistled *keek*, given singly or in series when agitated; song buzzy *pipipipipipi-chi-drrr*.

NESTING Deep sedge or grass-lined depression in sedge or grass; 4 eggs; 1 brood; May–June.

FEEDING Probes wet ground with "sewing-machine" motion for spiders, snails, worms, insects, and seeds.

FLIGHT: swift, direct flier with fast, powerful wingbeats.

TOUCHY FEELY
Sensitive touch-receptors at the tip of the bird's bill enable it to feel in the mud for food.

SIMILAR SPECIES

WILSON'S SNIPE see p.139

pale, central crown stripe

SHORT-BILLED DOWITCHER see p.136

slightly smaller overall

shorter legs

orangish underparts

OCCURRENCE
Breeds in wet, grassy meadows or coastal sedge tundra near freshwater pools. Migrates to Mexico and Central America, south to Panama, when found in freshwater habitats, including ponds, flooded fields, lake shores, also sheltered lagoons, saltmarsh pools, and tidal mudflats.

Length **9½–10in (24–26cm)**	Wingspan **18–20½in (46–52cm)**	Weight **3–4oz (85–125g)**
Social **Pairs/Flocks**	Lifespan **Unknown**	Status **Vulnerable**

DATE SEEN	WHERE	NOTES

| Order **Charadriiformes** | Family **Scolopacidae** | Species *Scolopax minor* |

American Woodcock

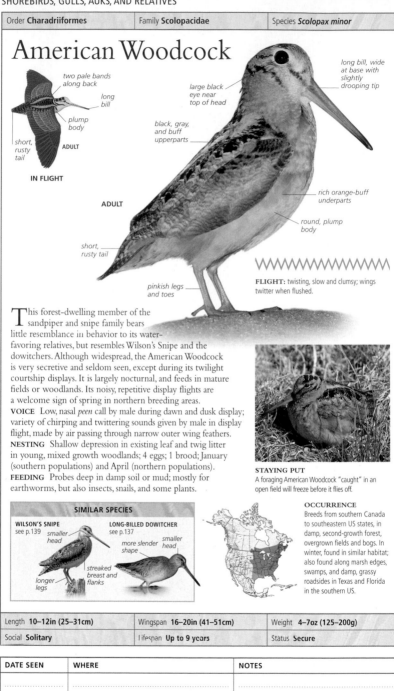

IN FLIGHT

two pale bands along back

long bill

plump body

short, rusty tail

ADULT

large black eye near top of head

long bill, wide at base with slightly drooping tip

black, gray, and buff upperparts

ADULT

rich orange-buff underparts

round, plump body

short, rusty tail

pinkish legs and toes

FLIGHT: twisting, slow and clumsy; wings twitter when flushed.

This forest-dwelling member of the sandpiper and snipe family bears little resemblance in behavior to its water-favoring relatives, but resembles Wilson's Snipe and the dowitchers. Although widespread, the American Woodcock is very secretive and seldom seen, except during its twilight courtship displays. It is largely nocturnal, and feeds in mature fields or woodlands. Its noisy, repetitive display flights are a welcome sign of spring in northern breeding areas.

VOICE Low, nasal *peen* call by male during dawn and dusk display; variety of chirping and twittering sounds given by male in display flight, made by air passing through narrow outer wing feathers.

NESTING Shallow depression in existing leaf and twig litter in young, mixed growth woodlands; 4 eggs; 1 brood; January (southern populations) and April (northern populations).

FEEDING Probes deep in damp soil or mud; mostly for earthworms, but also insects, snails, and some plants.

STAYING PUT
A foraging American Woodcock "caught" in an open field will freeze before it flies off.

SIMILAR SPECIES

WILSON'S SNIPE
see p.139

smaller head

streaked breast and flanks

longer legs

LONG-BILLED DOWITCHER
see p.137

smaller head

more slender shape

OCCURRENCE
Breeds from southern Canada to southeastern US states, in damp, second-growth forest, overgrown fields and bogs; in winter, found in similar habitat; also found along marsh edges, swamps, and damp, grassy roadsides in Texas and Florida in the southern US.

| Length **10–12in (25–31cm)** | Wingspan **16–20in (41–51cm)** | Weight **4–7oz (125–200g)** |
| Social **Solitary** | Lifespan **Up to 9 years** | Status **Secure** |

DATE SEEN	WHERE	NOTES

Order **Charadriiformes**	Family **Scolopacidae**	Species **Gallinago gallinago**

Wilson's Snipe

high-set large, dark eye

streaked face

long, tapered bill, slightly drooping at tip

white, vertical streaks

long, pointed, angled wings

long bill

short tail   **ADULT**

mostly brown upperparts

brown spots on breast and neck

IN FLIGHT

white underparts with barring on flanks

short russet tail

MALE

FLIGHT: extremely fast and zig zagging, rapid wingbeats; erratic-looking changes of direction.

RUSSET TAIL
Wilson's Snipe's russet-colored tail is usually hard to see, but it is evident on this preening bird.

This secretive and well camouflaged member of the sandpiper family has an unsettled taxonomic history, but is now classified individually. On its breeding grounds Wilson's Snipe produces rather eerie sounds during its aerial, mainly nocturnal, display flights. The birds fly up silently from the ground, then, from about 330ft (100m) up, they descend quickly, with their tail feathers spread, producing a unique, loud and vibrating sound through modified feathers. The North American populations belong to the subspecies *delicata*.
VOICE Alarm and overhead flight call raspy *kraitsch*; perched and low flying breeding birds give repetitive, monotonous *kup-kup-kup-kup* in alarm or aggression; distinctive whistling sound during territorial displays.
NESTING Elaborate woven nest lined with fine grass on ground, sedge, or moss; 4 eggs; 1 brood; May–June.
FEEDING Forages in mud or shallow water; probes deep into subsoil; diet includes mostly insect larvae, but also crustaceans, earthworms, and mollusks.

SIMILAR SPECIES		
AMERICAN WOODCOCK see p.138	**SHORT-BILLED DOWITCHER** see p.136	**LONG-BILLED DOWITCHER** see p.137
plump body / buffy orange underparts	smaller eye / orange tint to breast	no white streaks on back / longer legs

OCCURRENCE
Widespread from Alaska to Québec and Labrador south of the tundra zone; breeds in a variety of wetlands, including marshes, bogs, and open areas with rich soil. Winters farther south, where it prefers damp areas with vegetative cover, such as marshes, wet fields, and other bodies of water.

Length **10–11in (25–28cm)**	Wingspan **17–19in (43–48cm)**	Weight **2⅞–5oz (80–150g)**
Social **Solitary**	Lifespan **Up to 10 years**	Status **Secure**

DATE SEEN	WHERE	NOTES

SHOREBIRDS, GULLS, AUKS, AND RELATIVES

| Order **Charadriiformes** | Family **Scolopacidae** | Species *Actitis macularius* |

Spotted Sandpiper

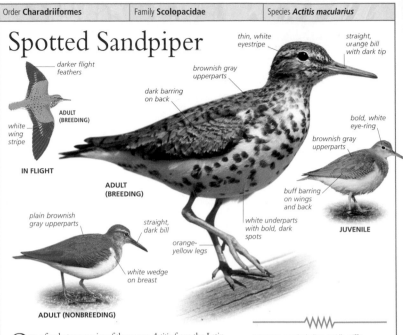

thin, white eyestripe

straight, orange bill with dark tip

darker flight feathers

brownish gray upperparts

dark barring on back

ADULT (BREEDING)

white wing stripe

IN FLIGHT

bold, white eye-ring

brownish gray upperparts

buff barring on wings and back

JUVENILE

ADULT (BREEDING)

plain brownish gray upperparts

straight, dark bill

orange-yellow legs

white underparts with bold, dark spots

white wedge on breast

ADULT (NONBREEDING)

One of only two species of the genus *Actitis*, from the Latin meaning "a coastal inhabitant," this small, short-legged sandpiper is the most widespread shorebird in North America. It is characterized by its quick walking pace, its habit of constantly teetering and bobbing its tail, and its unique style of flying low over water with stiff wingbeats. These birds have an unusual mating behavior, in which the females take on an aggressive role, defending territories and mating with three or more males per season.
VOICE Call a clear, ringing note *tee-tee-tee-tee*; flight song a monotonous *cree-cree-cree*.
NESTING Nest cup shaded by or scrape built under herbaceous vegetation; 3 eggs; 1–3 broods; May–June.
FEEDING Eats many items, including adult and larval insects, mollusks, small crabs, and worms.

FLIGHT: mostly shallow, rapidly, stiffly fluttering wingbeats, usually low above water.

BEHAVIORAL QUIRKS
This sandpiper "teeters," raising and lowering its tail while walking along the water's edge.

SIMILAR SPECIES

SOLITARY SANDPIPER ☾ see p.141
more slender body
longer legs
streaked breast

COMMON SANDPIPER
longer tail
more grayish green legs

OCCURRENCE
Breeds across North America in a wide variety of grassy, brushy, forested habitats near water, but not High Arctic tundra. During migration and in winter found in habitats near freshwater, including lake shores, rivers, streams, beaches, sewage ponds, ditches, seawalls, sometimes estuaries.

| Length **7¼–8in (18.5–20cm)** | Wingspan **15–16in (38–41cm)** | Weight **1⁹⁄₁₆–1¾oz (45–50g)** |
| Social **Small flocks** | Lifespan **Up to 12 years** | Status **Secure** |

DATE SEEN	WHERE	NOTES

| Order **Charadriiformes** | Family **Scolopacidae** | Species *Tringa solitaria* |

Solitary Sandpiper

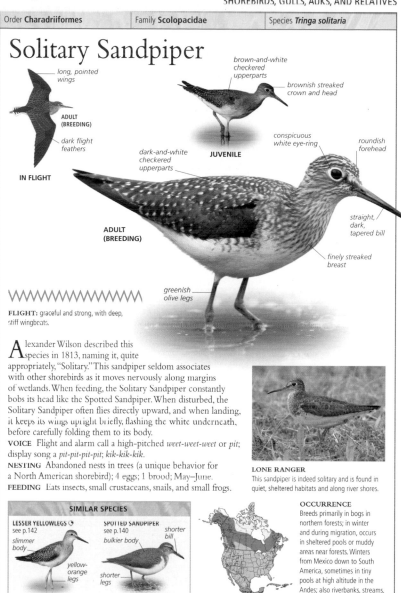

long, pointed wings

ADULT (BREEDING)

dark flight feathers

IN FLIGHT

brown-and-white checkered upperparts

brownish streaked crown and head

dark-and-white checkered upperparts

JUVENILE

conspicuous white eye-ring

roundish forehead

straight, dark, tapered bill

ADULT (BREEDING)

finely streaked breast

greenish olive legs

FLIGHT: graceful and strong, with deep, stiff wingbeats.

Alexander Wilson described this species in 1813, naming it, quite appropriately, "Solitary." This sandpiper seldom associates with other shorebirds as it moves nervously along margins of wetlands. When feeding, the Solitary Sandpiper constantly bobs its head like the Spotted Sandpiper. When disturbed, the Solitary Sandpiper often flies directly upward, and when landing, it keeps its wings upright briefly, flashing the white underneath, before carefully folding them to its body.

VOICE Flight and alarm call a high-pitched *weet-weet-weet* or *pit*; display song a *pit-pit-pit-pit; kik-kik-kik*.

NESTING Abandoned nests in trees (a unique behavior for a North American shorebird); 4 eggs; 1 brood; May–June.

FEEDING Eats insects, small crustaceans, snails, and small frogs.

LONE RANGER
This sandpiper is indeed solitary and is found in quiet, sheltered habitats and along river shores.

SIMILAR SPECIES

LESSER YELLOWLEGS ♂
see p.142
slimmer body
yellow-orange legs

SPOTTED SANDPIPER
see p.140
bulkier body
shorter bill
shorter legs

OCCURRENCE
Breeds primarily in bogs in northern forests; in winter and during migration, occurs in sheltered pools or muddy areas near forests. Winters from Mexico down to South America, sometimes in tiny pools at high altitude in the Andes; also riverbanks, streams, rain pools, and ditches.

| Length **7½–9in (19–23cm)** | Wingspan **22–23in (56–59cm)** | Weight **1⅟₁₆–2¼oz (30–65g)** |
| Social **Solitary/Small flocks** | Lifespan **Unknown** | Status **Secure** |

DATE SEEN	WHERE	NOTES

SHOREBIRDS, GULLS, AUKS, AND RELATIVES

Order **Charadriiformes**	Family **Scolopacidae**	Species *Tringa flavipes*

Lesser Yellowlegs 🔊

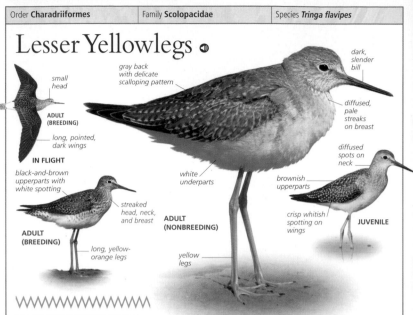

small head

gray back with delicate scalloping pattern

ADULT (BREEDING)

long, pointed, dark wings

IN FLIGHT

black-and-brown upperparts with white spotting

streaked head, neck, and breast

ADULT (BREEDING)

long, yellow-orange legs

white underparts

ADULT (NONBREEDING)

yellow legs

dark, slender bill

diffused, pale streaks on breast

diffused spots on neck

brownish upperparts

crisp whitish spotting on wings

JUVENILE

FLIGHT: straight and fast; with gliding and sideways banking; legs trail behind body.

With its smaller head, thinner bill, and smoother body shape, the Lesser Yellowlegs has a more elegant profile than the Greater Yellowlegs. It prefers smaller, freshwater, or brackish pools to open saltwater habitats, and it walks quickly and methodically while feeding. Although this species is a solitary feeder, it is often seen in small to large loose flocks in migration and winter.

VOICE Low, whistled *tu*, or *tu-tu* call; series of *tu* or *cuw* notes when agitated; display song a *pill-e-wee*, *pill-e-wee*, *pill-e-wee*.
NESTING Depression in ground or moss, lined with grass and leaves; 4 eggs; 1 brood; May–June.
FEEDING Eats a wide variety of aquatic and terrestrial insects, mollusks, and crustaceans, especially flies and beetles; also seeds.

READY TO FLY
This Lesser Yellowlegs raises its wings before takeoff.

SIMILAR SPECIES

GREATER YELLOWLEGS see p.144

SOLITARY SANDPIPER see p.141

larger and heavier

longer, thicker bill

shorter, greenish yellow legs

more defined breast streaks

OCCURRENCE
Breeds in northerly forest with clearings, and where forest meets tundra. In migration and in winter, uses wide variety of shallow wetlands, including flooded pastures and agricultural fields, swamps, lake and river shores, tidal creeks, and brackish mudflats. Winters from Mexico to Argentina.

Length **9–10in (23–25cm)**	Wingspan **23–25in (58–64cm)**	Weight **2–3⅜oz (55–95g)**
Social **Flocks**	Lifespan **Unknown**	Status **Secure**

DATE SEEN	WHERE	NOTES

142

Order **Charadriiformes**	Family **Scolopacidae**	Species *Tringa semipalmata*

Willet 🔊

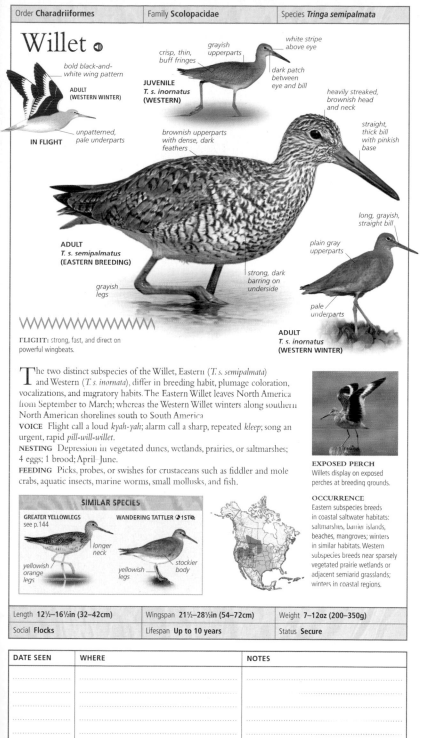

bold black-and-white wing pattern

ADULT (WESTERN WINTER)

IN FLIGHT

unpatterned, pale underparts

crisp, thin, buff fringes

grayish upperparts

JUVENILE T. s. inornatus (WESTERN)

white stripe above eye

dark patch between eye and bill

heavily streaked, brownish head and neck

straight, thick bill with pinkish base

brownish upperparts with dense, dark feathers

ADULT T. s. semipalmatus (EASTERN BREEDING)

grayish legs

strong, dark barring on underside

long, grayish, straight bill

plain gray upperparts

pale underparts

ADULT T. s. inornatus (WESTERN WINTER)

FLIGHT: strong, fast, and direct on powerful wingbeats.

The two distinct subspecies of the Willet, Eastern (*T. s. semipalmata*) and Western (*T. s. inornata*), differ in breeding habit, plumage coloration, vocalizations, and migratory habits. The Eastern Willet leaves North America from September to March; whereas the Western Willet winters along southern North American shorelines south to South America.
VOICE Flight call a loud *kyah-yah*; alarm call a sharp, repeated *kleep*; song an urgent, rapid *pill-will-willet*.
NESTING Depression in vegetated dunes, wetlands, prairies, or saltmarshes; 4 eggs; 1 brood; April–June.
FEEDING Picks, probes, or swishes for crustaceans such as fiddler and mole crabs, aquatic insects, marine worms, small mollusks, and fish.

EXPOSED PERCH
Willets display on exposed perches at breeding grounds.

OCCURRENCE
Eastern subspecies breeds in coastal saltwater habitats: saltmarshes, barrier islands, beaches, mangroves; winters in similar habitats. Western subspecies breeds near sparsely vegetated prairie wetlands or adjacent semiarid grasslands; winters in coastal regions.

SIMILAR SPECIES

GREATER YELLOWLEGS see p.144

yellowish / orange legs

longer neck

WANDERING TATTLER ❄1ST❄

yellowish legs

stockier body

Length **12½–16½in (32–42cm)**	Wingspan **21½–28½in (54–72cm)**	Weight **7–12oz (200–350g)**
Social **Flocks**	Lifespan **Up to 10 years**	Status **Secure**

DATE SEEN	WHERE		NOTES

| Order **Charadriiformes** | Family **Scolopacidae** | Species *Tringa melanoleuca* |

Greater Yellowlegs 🔊

long, pointed dark wings

ADULT (BREEDING)

IN FLIGHT

black-and-white checkered upperparts

heavily streaked head, neck, and breast

bold white eye-ring

slightly upturned bill

plain gray upperparts

variable pale gray base of bill

diffused gray streaks on neck and breast

ADULT (NONBREEDING)

long, yellow legs

ADULT (BREEDING)

diffused brown streaks on head and neck

brownish upperparts

JUVENILE

FLIGHT: direct, strong, and swift; legs trail behind tail.

This fairly large shorebird often runs frantically in many directions while pursuing small prey. It is one of the first northbound shorebird migrants in the spring, and one of the first to return south in late June or early July. Its plumage, a mixture of brown, black, and white checkered upperparts, and streaked underparts, is more streaked during the breeding season.
VOICE Call a loud, penetrating *tew-tew-tew*; agitated birds make repetitive *keu* notes; song a continuous *too-whee*.
NESTING Simple scrape in moss or peat, usually close to water; 4 eggs; 1 brood; May–June.
FEEDING Picks water surface and mud for small aquatic and terrestrial crustaceans and worms; also eats small fish, frogs, seeds, and berries.

EFFECTIVE METHOD
The Greater Yellowlegs often catches its prey by sweeping its bill sideways through water.

SIMILAR SPECIES		
LESSER YELLOWLEGS see p.142	**WILLET** see p.143 lacks checkered upperparts	heavier, thicker bill
less angular body contours	thinner, more pointed bill	

OCCURRENCE
Breeds in openings in northerly forests with bogs and wet meadows, a habitat called muskegs. In migration and winter, uses a wide variety of shallow water habitats, including freshwater and saltwater marshes, reservoirs, and tidal mudflats.

Length **11½–13in (29–33cm)**	Wingspan **28–29in (70–74cm)**	Weight **4–8oz (125–225g)**
Social **Solitary/Flocks**	Lifespan **Unknown**	Status **Secure**

DATE SEEN	WHERE	NOTES

| Order **Charadriiformes** | Family **Scolopacidae** | Species ***Phalaropus tricolor*** |

Wilson's Phalarope

reddish brown markings on sides of back

FEMALE (BREEDING)

grayish brown wings

IN FLIGHT

plain gray upperparts

yellowish legs

largely white face

white cheek

white underparts

JUVENILE (MOLTING TO 1ST WINTER)

gray and reddish brown back

black stripe from bill to nape

paler head markings

plain gray-and-black upperparts

MALE

white eyebrow

fairly long, straight bill

rust neck and throat

FEMALE (BREEDING)

A truly American phalarope, Wilson's is the largest of the three phalarope species. Unlike its two relatives, it does not breed in the Arctic, but in the shallow wetlands of western North America, and winters mainly in continental habitats of Bolivia and Argentina instead of in the ocean. This species can be found employing the feeding technique of spinning in shallow water to churn up adult and larval insects, or running in various directions on muddy wetland edges with its head held low to the ground while chasing and picking up insects. This bird is quite tolerant of humans on its breeding grounds, but this attitude changes immediately before migration, as it has gained weight and its movement is sluggish.

VOICE Flight call a low, nasal *werpf*; also higher, repetitive *emf, emf, emf, emf*, or *luk, luk, luk*.

NESTING Simple scrape lined with grass; 4 eggs; 1 brood; May–June.

FEEDING Eats brine shrimp, various insects, and insect larvae.

FLIGHT: fast and direct with quick wingbeats

ODD ONE OUT
Unlike its two essentially oceanic relatives, Wilson's Phalarope is also found in freshwater habitats.

SIMILAR SPECIES

LESSER YELLOWLEGS
see p.142

darker, spotted back

RED-NECKED PHALAROPE ♀
see p.146

streaked head and neck

black cheek patch

shorter bill

OCCURRENCE
Breeds in shallow, grassy wetlands of interior North America; during migration and winter, occurs in salty lakes and saline ponds as well as inland waterbodies. In winter, tens of thousands can be seen in the middle of Titicaca Lake in Bolivia.

| Length **8½–9½in (22–24cm)** | Wingspan **15½–17in (39–43cm)** | Weight **1¼–3oz (35–85g)** |
| Social **Large flocks** | Lifespan **Up to 10 years** | Status **Secure** |

DATE SEEN	WHERE	NOTES

| Order **Charadriiformes** | Family **Scolopacidae** | Species *Phalaropus lobatus* |

Red-necked Phalarope

pointed wings

narrow, white wing stripe

dark cap and cheek patch

dark upperparts with buff stripes

dark gray crown and face

black back with dull, white lines

JUVENILE

white throat

FEMALE (BREEDING)

IN FLIGHT

JUVENILE (WORN PLUMAGE)

dark upperparts with buff or rust feather edges

needle-like dark bill

rust neck and upper breast

FEMALE (BREEDING)

white underparts with dusky streaked flanks

This aquatic sandpiper spends much of its life in deep ocean waters feeding on tiny plankton; each year, after nine months at sea, it comes to nest in the Arctic. Its Latin name *lobatus* reflects the morphology of its toes, which are webbed (lobed). Both the Red-necked Phalarope and the Red Phalarope are oceanic birds that are found in large flocks or "rafts" far from shore. However, both species are occasionally found swimming inland, in freshwater habitats. Like the other two phalaropes, the Red-necked has a fascinating and unusual reversal of typical sex roles. The female is more brightly colored and slightly larger than the male; she will also pursue the male, compete savagely for him, and will migrate shortly after laying her eggs.

VOICE Flight call a hard, squeaky *pwit* or *kit*; on breeding grounds, vocalizations include variations of flight call notes.

NESTING Depression in wet sedge or grass; 3–4 eggs; 1–2 broods; May–June.

FEEDING Eats plankton; also insects, brine shrimp, and mollusks.

FLIGHT: fast and direct, with rapid wingbeats.

SINGLE FATHER
Male phalaropes perform all nesting and rearing duties after the female lays the eggs.

SIMILAR SPECIES
WILSON'S PHALAROPE ◑ see p.145 — *paler face*, *larger overall*
RED PHALAROPE ◑ see p.147 — *slightly thicker bill*, *larger head and thicker neck*

OCCURRENCE
Breeds in wet tundra, on raised ridges, or hummocks, but during migration and in winter, occurs far out at sea and away from shores, although sometimes found in freshwater habitats.

Length **7–7½in (18–19cm)**	Wingspan **12½–16in (32–41cm)**	Weight **1¹⁄₁₆–1⁹⁄₁₆oz (30–45g)**
Social **Flocks**	Lifespan **Unknown**	Status **Declining**

DATE SEEN	WHERE	NOTES

| Order **Charadriiformes** | Family **Scolopacidae** | Species *Phalaropus fulicarius* |

Red Phalarope

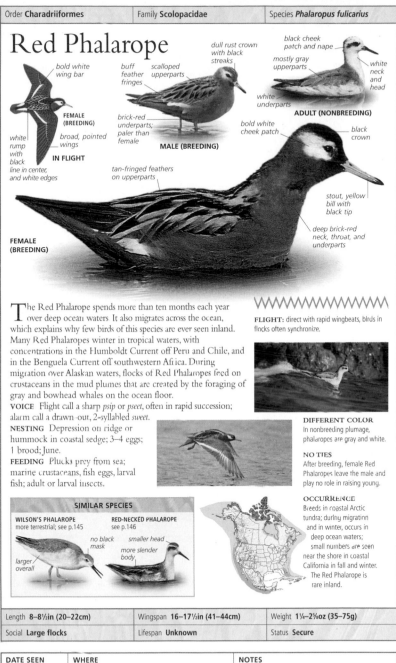

FEMALE (BREEDING)

bold white wing bar

IN FLIGHT

white rump with black line in center, and white edges

broad, pointed wings

dull rust crown with black streaks

buff feather fringes

scalloped upperparts

brick-red underparts; paler than female

tan-fringed feathers on upperparts

MALE (BREEDING)

black cheek patch and nape

mostly gray upperparts

white underparts

white neck and head

ADULT (NONBREEDING)

bold white cheek patch

black crown

stout, yellow bill with black tip

deep brick-red neck, throat, and underparts

FEMALE (BREEDING)

The Red Phalarope spends more than ten months each year over deep ocean waters. It also migrates across the ocean, which explains why few birds of this species are ever seen inland. Many Red Phalaropes winter in tropical waters, with concentrations in the Humboldt Current off Peru and Chile, and in the Benguela Current off southwestern Africa. During migration over Alaskan waters, flocks of Red Phalaropes feed on crustaceans in the mud plumes that are created by the foraging of gray and bowhead whales on the ocean floor.

VOICE Flight call a sharp *psip* or *pseet*, often in rapid succession; alarm call a drawn-out, 2-syllabled *sweet*.

NESTING Depression on ridge or hummock in coastal sedge; 3–4 eggs; 1 brood; June.

FEEDING Plucks prey from sea; marine crustaceans, fish eggs, larval fish; adult or larval insects.

FLIGHT: direct with rapid wingbeats, birds in flocks often synchronize.

DIFFERENT COLOR
In nonbreeding plumage, phalaropes are gray and white.

NO TIES
After breeding, female Red Phalaropes leave the male and play no role in raising young.

OCCURRENCE
Breeds in coastal Arctic tundra; during migration and in winter, occurs in deep ocean waters; small numbers are seen near the shore in coastal California in fall and winter. The Red Phalarope is rare inland.

SIMILAR SPECIES

WILSON'S PHALAROPE
more terrestrial; see p.145

larger overall

RED-NECKED PHALAROPE
see p.146

no black mask

smaller head

more slender body

| Length **8–8½in (20–22cm)** | Wingspan **16–17½in (41–44cm)** | Weight **1¼–2⅝oz (35–75g)** |
| Social **Large flocks** | Lifespan **Unknown** | Status **Secure** |

DATE SEEN	WHERE	NOTES

| Order **Charadriiformes** | Family **Stercorariidae** | Species ***Stercorarius pomarinus*** |

Pomarine Jaeger

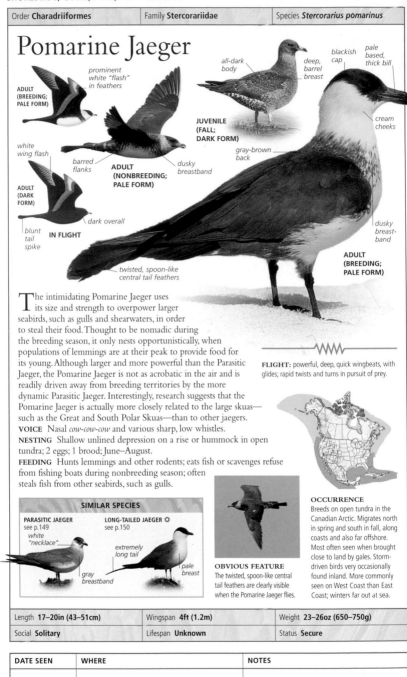

ADULT (BREEDING; PALE FORM)

prominent white "flash" in feathers

JUVENILE (FALL; DARK FORM)

all-dark body

deep, barrel breast

blackish cap

pale based, thick bill

cream cheeks

white wing flash

barred flanks

ADULT (NONBREEDING; PALE FORM)

dusky breastband

gray-brown back

ADULT (DARK FORM)

dark overall

blunt tail spike

IN FLIGHT

twisted, spoon-like central tail feathers

dusky breastband

ADULT (BREEDING; PALE FORM)

The intimidating Pomarine Jaeger uses its size and strength to overpower larger seabirds, such as gulls and shearwaters, in order to steal their food. Thought to be nomadic during the breeding season, it only nests opportunistically, when populations of lemmings are at their peak to provide food for its young. Although larger and more powerful than the Parasitic Jaeger, the Pomarine Jaeger is not as acrobatic in the air and is readily driven away from breeding territories by the more dynamic Parasitic Jaeger. Interestingly, research suggests that the Pomarine Jaeger is actually more closely related to the large skuas—such as the Great and South Polar Skuas—than to other jaegers.

VOICE Nasal *cow-cow-cow* and various sharp, low whistles.

NESTING Shallow unlined depression on a rise or hummock in open tundra; 2 eggs; 1 brood; June–August.

FEEDING Hunts lemmings and other rodents; eats fish or scavenges refuse from fishing boats during nonbreeding season; often steals fish from other seabirds, such as gulls.

FLIGHT: powerful, deep, quick wingbeats, with glides; rapid twists and turns in pursuit of prey.

OCCURRENCE
Breeds on open tundra in the Canadian Arctic. Migrates north in spring and south in fall, along coasts and also far offshore. Most often seen when brought close to land by gales. Storm-driven birds very occasionally found inland. More commonly seen on West Coast than East Coast; winters far out at sea.

SIMILAR SPECIES

PARASITIC JAEGER see p.149
white "necklace"
gray breastband

LONG-TAILED JAEGER ☼ see p.150
extremely long tail
pale breast

OBVIOUS FEATURE
The twisted, spoon-like central tail feathers are clearly visible when the Pomarine Jaeger flies.

| Length **17–20in (43–51cm)** | Wingspan **4ft (1.2m)** | Weight **23–26oz (650–750g)** |
| Social **Solitary** | Lifespan **Unknown** | Status **Secure** |

DATE SEEN	WHERE	NOTES

| Order **Charadriiformes** | Family **Stercorariidae** | Species *Stercorarius parasiticus* |

Parasitic Jaeger

pale cheek patch

ADULT (DARK FORM)

barring on wings

white wing patch

IN FLIGHT

mostly dark brown overall

dark cap

pale cheek

dark upperparts

ADULT (PALE FORM)

ADULT (DARK FORM)

long, pointed, central feathers

ADULT (INTERMEDIATE FORM)

dark legs and toes

wide, gray breastband

FLIGHT: swift wingbeats interspersed with fast glides, interrupted by twisting and climbing.

A true avian pirate of the high seas, the Parasitic Jaeger routinely seeks food by chasing, bullying, and forcing other seabirds to drop or regurgitate fish or other food they have caught. Unlike most jaegers, the Parasitic Jaeger is adaptable in its feeding habits so that it can forage and raise its young under a wide range of environmental conditions. Breeding on the Arctic tundra, it migrates to offshore areas during the nonbreeding season.

VOICE Variety of terrier-like yelps and soft squeals, often during interactions with other jaegers or predators, usually around nesting territories.

NESTING Shallow unlined depression on a rise or hummock in open tundra; 2 eggs; 1 brood; May–August.

FEEDING Steals fish and other aquatic prey from gulls and terns; catches small birds, eats eggs, or hunts small rodents on breeding grounds.

PARASITIC PIRATE
This Parasitic Jaeger is harrying a gull by pecking at it, to make it disgorge its hard-won meal.

SIMILAR SPECIES

POMARINE JAEGER
see p.148

two long, central, twisted tail feathers

LONG-TAILED JAEGER
see p.150

black cap

heavy hooked bill

longer pointed tail

OCCURRENCE
Breeds on tundra in northern Canada and Alaska (breeds farther south than other jaegers); during migration and in winter, uses both nearshore and offshore waters; rarely found inland in the US outside the breeding season.

Length **16–18½in (41–47cm)**	Wingspan **3ft 3in–3½ft (1–1.1m)**	Weight **13–18oz (375–500g)**
Social **Solitary/Small flocks**	Lifespan **Up to 18 years**	Status **Secure**

DATE SEEN	WHERE	NOTES

| Order **Charadriiformes** | Family **Stercorariidae** | Species *Stercorarius longicaudus* |

Long-tailed Jaeger

gray-and-black upperwing

ADULT (BREEDING)

IN FLIGHT

thin wings

slim, long body

IMMATURE (2ND SUMMER)

yellowish cream cheeks

dark cap

dark, grayish back

grayish brown

JUVENILE (DARK FORM)

extremely long tail streamers

ADULT (BREEDING)

pale breast, with no breastband

FLIGHT: direct, swift glides with rapid wingbeats; more buoyant and light than other jaegers.

This elegant and striking species is a surprisingly fierce Arctic and marine predator. Though the Long-tailed Jaeger occasionally steals food from small gulls and terns, it is much less proficient at such piracy than its larger relatives, and usually hunts for its own food. Indeed, the Long-tailed Jaeger is so dependent on there being an abundance of lemmings in the Arctic that in years when lemming numbers dip low, the bird may not even attempt to nest, because there would not be enough lemmings with which to feed its chicks.
VOICE Calls include a chorus of *kreek*, a loud *kreer* warning call, whistles, and high-pitched, sharp clicks.
NESTING Shallow, unlined depression on a rise or hummock in open tundra; 2 eggs; 1 brood; May–August.
FEEDING Hunts lemmings on tundra breeding grounds; takes fish, beetles, and mayflies from water surface; occasionally steals small fish from terns.

DEFENSIVE MOVES
This species protects its territory with angry calls, aggressive swoops, and distraction displays.

SIMILAR SPECIES

POMARINE JAEGER see p.148

long twisted feathers

PARASITIC JAEGER see p.149

thin bill

hooked bill

shorter tail

OCCURRENCE
Breeds on tundra in northern Canada and Alaska—generally the most northern breeding jaeger; on migration and in winter uses mostly offshore waters; very rarely seen inland in winter.

| Length **19–21in (48–53cm)** | Wingspan **3½ft (1.1m)** | Weight **10–11oz (275–300g)** |
| Social **Solitary/Flocks** | Lifespan **Up to 8 years** | Status **Secure** |

DATE SEEN	WHERE	NOTES

| Order **Charadriiformes** | Family **Alcidae** | Species *Alle alle* |

Dovekie

short, dark tail

dark wings

ADULT (BREEDING)
IN FLIGHT

dark head and upper breast

white triangle on side of breast

ADULT (BREEDING)

white collar at back of head

dark crown

small bill

dark back

white throat

white undertail

ADULT (NONBREEDING)

Also known widely as the Little Auk, the stocky and diminutive black-and-white Dovekie is a bird of the High Arctic. Most Dovekies breed in Greenland in large, noisy, crowded colonies (the largest one containing 15–20 million birds), but some breed in northeastern Canada, and others on a few islands in the Bering Sea off Alaska. On their breeding grounds, both adult and immature Dovekies are hunted ruthlessly by Glaucous Gulls, as well as mammalian predators, such as the Arctic Fox. Vast numbers of Dovekies winter on the Low Arctic waters off the northeastern North American seaboard, in immense flocks. Occasionally, severe onshore gales cause entire flocks to become stranded along the East Coast of North America.

VOICE Variety of calls at breeding colony, including high-pitched trilling that rises and falls; silent at sea.

NESTING Pebble nest in crack or crevice in boulder field or rocky outcrop; 1 egg; 1 brood; April–August.

FEEDING Mostly picks tiny crustaceans from just below the sea's surface.

FLIGHT: rapid, whirring wingbeats; flies in flocks low over the water's surface.

SOCIABLE LITTLE AUK
After initial squabbles over nest sites, Dovekies in breeding colonies become highly sociable.

OCCURRENCE
Breeds on islands inside the Arctic Circle; in Greenland, mostly, but also in northeastern Canada and the Bering Sea. Many birds remain just south of the Arctic pack ice throughout the winter; others fly south to winter off the northeastern seaboard of North America.

SIMILAR SPECIES

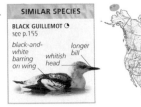

BLACK GUILLEMOT ♂
see p.155

black-and-white barring on wing

whitish head

longer bill

| Length **8½in (21cm)** | Wingspan **15in (38cm)** | Weight **6oz (175g)** |
| Social **Colonies** | Lifespan **Unknown** | Status **Secure** |

DATE SEEN	WHERE	NOTES

| Order **Charadriiformes** | Family **Alcidae** | Species *Uria aalge* |

Common Murre

black head

ADULT (BREEDING)

black wing

white eye-ring

white line extending backwards from eye

dark brown upperparts and breast

slender head and bill

long, straight, black bill

IN FLIGHT

ADULT (WHITE BRIDLED FORM)

curved, black line droops behind eye

white underparts

white face and throat

black back

ADULT (NONBREEDING)

ADULT (BREEDING)

grayish legs and toes

FLIGHT: fairly quick with rapid wingbeats; close to water's surface.

Abundant, penguin-like birds of the cooler northern oceans, Common Murres are often seen standing upright on cliffs. They are strong fliers and adept divers, to a depth of 500ft (150m). Their large nesting colonies, on rocky sea cliff ledges, are so densely packed that incubating adults may touch each other on both sides. Common Murre eggs are pointed at one end—when pushed, they roll around in a circle, reducing the risk of rolling off the nesting ledge. It has been suggested that unique egg markings may help adults recognize their own eggs.

VOICE Low-pitched, descending call given from cliffs or water, reminiscent of trumpeting elephant.

NESTING Directly on bare rock near shore, on wide cliff ledge, or large crevice; 1 egg; 1 brood; May–July.

FEEDING Pursues small schooling fish, such as herring, sand lance, and haddock; also crustaceans, marine worms, and squid.

BREEDING COLONY
Crowded together, Common Murres are not territorial but will defend a personal space.

SIMILAR SPECIES

THICK-BILLED MURRE
see p.153

thick, pale line between eye and bill

RAZORBILL ☼
see p.154

bill with white bar near tip

OCCURRENCE
Breeds close to rocky shorelines, nesting on coastal cliff ledges or flat rocks on top of sea stacks on both East and West Coasts. Found farther offshore during nonbreeding season, spending extended periods on the open ocean and in large bays. Winters at sea.

| Length **17½in (44cm)** | Wingspan **26in (65cm)** | Weight **35oz (1,000g)** |
| Social **Colonies** | Lifespan **At least 40 years** | Status **Localized** |

DATE SEEN	WHERE	NOTES

Order **Charadriiformes**	Family **Alcidae**	Species *Uria lomvia*

Thick-billed Murre

ADULT (BREEDING)

IN FLIGHT

hunched in flight

short, black tail

brownish black sides of head

white line along bill

white breast and underparts

all-blackish upperparts

ADULT (BREEDING)

reduced or absent white line on bill

more extensive white on throat

ADULT (NONBREEDING)

FLIGHT near the water surface with strong, rapid wingbeats.

Large and robust, the Thick-billed Murre is one of the most abundant seabirds in the whole of the Northern Hemisphere. Its dense, coastal cliff breeding colonies can be made up of around a million birds each. Chicks leave the colony when they are only about 25 percent of the adult's weight. Their growth is completed at sea, while being fed by the male parent alone. The Thick-billed Murre can dive to a remarkable 600ft (180m) to catch fish and squid.

VOICE Roaring, groaning, insistent sounding *aoorrr*; lower-pitched than the Common Murre.

NESTING Rocky coast or narrow sea cliff ledge in dense colony; 1 egg; 1 brood; March–September.

FEEDING Cod, herring, capelin, and sand lance in summer; also crustaceans, worms, and squid.

CLIFF HANGER
Thick-billed Murres breed in dense colonies on steep cliffs, often in very remote areas.

OCCURRENCE
Breeds on rocky shorelines, using the same nest each year. Winters at sea, spending extended periods of time on very cold, deep, and often remote ocean waters and pack ice edges or openings.

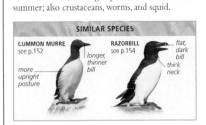

SIMILAR SPECIES

COMMON MURRE
see p.152

more upright posture

longer, thinner bill

RAZORBILL
see p.154

flat, dark bill

thick neck

Length **18in (46cm)**	Wingspan **28in (70cm)**	Weight **34oz (975g)**
Social **Colonies**	Lifespan **At least 25 years**	Status **Secure**

DATE SEEN	WHERE	NOTES

| Order **Charadriiformes** | Family **Alcidae** | Species *Alca torda* |

Razorbill

thin white line extends from bill to eye

large, round head

short neck

black upperparts

ADULT (BREEDING)

thick, black bill

long, black, pointed tail

IN FLIGHT

bill smaller than in breeding birds

brownish head

white underparts up to chin

ADULT (NONBREEDING)

ADULT (BREEDING)

snowy white underparts

blackish legs and toes

FLIGHT: agile with rapid wingbeats; long, pointed, black tail streamlines shape in flight.

This stocky, heavy-billed bird is the closest living relative of the extinct Great Auk. One of the rarest breeding seabirds in North America, the Razorbill is a strong flier and more agile in flight than many related species. Razorbills typically feed at depths of about 20ft (6m), but are sometimes known to dive to depths of more than 450ft (140m). On shore, Razorbills walk upright like penguins. They carry small fish at once to their chick, later male razorbills escort their flightless young to the sea to feed.

VOICE Deep, guttural, resonant croak, *hey al.*
NESTING Enclosed sites often built in crevices, among boulders, or in abandoned burrows; 1 egg; 1 brood; May–July.
FEEDING Dives for schooling fish, including capelin, herring, and sand lance; also consumes marine worms and crustaceans; sometimes steals fish from other auks.

IN FLIGHT
The razorbill flaps its wings constantly in flight as they are too small for the bird to glide.

SIMILAR SPECIES

THICK-BILLED MURRE
see p.153

more slender body

thick, pale line between eye and bill

COMMON MURRE ☼
see p.152

slimmer bill

more slender body

OCCURRENCE
Breeds on rocky islands and shorelines, or steep mainland cliffs in northeast North America, most of the world's population breeds in Iceland. Winters south of breeding range on ice-free coastal waters reaching New Jersey and Virginia. Forages in cool, shallower water, near shore.

| Length **17in (43cm)** | Wingspan **26in (65cm)** | Weight **26oz (725g)** |
| Social **Colonies** | Lifespan **At least 30 years** | Status **Localized** |

DATE SEEN	WHERE	NOTES

Order **Charadriiformes**	Family **Alcidae**	Species *Cepphus grylle*

Black Guillemot

ADULT (BREEDING)
broad, rounded wings
oval, snowy white upperwing patch

IN FLIGHT

gray bars in white wing patch
gray cap
gray neck

JUVENILE

large white patch

thin, straight bill

dark belly

scarlet legs and toes

ADULT (BREEDING)

round, black body

Black Guillemots, also known as "sea pigeons," are medium-sized auks with distinctive black plumage and white wing patches. Their striking scarlet legs and mouth lining help attract a mate during the breeding season. Like the other two species of the *Cepphus* genus, Black Guillemots prefer shallow, inshore waters to the open ocean. They winter near the shore, sometimes moving into the mouths of rivers.

VOICE Very high-pitched whistles and squeaks given on land and water near nesting habitat that resonate like an echo.
NESTING Shallow scrape in soil or pebbles within cave or crevice; site may be reused; 1–2 eggs, 1 brood; May–August.
FEEDING Dives under water near shore to hunt small, bottom-dwelling fish, such as rock eels, sand lance, and sculpin; propels down to depths of 59ft (18m) using partly opened wings, webbed toes as a rudder; feeds close to nesting islands.

FLIGHT: flies low over the water with very rapid wingbeats.

FOOD FOR CHICKS
The birds carry food for the chicks in their bills and often pause near the nest before dashing home.

SIMILAR SPECIES

DOVEKIE ❄
smaller;
see p.151

dark back

white patch behind eye

PIGEON GUILLEMOT ☼
dusky underwings in flight

black bar on white wing patch

OCCURRENCE
Primarily an Atlantic species. Breeds in crevices on remote rocky islands and cliffs that provide protection from predators. At sea prefers shallow waters, close to rocky coasts. At end of breeding season, adults and young move closer to shore to avoid pack ice.

Length **13in (33cm)**	Wingspan **21in (53cm)**	Weight **15oz (425g)**
Social **Colonies**	Lifespan **At least 20 years**	Status **Localized**

DATE SEEN	WHERE	NOTES

Order **Charadriiformes**	Family **Alcidae**	Species *Fratercula arctica*

Atlantic Puffin

IN FLIGHT — short tail — **ADULT (BREEDING)**

black back, collar, and underwings

blue-gray, orange, and red stripes on bill

orange legs and toes

ADULT (BREEDING)

dusky gray face — dull bill

ADULT (NONBREEDING)

gray face — red eye-ring — thick black line

stocky, rounded body

large, colorful, triangular bill

white breast

ADULT (BREEDING)

With its black-and-white "tuxedo," ungainly upright posture, and enormous, colorful bill, the Atlantic Puffin is often known as the "clown of the sea." Certainly it looks comical, whether strutting about or simply bobbing on the sea. It is seen in summer, when large breeding colonies gather on remote, rocky islands. To feed itself and its young, it can dive down to 200ft (60m) with partly folded wings, essentially "flying" underwater in pursuit of small schooling fish.

VOICE Rising and falling buzzy growl, resembling a chainsaw.
NESTING Underground burrow or deep rock crevice lined with grass and feathers; 1 egg; 1 brood; June–August.
FEEDING Dives deep for capelin, herring, hake, sand lance, and other small fish, which it swallows underwater, or stores crosswise in its bill to take back to its chicks.

FLIGHT: swift and direct, with rapid wingbeats; often circles breeding islands.

CATCH AND CARRY
When returning to breeding colonies to feed chicks, most birds carry more than one fish in their bill.

SIMILAR SPECIES

LONG-TAILED DUCK ♂ ❄
see p.54
long tail — white eye-ring — stubby bill — dark flanks

HORNED PUFFIN
fleshy "horn" above eye — yellow base to bill

OCCURRENCE
This northern North Atlantic seabird (found on both sides of the ocean) breeds in colonies on small, rocky, offshore islands, where it excavates nesting burrows or nests under boulders. Between breeding seasons, it heads for the high seas and remains far offshore, favoring cold, open waters.

Length **12½in (32cm)**	Wingspan **21in (53cm)**	Weight **12oz (350g)**
Social **Colonies**	Lifespan **At least 30 years**	Status **Localized**

DATE SEEN	WHERE	NOTES

| Order **Charadriiformes** | Family **Laridae** | Species *Rissa tridactyla* |

Black-legged Kittiwake

greenish yellow bill

white head

pale outer wing feathers

pale gray upperparts

black "M" pattern in wings

black bill

black tip to tail

ADULT

JUVENILE

IN FLIGHT

black wing tip

pale gray back feathers

ADULT

dark neck collar

dark wing bar

black legs and toes

JUVENILE

A kittiwake nesting colony is an impressive sight, with sometimes thousands of birds lined up along steep cliff ledges overlooking the sea. The ledges are often so narrow that the birds' tails stick out over the edge. Kittiwakes have sharper claws than other gulls, probably to give them a better grip on their ledges. In the late 20th century, the Black-legged Kittiwake population expanded greatly in the Canadian maritime provinces, with numbers doubling in the Gulf of St. Lawrence.

VOICE Repeated, nasal *kit-ti-wake, kit-ti-wake* call; vocal near nesting cliffs, usually silent in winter.

NESTING Mound of mud and vegetation on narrow cliff ledge; 1–3 eggs; 1 brood; April–August.

FEEDING Snatches small marine fish and invertebrates from the surface, or dives just below the water's surface; feeds in flocks.

FLIGHT: very stiff-winged; rapid, shallow wingbeats; overall more buoyant than most gulls.

LIVING ON THE EDGE
Young and adult kittiwakes pack together tightly on their precariously narrow cliff ledges.

SIMILAR SPECIES

RING-BILLED GULL
see p.164

RED-LEGGED KITTIWAKE

heavier, dark-marked bill

darker shoulder feathers

red legs

white spots in outer wing feathers

gray underwings

OCCURRENCE
Rarely seen far from the ocean; common in summer around sea cliffs, with ledges suitable for nesting, and nearby offshore waters; winters at sea; most likely to be seen from land during and after storms; strays have appeared throughout the interior.

| Length **15–16in (38–41cm)** | Wingspan **3ft 1in–4ft (0.95m–1.2m)** | Weight **11–18oz (300–500g)** |
| Social **Colonies** | Lifespan **Up to 26 years** | Status **Secure** |

DATE SEEN	WHERE	NOTES

| Order **Charadriiformes** | Family **Laridae** | Species *Xema sabini* |

Sabine's Gull

white triangle on wing

ADULT

black outer wing feathers

JUVENILE

black band on tail

IN FLIGHT

gray hood

red eye-ring

black border

yellow-tipped black bill

gray back

white underparts

ADULT (BREEDING)

black legs

barring on gray-brown back

black bill

JUVENILE

This strikingly patterned gull was discovered in Greenland by the English scientist Edward Sabine during John Ross's search for the Northwest Passage in 1818 (it was described in 1819). The distinctive wing pattern and notched tail make it unmistakable in all plumages—only juvenile kittiwakes are superficially similar. Previously thought to be related to the larger, but similarly patterned, Swallow-tailed Gull of the Galápagos, recent research indicates that Sabine's Gull is more closely related to the Ivory Gull. This species breeds in the Arctic and winters at sea, off the coasts of the Americas (south to Peru) and Africa (south to the Cape region).
VOICE Raucous, harsh *kyeer, kyeer, kyeer*; tern-like.
NESTING Shallow depression in marsh or tundra vegetation usually near water, lined with grass or unlined; 3–4 eggs; 1 brood; May–August.
FEEDING Catches aquatic insects from the water surface while swimming, wading, or flying during breeding season; winter diet mainly includes crustaceans, small fish, and plankton.

FLIGHT: wingbeats shallow and stiff; tern-like, buoyant.

STRIKING WING PATTERN
Juvenile Sabine's Gulls have a muted version of the distinctive triangular wing pattern seen in the adults.

SIMILAR SPECIES

BLACK-LEGGED KITTIWAKE ◐ see p.157
black wing bar
partial black collar

OCCURRENCE
In the summer, breeds near the Arctic Coast and on wet tundra in freshwater and brackish habitats, but also occurs near saltwater. Winters far offshore in tropical and subtropical waters; widespread in Pacific and Atlantic Oceans on migration.

| Length **13–14in (33–36 cm)** | Wingspan **35in–3ft 3in (90–100cm)** | Weight **5–9oz (150–250g)** |
| Social **Colonies** | Lifespan **At least 8 years** | Status **Secure** |

DATE SEEN	WHERE		NOTES

Order **Charadriiformes**	Family **Laridae**	Species *Chroicocephalus philadelphia*

Bonaparte's Gull

black wing tips

ADULT (NONBREEDING)

white flash on outer wings

IN FLIGHT

gray back

white head

blackish "ear" spot

gray neck

ADULT (NONBREEDING)

black hood

short bill

gray back and wings

brown patches on wing

IMMATURE (1ST WINTER)

white wedge on wing

orange-red legs

white underparts with rosy glow

ADULT (BREEDING)

Lighter and more delicate than the other North American gulls, Bonaparte's Gull is commonly distinguished in winter by the blackish smudge behind each eye and the large, white wing patch. It is one of America's most abundant gulls. In 1989, for example, more than 120,000 were estimated to have occurred in one harbor near Cleveland, Ohio. This species was named after the French ornithologist Charles Lucien Bonaparte (nephew of Napoleon), who lived in New Jersey in the 1820s.

VOICE Harsh *keek, keek*; can be vocal in feeding flocks, *kew, kew, kew*.

NESTING Stick nest of twigs, branches, tree bark, lined with mosses or lichens; usually in conifers 5–20ft (1.5–6m) above ground; also in rushes over water; 1–4 eggs; 1 brood; May–July.

FEEDING Catches insects in flight on breeding grounds; picks crustaceans, mollusks, and small fish from water's surface; also plunge-dives.

FLIGHT: graceful, light, and agile; rapid wingbeats; can be mistaken for a tern in flight.

TERN-LIKE GULL
Bonaparte's Gulls are very social and, flying in flocks, these pale, delicate birds look like terns.

WHITE UNDERWINGS
In all plumages, Bonaparte's Gulls have white underwings, unlike other similar small gulls.

OCCURRENCE
During breeding season, found in northern forest zone, in lakes, ponds, or bogs; on migration, may be found anywhere where there is water: ponds, lakes, sewage pools, or rivers. Winters on Great Lakes and along the coast; often found in large numbers at coastal inlets.

SIMILAR SPECIES

BLACK HEADED GULL see p.160
dark outer wing feathers
larger overall

LITTLE GULL see p.161
red bill
uniform gray upperwing
smaller overall

Length **11–12in (28–30cm)**	Wingspan **35in–3ft 3in (90–100cm)**	Weight **6–8oz (175–225g)**
Social **Flocks**	Lifespan **Up to 18 years**	Status **Secure**

DATE SEEN	WHERE	NOTES

159

| Order **Charadriiformes** | Family **Laridae** | Species *Chroicocephalus ridibundus* |

Black-headed Gull

brownish "crown-collar"

reddish bill

dark "ear" spot

gray back

white flash on outer wings

black trailing edge of wing

ADULT (NONBREEDING)

IN FLIGHT

black-tipped, red bill

brown spots on feathers

black-tipped orange bill

white nape

very pale gray back

chocolate brown hood

dark red bill

dark red legs

black tail tip

IMMATURE (1ST WINTER)

ADULT (BREEDING)

white underparts

bright red legs

ADULT (NONBREEDING)

An abundant breeder in Eurasia, the Black-headed Gull colonized North America in the 20th century. It was first seen in the 1920s, not long after nests were discovered in Iceland in 1911. It has become common in Newfoundland after being found nesting there in 1977, and has nested as far south as Cape Cod. However, it has not spread far to the West and remains an infrequent visitor or stray over most of the continent.

VOICE Loud laughing (its French name is Laughing Gull) or a chattering *kek kek keeaar*; very vocal at breeding sites.

NESTING Loose mass of vegetation, on ground or on top of other vegetation; may be a large mound in wet areas; 2–3 eggs; 1 brood; April–August.

FEEDING Picks insects, small crustaceans, and mollusks off water's surface while flying or hovering; eats some vegetation; also forages in plowed farm fields; raids garbage dumps.

FLIGHT: graceful, light, and buoyant; agile.

BEAUTIFUL BREEDING PLUMAGE
Most American birders never see the elegant summer plumage of the Black-headed Gull.

SIMILAR SPECIES

BONAPARTE'S GULL
see p.159

smaller and more delicate

white underwing

black bill

LITTLE GULL
see p.161

much smaller overall

all gray upperwing

OCCURRENCE
Rare breeder in northeastern North America; singles or a few individuals may be found along the coast, often with Bonaparte's Gulls, at harbors, inlets, bays, rivers, lakes, sewage outlets, or garbage dumps; strays may occur anywhere. One of the most common European gulls.

| Length **13½–14½in (34–37cm)** | Wingspan **3ft 3in–3½ft (1–1.1m)** | Weight **7–14oz (200–400g)** |
| Social **Colonies** | Lifespan **Up to 18 years** | Status **Localized** |

DATE SEEN	WHERE	NOTES

| Order **Charadriiformes** | Family **Laridae** | Species *Hydrocoloeus minutus* |

Little Gull

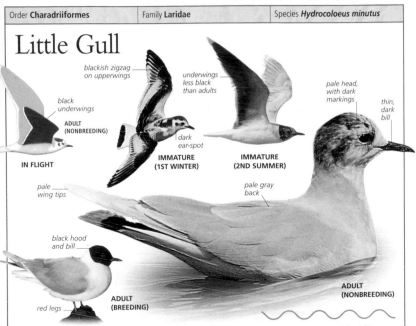

blackish zigzag on upperwings

black underwings

ADULT (NONBREEDING)

IN FLIGHT

underwings less black than adults

dark ear-spot

IMMATURE (1ST WINTER)

IMMATURE (2ND SUMMER)

pale head, with dark markings

thin, dark bill

pale wing tips

pale gray back

pale gray back

black hood and bill

ADULT (BREEDING)

red legs

ADULT (NONBREEDING)

A Eurasian species distributed from the Baltic to China, the Little Gull is the smallest gull in the world. Whether it is a recent immigrant to North America or has actually been here, unnoticed, in small numbers for many years remains a mystery. It was first recorded in North America in the early 1800s, but a nest was not found until 1962, in Ontario, Canada. Known nesting areas are still few, but winter numbers have been increasing steadily in recent decades.

VOICE Nasal *kek, kek, kek, kek*, reminiscent of a small tern.
NESTING Thick, floating mass of dry cattails, reeds, or other vegetation, in marshes and ponds; 3 eggs; 1 brood; May–August.
FEEDING Seizes prey from water's surface, while swimming or plunge-diving; typical prey includes flying insects, aquatic invertebrates such as shrimps, and small fish.

FLIGHT: quick wingbeats; light, nimble, and agile.

SIMPLE ELEGANCE
Its long, pale gray wings with a thin white border make this bird one of the most elegant gulls.

SIMILAR SPECIES

BLACK-HEADED GULL
see p.160

white flash in wing

red bill

BONAPARTE'S GULL
see p.159

larger overall

white flash in wing

OCCURRENCE
Breeds in extensive freshwater marshes in Hudson Bay and Great Lakes region, but the full extent of its breeding range in North America is unknown; can appear almost anywhere while migrating. Winters primarily along sea coasts, at sewage outfalls; often with groups of Bonaparte's Gulls.

| Length **10–12in (25–30cm)** | Wingspan **23½–26in (60–65cm)** | Weight **3½–5oz (100–150g)** |
| Social **Colonies** | Lifespan **Up to 6 years** | Status **Secure** |

DATE SEEN	WHERE	NOTES

Order **Charadriiformes**	Family **Laridae**	Species *Leucophaeus atricilla*

Laughing Gull 🔊

dark gray wings

ADULT (WINTER)

IN FLIGHT

brown wing feathers

white forehead

IMMATURE (1ST WINTER)

dark gray back

black wing tips

long, dark legs

broken white eye-ring

black head

long, slightly drooped bill

white neck

white underparts

ADULT (BREEDING)

gray nape

ADULT (WINTER)

The distinctive call of the Laughing Gull is a familiar sound in spring and summer along the East Coast. Already abundant when the Europeans arrived in North America, it was greatly reduced in the 19th century by egg collectors and the millinery trade. Its numbers increased in the 1920s, following protection, but declined again because of competition with larger gulls from the North. With the closing of landfills however, the Laughing Gull population has recovered.

VOICE Typical call strident laugh, *ha…ha…ha…ha…ha*; very vocal in breeding season; quiet in winter.

NESTING Mass of grass on dry land with heavy vegetation, sand, rocks, and saltmarshes; 2–4 eggs, 1 brood; April–July.

FEEDING Picks from surface while walking and swimming; feeds on various invertebrates: insects, earthworms, squid, crabs, crab eggs, and larvae; also eats small fish, garbage, and berries.

FLIGHT: strong and direct; graceful for a gull; agile enough to catch flying insects.

DARK WING TIPS
Unlike many gulls, the Laughing Gull usually shows little or no white in the wing tips.

OCCURRENCE
During breeding season usually found near saltwater. Post-breeders and juveniles wander widely; strays can turn up anywhere. Rare in winter in the Northeast. Small numbers once nested at the Salton Sea but only a visitor there for the last 50 years.

SIMILAR SPECIES

FRANKLIN'S GULL see p.163
white band in wing tips
short, straight bill

FRANKLIN'S GULL ♀ ☼ see p.163
short, straight bill
darker head
pink blush on underparts

Length **15½–18in (39–46cm)**	Wingspan **3¼–4ft (1–1.2m)**	Weight **7–13oz (200–375g)**
Social **Colonial**	Lifespan **Up to 20 years**	Status **Secure**

DATE SEEN	WHERE	NOTES

| Order **Charadriiformes** | Family **Laridae** | Species *Leucophaeus pipixcan* |

Franklin's Gull

black wing tips set-off by white band

dark gray wings

ADULT (WINTER)

IN FLIGHT

dark back of head

gray back

short, straight bill

ADULT (WINTER)

partial hood

IMMATURE (1ST SUMMER)

dark gray back

broken white eye crescent

black head

red bill

pink blush underneath

white in outer wing feathers

ADULT (SUMMER)

FLIGHT: stiff and direct; relatively fast wingbeats; agile flier.

Since its discovery, Franklin's Gull has carried a number of names: Prairie Dove, Rosy Dove, and Franklin's Rosy Gull—"Dove" alluding to its dainty appearance and "rosy" to the pink blush of its undersides. Its official name honors British Arctic explorer, John Franklin, on whose first expedition, the bird was discovered in 1823. Unlike other gulls, this species has two complete molts each year. As a result, its plumage usually looks fresh and it rarely has the scruffy look of some other gulls.

VOICE Nasal *weeh-a, weeh-a*; shrill *kuk kuk kuk kuk*; extremely vocal around breeding colonies.

NESTING Floating mass of bulrushes or other plants; material added as nest sinks; 2–4 eggs; 1 brood; April–July.

FEEDING Feeds mainly on earthworms and insects during breeding and some seeds, taken while walking or flying; opportunistic feeder during migration and winter.

PROMINENT EYES
In all plumages, Franklin's Gull has much more prominent white eye-crescents than similar species.

SIMILAR SPECIES

LAUGHING GULL
see p.162

longer, drooped bill

longer legs

LAUGHING GULL ♂ ✳
see p.162

smaller eye-crescents

longer, drooped bill

longer legs

OCCURRENCE
In summer, a bird of the high prairies; always nests over water. On migration often found in agricultural areas; large numbers frequent plowed fields or follows plows. Winters mainly along the Pacific Coast of South America.

| Length **12½–14in (32–36cm)** | Wingspan **33in–3ft 1in (85–95cm)** | Weight **8–11oz (225–325g)** |
| Social **Colonial** | Lifespan **At least 10 years** | Status **Declining** |

DATE SEEN	WHERE	NOTES

| Order **Charadriiformes** | Family **Laridae** | Species *Larus delawarensis* |

Ring-billed Gull

white wing spots

ADULT (BREEDING)

dark eye

mottled gray back

black-tipped, pink bill

white neck

IMMATURE (1ST WINTER)

heavily mottled back

mottled underparts

pink legs

black band on yellow bill

JUVENILE

IN FLIGHT

fine streaks on head

pale gray back

pale eye, with red eye-ring

IMMATURE (2ND WINTER)

pale gray back

gray back

olive-yellow legs

ADULT (NONBREEDING)

white markings on outer wing feathers

ADULT (BREEDING)

white underparts

yellowish or greenish legs

FLIGHT: quick, deep wingbeats; strong, direct flight, soaring on thermals.

One of the most common birds in North America, the medium-sized Ring-billed Gull is distinguished by the black band on its yellow bill. From the mid-19th to the early 20th century, population numbers crashed because of hunting and habitat loss. Protection allowed the species to make a spectacular comeback, and in the 1990s, there were an estimated 3–4 million birds. It can often be seen scavenging in parking lots at malls.
VOICE Call a slightly nasal and whiny *kee-ow* or *meee-ow*; series of 4–6 *kyaw* notes, higher pitched than Herring Gull.
NESTING Shallow cup of plant matter on ground in open areas, usually near low vegetation; 1–5 eggs; 1 brood; April–August.
FEEDING Picks food while walking; also dips and plunges in water; eats small fish, insects, grain, small rodents; also scavenges.

BLACK WING MARKING
The sharply demarcated black wing tips are prominent from both above and below.

SIMILAR SPECIES

MEW GULL see p.472
darker mantle
round head
small bill

MEW GULL 1ST
see p.472
less distinct streaks
round head
small bill

OCCURRENCE
Breeds in freshwater habitats in the interior of the continent. In winter, switches to mostly saltwater areas and along both the East and West Coasts; also along major river systems and reservoirs. Found year-round near the southern Great Lakes.

| Length **17–21½in (43–54cm)** | Wingspan **4–5ft (1.2–1.5m)** | Weight **11–25oz (300–700g)** |
| Social **Colonies** | Lifespan **Up to 32 years** | Status **Secure** |

DATE SEEN	WHERE	NOTES

| Order **Charadriiformes** | Family **Laridae** | Species *Larus argentatus* |

Herring Gull 🔊

white spots near wing tips
ADULT (BREEDING)

gray wings
IMMATURE (2ND WINTER)

light head
barred gray-brown overall

mottled brown back
barred brown body
white head and neck
IMMATURE (1ST WINTER)

large, yellow bill with red spot

gray back

streaked head
ADULT (NONBREEDING)

black outer wing feathers
IN FLIGHT

white underparts

pink legs
ADULT (BREEDING)

streaked head and neck
ADULT (NONBREEDING)

The Herring Gull is the archetypal, large "white-headed" gull to which nearly all other gulls are compared. When people mention "seagulls" they usually refer to the Herring Gull. The term, however, is misleading because the Herring Gull, like most other gulls, does not commonly go far out to sea—it is a bird of near-shore waters, coasts, lakes, rivers, and inland waterways. Now very common, the Herring Gull was nearly wiped out in the late 19th and early 20th century by plumage hunters and egg collectors.
VOICE Typical call a high-pitched, shrill, repeated *heyaa… heyaa…heyaa…heyaa*; vocal throughout the year.
NESTING Shallow bowl on ground lined with feathers, vegetation, detritus; 2–4 eggs; 1 brood; April–August.
FEEDING Eats fish, crustaceans, mollusks, worms; eggs and chicks of other seabirds; scavenges carrion, garbage; steals from other birds.

FLIGHT: steady, regular, slow wingbeats; also commonly soars and glides.

MASTER SCAVENGER
A common sight near any water body, the Herring Gull is an expert scavenger of carrion and trash.

OCCURRENCE
Found throughout North America along coasts and inland on lakes, rivers, and reservoirs; also frequents garbage dumps. Breeds in northeastern US and across Canada. Migrates southward across much of the continent to winter in coastal areas and along lakes and major rivers.

SIMILAR SPECIES	
RING-BILLED GULL see p.164	**CALIFORNIA GULL** see p.472
smaller overall	
black ring on bill	black-and-red spot on bill
yellow-green legs	greenish legs

| Length **22–26in (56–66cm)** | Wingspan **4–5ft (1.2–1.5m)** | Weight **28–42oz (800–1,200g)** |
| Social **Colonies** | Lifespan **At least 35 years** | Status **Secure** |

DATE SEEN	WHERE	NOTES

| Order **Charadriiformes** | Family **Laridae** | Species *Larus glaucoides* |

Iceland Gull

gray wing tips

pale brown plumage

ADULT (WINTER)

IMMATURE (1ST WINTER)

IN FLIGHT

wing tip white or marked with gray

short, pale yellow bill with red spot

markedly streaked head

gray back

gray wing tips

white belly

pink legs

brown barred plumage

blackish bill

head mostly white

pale, barred underparts

IMMATURE (1ST WINTER)

IMMATURE (2ND WINTER)

ADULT (WINTER)
L. g. kumlieni

Iceland Gulls of the subspecies *kumlieni* (seen in all the images here) are the most familiar form of this species in North America. They breed in the Canadian Arctic and winter farther south. Young birds have a dark tailband and brown streaks in the wing tip, while adults vary from white wing tips to gray with white spots. A darker subspecies, *thayeri,* breeds on Arctic islands west of the Kumlieni Gull's range, and has black-and-white wing tips like the Herring Gull and a darker eye. Thayer's Gull was considered to be a different species until 2017, when it was grouped with the Iceland Gull. The "Iceland" form of the gull, *L.g. glaucoides,* breeds in Greenland but is found farther eastward in winter, including in Iceland.

VOICE Call a *clew, clew, clew* or *kak-kak-kak*; vocal around breeding colonies; virtually silent on wintering grounds.
NESTING Loose nest of moss, vegetation, and feathers, usually on narrow rock ledge; 2–3 eggs; 1 brood; May–August.
FEEDING Grabs small fish from surface while in flight; also eats crustaceans, mollusks, carrion, and garbage.

FLIGHT: light and graceful; wings long in proportion to body.

WING TIP COLOR VARIATION
Some adult Iceland Gulls found in North America have wing tips that are almost pure white.

SIMILAR SPECIES
GLAUCOUS GULL
see p.168
much larger body
larger bill
white wing tips

OCCURRENCE
Usually nests on ledges on vertical cliffs overlooking the sea; winters where it finds regions of open water in frozen seas and along coast. A few wander to open water areas in the interior, such as the Niagara Falls, the Great Lakes and major rivers.

| Length **20½–23½in (52–60cm)** | Wingspan **4½–5ft (1.4–1.5m)** | Weight **21–39oz (600–1,100g)** |
| Social **Colonies** | Lifespan **Up to 33 years** | Status **Secure** |

DATE SEEN	WHERE	NOTES

Order **Charadriiformes**	Family **Laridae**	Species *Larus fuscus*

Lesser Black-backed Gull

black wing tips with white spot

ADULT (NONBREEDING)

IN FLIGHT

mottled, dark brown body

back turns dark gray

IMMATURE (1ST WINTER)

IMMATURE (2ND WINTER)

yellow eye

black bill

streaked head and neck

slate-gray back

white underparts

ADULT (NONBREEDNG)

white head

yellow bill with red spot

bright yellow legs

dull yellow legs

ADULT (BREEDING)

This European visitor was first discovered in North America on the New Jersey Coast on September 9, 1934 and in New York City a few months later. In recent decades, it has become an annual winter visitor. Nearly all the Lesser Black-backed Gulls found in North America are of the Icelandic and western European subspecies *L. f. graellsii*, with a slate-gray back. Another European subspecies, with a much darker back, has rarely been reported in North America, but it is probably only a matter of time before it nests here.

VOICE A *kyow…yow…yow…yow* call, similar to that of Herring Gull; also a deeper and throaty, repeated *gah-gah-gah-gah*.

NESTING Scrape on ground lined with dry lichens, dry grass, and feathers; 3 eggs; 1 brood; April–September.

FEEDING Eats mollusks, crustaceans, and various insects; also scavenges carrion and garbage.

FLIGHT: powerful and direct; regular wingbeats; long wings make it appear graceful.

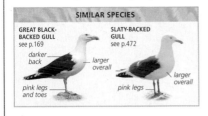

SIMILAR SPECIES

GREAT BLACK-BACKED GULL see p.169

darker back

pink legs and toes

larger overall

SLATY-BACKED GULL see p.472

larger overall

pink legs

EXCITING FIND
In recent years, gull enthusiasts and birdwatchers have found these birds visiting from Europe.

OCCURRENCE
Regular and increasingly common winter visitor to eastern North America, usually along the coast, but also in the interior; wherever gulls commonly concentrate such as harbors, lakeshores, landfills, and around fishing boats.

Length **20½–26in (52–67cm)**	Wingspan **4¼–5ft (1.3–1.5m)**	Weight **22–35oz (625–1,000g)**
Social **Colonies**	Lifespan **Up to 26 years**	Status **Secure**

DATE SEEN	WHERE	NOTES

| Order **Charadriiformes** | Family **Laridae** | Species *Larus hyperboreus* |

Glaucous Gull

ADULT (WINTER)

streaking on head

mottled white plumage

IMMATURE (1ST WINTER, FADED)

IN FLIGHT

white wing tips

light brownish plumage

IMMATURE (1ST WINTER)

mottled, pale brown back

IMMATURE (1ST WINTER)

pale brown underparts

white head

yellow bill with distinct red spot

pale gray upperparts

pale gray upperparts

white underparts

pink legs

ADULT (SUMMER)

FLIGHT: heavy, slow, and powerful; often glides and soars.

The Glaucous Gull is the largest of the "white-winged" gulls. Its large, pale shape is immediately apparent in a group of gulls as it appears like a large white spectre among its smaller, darker cousins. In the southern part of its US winter range, pale immatures are encountered more frequently than adults. In the Arctic, successful pairs of Glaucous Gulls maintain the bonds with their mates for years, often returning to the same nest site year after year.

VOICE Similar to that of the Herring Gull, but slightly harsher and deeper; hoarse, nasal *ku-ku-ku*.

NESTING Shallow cup lined with vegetation on ground, at edge of tundra pools, on cliffs and ledges and islands; 1–3 eggs; 1 brood; May–July.

FEEDING Eats fish, crustaceans, mollusks; also eggs and chicks of waterfowl, small seabirds, and small mammals.

NORTHERN VISITOR
This large gull is an uncommon visitor over most of North America during the winter months.

SIMILAR SPECIES

GLAUCOUS-WINGED GULL

dusky wing tips

ICELAND GULL see p.166

much smaller bill

much smaller overall

OCCURRENCE
Breeds along the High Arctic Coast, rarely inland; winters along northern Atlantic and Pacific Coasts and the Great Lakes; frequently seen at Niagara Falls. Strays, usually immatures, can occur inland anywhere where concentrations of gulls are found, such as trash sites dumps.

| Length **26–30in (65–75cm)** | Wingspan **5–6ft (1.5–1.8m)** | Weight **2¾–6lb (1.2–2.7kg)** |
| Social **Colonies** | Lifespan **Up to 21 years** | Status **Secure** |

DATE SEEN	WHERE	NOTES

| Order **Charadriiformes** | Family **Laridae** | Species *Larus marinus* |

Great Black-backed Gull 🔊

red eye-ring

large white spot on wing tips

ADULT (BREEDING)

white head with faint streaks

white underwings

white head and neck

yellow bill with red spot

ADULT (BREEDING)

black upperparts

IN FLIGHT

ADULT (NONBREEDING)

white underparts

white tips to outer feathers

whitish head

black bill

speckled back

ADULT (BREEDING)

pale pink legs and toes

IMMATURE (1ST WINTER)

The largest gull in North America, the Great Black-backed Gull is known for its bullying disposition. In breeding colonies, it is especially aggressive in the morning and early evening, and after chicks hatch; adults dive at ground predators and strike them with their wings and toes. Other birds benefit from this forceful behavior, for example eiders nesting in Great Black-backed Gull colonies suffer a low rate of nest predation.

VOICE Low, growling flight call, often repeated, low-pitched *heyaa…heyaa…heyaa…heyaa*, similar to the Herring Gull.

NESTING Shallow bowl on ground, lined with vegetation, feathers, and trash; 2–3 eggs; 1 brood; April–August.

FEEDING Scavenges and hunts fish, marine invertebrates, small mammals, eggs, chicks, adult seabirds, and waterfowl.

FLIGHT: heavy lumbering with deep wingbeats.

SOLITARY BIRDS
While all gulls are social animals, the Great Black-backed Gull is the most solitary.

SIMILAR SPECIES

LESSER BLACK-BACKED GULL ✳
see p.167

smaller body

slate-gray back

yellow legs

SLATY-BACKED GULL
see p.472

gray back

bright pink legs

OCCURRENCE
Breeds on natural and artificial islands, barrier beaches, saltmarshes, sand dunes; during winter, found along the coast, near shore water, major rivers, landfills, and harbors; in all seasons, often found together with Herring Gulls and Ring-billed Gulls. Also occurs in Europe.

| Length 28–31in (71–79cm) | Wingspan 5–5¼ft (1.5–1.6m) | Weight 2¾–4½lb (1.3–2kg) |
| Social **Pairs/Colonies** | Lifespan **Up to 27 years** | Status **Secure** |

DATE SEEN	WHERE	NOTES

| Order **Charadriiformes** | Family **Laridae** | Species *Sternula antillarum* |

Least Tern

dark outer wing feathers

streaked crown

patterned back

mostly dark bill

JUVENILE

forked tail

ADULT (BREEDING)

IN FLIGHT

black cap with white forehead

yellow bill

pale gray back

two dark outer wing feathers

white underparts

ADULT (BREEDING)

yellow legs

FLIGHT: extremely agile with stiff-winged, deep, rapid wingbeats; frequently hovers.

The Least Tern is the smallest of the North American terns and, in summer, its distinctive black cap and white forehead distinguish it from other members of its family. In the 19th century the population of Least Terns declined rapidly as its feathers were prized fashion accessories. Protected by the Migratory Bird Treaty of 1916, its numbers grew again, but it is still threatened by ongoing habitat loss.
VOICE Extremely vocal during breeding; a high-pitched *ki-deek, ki-deek*; also a rapid, almost nonstop chatter.
NESTING Shallow scrape on ground lined with dry vegetation, broken shells, and pebbles; 2–3 eggs; 1 brood; April–September.
FEEDING Plunge-dives, often after hovering, for fish and aquatic invertebrates, does not submerge completely; also skims surface for food; catches insects in flight.

COURTSHIP FEEDING
As with many other species of tern, Least Tern males offer fish to females during courtship.

SIMILAR SPECIES

COMMON TERN
see p.175
all-black cap
larger overall

black-tipped red bill

FORSTER'S TERN
larger overall; see p.177

black-tipped orange bill

longer tail

OCCURRENCE
Breeds along both coasts, major rivers, lakes, reservoirs, and in Great Plains wetlands; favors sandy areas such as barrier islands, beaches, sandbars, and nearby waters. Winters from Mexico to South America. Also breeds in the West Indies and Mexico.

| Length **8½–9in (21–23cm)** | Wingspan **19–21in (48–53cm)** | Weight **1¼–2oz (35–55g)** |
| Social **Colonies** | Lifespan **Up to 24 years** | Status **Endangered** |

DATE SEEN	WHERE	NOTES
....	....	....
....	....	....
....	....	....
....	....	....
....	....	....

| Order **Charadriiformes** | Family **Laridae** | Species *Gelochelidon nilotica* |

Gull-billed Tern

dark trailing edges on outer wing feathers

ADULT (BREEDING)

IN FLIGHT

white crown

small black "mask"

ADULT (NONBREEDING)

black cap

thick black bill

pale gray upperparts

ADULT (BREEDING)

white underparts

black legs and toes

With its relatively heavy build, thick bill, and broad wings, the Gull-billed Tern is more gull-like than any other North American tern. Also, unlike most other terns, it does not feed only on fish, and has a notably varied diet that enables foraging in a variety of different habitats, ranging from mudflats to desert scrub. It often nests in colonies with other terns—particularly Common and Caspian terns—and skimmers, and will occasionally hunt their chicks and steal their prey. During the 19th century, Gull-billed Terns were hunted ruthlessly for their eggs and feathers. Their numbers have at least partially recovered, but increasing human disturbance at nesting sites is a long-term conservation concern.

VOICE Short, two-noted, nasal yapping, *kay-wek, kay-wek*.

NESTING Simple, camouflaged scrape on ground, usually on sand, shell bank, or bare rock; shells and other debris used to build up nest; 2–3 eggs; 1 brood; April–July.

FEEDING Eats insects, lizards, small fish, and chicks. Catches insects in flight; plucks prey from ground or water's surface.

FLIGHT: buoyant and graceful; stiff-winged with shallow wingbeats.

LONG WINGS
The Gull-billed Tern has very long, pointed wings with a dusky edge on the outer feathers.

SIMILAR SPECIES

SANDWICH TERN ✿ see p.179

crest

yellow-tipped, thin, black bill

ROSEATE TERN ⚘ see p.174

thin bill

long, forked tail

smaller overall

OCCURRENCE
Rarely found away from saltwater. Historically considered a species of saltmarshes, but now breeds primarily on sandy beaches and barrier islands; most birds leave the US to winter in Central America, where they favor mudflats or flooded fields.

| Length **13–15in (33–38cm)** | Wingspan **3¼–4ft (1–1.2m)** | Weight **5–7oz (150–200g)** |
| Social **Colonies** | Lifespan **Up to 16 years** | Status **Localized** |

DATE SEEN	WHERE	NOTES

| Order **Charadriiformes** | Family **Laridae** | Species *Hydroprogne caspia* |

Caspian Tern

ADULT (BREEDING)

short tail

dark-tipped outer wing feathers

IN FLIGHT

streaked dark crown

ADULT (NONBREEDING)

slightly crested black cap

light gray back

dark markings on upperparts

JUVENILE

thick, red bill with dark tip

ADULT (BREEDING)

white underparts

black legs and toes

FLIGHT: strong, swift flier; heavy, powerful wingbeats; the most gull-like of North American terns.

Rivaling some of the gulls in size, the Caspian Tern is the world's largest tern. Unlike other "black-capped" terns, it never has a completely white forehead, even in winter. In nonbreeding plumage, when the cap is very heavily streaked. The Caspian Tern is known for its predatory habits, stealing prey from other seabirds, as well as snatching eggs from, and hunting the chicks of, other gulls and terns. It is aggressive in defending its nesting territory, giving hoarse alarm calls and rhythmically opening and closing its bill in a threatening display to intruders.

VOICE Hoarse, deep *kraaa, kraaa*; also barks at intruders; male's wings vibrate loudly in courtship flight.

NESTING Shallow scrape on ground; 2–3 eggs; 1 brood; May–August.

FEEDING Plunges into water to snatch fish, barnacles, and snails.

AGGRESSIVE BIRDS
The Caspian Tern is one of the most aggressive terns, though actual physical contact is rare.

OCCURRENCE
Found in a variety of aquatic habitats, freshwater and marine; rare offshore; breeds on interior lakes, saltmarsh, and on coastal barrier islands; winters on and near the coast. May be seen on marshes and wetlands during migration.

SIMILAR SPECIES

ELEGANT TERN
smaller overall

thin, orange-yellow bill

ROYAL TERN
see p.178

thinner, orange bill

slender build

| Length **18½–21½in (47–54cm)** | Wingspan **4¼–5ft (1.3–1.5m)** | Weight **19–27oz (525–775g)** |
| Social **Colonies/Pairs** | Lifespan **Up to 30 years** | Status **Secure** |

DATE SEEN	WHERE	NOTES

Order **Charadriiformes**	Family **Laridae**	Species ***Chlidonias niger***

Black Tern

dark gray wings

dark gray tail

ADULT (BREEDING)

IN FLIGHT

whitish underparts

ADULT (NONBREEDING)

white forehead

dark smudge on sides

gray upperparts

black head

black bill

black breast

ADULT (BREEDING)

white rump

black legs and toes

FLIGHT: very agile, but somewhat erratic-looking, bouncy flight; strong, deep wingbeats.

The Black Tern is a small, elegant, marsh-dwelling tern that undergoes a remarkable change in appearance from summer to winter—more so than any other regularly occurring North American tern. The Black Tern's breeding plumage can cause the bird to be confused with the closely related White-winged Tern, which is an accidental visitor to North America. The Black Tern's nonbreeding plumage is much paler than its breeding plumage—the head turns white with irregular black streaks, and the neck, breast, and belly become whitish gray.

VOICE Call nasal and harsh *krik*, *kip*, or *kik*; most vocal during breeding, but calls throughout the year.

NESTING Shallow cup on top of floating mass of vegetation, sometimes on top of muskrat lodges; usually 3 eggs; 1 brood; May–August.

FLOATING NEST
A floating nest is a dry place to lay eggs and raise chicks in a watery environment.

FEEDING Picks prey off water's surface or vegetation; rarely plunge dives; in summer, feeds on mainly insects, caught from the air or ground, also freshwater fish; in winter, eats mainly small sea fish.

SIMILAR SPECIES

SOOTY TERN ◐
see p.451

white spots on back

much larger overall

OCCURRENCE
Freshwater marshes in summer, but nonbreeding plumaged birds—probably young—occasionally seen along the coast. During migration, can be found almost anywhere near water. Winters in the marine coastal waters of Central and South America.

Length **9–10in (23–26cm)**	Wingspan **25–35in (63–88cm)**	Weight **1¾–2½ oz (50–70g)**
Social **Colonies**	Lifespan **Up to 9 years**	Status **Vulnerable**

DATE SEEN	WHERE	NOTES

| Order **Charadriiformes** | Family **Laridae** | Species *Sterna dougallii* |

Roseate Tern

scalloped appearance to upperparts

dark legs

JUVENILE

long tail feathers

red base to black bill

pale gray underwings

ADULT (LATE SUMMER)

IN FLIGHT

black cap

ADULT (SPRING)

pale gray upperparts

black bill

long, forked tail

FLIGHT: strong and fairly swift; stiffer-winged than terns of similar size.

white underparts

ADULT (SPRING)

Mostly found nesting with Common Tern, the Roseate Tern is paler and more slender. Its slim bill is black only for a short time in the spring before turning at least half red during the nesting season. At breeding colonies, these terns engage in distinctive courtship flights, with pairs gliding down from hundreds of feet in the air, swaying side to side with each other. Some birds nest as trios—two females and a male—all taking part in incubating the eggs and raising the young.

VOICE Most common calls *keek* or *ki-rik* given in flight and around nesting colony.

NESTING Simple scrape, often under vegetation or large rocks; adds twigs and dry grass during incubation; 1–3 eggs; 1 brood; May–August.

FEEDING Catches small fish with its bill by diving from a height of 3–20ft (1–6m); carries whole fish to young.

GRACEFUL COURTSHIP
Roseate Tern pairs engage in elegant, graceful courtship displays before mating.

SIMILAR SPECIES

SANDWICH TERN ☼
yellow-tipped bill;
see p.179

COMMON TERN ☼
shorter tail; see p.175

larger overall

darker gray overall

OCCURRENCE
Breeds almost exclusively in coastal areas in the Northeast from Long Island, New York, to Nova Scotia, with another small population in the outer Florida Keys. Typically nests on beaches and offshore islands. Not often seen far from breeding sites.

| Length **13–16in (33–41cm)** | Wingspan **28in (70cm)** | Weight **3–5oz (85–150g)** |
| Social **Colonies** | Lifespan **Up to 26 years** | Status **Endangered** |

DATE SEEN	WHERE	NOTES

Order **Charadriiformes**	Family **Laridae**	Species *Sterna hirundo*

Common Tern 🔊

dark wedge on outer feathers

brown bars on upperparts

whitish forehead

dark bill with red-orange base

black wing bar

ADULT (BREEDING)

JUVENILE

white forehead

bill mostly dark

blackish leg

ADULT (NONBREEDING)

IN FLIGHT

black cap

gray upperparts

forked tail

FLIGHT: graceful, steady and strong; wingbeats relatively deep.

pale gray-white underparts

black-tipped red bill

red leg

ADULT (BREEDING)

One of North America's most widespread terns, the Common Tern was nearly wiped out in the late 19th century by hunters seeking its feathers. The 1918 Migratory Bird Treaty helped protect it, and numbers increased, but populations have declined again in recent decades because of human disturbance, habitat loss, and pollution.

VOICE Common call loud *keee-aarr* descending at end; emits *kek-kek-kek kek* call when attacking intruders; vocal in colonies; also calls elsewhere.

NESTING Shallow scrape on bare sand, often gravel or similar surface, dry vegetation and debris used during incubation; 2–3 eggs; 1 brood; May–August.

FEEDING Plunges for prey, snatches from water's surface, catches insects in flight; mainly eats fish but also crustaceans, squid, and insects.

SIMILAR SPECIES

ARCTIC TERN ☼
see p.176

shorter red bill

shorter neck

shorter legs

FORSTER'S TERN
see p.177

paler wings

longer tail

FEEDING FLOCK
A flock of Common Terns focus on a school of fish, diving to catch them. Fishermen watch for such flocks to locate fish.

OCCURRENCE
Found almost anywhere with water during migration. Winters in Central and South America. One population breeds along the barrier beaches and coasts northward from the Carolinas, a second population occurs around lakes and wetland areas in the northern interior.

Length **12–14in (31–35cm)**	Wingspan **30–31in (75–80cm)**	Weight **3⅜–5oz (95–150g)**
Social **Colonies**	Lifespan **Up to 26 years**	Status **Endangered**

DATE SEEN	WHERE	NOTES

Order **Charadriiformes**	Family **Laridae**	Species *Sterna paradisaea*

Arctic Tern

barring on upperparts

white forehead

short, dark bill

ADULT (BREEDING)

dark tips to translucent outer wing feathers

long, forked tail

short, red bill

IN FLIGHT

JUVENILE

black cap extends to nape

short, blood-red bill

short neck

white cheek

gray upperparts

ADULT (BREEDING)

long wings

pale gray underparts

short, red legs and toes

The majority of these remarkable birds breed in the Arctic, then migrate to the Antarctic seas for the Southern Hemisphere summer before returning north. On this round-trip, the Arctic Tern travels at least 25,000 miles (40,000km). Apart from during migration, it spends its life in areas of near continuous daylight and rarely comes to land, except to nest. It looks fairly similar to the Common Tern, but the former has a comparatively smaller bill, shorter legs, and a shorter neck.

VOICE Descending *keeyaar* call; nearly all calls similar to Common Tern, but higher-pitched and harsher.

NESTING Shallow scrape on bare ground or low vegetation in open areas; 2 eggs; 1 brood; May–August.

FEEDING Mostly plunge-dives for small fish and crustaceans, including crabs and shrimps; will also take prey from surface, sometimes catches insects in flight.

FLIGHT: downstroke slower than upstroke; buoyant and elegant with regular wingbeats.

FEEDING THE YOUNG
Both parents feed chicks—males bring more food than females, especially right after hatching.

TRANSLUCENT FEATHERS
The translucent outer wing feathers of the Arctic Tern are evident on these two flying birds.

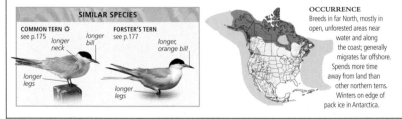

SIMILAR SPECIES

COMMON TERN ✿
see p.175

longer neck

longer legs

longer bill

FORSTER'S TERN
see p.177

longer, orange bill

longer legs

OCCURRENCE
Breeds in far North, mostly in open, unforested areas near water and along the coast; generally migrates far offshore. Spends more time away from land than other northern terns. Winters on edge of pack ice in Antarctica.

Length **11–15½in (28–39cm)**	Wingspan **26–30in (65–75cm)**	Weight **3⅛–4oz (90–125g)**
Social **Colonies**	Lifespan **Up to 34 years**	Status **Vulnerable**

DATE SEEN	WHERE	NOTES
....	....	....
....	....	....
....	....	....
....	....	....
....	....	....

| Order **Charadriiformes** | Family **Laridae** | Species *Sterna forsteri* |

Forster's Tern

deeply forked tail

gray wings with slightly darker wing tips

IN FLIGHT

shorter tail

ADULT (NONBREEDING)

large, black ear patch

shorter tail

JUVENILE

plain gray wings

dark bill

ADULT (NONBREEDING)

black cap and nape

pale gray upperparts

orange-red bill with dark tip

long, gray tail with white outer margins

snowy white underparts

ADULT (BREEDING)

FLIGHT: graceful and agile, with shallow wingbeats.

This medium-sized tern is very similar in appearance to the Common Tern. The features that differentiate it from the Common Tern are its lighter outer wing feathers and longer tail. Early naturalists could not tell the two species apart until 1834 when English botanist Thomas Nuttall made the distinction. He named this tern after Johann Reinhold Forster, a naturalist who accompanied the English explorer Captain Cook on his epic second voyage (1772–75).
VOICE Harsh, descending *kyerr*; more nasal than Common Tern.
NESTING Shallow scrape in mud or sand, but occasionally nests on top of muskrat lodge or on old grebe nest; sometimes constructs raft of floating vegetation; 2–3 eggs; 1 brood; May–August.
FEEDING Catches fish and crustaceans with shallow plunge-diving, often only head submerges; also catches insects in flight.

BLACK EARS
With its black ear patch, Forster's Tern is more distinctive in nonbreeding than breeding plumage.

OCCURRENCE
Breeds in northeastern Mexico, in freshwater and saltwater marshes with large stretches of open water. Winters on both coasts and across southern US states, unlike the Common Tern, which primarily winters in South America.

SIMILAR SPECIES

COMMON TERN
see p.175

shorter tail

redder bill

ARCTIC TERN
see p.176

shorter neck

shorter red bill

shorter legs

| Length **13–14in (33–36cm)** | Wingspan **29–32in (73–82cm)** | Weight **4–7oz (125–190g)** |
| Social **Colonies** | Lifespan **Up to 16 years** | Status **Secure** |

DATE SEEN	WHERE	NOTES

Order **Charadriiformes**	Family **Laridae**	Species *Thalasseus maximus*

Royal Tern

white underwings

white flanks

black forehead and crown

ADULT (BREEDING)

darker gray tips on outer flight feathers

darker pattern on wings

shaggy crest

ADULT (BREEDING)

JUVENILE

pale gray wings

light gray upperparts

strong, orange bill

IN FLIGHT

ADULT (BREEDING)

forked tail

white underparts

shaggy coat

white forehead

black legs

FLIGHT: wingbeats shallow, but powerful; less rapid and buoyant than other large terns.

Royal Terns have a full black cap for only a very short time at the beginning of the breeding season; for most of the year, they have white foreheads. The color of a Royal Tern's bill is quite variable, ranging from yellowish orange to red. Some possess a reddish bill similar to that of the Caspian Tern, but the latter does not have a pure white forehead and its bill is thicker. Perhaps it was these red-billed Royal Terns that caused the renowned ornithologist, John James Audubon, to confuse the two species.

ADULT (NONBREEDING)

VOICE Call *keer-reet*, usually during courtship; higher pitched and less raspy than Caspian Tern; more vocal around colonies.

NESTING Shallow scrape on bare ground, usually unlined, rim of guano reinforces nest; 1 egg; 1 brood; April–August.

FEEDING Mostly plunge-dives, but also plucks prey from surface while flying; sometimes skims surface; almost exclusively eats fish and crustaceans, such as crabs and barnacles.

BREEDING HABITS
Royal Terns appear monogamous, but it is unclear whether the pair bond is kept between seasons.

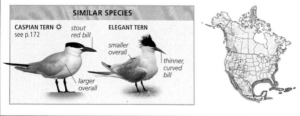

SIMILAR SPECIES		
CASPIAN TERN ☼ see p.172	stout red bill	**ELEGANT TERN** smaller overall
	larger overall	thinner, curved bill

OCCURRENCE
Normally restricted to warm saltwater habitats. Breeds in dense colonies, often on barrier islands; post-breeders wander north of regular breeding range; some are carried north by tropical storms and hurricanes, and may be found in the interior of the US.

Length **17½–19½in (45–50cm)**	Wingspan **4–4¼ft (1.2–1.3m)**	Weight **12–16oz (350–450g)**
Social **Colonies**	Lifespan **Up to 29 years**	Status **Secure**

DATE SEEN	WHERE	NOTES

| Order **Charadriiformes** | Family **Laridae** | Species *Thalasseus sandvicensis* |

Sandwich Tern

dark spots on wings

pale forehead

IMMATURE (1ST WINTER)

dark-edged tail

indistinct barring above

JUVENILE

white forehead

no shaggy crest

ADULT (NONBREEDING)

long, slender wings

ADULT (BREEDING)

dark wedge in outer feathers

IN FLIGHT

black cap

shaggy crest

very pale gray back

long, yellow-tipped black bill

white underparts

ADULT (BREEDING)

FLIGHT: shallow, relatively rapid wingbeats; strong and agile.

black legs and toes

The Sandwich Tern is the only North American tern to possess both a crest and a mostly black bill. Up close it is possible to spot the yellow tip on its black bill, which is also a unique feature among North American terns. This species nests in dense breeding colonies along with Royal Terns and Laughing Gulls. It is not an aggressive species and, like the Elegant Tern, is thought to benefit from the protection the other, more aggressive species offer it from potential predators. Worldwide, there are three subspecies of Sandwich Tern, but only one of these inhabits North America.

VOICE Loud, harsh two-syllabled *kirr-ick*; vocal when breeding, less elsewhere.

NESTING Shallow scrape on bare ground in open area, often alongside other tern species; debris added during incubation, but sometimes unlined; 1–2 eggs; 1 brood; April–August.

FEEDING Plunge-dives from medium height to catch fish, squid, and crustaceans; also snatches prey from surface and catches insects in flight.

SIMILAR SPECIES

GULL-BILLED TERN see p.171

stout, all black bill

more compact body

ROSEATE TERN see p.174

no yellow tip on bill

smaller overall

CLOSE NESTING
Sandwich Terns often nest in extremely dense colonies with nests packed closely together.

OCCURRENCE
An East Coast and Caribbean species, it is rarely far from saltwater; breeds on barrier beaches, barrier islands, and manmade dredge islands. Winters in similar areas; roosts on sandbars. May occur north of normal range after tropical storms and hurricanes.

| Length **13½–17½in (34–45cm)** | Wingspan **3ft 1in–3ft 4in (95–105cm)** | Weight **6–11oz (175–300g)** |
| Social **Colonies** | Lifespan **Up to 22 years** | Status **Secure** |

DATE SEEN	WHERE	NOTES

Order **Charadriiformes**	Family **Laridae**	Species **Rynchops niger**

Black Skimmer

long wing

ADULT (BREEDING)

short, forked tail

IN FLIGHT

mottled brown upperparts

bill duller than adult

JUVENILE

black upperparts

white forehead

orange-red and black bill

lower half of bill longer than upper

long, thick neck

ADULT (BREEDING)

white underparts

orange-red legs

With its long, orange-red and black bill, the Black Skimmer is quite unmistakable. Compressed laterally into a knife-like shape, the bill's lower mandible is about 1in (2.5cm) longer than the upper part. The unique bill and feeding behavior of the world's three skimmer species have led some to place them in their own family, although they are usually grouped with gulls and terns. When disturbed, Black Skimmer chicks kick up sand with their toes, forming a depression and throwing sand over their backs, which helps to camouflage them.

VOICE Calls given by both sexes, more often at night; distinctive sound like the yapping of a small dog.

NESTING Shallow scrape or depression on sandy beach or dead saltmarsh vegetation, also on gravel rooftops; 1–5 eggs; 1 brood; May–August.

FEEDING Skims surface with the lower part of its bill in water; bill snaps shut when prey is within reach; catches small fish in relatively calm waters.

FLIGHT: mostly low and buoyant with slow wingbeats; often glides when feeding.

GREGARIOUS BIRDS
The Black Skimmer is often seen in flocks on sandy beaches and mudflats.

SLICING THE SURFACE
The unique way in which skimmers such as the Black Skimmer feed gave rise to the old common name for these birds—Cutwaters.

OCCURRENCE
Breeds on East Coast from Massachusetts south to Mexico; West Coast only in southern California, including Salton Sea; rarely found far from saltwater. Found on beaches; feeds in bays, estuaries, lagoons, and areas with relatively calm waters. Winters in Central America.

Length **15½–19½in (40–50cm)**	Wingspan **3½–4¼ft (1.1–1.3m)**	Weight **8–14oz (225–400g)**
Social **Colonies**	Lifespan **Up to 20 years**	Status **Endangered**

DATE SEEN	WHERE	NOTES

LOONS

WORLDWIDE THERE ARE only five species of loons, comprising a single genus (*Gavia*), a single family (the Gaviidae), and a single order (the Gaviiformes). The five species are limited to the Northern Hemisphere, where they are found in both northern North America and northern Eurasia. One feature of loons is that their legs are positioned so far to the rear of their body that they must shuffle on their bellies when they go from water to land. Not surprisingly, therefore, loons are almost entirely aquatic birds. In summer they are found on rivers, lakes, and ponds, where they nest close to the water's edge. After breeding, they occur along coasts, often after flying hundreds of miles away from their freshwater breeding grounds. Excellent swimmers and divers, loons are unusual among birds in that their bones are less hollow than those of other groups. Consequently, they can expel air from their lungs and compress their body feathers until they slowly sink beneath the surface. They can remain submerged like this for several minutes. A loon's wings are relatively small in proportion to its body weight. This means that they have to run a long way across the surface of the water, flapping energetically, before they can get airborne. Once in the air, they keep on flapping, and can fly at up to 60mph (95kmh).

WIDESPREAD
The Common Loon has the widest range of any loon in North America.

PROVIDING FOR THE FUTURE
A Red-throated Loon gives a fish to its chick to gulp down headfirst and whole.

TUBENOSES

THE NAME "TUBENOSES" IS given to several families of seabirds with tubular nostrils, which help get rid of excess salt and may enhance their sense of smell. Tubenoses are all members of the order Procellariiformes.

STORM-PETRELS

The smallest tubenoses in North American waters, the storm-petrels (families Oceanitidae, Hydrobatidae) are also the most agile fliers. They often patter or "dance" as they fly low over the surface of the ocean in search of small fish, squid, and crustaceans. Storm-petrels spend most of their lives flying over the open sea, only visiting land in the breeding season, when they form huge colonies.

SHEARWATERS AND PETRELS

Shearwaters and gadfly petrels (family Procellariidae) are smaller than their larger cousins, albatrosses (family Diomedeidae). Like albatrosses, they are excellent gliders, but their lighter weight and proportionately shorter wings mean that they use more powered flight. They range over all the world's oceans. With its far more numerous islands, the Pacific Ocean is home to a greater variety of these seabirds than the Atlantic. During and after storms are the best times to look for these birds from land, as this is when they have been drifting away from the deep sea because of wind and waves.

FLAP AND GLIDE
Shearwaters alternate stiff winged flapping with gliding just over the ocean's surface.

| Order **Gaviiformes** | Family **Gaviidae** | Species *Gavia stellata* |

Red-throated Loon

white speckled back

white face

ADULT (NONBREEDING)

humped back

head lower than body

white underparts

ADULT (BREEDING)

ADULT (NONBREEDING)

IN FLIGHT

upturned bill

pale dusky face

IMMATURE

upturned gray bill

gray face and neck

all-brown back

striped gray nape

tapering dark reddish brown throat patch

ADULT (BREEDING)

Even when seen from a distance, this elegant loon is almost unmistakable, with a pale, slim body, upward-tilted head, and a thin, upturned bill. Unlike other Loons, the Red-throated Loon can leap straight into the air from both land and water, although most of the time it needs a "runway." The Red-throated Loon has an elaborate breeding ritual—side by side, a pair of birds races upright across the surface of water. Downy chicks climb onto the parents back only when very young.
VOICE High gull-like or even cat-like wail and low goose-like growl; vocal on breeding grounds, otherwise silent.
NESTING Scrape with mud and vegetation added during incubation, placed at water's edge in coastal and lake bays, shallow ponds, often at high altitudes; 2 eggs; 1 brood; April–July.
FEEDING Mainly eats fish; also spiders, crustaceans, and mollusks; flies long distances from shallow ponds when food is scarce.

FLIGHT: very direct; fast, with constant wingbeats; head held lower than other loons.

TAKING OFF
While this bird is using the water's surface to takeoff, it can leap directly into flight from water or land.

SIMILAR SPECIES

YELLOW-BILLED LOON ❊
see p.471

massive, light-colored bill

larger overall

RED-NECKED GREBE ❊
see p.77

yellow in bill

darker back

smaller overall

OCCURRENCE
Lives in open areas within northern boreal forest, muskeg, and tundra; in Canadian Arctic Archipelago, sometimes in areas almost devoid of vegetation. Winters on the Great Lakes, and both coasts southward to Florida and northern Mexico.

| Length **24–27in (61–69cm)** | Wingspan **3½ft (1.1m)** | Weight **3¼lb (1.5kg)** |
| Social **Solitary/Loose flocks** | Lifespan **Up to 23 years** | Status **Declining** |

DATE SEEN	WHERE	NOTES

| Order **Gaviiformes** | Family **Gaviidae** | Species *Gavia immer* |

Common Loon 🔊

checkered back pattern

ADULT (BREEDING)

humped back

head held low

ADULT (NONBREEDING)

IN FLIGHT

spotted wings

scalloped pattern on back

barely visible eye

light, partial collar

ADULT (NONBREEDING)

brownish head

JUVENILE

iridescent green on head and neck

white lines on sides of neck

white "necklace" on throat

ADULT (BREEDING)

The Common Loon has the largest range of all loons in North America and is the only species to nest in a few of the northern states. It is slightly smaller than the Yellow-billed Loon but larger than the other three loons. It can remain underwater for well over 10 minutes, although it usually stays submerged for 40 seconds to 2 minutes while fishing, or a few more minutes if it is being pursued. Evidence shows that, occasionally, it interbreeds with its closest relative, the Yellow-billed Loon, in addition to the Arctic and Pacific Loons.

VOICE Most recognized call a 3–10 note falsetto yodel, rising, then fading; other calls similar in quality.

NESTING Simple scrape in large mound of vegetation, a few feet from open water; 2 eggs; 1 brood; April–June.

FEEDING Feeds primarily on fish underwater; also eats crustaceans, mollusks, amphibians, leeches, insects, and aquatic plants.

FLIGHT: fast, direct, with constant wingbeats; head and neck held just above belly.

COZY RIDE
Downy Common Loon chicks climb up the backs of male and female adults for a safe ride.

BATHING RITUAL
Common Loons often shake their wings after bathing.

OCCURRENCE
Breeds across North America, Canada, and south to northern US. Winters on large ice-free lakes in Canada and the US, and along the Pacific and Atlantic Coasts, south to Baja California and Florida. In the Old World breeds only in Iceland.

SIMILAR SPECIES

YELLOW-BILLED LOON
see p.471

large, whitish or yellow bill

larger, checkered back pattern

RED-NECKED GREBE ❀
see p.77

much smaller overall

yellowish bill

brownish gray cheeks

| Length **26–36in (66–91cm)** | Wingspan **4¼–5ft (1.3–1.5m)** | Weight **4½–18lb (2–8kg)** |
| Social **Family groups** | Lifespan **Up to 30 years** | Status **Vulnerable** |

DATE SEEN	WHERE	NOTES

Order **Procellariiformes**	Family **Oceanitidae**	Species *Oceanites oceanicus*

Wilson's Storm-Petrel

broad, pointed wings

white rump and lower flanks

ADULT

pale bar on upperwing

ADULT

IN FLIGHT

"walking" on water

dark wings and body

small, black "tube nose"

ADULT

short, square tail

yellow webbing between toes

Named after Alexander Wilson, often called the "father of North American ornithology," Wilson's Storm-Petrel is the quintessential small oceanic petrel. It is an extremely abundant species and breeds in the many millions on the Antarctic Peninsula and islands in Antarctica. After breeding, many move north to spend the summer off the Atlantic Coast of North America. Here, they are a familiar sight to fishermen and birders at sea. By August they can be seen lingering, but by October they have flown south.
VOICE At sea, soft rasping notes; at breeding sites a variety of *coos*, *churrs*, and twitters during the night.
NESTING Mostly in rock crevices; also burrows where there is peaty soil; 1 egg; 1 brood; November–March.
FEEDING Patters on the water's surface, legs extended, picking up tiny crustaceans; also carrion, droplets of oil.

FLIGHT: flutters, low to ocean's surface, often "stalling" to drop to the surface and glean food.

FEEDING FLOCK
While flying, this bird "walks" on water, simultaneously picking food from the surface.

SIMILAR SPECIES

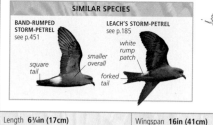

BAND-RUMPED STORM-PETREL see p.451

square tail

smaller overall

LEACH'S STORM-PETREL see p.185

white rump patch

forked tail

OCCURRENCE
Breeds on the Antarctic Peninsula, many sub-Antarctic islands, and islands in the Cape Horn Archipelago. April –September or October, moves north, and is abundant off the coasts of New England, New York, and New Jersey July– September. With inshore winds, can often be seen from land.

Length **6¾in (17cm)**	Wingspan **16in (41cm)**	Weight **1¹⁄₁₆–1⁷⁄₁₆oz (30–40g)**
Social **Flocks**	Lifespan **Up to 10 years**	Status **Secure**

DATE SEEN	WHERE	NOTES

Order **Procellariiformes**	Family **Hydrobatidae**	Species *Hydrobates leucorhous*

Leach's Storm-Petrel

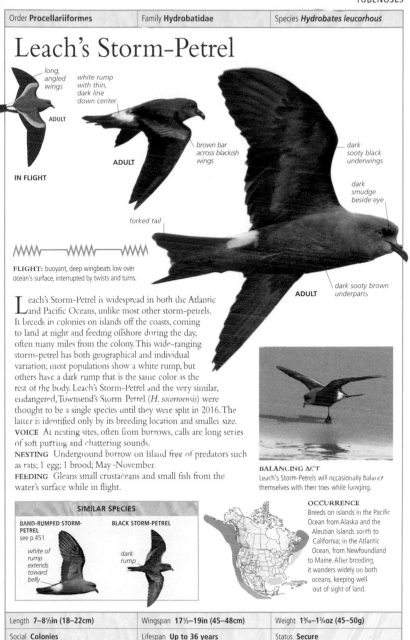

long, angled wings

ADULT

white rump with thin, dark line down center

ADULT

IN FLIGHT

brown bar across blackish wings

dark sooty black underwings

dark smudge beside eye

forked tail

FLIGHT: buoyant, deep wingbeats low over ocean's surface, interrupted by twists and turns.

dark sooty brown underparts

ADULT

Leach's Storm-Petrel is widespread in both the Atlantic and Pacific Oceans, unlike most other storm-petrels. It breeds in colonies on islands off the coasts, coming to land at night and feeding offshore during the day, often many miles from the colony. This wide-ranging storm-petrel has both geographical and individual variation; most populations show a white rump, but others have a dark rump that is the same color as the rest of the body. Leach's Storm-Petrel and the very similar, endangered, Townsend's Storm Petrel (*H. socorroensis*) were thought to be a single species until they were split in 2016. The latter is identified only by its breeding location and smaller size.
VOICE At nesting sites, often from burrows, calls are long series of soft purring and chattering sounds.
NESTING Underground burrow on island free of predators such as rats; 1 egg; 1 brood; May–November.
FEEDING Gleans small crustaceans and small fish from the water's surface while in flight.

BALANCING ACT
Leach's Storm-Petrels will occasionally balance themselves with their toes while foraging.

SIMILAR SPECIES		
BAND-RUMPED STORM-PETREL see p.451	**BLACK STORM-PETREL**	
white of rump extends toward belly	*dark rump*	

OCCURRENCE
Breeds on islands in the Pacific Ocean from Alaska and the Aleutian Islands south to California; in the Atlantic Ocean, from Newfoundland to Maine. After breeding, it wanders widely on both oceans, keeping well out of sight of land.

Length **7–8½in (18–22cm)**	Wingspan **17½–19in (45–48cm)**	Weight **1⁹⁄₁₆–1¾oz (45–50g)**
Social **Colonies**	Lifespan **Up to 36 years**	Status **Secure**

DATE SEEN	WHERE	NOTES

Order **Procellariiformes**	Family **Procellariidae**	Species **Fulmarus glacialis**

Northern Fulmar

white patch on wing

ADULT (ATLANTIC FORM)

IN FLIGHT

paddle-like wings

dark gray overall

ADULT (DARK PACIFIC FORM)

gray back

small dark patch in front of eye

white head

thick, yellow bill

short, rounded, gray tail

ADULT (LIGHT PACIFIC FORM)

white underparts

ADULT (ATLANTIC FORM)

Possessing paddle-shaped wings and distinctive color patterns ranging from almost all-white to all-gray, the Northern Fulmar is among the most common seabirds in places like the Bering Sea. It breeds at high latitudes, then disperses south to offshore waters along both coasts of the continent. The Northern Fulmar can sometimes be seen in large mixed flocks containing albatrosses, shearwaters, and small petrels.

VOICE Mostly silent at sea; occasionally utters cackles and grunts.

NESTING Scrape in rock or soil on edge of cliff; 1 egg; 1 brood; May–October.

FEEDING Picks fish and offal from the surface of the ocean; also dives underwater to catch fish.

FLIGHT: snappy wingbeats and long glides near the surface of the ocean.

FEEDING FRENZY
Large numbers of Northern Fulmars compete for the offal discarded by fishing trawlers.

SIMILAR SPECIES

SOOTY SHEARWATER see p.188	GREAT SHEARWATER see p.189
more slender wings	more slender wings
dark bill	dark cap
dark overall	white collar

OCCURRENCE
Breeds on remote, high, coastal cliffs in Alaska and Canada; winters at sea in offshore Pacific and Atlantic waters, generally farther north than most other seabirds. Breeds in Europe, northward to Greenland, Svalbard; also parts of Russia.

Length **17½–19½in (45–50cm)**	Wingspan **3¼–3½ft (1–1.1m)**	Weight **16–35oz (0.45–1kg)**
Social **Flocks**	Lifespan **Up to 50 years**	Status **Secure**

DATE SEEN	WHERE	NOTES

Order **Procellariiformes**	Family **Procellariidae**	Species *Calonectris diomedea*

Cory's Shearwater

long, pointed wings

pale rump

ADULT

IN FLIGHT

dark wingtip and trailing edge

clean white underwing

all white belly

ADULT

scalloped pattern

grayish head and chin

yellow bill with dark tip

ADULT

white breast, with sooty-gray sides

Close observation of flocks of Cory's Shearwaters off the Atlantic Coast has suggested the presence of two subspecies. The more common one, *C. d. borealis*, nests in the eastern Atlantic and is chunkier, with less white on the underwing. The other subspecies, *C. d. diomedea*, breeds in the Mediterranean, has a more slender build and a thinner bill, and more white on the underwing. Both subspecies of Cory's Shearwater have a relatively "languid" flight style that differs from that of other shearwaters in North Atlantic waters.

VOICE Mostly silent at sea; descending, lamb-like bleating.
NESTING Nests in burrow or rocky crevice; 1 egg; 1 brood; May–September.
FEEDING Dives into water or picks at surface for small schooling fish, and marine invertebrates such as squid.

FLIGHT: slow, deliberate wingbeats interspersed with long glides; often arcs strongly on bent wings.

LAZY FLIERS
In calm weather Cory's Shearwaters look heavy and fly low, swooping higher in strong winds.

SIMILAR SPECIES

AUDUBON'S SHEARWATER see p.452

dark brown overall

GREAT SHEARWATER see p.189

dark head

brownish overall

white neck

OCCURRENCE
This species breeds in the Mediterranean and on islands of the eastern Atlantic, including the Azores, the Salvages, Madeira, and the Canaries. When nonbreeding, Cory's Shearwaters disperse widely over the Atlantic Ocean and the Gulf of Mexico.

Length **18in (46cm)**	Wingspan **3½ft (1.1m)**	Weight **28oz (800g)**
Social **Flocks**	Lifespan **Unknown**	Status **Secure**

DATE SEEN	WHERE	NOTES

Order **Procellariiformes**	Family **Procellariidae**	Species *Ardenna grisea*

Sooty Shearwater

silvery white patch along underwing

ADULT

all-dark underparts

IN FLIGHT

long, slender wings

ADULT

ADULT

all-dark upperparts

sooty head

long, hooked bill

FLIGHT: rapid, stiff wingbeats, interspersed with glides; arcs up highly in strong winds.

Sooty Shearwaters are extremely long-distance migrants, with both Atlantic and Pacific populations undergoing lengthy circular migrations. Pacific birds in particular travel as far as 300 miles (480km) per day and an extraordinary 45,000 miles (72,500km) or more per year. Huge flocks of this species are often seen off the coast of California. It is fairly easy to identify off the East Coast of the US, as it is the only all-dark shearwater found there.

VOICE Silent at sea; occasionally gives varied, agitated vocalizations when feeding, very loud calls at breeding colonies.

NESTING In burrow or rocky crevice; 1 egg; 1 brood; October–May.

FEEDING Dives and picks at surface for small schooling fish and mollusks such as squid.

HUGE FLOCKS
Sooty Shearwaters are often found in "rafts" numbering many thousands of birds.

TUBENOSE
Shearwaters are tubenoses, so-called for the salt-excreting tubes on their bills.

SIMILAR SPECIES

SHORT-TAILED SHEARWATER

dark upperparts

GREAT SHEARWATER
see p.189

dark cap

white tail band

shorter bill

pale throat

white collar

OCCURRENCE
Sooty Shearwaters breed on islands in the southern Ocean and nearby waters, some colonies numbering thousands of pairs. Postbreeding movements take them north into the Pacific and Atlantic Ocean, on 8-shaped migrations.

Length **18in (46cm)**	Wingspan **3ft 3in (1m)**	Weight **27oz (775g)**
Social **Flocks**	Lifespan **Unknown**	Status **Secure**

DATE SEEN	WHERE	NOTES

| Order **Procellariiformes** | Family **Procellariidae** | Species *Ardenna gravis* |

Great Shearwater

ADULT

dark, half "necklace" at sides of neck

dark smudge on center of belly

IN FLIGHT

darker outer wing feathers

brownish upperwings

white collar

dark cap

thin, black bill

thin, white band on rump

ADULT

A common species in North Atlantic waters, from northern Canada to Florida, the Great Shearwater is similar in size to Cory's Shearwater and the birds scavenge together for scraps around fishing boats. However, their plumages and flight styles are quite different. While Cory's Shearwater has slow, labored wingbeats, and glides high on broad, bowed, swept-back wings, Great Shearwaters keep low, flapping hurriedly between glides on straight, narrow wings. The brown smudges on the belly (not always visible) and paler underwings of the Great Shearwater also help distinguish the species.

VOICE Silent at sea; descending, lamb-like bleating at breeding sites.

NESTING Digs deep burrow in peaty or boggy soil; 1 egg; 1 brood; September–March.

FEEDING Feeds either from the surface, picking up items such as fish and squid, or makes shallow dives with open wings.

FLIGHT: fast, stiff wingbeats interspersed with gliding; arcs high in windy conditions.

WHITE COLLAR
The Great Shearwater's white collar is highly visible between its black cap and sooty back.

SIMILAR SPECIES

BLACK-CAPPED PETREL
see p.451

large, white rump

white forehead

MANX SHEARWATER
see p.190

darker plumage

smaller overall

OCCURRENCE
Nests on just a few islands in the middle of the South Atlantic. Total population probably well over 200 million. Postbreeding birds make a very long 8-shaped migration around the Atlantic, spending late July–September in North Atlantic waters, usually offshore.

| Length **18in (46cm)** | Wingspan **3½ft (1.1m)** | Weight **30oz (850g)** |
| Social **Flocks** | Lifespan **At least 25 years** | Status **Secure** |

DATE SEEN	WHERE	NOTES

189

Order **Procellariiformes**	Family **Procellariidae**	Species **Puffinus puffinus**

Manx Shearwater

long, pointed wings

black edge of wing

IN FLIGHT

very dark brownish black upperparts

head is black above, white below

long, thin, hooked bill

crisp white underwings

white undertail feathers

snow white underparts

dark upperwings

small head

dark, hooked bill

short tail

white throat

Most shearwaters are little known because of their nocturnal and oceanic habits, but the Manx is an exception. It is common in the British Isles, and ornithologists have been studying it there for decades. Long-term banding programs revealed that one bird flew more than 3,000 miles (4,800km) from Massachusetts to its nesting burrow in Wales in just 12½ days, and that another was captured 56 years after it was first banded, making its accumulated migration-only mileage around 600,000 miles (1,000,000km).

VOICE Usually silent at sea, but at breeding sites, produces loud and raucous series of cries, *kah-kah-kah-kah-kah-HOWW*.

NESTING In burrow, in peaty soil, or rocky crevice; 1 egg; 1 brood; April–October.

FEEDING Dives into water, often with open wings and stays underwater, or picks at surface for small schooling fish and squid.

FLIGHT: rapid, stiff wingbeats interspersed with glides; arcs high in strong winds.

PITTER-PATTER
Unlike gulls, shearwaters have to patter along the surface with their legs and toes to achieve lift-off speed.

SIMILAR SPECIES

BLACK-VENTED SHEARWATER

brownish upperparts

paler head

AUDUBON'S SHEARWATER
see p.452

longer tail

slightly smaller overall

OCCURRENCE
Breeds on many islands in eastern North Atlantic; restricted to islands off Newfoundland in North America. Regularly occurs off US East Coast as far south as Florida. Rare in Gulf of Mexico and off the West Coast. Rarely seen from shore; cold-water shearwater.

Length **13½in (34cm)**	Wingspan **33in (83cm)**	Weight **14–20oz (400–575g)**
Social **Migrant flocks**	Lifespan **Up to 55 years**	Status **Secure**

DATE SEEN	WHERE	NOTES

STORKS

STORKS ARE LARGE, LONG-LEGGED, mainly wetland birds. They fly with their long necks extended and their legs trailing behind them. The wings are "fingered" at the tips, similar to those of vultures, among others, which aids them in soaring flight by providing extra lift, particularly when using thermals. Storks are able to travel very long distances in the right conditions, with very little effort. Storks feed in marshy places and open grasslands. They prey on a variety of amphibians, small reptiles, and rodents, as well as large insect prey.

BARE HEADS
Wood Storks have bare heads with wrinkled, blackish skin, and bills that are tapered and drooped.

FRIGATEBIRDS, GANNETS, CORMORANTS, AND ANHINGAS

FRIGATEBIRDS
Frigatebirds are large seabirds characterized by very long, angular wings, lengthy, deeply forked tails, and extended, sturdy, and sharply hooked bills. Although they feed over the ocean, catching flying fish or forcing other birds to disgorge food, frigatebirds have neither fully webbed toes nor thoroughly waterproof plumage, so they rarely settle on water.

GANNETS AND BOOBIES
Gannets, and the related boobies of the tropics, have pointed bills, long wings, and fully webbed toes. Their eyes face well forward and air sacs beneath the skin of the head and neck provide protection when they dive headlong from the air to catch fish. They breed in large colonies—gannets on cliffs and islands, and boobies also in trees.

CORMORANTS AND ANHINGAS
The birds in this group also have four fully webbed toes. Their long, angular wings resemble those of gannets but are less pointed. Cormorants, which have slightly hooked bills, comprise both marine and freshwater species. Anhingas, or darters, are also known as "snakebirds," which describes them well as they swim with their bodies submerged and heads raised. Their heads are barely wider than their necks, and their bills are long and pointed, giving them a snake-like appearance.

SEEKING ATTENTION
A male Magnificent Frigatebird inflates his red gular pouch, a strip of bare skin beneath the base of the bill, to attract a female.

| Order **Ciconiiformes** | Family **Ciconiidae** | Species **Mycteria americana** |

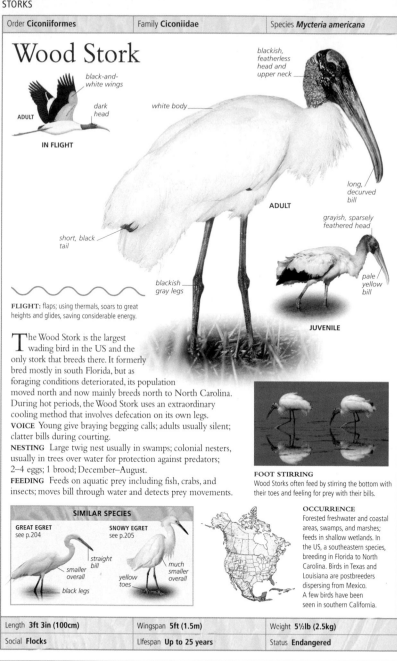

Wood Stork

IN FLIGHT

black-and-white wings

ADULT

dark head

blackish, featherless head and upper neck

white body

long, decurved bill

ADULT

grayish, sparsely feathered head

short, black tail

blackish gray legs

pale yellow bill

JUVENILE

FLIGHT: flaps; using thermals, soars to great heights and glides, saving considerable energy.

The Wood Stork is the largest wading bird in the US and the only stork that breeds there. It formerly bred mostly in south Florida, but as foraging conditions deteriorated, its population moved north and now mainly breeds north to North Carolina. During hot periods, the Wood Stork uses an extraordinary cooling method that involves defecation on its own legs.

VOICE Young give braying begging calls; adults usually silent; clatter bills during courting.

NESTING Large twig nest usually in swamps; colonial nesters, usually in trees over water for protection against predators; 2–4 eggs; 1 brood; December–August.

FEEDING Feeds on aquatic prey including fish, crabs, and insects; moves bill through water and detects prey movements.

FOOT STIRRING
Wood Storks often feed by stirring the bottom with their toes and feeling for prey with their bills.

SIMILAR SPECIES

GREAT EGRET
see p.204

straight bill

smaller overall

black legs

SNOWY EGRET
see p.205

much smaller overall

yellow toes

OCCURRENCE
Forested freshwater and coastal areas, swamps, and marshes; feeds in shallow wetlands. In the US, a southeastern species, breeding in Florida to North Carolina. Birds in Texas and Louisiana are postbreeders dispersing from Mexico. A few birds have been seen in southern California.

| Length **3ft 3in (100cm)** | Wingspan **5ft (1.5m)** | Weight **5½lb (2.5kg)** |
| Social **Flocks** | Lifespan **Up to 25 years** | Status **Endangered** |

DATE SEEN	WHERE	NOTES
....	....	....
....	....	....
....	....	....
....	....	....
....	....	....

Order **Suliformes**	Family **Fregatidae**	Species *Fregata magnificens*

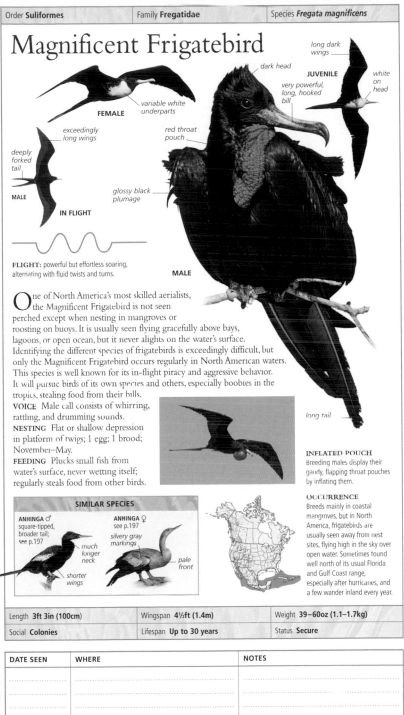

Magnificent Frigatebird

long dark wings

dark head

JUVENILE

very powerful, long, hooked bill

white on head

variable white underparts

FEMALE

exceedingly long wings

red throat pouch

deeply forked tail

glossy black plumage

MALE

IN FLIGHT

FLIGHT: powerful but effortless soaring, alternating with fluid twists and turns.

MALE

One of North America's most skilled aerialists, the Magnificent Frigatebird is not seen perched except when nesting in mangroves or roosting on buoys. It is usually seen flying gracefully above bays, lagoons, or open ocean, but it never alights on the water's surface. Identifying the different species of frigatebirds is exceedingly difficult, but only the Magnificent Frigatebird occurs regularly in North American waters. This species is well known for its in-flight piracy and aggressive behavior. It will pursue birds of its own species and others, especially boobies in the tropics, stealing food from their bills.

VOICE Male call consists of whirring, rattling, and drumming sounds.

NESTING Flat or shallow depression in platform of twigs; 1 egg; 1 brood; November–May.

FEEDING Plucks small fish from water's surface, never wetting itself; regularly steals food from other birds.

long tail

INFLATED POUCH
Breeding males display their gaudy, flapping throat pouches by inflating them.

OCCURRENCE
Breeds mainly in coastal mangroves, but in North America, frigatebirds are usually seen away from nest sites, flying high in the sky over open water. Sometimes found well north of its usual Florida and Gulf Coast range, especially after hurricanes, and a few wander inland every year.

SIMILAR SPECIES

ANHINGA ♂
square-tipped, broader tail;
see p.197

much longer neck

shorter wings

ANHINGA ♀
see p.197

silvery gray markings

pale front

Length **3ft 3in (100cm)**	Wingspan **4½ft (1.4m)**	Weight **39–60oz (1.1–1.7kg)**
Social **Colonies**	Lifespan **Up to 30 years**	Status **Secure**

DATE SEEN	WHERE	NOTES

| Order **Suliformes** | Family **Sulidae** | Species ***Morus bassanus*** |

Northern Gannet

light blue eye

yellow tinge to back of head

dark brown overall

ADULT

IMMATURE (1ST YEAR)

black wing tip

ADULT

white upperparts

black wing tip

long, pointed wing

IN FLIGHT

black wing tip

upper wings and white back mottled with black

pointed gray bill

IMMATURE (3RD YEAR)

yellow-orange nape

black-and-white mottled upperparts

white underparts

ADULT

IMMATURE (2ND YEAR)

pointed tail

FLIGHT: strong, direct flight with deep, powerful wingbeats and short glides.

The Northern Gannet is known for its spectacular headfirst dives during frantic, voracious foraging in flocks of hundreds to thousands for surface-schooling fish. In North America, this bird nests in just six locations in northeastern Canada. It was the first species to have its total world population estimated, at 83,000 birds in 1939. Numbers have since increased.

VOICE Loud landing call by both sexes *arrrr, arrah,* or *urrah rah rah;* hollow groan *oh-ah* uttered during takeoff; *krok* call at sea.

NESTING Large pile of mud, seaweed, and rubbish, glued with guano, on bare rock or soil; 1 egg; 1 brood; April–November.

FEEDING Plunge-dives headfirst into water and often swims underwater to catch fish; eats mackerel, herring, capelin, and cod.

NESTING SITE
Northern Gannets prefer to nest in huge, noisy colonies on isolated rocky slopes or cliffs.

SIMILAR SPECIES

LAYSAN ALBATROSS
more rounded tail
white underwing with black patches

MASKED BOOBY
see p.471
pinkish bill
long, pointed wings
black "mask"
yellow bill
black inner wing feathers

OCCURRENCE
Breeds on isolated rock stacks, on small uninhabited islands in the eastern North Atlantic, or on steep, inaccessible cliffs in marine areas of northeastern North America; during migration and in winter, occurs in the waters of the continental shelf of the Gulf and Atlantic Coast.

| Length 2¾–3½ft (0.8–1.1m) | Wingspan 5½ft (1.7m) | Weight 5–8lb (2.2–3.6kg) |
| Social **Flocks** | Lifespan **Up to 20 years** | Status **Localized** |

DATE SEEN	WHERE	NOTES

| Order **Suliformes** | Family **Phalacrocoracidae** | Species *Phalacrocorax auritus* |

Double-crested Cormorant

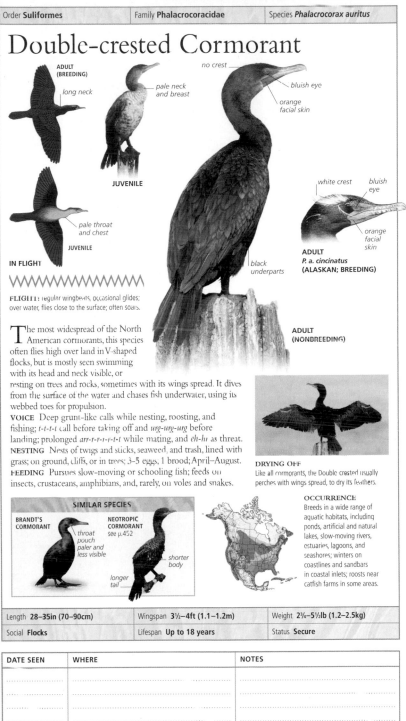

ADULT (BREEDING)

long neck

pale neck and breast

JUVENILE

no crest

bluish eye

orange facial skin

pale throat and chest

JUVENILE

IN FLIGHT

FLIGHT: regular wingbeats, occasional glides; over water, flies close to the surface; often soars.

white crest

bluish eye

orange facial skin

ADULT
P. a. cincinatus
(ALASKAN; BREEDING)

black underparts

ADULT (NONBREEDING)

The most widespread of the North American cormorants, this species often flies high over land in V-shaped flocks, but is mostly seen swimming with its head and neck visible, or resting on trees and rocks, sometimes with its wings spread. It dives from the surface of the water and chases fish underwater, using its webbed toes for propulsion.

VOICE Deep grunt-like calls while nesting, roosting, and fishing; *t-t-t-t* call before taking off and *urg-urg-urg* before landing; prolonged *arr-r-r-r-r-t-t* while mating, and *eh-lu* as threat.

NESTING Nests of twigs and sticks, seaweed, and trash, lined with grass; on ground, cliffs, or in trees; 3–5 eggs, 1 brood; April–August.

FEEDING Pursues slow-moving or schooling fish; feeds on insects, crustaceans, amphibians, and, rarely, on voles and snakes.

DRYING OFF
Like all cormorants, the Double-crested usually perches with wings spread, to dry its feathers.

SIMILAR SPECIES

BRANDT'S CORMORANT

throat pouch paler and less visible

NEOTROPIC CORMORANT
see p.452

shorter body

longer tail

OCCURRENCE
Breeds in a wide range of aquatic habitats, including ponds, artificial and natural lakes, slow-moving rivers, estuaries, lagoons, and seashores; winters on coastlines and sandbars in coastal inlets; roosts near catfish farms in some areas.

| Length **28–35in (70–90cm)** | Wingspan **3½–4ft (1.1–1.2m)** | Weight **2¾–5½lb (1.2–2.5kg)** |
| Social **Flocks** | Lifespan **Up to 18 years** | Status **Secure** |

DATE SEEN	WHERE		NOTES

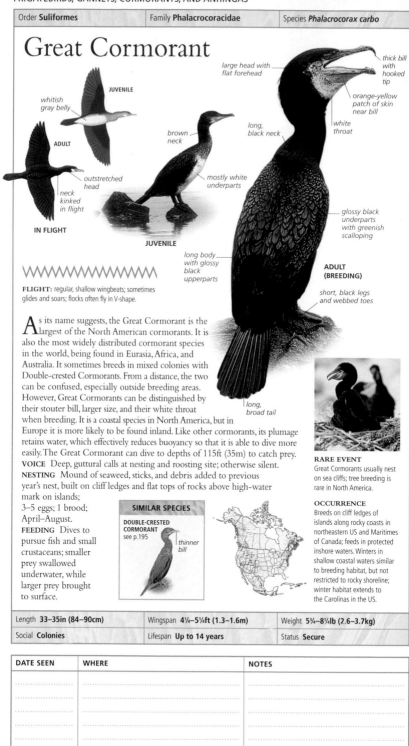

| Order **Suliformes** | Family **Phalacrocoracidae** | Species *Phalacrocorax carbo* |

Great Cormorant

JUVENILE

whitish gray belly

ADULT

outstretched head

neck kinked in flight

IN FLIGHT

brown neck

mostly white underparts

JUVENILE

large head with flat forehead

thick bill with hooked tip

orange-yellow patch of skin near bill

long, black neck

white throat

glossy black underparts with greenish scalloping

long body with glossy black upperparts

ADULT (BREEDING)

short, black legs and webbed toes

FLIGHT: regular, shallow wingbeats; sometimes glides and soars; flocks often fly in V-shape.

long, broad tail

As its name suggests, the Great Cormorant is the largest of the North American cormorants. It is also the most widely distributed cormorant species in the world, being found in Eurasia, Africa, and Australia. It sometimes breeds in mixed colonies with Double-crested Cormorants. From a distance, the two can be confused, especially outside breeding areas. However, Great Cormorants can be distinguished by their stouter bill, larger size, and their white throat when breeding. It is a coastal species in North America, but in Europe it is more likely to be found inland. Like other cormorants, its plumage retains water, which effectively reduces buoyancy so that it is able to dive more easily. The Great Cormorant can dive to depths of 115ft (35m) to catch prey.

VOICE Deep, guttural calls at nesting and roosting site; otherwise silent.

NESTING Mound of seaweed, sticks, and debris added to previous year's nest, built on cliff ledges and flat tops of rocks above high-water mark on islands; 3–5 eggs; 1 brood; April–August.

FEEDING Dives to pursue fish and small crustaceans; smaller prey swallowed underwater, while larger prey brought to surface.

RARE EVENT
Great Cormorants usually nest on sea cliffs; tree breeding is rare in North America.

OCCURRENCE
Breeds on cliff ledges of islands along rocky coasts in northeastern US and Maritimes of Canada; feeds in protected inshore waters. Winters in shallow coastal waters similar to breeding habitat, but not restricted to rocky shoreline; winter habitat extends to the Carolinas in the US.

SIMILAR SPECIES

DOUBLE-CRESTED CORMORANT
see p.195

thinner bill

| Length **33–35in (84–90cm)** | Wingspan **4¼–5¼ft (1.3–1.6m)** | Weight **5¾–8¼lb (2.6–3.7kg)** |
| Social **Colonies** | Lifespan **Up to 14 years** | Status **Secure** |

DATE SEEN	WHERE	NOTES

| Order **Suliformes** | Family **Anhingidae** | Species *Anhinga anhinga* |

Anhinga

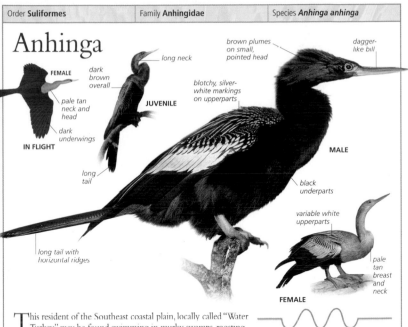

FEMALE

dark brown overall

long neck

brown plumes on small, pointed head

dagger-like bill

JUVENILE

blotchy, silver-white markings on upperparts

pale tan neck and head

dark underwings

IN FLIGHT

long tail

MALE

long tail with horizontal ridges

black underparts

variable white upperparts

pale tan breast and neck

FEMALE

This resident of the Southeast coastal plain, locally called "Water Turkey," may be found swimming in murky swamps, roosting on tall trees, or soaring high overhead. The Anhinga is also known as the "snake bird"—a reference to its habit of swimming with its body immersed so deeply that only its long, thin, sinuous neck, pointed head, and sharp bill stick out above the water. Although they superficially resemble cormorants, the four species of darters, including the Anhinga, stand apart in many ways—particularly their sharply pointed bills and long tails with horizontally ridged feathers.

VOICE Silent most of the time, but pairs may give various calls around nest; these vocalizations consist of soft rattles and trills, but are sometimes quite noisy, repeated *Krah-Krah*.

NESTING Loose platform of sticks in trees above water; 3–5 eggs, 1 brood, February–June.

FEEDING Jabs suddenly with its dagger-like bill, mostly for fish in calm freshwater habitats; also eats insects and shrimp.

FLIGHT: strong flier; neck and tail outstretched and wings held flat; often soars.

HANGING OUT TO DRY
Anhingas do not have waterproof plumage and so spend a lot of time drying off their wings.

SIMILAR SPECIES

DOUBLE-CRESTED CORMORANT see p.195

hooked bill

shorter tail

DOUBLE-CRESTED CORMORANT ♀ see p.195

dark upperwings

shorter tail

OCCURRENCE
An inhabitant of southeastern wetlands south all the way to Argentina. Greatest concentrations in wooded wetlands, calm waters in swamps; often also seen in habitats far from open water. The second species occurs in the Old World tropics.

| Length **35in (89cm)** | Wingspan **3½ft (1.1m)** | Weight **2¾lb (1.3kg)** |
| Social **Colonies** | Lifespan **Up to 10 years** | Status **Secure** |

DATE SEEN	WHERE	NOTES

PELICANS, HERONS, IBISES, AND RELATIVES

THESE RELATED WATERBIRDS exploit a diversity of water and waterside habitats in different ways, from plunge-diving in the ocean to wading at the edge of mangroves and freshwater swamps, from scooping up fish to stealthy and patient hunting from overhanging branches.

PELICANS
Pelicans are large fish-eating birds, bulky but buoyant on water. Brown Pelicans dive head first to catch fish, while White Pelicans work together to herd fish into shallow bays, and scoop them up in flexible pouches beneath their long bills.

HERONS, EGRETS, AND BITTERNS
These waterside birds have long toes, which enable them to walk on wet mud and wade among reed stems. Their long toes also aid their balance as they lean forward in search of fish and when catching prey in their long,

pointed bills. Herons and egrets have slender, feathered necks with a distinct kink that gives a lightning forward thrust when catching prey. Most herons and egrets make bulky nests in treetop colonies, whereas bitterns nest on the ground in marshes. Unlike storks (p.191) and cranes, they all fly with their heads withdrawn into their shoulders.

EVER ALERT
The Green Heron catches fish by waiting and watching patiently until prey is near.

IBISES AND SPOONBILL
Ibises and the related spoonbill are long-legged, waterside or dry-land birds. Ibises have long, decurved bills that are adapted to picking insects, worms, small mollusks, and crustaceans from wet mud. Spoonbills have a unique flat, spatula-shaped bill that they sweep from side to side in shallow water to catch aquatic prey.

WATER BIRD
Webbed toes help the Brown Pelican negotiate water with ease, while strong wings allow easy takeoffs.

Order **Pelecaniformes**	Family **Pelecanidae**	Species *Pelecanus erythrorhynchos*

American White Pelican

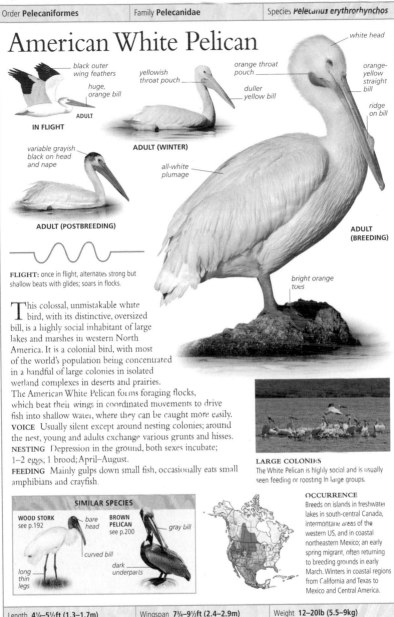

black outer wing feathers

huge, orange bill

ADULT

IN FLIGHT

yellowish throat pouch

ADULT (WINTER)

duller yellow bill

orange throat pouch

white head

orange-yellow straight bill

ridge on bill

variable grayish black on head and nape

ADULT (POSTBREEDING)

all-white plumage

ADULT (BREEDING)

FLIGHT: once in flight, alternates strong but shallow beats with glides; soars in flocks.

bright orange toes

This colossal, unmistakable white bird, with its distinctive, oversized bill, is a highly social inhabitant of large lakes and marshes in western North America. It is a colonial bird, with most of the world's population being concentrated in a handful of large colonies in isolated wetland complexes in deserts and prairies. The American White Pelican forms foraging flocks, which beat their wings in coordinated movements to drive fish into shallow water, where they can be caught more easily.

VOICE Usually silent except around nesting colonies; around the nest, young and adults exchange various grunts and hisses.

NESTING Depression in the ground, both sexes incubate; 1–2 eggs; 1 brood; April–August.

FEEDING Mainly gulps down small fish, occasionally eats small amphibians and crayfish.

LARGE COLONIES
The White Pelican is highly social and is usually seen feeding or roosting in large groups.

SIMILAR SPECIES

WOOD STORK see p.192

bare head

curved bill

long thin legs

BROWN PELICAN see p.200

gray bill

dark underparts

OCCURRENCE
Breeds on islands in freshwater lakes in south-central Canada, intermontane areas of the western US, and in coastal northeastern Mexico; an early spring migrant, often returning to breeding grounds in early March. Winters in coastal regions from California and Texas to Mexico and Central America.

Length 4¼–5½ft (1.3–1.7m)	Wingspan 7¾–9½ft (2.4–2.9m)	Weight 12–20lb (5.5–9kg)
Social **Colonies**	Lifespan **Up to 26 years**	Status **Vulnerable**

DATE SEEN	WHERE	NOTES

Order **Pelecaniformes**	Family **Pelecanidae**	Species *Pelecanus occidentalis*

Brown Pelican

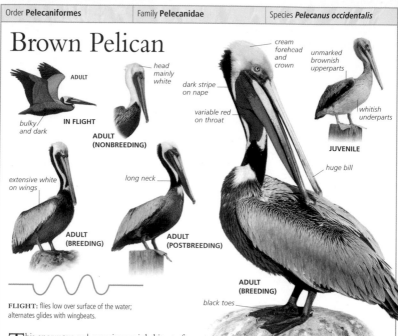

ADULT

bulky and dark — **IN FLIGHT**

head mainly white — **ADULT (NONBREEDING)**

cream forehead and crown

unmarked brownish upperparts

dark stripe on nape

variable red on throat

whitish underparts

JUVENILE

huge bill

extensive white on wings — **ADULT (BREEDING)**

long neck — **ADULT (POSTBREEDING)**

ADULT (BREEDING)

black toes

FLIGHT: flies low over surface of the water; alternates glides with wingbeats.

This enormous and conspicuous inhabitant of warm coastal regions is an ungainly species on land but is amazingly graceful in flight. Sadly, numbers plummeted in the 1960s when DDT was used widely as a pesticide, but it rapidly recovered in recent decades, and is now expanding its range northward along both coasts. The color of its throat varies according to geographic location and time of year.

VOICE Silent most of the time; vocal at nest colonies; adults and juveniles communicate with grunts and hisses; courting birds give a strange, deliberate *heart-hark*, repeated slowly.

NESTING Pile of debris, usually on ground; 2–3 eggs; 1 brood; February–August.

FEEDING Adults plunge headfirst into water to scoop up fish near the surface; does not herd fish, unlike the American White Pelican.

RESTING TOGETHER
Brown Pelicans are social most of the year, and can often be seen roosting in groups.

SIMILAR SPECIES

BLACK-FOOTED ALBATROSS

long, pointed wings

short bill

AMERICAN WHITE PELICAN see p.199

orange bill

white plumage

OCCURRENCE
Found in and around warm coastal waters, flying above the water's surface over the cresting waves; small numbers breed in the interior US; individuals and small flocks can be found around docks and marinas.

Length **4–4¼ft (1.2–1.3m)**	Wingspan **6½–7ft (2–2.1m)**	Weight **4–8¾lb (1.8–4kg)**
Social **Colonies**	Lifespan **Up to 10 years**	Status **Secure**

DATE SEEN	WHERE	NOTES
....	....	....
....	....	....
....	....	....
....	....	....
....	....	....

| Order **Pelecaniformes** | Family **Ardeidae** | Species *Botaurus lentiginosus* |

American Bittern

dark outer wing feathers

ADULT

trailing legs

IN FLIGHT

rusty brown crown

long, straight bill

black streak on side of neck

duller crown

no large black patch on neck

brown back

brown streaks on chest

JUVENILE

short tail

greenish legs

ADULT

The American Bittern's camouflaged plumage and secretive behavior help it to blend into the thick vegetation of its freshwater wetland habitat. It is heard much more often than it is seen; its call is unmistakable and has given rise to many evocative colloquial names, such as "thunder pumper."

VOICE Deep, resonant *pump-er-unk*, *pump-er-unk*; calls mainly at dawn, dusk, and nighttime, but also during the day in the early mating season.

NESTING Platform or mound constructed of available marsh vegetation, usually over shallow water; 2–7 eggs; 1 brood; April–August.

FEEDING Stands still or moves slowly, then strikes downward with bill to catch prey; eats fish, insects, crustaceans, snakes, amphibians, and small mammals.

FLIGHT steady, deep, slightly stiff wingbeats; usually flies relatively low and direct.

LOOKING UP
Bitterns are secretive birds, but can occasionally be found walking slowly through reeds.

OCCURRENCE
Breeds in heavily vegetated freshwater wetlands across the northern US and southern Canada; also occasionally in estuarine wetlands; winters in southern and coastal wetlands where temperatures stay above freezing; can appear in any wetland habitat during migration.

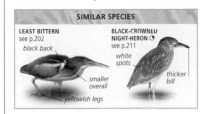

SIMILAR SPECIES		
LEAST BITTERN see p.202	**BLACK-CROWNED NIGHT-HERON ☾** see p.211	
black back	white spots	
smaller overall	thicker bill	
yellowish legs		

Length **23½–31in (60–80cm)**	Wingspan **3½–4¼ft (1.1–1.3m)**	Weight **13–20oz (375–575g)**
Social **Solitary**	Lifespan **At least 8 years**	Status **Declining**

DATE SEEN	WHERE	NOTES

| Order **Pelecaniformes** | Family **Ardeidae** | Species *Ixobrychus exilis* |

Least Bittern

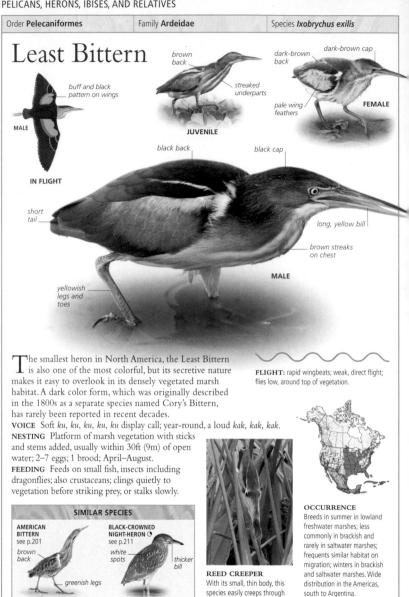

buff and black pattern on wings

MALE

IN FLIGHT

brown back

streaked underparts

JUVENILE

dark-brown cap

dark-brown back

pale wing feathers

FEMALE

black back

black cap

short tail

long, yellow bill

brown streaks on chest

MALE

yellowish legs and toes

The smallest heron in North America, the Least Bittern is also one of the most colorful, but its secretive nature makes it easy to overlook in its densely vegetated marsh habitat. A dark color form, which was originally described in the 1800s as a separate species named Cory's Bittern, has rarely been reported in recent decades.

VOICE Soft *ku, ku, ku, ku, ku* display call; year-round, a loud *kak, kak, kak*.

NESTING Platform of marsh vegetation with sticks and stems added, usually within 30ft (9m) of open water; 2–7 eggs; 1 brood; April–August.

FEEDING Feeds on small fish, insects including dragonflies; also crustaceans; clings quietly to vegetation before striking prey, or stalks slowly.

FLIGHT: rapid wingbeats; weak, direct flight; flies low, around top of vegetation.

SIMILAR SPECIES

AMERICAN BITTERN
see p.201

brown back

greenish legs

BLACK-CROWNED NIGHT-HERON ◖
see p.211

white spots

thicker bill

REED CREEPER
With its small, thin body, this species easily creeps through dense reeds in search of prey.

OCCURRENCE
Breeds in summer in lowland freshwater marshes; less commonly in brackish and rarely in saltwater marshes; frequents similar habitat on migration; winters in brackish and saltwater marshes. Wide distribution in the Americas, south to Argentina.

| Length **11–14in (28–36cm)** | Wingspan **15½–18in (40–46cm)** | Weight **2⅝–3⅜oz (75–95g)** |
| Social **Solitary/Small flocks** | Lifespan **Unknown** | Status **Secure** |

DATE SEEN	WHERE	NOTES

| Order **Pelecaniformes** | Family **Ardeidae** | Species *Ardea herodias* |

Great Blue Heron

ADULT

- dark wing tips
- dark tail
- brownish body
- white face
- dark bill
- gray neck
- yellowish bill
- crooked neck
- **JUVENILE**
- blue-gray body

IN FLIGHT

- lighter-colored neck, almost beige
- light bill
- large, white bird
- overall similar to Great Blue
- shaggy plumes
- light legs

MALE

- dark legs

WURDEMANN'S HERON (WHITE-HEADED FORM)

GREAT WHITE HERON (WHITE FORM)

FLIGHT: deep-flapping, regular wingbeats.

This is one of the world's largest herons, slightly smaller than Africa's Goliath Heron but of similar stature to the more closely related Gray Heron of Eurasia and Cocoi Heron of South America. The Great Blue Heron is a common inhabitant of a variety of North American waterbodies, from marshes to swamps, as well as along sea coasts. Its majestic, deliberate flight is wonderful to behold.

VOICE Mostly silent; gives a loud, barking squawk or *crank* in breeding colonies or when disturbed.

NESTING Nest of twigs and branches; usually in colonies, but also singly; in trees, often over water, but also over ground; 2–4 eggs; 1–2 broods; February–August.

FEEDING Catches prey with quick jab of bill; primarily fish.

LOFTY ABODE
Great Blue Herons nest in small colonies in trees, and often roost in them.

SIMILAR SPECIES

TRICOLORED HERON
see p.207
smaller overall
- dark bill
- white underparts

LITTLE BLUE HERON
smaller overall;
see p.206
- greenish legs
- darker overall

OCCURRENCE
Across southern Canada and the US in wetlands, such as marshes, lake edges, and along rivers and swamps; also in marine habitats, especially tidal grass flats. The Great White Heron is common in mangroves in the Florida Keys; also West Indies and Yucatán.

| Length **2¾–4¼ft (0.9–1.3m)** | Wingspan **5¼–6½ft (1.6–2m)** | Weight **4¾–5½lb (2.1–2.5kg)** |
| Social **Solitary/Flocks** | Lifespan **Up to 20 years** | Status **Secure** |

DATE SEEN	WHERE	NOTES

Order **Pelecaniformes**	Family **Ardeidae**	Species *Ardea alba*

Great Egret 🔊

large size

SUMMER

white overall

IN FLIGHT

long, yellow bill

long, S-curved neck

all-white plumage

long, black plumes

black legs and toes

ADULT (NONBREEDING)

lime-green patch between eye and bill

ADULT (BREEDING)

〰️〰️〰️〰️〰️

FLIGHT: flies with regular, deep wingbeats.

This large white heron is found on every continent except Antarctica. When feeding, the Great Egret would apparently rather forage alone than in flocks—it maintains space around itself, and will defend a territory of 10ft (3m) in diameter from other wading birds. This territory "moves" with the bird as it feeds. In years of scarce food supplies, a chick may kill a sibling, permitting the survival of at least one bird.

VOICE Largely vocal during courtship and breeding; otherwise, *kraak* or *cuk-cuk-cuk* when disturbed or in a combative encounter.

NESTING Nest of twigs in trees, over land or water; 2–4 eggs; 1 brood; March–July.

FEEDING Catches prey with quick thrust of bill; feeds on aquatic prey, primarily fish, also crustaceans.

TREE PERCHES
Great Egrets nest in trees and regularly perch in them when not feeding.

SIMILAR SPECIES

LITTLE BLUE HERON 🌙
see p.206

two-toned bill

smaller overall

yellow-green legs

SNOWY EGRET
black bill;
see p.205

smaller overall

yellow toes

OCCURRENCE
Breeds in trees over water or on islands; forages in almost all types of freshwater and marine wetlands from marshes and ponds to rivers. Migratory over much of its North American range; more southerly populations resident. Distance migrated depends on severity of winter.

Length **3¼ft (1m)**	Wingspan **6ft (1.8m)**	Weight **1¾–3¼ft (0.8–1.5kg)**
Social **Solitary**	Lifespan **Up to 25 years**	Status **Secure**

DATE SEEN	WHERE	NOTES

| Order **Pelecaniformes** | Family **Ardeidae** | Species *Egretta thula* |

Snowy Egret

paler patch of skin at base of bill

plumes on head

all-white plumage

yellow patch between eye and bill

black bill

wispy breast plumes

long, extended legs

ADULT

IN FLIGHT

red patch between eye and bill

greenish yellow legs

JUVENILE

ADULT (HIGH BREEDING)

orangish legs

black legs

ADULT (BREEDING)

yellow toes

FLIGHT: flies with deep wingbeats; gliding descent before landing.

A New World species, the Snowy Egret is similar to an Old World species, the Little Egret. It is very adaptable in estuarine and freshwater habitats. When foraging, it uses a wide variety of behaviors, including wing-flicking, foot-stirring, and foot-probing to get its prey moving, making it easier to capture.

VOICE High-pitched *Aargaarg* when flushed; low-pitched *Arg* and *Raah* aggressive calls; *Aarg* call during attacks and pursuits.

NESTING Small sticks, branches, and rushes over water or on land; also on ground, in shrubs, mangroves, and other trees; 3–5 eggs; 1 brood; March–August.

FEEDING Feeds on aquatic prey, from invertebrates, such as insects, shrimp, and prawns, to small fish, amphibians, and snakes.

WIDESPREAD SPECIES
Snowy Egrets feed in a wide variety of wetland habitats, using different foraging techniques.

SIMILAR SPECIES

GREAT EGRET see p.204

yellow bill

black legs and toes

LITTLE BLUE HERON see p.206

black legs and toes

OCCURRENCE
Found in a wide variety of wetlands throughout North and South America: from mangroves in Florida to marshlands in New England and the western US. Highly adaptable and widely found. Sites of breeding colonies may change from year to year within a set range.

| Length **24in (62cm)** | Wingspan **3½ft (1.1m)** | Weight **12oz (350g)** |
| Social **Solitary** | Lifespan **Up to 22 years** | Status **Declining** |

DATE SEEN	WHERE	NOTES

| Order **Pelecaniformes** | Family **Ardeidae** | Species *Egretta caerulea* |

Little Blue Heron

ADULT

short tail

coiled neck

IN FLIGHT

white plumage

pale, black-tipped bill

JUVENILE

pale greenish legs

slate-gray back

purplish maroon neck

gray bill with black tip

long, slender neck

ADULT

yellowish to greenish legs

blotchy, blue-and-white plumage

IMMATURE (1ST SPRING)

The shy and retreating Little Blue Heron is often overlooked because of its blue-gray color and secretive eating habits. First-year birds, which may be mistaken for Snowy Egrets, are white, and gradually acquire blue-gray, mottled feathers before eventually molting into their all-dark adult plumage. Immature birds are seen feeding together in open wetlands while adults feed alone in denser habitats, such as swamps and thick wetlands.
VOICE Vocal during courtship; generally silent.
NESTING Uses sticks and twigs, in trees or reeds, in wetlands or terrestrial habitats nearby; 2–4 eggs; 1 brood; April–September.
FEEDING Eats small fish, amphibians, crustaceans, and insects; stalks its prey, wading slowly in shallow waters or along the water's edge.

FLIGHT: deep and continuous wingbeats; glides when descending and landing.

UNIQUE TRANSFORMATION
No other heron species undergoes such a complete change from an all-white juvenile to all-dark adult.

SIMILAR SPECIES

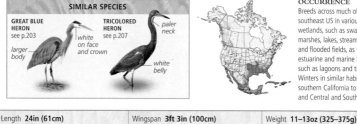

GREAT BLUE HERON see p.203

larger body

white on face and crown

TRICOLORED HERON see p.207

paler neck

white belly

OCCURRENCE
Breeds across much of southeast US in various wetlands, such as swamps, marshes, lakes, streams, rivers, and flooded fields, as well as estuarine and marine habitats, such as lagoons and tidal flats. Winters in similar habitat from southern California to Mexico and Central and South America.

| Length **24in (61cm)** | Wingspan **3ft 3in (100cm)** | Weight **11–13oz (325–375g)** |
| Social **Solitary** | Lifespan **10–20 years** | Status **Secure** |

DATE SEEN	WHERE	NOTES

Order **Pelecaniformes**	Family **Ardeidae**	Species *Egretta tricolor*

Tricolored Heron

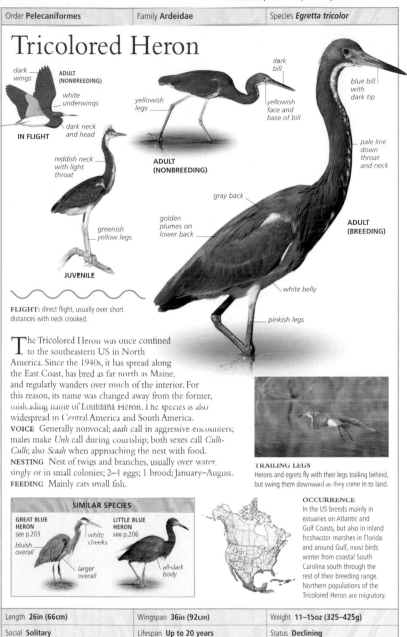

ADULT (NONBREEDING)

dark wings

white underwings

dark neck and head

IN FLIGHT

yellowish legs

ADULT (NONBREEDING)

dark bill

yellowish face and base of bill

blue bill with dark tip

pale line down throat and neck

reddish neck with light throat

gray back

golden plumes on lower back

ADULT (BREEDING)

greenish yellow legs

white belly

JUVENILE

pinkish legs

FLIGHT: direct flight, usually over short distances with neck crooked.

The Tricolored Heron was once confined to the southeastern US in North America. Since the 1940s, it has spread along the East Coast, has bred as far north as Maine, and regularly wanders over much of the interior. For this reason, its name was changed away from the former, misleading name of Louisiana Heron. The species is also widespread in Central America and South America.

VOICE Generally nonvocal; *aaah* call in aggressive encounters; males make *Unh* call during courtship; both sexes call *Culh-Culh*; also *Scaah* when approaching the nest with food.

NESTING Nest of twigs and branches, usually over water, singly or in small colonies; 2–4 eggs; 1 brood; January–August.

FEEDING Mainly eats small fish.

TRAILING LEGS
Herons and egrets fly with their legs trailing behind, but swing them downward as they come in to land.

SIMILAR SPECIES

GREAT BLUE HERON see p.203	LITTLE BLUE HERON see p.206
bluish overall	white cheeks
larger overall	all-dark body

OCCURRENCE
In the US breeds mainly in estuaries on Atlantic and Gulf Coasts, but also in inland freshwater marshes in Florida and around Gulf; most birds winter from coastal South Carolina south through the rest of their breeding range. Northern populations of the Tricolored Heron are migratory.

Length **26in (66cm)**	Wingspan **36in (92cm)**	Weight **11–15oz (325–425g)**
Social **Solitary**	Lifespan **Up to 20 years**	Status **Declining**

DATE SEEN	WHERE	NOTES

| Order **Pelecaniformes** | Family **Ardeidae** | Species *Egretta rufescens* |

Reddish Egret

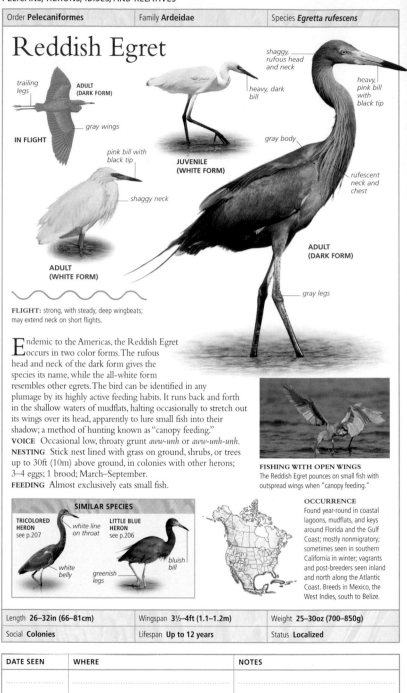

trailing legs

ADULT (DARK FORM)

gray wings

IN FLIGHT

shaggy, rufous head and neck

heavy, dark bill

heavy, pink bill with black tip

gray body

pink bill with black tip

JUVENILE (WHITE FORM)

rufescent neck and chest

shaggy neck

gray legs

ADULT (WHITE FORM)

ADULT (DARK FORM)

FLIGHT: strong, with steady, deep wingbeats; may extend neck on short flights.

Endemic to the Americas, the Reddish Egret occurs in two color forms. The rufous head and neck of the dark form gives the species its name, while the all-white form resembles other egrets. The bird can be identified in any plumage by its highly active feeding habits. It runs back and forth in the shallow waters of mudflats, halting occasionally to stretch out its wings over its head, apparently to lure small fish into their shadow; a method of hunting known as "canopy feeding."
VOICE Occasional low, throaty grunt *aww-unh* or *aww-unh-unh.*
NESTING Stick nest lined with grass on ground, shrubs, or trees up to 30ft (10m) above ground, in colonies with other herons; 3–4 eggs; 1 brood; March–September.
FEEDING Almost exclusively eats small fish.

FISHING WITH OPEN WINGS
The Reddish Egret pounces on small fish with outspread wings when "canopy feeding."

SIMILAR SPECIES

TRICOLORED HERON see p.207

white line on throat

LITTLE BLUE HERON see p.206

bluish bill

white belly

greenish legs

OCCURRENCE
Found year-round in coastal lagoons, mudflats, and keys around Florida and the Gulf Coast; mostly nonmigratory; sometimes seen in southern California in winter; vagrants and post-breeders seen inland and north along the Atlantic Coast. Breeds in Mexico, the West Indies, south to Belize.

| Length **26–32in (66–81cm)** | Wingspan **3½–4ft (1.1–1.2m)** | Weight **25–30oz (700–850g)** |
| Social **Colonies** | Lifespan **Up to 12 years** | Status **Localized** |

DATE SEEN	WHERE	NOTES

| Order **Pelecaniformes** | Family **Ardeidae** | Species **Bubulcus ibis** |

Cattle Egret

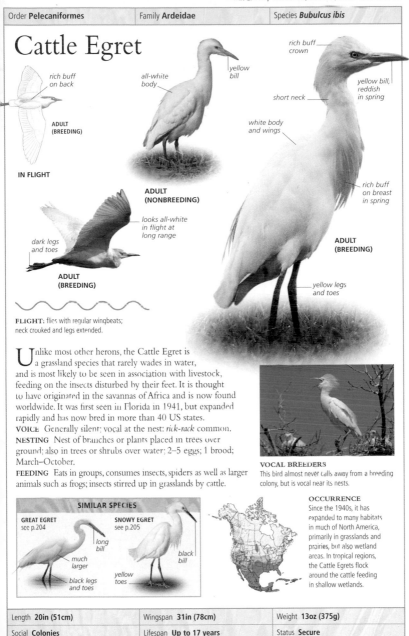

rich buff
on back

**ADULT
(BREEDING)**

IN FLIGHT

all-white
body

yellow
bill

rich buff
crown

yellow bill,
reddish
in spring

short neck

white body
and wings

rich buff
on breast
in spring

**ADULT
(NONBREEDING)**

looks all-white
in flight at
long range

dark legs
and toes

**ADULT
(BREEDING)**

**ADULT
(BREEDING)**

yellow legs
and toes

FLIGHT: flies with regular wingbeats;
neck crooked and legs extended.

Unlike most other herons, the Cattle Egret is
a grassland species that rarely wades in water,
and is most likely to be seen in association with livestock,
feeding on the insects disturbed by their feet. It is thought
to have originated in the savannas of Africa and is now found
worldwide. It was first seen in Florida in 1941, but expanded
rapidly and has now bred in more than 40 US states.
VOICE Generally silent; vocal at the nest: *rick-rack* common.
NESTING Nest of branches or plants placed in trees over
ground; also in trees or shrubs over water; 2–5 eggs; 1 brood;
March–October.
FEEDING Eats in groups, consumes insects, spiders as well as larger
animals such as frogs; insects stirred up in grasslands by cattle.

VOCAL BREEDERS
This bird almost never calls away from a breeding
colony, but is vocal near its nests.

SIMILAR SPECIES

GREAT EGRET
see p.204

long
bill

much
larger

black legs
and toes

SNOWY EGRET
see p.205

black
bill

yellow
toes

OCCURRENCE
Since the 1940s, it has
expanded to many habitats
in much of North America,
primarily in grasslands and
prairies, but also wetland
areas. In tropical regions,
the Cattle Egrets flock
around the cattle feeding
in shallow wetlands.

| Length **20in (51cm)** | Wingspan **31in (78cm)** | Weight **13oz (375g)** |
| Social **Colonies** | Lifespan **Up to 17 years** | Status **Secure** |

DATE SEEN	WHERE	NOTES

| Order **Pelecaniformes** | Family **Ardeidae** | Species *Butorides virescens* |

Green Heron 🔊

ADULT (BREEDING)

greenish back

IN FLIGHT

greenish black cap

short, rufous neck

white chin

cream streak extends from throat to belly

yellowish legs and toes

ADULT (NONBREEDING)

white speckles on wings

paler bill

JUVENILE

thin, straight, black bill

long back plumes

glossy orange legs

ADULT (BREEDING)

A small, solitary, and secretive bird of dense thicketed wetlands, the Green Heron can be difficult to observe. This dark, crested heron is most often seen flying away from a perceived threat, emitting a loud squawk. While the Green Heron of North and Central America has now been recognized as a separate species, it was earlier grouped with what is now the Striated Heron (*B. striata*), which is found in the tropics and subtropics throughout the world.

VOICE Squawking *keow* when flying from disturbance.
NESTING Nest of twigs often in bushes or trees, often over water but also on land; 1–2 broods; 3–5 eggs; March–July.
FEEDING Stands quietly on the shore or in shallow water and strikes quickly; mainly fish, but also frogs, insects, and spiders.

FLIGHT: direct, a bit plodding, and usually over short distances.

READY TO STRIKE
Green Herons usually catch their prey by lunging forward and downward with their whole body.

SIMILAR SPECIES

BLACK-CROWNED NIGHT-HERON ↻
see p.211
larger overall
thicker bill

YELLOW-CROWNED NIGHT-HERON ↻
see p.212
larger overall

OCCURRENCE
An inhabitant of swampy thickets, but occasionally dry land close to water across much of North America, but missing in the plains, the Rocky Mountains, and the western deserts that do not provide appropriate wetlands. Winters in coastal wetlands.

| Length **14½–15½in (37–39cm)** | Wingspan **25–27in (63–68cm)** | Weight **7–9oz (200–250g)** |
| Social **Solitary/Pairs/Small flocks** | Lifespan **Up to 10 years** | Status **Secure** |

DATE SEEN	WHERE	NOTES

Order **Pelecaniformes**	Family **Ardeidae**	Species *Nycticorax nycticorax*

Black-crowned Night-Heron 🔊

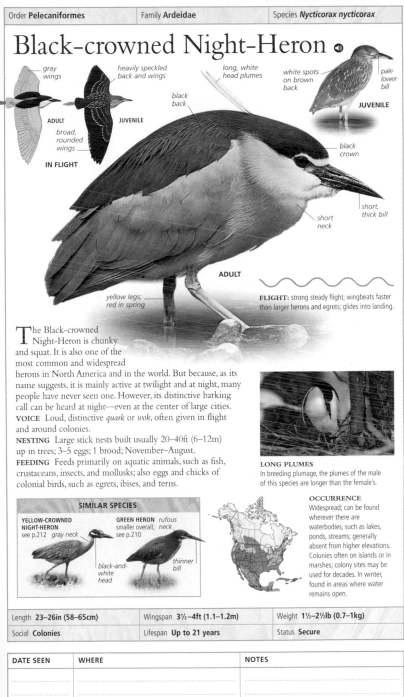

gray wings

heavily speckled back and wings

long, white head plumes

white spots on brown back

pale lower bill

JUVENILE

ADULT

JUVENILE

black back

broad, rounded wings

black back

black crown

IN FLIGHT

short, thick bill

short neck

ADULT

yellow legs; red in spring

FLIGHT: strong steady flight; wingbeats faster than larger herons and egrets; glides into landing.

The Black-crowned Night-Heron is chunky and squat. It is also one of the most common and widespread herons in North America and in the world. But because, as its name suggests, it is mainly active at twilight and at night, many people have never seen one. However, its distinctive barking call can be heard at night—even at the center of large cities.

VOICE Loud, distinctive *quark* or *wok*, often given in flight and around colonies.

NESTING Large stick nests built usually 20–40ft (6–12m) up in trees; 3–5 eggs; 1 brood; November–August.

FEEDING Feeds primarily on aquatic animals, such as fish, crustaceans, insects, and mollusks; also eggs and chicks of colonial birds, such as egrets, ibises, and terns.

LONG PLUMES
In breeding plumage, the plumes of the male of this species are longer than the female's.

SIMILAR SPECIES

YELLOW-CROWNED NIGHT-HERON
see p.212 *gray neck*

black-and-white head

GREEN HERON *rufous smaller overall; neck*
see p.210

thinner bill

OCCURRENCE
Widespread; can be found wherever there are waterbodies, such as lakes, ponds, streams; generally absent from higher elevations. Colonies often on islands or in marshes; colony sites may be used for decades. In winter, found in areas where water remains open.

Length **23–26in (58–65cm)**	Wingspan **3½–4ft (1.1–1.2m)**	Weight **1½–2½lb (0.7–1kg)**
Social **Colonies**	Lifespan **Up to 21 years**	Status **Secure**

DATE SEEN	WHERE	NOTES

Order **Pelecaniformes**	Family **Ardeidae**	Species *Nyctanassa violacea*

Yellow-crowned Night-Heron

short tail

ADULT

uniform gray back and wings

IN FLIGHT

white cheek patches

long, white plumes extending from crown

yellowish white crown

thick, black bill

slender neck

ADULT

no white on face

fine speckling on back and wings

brown streaks on underparts

JUVENILE

long, yellow legs

More slender and elegant than its more common cousin, the Black-crowned Night-Heron, the Yellow-crowned Night-Heron was unaffected by the plume hunting trade that decimated many heron species in the 19th century. It then expanded northward in the 20th century, but has retreated slightly from the northern edge of its range in recent decades. It can be seen in wooded areas.
VOICE Call an abrupt *quark* or *wok*, higher-pitched than Black-crowned Night-Heron; most vocal in mornings, evenings, and at night.
NESTING Platform of sticks in tree, tall shrubs, often 40–60ft (12–18m) above ground, away from main trunk; 2–6 eggs; 1 brood; March–August.
FEEDING Stands motionless or slowly stalks prey and then lunges; mostly eats crabs and crayfish; also insects, small mollusks, and fish.

FLIGHT: strong and steady, with neck drawn up close to body; legs trailing.

SIMILAR SPECIES

BLACK-CROWNED NIGHT-HERON see p.211

black back

white throat

GREEN HERON see p.210

blue-green upperparts

thinner bill

DARKER JUVENILE
A juvenile Yellow-crowned has darker plumage than its Black-crowned counterpart.

OCCURRENCE
Breeds near wetlands along the East Coast, across the Southeast and the Midwest; often nests and roosts near houses in wooded neighborhoods. Found in similar habitats during migration; mainly coastal in winter.

Length **19½–28in (50–70cm)**	Wingspan **3¼–3½ft (1–1.1m)**	Weight **23–28oz (650–800g)**
Social **Colonies**	Lifespan **At least 6 years**	Status **Secure (p)**

DATE SEEN	WHERE	NOTES

Order **Pelecaniformes**	Family **Threskiornithidae**	Species *Eudocimus albus*

White Ibis

red or pink facial skin

pale bluish eye

white overall

curved, red bill with dark tip

ADULT (BREEDING)

red legs and toes

long, white neck

trailing legs

ADULT (BREEDING)

black wing tips

IN FLIGHT

streaked neck

mottled brown-and-white upperparts

curved, yellowish bill

white underparts

yellow legs

IMMATURE (1ST SPRING)

short tail

It is the bill shape that hints at the close relationship between the White Ibis and the darker Glossy and White-faced Ibises. Depending on the season, the White Ibis has a pink face, bill, and legs set against its white plumage and black wing tips. When breeding, however, the legs, bill, and bare facial skin turn a vivid red. The 20,000–30,000 birds living in the southeastern US breed from Florida north to South Carolina, and along the Gulf Coast to Louisiana and Texas. The population moves around within this area, as do other large waders, depending on the water level.

VOICE Hoarse, croaking *knaah*; high-pitched calls during courtship.
NESTING Platform of sticks placed in trees or shrubs, often mangroves, over water; 2–4 eggs; 1 brood; March–October.
FEEDING Eats small crustaceans such as crayfish, small fish, and frogs; feeds in flocks in both estuarine and freshwater wetlands.

FLIGHT: rapid wingbeats alternating with glides; soars on thermals to save energy.

HIGHLY GREGARIOUS
White Ibises are extremely social birds, flying, breeding, feeding, and roosting in large flocks.

SIMILAR SPECIES

GREAT EGRET see p.204
larger overall
black legs

SNOWY EGRET see p.205
shorter, straight bill
black bill
black legs
yellow toes

OCCURRENCE
Found in estuaries along the coast, also in freshwater marshes, swamps, and rice fields; breeds in colonies with other wading birds. Also occurs throughout Central America and northern South America from Venezuela to Colombia.

Length **25in (64cm)**	Wingspan **3ft 2in (96cm)**	Weight **32oz (900g)**
Social **Flocks/Colonies**	Lifespan **Up to 16 years**	Status **Secure**

DATE SEEN	WHERE	NOTES
....	....	....
....	....	....
....	....	....
....	....	....
....	....	....

| Order **Pelecaniformes** | Family **Threskiornithidae** | Species *Plegadis falcinellus* |

Glossy Ibis

finely streaked head and neck

ADULT (NONBREEDING)

iridescent crown

dark brown eye

dark maroon neck

curved, gray-brown bill

outstretched neck

trailing legs

ADULT (BREEDING)

iridescent bronze-green feathers on inner wing

IN FLIGHT

chestnut or maroon underparts

ADULT (BREEDING)

gray-green legs and toes

FLIGHT: alternate wingbeats and glides; flies with neck outstretched, legs extended beyond tail.

With its long, curved bill, the dark, long-legged Glossy Ibis is similar to the White-faced Ibis. It is well known for its wandering tendencies and can also be found in southern Europe, Asia, Australia, and Africa. Despite being found in the US in the mid-19th century, the Glossy Ibis was not discovered nesting in Florida until 1886. Confined to Florida until the mid-20th century, it then started spreading northward, eventually as far as New England.

VOICE Crow-like croak; subdued nasal chatter in flocks; mostly silent.

NESTING Platform of twigs and reeds in trees, shrubs, or reeds, on ground or over water; 3–4 eggs; 1 brood; April–July.

FEEDING Forages by feel, puts bill in soil and mud to catch prey, including snails, insects, leeches, frogs, and crayfish.

MARSH FEEDER
The Glossy Ibis regularly feeds in shallow pools and along the waterways of coastal marshes.

SIMILAR SPECIES

WHITE-FACED IBIS
see p.215

pink legs

white mask on pink face

BLACK-CROWNED NIGHT-HERON ↺
see p.211

brown body

thick, straight bill

OCCURRENCE
Common from New England south to Florida. Occurs in brackish and freshwater marshes and in flooded or plowed fields; feeds with other waders in inland freshwater wetlands as well as coastal lagoons and estuaries.

| Length **23in (59cm)** | Wingspan **36in (92cm)** | Weight **13oz (375g)** |
| Social **Flocks/Colonies** | Lifespan **15–20 years** | Status **Secure (p)** |

DATE SEEN	WHERE	NOTES

| Order **Pelecaniformes** | Family **Threskiornithidae** | Species *Plegadis chihi* |

White-faced Ibis

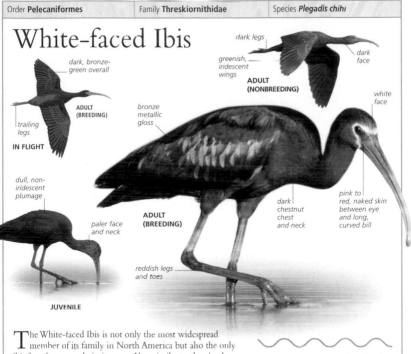

dark legs

greenish, iridescent wings

dark face

ADULT (NONBREEDING)

dark, bronze-green overall

ADULT (BREEDING)

trailing legs

IN FLIGHT

bronze metallic gloss

white face

dull, non-iridescent plumage

paler face and neck

ADULT (BREEDING)

dark chestnut chest and neck

pink to red, naked skin between eye and long, curved bill

reddish legs and toes

JUVENILE

The White-faced Ibis is not only the most widespread member of its family in North America but also the only ibis found commonly in its range. Very similar to the closely related Glossy Ibis, it is separable in winter only by its reddish eye and the absence of a thin blue line around the face, though the two are only likely to be seen together in the Louisiana area.
VOICE Generally silent; soft calls at the nest, including feeding calls, vocalizations after mating, and greeting calls to mates and chicks; outside breeding, a raucous *khah* or *krah*.
NESTING Flat or columnar nest lined with plant matter, such as cattail, or bulrush in low trees or shrubs over shallow water, or on ground on small islands; 2–5 eggs; 1 brood; May–July.
FEEDING Captures prey below soil by probing with bill; eats aquatic prey such as crayfish, small fish, and frogs.

FLIGHT: strong and direct, with rapid wingbeats, alternating with glides; soars on thermals.

LARGE FLOCKS
The White-faced Ibis is social, feeding and traveling in flocks, which can be large.

SIMILAR SPECIES

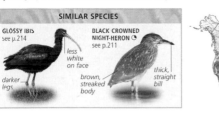

GLOSSY IBIS
see p.214

less white on face

darker legs

BLACK CROWNED NIGHT-HERON ♀
see p.211

brown, streaked body

thick, straight bill

OCCURRENCE
Found in freshwater wetlands, especially in flooded fields, marshes, and lake edges with cattails and bulrushes. Although birds may disperse farther east after breeding, they are, for the most part, restricted to the western part of the United States, and in Central and South America.

| Length **23in (59cm)** | Wingspan **36in (92cm)** | Weight **22oz (625g)** |
| Social **Flocks/Colonies** | Lifespan **Up to 14 years** | Status **Secure** |

DATE SEEN	WHERE	NOTES

Order **Pelecaniformes**	Family **Threskiornithidae**	Species *Platalea ajaja*

Roseate Spoonbill

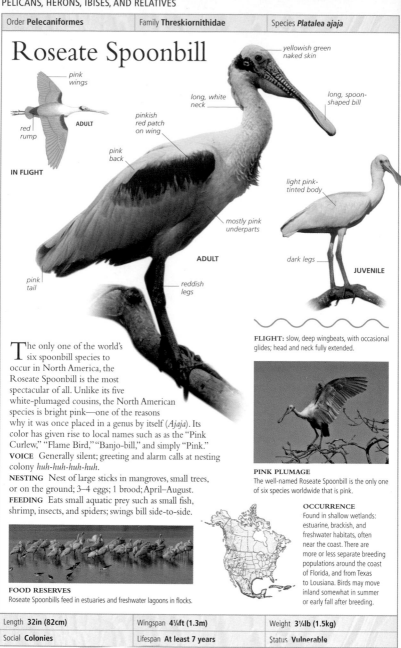

yellowish green
naked skin

pink
wings

ADULT

red
rump

IN FLIGHT

long, white
neck

pinkish
red patch
on wing

pink
back

long, spoon-
shaped bill

light pink-
tinted body

mostly pink
underparts

ADULT

dark legs

JUVENILE

pink
tail

reddish
legs

The only one of the world's six spoonbill species to occur in North America, the Roseate Spoonbill is the most spectacular of all. Unlike its five white-plumaged cousins, the North American species is bright pink—one of the reasons why it was once placed in a genus by itself (*Ajaja*). Its color has given rise to local names such as as the "Pink Curlew," "Flame Bird," "Banjo-bill," and simply "Pink."
VOICE Generally silent; greeting and alarm calls at nesting colony *huh-huh-huh-huh*.
NESTING Nest of large sticks in mangroves, small trees, or on the ground; 3–4 eggs; 1 brood; April–August.
FEEDING Eats small aquatic prey such as small fish, shrimp, insects, and spiders; swings bill side-to-side.

FLIGHT: slow, deep wingbeats, with occasional glides; head and neck fully extended.

PINK PLUMAGE
The well-named Roseate Spoonbill is the only one of six species worldwide that is pink.

FOOD RESERVES
Roseate Spoonbills feed in estuaries and freshwater lagoons in flocks.

OCCURRENCE
Found in shallow wetlands: estuarine, brackish, and freshwater habitats, often near the coast. There are more or less separate breeding populations around the coast of Florida, and from Texas to Lousiana. Birds may move inland somewhat in summer or early fall after breeding.

Length **32in (82cm)**	Wingspan **4¼ft (1.3m)**	Weight **3¼lb (1.5kg)**
Social **Colonies**	Lifespan **At least 7 years**	Status **Vulnerable**

DATE SEEN	WHERE	NOTES

NEW WORLD VULTURES

NEW WORLD VULTURES are not related to Old World vultures, although they look somewhat similar, having long, broad wings with "fingered" tips. Their heads and necks are more or less bare, which helps prevent meat and bacteria from collecting in their feathers when they feed on carcasses. Their bills are large and hooked, to tear flesh, but their toes are unspecialized, with short claws, and not used for capturing prey. All the birds in this group have exceptional eyesight and find their food by sight while soaring high over open ground. The Turkey Vulture, a common sight in many areas, also has a keen sense of smell and can even find dead animals inside woodland. The largest species in this group is the California Condor, a scavenger that was recently on the verge of extinction, before conservation efforts turned things around.

WEAK TOOL
In spite of its sharp bill, the Turkey Vulture cannot always break the skin of carcasses.

HAWKS, EAGLES, AND RELATIVES

THESE DIURNAL BIRDS OF prey include several loosely related groups. All have hooked bills and large eyes, but their shapes and lifestyles are varied.

OSPREY
The sole member of the Pandionidae family, the Osprey catches fish in a headlong dive from a hover. It has long, curved claws and toes equipped with sharp scales to give extra grip.

HAWKS, KITES, AND EAGLES
The Accipitridae family covers a range of raptors with much variation in shape, size, and habitat. Graceful, long-winged kites and harriers are medium-sized birds that feed in open spaces or over marshes. Huge, powerful eagles of mountains and open country have long, broad wings and feathered legs. "Sea-eagles" such as the Bald Eagle have massive bills and long wings but very short tails and bare legs. Sea-eagles feed on fish as well as birds, mammals, and carrion. Bird-eating hawks (in the genus *Accipiter*) have rounded wings and slender tails and long claws for catching prey with their toes. Other hawks (in the genus *Buteo*) are more like small eagles, with small but powerful bills. Some are more widespread than eagles, and are found in a broader range of habitats.

DOUBLE SHOT
With lots of fish running in a tight school, this Osprey has the strength and skill to catch two with one dive.

| Order **Cathartiformes** | Family **Cathartidae** | Species *Coragyps atratus* |

Black Vulture

naked, wrinkled, gray skin

yellowish tip of bill

broad wings, spread at roost

silvery white patch on wing

ADULT

short, rounded tail

ADULT

black upperparts

IN FLIGHT

black underparts

ADULT

FLIGHT: rapid wingbeats followed by glides on flat wings; soars using rising air currents.

long, grayish legs and toes

Common in the southern and eastern states, the Black Vulture is often seen in large communal roosts in the evening. Communal roosts act as meeting places for adults and young, and possibly serve as information centers, where food locations are communicated. Maintaining long pair-bonds, Black Vultures remain together year-round. According to one study, parents will continue to feed their young for as long as eight months after fledging. When not feeding on roadkills along highways, Black Vultures spend time soaring above the landscape, in search of carrion.

VOICE Usually silent; hisses and barks occasionally.
NESTING No nest; lays eggs on ground in thickets or under stumps, in piles of rocks, seldom in old buildings; 2 eggs; 1 brood; January–August.
FEEDING Generally eats carrion (mostly large mammals) on the ground; also consumes live prey.

SIMILAR SPECIES

TURKEY VULTURE see p.219 — red head
long tail

TURKEY VULTURE see p.219 — brownish head, brownish body

DOMINANT SCAVENGER
The more aggressive Black Vultures often displace the Turkey Vultures at carcasses.

OCCURRENCE
Breeds in dense woodlands, caves, old buildings; forms roosts in stands of tall trees; forages in open habitats and near roads and highways; year-round resident throughout its range in southern and eastern states. Range expanding in the northeastern US. Also widespread in Central and South America.

| Length **24–27in (61–68cm)** | Wingspan **4½–5ft (1.4–1.5m)** | Weight **3½–5lb (1.6–2.2kg)** |
| Social **Loose colonies** | Lifespan **Up to 26 years** | Status **Secure** |

DATE SEEN	WHERE	NOTES

| Order **Cathartiformes** | Family **Cathartidae** | Species *Cathartes aura* |

Turkey Vulture

long wings

silvery gray flight feathers

ADULT

IN FLIGHT

blackish back feathers, edged brown

brownish gray head

JUVENILE

brownish back

naked skin

small, red head

SUB-ADULT

black underparts

long tail

pink legs

FLIGHT: seldom flaps; mostly soars with wings held in a V-shape, gently tipping from side to side.

The most widely distributed vulture in North America, the Turkey Vulture is found in most of the US and has expanded its range into southern Canada. It possesses a better sense of smell than the Black Vulture, which often follows it and displaces it from carcasses. The Turkey Vulture's habit of defecating down its legs, which it shares with the Wood Stork, may serve to cool it or to kill bacteria with its ammonia content.

VOICE Silent, but will hiss at intruders; also grunts.

NESTING Dark recesses, such as under large rocks or stumps, on rocky ledges in caves, and crevices, in mammal burrows and hollow logs, and abandoned buildings; 1–3 eggs; 1 brood; March–August.

FEEDING Feeds on a wide range of wild and domestic carrion, mostly mammals, but also birds, reptiles, amphibians, and fish; occasionally takes live prey such as nestlings or trapped birds.

SOAKING UP THE SUN
Turkey Vultures often spread their wings to sun themselves and increase their body temperature.

SIMILAR SPECIES

BLACK VULTURE
see p.218

shorter tail

all-black body

OCCURRENCE
Generally forages and migrates over mixed farmland and forest; prefers to nest in forested or partly forested hillsides; roosts in large trees on rocky outcrops, and on power line transmission towers; some winter in urban areas and near landfills. Also widespread in the Caribbean, and in Central and South America.

| Length **25–32in (64–81cm)** | Wingspan **5½–6ft (1.7–1.8m)** | Weight **4½lb (2kg)** |
| Social **Flocks** | Lifespan **At least 17 years** | Status **Secure** |

DATE SEEN	WHERE	NOTES

Order **Accipitriformes**	Family **Pandionidae**	Species *Pandion haliaetus*

Osprey 🔊

wing tips at slight backward angle

dark band running across wing

barred tail

ADULT

black eye stripe

dark brown upperparts

IN FLIGHT

wings bowed while soaring

ADULT

finely barred underwings

crest on head

black mask on face

speckled chest

black bill

white underparts

pale gray legs and toes

ADULT

FLIGHT: stiff wingbeats interspersed with glides; occasionally soars on migration.

Sometimes referred to as the "fish hawk" or "fish eagle," the Osprey is the only bird of prey in North America that feeds almost exclusively on live fish. Sharp spicules (tiny, spike-like growths) on the pads of its toes, its reversible outer toes, and an ability to lock its talons in place enable it to hold onto slippery fish. Some populations declined between the 1950s and 1980s due to the use of dangerous pesticides. However, the ban on use of these chemicals, along with availability of artificial nest sites and a tolerance of nearby human activity has allowed the Osprey to return to its former numbers. The Osprey is Nova Scotia's official bird.
VOICE Slow, whistled notes, falling in pitch: *tiooop, tioooop, tiooop*; also screams by displaying male.
NESTING Twig nest on tree, cliff, rock pinnacles, boulders, ground; 1–4 eggs; 1 brood; March–August.
FEEDING Dives to catch fish up to top 3ft (90cm) of water.

IMPROVING AERODYNAMICS
Once caught, a fish is held with its head pointing forward reducing drag as the bird flies.

SIMILAR SPECIES

BALD EAGLE (2ND YEAR) see p.228

no crook in wings during flight

paler tail

GOLDEN EAGLE see p.223

dark brown head

brown, feathered legs

OCCURRENCE
Breeds in a wide variety of habitats: northern forests, near shallow reservoirs, along freshwater rivers and large lakes, estuaries and saltmarshes, coastal deserts and desert saltflat lagoons. Migrates through and winters in similar habitats.

Length **21–23in (53–58cm)**	Wingspan **5–6ft (1.5–1.8m)**	Weight **3–4½lb (1.4–2kg)**
Social **Solitary/Pairs**	Lifespan **Up to 25 years**	Status **Secure**

DATE SEEN	WHERE	NOTES

| Order **Accipitriformes** | Family **Accipitridae** | Species ***Elanus leucurus*** |

White-tailed Kite

dark gray wing tips

ADULT

square or notched tail tip

IN FLIGHT

JUVENILE

pale eye

splashes of sandy rufous around neck and breast

dark wrist mark

dusky wing tips

gray upperparts, black triangle on shoulder

white head and neck

orange eye

thin, shapely black bill

dusky gray wing tips

whitish underside

ADULT

white sided tail

FLIGHT: fast, shallow wingbeats interspersed with glides; hovers with tail down.

Formerly known as the Black shouldered Kite, the White-tailed Kite almost disappeared from North America because of hunting and egg-collecting, but its numbers have rebounded in California. It is also found in Oregon, Washington, Florida, southern Texas, and from Mexico to Central and South America. These birds can be easily identified by their falcon-like shape, gray-and-white plumage, and hovering behavior when hunting for rodents in open grasslands When not breeding, White-tailed Kites roost communally in groups of about 100. The species is largely sedentary, but dispersal takes place after breeding, especially of young birds.

VOICE Whistle-like *kewt* and an *eee-grack* call.
NESTING Twig nest lined with grass or hay; 4 eggs; 1–2 broods; February–August.
FEEDING Captures rodents such as voles and field mice; also birds, lizards, and insects from a hovering position.

A HIGH PERCH IS BEST
The White-tailed Kite likes to perch as high up in trees as possible.

SIMILAR SPECIES

MISSISSIPPI KITE
see p.229

darker body

deep red eyes

NORTHERN HARRIER ♂
see p.224

dark grayish wings

marked underparts

OCCURRENCE
Limited range in the US, breeds and winters in a restricted range; found in open grassland areas, and over large agricultural fields, as well as in rough wetlands with low, reedy, or rushy growth, open oak woodland and light savanna woods. Especially fond of damp, riverside areas.

| Length **13–15in (33–38cm)** | Wingspan **3ft 3in–3½ft (1–1.1m)** | Weight **11–12oz (300–350g)** |
| Social **Colonies** | Lifespan **Up to 6 years** | Status **Secure** |

DATE SEEN	WHERE	NOTES

| Order **Accipitriformes** | Family **Accipitridae** | Species *Elanoides forficatus* |

Swallow-tailed Kite

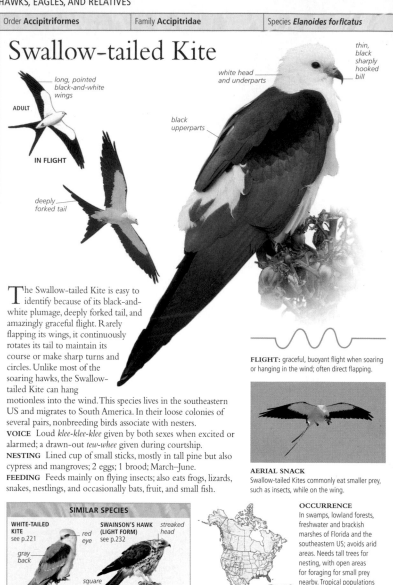

thin, black sharply hooked bill

white head and underparts

long, pointed black-and-white wings

ADULT

black upperparts

IN FLIGHT

deeply forked tail

The Swallow-tailed Kite is easy to identify because of its black-and-white plumage, deeply forked tail, and amazingly graceful flight. Rarely flapping its wings, it continuously rotates its tail to maintain its course or make sharp turns and circles. Unlike most of the soaring hawks, the Swallow-tailed Kite can hang motionless into the wind. This species lives in the southeastern US and migrates to South America. In their loose colonies of several pairs, nonbreeding birds associate with nesters.

VOICE Loud *klee-klee-klee* given by both sexes when excited or alarmed; a drawn-out *tew-whee* given during courtship.

NESTING Lined cup of small sticks, mostly in tall pine but also cypress and mangroves; 2 eggs; 1 brood; March–June.

FEEDING Feeds mainly on flying insects; also eats frogs, lizards, snakes, nestlings, and occasionally bats, fruit, and small fish.

FLIGHT: graceful, buoyant flight when soaring or hanging in the wind; often direct flapping.

AERIAL SNACK
Swallow-tailed Kites commonly eat smaller prey, such as insects, while on the wing.

SIMILAR SPECIES

WHITE-TAILED KITE
see p.221

gray back
red eye

SWAINSON'S HAWK (LIGHT FORM)
see p.232

streaked head

square tail

OCCURRENCE
In swamps, lowland forests, freshwater and brackish marshes of Florida and the southeastern US; avoids arid areas. Needs tall trees for nesting, with open areas for foraging for small prey nearby. Tropical populations are found from Central America south to Argentina.

| Length **20–25in (51–64cm)** | Wingspan **4ft (1.2m)** | Weight **13–21oz (375–600g)** |
| Social **Colonies** | Lifespan **Unknown** | Status **Secure** |

DATE SEEN	WHERE	NOTES

| Order **Accipitriformes** | Family **Accipitridae** | Species *Aquila chrysaetos* |

Golden Eagle

long, narrow white wing patches

IMMATURE   **ADULT**

holds wings in distinctive "V"

golden feathers on long neck

flat, broad head merges into heavy bill

brown overall

dark brown underparts

black tail band

IN FLIGHT

large, powerful bill

pale head

ADULT

heavy feathering on legs

dark plumage with variable white

white tail feathers

FLIGHT: slow, steady wingbeats; most often seen gliding or soaring.

JUVENILE

Perhaps the most formidable of all North American birds of prey, the Golden Eagle is found mostly in the western part of the continent. It defends large territories ranging from 8 to 12 square miles (20–30 square kilometers), containing up to 14 nests. Although its appears sluggish, it is amazingly swift and agile, and employs a variety of hunting techniques to catch specific prey. Shot and poisoned by ranchers and trappers, it is unfortunately also faced with dwindling habitat and food sources because of human development.
VOICE Mostly silent, but breeding adults yelp and mew.
NESTING Large pile of sticks and vegetation on cliffs, in trees, and on manmade structures; 1–3 eggs; 1 brood; April–August.
FEEDING Eats mammals, such as hares, rabbits, ground squirrels, prairie dogs, marmots, foxes, and coyotes; also birds.

POWER AND STRENGTH
The Golden Eagle symbolizes all birds of prey, with its sharp talons, hooked bill, and large size.

SIMILAR SPECIES

BALD EAGLE 🦅
see p.228
white head
and neck

FERRUGINOUS HAWK 🦅
(DARK FORM)
see p.454

no golden tinge

some pale wing feathers

smaller overall

OCCURRENCE
In North America occurs mostly in grasslands, wetlands, and rocky areas; breeds south to Mexico, in open and semi-open habitats from sea level to 12,000ft (3,500m) including tundra, shrublands, grasslands, coniferous forests, farmland, areas close to streams or rivers; winters in open habitat.

| Length **28–33in (70–84cm)** | Wingspan **6–7¼ft (1.8–2.2m)** | Weight **6½–13lb (3–6kg)** |
| Social **Solitary/Pairs** | Lifespan **Up to 39 years** | Status **Declining (p)** |

DATE SEEN	WHERE	NOTES

Order **Accipitriformes**	Family **Accipitridae**	Species *Circus hudsonius*

Northern Harrier

MALE — black wing tips
wings held in V-shape
white rump

IN FLIGHT

FEMALE — dark barring on silver-gray underwings

bluish gray upperparts

bluish gray head

dark bill with yellow shin at base of bill

reddish underparts

JUVENILE

gray uppertail with light undertail feathers

white underparts with reddish brown markings

ADULT MALE

white ring around face

brown upperparts

FEMALE

Found nearly all over North America, the Northern Harrier is most often seen flying buoyantly low in search of food. A white rump, V-shaped wings, and tilting flight make this species easily identifiable. The blue-gray males are quite different to the dark-brown females. The bird's most recognizable characteristic is its owl-like face, which contains stiff feathers to help channel in sounds from prey. Northern Harriers are highly migratory throughout their range.

VOICE Call given by both sexes in rapid succession at nest: *kek* becomes more high-pitched when intruders are spotted.

NESTING Platform of sticks on ground in open, wet field; 4–6 eggs; 1 brood; April–September.

FEEDING Mostly hunts rodents like mice and muskrats; also birds, frogs, reptiles; occasionally takes larger prey such as rabbits.

FLIGHT: low and slow with lazy flaps, alternating with buoyant, brusquely tilting glides.

WATERY DWELLING
To avoid predators, Northern Harriers prefer to raise their young on wet sites in tall, dense vegetation.

SIMILAR SPECIES

MISSISSIPPI KITE see p.229
whitish head
gray underparts
dark eye patch

ROUGH-LEGGED HAWK see p.234
broader wings
shorter tail

OCCURRENCE
Breeds in a variety of open wetlands: marshes, meadows, pastures, fallow fields across most of North America; winters in open habitats like deserts, coastal sand dunes, cropland, grasslands, marshy, and riverside areas.

Length **18–20in (46–51cm)**	Wingspan **3½–4ft (1.1m–1.2m)**	Weight **11–26oz (300–750g)**
Social **Solitary/Pairs/Colonies**	Lifespan **Up to 16 years**	Status **Secure**

DATE SEEN	WHERE	NOTES

| Order **Accipitriformes** | Family **Accipitridae** | Species *Accipiter striatus* |

Sharp-shinned Hawk

grayish blue crown

reddish yellow eye

JUVENILE
square-tipped tail
short, rounded wings
head appears small

grayish blue upperparts

slightly browner upperparts than male

IN FLIGHT
wide, dark, horizontal bars on gray tail

yellow legs and toes

MALE

reddish brown bars on underparts

ADULT
dark brown upperparts
light yellowish eye
wide, brown streaks on underparts

white, fluffy undertail feathers

JUVENILE FEMALE

FEMALE

This small and swift hawk is quite adept at capturing birds, occasionally even taking species larger than itself. The Sharp-shinned Hawk's short, rounded wings and long tail allow it to make abrupt turns and lightning-fast dashes in thick woods and dense shrubby terrain. With needle-like talons, long, spindle-thin legs, and long toes, this hawk is well adapted to snatching birds in flight. The prey is plucked before being consumed or fed to the nestlings.

VOICE High-pitched, repeated *kiu kiu kiu* call; sometimes makes squealing sound when disturbed at nest.

NESTING Sturdy nest of sticks lined with twigs or pieces of bark; sometimes an old crow or squirrel nest; 3–4 eggs; 1 brood; March–June.

FEEDING Catches small birds, such as sparrows and wood warblers, on the wing, or takes them unaware while perched.

FLIGHT: rapid, direct, and strong; nimble enough to maneuver in dense forest; soars during migration.

HUNTING BIRDS
A Sharp-shinned Hawk pauses on the ground with a freshly captured sparrow in its talons

SIMILAR SPECIES

MERLIN see p.262
light eye-stripe
long, pointed wings

COOPER'S HAWK see p.226
larger overall
rounded tip of tail

OCCURRENCE
Deep coniferous forests and mixed hardwood–conifer woodlands across North America from the tree limit in northern Canada to the Gulf states. During fall migration sometimes seen in flocks of hundreds of individuals. Winters in Central America from Guatemala to Panama.

| Length **11in (28cm)** | Wingspan **23in (58cm)** | Weight **3½–6oz (100–175g)** |
| Social **Solitary/Flocks** | Lifespan **At least 10 years** | Status **Secure** |

DATE SEEN	WHERE	NOTES

| Order **Accipitriformes** | Family **Accipitridae** | Species *Accipiter cooperii* |

Cooper's Hawk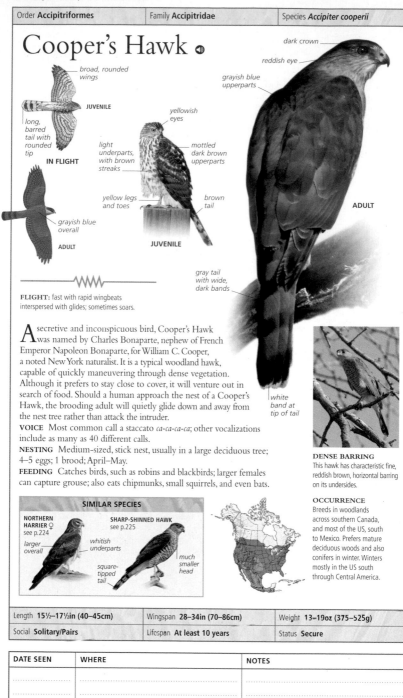

dark crown
reddish eye

grayish blue upperparts

broad, rounded wings

JUVENILE

long, barred tail with rounded tip
IN FLIGHT

yellowish eyes

light underparts, with brown streaks

mottled dark brown upperparts

yellow legs and toes
brown tail

grayish blue overall
ADULT

JUVENILE

ADULT

gray tail with wide, dark bands

FLIGHT: fast with rapid wingbeats interspersed with glides; sometimes soars.

A secretive and inconspicuous bird, Cooper's Hawk was named by Charles Bonaparte, nephew of French Emperor Napoleon Bonaparte, for William C. Cooper, a noted New York naturalist. It is a typical woodland hawk, capable of quickly maneuvering through dense vegetation. Although it prefers to stay close to cover, it will venture out in search of food. Should a human approach the nest of a Cooper's Hawk, the brooding adult will quietly glide down and away from the nest tree rather than attack the intruder.

white band at tip of tail

VOICE Most common call a staccato *ca-ca-ca-ca*; other vocalizations include as many as 40 different calls.

NESTING Medium-sized, stick nest, usually in a large deciduous tree; 4–5 eggs; 1 brood; April–May.

FEEDING Catches birds, such as robins and blackbirds; larger females can capture grouse; also eats chipmunks, small squirrels, and even bats.

DENSE BARRING
This hawk has characteristic fine, reddish brown, horizontal barring on its undersides.

OCCURRENCE
Breeds in woodlands across southern Canada, and most of the US, south to Mexico. Prefers mature deciduous woods and also conifers in winter. Winters mostly in the US south through Central America.

SIMILAR SPECIES

NORTHERN HARRIER ♀
see p.224
larger overall

SHARP-SHINNED HAWK
see p.225
whitish underparts
much smaller head
square-tipped tail

| Length **15½–17½in (40–45cm)** | Wingspan **28–34in (70–86cm)** | Weight **13–19oz (375–525g)** |
| Social **Solitary/Pairs** | Lifespan **At least 10 years** | Status **Secure** |

DATE SEEN	WHERE	NOTES

| Order **Accipitriformes** | Family **Accipitridae** | Species *Accipiter gentilis* |

Northern Goshawk

speckled back

light yellow iris

buff underparts with vertical streaks

JUVENILE

fairly short, rounded wings

ADULT

barred underwings

JUVENILE

conspicuous white stripe above eye

yellow to orange eye

slate-gray upperparts

long tail

brown bars on tail

IN FLIGHT

slate-gray tail

ADULT

conspicuous dark barring on underparts

yellow legs and toes

FLIGHT: fast, direct flight with swift wingbeats and alternating glides; occasionally soars.

The powerful and agile Northern Goshawk is secretive by nature and not easily observed, even in regions where it is common. It has few natural enemies, but will defend its territories, nests, and young fiercely, by repeatedly diving and screaming at intruders that get too close. Spring hikers and turkey-hunters occasionally discover Northern Goshawks by wandering into their territory and being driven off by the angry occupants.

VOICE Loud, high-pitched *gek-gek-gek* when agitated.
NESTING Large stick structures lined with bark and plant matter in the mid- to lower region of trees; 1–3 eggs; 1 brood; May–June.
FEEDING Sits and waits on perch before diving rapidly; preys on birds as large as grouse and pheasants; also mammals, including hares and squirrels.

OCCASIONAL SOARER
A juvenile Northern Goshawk takes advantage of a thermal, soaring over its territory.

OCCURRENCE
Breeds in deep deciduous, coniferous, and mixed woodlands in northern North America, from the tundra–taiga border south to California, northern Mexico, and Pennsylvania in the eastern US, absent from east-central US. The Northern Goshawk is widespread in northern Eurasia.

SIMILAR SPECIES

GYRFALCON (GRAY FORM) see p.263

longer, pointed wings

COOPER'S HAWK see p.226

no streaks on underparts

brownish upperparts

streaked underparts

| Length **21in (53cm)** | Wingspan **3½ft (1.1m)** | Weight **2–3lb (0.9–1.4kg)** |
| Social **Solitary/Pairs** | Lifespan **Up to 20 years** | Status **Secure** |

DATE SEEN	WHERE	NOTES

| Order **Accipitriformes** | Family **Accipitridae** | Species *Haliaeetus leucocephalus* |

Bald Eagle 🔊

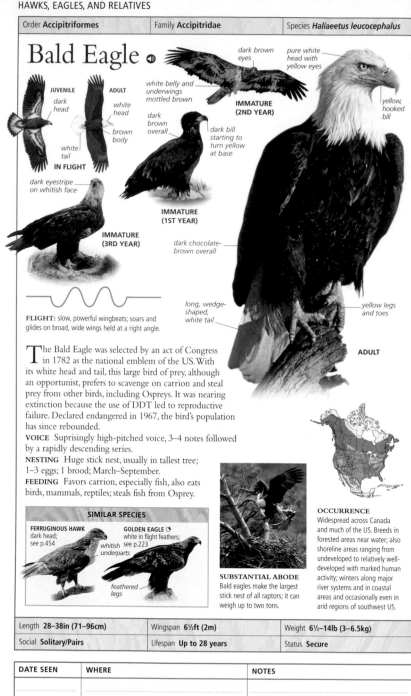

dark brown eyes

pure white head with yellow eyes

white belly and underwings mottled brown

IMMATURE (2ND YEAR)

yellow, hooked bill

JUVENILE dark head

ADULT white head

brown body

white tail

IN FLIGHT

dark brown overall

dark bill starting to turn yellow at base

IMMATURE (1ST YEAR)

dark eyestripe on whitish face

IMMATURE (3RD YEAR)

dark chocolate-brown overall

long, wedge-shaped, white tail

yellow legs and toes

ADULT

FLIGHT: slow, powerful wingbeats; soars and glides on broad, wide wings held at a right angle.

The Bald Eagle was selected by an act of Congress in 1782 as the national emblem of the US. With its white head and tail, this large bird of prey, although an opportunist, prefers to scavenge on carrion and steal prey from other birds, including Ospreys. It was nearing extinction because the use of DDT led to reproductive failure. Declared endangered in 1967, the bird's population has since rebounded.

VOICE Suprisingly high-pitched voice, 3–4 notes followed by a rapidly descending series.

NESTING Huge stick nest, usually in tallest tree; 1–3 eggs; 1 brood; March–September.

FEEDING Favors carrion, especially fish, also eats birds, mammals, reptiles; steals fish from Osprey.

SUBSTANTIAL ABODE Bald eagles make the largest stick nest of all raptors; it can weigh up to two tons.

OCCURRENCE Widespread across Canada and much of the US. Breeds in forested areas near water; also shoreline areas ranging from undeveloped to relatively well-developed with marked human activity; winters along major river systems and in coastal areas and occasionally even in arid regions of southwest US.

SIMILAR SPECIES

FERRUGINOUS HAWK dark head; see p.454

whitish underparts

GOLDEN EAGLE ☉ white in flight feathers; see p.223

feathered legs

| Length **28–38in (71–96cm)** | Wingspan **6½ft (2m)** | Weight **6½–14lb (3–6.5kg)** |
| Social **Solitary/Pairs** | Lifespan **Up to 28 years** | Status **Secure** |

DATE SEEN	WHERE	NOTES

| Order **Accipitriformes** | Family **Accipitridae** | Species ***Ictinia mississippiensis*** |

Mississippi Kite

white patch on inner wing feathers

unbarred, black tail

ADULT

flecked, brownish gray overall

dark gray upperparts

JUVENILE

pale gray head with conspicuous dark eye patch

brick-red eye

dark gray upperparts

brownish upperparts

JUVENILE

IN FLIGHT

long wings

SUB-ADULT

FLIGHT: regular wingbeats interspersed with glides; often soars with flight feathers extended.

The Mississippi Kite is locally abundant and nests in colonies in the central and southern Great Plains, but is less common and less colonial in the southeastern US. Foraging flocks of 25 or more individuals are common, and groups of ten or more roost near nests. In the West, the species nests in urban habitats, including city parks and golf courses. These urban birds can be aggressive, even attacking humans who venture too close to their nest. This graceful bird pursues its insect prey in flight. Mississippi Kites are long-distance migrants, wintering in South America.

VOICE High-pitched *phee-phew*; also multisyllabled *phee-ti-ti*.
NESTING Circular to oval nest of dead twigs, built in dead or well-foliaged tree; 1–3 eggs; 1 brood; March–July.
FEEDING Eats medium to large insects; also frogs, toads, lizards, box turtles, snakes, small birds, terrestrial mammals, and bats.

HIGH FLYING
Despite their falcon-like shape, these birds spend much of their time soaring, rather than perched

SIMILAR SPECIES

PEREGRINE FALCON see p.264

dark head

prominent black "mustache"

larger overall

WHITE-TAILED KITE see p.221

dark shoulder patch

white underparts

OCCURRENCE
In the East, mostly mature bottomland forest or riverside woodland with open habitat nearby for foraging. Birds in the central and southern Great Plains prefer areas with numerous shelterbelts (windbreaks). Western birds use both rural woodland and suburban or urban habitat.

| Length **13–15in (33–38cm)** | Wingspan **35in (89cm)** | Weight **8–14oz (225–400g)** |
| Social **Colonies** | Lifespan **At least 8 years** | Status **Secure** |

DATE SEEN	WHERE	NOTES

| Order **Accipitriformes** | Family **Accipitridae** | Species *Buteo lineatus* |

Red-shouldered Hawk 🔊

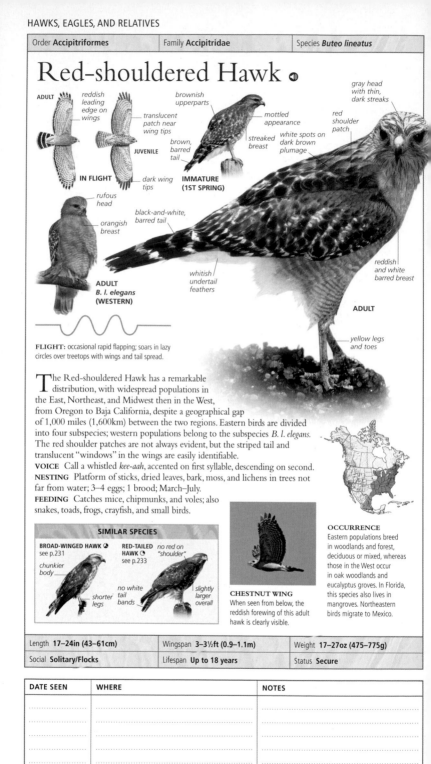

ADULT

reddish leading edge on wings

translucent patch near wing tips

JUVENILE

brown, barred tail

IN FLIGHT

dark wing tips

brownish upperparts

mottled appearance

streaked breast

white spots on dark brown plumage

IMMATURE (1ST SPRING)

gray head with thin, dark streaks

red shoulder patch

rufous head

orangish breast

black-and-white, barred tail

whitish undertail feathers

ADULT
B. l. elegans
(WESTERN)

reddish and white barred breast

ADULT

yellow legs and toes

FLIGHT: occasional rapid flapping; soars in lazy circles over treetops with wings and tail spread.

The Red-shouldered Hawk has a remarkable distribution, with widespread populations in the East, Northeast, and Midwest then in the West, from Oregon to Baja California, despite a geographical gap of 1,000 miles (1,600km) between the two regions. Eastern birds are divided into four subspecies; western populations belong to the subspecies *B. l. elegans*. The red shoulder patches are not always evident, but the striped tail and translucent "windows" in the wings are easily identifiable.

VOICE Call a whistled *kee-aah*, accented on first syllable, descending on second.
NESTING Platform of sticks, dried leaves, bark, moss, and lichens in trees not far from water; 3–4 eggs; 1 brood; March–July.
FEEDING Catches mice, chipmunks, and voles; also snakes, toads, frogs, crayfish, and small birds.

SIMILAR SPECIES

BROAD-WINGED HAWK 🔊
see p.231

chunkier body

shorter legs

RED-TAILED HAWK 🔊
see p.233

no red on "shoulder"

no white tail bands

slightly larger overall

CHESTNUT WING
When seen from below, the reddish forewing of this adult hawk is clearly visible.

OCCURRENCE
Eastern populations breed in woodlands and forest, deciduous or mixed, whereas those in the West occur in oak woodlands and eucalyptus groves. In Florida, this species also lives in mangroves. Northeastern birds migrate to Mexico.

| Length **17–24in (43–61cm)** | Wingspan **3–3½ft (0.9–1.1m)** | Weight **17–27oz (475–775g)** |
| Social **Solitary/Flocks** | Lifespan **Up to 18 years** | Status **Secure** |

DATE SEEN	WHERE	NOTES

| Order **Accipitriformes** | Family **Accipitridae** | Species *Buteo platypterus* |

Broad-winged Hawk

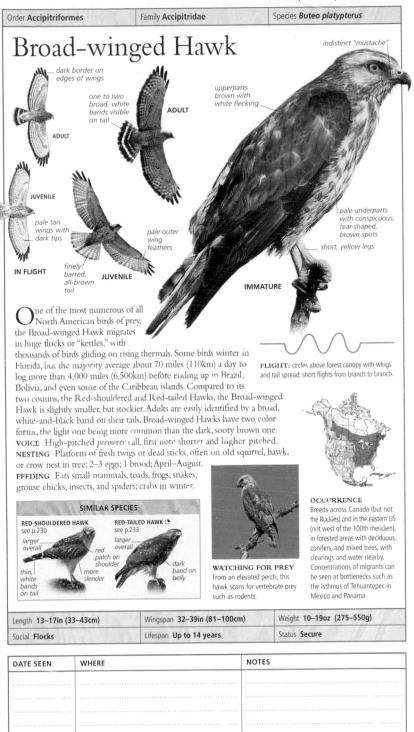

indistinct "mustache"

dark border on edges of wings

ADULT

one to two broad, white bands visible on tail

upperparts brown with white flecking

ADULT

JUVENILE

pale tan wings with dark tips

pale outer wing feathers

pale underparts with conspicuous, tear-shaped, brown spots

short, yellow legs

IN FLIGHT

finely barred, all-brown tail

JUVENILE

IMMATURE

One of the most numerous of all North American birds of prey, the Broad-winged Hawk migrates in huge flocks or "kettles," with thousands of birds gliding on rising thermals. Some birds winter in Florida, but the majority average about 70 miles (110km) a day to log more than 4,000 miles (6,500km) before ending up in Brazil, Bolivia, and even some of the Caribbean islands. Compared to its two cousins, the Red-shouldered and Red-tailed Hawks, the Broad-winged Hawk is slightly smaller, but stockier. Adults are easily identified by a broad, white-and-black band on their tails. Broad-winged Hawks have two color forms, the light one being more common than the dark, sooty brown one.
VOICE High-pitched *peeoweee* call, first note shorter and higher pitched.
NESTING Platform of fresh twigs or dead sticks, often on old squirrel, hawk, or crow nest in tree; 2–3 eggs; 1 brood; April–August.
FEEDING Eats small mammals, toads, frogs, snakes, grouse chicks, insects, and spiders; crabs in winter.

FLIGHT: circles above forest canopy with wings and tail spread; short flights from branch to branch.

SIMILAR SPECIES

RED-SHOULDERED HAWK
see p.230

larger overall

thin, white bands on tail

red patch on shoulder

RED-TAILED HAWK ◐
see p.233

larger overall

more slender

dark band on belly

WATCHING FOR PREY
From an elevated perch, this hawk scans for vertebrate prey such as rodents.

OCCURRENCE
Breeds across Canada (but not the Rockies) and in the eastern US (not west of the 100th meridian), in forested areas with deciduous, conifers, and mixed trees, with clearings and water nearby. Concentrations of migrants can be seen at bottlenecks such as the Isthmus of Tehuantepec in Mexico and Panama.

| Length **13–17in (33–43cm)** | Wingspan **32–39in (81–100cm)** | Weight **10–19oz (275–550g)** |
| Social **Flocks** | Lifespan **Up to 14 years** | Status **Secure** |

DATE SEEN	WHERE	NOTES

Order **Accipitriformes**	Family **Accipitridae**	Species *Buteo swainsoni*

Swainson's Hawk

long pointed wings

dark wing tips

ADULT (LIGHT FORM)

JUVENILE (LIGHT FORM)

dark chest

IN FLIGHT

whitish head

spotted underparts

JUVENILE (LIGHT FORM)

reddish breast and belly

slender shape overall

white face and chin

dark brown head and breast

spotted underparts

ADULT (DARK FORM)

ADULT (INTERMEDIATE FORM)

longish tail

wing tips reach end of tail when perched

pale reddish upper chest

white underbelly

ADULT (LIGHT FORM)

FLIGHT: soaring, buoyant flight with deep wingbeats; will often hover and hang motionless.

Swainson's Hawk is perhaps most famous for its spectacular 6,000-mile (9,650km) fall migration from the Canadian prairies to the lower regions of South America, when thousands can be observed soaring in the air at any one time. While migrating, this hawk averages 125 miles (200km) a day. There are three color forms: light, dark, and an intermediate form between the two.

VOICE Alarm call a shrill, plaintive scream *kreeeee* given by both sexes; high-pitched *keeeoooo* fading at the end.

NESTING Bulky, flimsy pile of sticks or various debris, in solitary tree or on utility poles; 1–4 eggs; 1 brood; April–July.

FEEDING Eats ground squirrels, pocket gophers, mice, voles, bats, rabbits; also snakes, lizards, songbirds.

SIMILAR SPECIES

HARRIS'S HAWK
see p.453

RED-TAILED HAWK
see p.233

bulkier overall

chestnut thighs and wing patches

shorter wings

long legs

white on tail

red tail

ON THE LOOKOUT
This slim, elegant species will perch before diving for its prey.

OCCURRENCE
Breeds in scattered trees along streams; found in areas of open woodland, sparse shrubland, grasslands, and agricultural land; winters in native Argentinian grassland, and in harvested fields where grasshoppers are found abundantly.

Length **19–22in (48–56cm)**	Wingspan **4½ft (1.4m)**	Weight **1½–3lb (0.7–1.4kg)**
Social **Solitary/Pairs/Flocks**	Lifespan **Up to 19 years**	Status **Declining (p)**

DATE SEEN	WHERE	NOTES

| Order **Accipitriformes** | Family **Accipitridae** | Species ***Buteo jamaicensis*** |

Red-tailed Hawk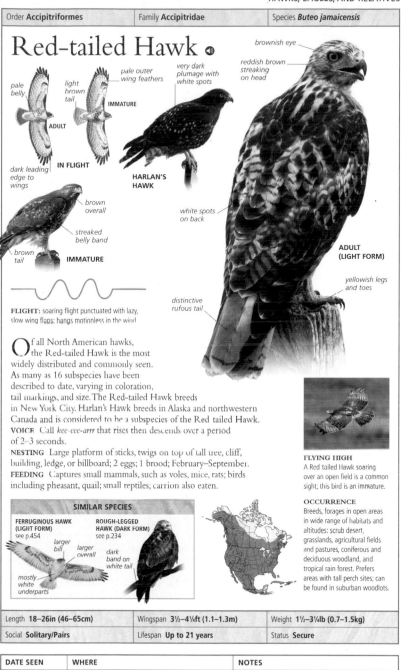

brownish eye

reddish brown streaking on head

IN FLIGHT

pale belly

light brown tail

pale outer wing feathers

very dark plumage with white spots

ADULT

IMMATURE

dark leading edge to wings

brown overall

HARLAN'S HAWK

white spots on back

streaked belly band

brown tail **IMMATURE**

ADULT (LIGHT FORM)

yellowish legs and toes

distinctive rufous tail

FLIGHT: soaring flight punctuated with lazy, slow wing flaps; hangs motionless in the wind

Of all North American hawks, the Red-tailed Hawk is the most widely distributed and commonly seen. As many as 16 subspecies have been described to date, varying in coloration, tail markings, and size. The Red-tailed Hawk breeds in New York City. Harlan's Hawk breeds in Alaska and northwestern Canada and is considered to be a subspecies of the Red-tailed Hawk.

VOICE Call *kee-eee-arrr* that rises then descends over a period of 2–3 seconds.

NESTING Large platform of sticks, twigs on top of tall tree, cliff, building, ledge, or billboard; 2 eggs; 1 brood; February–September.

FEEDING Captures small mammals, such as voles, mice, rats; birds including pheasant, quail; small reptiles; carrion also eaten.

FLYING HIGH
A Red-tailed Hawk soaring over an open field is a common sight; this bird is an immature.

SIMILAR SPECIES

FERRUGINOUS HAWK (LIGHT FORM) see p.454

larger bill

mostly white underparts

larger overall

ROUGH-LEGGED HAWK (DARK FORM) see p.234

dark band on white tail

OCCURRENCE
Breeds, forages in open areas in wide range of habitats and altitudes: scrub desert, grasslands, agricultural fields and pastures, coniferous and deciduous woodland, and tropical rain forest. Prefers areas with tall perch sites; can be found in suburban woodlots.

| Length **18–26in (46–65cm)** | Wingspan **3½–4¼ft (1.1–1.3m)** | Weight **1½–3¼lb (0.7–1.5kg)** |
| Social **Solitary/Pairs** | Lifespan **Up to 21 years** | Status **Secure** |

DATE SEEN	WHERE	NOTES

| Order **Accipitriformes** | Family **Accipitridae** | Species ***Buteo lagopus*** |

Rough-legged Hawk

dark wing tips

ADULT

dark tail band

IN FLIGHT

bold black patch

FEMALE

black trailing edge

one line before tail tip

pale forehead

short, broad head

MALE

JUVENILE

black belly

barred underparts

thin bands near tail tip

white tail with faint black band at tip

plain gray brown or frosty feather edges

MALE

FLIGHT: strong wingbeats; usually soars on thermals; frequently hovers in one spot.

The Rough-legged Hawk is known for its extensive variation in plumage—some individuals are almost completely black, whereas others are much paler, very nearly cream or white. The year to year fluctuation in numbers of breeding pairs in a given region strongly suggest that this species is nomadic, moving about as a response to the availability of its rodent prey.

VOICE Wintering birds silent; breeding birds utter loud, cat-like mewing or thin whistles, slurred downward when alarmed.

NESTING Bulky mass of sticks, lined with grasses, sedges, feathers and fur from prey, constructed on cliff ledge; 2–6 eggs; 1 brood; April–August.

FEEDING Hovers in one spot over fields in search of prey; lemmings and voles in spring and summer; mice and shrews in winters; variety of birds, ground squirrels, and rabbits year-round.

ABUNDANT FOOD SUPPLY
When small mammals are abundant, these hawks produce large broods on cliff ledges in the tundra.

SIMILAR SPECIES

NORTHERN HARRIER ♂
see p.224

reddish underparts

longer wings

FERRUGINOUS HAWK
see p.454

reddish upperparts

white underparts

OCCURRENCE
Breeds in rough, open country with low crags and cliffs, in high subarctic and Arctic regions; found on the edge of extensive forest or forest clearings, and in treeless tundra, uplands, and alpine habitats. Winters in open areas with fields, marshes, and rough grasslands.

| Length **19–20in (48–51cm)** | Wingspan **4¼–4½ft (1.3–1.4m)** | Weight **1½–3lb (0.7–1.4kg)** |
| Social **Solitary** | Lifespan **Up to 18 years** | Status **Secure** |

DATE SEEN	WHERE	NOTES

OWLS

OWLS HAVE FASCINATED humans throughout history, partly because of their nocturnal habits and eerie cries. They are placed in the order Strigiformes, and two families are represented in North America: the Barn Owl is classified in Tytonidae, other North American owl species are in the Strigidae. Most owls are active primarily at night and have developed adaptations for living in low-light environments. Their large eyes are sensitive enough to see in the dark, and face forward to maximize binocular vision. Since the eyes are fixed in their sockets, a flexible neck helps owls turn

OWL AT TWILIGHT
The best time to see the nocturnal Barn Owl is often at dawn or dusk.

their heads almost 180° toward a direction of interest. Ears are offset on each side of the head to help identify the source of a sound. A few species have "ear" tufts but they are for visual effect only and are unrelated to hearing. Many owls have serrations on the forward edges of their flight feathers to cushion airflow, so their flight is silent while stalking prey. All North American owls are predatory to some degree and they inhabit most areas of the continent. The Burrowing Owl is unique in that it hunts during the day and nests underground.

BIG HORNS
The "ear" tufts of the Great Horned Owl are taller than those of other "tufted" owls.

SNOW SWOOP
The Great Gray Owl can hunt by sound alone, allowing it to locate and capture prey hidden even beneath a thick snow cover.

Order **Strigiformes**	Family **Tytonidae**	Species **Tyto alba**

Barn Owl 🔊

barring on wings and tail

ADULT

head lacks "ear" tufts

long wings

ADULT

IN FLIGHT

dark eyes

ruff surrounds facial disk

ADULT

relatively small eyes

rounded, heart-shaped facial disk

pale buff upperparts

gray and black spots

white underparts

feathered legs

FLIGHT: irregular bursts of flapping, interspersed with short glides, banking, doubling back, fluttering.

Aptly named, the Barn Owl inhabits old sheds, sheltered rafters, and empty buildings in rural fields. With its affinity for human settlement, and 32 subspecies, this owl has an extensive range covering every continent except Antarctica. Although widespread, the Barn Owl is secretive. Primarily nocturnal, it can fly undetected until its screeching call pierces the air. The Barn Owl is endangered in several Midwestern states as a result of modern farming practices, which have decimated prey populations and reduced the number of barns for nesting.

VOICE Typical call loud, raspy, screeching shriek, *shkreee,* often given in flight; also clicking sounds associated with courtship.

NESTING Unlined cavity in tree, cave, building, hay bale, or nest box; 5–7 eggs; 1–2 broods; March–September.

FEEDING Hunts on the wing for small rodents such as mice; research reveals it can detect the slightest rustle made by prey even in total darkness.

NOCTURNAL HUNTER
The Barn Owl hunts at night for small rodents, but may be seen before sunset feeding its young.

OCCURRENCE
In North America breeds from northwestern and northeastern US south to Mexico. Resident in all except very north of range. Prefers open habitats, such as desert, grassland, and fields, wherever prey and suitable nest sites are available. Generally not found in mountainous or heavily forested areas.

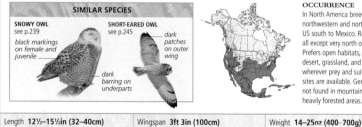

SIMILAR SPECIES

SNOWY OWL
see p.239

black markings on female and juvenile

SHORT-EARED OWL
see p.245

dark patches on outer wing

dark barring on underparts

Length **12½–15½in (32–40cm)**	Wingspan **3ft 3in (100cm)**	Weight **14–25oz (400–700g)**
Social **Solitary**	Lifespan **Up to 8 years**	Status **Declining**

DATE SEEN	WHERE	NOTES
....	....	....
....	....	....
....	....	....
....	....	....
....	....	....

| Order **Strigiformes** | Family **Strigidae** | Species *Megascops asio* |

Eastern Screech-Owl 🔊

"ear" tufts

yellow eyes

dark gray bars on short, rounded wings

ADULT

white spots on inner wing feathers

short tail **IN FLIGHT**

streaked underparts

ADULT (GRAY FORM)

feathered legs

FLIGHT: direct, purposeful flight; straight with steady wingbeats, typically below tree cover.

This widespread little owl has adapted to suburban areas, and its distinctive call is a familiar sound across the eastern US at almost any time of the year. An entirely nocturnal species, it may be found roosting (and hidden) during the day in a birdhouse or tree cavity. With gray and red color forms, this species shows considerable plumage variation. The relatively high mortality rate of Eastern Screech-Owls, especially juveniles, is caused in part by predation by Great Horned Owls and collisions with motor vehicles.

VOICE Most familiar call a descending whinny and often used in movie soundtracks, also an even trill; occasional barks and screeches; female higher-pitched than male.
NESTING No nest; lays eggs in cavity in tree, woodpecker hole, rotted snag, nest box; 2–6 eggs; 1 brood; March–August.
FEEDING Captures prey with toes; eats insects, earthworms, rodents, songbirds, crayfish, small fish, frogs, snakes, and lizards.

STANDING OUT
The striking red color form of the Eastern Screech-Owl is less common than the gray.

SIMILAR SPECIES

BOREAL OWL see p.246
brown back

no ear tufts

NORTHERN SAW-WHET OWL see p.247
white spots
long brown streaks

OCCURRENCE
In the US and southern Canada, breeds in a variety of lowland wooded areas east of the Rockies. Also breeds south to northeastern Mexico. Can be found in suburban and urban parks and gardens; avoids mountain forests above 1,000ft (300m).

| Length **6½–10in (16–25cm)** | Wingspan **19–24in (48–61cm)** | Weight **5–7oz (150–200g)** |
| Social **Solitary** | Lifespan **Up to 13 years** | Status **Secure** |

DATE SEEN	WHERE	NOTES

Order **Strigiformes**	Family **Strigidae**	Species ***Bubo virginianus***

Great Horned Owl 🔊

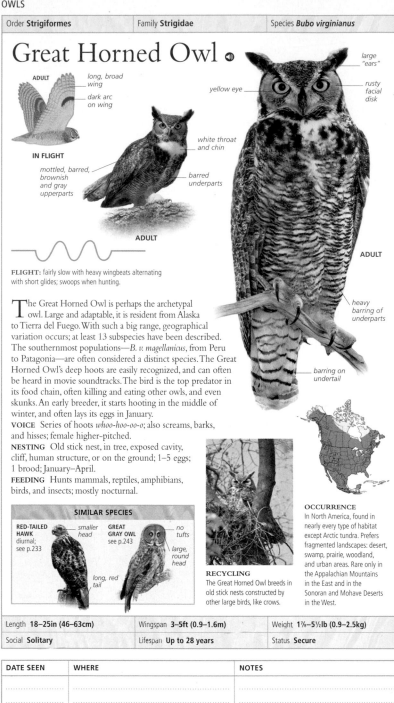

large "ears"

ADULT

long, broad wing

dark arc on wing

yellow eye

rusty facial disk

IN FLIGHT

white throat and chin

mottled, barred, brownish and gray upperparts

barred underparts

ADULT

ADULT

heavy barring of underparts

barring on undertail

FLIGHT: fairly slow with heavy wingbeats alternating with short glides; swoops when hunting.

The Great Horned Owl is perhaps the archetypal owl. Large and adaptable, it is resident from Alaska to Tierra del Fuego. With such a big range, geographical variation occurs; at least 13 subspecies have been described. The southernmost populations—*B. v. magellanicus*, from Peru to Patagonia—are often considered a distinct species. The Great Horned Owl's deep hoots are easily recognized, and can often be heard in movie soundtracks. The bird is the top predator in its food chain, often killing and eating other owls, and even skunks. An early breeder, it starts hooting in the middle of winter, and often lays its eggs in January.

VOICE Series of hoots *whoo-hoo-oo-o*; also screams, barks, and hisses; female higher-pitched.

NESTING Old stick nest, in tree, exposed cavity, cliff, human structure, or on the ground; 1–5 eggs; 1 brood; January–April.

FEEDING Hunts mammals, reptiles, amphibians, birds, and insects; mostly nocturnal.

SIMILAR SPECIES

RED-TAILED HAWK diurnal; see p.233

smaller head

long, red tail

GREAT GRAY OWL see p.243

no tufts

large, round head

RECYCLING
The Great Horned Owl breeds in old stick nests constructed by other large birds, like crows.

OCCURRENCE
In North America, found in nearly every type of habitat except Arctic tundra. Prefers fragmented landscapes: desert, swamp, prairie, woodland, and urban areas. Rare only in the Appalachian Mountains in the East and in the Sonoran and Mohave Deserts in the West.

Length **18–25in (46–63cm)**	Wingspan **3–5ft (0.9–1.6m)**	Weight **1¾–5½lb (0.9–2.5kg)**
Social **Solitary**	Lifespan **Up to 28 years**	Status **Secure**

DATE SEEN	WHERE	NOTES
....	....	....
....	....	....
....	....	....
....	....	....
....	....	....

| Order **Strigiformes** | Family **Strigidae** | Species *Bubo scandiacus* |

Snowy Owl

white face

flecked gray-brown

IMMATURE

IN FLIGHT

variably barred underparts

large round head

yellow eyes

dusky barring

JUVENILE

variable barring on wings

nearly all-white breast

feathered legs and toes

ADULT (FEMALE)

FLIGHT: slow, steady flight with strong, deep wingbeats; flaps interspersed with glides.

An icon of the far north and Québec's Provincial Bird, the Snowy Owl occasionally appears far to the south of its usual range, making an eyecatching addition to the local landscape. This is a bird of the open tundra, where it hunts from headlands or hummocks and nests on the ground. In such a harsh environment, the Snowy Owl largely depends on lemmings for prey. It is fiercely territorial, and will valiantly defend its young in the nest even against larger animals, such as the Arctic Fox.

VOICE Deep hoots, doubled or given in a short series, usually by male; also rattles, whistles, and hisses.

NESTING Scrape in ground vegetation or dirt, with no lining; 3–12 eggs; 1 brood; May–September.

FEEDING Mostly hunts lemmings, but takes whatever other small mammals, birds, and occasionally fish it can find.

SNOWY MALE
Some adult males show no barring at all and have pure white plumage.

SIMILAR SPECIES

BARN OWL
see p.236

black eyes

golden brown

SHORT-EARED OWL
see p.245

mottled brown markings

larger overall

OCCURRENCE
Breeds in the tundra of Eurasia and northern North America, north to Ellesmere Island; North American birds winter south to the Great Plains. In some years, many North American birds winter south of their normal range, including in dunes, marshes, and airfields, as far south as Florida and California.

| Length **20–27in (51–68cm)** | Wingspan **4¼–5¼ft (1.3–1.6m)** | Weight **3½–6½lb (1.6–2.9kg)** |
| Social **Solitary** | Lifespan **Up to 9 years** | Status **Vulnerable** |

DATE SEEN	WHERE	NOTES

Order **Strigiformes**	Family **Strigidae**	Species *Surnia ulula*

Northern Hawk Owl

fine spotting on forehead and crown

yellowish eyes

black line around white face

brownish black upperparts

heavy white marking

ADULT

long wings

patterned face

whitish facial disks

long tail **IN FLIGHT**

heavy barring below

ADULT

regularly barred underparts

ADULT

Whether swooping low through a bog or perching at the tip of a branch, the Northern Hawk Owl is as falcon-like as it is owl-like, being streamlined, a powerful flier, and an active daytime hunter. It is patchily distributed across the northern North American forests, far from most human settlements, so is seldom seen—and is not well studied—on its breeding grounds. In winter, the bird is somewhat nomadic and is occasionally seen south of its breeding range for a few days or weeks in southern Canada and the northern US.

VOICE Ascending, whistled, drawn-out trill; also chirps, screeches, and yelps.

NESTING Cavities, hollows, broken-off branches, old stick nests, nest boxes; 3–13 eggs; 1 brood; April–August.

FEEDING Swoops like a falcon, from an elevated perch, to pounce on prey; preys mainly on rodents in summer, and on grouse and ptarmigan in winter.

FLIGHT: powerful, deep wingbeats; glides; highly maneuverable, occasionally soars.

KEEN-EYED OWL
This owl hunts mainly by sight, swooping down on prey spotted from a high perch.

OCCURRENCE
Breeds across the forests of northern Canada, from Alaska to Québec and Newfoundland, in sparse woodland or mixed conifer forest with swamps, bogs, burned areas, or storm damage. In winter occasionally moves south to southern Canada, Great Lakes region and New England.

SIMILAR SPECIES		
MERLIN see p.262 *small head* *smaller overall* *buffy orange underneath*	**GREAT HORNED OWL** see p.238 *chunky shape*	*"ear" tufts* *much larger overall*

Length **14–17½in (36–44cm)**	Wingspan **31in (80cm)**	Weight **11–12oz (300–350g)**
Social **Family groups**	Lifespan **Up to 10 years**	Status **Secure**

DATE SEEN	WHERE	NOTES

Order **Strigiformes**	Family **Strigidae**	Species *Athene cunicularia*

Burrowing Owl

short, rounded wings

ADULT

white streaking on forehead and crown

IN FLIGHT

brown ear feathers

short tail

ADULT

chest spotted with white

short tail

yellow eyes

white contrasting with dark brown band below

brown upperparts with white spotting

white spots

brown streaks on lower belly

ADULT

short tail

long, feathered legs

FLIGHT. buoyant, often undulating; close to ground; sometimes hovers while hunting.

The Burrowing Owl is unique among North American owls in nesting underground. Usually it uses the abandoned burrows of prairie dogs, ground squirrels, armadillos, badgers, and other mammals. Where such burrows are scarce, however—in built-up areas of Florida, notably—it excavates its own burrow, digging out the soil with its bill and scraping it away with its toes. Usually it nests in loose colonies, too. Active by day or night, the Burrowing Owl hunts prey on foot or on the wing. Populations of the bird in southern areas of North America tend to stay there year-round, but those farther north move south to Mexico for the winter.

VOICE *Coo-cooo*, or *ha-haaa*, with accent on second syllable; also clucks, chatters, warbles, and screams.

NESTING Cavity lined with grass, feathers, sometimes animal dung, at end of burrow; 8–10 eggs; 1 brood; March–August.

FEEDING Walks, hops, runs, hovers, or flies from perch to capture mainly insects, and occasionally small mammals, birds, reptiles, and amphibians.

ON THE ALERT
A Burrowing Owl keeps watch from the entrance of its burrow, which can be 10ft (3m) long.

SIMILAR SPECIES

SHORT-EARED OWL
see p.245
larger overall

streaked below

OCCURRENCE
Breeds in Florida, the western US, and southwestern Canada, in a wide range of open, well-drained habitats not prone to flooding, including pastures, plains, deserts, grasslands, and steppes, but also developed area, up to about 6,500ft (2,000m). Partial migrant.

Length **7½–10in (19–25cm)**	Wingspan **21½in (55cm)**	Weight **5oz (150g)**
Social **Loose colonies**	Lifespan **Up to 9 years**	Status **Declining**

DATE SEEN	WHERE	NOTES

| Order **Strigiformes** | Family **Strigidae** | Species *Strix varia* |

Barred Owl 🔊

rounded wings

ADULT

IN FLIGHT

large round head

dark eyes

conspicuously yellowish bill

brown upperparts

heavy white spotting

ADULT

barred tail

barring on breast

streaking on belly

ADULT

FLIGHT: glides silently among trees, interspersed with flaps; rarely hovers.

The Barred Owl is more adaptable and aggressive than its close relative the Spotted Owl. Recent range expansions have brought the two species into closer contact, which has resulted in the Barred Owl displacing the Spotted Owl, as well as occasional interbreeding. The Barred Owl is mostly nocturnal, but may also call or hunt during the day.

VOICE Series of hoots in rhythm: *who-cooks-for-you*, *who-cooks-for-you-all*; also pair duetting (at different pitches), cawing, cackling, and guttural sounds.

NESTING No nest; lays eggs in broken-off branches, cavities, old stick nests; 1–5 eggs; 1 brood; January–September.

FEEDING Perches quietly and waits to spot prey below, then pounces; eats small mammals, birds, amphibians, reptiles, insects, and spiders.

WOODED HABITATS
The Barred Owl is very much at home in dense woodlands, including conifer forests.

OCCURRENCE
Widespread, though not evenly so, in North America from British Columbia across to the Maritimes and much of the eastern US. Found in a variety of wooded habitats— from cypress swamps in the South to conifer rain forest in the Northwest—and in mixed hardwoods.

SIMILAR SPECIES

GREAT HORNED OWL
see p.238

"ear" tufts

SPOTTED OWL

yellow eyes

larger overall

horizontal barring on underparts

pale oval bars

longer tail

| Length **17–19½in (43–50cm)** | Wingspan **3½ft (1.1m)** | Weight **17–37oz (475–1,050g)** |
| Social **Solitary** | Lifespan **Up to 18 years** | Status **Secure** |

DATE SEEN	WHERE	NOTES

| Order **Strigiformes** | Family **Strigidae** | Species ***Strix nebulosa*** |

Great Gray Owl

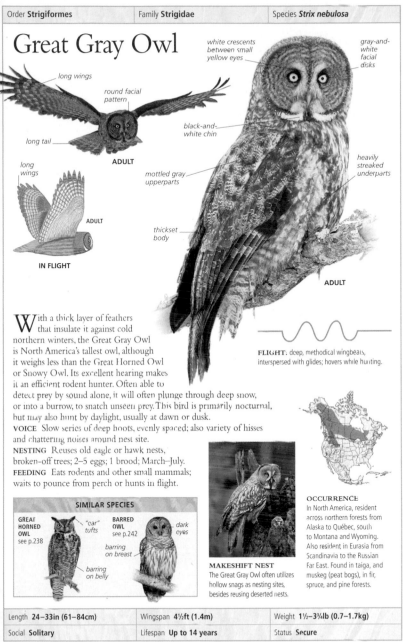

white crescents between small yellow eyes

gray-and-white facial disks

long wings

round facial pattern

black-and-white chin

long tail

ADULT

long wings

heavily streaked underparts

mottled gray upperparts

ADULT

IN FLIGHT

thickset body

ADULT

With a thick layer of feathers that insulate it against cold northern winters, the Great Gray Owl is North America's tallest owl, although it weighs less than the Great Horned Owl or Snowy Owl. Its excellent hearing makes it an efficient rodent hunter. Often able to detect prey by sound alone, it will often plunge through deep snow, or into a burrow, to snatch unseen prey. This bird is primarily nocturnal, but may also hunt by daylight, usually at dawn or dusk.

FLIGHT. deep, methodical wingbeats, interspersed with glides; hovers while hunting.

VOICE Slow series of deep hoots, evenly spaced; also variety of hisses and chattering noises around nest site.
NESTING Reuses old eagle or hawk nests, broken-off trees; 2–5 eggs; 1 brood; March–July.
FEEDING Eats rodents and other small mammals; waits to pounce from perch or hunts in flight.

SIMILAR SPECIES

| GREAT HORNED OWL see p.238 | "ear" tufts | BARRED OWL see p.242 | dark eyes |

barring on breast

barring on belly

MAKESHIFT NEST
The Great Gray Owl often utilizes hollow snags as nesting sites, besides reusing deserted nests.

OCCURRENCE
In North America, resident across northern forests from Alaska to Québec, south to Montana and Wyoming. Also resident in Eurasia from Scandinavia to the Russian Far East. Found in taiga, and muskeg (peat bogs), in fir, spruce, and pine forests.

| Length **24–33in (61–84cm)** | Wingspan **4½ft (1.4m)** | Weight **1½–3¾lb (0.7–1.7kg)** |
| Social **Solitary** | Lifespan **Up to 14 years** | Status **Secure** |

DATE SEEN	WHERE	NOTES

Order **Strigiformes**	Family **Strigidae**	Species *Asio otus*

Long-eared Owl

IN FLIGHT

- tan patch on outer wing
- dark wrist patch
- gray tips

- long "ear" tufts
- rusty face disks
- slender body
- finely streaked underparts

ADULT

- white eyebrows
- conspicuous "ear" tufts
- dark eye-ring
- yellow eye
- black bill
- mottled upperwings

ADULT

FLIGHT: quick, deep wingbeats and long glides; often hovers while hunting.

Although widely distributed across Eurasia and North America, the Long-eared Owl is seldom seen, being secretive and nocturnal. By day it roosts high up and out of sight in thick cover. Only at nightfall does it fly out to hunt on the wing over open areas, patrolling for small mammals. Its wing feathers, like those of many other owls, have sound-suppressing structures that allow it to fly almost silently.

VOICE Evenly spaced *hooo* notes, continuously repeated, about 3 seconds apart, typically 10–50 per series, sometimes more; barks when alarmed.

NESTING Old stick nests of ravens, crows, magpies, and hawks; 2–7 eggs; 1 brood; March–July.

FEEDING Preys mainly on mice and other small rodents, occasionally small birds.

OWL ON THE WING
In flight this bird's "ear" tufts are flattened back and not visible, but the face and underwing markings are clearly revealed.

SIMILAR SPECIES

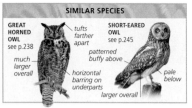

GREAT HORNED OWL
see p.238
- much larger overall

- tufts farther apart

SHORT-EARED OWL
see p.245
- patterned buffy above
- pale below
- horizontal barring on underparts
- larger overall

OCCURRENCE
Breeds in old nests, especially in dense stands of cottonwood, willow, juniper, and conifers near open areas suitable for hunting. Occasionally uses old nests in tree holes, cliffs, or on ground in dense vegetation; in winter, up to 100 birds in roosts. Northern birds move south for winter; some western birds resident.

Length **14–15½in (35–40cm)**	Wingspan **34–39in (86–98cm)**	Weight **8–15oz (225–425g)**
Social **Solitary/Winter flocks**	Lifespan **Up to 27 years**	Status **Secure**

DATE SEEN	WHERE	NOTES

| Order **Strigiformes** | Family **Strigidae** | Species *Asio flammeus* |

Short-eared Owl

short "ear" tufts, usually not visible

large, round head

blackish eye-ring

yellow eyes

pale face disks

whitish underwing

narrow, dark bar

complex, buff marbling on upperparts

ADULT

black wing tips

white belly

row of pale spots along sides of back

black wing tips

fine dark streaks

dark wrist patch

whitish buff underparts

orange-buff to yellowish outer wings

ADULT

IN FLIGHT

FLIGHT: light, slow, buoyant, harrier-like, maneuverable; often hovers, sometimes soars.

This owl is often seen on cloudy days or toward dusk, floating above and patrolling low, back and forth, over open fields, looking and listening for prey, sometimes with Northern Harriers. Although territorial in the breeding season, it may winter in communal roosts of up to 200 birds, occasionally alongside Long-eared Owls. About 10 subspecies are widely distributed across five continents and numerous island groups, including the Greater Antilles, Galápagos, the Falklands, and Hawaii. Unlike other North American owls, the Short-eared Owl builds its own nest.
VOICE Usually silent; male courtship call a rapid *hoo hoo hoo*, often given during display flights; about 16 notes in 3 seconds; also barking, *chee-oww*.
NESTING Scrape lined with grass and feathers on ground; 4–7 eggs; 1–2 broods; March–June.
FEEDING Eats small mammals and some birds.

SIMILAR SPECIES

NORTHERN HARRIER
see p.224

gray upperparts

whitish underparts

long tail

LONG-EARED OWL
see p.244

"ear" tufts

rusty face disks

LOOKOUT POST
Perched on a branch, a Short-eared Owl keeps a wary eye on any intruder on its territory.

OCCURRENCE
Breeds in open areas, including prairie, grasslands, tundra, fields, and marshes across northern North America, from Alaska, the Yukon, and British Columbia to Québec, and Newfoundland, south to the western and central prairies, and east to New England. Northern populations move south in winter.

| Length **13½–16in (34–41cm)** | Wingspan **2¾–3½ft (0.9–1.1m)** | Weight **11–13oz (325–375g)** |
| Social **Solitary/Winter flocks** | Lifespan **Up to 13 years** | Status **Vulnerable** |

DATE SEEN	WHERE	NOTES

Order **Strigiformes**	Family **Strigidae**	Species *Aegolius funereus*

Boreal Owl

ADULT

rounded wings

IN FLIGHT

white and brown streaked underparts

ADULT

finely spotted crown

black border around face

short tail

usually flat-topped head, with fine white spots

yellow eyes

pale bill

ADULT

WWWWWWWWWWWW

FLIGHT: quick, strong wingbeats; adept at maneuvering; glides down to attack prey.

The female Boreal Owl is bigger than the male. Males will mate with two or three females in years when voles and other small rodents are abundant. The Boreal Owl roosts on an inconspicuous perch by day and hunts at night, detecting its prey by sound. In the US it is elusive and rarely seen, as it breeds at high elevations in isolated western mountain ranges. White spotting on the crown, a grayish bill, and a black facial disk distinguish the Boreal Owl from the Northern Saw-whet Owl.

VOICE Prolonged series of whistles, usually increasing in volume and intensity toward the end; also screeches and hisses; can be heard from afar.

NESTING Natural and woodpecker-built tree cavities, also nest boxes; 3–6 eggs; 1 brood; March–July.

FEEDING Mainly eats small mammals, occasionally birds and insects; pounces from elevated perch; sometimes stores prey.

DAYTIME ROOSTING
The Boreal Owl roosts in dense vegetation by day, even when the branches are laden with snow.

SIMILAR SPECIES

NORTHERN PYGMY-OWL

black streaks on belly

longer tail

NORTHERN SAW-WHET OWL
see p.247

lacks dark frame to facial disk

dark bill

OCCURRENCE
Breeds in northern forests from Alaska to Newfoundland and Québec, south into the Rockies to Colorado and New Mexico. Largely sedentary, but irregular movements take place south of the breeding range, southward to New England and New York. In the Old World it is called Tengmalm's Owl.

Length **8½–11in (21–28cm)**	Wingspan **21½–24in (54–62cm)**	Weight **3⅜–8oz (90–225g)**
Social **Solitary**	Lifespan **Up to 11 years**	Status **Secure**

DATE SEEN	WHERE	NOTES
....	....	....
....	....	....
....	....	....
....	....	....
....	....	....

Order **Strigiformes**	Family **Strigidae**	Species *Aegolius acadicus*

Northern Saw-whet Owl

white patch
between eyes

ADULT

rounded
wings

thin white streaks on
forehead and crown

whitish
eyebrows

yellow eyes

dark
bill

chestnut-
brown
upperparts
with white
spots

short
tail
IN FLIGHT

brown
streaks

ADULT

ADULT

FLIGHT: swift and direct; low to ground
with quick wingbeats; swoops up to perch.

unmarked white
undertail feathers

One of the most secretive yet common and widespread owls
in North America, the Northern Saw-whet Owl is much
more often heard than seen. Strictly nocturnal, it is concealed as
it sleeps by day in thick vegetation, usually in conifers. Although
the same site may be used for months if it remains undisturbed,
it is never an easy bird to locate and, like most owls, it is elusive,
even though it sometimes roosts in large garden trees. When it is
discovered, the Northern Saw-whet Owl "freezes," and relies on
its camouflage rather than flying off. At night it watches intently
from a perch, before swooping down to snatch its prey.
VOICE Series of rapid whistled notes, on constant pitch; can
continue for minutes on end; also whines and squeaks.
NESTING Unlined cavity in tree, usually old woodpecker hole
or nest box; 4–7 eggs; 1 brood; March–July
FEEDING Hunts from elevated perch; eats small mammals,
including mice and voles; also eats insects and small birds.

RARE SIGHT
Despite being abundant in its range, this shy
species is rarely seen.

SIMILAR SPECIES

ELF OWL
see p.454
gray
back

smaller
overall

BOREAL OWL
see p.246
darker
face

spotted
crown

black
facial
border

OCCURRENCE
Breeds from Alaska and British
Columbia to Maritimes; in West,
south to Mexico; in East, south
to Appalachians; coniferous and
mixed deciduous forests, swampy
forests, wooded wetlands,
bogs. Winters in southern
to central states, in open
woodlands, pine plantations,
and shrubby areas.

Length **7–8½in (18–21cm)**	Wingspan **16½–19in (42–48cm)**	Weight **3½oz (100g)**
Social **Solitary**	Lifespan **Up to 10 years**	Status **Secure**

DATE SEEN	WHERE	NOTES

KINGFISHERS

K INGFISHERS ARE primarily
a tropical family
(Alcedinidae) that apparently
originated in the Australasian
region. Three species arefound
in North America, but only
one, the Belted Kingfisher, is
widespread. Like most species
of kingfishers, these birds are
large-headed and large-billed but
have comparatively short legs and toes.
Although North American kingfishers
lack the array of bright blues, greens, and
reds associated with their tropical and
European counterparts, they are striking
birds, distinguished by chestnut-colored
chest bands and white underparts. While they
also eat frogs and crayfish, North American
species are primarily fish-eaters. After catching
a fish, they routinely stun their prey by beating
it against a perch before turning the fish around
so that it can be eaten head first. Smaller species
such as the Green Kingfisher are shy and not
often seen.

FISH DINNER
A female Belted Kingfisher
uses its large bill to catch
and hold slippery prey.

WOODPECKERS

W OODPECKERS ARE FOUND throughout
North America except in the tundra.
They are adapted to gripping upright tree
trunks, using the tail as a support or prop.
Most woodpeckers have two toes facing
forward and two facing backward, to give
an extra strong grip on a rounded branch.
Unlike nuthatches, they do not perch upside-
down but they can cling to the underside of
angled branches. They have striking plumage
patterns with simple, bold colors. Many
proclaim their territory by instrumental,
rather than vocal, means, hammering the
bill against a hard surface to give a brief but
rapid "drumroll." The bill is also used for
chipping into bark and excavating deep
nestholes in solid wood. Sapsuckers also
make rows or rings of small holes on tree
trunks, allowing sap to ooze freely: they feed
on the sap and also on the insects that are
attracted to it. Several species, especially the
flickers, also feed on the ground, probing
inside ant nests for larvae, with catching
them with their long, sticky tongues.

RED ALERT
With its crimson head, the
Red-headed Woodpecker
is an instantly recognizable
North American bird.

| Order **Coraciiformes** | Family **Alcedinidae** | Species *Megaceryle alcyon* |

Belted Kingfisher 🔊

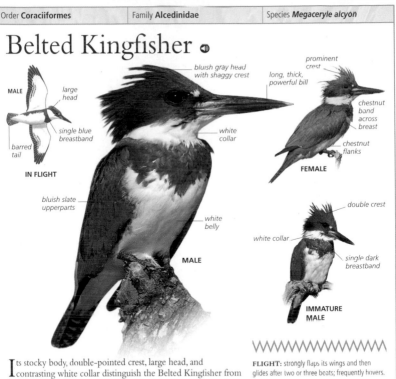

MALE

large head

single blue breastband

barred tail

IN FLIGHT

bluish gray head with shaggy crest

white collar

bluish slate upperparts

white belly

MALE

prominent crest

long, thick, powerful bill

chestnut band across breast

chestnut flanks

FEMALE

double crest

white collar

single dark breastband

IMMATURE MALE

Its stocky body, double-pointed crest, large head, and contrasting white collar distinguish the Belted Kingfisher from other species in its range. This kingfisher's loud and far-carrying rattles are heard more often than the bird is seen. Interestingly, it is one of the few birds in North America in which the female is more colorful than the male. The Belted Kingfisher can be found in a large variety of aquatic habitats, both coastal and inland, vigorously defending its territory all year round.

VOICE Harsh mechanical rattle given in flight or from a perch; sometimes emits screams or trill-like warble during breeding.

NESTING Unlined chamber in subterranean burrow 3–6ft (1–2m) deep, excavated in earthen bank usually over water, but sometimes in ditches, sand, or gravel pits; 6–7 eggs; 1 brood; March–July.

FEEDING Plunge-dives from branches or wires to catch a wide variety of fish near the surface, including sticklebacks and trout; also takes crustaceans, such as crayfish.

FLIGHT: strongly flaps its wings and then glides after two or three beats; frequently hovers.

SIMILAR SPECIES

RINGED KINGFISHER ♂
see p.455

larger overall

chestnut belly

CATCH OF THE DAY
The female's chestnut belly band and flanks are clearly visible here as she perches with her catch.

OCCURRENCE
Breeds and winters around clear, open waters of streams, rivers, lakes, estuaries, and protected marine shorelines, where perches are available and prey is visible. Avoids water with emergent vegetation. Northern populations migrate south to Mexico, Central America, and the West Indies.

| Length **11–14in (28–35cm)** | Wingspan **19–23in (48–58cm)** | Weight **5–6oz (150–175g)** |
| Social **Solitary** | Lifespan **Unknown** | Status **Secure** |

DATE SEEN	WHERE	NOTES

| Order **Piciformes** | Family **Picidae** | Species ***Melanerpes erythrocephalus*** |

Red-headed Woodpecker

white rump

red head

ADULT

IN FLIGHT

bright red head

bluish gray bill

upperparts black with bluish sheen

narrow black "necklace"

ADULT

brownish head

wing feathers white with black barring

JUVENILE

white secondary wing feathers

The Red-headed Woodpecker is the only member of this family that has a completely red head, and is therefore easy to identify. Unlike most other woodpecker species, it forages for food—both insects and nuts—and stores it for eating at a later time. It is one of the most skilled flycatchers in the woodpecker family. Its numbers have declined, largely because of the destruction of its habitat, especially the removal of dead trees in urban and rural areas, and clearing and cutting of trees for firewood in rural areas. The Red-headed Woodpecker is a truly North American bird, not extending south of the Rio Grande.

VOICE Primary call an extremely harsh and loud *churr*, also produces breeding call and alarm; no song; active drummer.

NESTING Excavates cavity in dead wood; 3–5 eggs; 1–2 broods; May–August.

FEEDING Forages in flight, on ground, and in trees; feeds on a variety of insects, spiders, nuts seeds, berries, and fruit, and, in rare cases, small mammals such as mice.

WORK IN PROGRESS
The Red-headed Woodpecker excavates its breeding cavities in tree trunks and stumps.

FLIGHT: strong flapping; undulation not as marked as in other woodpecker species.

OCCURRENCE
Breeds in a variety of habitats, especially open deciduous woodlands, including riverside areas, orchards, municipal parks, agricultural areas, forest edges, and forests affected by fire. Uses the same habitats during the winter and in the breeding season.

Length **8½–9½in (22–24cm)**	Wingspan **16–18in (41–46cm)**	Weight **2–3oz (55–85g)**
Social **Solitary**	Lifespan **At least 10 years**	Status **Declining**

DATE SEEN	WHERE	NOTES

Order **Piciformes**	Family **Picidae**	Species *Melanerpes carolinus*

Red-bellied Woodpecker 🔊

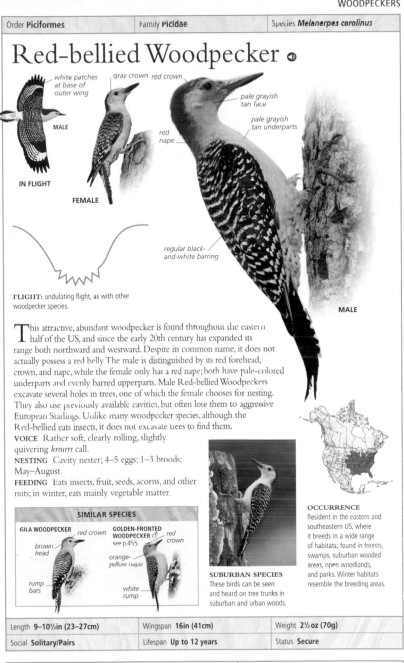

white patches at base of outer wing

MALE

IN FLIGHT

gray crown red crown

red nape

FEMALE

red crown

pale grayish tan face

pale grayish tan underparts

regular black-and-white barring

MALE

FLIGHT: undulating flight, as with other woodpecker species.

This attractive, abundant woodpecker is found throughout the eastern half of the US, and since the early 20th century has expanded its range both northward and westward. Despite its common name, it does not actually possess a red belly. The male is distinguished by its red forehead, crown, and nape, while the female only has a red nape; both have pale-colored underparts and evenly barred upperparts. Male Red-bellied Woodpeckers excavate several holes in trees, one of which the female chooses for nesting. They also use previously available cavities, but often lose them to aggressive European Starlings. Unlike many woodpecker species, although the Red-bellied eats insects, it does not excavate trees to find them.

VOICE Rather soft, clearly rolling, slightly quivering *krrurrr* call.

NESTING Cavity nester; 4–5 eggs; 1–3 broods; May–August.

FEEDING Eats insects, fruit, seeds, acorns, and other nuts; in winter, eats mainly vegetable matter.

SIMILAR SPECIES	
GILA WOODPECKER red crown brown head rump bars	**GOLDEN-FRONTED WOODPECKER ♂** see p.455 red crown orange-yellow nape white rump

SUBURBAN SPECIES
These birds can be seen and heard on tree trunks in suburban and urban woods.

OCCURRENCE
Resident in the eastern and southeastern US, where it breeds in a wide range of habitats; found in forests, swamps, suburban wooded areas, open woodlands, and parks. Winter habitats resemble the breeding areas.

Length **9–10½in (23–27cm)**	Wingspan **16in (41cm)**	Weight **2½oz (70g)**
Social **Solitary/Pairs**	Lifespan **Up to 12 years**	Status **Secure**

DATE SEEN	WHERE	NOTES

| Order **Piciformes** | Family **Picidae** | Species *Sphyrapicus varius* |

Yellow-bellied Sapsucker ◉

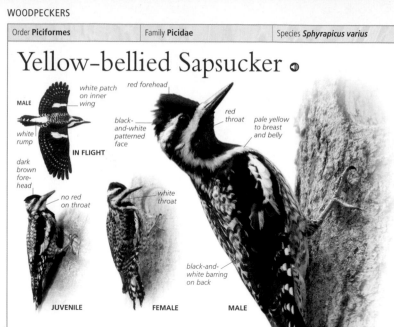

MALE

white patch on inner wing

IN FLIGHT

white rump

dark brown fore-head

red forehead

black-and-white patterned face

red throat

pale yellow to breast and belly

no red on throat

white throat

black-and-white barring on back

JUVENILE **FEMALE** **MALE**

The Yellow-bellied Sapsucker, with its red, black, and white coloring and soft yellow wash on its underparts, is a striking bird. Like its relatives, the Red-breasted Sapsucker and the Red-naped Sapsucker, it drills holes in trees to drink sap. It was not until 1983 that the sapsuckers were allocated to four separate species. Sapsuckers are the only wholly migratory woodpeckers; female Yellow-bellied Sapsuckers move farther south than males. The other is the Red-naped Sapsucker, in the West.

VOICE Primary call a mewing *wheer-wheer-wheer*.

NESTING Cavities in dead trees; 5–6 eggs; 1 brood; May–June.

FEEDING Drinks sap; eats ants and other small insects; feeds on the inner bark of trees, also a variety of fruit.

FLIGHT: typical woodpecker, undulating flight pattern with intermittent flapping and gliding.

STRIKING SPECIES
The Yellow-bellied Sapsucker's white rump and black-and-white forked tail are clearly evident here.

SIMILAR SPECIES

WILLIAMSON'S SAPSUCKER ♀ brown head

more extensive barring on back

RED-NAPED SAPSUCKER

red patch on forehead

two rows of white bars on back

OCCURRENCE
Breeds in eastern Alaska, Canada, and south to the Appalachians. Prefers either deciduous forests or mixed deciduous-coniferous forests; preferably young forests. In winter, it is found in open wooded areas in southeastern states, Caribbean islands, and Central America.

| Length **8–9in (20–23cm)** | Wingspan **16–18in (41–46cm)** | Weight **1¾oz (50g)** |
| Social **Solitary/Pairs** | Lifespan **Up to 7 years** | Status **Secure** |

DATE SEEN	WHERE	NOTES
....	....	....
....	....	....
....	....	....
....	....	....
....	....	....

Order **Piciformes**	Family **Picidae**	Species *Picoides dorsalis*

American Three-toed Woodpecker

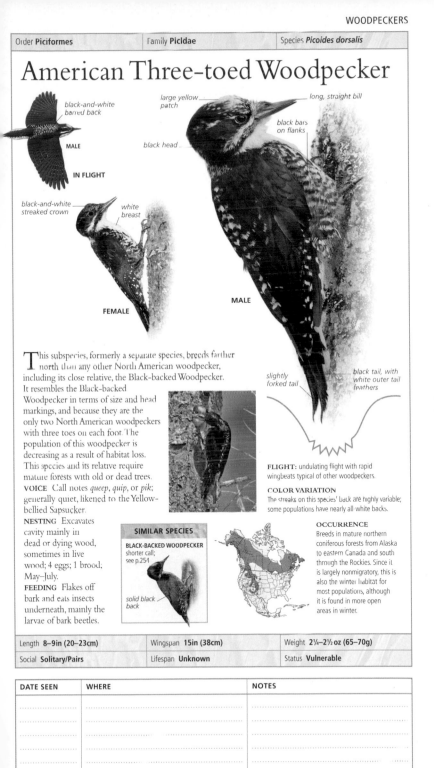

black-and-white barred back

MALE

IN FLIGHT

large yellow patch

long, straight bill

black bars on flanks

black head

black-and-white streaked crown

white breast

FEMALE

MALE

slightly forked tail

black tail, with white outer tail feathers

FLIGHT: undulating flight with rapid wingbeats typical of other woodpeckers.

COLOR VARIATION
The streaks on this species' back are highly variable; some populations have nearly all-white backs.

This subspecies, formerly a separate species, breeds farther north than any other North American woodpecker, including its close relative, the Black-backed Woodpecker. It resembles the Black-backed Woodpecker in terms of size and head markings, and because they are the only two North American woodpeckers with three toes on each foot. The population of this woodpecker is decreasing as a result of habitat loss. This species and its relative require mature forests with old or dead trees.
VOICE Call notes *queep*, *quip*, or *pik*; generally quiet, likened to the Yellow-bellied Sapsucker.
NESTING Excavates cavity mainly in dead or dying wood, sometimes in live wood; 4 eggs; 1 brood; May–July.
FEEDING Flakes off bark and eats insects underneath, mainly the larvae of bark beetles.

SIMILAR SPECIES

BLACK-BACKED WOODPECKER
shorter call; see p.254

solid black back

OCCURRENCE
Breeds in mature northern coniferous forests from Alaska to eastern Canada and south through the Rockies. Since it is largely nonmigratory, this is also the winter habitat for most populations, although it is found in more open areas in winter.

Length **8–9in (20–23cm)**	Wingspan **15in (38cm)**	Weight **2¼–2½ oz (65–70g)**
Social **Solitary/Pairs**	Lifespan **Unknown**	Status **Vulnerable**

DATE SEEN	WHERE	NOTES

| Order **Piciformes** | Family **Picidae** | Species *Picoides arcticus* |

Black-backed Woodpecker

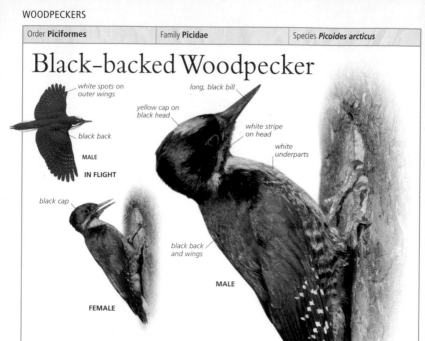

white spots on
outer wings

long, black bill

yellow cap on
black head

white stripe
on head

black back

white
underparts

MALE

IN FLIGHT

black cap

black back
and wings

MALE

FEMALE

Formerly called the Black-backed Three-toed Woodpecker, this species has a black back and heavily barred flanks. Despite a widespread distribution from central Alaska to the western US mountains and east to Newfoundland and the northeastern US, this bird is difficult to find. It often occurs in areas of burned forest, eating wood-boring beetles that occur after outbreaks of fire. This diet is very specialized, and the species is greatly affected by forestry programs, which prevent the spread of fire. Although it overlaps geographically with the American Three-toed Woodpecker, the two are rarely found together in the same locality.

VOICE Main call a single *pik*.

NESTING Cavity excavated in tree; 3–4 eggs; 1 brood; May–July.

FEEDING Eats beetles, especially larvae of wood-boring beetles, by flaking off bark.

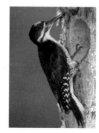

FLIGHT: typical undulating flight of woodpeckers.

FREQUENT MOVING
This bird excavates a new nest cavity each year, rarely returning in subsequent years.

SIMILAR SPECIES

AMERICAN THREE-
TOED WOODPECKER
see p.253

black-and-
white barred
upperparts

OCCURRENCE
Inhabitant of northern and mountain coniferous forests that require fire for renewal. Breeding occurs soon after sites are burned as new colonies are attracted to the habitat. In Michigan's Upper Peninsula, the bird uses trees similar to those in its northern habitat.

| Length **9–9½in (23–24cm)** | Wingspan **15–16in (38–41cm)** | Weight **2½oz (70g)** |
| Social **Pairs** | Lifespan **Unknown** | Status **Secure** |

DATE SEEN	WHERE	NOTES
....	....	....
....	....	....
....	....	....
....	....	....
....	....	....

| Order **Piciformes** | Family **Picidae** | Species **Dryobates pubescens** |

Downy Woodpecker 🔊

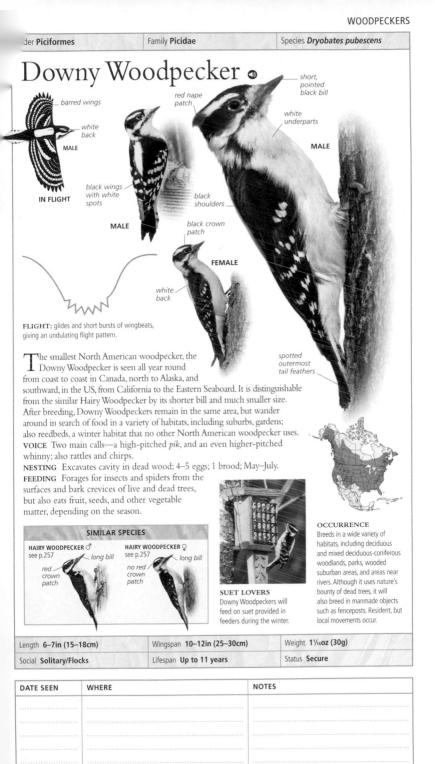

barred wings

white back

MALE

IN FLIGHT

red nape patch

short, pointed black bill

white underparts

MALE

black wings with white spots

black shoulders

MALE

black crown patch

FEMALE

white back

spotted outermost tail feathers

FLIGHT: glides and short bursts of wingbeats, giving an undulating flight pattern.

The smallest North American woodpecker, the Downy Woodpecker is seen all year round from coast to coast in Canada, north to Alaska, and southward, in the US, from California to the Eastern Seaboard. It is distinguishable from the similar Hairy Woodpecker by its shorter bill and much smaller size. After breeding, Downy Woodpeckers remain in the same area, but wander around in search of food in a variety of habitats, including suburbs, gardens; also reedbeds, a winter habitat that no other North American woodpecker uses.

VOICE Two main calls—a high-pitched *pik*, and an even higher-pitched whinny; also rattles and chirps.

NESTING Excavates cavity in dead wood; 4–5 eggs; 1 brood; May–July.

FEEDING Forages for insects and spiders from the surfaces and bark crevices of live and dead trees, but also eats fruit, seeds, and other vegetable matter, depending on the season.

SIMILAR SPECIES

HAIRY WOODPECKER ♂
see p.257
long bill
red crown patch

HAIRY WOODPECKER ♀
see p.257
long bill
no red crown patch

SUET LOVERS
Downy Woodpeckers will feed on suet provided in feeders during the winter.

OCCURRENCE
Breeds in a wide variety of habitats, including deciduous and mixed deciduous-coniferous woodlands, parks, wooded suburban areas, and areas near rivers. Although it uses nature's bounty of dead trees, it will also breed in manmade objects such as fenceposts. Resident, but local movements occur.

| Length **6–7in (15–18cm)** | Wingspan **10–12in (25–30cm)** | Weight **1¹⁄₁₆oz (30g)** |
| Social **Solitary/Flocks** | Lifespan **Up to 11 years** | Status **Secure** |

DATE SEEN	WHERE	NOTES

Order **Piciformes**	Family **Picidae**	Species ***Dryobates borealis***

Red-cockaded Woodpecker

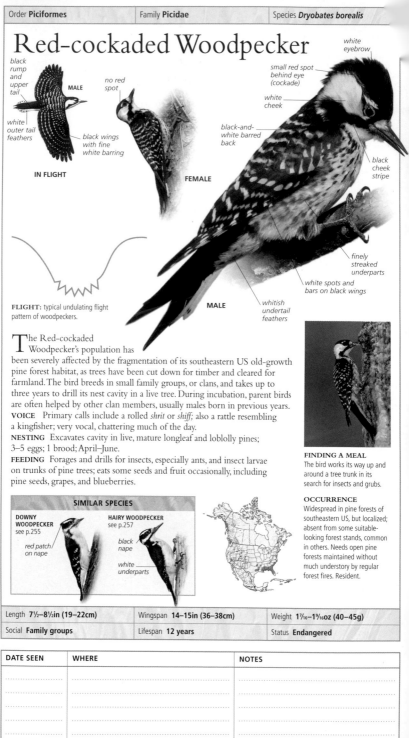

black rump and upper tail

MALE

white outer tail feathers

IN FLIGHT

no red spot

black wings with fine white barring

FEMALE

white eyebrow

small red spot behind eye (cockade)

white cheek

black-and-white barred back

black cheek stripe

finely streaked underparts

white spots and bars on black wings

whitish undertail feathers

MALE

FLIGHT: typical undulating flight pattern of woodpeckers.

The Red-cockaded Woodpecker's population has been severely affected by the fragmentation of its southeastern US old-growth pine forest habitat, as trees have been cut down for timber and cleared for farmland. The bird breeds in small family groups, or clans, and takes up to three years to drill its nest cavity in a live tree. During incubation, parent birds are often helped by other clan members, usually males born in previous years.

VOICE Primary calls include a rolled *shrit* or *shiff;* also a rattle resembling a kingfisher; very vocal, chattering much of the day.

NESTING Excavates cavity in live, mature longleaf and loblolly pines; 3–5 eggs; 1 brood; April–June.

FEEDING Forages and drills for insects, especially ants, and insect larvae on trunks of pine trees; eats some seeds and fruit occasionally, including pine seeds, grapes, and blueberries.

FINDING A MEAL
The bird works its way up and around a tree trunk in its search for insects and grubs.

OCCURRENCE
Widespread in pine forests of southeastern US, but localized; absent from some suitable-looking forest stands, common in others. Needs open pine forests maintained without much understory by regular forest fires. Resident.

SIMILAR SPECIES		
DOWNY WOODPECKER see p.255	**HAIRY WOODPECKER** see p.257	
red patch on nape	black nape	
	white underparts	

Length **7½–8½in (19–22cm)**	Wingspan **14–15in (36–38cm)**	Weight **1⁷⁄₁₆–1⁹⁄₁₆oz (40–45g)**
Social **Family groups**	Lifespan **12 years**	Status **Endangered**

DATE SEEN	WHERE	NOTES

| Piciformes | Family **Picidae** | Species ***Dryobates villosus*** |

Hairy Woodpecker 🔊

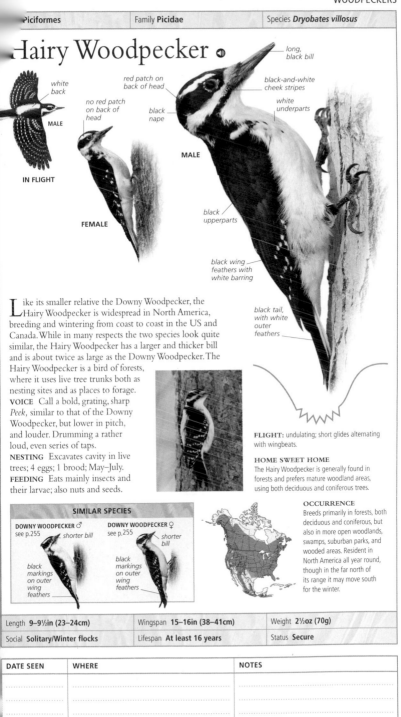

white back

MALE

IN FLIGHT

no red patch on back of head

black nape

FEMALE

red patch on back of head

long, black bill

black-and-white cheek stripes

white underparts

MALE

black upperparts

black wing feathers with white barring

black tail, with white outer feathers

Like its smaller relative the Downy Woodpecker, the Hairy Woodpecker is widespread in North America, breeding and wintering from coast to coast in the US and Canada. While in many respects the two species look quite similar, the Hairy Woodpecker has a larger and thicker bill and is about twice as large as the Downy Woodpecker. The Hairy Woodpecker is a bird of forests, where it uses live tree trunks both as nesting sites and as places to forage.

VOICE Call a bold, grating, sharp *Peek*, similar to that of the Downy Woodpecker, but lower in pitch, and louder. Drumming a rather loud, even series of taps.

NESTING Excavates cavity in live trees; 4 eggs; 1 brood; May–July.

FEEDING Eats mainly insects and their larvae; also nuts and seeds.

FLIGHT: undulating; short glides alternating with wingbeats.

HOME SWEET HOME
The Hairy Woodpecker is generally found in forests and prefers mature woodland areas, using both deciduous and coniferous trees.

OCCURRENCE
Breeds primarily in forests, both deciduous and coniferous, but also in more open woodlands, swamps, suburban parks, and wooded areas. Resident in North America all year round, though in the far north of its range it may move south for the winter.

SIMILAR SPECIES

DOWNY WOODPECKER ♂
see p.255

shorter bill

black markings on outer wing feathers

DOWNY WOODPECKER ♀
see p.255

shorter bill

black markings on outer wing feathers

Length **9–9½in (23–24cm)**	Wingspan **15–16in (38–41cm)**	Weight **2½oz (70g)**
Social **Solitary/Winter flocks**	Lifespan **At least 16 years**	Status **Secure**

DATE SEEN	WHERE	NOTES

| Order **Piciformes** | Family **Picidae** | Species ***Colaptes auratus*** |

Northern Flicker 🔊

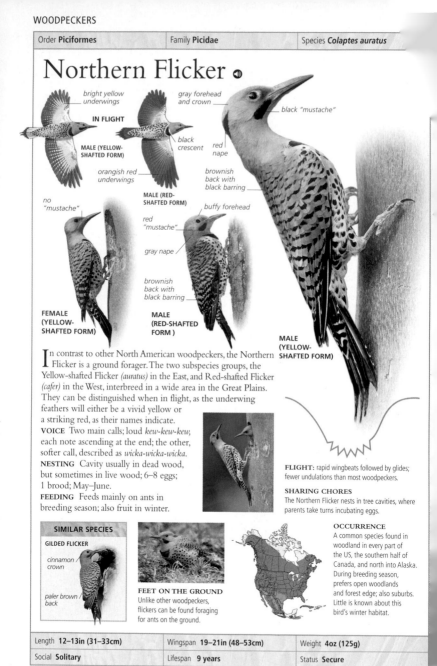

bright yellow underwings

IN FLIGHT

MALE (YELLOW-SHAFTED FORM)

gray forehead and crown

black "mustache"

black crescent

red nape

orangish red underwings

MALE (RED-SHAFTED FORM)

brownish back with black barring

no "mustache"

buffy forehead

red "mustache"

gray nape

brownish back with black barring

FEMALE (YELLOW-SHAFTED FORM)

MALE (RED-SHAFTED FORM)

MALE (YELLOW-SHAFTED FORM)

In contrast to other North American woodpeckers, the Northern Flicker is a ground forager. The two subspecies groups, the Yellow-shafted Flicker *(auratus)* in the East, and Red-shafted Flicker *(cafer)* in the West, interbreed in a wide area in the Great Plains. They can be distinguished when in flight, as the underwing feathers will either be a vivid yellow or a striking red, as their names indicate.

VOICE Two main calls; loud *kew-kew-kew*, each note ascending at the end; the other, softer call, described as *wicka-wicka-wicka*.

NESTING Cavity usually in dead wood, but sometimes in live wood; 6–8 eggs; 1 brood; May–June.

FEEDING Feeds mainly on ants in breeding season; also fruit in winter.

FLIGHT: rapid wingbeats followed by glides; fewer undulations than most woodpeckers.

SHARING CHORES
The Northern Flicker nests in tree cavities, where parents take turns incubating eggs.

SIMILAR SPECIES

GILDED FLICKER

cinnamon crown

paler brown back

FEET ON THE GROUND
Unlike other woodpeckers, flickers can be found foraging for ants on the ground.

OCCURRENCE
A common species found in woodland in every part of the US, the southern half of Canada, and north into Alaska. During breeding season, prefers open woodlands and forest edge; also suburbs. Little is known about this bird's winter habitat.

| Length **12–13in (31–33cm)** | Wingspan **19–21in (48–53cm)** | Weight **4oz (125g)** |
| Social **Solitary** | Lifespan **9 years** | Status **Secure** |

DATE SEEN	WHERE	NOTES

| Order **Piciformes** | Family **Picidae** | Species **_Dryocopus pileatus_** |

Pileated Woodpecker 🔊

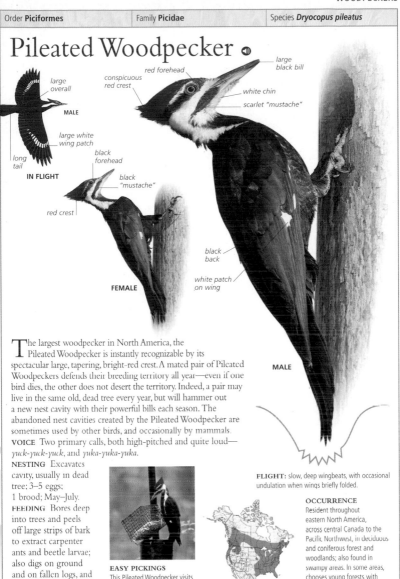

- large overall
- **MALE**
- large white wing patch
- long tail
- **IN FLIGHT**
- red forehead
- conspicuous red crest
- large black bill
- white chin
- scarlet "mustache"
- black forehead
- black "mustache"
- red crest
- **FEMALE**
- black back
- white patch on wing
- **MALE**

The largest woodpecker in North America, the Pileated Woodpecker is instantly recognizable by its spectacular large, tapering, bright-red crest. A mated pair of Pileated Woodpeckers defends their breeding territory all year—even if one bird dies, the other does not desert the territory. Indeed, a pair may live in the same old, dead tree every year, but will hammer out a new nest cavity with their powerful bills each season. The abandoned nest cavities created by the Pileated Woodpecker are sometimes used by other birds, and occasionally by mammals.

VOICE Two primary calls, both high-pitched and quite loud— _yuck-yuck-yuck_, and _yuka-yuka-yuka_.

NESTING Excavates cavity, usually in dead tree; 3–5 eggs; 1 brood; May–July.

FEEDING Bores deep into trees and peels off large strips of bark to extract carpenter ants and beetle larvae; also digs on ground and on fallen logs, and opportunistically eats fruit and nuts.

EASY PICKINGS
This Pileated Woodpecker visits a feeder to supplement its natural diet.

FLIGHT: slow, deep wingbeats, with occasional undulation when wings briefly folded.

OCCURRENCE
Resident throughout eastern North America, across central Canada to the Pacific Northwest, in deciduous and coniferous forest and woodlands; also found in swampy areas. In some areas, chooses young forests with dead trees but in other places, old-growth forests.

| Length **16–18in (41–46cm)** | Wingspan **26–30in (66–76cm)** | Weight **10oz (275g)** |
| Social **Pairs** | Lifespan **Up to 9 years** | Status **Secure** |

DATE SEEN	WHERE	NOTES

FALCONS

FALCONS INCLUDE birds that catch insects on the wing, others that hover to search for prey below, and yet others that are more dramatic aerial hunters. Some use high-speed "stoops" from above, seizing birds up to their own size, while larger species such as the Gyrfalcon can kill prey much heavier than themselves. They are distinguished from bird-eating hawks in the genus *Accipiter* by their dark eyes and their hunting styles: both use their toes to catch prey, but while falcons kill primarily with their bills, hawks kill with their toes. Falcons' bills are equipped with a notch or "tooth" on the upper mandible. Unlike hawks and eagles, falcons do not build nests, but some use old nests of other birds.

PRECISION LANDING
A Peregrine Falcon swoops down to settle on the branch, thrusting out its toes to absorb the shock of landing.

PARAKEETS AND PARROTS

PARROTS AND PARAKEETS have a large but short, hooked bill, a stocky head and neck, very short legs, and two backward-pointing toes. They grasp twigs and branches and can be very acrobatic feeders despite their "neckless" shape. Most are brightly colored with much green and various patches of red, yellow, and orange. They are easy to hear but often difficult to see in dense foliage. Introduced or escaped species frequently become familiar visitors to backyard feeders and birdhouses.

POPULAR PET
The Monk Parakeet is native to South America, but escaped pets breed locally in North America.

| Order **Falconiformes** | Family **Falconidae** | Species **_Falco sparverius_** |

American Kestrel 🔊

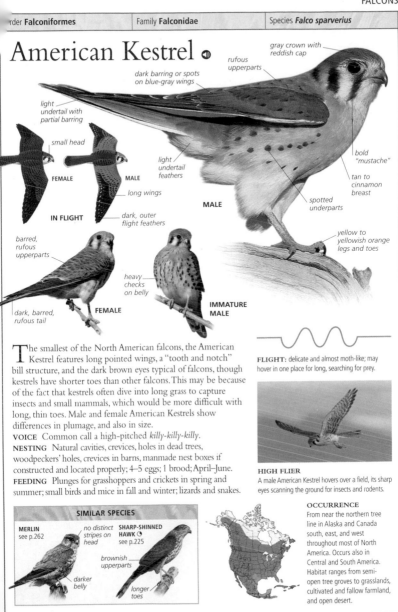

gray crown with reddish cap

rufous upperparts

dark barring or spots on blue-gray wings

light undertail with partial barring

small head

light undertail feathers

FEMALE **MALE**

long wings

IN FLIGHT

dark, outer flight feathers

MALE

bold "mustache"

tan to cinnamon breast

spotted underparts

yellow to yellowish orange legs and toes

barred, rufous upperparts

heavy checks on belly

dark, barred, rufous tail **FEMALE**

IMMATURE MALE

The smallest of the North American falcons, the American Kestrel features long pointed wings, a "tooth and notch" bill structure, and the dark brown eyes typical of falcons, though kestrels have shorter toes than other falcons. This may be because of the fact that kestrels often dive into long grass to capture insects and small mammals, which would be more difficult with long, thin toes. Male and female American Kestrels show differences in plumage, and also in size.

VOICE Common call a high-pitched _killy-killy-killy_.
NESTING Natural cavities, crevices, holes in dead trees, woodpeckers' holes, crevices in barns, manmade nest boxes if constructed and located properly; 4–5 eggs; 1 brood; April–June.
FEEDING Plunges for grasshoppers and crickets in spring and summer; small birds and mice in fall and winter; lizards and snakes.

FLIGHT: delicate and almost moth-like; may hover in one place for long, searching for prey.

HIGH FLIER
A male American Kestrel hovers over a field, its sharp eyes scanning the ground for insects and rodents.

SIMILAR SPECIES

MERLIN see p.262

no distinct stripes on head

darker belly

SHARP-SHINNED HAWK ↻ see p.225

brownish upperparts

longer toes

OCCURRENCE
From near the northern tree line in Alaska and Canada south, east, and west throughout most of North America. Occurs also in Central and South America. Habitat ranges from semi-open tree groves to grasslands, cultivated and fallow farmland, and open desert.

| Length **9in (23cm)** | Wingspan **22in (56cm)** | Weight **3½–4oz (100–125g)** |
| Social **Family groups** | Lifespan **10–15 years** | Status **Vulnerable** |

DATE SEEN	WHERE	NOTES

| Order **Falconiformes** | Family **Falconidae** | Species *Falco columbarius* |

Merlin

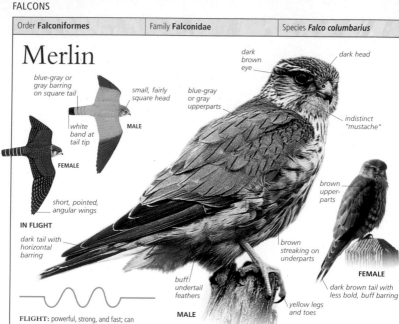

dark brown eye

dark head

blue-gray or gray barring on square tail

small, fairly square head

blue-gray or gray upperparts

white band at tail tip

MALE

indistinct "mustache"

FEMALE

short, pointed, angular wings

brown upperparts

IN FLIGHT

dark tail with horizontal barring

brown streaking on underparts

FEMALE

buff undertail feathers

dark brown tail with less bold, buff barring

yellow legs and toes

MALE

FLIGHT: powerful, strong, and fast; can abruptly turn to the left or right in pursuit of prey.

Merlins are small, fast-flying falcons that were formerly known as "pigeon hawks," because their shape and flight are similar to those strong fliers. Merlins can overtake and capture a wide variety of prey. They can turn on a dime, and use their long, thin toes, typical of falcons, to pluck birds from the air after launching a direct attack. Males are smaller than females, and different in color. Both males and females show geographical color variations.
VOICE Male call a high-pitched *ki-ki-ki-ki*; female call a low-pitched *kek-ek-ek-ek-ek*.
NESTING Small scrapes on ground in open country, or abandoned nests of other species, such as crows, in forested areas; 4–6 eggs; 1 brood; April–June.
FEEDING Catches small birds in midair, and occasionally birds as large as doves; also feeds on small mammals, including bats.

ABOUT TO ROUSE
An adult female Merlin sits on a moss-covered rock, about to "rouse," or fluff out and shake her feathers.

SIMILAR SPECIES

AMERICAN KESTREL see p.261

cinnamon flanks

tan breast

SHARP-SHINNED HAWK see p.225

rounder wings

barred underparts

longer tail

OCCURRENCE
In North America breeds throughout Alaska and Canada. Highly migratory, winters throughout the US south to northern South America. Merlins can be seen hunting along coastlines, over marshlands and open fields, and in desert areas.

| Length **10in (25cm)** | Wingspan **24in (61cm)** | Weight **5–7oz (150–200g)** |
| Social **Pairs/Family groups** | Lifespan **10–15 years** | Status **Secure** |

DATE SEEN	WHERE	NOTES

| Order **Falconiformes** | Family **Falconidae** | Species *Falco rusticolus* |

Gyrfalcon

yellow patch of skin near bill

pointed tips

dark brown to black all over

almost completely white

JUVENILE (GRAY FORM)

paler upperparts with brown barring

dark brown iris

ADULT (DARK FORM)

darker wing linings

gray, barred upperparts

paler flight feathers

heavily streaked head

yellow bill

ADULT (WHITE FORM)

IN FLIGHT

blue bill with dark tip

lighter underparts with spots

yellow toes and legs

ADULT (GRAY FORM)

long, barred tail

ADULT (GRAY FORM)

Arctic bred, the Gyrfalcon is used to harsh environments. It is the largest of all the falcons and one of the most majestic species of bird in the world. For centuries, the Gyrfalcon has been sought by both the nobility and falconers for its power, beauty, and gentle nature; today, it is also the mascot of the US Air Force Academy. It uses its speed to pursue prey in a "tail chase," sometimes striking its quarry on the ground, but also in flight. Three forms are known, ranging from almost pure white to gray and dark.

VOICE Loud, harsh *KYHa-KYHa-KYHa*.
NESTING Scrape on cliff, or old Common Ravens' nests; 2–7 eggs; 1 brood; April–July.
FEEDING Feeds mostly on large birds such as ptarmigan, pigeons, grouse; may also hunt mammals, such as lemmings.

FLIGHT: powerful and direct; continuous, rapid, stiff wingbeats.

SNOWY PLUMAGE
A Gyrfalcon stands on an Arctic hillside. From a distance, it might be mistaken for a patch of snow.

SIMILAR SPECIES

PRAIRIE FALCON light, sandy brown upperparts; see p.265

PEREGRINE FALCON see p.264

dark "hood" on head

smaller overall

light, brown-spotted underparts

light, barred underparts

OCCURRENCE
Breeds in Alaska and Arctic Canada. In winter some birds move south as far as the northern US. A truly Arctic species found in the most barren regions of the tundra, high mountains and foothills of the tundra, and Arctic and subarctic evergreen forests and woodlands. Not common outside its breeding range.

| Length **22in (56cm)** | Wingspan **4ft (1.2m)** | Weight **2¾–4lb (1.2–1.8kg)** |
| Social **Solitary/Pairs** | Lifespan **15–30 years** | Status **Localized** |

DATE SEEN	WHERE	NOTES

| Order **Falconiformes** | Family **Falconidae** | Species *Falco peregrinus* |

Peregrine Falcon

IN FLIGHT
- long, pointed wings
- short tail

ADULT
- streaked underparts

JUVENILE
- brown upperparts
- dark spots on light buff breast
- light yellow or bluish gray legs and toes

ADULT
- barred underwings
- barred undertail feathers
- prominent dark "mustache"
- light underparts with horizontal barring

- dark "hood" on head
- yellow eye-ring
- bluish gray upperparts

ADULT
- yellow toes and legs

FLIGHT: powerful and direct; faster, deeper wingbeats during pursuit; also soars.

Peregrine Falcons are distributed worldwide and are long-distance travelers—"Peregrine" means "wanderer." It has been shown to dive from great heights at speeds of up to 200mph (320kmph)—a technique known as "stooping." Like all true falcons, this species has a pointed "tooth" on its upper bill and a "notch" on the lower one, and it instinctively bites the neck of captured prey to kill it. From the 1950s to the 1980s, its breeding ability was reduced by the insecticide DDT, which resulted in thin eggshells that could easily be crushed by the parent. Peregrines were then bred in captivity, and later released into the wild. Their status is now secure.

VOICE Sharp *hek-hek-hek* when alarmed.

NESTING Shallow scrape on cliff or building (nest sites are used year after year); 2–5 eggs; 1 brood; March–June.

FEEDING Dives on prey—birds of various sizes in flight; now feeds on pigeons in cities.

PARENTAL CARE
An adult Peregrine gently feeds a hatchling bits of meat; the remaining egg is likely to hatch soon.

SIMILAR SPECIES

GYRFALCON see p.263
- larger and stockier
- longer tail
- less defined "hood"
- light sandy brown upperparts

PRAIRIE FALCON see p.265
- lighter head color

OCCURRENCE
A variety of habitats across northern North America, ranging from open valleys to cities with tall buildings. Peregrines prefer to inhabit cliffs along sea coasts, in addition to inland mountain ranges, but also occur in open country such as scrubland and saltmarshes.

| Length **16in (41cm)** | Wingspan **3¼–3½ft (1–1.1m)** | Weight **22–35oz (620–1,000g)** |
| Social **Solitary/Pairs** | Lifespan **15–20 years** | Status **Secure** |

DATE SEEN	WHERE	NOTES

| Order **Falconiformes** | Family **Falconidae** | Species *Falco mexicanus* |

Prairie Falcon

yellow eye-ring

yellow patch of skin near bill

light head and "mustache"

ADULT

long, pointed wings

light, sandy brown upperparts with incomplete barring

white cheek

longish tail

distinctive, triangle-shaped patch on wingpit feathers

IN FLIGHT

light underparts with brown spots

ADULT

yellow legs and toes

light undertail feathers

Prairie Falcons are light-colored, buoyant residents of the arid regions of North America. They blend in well with their surroundings (cliff faces and dry grass), where they are invisible to their prey. Prairie Falcons chase their prey close to the ground and do not often dive or "stoop" on prey from a great height. Ground squirrels are important prey items in some areas, and breeding is often linked with the squirrels' emergence. The sexes are very similar in coloration, though juveniles have a streaked rather than spotted breast. The underwing pattern with almost black feathers in the "wingpits" is distinctive; no other North American falcon shows this mark.

VOICE Repeated shrill *kik-kik-kik kik-kik*.

NESTING Slight, shallow scrapes, almost always located on high cliff ledges or bluffs; 3–6 eggs; 1 brood; March–July.

FEEDING Feeds on small to medium-sized birds and small mammals, such as ground squirrels.

FLIGHT: fast flight; capable of soaring and diving; usually chases prey low above the ground.

STRIKING MUSTACHE
An inquisitive Prairie Falcon stares at the camera. The white cheek is obvious from this angle.

SIMILAR SPECIES

MERLIN
see p.262

smaller overall

heavily streaked underparts

PEREGRINE FALCON ♀
see p.264

darker head

streaked underparts

yellow or bluish gray legs and toes

OCCURRENCE
Interior North America, from central British Columbia east to western North Dakota and south to southern California, and Mexico, Arizona, northern Texas. Found in open plains, prairies, and grasslands, dotted with buttes or cliffs. A partial migrant, it moves east of its breeding range in winter.

| Length **16in (41cm)** | Wingspan **3¼ft (1m)** | Weight **22–30oz (625–850g)** |
| Social **Solitary/Pairs** | Lifespan **10–20 years** | Status **Localized** |

DATE SEEN	WHERE	NOTES

Order **Psittaciformes**	Family **Psittacidae**	Species *Myiopsitta monachus*

Monk Parakeet

long, pointed tail

green inner wing feathers

gray face

dark blue-black outer wing feathers

IN FLIGHT

green upperparts

hooked, orangish bill

gray face and forehead

gray breast

yellowish belly

two forward- and two backward-pointing toes

long, green tail

FLIGHT: swift and direct; short glides on bowed wings; often changes direction, usually in flocks.

PLANT FEEDER
Monk Parakeets feed on a wide variety of plant material, including bottlebrush flowers.

Monk Parakeets, native to southern South America, have been introduced to a number of places in the United States. They are the most abundant and widespread species of introduced parrot in North America, locally breeding in huge colonies. Their large communal nests of sticks are unique among parrots and parakeets. These nests are used both for breeding and for roosting. If food is abundant, Monk Parakeets are perfectly capable of surviving cold winters in places such as Chicago or New York City, although supplementary food from feeders is welcome.
VOICE Wide variety of calls, mostly loud and grating squawks, can mimic human voice and other sounds.
NESTING Large, bulky stick nests placed in trees, palms, or on manmade structures; 5–8 eggs; 2 broods; March–July.
FEEDING Eats seeds, buds, flowers, fruit, nuts; occasionally eats insects; visits birdfeeders.

SIMILAR SPECIES

GREEN PARAKEET
see p.456

green breast and face

green upperparts and flight feathers

ACROBATIC FLIGHT
Flocks of vividly colored Monk Parakeets twist and turn in flight, and are notoriously vocal.

OCCURRENCE
In North America mainly restricted to urban or suburban habitats, where nests can be built in palms, deciduous trees, telephone poles, or electrical substations. Common in southern Florida; found in several other areas, north to New York City, Chicago, and Portland, Oregon.

Length **11½in (29cm)**	Wingspan **21in (53cm)**	Weight **3½oz (100g)**
Social **Flocks/Colonies**	Lifespan **Up to 6 years**	Status **Localized**

DATE SEEN	WHERE	NOTES

NEW WORLD FLYCATCHERS

BIRDS POPULARLY known as "flycatchers" occur in many parts of the world; however several different families of songbirds have this name. With the exception of some Old World species that stray into Alaska, the North American flycatchers are members of a single family—the Tyrant Flycatchers (Tyrannidae). With about 400 species, this is the largest bird family in the New World. These birds are uniform in appearance, with only a hint of the diversity in the family that is found in Central and South America. Most are drab-colored, olive-green or gray birds, sometimes with yellow underparts. The Vermilion Flycatcher is a striking exception, as is the gray and salmon-pink

BIG MOUTHS
Young Dusky Flycatchers display the wide bills that help them catch flying insects as adults.

Scissor-tailed Flycatcher, which also has elongated outer tail feathers. Members of the genus *Empidonax* include some of the most difficult birds to identify in North America; they are best distinguished by their songs. Typical flycatcher feeding behavior is to sit on a branch or exposed perch, then sally to catch flying insects. Tyrannid flycatchers are found across North America, except in Arctic regions. Most are found in wooded habitats, though others prefer woodland edges and deserts. Nearly all flycatchers are long-distance migrants and spend the northern winter in Central and South America.

TYRANT BEHAVIOR
Such aggressive display by Couch's Kingbird reflects its English and generic names. Couch's Kingbird is rare in the East.

ERECT STANCE
A large-headed look and erect posture are typical of this Eastern Phoebe.

| Order **Passeriformes** | Family **Tyrannidae** | Species **Myiarchus crinitus** |

Great Crested Flycatcher 🔊

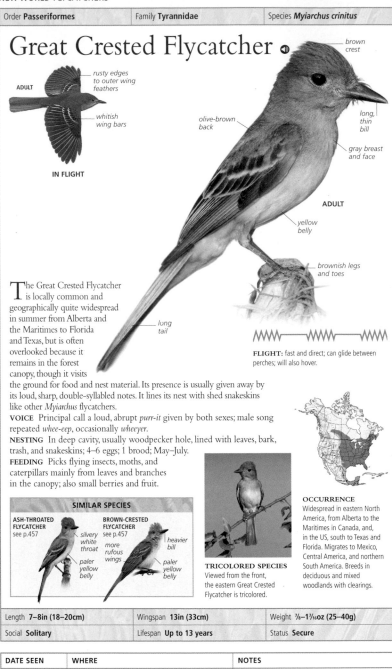

brown
crest

ADULT

rusty edges
to outer wing
feathers

whitish
wing bars

olive-brown
back

long,
thin
bill

gray breast
and face

IN FLIGHT

ADULT

yellow
belly

brownish legs
and toes

long
tail

WWW ——— WWW ——— WWW

FLIGHT: fast and direct; can glide between
perches; will also hover.

The Great Crested Flycatcher is locally common and geographically quite widespread in summer from Alberta and the Maritimes to Florida and Texas, but is often overlooked because it remains in the forest canopy, though it visits the ground for food and nest material. Its presence is usually given away by its loud, sharp, double-syllabled notes. It lines its nest with shed snakeskins like other *Myiarchus* flycatchers.

VOICE Principal call a loud, abrupt *purr-it* given by both sexes; male song repeated *whee-eep*, occasionally *wheeyer*.

NESTING In deep cavity, usually woodpecker hole, lined with leaves, bark, trash, and snakeskins; 4–6 eggs; 1 brood; May–July.

FEEDING Picks flying insects, moths, and caterpillars mainly from leaves and branches in the canopy; also small berries and fruit.

SIMILAR SPECIES

**ASH-THROATED
FLYCATCHER**
see p.457

silvery
white
throat

paler
yellow
belly

**BROWN-CRESTED
FLYCATCHER**
see p.457

more
rufous
wings

heavier
bill

paler
yellow
belly

TRICOLORED SPECIES
Viewed from the front,
the eastern Great Crested
Flycatcher is tricolored.

OCCURRENCE
Widespread in eastern North America, from Alberta to the Maritimes in Canada, and, in the US, south to Texas and Florida. Migrates to Mexico, Central America, and northern South America. Breeds in deciduous and mixed woodlands with clearings.

| Length **7–8in (18–20cm)** | Wingspan **13in (33cm)** | Weight **⅞–1⁷⁄₁₆oz (25–40g)** |
| Social **Solitary** | Lifespan **Up to 13 years** | Status **Secure** |

DATE SEEN	WHERE	NOTES

| Order **Passeriformes** | Family **Tyrannidae** | Species *Tyrannus verticalis* |

Western Kingbird 🔊

- olive-gray back
- **ADULT**
- white-edged tail
- **IN FLIGHT**
- dark wing with no wing bars
- white edge to outer tail feathers
- strong, dark eye-line
- small bill
- white chin
- gray chest
- gray back
- yellow belly
- gray head
- **ADULT**
- notched tail
- **ADULT**

A conspicuous summer breeder in the US, the Western Kingbird occurs in open habitats in much of western North America. The white outer edges on its outer tail feathers distinguish it from other kingbirds. Its population has expanded eastward over the last 100 years. A large, loosely defined territory is defended against other kingbirds when breeding begins in spring; a smaller core area is defended as the season progresses.

VOICE Calls include *whit*, *pwee-t*, and chatter; song, regularly repeated sharp *kip* notes and high-pitched notes.

NESTING Open, bulky cup of grass, rootlets, and twigs in tree, shrub, utility pole; 2–7 eggs; 1 brood; April–July.

FEEDING Feeds on a wide variety of insects; also berries and fruit.

FLIGHT: agile, fast, direct, flapping flight; flies to catch insects; hovers to pick bugs on vegetation.

FENCE POST
A favorite place for the Western Kingbird to perch, and look around, is on fenceposts.

QUENCHING THIRST
A juvenile Western Kingbird drinks at the edge of a shallow pool of water.

SIMILAR SPECIES

TROPICAL KINGBIRD see p.457
- heavier bill
- olive-yellow chest

CASSIN'S KINGBIRD
- paler wings
- gray tip to tail

OCCURRENCE
Widespread in southwestern Canada and the western US, in open habitats such as grasslands, prairie, desert shrub, pastures, and cropland, near elevated perches; particularly near water. Winters in similar habitats and in tropical forest and shrubbery from Mexico to Costa Rica.

| Length **8–9in (20–23cm)** | Wingspan **15–16in (38–41cm)** | Weight **1¼–1⁹⁄₁₆oz (35–45g)** |
| Social **Solitary** | Lifespan **Up to 6 years** | Status **Secure** |

DATE SEEN	WHERE	NOTES

Order **Passeriformes**	Family **Tyrannidae**	Species *Tyrannus tyrannus*

Eastern Kingbird 🔊

dark eyes

ADULT

dark crown and cheeks, almost black

white throat

white-tipped tail

faint gray "necklace"

white throat and underparts

relatively short, thick bill

slate-gray back

IN FLIGHT

pale edges to wing feathers

ADULT

white belly

black legs and toes

white undertail feathers

black tail with white tip

ADULT

The Eastern Kingbird is a tame and widely distributed bird. It is a highly territorial species and is known for its aggressive behavior toward potential predators, particularly crows and hawks, which it pursues relentlessly. It is able to identify and remove the eggs of the Brown-headed Cowbird when they are laid in its nest. The Eastern Kingbird is generally monogamous and pairs will return to the same territory in subsequent years. This species winters in tropical South America, where it forages for fruit in the treetops of evergreen forests.

VOICE Principal call is loud, metallic *chatter-zeer*; song rapid, electric *kdik-kdik-kdik-pika-pika-pika-kzeeeer*.

NESTING Open cup of twigs, roots, stems in hawthorn, elm, stump, fence, or post; 2–5 eggs; 1 brood; May–August.

FEEDING Catches flying insects from elevated perch or gleans insects from foliage; eats berries and fruit, except in spring.

FLIGHT: strong, direct, and very agile with vigorous, rapid wingbeats; hovers and sails.

WHITE-TIPPED
The white-tipped tails of these two Eastern Kingbirds are conspicuous as they sit on a budding twig.

SIMILAR SPECIES

THICK-BILLED KINGBIRD

dark mask

thicker bill

yellowish belly

GRAY KINGBIRD see p.458

larger bill

gray crown and back

no white on tail

OCCURRENCE
Breeds across much of North America in a variety of open habitats, including urban areas, parks, golf courses, fields with scattered shrubs, beaver ponds, and along forest edges. Long-distance migrant; winters in South America, south to Argentina.

Length **7–9in (18–23cm)**	Wingspan **13–15in (33–38cm)**	Weight **1¹⁄₁₆–2oz (30–55g)**
Social **Solitary/Pairs**	Lifespan **Up to 7 years**	Status **Secure**

DATE SEEN	WHERE	NOTES

| Order **Passeriformes** | Family **Tyrannidae** | Species *Tyrannus forficatus* |

Scissor-tailed Flycatcher

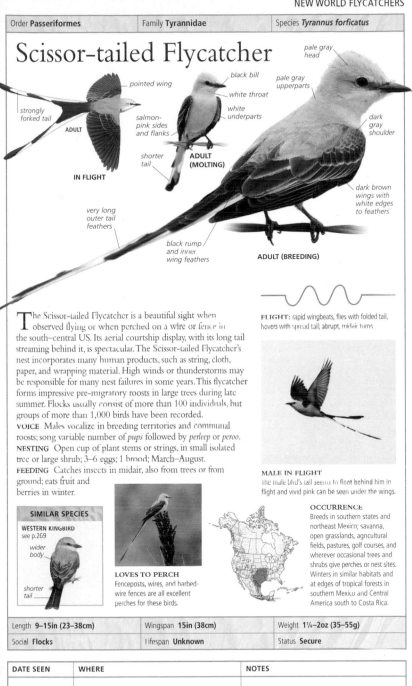

pale gray head

pointed wing

black bill

white throat

pale gray upperparts

strongly forked tail

ADULT

salmon-pink sides and flanks

white underparts

dark gray shoulder

shorter tail

ADULT (MOLTING)

IN FLIGHT

dark brown wings with white edges to feathers

very long outer tail feathers

black rump and inner wing feathers

ADULT (BREEDING)

The Scissor-tailed Flycatcher is a beautiful sight when observed flying or when perched on a wire or fence in the south–central US. Its aerial courtship display, with its long tail streaming behind it, is spectacular. The Scissor-tailed Flycatcher's nest incorporates many human products, such as string, cloth, paper, and wrapping material. High winds or thunderstorms may be responsible for many nest failures in some years. This flycatcher forms impressive pre-migratory roosts in large trees during late summer. Flocks usually consist of more than 100 individuals, but groups of more than 1,000 birds have been recorded.

VOICE Males vocalize in breeding territories and communal roosts; song variable number of *pups* followed by *perleep* or *peroo*.

NESTING Open cup of plant stems or strings, in small isolated tree or large shrub; 3–6 eggs; 1 brood; March–August.

FEEDING Catches insects in midair, also from trees or from ground; eats fruit and berries in winter.

FLIGHT: rapid wingbeats, flies with folded tail, hovers with spread tail; abrupt, midair turns.

MALE IN FLIGHT
The male bird's tail seems to float behind him in flight and vivid pink can be seen under the wings.

SIMILAR SPECIES

WESTERN KINGBIRD
see p.269

wider body

shorter tail

LOVES TO PERCH
Fenceposts, wires, and barbed-wire fences are all excellent perches for these birds.

OCCURRENCE
Breeds in southern states and northeast Mexico; savanna, open grasslands, agricultural fields, pastures, golf courses, and wherever occasional trees and shrubs give perches or nest sites. Winters in similar habitats and at edges of tropical forests in southern Mexico and Central America south to Costa Rica.

| Length **9–15in (23–38cm)** | Wingspan **15in (38cm)** | Weight **1¼–2oz (35–55g)** |
| Social **Flocks** | Lifespan **Unknown** | Status **Secure** |

DATE SEEN	WHERE	NOTES

| Order **Passeriformes** | Family **Tyrannidae** | Species ***Contopus cooperi*** |

Olive-sided Flycatcher 🔊

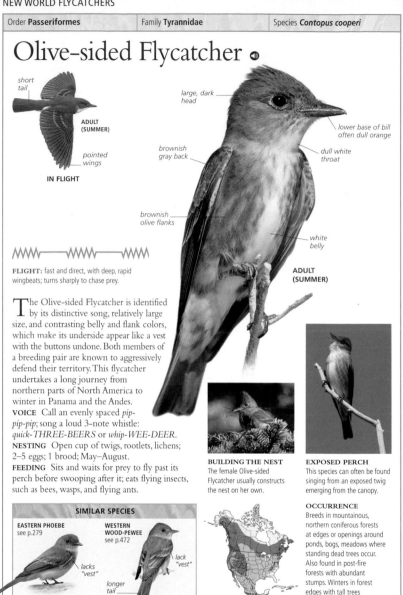

short tail

ADULT (SUMMER)

pointed wings

IN FLIGHT

large, dark head

lower base of bill often dull orange

dull white throat

brownish gray back

brownish olive flanks

white belly

ADULT (SUMMER)

FLIGHT: fast and direct, with deep, rapid wingbeats; turns sharply to chase prey.

The Olive-sided Flycatcher is identified by its distinctive song, relatively large size, and contrasting belly and flank colors, which make its underside appear like a vest with the buttons undone. Both members of a breeding pair are known to aggressively defend their territory. This flycatcher undertakes a long journey from northern parts of North America to winter in Panama and the Andes.

VOICE Call an evenly spaced *pip-pip-pip*; song a loud 3-note whistle: *quick-THREE-BEERS* or *whip-WEE-DEER*.

NESTING Open cup of twigs, rootlets, lichens; 2–5 eggs; 1 brood; May–August.

FEEDING Sits and waits for prey to fly past its perch before swooping after it; eats flying insects, such as bees, wasps, and flying ants.

BUILDING THE NEST
The female Olive-sided Flycatcher usually constructs the nest on her own.

EXPOSED PERCH
This species can often be found singing from an exposed twig emerging from the canopy.

OCCURRENCE
Breeds in mountainous, northern coniferous forests at edges or openings around ponds, bogs, meadows where standing dead trees occur. Also found in post-fire forests with abundant stumps. Winters in forest edges with tall trees and stumps.

SIMILAR SPECIES

EASTERN PHOEBE
see p.279

lacks "vest"

WESTERN WOOD-PEWEE
see p.472

lack "vest"

longer tail

| Length **7–8in (18–20cm)** | Wingspan **13in (33cm)** | Weight **1¹⁄₁₆–1¼oz (30–35g)** |
| Social **Solitary** | Lifespan **Up to 7 years** | Status **Declining** |

DATE SEEN	WHERE	NOTES

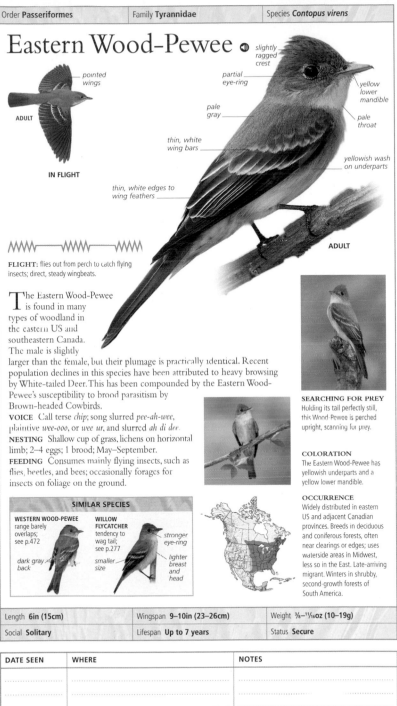

| Order **Passeriformes** | Family **Tyrannidae** | Species *Contopus virens* |

Eastern Wood-Pewee

slightly ragged crest

pointed wings

partial eye-ring

yellow lower mandible

pale gray

pale throat

ADULT

thin, white wing bars

yellowish wash on underparts

IN FLIGHT

thin, white edges to wing feathers

ADULT

FLIGHT: flies out from perch to catch flying insects; direct, steady wingbeats.

The Eastern Wood-Pewee is found in many types of woodland in the eastern US and southeastern Canada. The male is slightly larger than the female, but their plumage is practically identical. Recent population declines in this species have been attributed to heavy browsing by White-tailed Deer. This has been compounded by the Eastern Wood-Pewee's susceptibility to brood parasitism by Brown-headed Cowbirds.

VOICE Call terse *chip*; song slurred *pee-ah-wee*, plaintive *wee-ooo*, or *wee ur*, and slurred *ah di dee*.

NESTING Shallow cup of grass, lichens on horizontal limb; 2–4 eggs; 1 brood; May–September.

FEEDING Consumes mainly flying insects, such as flies, beetles, and bees; occasionally forages for insects on foliage on the ground.

SEARCHING FOR PREY
Holding its tail perfectly still, this Wood-Pewee is perched upright, scanning for prey.

COLORATION
The Eastern Wood-Pewee has yellowish underparts and a yellow lower mandible.

OCCURRENCE
Widely distributed in eastern US and adjacent Canadian provinces. Breeds in deciduous and coniferous forests, often near clearings or edges; uses waterside areas in Midwest, less so in the East. Late-arriving migrant. Winters in shrubby, second-growth forests of South America.

SIMILAR SPECIES

WESTERN WOOD-PEWEE
range barely overlaps; see p.472

dark gray back

WILLOW FLYCATCHER
tendency to wag tail; see p.277

stronger eye-ring

smaller size

lighter breast and head

| Length **6in (15cm)** | Wingspan **9–10in (23–26cm)** | Weight **⅜–¹¹⁄₁₆oz (10–19g)** |
| Social **Solitary** | Lifespan **Up to 7 years** | Status **Secure** |

DATE SEEN	WHERE	NOTES

| Order **Passeriformes** | Family **Tyrannidae** | Species *Empidonax flaviventris* |

Yellow–bellied Flycatcher

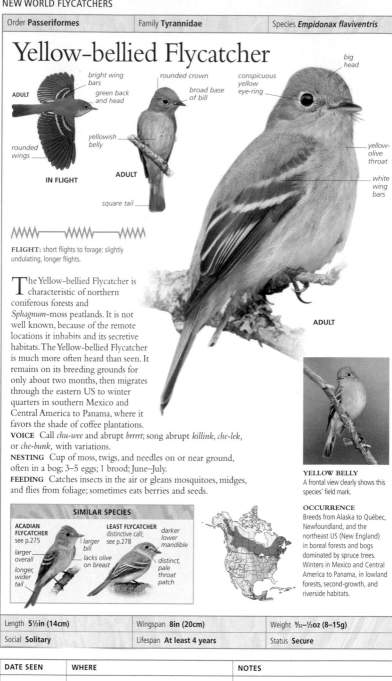

ADULT

bright wing
bars

green back
and head

rounded
wings

IN FLIGHT

rounded crown

broad base
of bill

yellowish
belly

ADULT

square tail

big
head

conspicuous
yellow
eye-ring

yellow-
olive
throat

white
wing
bars

ADULT

FLIGHT: short flights to forage; slightly
undulating, longer flights.

The Yellow-bellied Flycatcher is
characteristic of northern
coniferous forests and
Sphagnum-moss peatlands. It is not
well known, because of the remote
locations it inhabits and its secretive
habitats. The Yellow-bellied Flycatcher
is much more often heard than seen. It
remains on its breeding grounds for
only about two months, then migrates
through the eastern US to winter
quarters in southern Mexico and
Central America to Panama, where it
favors the shade of coffee plantations.
VOICE Call *chu-wee* and abrupt *brrrrt*; song abrupt *killink, che-lek,*
or *che-bunk,* with variations.
NESTING Cup of moss, twigs, and needles on or near ground,
often in a bog; 3–5 eggs; 1 brood; June–July.
FEEDING Catches insects in the air or gleans mosquitoes, midges,
and flies from foliage; sometimes eats berries and seeds.

YELLOW BELLY
A frontal view clearly shows this
species' field mark.

OCCURRENCE
Breeds from Alaska to Québec,
Newfoundland, and the
northeast US (New England)
in boreal forests and bogs
dominated by spruce trees.
Winters in Mexico and Central
America to Panama, in lowland
forests, second-growth, and
riverside habitats.

SIMILAR SPECIES		
ACADIAN FLYCATCHER see p.275 larger overall longer, wider tail	larger bill **LEAST FLYCATCHER** distinctive call; see p.278 lacks olive on breast	darker lower mandible distinct, pale throat patch

Length **5½in (14cm)**	Wingspan **8in (20cm)**	Weight **⁹⁄₃₂–½oz (8–15g)**
Social **Solitary**	Lifespan **At least 4 years**	Status **Secure**

DATE SEEN	WHERE	NOTES

Order **Passeriformes**	Family **Tyrannidae**	Species ***Empidonax virescens***

Acadian Flycatcher

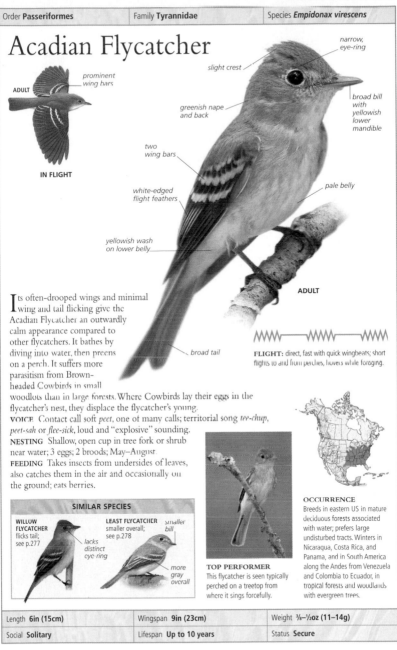

narrow, eye-ring

slight crest

ADULT

prominent wing bars

greenish nape and back

broad bill with yellowish lower mandible

two wing bars

IN FLIGHT

white-edged flight feathers

pale belly

yellowish wash on lower belly

ADULT

Its often-drooped wings and minimal wing and tail flicking give the Acadian Flycatcher an outwardly calm appearance compared to other flycatchers. It bathes by diving into water, then preens on a perch. It suffers more parasitism from Brown-headed Cowbirds in small woodlots than in large forests. Where Cowbirds lay their eggs in the flycatcher's nest, they displace the flycatcher's young.

broad tail

FLIGHT: direct, fast with quick wingbeats; short flights to and from perches, hovers while foraging.

VOICE Contact call soft *peet*, one of many calls; territorial song *tee-chup*, *peet-sah* or *flee-sick*, loud and "explosive" sounding.

NESTING Shallow, open cup in tree fork or shrub near water; 3 eggs; 2 broods; May–August.

FEEDING Takes insects from undersides of leaves, also catches them in the air and occasionally on the ground; eats berries.

TOP PERFORMER
This flycatcher is seen typically perched on a treetop from where it sings forcefully.

OCCURRENCE
Breeds in eastern US in mature deciduous forests associated with water; prefers large undisturbed tracts. Winters in Nicaragua, Costa Rica, and Panama, and in South America along the Andes from Venezuela and Colombia to Ecuador, in tropical forests and woodlands with evergreen trees.

SIMILAR SPECIES

WILLOW FLYCATCHER
flicks tail;
see p.277

lacks distinct eye-ring

LEAST FLYCATCHER
smaller overall;
see p.278

smaller bill

more gray overall

Length **6in (15cm)**	Wingspan **9in (23cm)**	Weight **⅜–½oz (11–14g)**
Social **Solitary**	Lifespan **Up to 10 years**	Status **Secure**

DATE SEEN	WHERE	NOTES

Order **Passeriformes**	Family **Tyrannidae**	Species *Empidonax alnorum*

Alder Flycatcher

ADULT
two white wing bars

rounded wings

IN FLIGHT

white eye-ring

brownish olive head

dark upper mandible

paler lower mandible

brownish olive upperparts

whitish throat and breast

ADULT

dark legs and toes

FLIGHT: short bursts, with twists and turns; weak over long distances.

Until 1973 the Alder Flycatcher and the Willow Flycatcher were considered to be one species called Traill's Flycatcher. The two species cannot be reliably identified by sight, but they do have distinctive songs. The Alder Flycatcher also breeds farther north than the Willow Flycatcher, arriving late in spring and leaving early in fall. Its nests are extremely hard to locate, and much remains to be learned about this bird's breeding habits.

long, dark tail

VOICE Calls include flat *pit* or *pip-peep-tip*, also *wee-oo* and *churr*; male sings characteristic *fee-bee-o* song while breeding, and occasionally during spring migration.

NESTING Coarse and loosely structured nest low in fork of deciduous shrub; 3–4 eggs; 1 brood; June–July.

FEEDING Mostly eats insects, caught mainly in flight, but some gleaned from foliage; eats fruit in winter.

ON THE ALERT
Attentive to potential meals, an Alder Flycatcher will swiftly pursue prey as soon as it flies by.

SIMILAR SPECIES

ACADIAN FLYCATCHER see p.275

greener back

longer, deeper bill

WILLOW FLYCATCHER see p.277

fainter eye-ring

slightly longer bill

OCCURRENCE
Breeds at low density across northern North America, in wet shrubby habitats with alder or willow thickets, often close to streams. Winters at low elevations in South America in tropical second-growth forest and forest edges.

Length **5¾in (14.5cm)**	Wingspan **8½in (22cm)**	Weight **½oz (14g)**
Social **Solitary**	Lifespan **At least 3 years**	Status **Secure**

DATE SEEN	WHERE	NOTES

Order **Passeriformes**	Family **Tyrannidae**	Species *Empidonax traillii*

Willow Flycatcher

square tail

two buff to yellow wing bars

ADULT

IN FLIGHT

thin eye ring

brown eye

dark upper mandible

paler lower mandible

grayish green upperparts

yellow-tinged flanks

whitish belly

ADULT

dark legs and toes

FLIGHT: weak and fluttering; swoops and hovers when pursuing insects.

dark tail

The Willow Flycatcher is only distinguished from the nearly identical Alder Flycatcher by its song. It is a strongly territorial bird, spreading its tail and flicking it upward during aggressive encounters. The Willow Flycatcher is, however, a frequent victim of brood parasitism by the Brown-headed Cowbird, which lays its eggs in the flycatcher's nest and removes the eggs that were already inside. Compounded by loss of suitable breeding habitat, this may be a major reason for the Willow Flycatcher's decline, especially in the case of the southwestern subspecies, *E. t. extimus*, which is now considered endangered.

VOICE Calls include soft, dry *whit* and several buzzy notes; song sharp *fitz-bew* with accent on the first syllable; also *creet*.

NESTING Rather loose and untidy cup in base of shrub near water; 3–4 eggs; 1 brood; May–August.

FEEDING Eats insects, mostly caught in flight; eats fruit in winter.

UNEVEN WORKLOAD
Although both parents feed their young, the female Willow Flycatcher does so the most.

SIMILAR SPECIES

ALDER FLYCATCHER different song; see p.276

bolder wing bars

LEAST FLYCATCHER see p.278

larger head

bold white eye-ring

OCCURRENCE
Breeds from southern Canada to eastern and southwestern US, mainly in willow thickets and other moist shrubby areas along watercourses. On winter grounds, it favors lighter woodland, shrubby clearings, and brush near water in coastal areas.

Length **5–6¾in (13–17cm)**	Wingspan **7½–9½in (19–24cm)**	Weight **⅜–⁹⁄₁₆oz (11–16g)**
Social **Solitary**	Lifespan **Up to 11 years**	Status **Declining**

DATE SEEN	WHERE	NOTES

| Order **Passeriformes** | Family **Tyrannidae** | Species *Empidonax minimus* |

Least Flycatcher 🔊

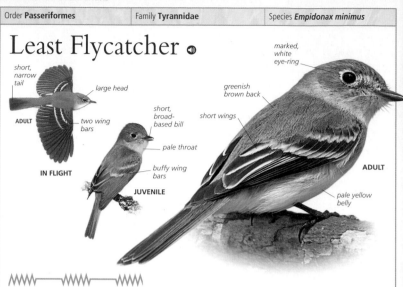

short, narrow tail

large head

ADULT

two wing bars

IN FLIGHT

short, broad-based bill

pale throat

buffy wing bars

JUVENILE

marked, white eye-ring

greenish brown back

short wings

ADULT

pale yellow belly

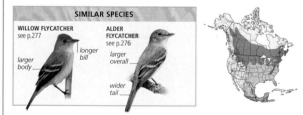

FLIGHT: direct, short forays with rapid wingbeats to catch prey; sometimes hovers briefly.

The smallest eastern member of the *Empidonax* genus is a solitary bird and is very aggressive toward intruders encroaching upon its breeding territory, including other species of flycatchers. This combative behavior reduces the likelihood of acting as unwitting host parents to eggs laid by the Brown-headed Cowbird. The Least Flycatcher is very active, and frequently flicks its wings and tail upward. Common in the eastern US in mixed and deciduous woodland, especially at the edges, it spends a short time—up to only two months—on its northern breeding grounds before migrating south. Adults molt in winter, while young molt before and during fall migration.

VOICE Call soft, short *whit*; song frequent, persistent, characteristic *tchebeck*, sings during spring migration and breeding season.

NESTING Compact cup of tightly woven bark strips and plant fibers in fork of deciduous tree; 3–5 eggs; 1 brood; May–July.

FEEDING Feeds principally on insects, such as flies, midges, beetles, ants, butterflies, and larvae; occasionally eats berries and seeds.

YELLOW TINGE
The subtle yellow tinge to its underparts and white undertail feathers are evident here.

SIMILAR SPECIES

WILLOW FLYCATCHER see p.277

larger body

longer bill

ALDER FLYCATCHER see p.276

larger overall

wider tail

OCCURRENCE
Breeds in coniferous and mixed deciduous forests across North America, east of Rockies to East Coast; occasionally in conifer groves or wooded wetlands, often near openings or edges. Winters in Central America in varied habitat from second-growth evergreen woodland to arid scrub.

| Length **5¼in (13.5cm)** | Wingspan **7¾in (19.5cm)** | Weight **⁹⁄₃₂–⁷⁄₁₆oz (8–13g)** |
| Social **Solitary** | Lifespan **Up to 6 years** | Status **Secure** |

DATE SEEN	WHERE	NOTES

| Order **Passeriformes** | Family **Tyrannidae** | Species *Sayornis phoebe* |

Eastern Phoebe 🔊

round, dark-capped head

ADULT
rounded wings with two faint wing bars

white throat

dark eye

IN FLIGHT

ADULT (FALL)
yellowish tint on lower belly

olive tint to sides and breast

long, dark tail

ADULT (BREEDING)

The Eastern Phoebe is an early spring migrant that tends to nest under bridges, culverts, and on buildings, in addition to rocky outcroppings. Not shy, it is also familiar because of its *fee-bee* vocalization and constant tail wagging. By tying a thread on the leg of several Eastern Phoebes, ornithologist John James Audubon established that individuals return from the south to a previously used nest site. Although difficult to tell apart, males tend to be slightly larger and darker than females.
VOICE Common call a clear, weak *chip*; song an emphatic *fee-bee* or *fee-b be bee*.
NESTING Open cup of mud, moss, and leaves, almost exclusively on manmade structures; 3–5 eggs; 2 broods; April–July.
FEEDING Feeds mainly on flying insects; also consumes small fruit from fall through winter.

FLIGHT: direct, with steady wingbeats; hovers occasionally; approaches nest with a low swoop.

PALE EDGES
Perched on a twig, a male shows off the pale margins of his wing feathers.

LIGHTER FEMALE
They are difficult to distinguish, but the female is slightly lighter overall than the male.

OCCURRENCE
Found in open woodland and along deciduous or mixed forest edges, in gardens and parks, near water. Breeds across Canada from the Northwest Territories south of the tundra belt and in the eastern half of the US. Winters in the southeast US and Mexico.

SIMILAR SPECIES

EASTERN WOOD-PEWEE
lacks tail-wag; see p.273
distinct wing bars

WILLOW FLYCATCHER
flicks tail upward; see p.277
often has eye-ring
more distinct wing bars
smaller overall

| Length **5½–7in (14–17cm)** | Wingspan **10½in (27cm)** | Weight **¹¹⁄₁₆oz (20g)** |
| Social **Solitary** | Lifespan **Up to 9 years** | Status **Secure** |

DATE SEEN	WHERE	NOTES

SHRIKES AND VIREOS

SHRIKES

Two of the thirty species of shrikes (Laniidae) occur in Canada and the United States. The Loggerhead Shrike is truly North American, but the other North American species, the Northern (or Gray) Shrike, is also widespread in Europe and western Asia. Shrikes have a strongly hooked bill, almost like a bird of prey. In fact, shrikes capture not only insects, but also birds, rodents, and lizards, which they impale on a thorn in a shrub (a larder). Shrikes pounce down on their prey from high perches in trees or on fenceposts, catching it on or near the ground. Many shrike species are declining.

KEEN SONGSTER
The White-eyed Vireo sings almost continuously, even on the hottest of summer days.

VIREOS

Vireos are a family of songbirds restricted to the New World, with about 15 species occurring in the United States and Canada. Their classification has long been problematic—traditionally they were associated with warblers, but recent molecular studies suggest that they are actually related to crow-like birds. Vireo plumage is drab, often predominantly greenish or grayish above and whitish below, augmented by eye-rings, ("spectacles,") eyestripes, and wing bars. Most vireos have a preference for broadleaved habitats, where they move about deliberately, hopping and climbing as they slowly forage for their prey. They are mainly insect-eaters. Most species are mid- to long-distance migrants, retreating to warmer climes in winter, when insects are dormant. Vireos are most often detected by the male's loud and clear territorial song, which is repetitive and persistent.

SEPARATE SPECIES
The Blue-headed Vireo is one of three species, formerly known as just one species, the Solitary Vireo.

JAYS AND CROWS

ALTHOUGH JAYS AND crows belong to a highly diverse family, the Corvidae, most members share some important characteristics. They are remarkably social, some species even breed cooperatively, but at the same time they can be quiet and stealthy. Always opportunistic, corvids use strong bills and toes to obtain a varied, omnivorous diet. Ornithologists have shown that ravens, magpies, and crows are among the most intelligent birds. They exhibit self-awareness when looking into mirrors, can make tools, and successfully tackle difficult counting and problem-solving. As a rule, most corvid plumage comes in shades of blue, black, and white. The plumage of adult corvids does not vary by season. Corvidae are part of an ancient bird lineage (Corvoidea) that originated in Australasia. Crows and jays were among the birds most affected by the spread of West Nile virus in the early 2000s, but most populations seem to have recovered quickly.

WHITE AND BLUE
Everybody knows at least one bird, and it is likely to be the Blue Jay.

| Order **Passeriformes** | Family **Laniidae** | Species *Lanius ludovicianus* |

Loggerhead Shrike 🔊

ADULT

white flash in wings

white edges to tail

IN FLIGHT

black wings

pale undertail feathers

JUVENILE

gray crown

black "mask"

hooked bill

unstreaked, gray underparts

ADULT

rounded tail

FLIGHT: fast with rapid wingbeats, sometimes interspersed with glides; swoops from perches.

Although a songbird, the Loggerhead Shrike behaves like a small bird of prey and has a hooked bill and strong, sharp, curved claws. It sits atop posts or tall trees, swooping down to catch prey on the ground. It has the unusual habit of then impaling its prey on thorns, barbed wire, or sharp twigs, which is the reason for the nickname "butcher bird." Unfortunately, the Loggerhead Shrike is declining, principally because of human alteration of its habitat.

VOICE Quiet warbles, trills, and harsh notes; song harsh notes singly or in series: *chaa chaa chaa.*
NESTING Open cup of vegetation, placed in thorny tree; 5 eggs; 1 brood; March–June.
FEEDING Kills large insects and small vertebrates—rodents, birds, reptiles—with powerful bill.

GEARED FOR HUNTING
The Loggerhead Shrike perches upright on tall shrubs or small trees, where it scans for prey.

OCCURRENCE
Found in semi-open country with scattered perches, but its distribution is erratic, occurring in relatively high densities in certain areas, but absent from seemingly suitable habitat. Occurs in congested residential areas in some regions (south Florida), but generally favors fairly remote habitats.

SIMILAR SPECIES

NORTHERN SHRIKE see p.282

smaller bill

lighter upperparts

NORTHERN MOCKINGBIRD see p.334

darker upperparts

longer tail

| Length **9in (23cm)** | Wingspan **12in (31cm)** | Weight **1¼–2⅛oz (35–60g)** |
| Social **Solitary** | Lifespan **Unknown** | Status **Declining** |

DATE SEEN	WHERE	NOTES

| Order **Passeriformes** | Family **Laniidae** | Species **Lanius borealis** |

Northern Shrike

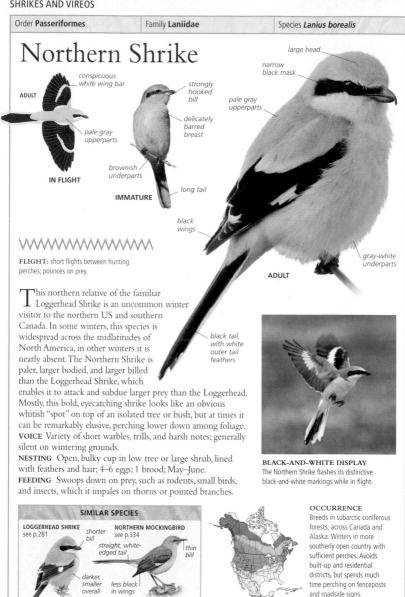

ADULT

conspicuous white wing bar

IN FLIGHT

pale gray upperparts

strongly hooked bill

delicately barred breast

brownish underparts

long tail

IMMATURE

large head

narrow black mask

pale gray upperparts

black wings

gray-white underparts

ADULT

black tail, with white outer tail feathers

FLIGHT: short flights between hunting perches; pounces on prey.

This northern relative of the familiar Loggerhead Shrike is an uncommon winter visitor to the northern US and southern Canada. In some winters, this species is widespread across the midlatitudes of North America, in other winters it is nearly absent. The Northern Shrike is paler, larger bodied, and larger billed than the Loggerhead Shrike, which enables it to attack and subdue larger prey than the Loggerhead. Mostly, this bold, eyecatching shrike looks like an obvious whitish "spot" on top of an isolated tree or bush, but at times it can be remarkably elusive, perching lower down among foliage. **VOICE** Variety of short warbles, trills, and harsh notes; generally silent on wintering grounds. **NESTING** Open, bulky cup in low tree or large shrub, lined with feathers and hair; 4–6 eggs; 1 brood; May–June. **FEEDING** Swoops down on prey, such as rodents, small birds, and insects, which it impales on thorns or pointed branches.

BLACK-AND-WHITE DISPLAY
The Northern Shrike flashes its distinctive black-and-white markings while in flight.

SIMILAR SPECIES

LOGGERHEAD SHRIKE see p.281

shorter bill

darker, smaller overall

NORTHERN MOCKINGBIRD see p.334

straight, white-edged tail

thin bill

less black in wings

OCCURRENCE
Breeds in subarctic coniferous forests, across Canada and Alaska. Winters in more southerly open country with sufficient perches. Avoids built-up and residential districts, but spends much time perching on fenceposts and roadside signs.

| Length **10in (25cm)** | Wingspan **14in (35cm)** | Weight **1¾–2⅝oz (50–75g)** |
| Social **Solitary** | Lifespan **Unknown** | Status **Vulnerable** |

DATE SEEN	WHERE	NOTES

| Order **Passeriformes** | Family **Vireonidae** | Species *Vireo griseus* |

White-eyed Vireo 🔊

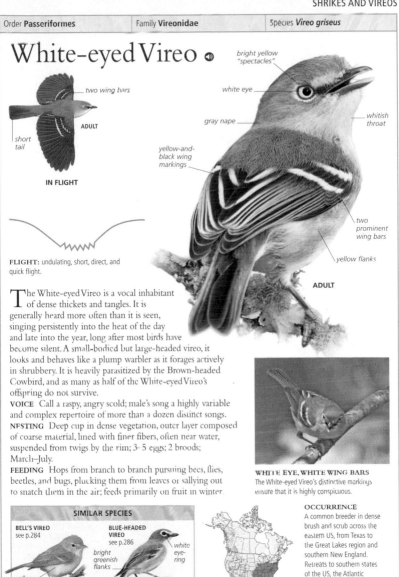

two wing bars

ADULT

short tail

IN FLIGHT

FLIGHT: undulating, short, direct, and quick flight.

bright yellow "spectacles"

white eye

gray nape

yellow-and-black wing markings

whitish throat

two prominent wing bars

yellow flanks

ADULT

The White-eyed Vireo is a vocal inhabitant of dense thickets and tangles. It is generally heard more often than it is seen, singing persistently into the heat of the day and late into the year, long after most birds have become silent. A small-bodied but large-headed vireo, it looks and behaves like a plump warbler as it forages actively in shrubbery. It is heavily parasitized by the Brown-headed Cowbird, and as many as half of the White-eyed Vireo's offspring do not survive.

VOICE Call a raspy, angry scold; male's song a highly variable and complex repertoire of more than a dozen distinct songs.

NESTING Deep cup in dense vegetation, outer layer composed of coarse material, lined with finer fibers, often near water, suspended from twigs by the rim; 3–5 eggs; 2 broods; March–July.

FEEDING Hops from branch to branch pursuing bees, flies, beetles, and bugs, plucking them from leaves or sallying out to snatch them in the air; feeds primarily on fruit in winter.

WHITE EYE, WHITE WING BARS
The White-eyed Vireo's distinctive markings ensure that it is highly conspicuous.

SIMILAR SPECIES

BELL'S VIREO
see p.284

BLUE-HEADED VIREO
see p.286

bright greenish flanks

yellow flanks

white eye-ring

OCCURRENCE
A common breeder in dense brush and scrub across the eastern US, from Texas to the Great Lakes region and southern New England. Retreats to southern states of the US, the Atlantic slope of Mexico, Cuba, and the Bahamas in winter.

| Length **5in (13cm)** | Wingspan **7½in (19cm)** | Weight **⅜oz (10g)** |
| Social **Solitary** | Lifespan **Up to 7 years** | Status **Secure** |

DATE SEEN	WHERE	NOTES

| Order **Passeriformes** | Family **Vireonidae** | Species *Vireo bellii* |

Bell's Vireo

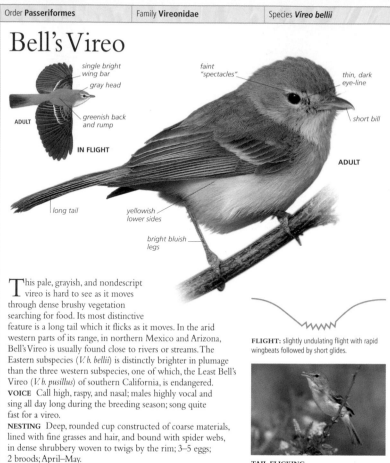

IN FLIGHT

- single bright wing bar
- gray head
- greenish back and rump

ADULT

- faint "spectacles"
- thin, dark eye-line
- short bill

ADULT

- long tail
- yellowish lower sides
- bright bluish legs

This pale, grayish, and nondescript vireo is hard to see as it moves through dense brushy vegetation searching for food. Its most distinctive feature is a long tail which it flicks as it moves. In the arid western parts of its range, in northern Mexico and Arizona, Bell's Vireo is usually found close to rivers or streams. The Eastern subspecies (*V. b. bellii*) is distinctly brighter in plumage than the three western subspecies, one of which, the Least Bell's Vireo (*V. b. pusillus*) of southern California, is endangered.

VOICE Call high, raspy, and nasal; males highly vocal and sing all day long during the breeding season; song quite fast for a vireo.

NESTING Deep, rounded cup constructed of coarse materials, lined with fine grasses and hair, and bound with spider webs, in dense shrubbery woven to twigs by the rim; 3–5 eggs; 2 broods; April–May.

FEEDING Actively gleans its insect and spider prey from leaves and twigs, hopping from branch to branch in brushy vegetation.

FLIGHT: slightly undulating flight with rapid wingbeats followed by short glides.

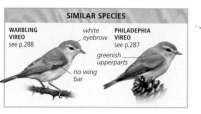

TAIL FLICKING
Unlike other vireos, Bell's Vireo is known for flicking its long tail as it sings.

SIMILAR SPECIES

WARBLING VIREO see p.288
- white eyebrow
- no wing bar

PHILADELPHIA VIREO see p.287
- greenish upperparts

OCCURRENCE
Fairly common breeder in the bushy habitats of the central US, and the riverside thickets of the southwestern US, southward into northern Mexico. Winters along the Pacific slopes of Mexico.

| Length **4¾in (12cm)** | Wingspan **7in (18cm)** | Weight **⁵⁄₁₆oz (9g)** |
| Social **Solitary** | Lifespan **Up to 8 years** | Status **Vulnerable** |

DATE SEEN	WHERE	NOTES

| Order **Passeriformes** | Family **Vireonidae** | Species **Vireo flavifrons** |

Yellow-throated Vireo 🔊

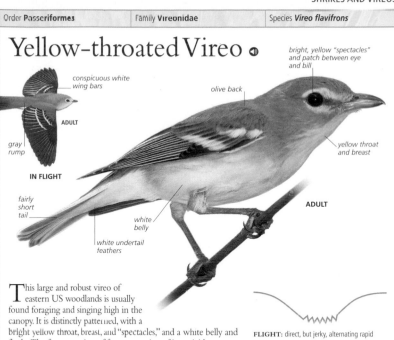

conspicuous white wing bars

ADULT

gray rump

IN FLIGHT

olive back

bright, yellow "spectacles" and patch between eye and bill

yellow throat and breast

ADULT

fairly short tail

white belly

white undertail feathers

This large and robust vireo of eastern US woodlands is usually found foraging and singing high in the canopy. It is distinctly patterned, with a bright yellow throat, breast, and "spectacles," and a white belly and flanks. The fragmentation of forests, spraying of insecticides, and cowbird parasitism have led to regional declines in Yellow-throated Vireo populations, but the bird's range, as a whole, has actually expanded.

VOICE Scolding, hoarse, rapid calls; male song a slow, repetitive, two- or three-note phrase, separated by long pauses.

NESTING Rounded cup of plant and animal fibers bound with spider webs, usually located toward the top of a large tree and hung by the rim; 3–5 eggs; 1 brood; April–July.

FEEDING Forages high in trees, picking spiders and insects from the branches; also eats fruit when available.

FLIGHT: direct, but jerky, alternating rapid wingbeats with brief pauses.

CANOPY SINGER
The Yellow-throated Vireo sings from the very tops of tall trees.

HIGH FORAGER
This bird finds much of its food in the peeling bark of mature trees.

OCCURRENCE
Breeds in extensive, mature deciduous, and mixed woodlands in the eastern half of the US, and extreme southern Canada. Winters mainly from southern Mexico to northern South America, primarily in wooded areas.

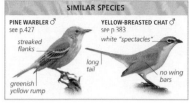

SIMILAR SPECIES

PINE WARBLER ♂ see p.427
streaked flanks
greenish yellow rump

YELLOW-BREASTED CHAT ♂ see p.383
white "spectacles"
long tail
no wing bars

| Length **5½in (14cm)** | Wingspan **9½in (24cm)** | Weight **⅝oz (18g)** |
| Social **Solitary/Pairs** | Lifespan **Up to 6 years** | Status **Secure** |

DATE SEEN	WHERE	NOTES

| Order **Passeriformes** | Family **Vireonidae** | Species *Vireo solitarius* |

Blue-headed Vireo 🔊

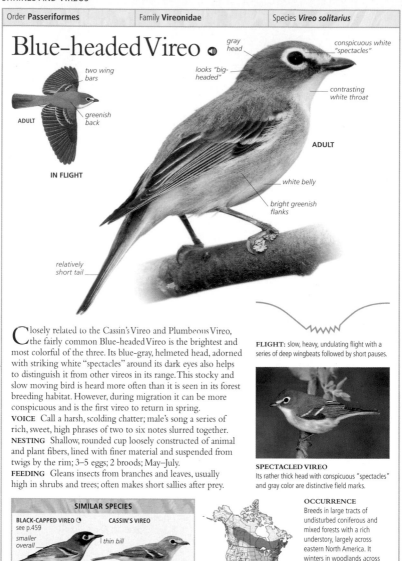

gray head

looks "big-headed"

conspicuous white "spectacles"

contrasting white throat

two wing bars

greenish back

ADULT

IN FLIGHT

ADULT

white belly

bright greenish flanks

relatively short tail

Closely related to the Cassin's Vireo and Plumbeous Vireo, the fairly common Blue-headed Vireo is the brightest and most colorful of the three. Its blue-gray, helmeted head, adorned with striking white "spectacles" around its dark eyes also helps to distinguish it from other vireos in its range. This stocky and slow moving bird is heard more often than it is seen in its forest breeding habitat. However, during migration it can be more conspicuous and is the first vireo to return in spring.

VOICE Call a harsh, scolding chatter; male's song a series of rich, sweet, high phrases of two to six notes slurred together.
NESTING Shallow, rounded cup loosely constructed of animal and plant fibers, lined with finer material and suspended from twigs by the rim; 3–5 eggs; 2 broods; May–July.
FEEDING Gleans insects from branches and leaves, usually high in shrubs and trees; often makes short sallies after prey.

FLIGHT: slow, heavy, undulating flight with a series of deep wingbeats followed by short pauses.

SPECTACLED VIREO
Its rather thick head with conspicuous "spectacles" and gray color are distinctive field marks.

SIMILAR SPECIES

BLACK-CAPPED VIREO ◔
see p.459
smaller overall

CASSIN'S VIREO
thin bill
duller overall

OCCURRENCE
Breeds in large tracts of undisturbed coniferous and mixed forests with a rich understory, largely across eastern North America. It winters in woodlands across the southeastern US from Virginia to Texas, as well as in Mexico and northern Central America to Costa Rica.

| Length **5½in (14in)** | Wingspan **9½in (24cm)** | Weight **⁹⁄₁₆oz (16g)** |
| Social **Solitary/Pairs** | Lifespan **Up to 7 years** | Status **Secure** |

DATE SEEN	WHERE	NOTES

| Order **Passeriformes** | Family **Vireonidae** | Species *Vireo philadelphicus* |

Philadelphia Vireo

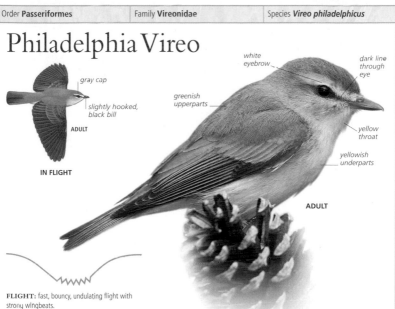

white eyebrow

dark line through eye

gray cap

greenish upperparts

slightly hooked, black bill

ADULT

yellow throat

yellowish underparts

IN FLIGHT

ADULT

FLIGHT: fast, bouncy, undulating flight with strong wingbeats.

Despite being widespread, the Philadelphia Vireo remains rather poorly studied. It shares its breeding habitat with the similar looking, but larger and more numerous, Red-eyed Vireo, and, interestingly, it modifies its behavior to avoid competition. It is the most northerly breeding vireo, with its southernmost breeding range barely reaching the US. Its scientific and English names derive from the fact that the bird was first discovered near Philadelphia in the mid-19th century.

VOICE Song a series of two and four note phrases, remarkably similar to the song of the Red-eyed Vireo.

NESTING Rounded cup of plant fibers bound by spider webs, hanging between forked twigs that narrows at the rim; 3–5 eggs; 1–2 broods; June–August.

FEEDING Gleans caterpillars, bees, flies, and bugs from leaves; usually forages high in trees, moving with short hops and flights.

DISTINGUISHED APPEARANCE
The Philadelphia Vireo's gentle expression and pudgy appearance help separate it from its neighbor, the Red-eyed Vireo.

SIMILAR SPECIES

BELL'S VIREO
see p.284
faint wing bar
longer tail

WARBLING VIREO
see p.288
plainer face
less yellow below

OCCURRENCE
Breeds in deciduous woodlands, mixed woodlands, and woodland edges, in a wide belt across Canada, reaching the Great Lakes and northern New England. The Philadelphia Vireo winters from Mexico to Panama and northern Colombia.

| Length **5¼in (13.5cm)** | Wingspan **8in (20cm)** | Weight **⁷⁄₁₆oz (12g)** |
| Social **Solitary/Pairs** | Lifespan **Up to 8 years** | Status **Secure** |

DATE SEEN	WHERE	NOTES

Order **Passeriformes**	Family **Vireonidae**	Species **Vireo gilvus**

Warbling Vireo 🔊

pale brownish
crown contrasts
with darker back

grayish green
upperparts

white
eyebrow

grayish
behind eye

blackish
bill

ADULT

**ADULT
(FALL)**

IN FLIGHT

grayish
overall

pale
patch
between
eye
and bill

yellowish
flanks

ADULT

FLIGHT: fast and undulating; rapid wingbeats
followed by brief, closed-wing glides.

Widely distributed across North America, this rather drab vireo is better known for its cheerful warbling song than for its plumage, and coincidentally, its thin bill and longish tail give this rather active vireo a somewhat warbler-like appearance. Eastern and western Warbling Vireos are quite different and may in fact be separate species. Eastern birds are heavier and have a larger bill. Out of all the vireos, the Warbling Vireo is most likely to breed in human developments, such as city parks, suburbs, and orchards.

VOICE Harsh, raspy scold call; male's persistent song a high, rapid, and highly variable warble.

NESTING Rough cup placed high in a deciduous tree, hung from the rim between forked twigs; 3–5 eggs; 2 broods; March–July.

FEEDING Gleans a variety of insects, including grasshoppers, aphids, and beetles from leaves; eats fruit in winter.

PLAIN-LOOKING SONGSTER
The Warbling Vireo makes up for its plain appearance by its colorful voice, full of rounded notes and melodious warbles.

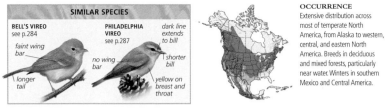

SIMILAR SPECIES		

BELL'S VIREO
see p.284

faint wing
bar

longer
tail

**PHILADELPHIA
VIREO**
see p.287

no wing
bar

dark line
extends
to bill

shorter
bill

yellow on
breast and
throat

OCCURRENCE
Extensive distribution across most of temperate North America, from Alaska to western, central, and eastern North America. Breeds in deciduous and mixed forests, particularly near water. Winters in southern Mexico and Central America.

Length **5½in (14cm)**	Wingspan **8½in (21cm)**	Weight **⁷⁄₁₆oz (12g)**
Social **Solitary/Pairs**	Lifespan **Up to 13 years**	Status **Secure**

DATE SEEN	WHERE	NOTES

| Order **Passeriformes** | Family **Vireonidae** | Species **Vireo olivaceus** |

Red-eyed Vireo 🔊

generally olive above

head held at downward angle

ADULT

IN FLIGHT

gray crown

white eyestripe with black upper border

heavy eye-line

long bill

deep red eye

ADULT

bird appears long and slender

whitish underparts

bluish legs and toes

FLIGHT: fast, strong, and undulating with the body angled upward.

Probably the most common songbird of northern and eastern North America, the Red-eyed Vireo is perhaps the quintessential North American vireo, although it is heard far more often than it is seen. It sings persistently and monotonously all day long and late into the season, long after other species have stopped singing. It generally stays high in the canopy of the deciduous and mixed woodlands where it breeds. The entire population migrates to central South America in winter. To reach their Amazonian winter habitats, Red-eyed Vireos migrate in fall (August–October) through Central America, Caribbean Islands, and northern South America to Ecuador, Peru, and Brazil.

VOICE Nasal mewing call; male song consists of slurred three-note phrases.

NESTING Open cup nest hanging on horizontal fork of tree branch; built with plant fibers bound with spider's web; exterior is sometimes decorated with lichen; 3–5 eggs; 1 brood; May–July.

FEEDING Gleans insects from leaves, hopping methodically in the canopy and sub-canopy of deciduous trees; during fall and winter, primarily feeds on fruit.

HOPPING BIRD
The Red-eyed Vireo's primary form of locomotion is hopping, at ground level and in trees.

OCCURRENCE
Breeds across North America from the Yukon and British Columbia east to the Canadian maritimes, and from Washington to eastern and southeastern US. Inhabits the canopy of deciduous forests and pine hardwood forests.

SIMILAR SPECIES

BLACK-WHISKERED VIREO
see p.460

faint black "mustache"

duller green upperparts

BROWN EYES
Immature Red-eyed Vireos have brown eyes, but those of the adult birds are red.

| Length **6in (15cm)** | Wingspan **10in (25cm)** | Weight **⅝oz (17g)** |
| Social **Solitary/Pairs** | Lifespan **Up to 10 years** | Status **Secure** |

DATE SEEN	WHERE	NOTES

| Order **Passeriformes** | Family **Corvidae** | Species *Perisoreus canadensis* |

Canada Jay

ADULT — dark gray upperparts

long tail with white corners

IN FLIGHT

brownish back with white streaks

ADULT
P. c. obscurus
(NORTHWESTERN USA)

white collar

gray overall, darker upperparts

dark crown

white forehead

short bill

whitish "mustache"

JUVENILE — uniform medium to dark gray

dark, smoky-gray tail and wings

black legs and toes

ADULT
P. c. canadensis
(NORTHERN AND EASTERN)

F earless and cunning, the Canada Jay can often be a
nuisance to campers because of its inquisitive behavior.
It is particularly adept at stealing food and shiny metal objects,
which has earned it the colloquial name of "Camp Robber."
One of the interesting aspects of its behavior is the way it stores
food for later use by sticking it to trees with its viscous saliva.
This is thought to be one of the reasons that enable it to survive
the long northern winters. Canada Jays can often gather in noisy
groups of three to six birds in order to investigate intruders
encroaching upon their territory.
VOICE Mostly silent, but also produces variety of odd clucks
and screeches; sometimes Blue Jay-like *jay!* and eerie whistles,
including bisyllabic *whee-oo* or *ew*.
NESTING Bulky platform of sticks with cocoons on south side
of coniferous tree; 2–5 eggs; 1 brood; February–May.
FEEDING Forages for insects and berries; also raids birds' nests.

FLIGHT: hollow-sounding wingbeats followed by slow, seemingly awkward, rocking glides.

BUILT FOR COLD
The Canada Jay's short extremities and dense, fluffy plumage are perfect for long, harsh winters.

OCCURRENCE
Northern forests, especially lichen-festooned areas with firs and spruce. Found in coniferous forests across northern North America from Alaska to Newfoundland, the Maritimes, and northern New York and New England; south to western mountains; an isolated population in the Black Hills.

SIMILAR SPECIES

CLARK'S NUTCRACKER

white wing patch

longer bill

NORTHERN MOCKINGBIRD
see p.334

no dark crown

white wing patch

longer tail

| Length **10–11½in (25–29cm)** | Wingspan **18in (46cm)** | Weight **2⅛–2⅞ oz (60–80g)** |
| Social **Family groups** | Lifespan **Up to 10 years** | Status **Secure** |

DATE SEEN	WHERE	NOTES

| Order **Passeriformes** | Family **Corvidae** | Species *Cyanocitta cristata* |

Blue Jay 🔊

long tail with white corners
white streak in blue wings
ADULT
white trailing edge feathers
IN FLIGHT
black bars on tail

blue wings and tail
black legs and toes
black bars on tail

blue crest
black patch between eye and bill
black collar
plain blue mantle
long, black bill
whitish throat
ADULT
grayish underparts

The Blue Jay is one of the best known birds in North America; it is loud, flashy, and common in rural and suburban backyards across the eastern US and southern Canada. Beautiful as it is, this bird has a darker side. It often raids the nests of smaller birds for eggs and nestlings. Although usually thought of as a nonmigratory species, some Blue Jays undergo impressive migrations, with loose flocks sometimes numbering in the hundreds visible overhead in spring and fall.

VOICE Harsh, screaming *jay! jay!*; other common call an odd ethereal, chortling *queedle-ee-dee*; soft clucks when feeding.

NESTING Cup of strong twigs at variable height in trees or shrubs; 3–6 eggs; 1 brood; March–July.

FEEDING Eats insects, acorns, small vertebrates, such as lizards, rodents, bird eggs, birds, tree frogs; fruit and seeds.

FLIGHT: bursts of flapping followed by long glides on flat wings.

UNIQUE FEATURES
The Blue Jay is unique among American jays in having white patches on its wings and tail.

VERSATILE BIRD
Blue Jays are true omnivores, eating almost anything they can find. They are also excellent imitators of other bird calls.

SIMILAR SPECIES

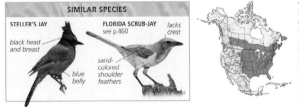

STELLER'S JAY
black head and breast
blue belly

FLORIDA SCRUB-JAY
see p.460
lacks crest
sand-colored shoulder feathers

OCCURRENCE
Native to eastern deciduous, coniferous, and mixed woodlands, but also at home in suburban vegetation; often found in backyards. The Blue Jay is fond of oak trees and their acorns. Blue Jays from northeast Canada and northeast US migrate in the fall to more southern locations.

| Length **9½–12in (24–30cm)** | Wingspan **16in (41cm)** | Weight **2¼–3½oz (65–100g)** |
| Social **Small flocks** | Lifespan **Up to 7 years** | Status **Secure** |

DATE SEEN	WHERE	NOTES

| Order **Passeriformes** | Family **Corvidae** | Species *Pica hudsonia* |

Black-billed Magpie 🔊

large, white patches on outer wings

white shoulders

ADULT

IN FLIGHT

blue-green iridescence to wings and tail

black back and head

thick, black bill

black breast

ADULT

white belly

long black tail

L oud, flashy, and conspicuous, the Black-billed Magpie is abundant in the northwestern quarter of the continent, from Alaska to interior US. It has adapted to suburbia, confidently strutting across front lawns locally. Until recently, it was considered the same species as the Eurasian Magpie (*P. pica*), and even though they look nearly identical, scientific evidence points instead to a close relationship with the other North American magpie, the Yellow-billed Magpie. Its long tail enables it to make rapid changes in direction in flight. The male uses his tail to display while courting a female. Why the Black-billed Magpie does not occur widely in eastern North America is a biological mystery.

VOICE Common call a questioning, nasal *ehnk*; also raspy *shenk, shenk, shenk*, usually in series.

NESTING Large, domed, often made of thorny sticks; 5–8 eggs; 1 brood; March–June.

FEEDING Omnivorous; forages on ground, mainly for insects, worms, seeds and carrion; even picks ticks from mammals.

FLIGHT: direct, with slow, steady, and often shallow wingbeats; occasional shallow glides.

IRIDESCENT SHEEN
In bright sunlight, beautiful iridescent blues, greens, golds, and purples appear on the wings and tail.

SIMILAR SPECIES

YELLOW-BILLED MAGPIE

yellow bill

yellow patch around eye

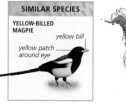

OCCURRENCE
Found in open habitats, foothills, and plains of the western US and Canada; nests in streamside vegetation; persecution has made it wary and restricted to wilderness in some areas, but in others it has adapted to suburbs of towns and cities.

| Length **17–19½in (43–50cm)** | Wingspan **25in (63cm)** | Weight **6–7oz (175–200g)** |
| Social **Small flocks** | Lifespan **Up to 15 years** | Status **Secure** |

DATE SEEN	WHERE	NOTES

| Order **Passeriformes** | Family **Corvidae** | Species ***Corvus brachyrhynchos*** |

American Crow 🔊

black overall

ADULT

IN FLIGHT

black overall with greenish sheen

long, black bill

ADULT

strong legs and toes

dull black overall

shorter bill

JUVENILE

One of the most widespread and familiar of North American birds, the American Crow is common in almost all habitats—from wilderness to urban centers. Like most birds with large ranges, there is substantial geographical variation in this species. Birds are black across the whole continent, but size and bill shape vary from region to region. Birds from western Canada and western USA (*C. b. hesperis*), are on average smaller and have a lower pitched voice; birds from southern Florida (*C. b. pascuus*) are more solitary and more wary.

VOICE Call a loud, familiar *caw!*; juveniles' call higher-pitched.
NESTING Stick base with finer inner cup, 3–7 eggs; 1 brood; April–June.
FEEDING Feeds omnivorously on fruit, carrion, garbage, insects, spiders; raids nests.

FLIGHT: direct and level with slow, steady flapping; does not soar.

LOOKING AROUND
Extremely inquisitive, American Crows are always on the lookout for food or something of interest.

OCCURRENCE
Often seen converging at dusk toward favored roosting areas; most numerous in relatively open areas with large and widely spaced trees; has become abundant in some cities; a partial migrant, some populations are more migratory than others.

SIMILAR SPECIES

FISH CROW
higher, more nasal call; see p.294
slightly smaller overall

smaller head
CHIHUAHUAN RAVEN
see p.461
larger overall
larger bill
wedge-shaped tail

Length **15½–19½in (39–49cm)**	Wingspan **3ft (1m)**	Weight **15–22oz (425–625g)**
Social **Social**	Lifespan **Up to 15 years**	Status **Secure**

DATE SEEN	WHERE	NOTES

| Order **Passeriformes** | Family **Corvidae** | Species ***Corvus ossifragus*** |

Fish Crow

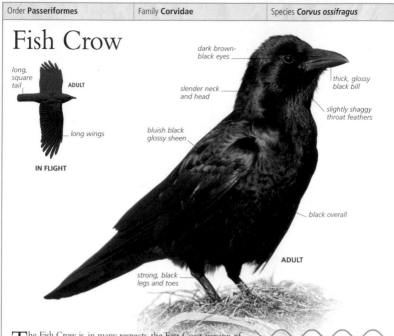

long, square tail

ADULT

long wings

IN FLIGHT

dark brown-black eyes

slender neck and head

bluish black glossy sheen

thick, glossy black bill

slightly shaggy throat feathers

black overall

ADULT

strong, black legs and toes

The Fish Crow is, in many respects, the East Coast version of the Northwestern Crow. Like the Northwestern Crow, it is a highly social species, and not only forages in flocks but also breeds in small colonies. The Fish Crow is common along the eastern seaboard of the US, where it occurs alongside the nearly identical, but slightly larger, American Crow. The Fish Crow is also distinguishable as it has a higher-pitched and more nasal call. Its Latin species name *ossifragus* translates as "bone-breaker."
VOICE Call a paired *ehn uhn* with the second note lower.
NESTING Bulky stick platform with finer inner bowl in fork of tree, often high up; 3–5 eggs; 1 brood; April–August.
FEEDING Takes arthropods such as crabs and insects, small live fish and reptiles, nestling birds, bird and turtle eggs, fruit, carrion, and garbage; notorious for raiding nests in heron rookeries.

FLIGHT: rowing motion with quick, snappy wingbeats; soars occasionally.

OMNIVORE
Fish Crows are numerous along coastlines and riverbanks where they eat virtually anything edible.

SIMILAR SPECIES

AMERICAN CROW lower-pitched, huskier voice; see p.293

shorter head

larger body

shorter tail

COMMON RAVEN see p.295

massive bill

wedge-shaped tail

shaggier throat feathers

OCCURRENCE
Found in lowland coastal and riverbank habitats such as beaches, estuaries, and marshes; also found inland and near human structures such as parking lots in suburban malls. Northern populations appear to be migratory.

| Length **14–16in (36–41cm)** | Wingspan **36in (91cm)** | Weight **8–11oz (225–325g)** |
| Social **Flocks** | Lifespan **Up to 15 years** | Status **Secure** |

DATE SEEN	WHERE	NOTES

| Order **Passeriformes** | Family **Corvidae** | Species *Corvus corax* |

Common Raven 🔊

long wings

flared outer wing feathers

ADULT

large, protruding head

black upperparts, with purplish gloss

thick, long bill, with pronounced curvature

shaggy throat

black neck and underparts

IN FLIGHT

wedge-shaped tail

ADULT

long, black legs and toes

The Common Raven, twice the size of the American Crow, is a bird of Viking legend, literature, and scientific wonder, and the Yukon Official Bird. Its Latin name, *Corvus corax*, means "crow of crows." Ravens are perhaps the most intelligent of all birds: they learn quickly, adapt to new circumstances with remarkable mental agility, and communicate with each other through an array of vocal and motional behaviors. They are master problem solvers and deceivers, tricking each other with ingenious methods.
VOICE Varied and numerous vocalizations, including hoarse, rolling *krruuk*, twangy peals, guttural clicks, and resonant *bonks*.
NESTING Platform of sticks with fine inner material on trees, cliffs, or manmade structure; 4–5 eggs; 1 brood; March–June.
FEEDING Feeds omnivorously on carrion, small crustaceans, fish, rodents, fruit, grain, and garbage; also raids nests.

FLIGHT: slow, steady, powerful, and direct; can also be quite acrobatic; commonly soars.

SHARING INFORMATION
Ravens in flocks can communicate information about food sources.

SIMILAR SPECIES

AMERICAN CROW lacks shaggy throat feathers; see p.293

lacks wedge-shaped tail

CHIHUAHUAN RAVEN see p.461

smaller bill

much smaller overall

slightly smaller overall

OCCURRENCE
Found in almost every kind of habitat, including tundra, mountains, northern forest, woodlands, prairies, arid regions, coasts, and around human settlements; has recently recolonized areas at southern edge of range, from which it was once expelled by humans.

| Length **23½–27in (60–69cm)** | Wingspan **4½ft (1.4m)** | Weight **2½–3¼lb (1–1.5kg)** |
| Social **Solitary/Pairs/Small flocks** | Lifespan **Up to 15 years** | Status **Secure** |

DATE SEEN	WHERE	NOTES
....	....	....
....	....	....
....	....	....
....	....	....
....	....	....

SWALLOWS

SWALLOWS ARE A COSMOPOLITAN family of birds with species found nearly everywhere, except in the polar regions and some of the largest deserts, although during migration they fly over some of the world's harshest deserts, including the Sahara and Atacama. Most species have relatively short, notched tails but some have elongated outer tail feathers. Among these latter species, females appear to prefer males with the longest tails as mates. The Bank Swallow and the Barn Swallow, which are also found across Eurasia, are the most widespread. All North American swallows are migratory, and most of them winter in Central and South America, where they feed on flying insects that occur year-round. They are all superb fliers, and skilled at aerial pursuit and capture of flying insects. They are sometimes confused with swifts, which belong to a different family and order, and have a different style of flight. Swallows have relatively shorter, broader wings and less stiff wingbeats.

SURFACE SKIMMER
This Tree Swallow flies low over freshwater to catch insects as they emerge into the air.

CHICKADEES AND TITMICE

CHICKADEES AND TITMICE may be some of the most well-known and widespread birds in North America. Once considered to be in the same genus, recent genetic studies have placed titmice and chickadees in different genera.

CHICKADEES
Chickadees are readily distinguished from titmice by their smooth-looking, dark caps and black bibs. Some chickadees are frequent visitors to backyards. The name "chickadee" is derived from the common calls of several species. Highly social outside the breeding season and generally tolerant of people, these energetic little birds form flocks in winter. Some species, such as the Black-capped Chickadee, can lower their body temperature to survive the cold, but others, like the similar-looking Carolina Chickadee, have a high winter mortality rate. Most species eat a combination of insects and plant material.

TITMICE
Titmice are distinguished from chickadees by their crests; most, like the familiar Tufted Titmouse, also have plain throats. Like chickadees, titmice are highly territorial and insectivorous during the breeding season, then become gregarious seed-eaters afterward. At that time they often form mixed-species flocks with other small birds, like kinglets, as they move through woodlands searching for food. Titmice are nonmigratory.

TAME BIRDS
Black-capped Chickadees have distinctive black-and-white markings and are often very tame.

| Order **Passeriformes** | Family **Alaudidae** | Species *Eremophila alpestris* |

Horned Lark

muted facial markings

tiny "horns"

bold black-and-yellow face

brown wings

variable brown on upperparts

dark streaks on reddish brown upperparts

ADULT

IN FLIGHT

ADULT (POSTBREEDING)

whitish underparts

streaked upperparts

black tail with narrow, white edges to outer feathers

JUVENILE

short legs

ADULT (BREEDING)

FLIGHT: undulating, with wings folded in after every few beats.

The Horned Lark is a bird of open country, especially places with extensive bare ground. The species is characteristic of arid, alpine, and Arctic regions; in these areas, it flourishes in the bleakest of habitats imaginable, from sun-scorched, arid lakeshores in the Great Basin, to windswept tundra north of the timberline. In some places, the only breeding bird species are the Horned Lark and the equally resilient Common Raven. In Europe and Asia, this species is known as the Shorelark.

GROUND FORAGER
With its short legs bent under its body, an adult looks for insects and seeds.

VOICE Flight call a sharp *sweet* or *soo-weet*; song, either in flight or from the ground, pleasant, musical tinkling series, followed by *sweet... swit... sweet... s'sweea'weea'witta'swit.*

NESTING In depression in bare ground, somewhat sheltered by grass or low shrubs, lined with plant matter; 2–5 eggs; 1–3 broods, March–July.

FEEDING Survives exclusively on seeds of grasses and sedges in winter; eats mostly insects in summer.

SIMILAR SPECIES		
SPRAGUE'S PIPIT see p.342 / shorter tail	**EURASIAN SKYLARK** / shorter wings	streaked crest / streaked overall

VERY VOCAL
The Horned Lark is a highly vocal bird, singing from the air, the ground, or low shrubs.

OCCURRENCE
Breeds widely, in any sort of open, even barren habitat with extensive bare ground, especially short-grass prairies and deserts. Winters wherever there are snow-free openings, including along beaches and roads. Winters from southern Canada southward to Florida and Mexico.

| Length **7in (18cm)** | Wingspan **12in (30cm)** | Weight **1¹⁄₁₆oz (30g)** |
| Social **Winter flocks** | Lifespan **Up to 8 years** | Status **Secure** |

DATE SEEN	WHERE	NOTES

| Order **Passeriformes** | Family **Hirundinidae** | Species *Riparia riparia* |

Bank Swallow

ADULT

dark breastband

white belly

IN FLIGHT

dark brown head

dark brown upperparts

whitish chin and throat

complete breastband

brownish cheeks

forked tail

whitish underparts

ADULT

ADULT

wings dark underneath

The Bank Swallow, known in the UK as the Sand Martin, is the slimmest and smallest of North American swallows. As its scientific name *riparia* (meaning "riverbanks") and common names suggest, the Bank Swallow nests in the banks and bluffs of rivers, streams, and lakes. It also favors sand and gravel quarries in the East. It is widely distributed across North America, breeding from south of the tundra–taiga line south to the central US. Nesting colonies can range from as few as 10 pairs to as many as 2,000, which are quite busy and noisy when all the birds are calling or coming in simultaneously to feed the young.
VOICE Call a soft *brrrrr* or *breee* often issued in pairs; song a harsh twittering or continuous chatter.
NESTING Both sexes excavate burrows in sandy banks containing a flat platform of grass, feathers, and twigs; 2–6 eggs; 1 brood; April–August.
FEEDING Catches insects, such as flies, moths, dragonflies, and bees in flight, but occasionally skims aquatic insects or their larvae off the water or terrestrial insects from the ground.

FLIGHT: fast, frantic, butterfly-like flight with glides, twists, and turns; shallow, rapid wingbeats.

WAITING FOR MOM OR DAD
Hungry youngsters still expect to be fed, even when they're ready to fledge.

SIMILAR SPECIES

TREE SWALLOW ♂
larger; gray-brown upperparts with greenish tinge; see p.299

incomplete breastband

NORTHERN ROUGH-WINGED SWALLOW
larger overall; see p.300

uniformly colored upperparts

OCCURRENCE
Widespread in North America. Breeds in lowland habitats associated with rivers, streams, lakes, reservoirs, and coasts, as well as in sand and gravel quarries. Often prefers manmade sites; winters in grasslands, open farm habitat, and freshwater areas in South America, south to Chile and Argentina.

| Length **4¾–5½in (12–14cm)** | Wingspan **10–11in (25–28cm)** | Weight **⅜–¹¹⁄₁₆oz (10–19g)** |
| Social **Colonies** | Lifespan **Up to 9 years** | Status **Secure** |

DATE SEEN	WHERE	NOTES

| Order **Passeriformes** | Family **Hirundinidae** | Species *Tachycineta bicolor* |

Tree Swallow 🔊

MALE

dark, pointed wings

IN FLIGHT

slightly forked tail

iridescent bluish green upperparts

blackish flight feathers

small black bill

no blue on head or upperparts

white throat

partial grayish brown breastband

brilliant white underparts

JUVENILE

bluish back

brownish cap

SECOND-YEAR BIRD

MALE

reddish brown legs and toes

brownish primaries

FLIGHT: rapid, deep, fluttery wingbeats without pause; quick turns and twists.

One of the most common North American swallows, the Tree Swallow is found from coast to coast in the northern two-thirds of the continent, all the way north to Alaska. As its Latin name *bicolor* suggests, it is a two-toned bird, with iridescent bluish green upperparts and white underparts. Juveniles can be confused with the smaller Bank Swallow, which has a more complete breastband. The Tree Swallow lives in a variety of habitats, but its hole-nesting habit makes it dependent on crevices in old trees, abandoned woodpecker cavities, and on artificial "housing" such as nest boxes. The size of the population fluctuates according to the availability of nesting sites.

VOICE Ranges from variable high, chirping notes to chatters and soft trills; also complex high and clear 2-note whistle phrases.

NESTING Layer of fine plant matter in abandoned woodpecker hole or nest box, lined with feathers; 4–6 eggs; 1 brood; May–July.

FEEDING Swoops after flying insects from dawn to dusk; also takes bayberries.

KEEPING LOOKOUT
This species uses nest boxes, which the males occupy and defend as soon as they arrive.

OCCURRENCE
Typically breeds close to water in open habitat such as fields, marshes, lakes, and swamps, especially those with standing dead wood for cavity-nesting. Winters in roosts of hundreds of thousands of birds in marshes, in the southern US, and from Mexico to Panama; also Cuba.

SIMILAR SPECIES

BANK SWALLOW
paler brown rump;
see p.298

distinct dusky breastband

VIOLET-GREEN SWALLOW
white flank patch;

white eye patch

violet-green upperparts

| Length **5–6in (13–15cm)** | Wingspan **12–14in (30–35cm)** | Weight **⅝–⅞oz (17–25g)** |
| Social **Large flocks** | Lifespan **Up to 11 years** | Status **Secure** |

DATE SEEN	WHERE	NOTES

| Order **Passeriformes** | Family **Hirundinidae** | Species *Stelgidopteryx serripennis* |

Northern Rough-winged Swallow 🔊

light crescent from cheek to crown

brown head

dark brown overall

black eye

square tail

ADULT

JUVENILE

tan-buffy wing bars

dark face

pale brown breast

pale underparts

IN FLIGHT

pale brown breast

pale, grayish brown belly

long, brown wings

ADULT

Given the name *serripennis*—"saw feather"—by Audubon in 1888, and characterized by the stiff barbs on the leading edges of its outer wing feathers, this species is otherwise somewhat drab in color and aspect. The Northern Rough-winged Swallow has a broad distribution in North America, across southern Canada and throughout the US. This brown-backed, dusky-throated swallow can be spotted hunting insects over water. In size and habit, the Northern Rough-winged Swallow shares many similarities with the Bank Swallow, including breeding habits and color, but the latter's notched tail and smaller size help tell them apart.

VOICE Steady repetition of short, rapid *brrrt* notes inflected upward; sometimes a buzzy *jee-jee-jee* or high-pitched *brzzzzzt*.

NESTING Loose cup of twigs and straw in a cavity or burrow in a bank, such as road cuts; 4–7 eggs; 1 brood; May–July.

FEEDING Captures flying insects, including flies, wasps, bees, damselflies, and beetles in the air; more likely to feed over water and at lower altitudes than other swallows.

FLIGHT: slow, deliberate wingbeats; short to long glides; long, straight flight, ends in steep climb.

BROWN BIRD
This swallow is brownish above and grayish below, with a brown smudge on the sides of its neck.

SIMILAR SPECIES

BANK SWALLOW
see p.298
smaller overall
whitish belly and throat
long, notched tail
brownish breastband
white belly

TREE SWALLOW 🔊
see p.299
white throat
grayish breast-band
white belly

OCCURRENCE
In North America widespread from coast to coast. Nests at a wide variety of altitudes, prefers exposed banks of clay, sand, or gravel such as gorges, shale banks, and gravel pits. Forages along watercourses where aerial insects are plentiful. Breeds south to Costa Rica. Winters in Central America.

| Length **4¾–6in (12–15cm)** | Wingspan **11–12in (28–30cm)** | Weight **⅜–⅝oz (10–18g)** |
| Social **Solitary** | Lifespan **Unknown** | Status **Secure** |

DATE SEEN	WHERE	NOTES

| Order **Passeriformes** | Family **HIrundinidae** | Species *Progne subis* |

Purple Martin

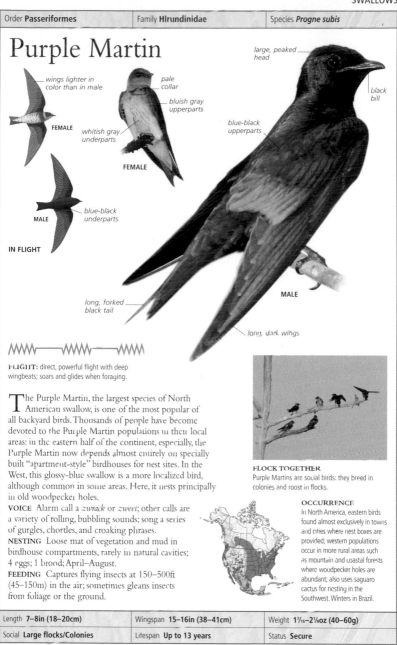

large, peaked head

wings lighter in color than in male

pale collar

bluish gray upperparts

FEMALE

whitish gray underparts

blue-black upperparts

black bill

FEMALE

blue-black underparts

MALE

IN FLIGHT

blue-black upperparts

long, forked black tail

MALE

long, dark wings

FLIGHT: direct, powerful flight with deep wingbeats; soars and glides when foraging.

The Purple Martin, the largest species of North American swallow, is one of the most popular of all backyard birds. Thousands of people have become devoted to the Purple Martin populations in their local areas: in the eastern half of the continent, especially, the Purple Martin now depends almost entirely on specially built "apartment-style" birdhouses for nest sites. In the West, this glossy-blue swallow is a more localized bird, although common in some areas. Here, it nests principally in old woodpecker holes.

VOICE Alarm call a *zwrack* or *zweet*; other calls are a variety of rolling, bubbling sounds; song a series of gurgles, chortles, and croaking phrases.

NESTING Loose mat of vegetation and mud in birdhouse compartments, rarely in natural cavities; 4 eggs; 1 brood; April–August.

FEEDING Captures flying insects at 150–500ft (45–150m) in the air; sometimes gleans insects from foliage or the ground.

FLOCK TOGETHER
Purple Martins are social birds: they breed in colonies and roost in flocks.

OCCURRENCE
In North America, eastern birds found almost exclusively in towns and cities where nest boxes are provided; western populations occur in more rural areas such as mountain and coastal forests where woodpecker holes are abundant; also uses saguaro cactus for nesting in the Southwest. Winters in Brazil.

| Length **7–8in (18–20cm)** | Wingspan **15–16in (38–41cm)** | Weight **1⁷⁄₁₆–2⅛oz (40–60g)** |
| Social **Large flocks/Colonies** | Lifespan **Up to 13 years** | Status **Secure** |

DATE SEEN	WHERE	NOTES

| Order **Passeriformes** | Family **Hirundinidae** | Species *Hirundo rustica* |

Barn Swallow 🔊

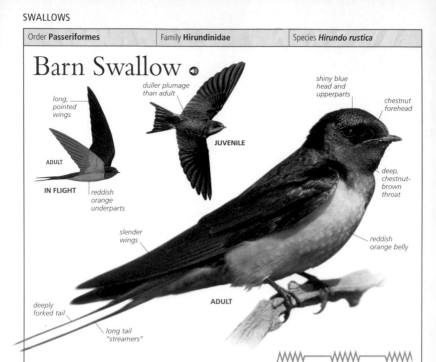

long, pointed wings

duller plumage than adult

JUVENILE

shiny blue head and upperparts

chestnut forehead

ADULT

IN FLIGHT

reddish orange underparts

slender wings

deep, chestnut-brown throat

reddish orange belly

deeply forked tail

long tail "streamers"

ADULT

The most widely distributed and abundant swallow in the world, the Barn Swallow is found just about everywhere in North America south of the Arctic timberline. Originally a cave-nester before Europeans settlers came to the New World, the Barn Swallow readily adapted to nesting under the eaves of houses, under bridges, and inside buildings such as barns. It is now rare to find this elegant swallow breeding in a natural site. Steely blue upperparts, reddish underparts, and a deeply forked tail identify the Barn Swallow. North American breeders have deep, reddish orange underparts, but birds from Eurasia are white-bellied.

VOICE High-pitched, squeaky *chee-chee* call; song a long series of chatty, pleasant churrs, squeaks, chitterings, and buzzes.

NESTING Deep cup of mud and grass-stems attached to vertical surfaces or on ledges; 4–6 eggs; 1–2 broods; May–September.

FEEDING Snatches flying insects, such as flies, mosquitoes, wasps, and beetles in the air at lower altitudes than other swallows; sometimes eats wild berries and seeds.

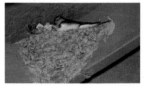

FLIGHT: bursts of straight flight; close to the ground; weaves left and right, with sharp turns.

WELL PROTECTED
Whether in a barn or other structure, a Barn Swallow nest is totally protected from wind and rain.

SIMILAR SPECIES

TREE SWALLOW ♂
see p.299

lacks forked tail and dark breast-band

white underparts

OCCURRENCE
Breeds across North America south to central Mexico. Prefers agricultural regions and towns. Winters near sugarcane fields, grain fields, and marshes, south in South America as far as Patagonia. Hundreds of thousands winter in marshes of northern Argentina.

| Length **6–7½in (15–19cm)** | Wingspan **11½–13in (29–33cm)** | Weight **⅝–¹¹⁄₁₆oz (17–20g)** |
| Social **Small colonies/Flocks** | Lifespan **Up to 8 years** | Status **Secure** |

DATE SEEN	WHERE	NOTES

| Order **Passeriformes** | Family **Hirundinidae** | Species *Petrochelidon pyrrhonata* |

Cliff Swallow 🔊

long, roundish wings

brown-tinged, black back

rusty cheek patch

mottled throat

JUVENILE

bluish black back

ADULT

IN FLIGHT

rusty-brown cheeks

pale hind neck collar

bluish black cap

whitish forehead

dark throat

ADULT

pale underparts

slight notch in squared tail

pale reddish rump

The Cliff Swallow is one of North America's most social land birds, sometimes nesting in colonies of more than 3,500 pairs, especially in the western US. It is more locally distributed in the East. It can be distinguished from other North American swallows by its square tail and orange rump, but it resembles its close relative, the Cave Swallow, in color, pattern, and in affixing its mud nests to the sides of highway culverts, bridges, and buildings. The considerable increase in such structures has allowed the species to expand its range from the West to breed almost everywhere except in dense forests and desert habitats.
VOICE Gives *purr* and *churr* calls when alarmed; song a low, squeaky, 6-second twitter given in flight and near nests.
NESTING Domed nests of mud pellets on cave walls, buildings, culverts, bridges, and dams; 3–5 eggs; 1–2 broods; April–August.
FEEDING Catches flying insects (often swarming varieties) while on the wing; sometimes forages on the ground; ingests grit to aid digestion.

FLIGHT: strong, fast wingbeats; glides more often but less acrobatically than other swallows.

GATHERING MUD
The Cliff Swallow gathers wet mud from puddles, pond edges, and streamsides to build its nest.

SIMILAR SPECIES

CAVE SWALLOW see p.304

brighter orange cheek

paler overall

INDIVIDUAL HOMES
In a Cliff Swallow colony, each nest has a single opening.

OCCURRENCE
Breeds in North America from Alaska to Mexico. Prefers walls, culverts, buildings, cliffs, and undersides of piers on which to affix mud nests. Migrates to South America. Hundreds of thousands winter in marshes of northern Argentina.

| Length **5in (13cm)** | Wingspan **11–12in (28–30cm)** | Weight **¹¹⁄₁₆–1¼oz (20–35g)** |
| Social **Colonies** | Lifespan **Up to 11 years** | Status **Secure** |

DATE SEEN	WHERE	NOTES

Order **Passeriformes**	Family **Hirundinidae**	Species **Petrochelidon fulva**

Cave Swallow

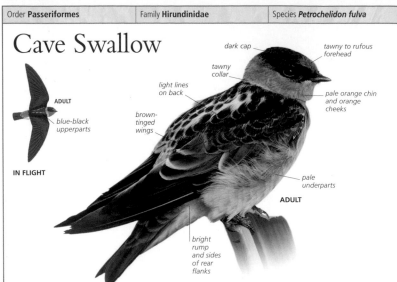

dark cap

tawny to rufous forehead

tawny collar

light lines on back

ADULT

brown-tinged wings

pale orange chin and orange cheeks

blue-black upperparts

IN FLIGHT

pale underparts

ADULT

bright rump and sides of rear flanks

D istinguished from its close relative, the Cliff Swallow, by a pale rather than black throat and rufous rather than white forehead, the buffy-rumped Cave Swallow is limited in its breeding range to parts of New Mexico, Arizona, Texas, and southern Florida. As its name suggests, the Cave Swallow cements its cup nest to the walls of caves, which it often shares with bats; it also builds nests on bridges, water culverts, and buildings. The Cave Swallow was once rare in North America, but in recent years it has expanded both geographically and numerically because it has adapted to nesting on manmade structures. In winter the US Cave Swallow population moves south to Mexico.

VOICE Call a low *wheet*; song a series of bubbly sounds blending into warbling trill, ending in series of double-toned notes.

NESTING Open flat cup with tall, broad rim, made of mud and guano, glued to concrete structure or cave wall; 3–5 eggs; 1–2 broods; April–July.

FEEDING Captures a variety of flying insects while on the wing, including beetles, flies, and bees; sometimes flushes its prey out into the air by flying into vegetation.

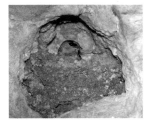

FLIGHT: uses rapid wingbeats to swoop and dive, but also likes to glide.

MUD BOWL NEST
Cave Swallow nests are cup-like, and not domed like those of the Cliff Swallow.

SIMILAR SPECIES

CLIFF SWALLOW see p.303

light forehead

dark throat

OCCURRENCE
In US, breeds in the arid central West (Arizona, Texas) and southern Florida, wherever nests can be attached to walls of caves, sinkholes, bridges, buildings, and culverts; preferably near open water for feeding on flying insects. Outside US, breeds in Mexico and the Greater Antilles.

Length **5½in (14cm)**	Wingspan **13in (33cm)**	Weight **⅝– ⅞oz (17–25g)**
Social **Colonies**	Lifespan **Up to 9 years**	Status **Localized**

DATE SEEN	WHERE	NOTES

| Order **Passeriformes** | Family **Paridae** | Species *Poecile carolinensis* |

Carolina Chickadee 🔊

ADULT

plain gray upperparts

conspicuous black-and-white head

IN FLIGHT

pale gray edges on inner wing feathers

white cheeks

short black bill

sharp-edged bib margin

ADULT

short, slightly notched tail

buffy flanks

FLIGHT: fast, undulating, with quick wingbeats.

The Carolina Chickadee is the only chickadee found in the southeastern US, and was first described and named by John James Audubon in 1834, when he was in South Carolina. Its northern range limit locally overlaps the Black-capped Chickadee's southern limit in a narrow band from Kansas to New Jersey, where the two species interbreed regularly, creating hybrids with mixed plumage that are hard to identify. The Carolina Chickadee hides food in caches under branches or even within curled dead leaves, returning for it within a few days. It has a strong preference for sunflower seeds, and can be seen at birdfeeders along with the Black-capped Chickadee, where the Carolina's characteristic call is the easiest way to distinguish the two species.

VOICE Fast *dee-dee-dee* call; song clear, whistled, 4-note sequence *wee-bee wee-bay*, second note lower in pitch.
NESTING Cavity lined with moss, fur, hair, plant down in soft, rotting tree; 5–8 eggs, 1–2 broods; April–May.
FEEDING Forages for insects and spiders; visits birdfeeders in winter.

DULL EXTREME
In worn plumage, and in its southwestern range, this bird has grayish white flanks.

BRIGHT EXTREME
In fresh plumage, some Carolina Chickadees have brighter, buffy flanks.

OCCURRENCE
Year-round dweller in deciduous, mixed and conifer woodlands, urban parks, and suburbs. In the Appalachians, prefers lower elevations than Black-capped. Range is expanding northward, especially in Ohio and Pennsylvania, where it is gradually replacing Black-capped as the resident species.

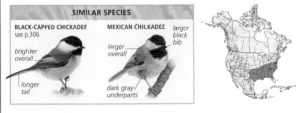

SIMILAR SPECIES

BLACK-CAPPED CHICKADEE
see p.306

brighter overall

longer tail

MEXICAN CHICKADEE

larger overall

dark gray underparts

larger black bib

| Length **4¾in (12cm)** | Wingspan **7½in (19cm)** | Weight **⅜oz (11g)** |
| Social **Mixed flocks** | Lifespan **Up to 10 years** | Status **Secure** |

DATE SEEN	WHERE	NOTES

Order **Passeriformes**	Family **Paridae**	Species *Poecile atricapillus*

Black-capped Chickadee 🔊

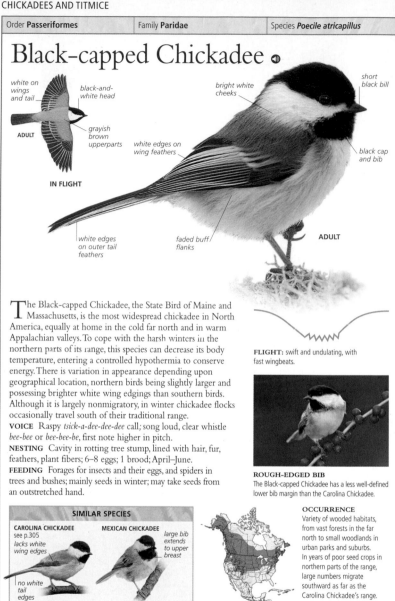

white on wings and tail

black-and-white head

grayish brown upperparts

ADULT

IN FLIGHT

bright white cheeks

short black bill

black cap and bib

white edges on wing feathers

white edges on outer tail feathers

faded buff flanks

ADULT

The Black-capped Chickadee, the State Bird of Maine and Massachusetts, is the most widespread chickadee in North America, equally at home in the cold far north and in warm Appalachian valleys. To cope with the harsh winters in the northern parts of its range, this species can decrease its body temperature, entering a controlled hypothermia to conserve energy. There is variation in appearance depending upon geographical location, northern birds being slightly larger and possessing brighter white wing edgings than southern birds. Although it is largely nonmigratory, in winter chickadee flocks occasionally travel south of their traditional range.

VOICE Raspy *tsick-a-dee-dee-dee* call; song loud, clear whistle *bee-bee* or *bee-bee-be*, first note higher in pitch.

NESTING Cavity in rotting tree stump, lined with hair, fur, feathers, plant fibers; 6–8 eggs; 1 brood; April–June.

FEEDING Forages for insects and their eggs, and spiders in trees and bushes; mainly seeds in winter; may take seeds from an outstretched hand.

FLIGHT: swift and undulating, with fast wingbeats.

ROUGH-EDGED BIB
The Black-capped Chickadee has a less well-defined lower bib margin than the Carolina Chickadee.

SIMILAR SPECIES

CAROLINA CHICKADEE
see p.305
lacks white wing edges

no white tail edges

MEXICAN CHICKADEE

large bib extends to upper breast

OCCURRENCE
Variety of wooded habitats, from vast forests in the far north to small woodlands in urban parks and suburbs. In years of poor seed crops in northern parts of the range, large numbers migrate southward as far as the Carolina Chickadee's range.

Length **5¼in (13.5cm)**	Wingspan **8½in (22cm)**	Weight **⅜oz (11g)**
Social **Mixed flocks**	Lifespan **Up to 12 years**	Status **Secure**

DATE SEEN	WHERE	NOTES

| Order **Passeriformes** | Family **Paridae** | Species *Poecile hudsonicus* |

Boreal Chickadee

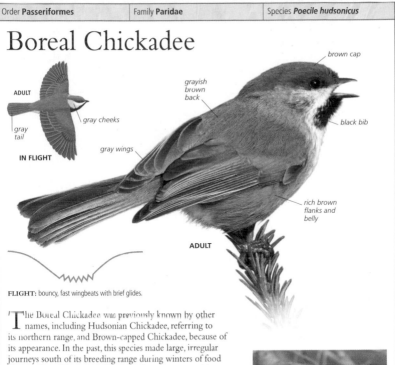

brown cap

grayish brown back

ADULT

gray cheeks

black bib

gray tail

IN FLIGHT

gray wings

rich brown flanks and belly

ADULT

FLIGHT: bouncy, fast wingbeats with brief glides.

The Boreal Chickadee was previously known by other names, including Hudsonian Chickadee, referring to its northern range, and Brown-capped Chickadee, because of its appearance. In the past, this species made large, irregular journeys south of its breeding range during winters of food shortage, but this pattern of invasions has not occurred in recent decades. Its back color is an interesting example of geographic variation—grayish in the West and brown in the central and eastern portions of its range.

VOICE Call a low-pitched, buzzy, and rather slow *tsee-day-day*; also a high-pitched trill, *didididididi*; no whistled song.

NESTING Cavity lined with fur, hair, plant down; in natural, excavated, or old woodpecker hole; 4–9 eggs; 1 brood; May–June.

FEEDING Gleans insects, conifer seeds; hoards larvae and seeds in bark crevices in fall in preparation for winter.

IDENTIFICATION TIP
A brown back or flank help distinguish a Boreal Chickadee from a Black-capped Chickadee.

SIMILAR SPECIES

CHESTNUT-BACKED CHICKADEE narrow, white cheeks

chestnut sides

ACROBATIC FORAGER
This acrobatic feeder is able to cling on to conifer needles as it searches for insects and spiders.

OCCURRENCE
Found across the vast northern spruce-fir forests from Alaska to Newfoundland, and from the treeline at the tundra south to the northeastern and northwestern states. The southern edge of the range appears to be retracting, for unknown reasons.

| Length **5½in (14cm)** | Wingspan **8½in (21cm)** | Weight **⅜oz (10g)** |
| Social **Flocks** | Lifespan **Up to 5 years** | Status **Secure** |

DATE SEEN	WHERE	NOTES

| Order **Passeriformes** | Family **Paridae** | Species *Baeolophus bicolor* |

Tufted Titmouse 🔊

ADULT

crest may be flattened

gray wings

IN FLIGHT

tufted dark gray head

conspicuous black eye in whitish face

black forehead

orange flanks

gray tail

ADULT

gray-black legs and toes

gray underparts

FLIGHT: swift and undulating, with irregular wingbeats; usually across short distances.

A familiar and friendly sight, the Tufted Titmouse is widespread in eastern North America. Its lack of fear of people has enabled the Tufted Titmouse to adapt to human surroundings. In the last century its range has expanded significantly northward to southern Canada, probably because of the increased numbers of birdfeeders, which allow the Tufted Titmouse to survive cold northern winters. Its loud and cheerful song is a sure sign of spring!

VOICE Call a loud, harsh *pshurr, pshurr, pshurr*; song a ringing, far-carrying *peto peto peto*, sometimes shortened to *peer peer peer*.

NESTING Tree cavities, old woodpecker holes, and nest boxes, lined with damp leaves, moss, grass, hair; 5–6 eggs; 1 brood; March–May.

FEEDING Forages actively in trees and shrubs for insects, spiders, and their eggs; in winter, corn kernels, seeds, and small fruit, can split an acorn by hammering it with its bill.

COLOR VARIATION
The orange on an adult's flanks varies from bright in freshly molted feathers to dull in worn plumage.

SIMILAR SPECIES

BLACK-CRESTED TITMOUSE see p.462

high, black crest

pale forehead

BLUE-GRAY GNATCATCHER see p.320

lacks crest

smaller, slimmer body

OCCURRENCE
Lives year-round in areas of large and small deciduous and coniferous woodlands in the eastern half of the US. It has flourished in parks and gardens and can often be found using nest boxes in suburban backyards.

| Length **6½in (16cm)** | Wingspan **10in (25cm)** | Weight **¹¹⁄₁₆ oz (20g)** |
| Social **Mixed flocks** | Lifespan **Up to 13 years** | Status **Secure** |

DATE SEEN	WHERE	NOTES

NUTHATCHES

COMMON WOODLAND BIRDS, nuthatches are easily recognized by their distinctive shape and characteristic feeding techniques, and often located by loud squeaky calls. They are tree dwellers, feeding around branches and nesting in small tree holes. Nuthatches are quite plump-bodied, short-tailed but large-headed birds, with strong, pointed bills and short legs, strong toes, and arched claws. Unlike woodpeckers and creepers, which mostly climb in an upward direction, they do not need to use the tail as a prop when exploring a tree's bark. These birds rely solely on their strong and secure grip to hop and shuffle in all directions, frequently hanging upside down. They feed on spiders and also probe for insects and their larvae in the cracks of tree bark. They also eat seeds and nuts, which they may wedge into a crevice and break open with noisy taps of the bill—hence, the name "nuthatch."

ACROBATIC POSE
Downward-facing nuthatches such as this White-breasted Nuthatch, often lift their heads in a characteristic pose.

WRENS

WITH ONE EXCEPTION, the Eurasian Winter Wren, wrens are small American songbirds. They are sharp-billed birds with short- or medium-length tails that are frequently cocked. Wrens are intricately patterned, mostly with dark bars and streaks, and pale spots on buff and rusty backgrounds. Their family name, *Troglodytidae*, derives from a Greek word for "cave-dweller"—while they do not really inhabit caves, the description is apt as some North American species, such as the Winter and Pacific Wrens, forage deep inside thick cover of all kinds, from scrub to upturned tree roots and overgrown stumps, or in dense growth inside ditches. Marsh Wrens are found in marshes and Sedge Wrens in sedge meadows. Wrens are often best located by their calls, which are fairly loud for such small birds. There are some species that sing precisely synchronized duets.

COCKED TAIL
As they sing, Winter Wrens often hold their tails upward in a near-vertical position.

Order **Passeriformes**	Family **Sittidae**	Species *Sitta canadensis*

Red-breasted Nuthatch

rounded wings

MALE

white bands on tail

IN FLIGHT

slightly muted head pattern

dark blue-gray crown and eyestripe

pale orange underparts

FEMALE

blue-gray upperparts

bold black-and-white head pattern

pointed, chisel-like bill

black eyestripe

white cheeks

blue-gray, short tail, with black side feathers

rusty underparts

compact body shape

MALE

FLIGHT: short, swift dashes across forest clearings; irregular, undulating motion.

This inquisitive nuthatch, with its distinctive black eyestripe, breeds in conifer forests across North America. The bird inhabits mountains in the West; in the East, it is found in lowlands and hills. However, sometimes it breeds in conifer groves away from its core range. Each fall, birds move from their main breeding grounds, but the extent of this exodus varies from year to year, depending on population cycles and food availability.

VOICE Call a one-note tooting sound, often repeated, with strong nasal yet musical quality: *aaank, enk, ink*, rather like a horn.

NESTING Excavates cavity in pine tree; nest of grass lined with feathers, with sticky pine resin applied to entrance; 5–7 eggs, 1 brood; May–July.

FEEDING Probes bark for beetle grubs; also eats insect larvae found on conifer needles; seeds in winter.

TASTY GRUB
This nuthatch has just extracted its dinner from the bark of a tree, a favorite foraging habitat.

SIMILAR SPECIES

BROWN-HEADED NUTHATCH
see p.312
brown nape
slightly smaller overall
pale gray

WHITE-BREASTED NUTHATCH
see p.311
larger overall
lacks black eyestripe
white belly
chestnut undertail

OCCURRENCE
Found year-round in coniferous and mixed hardwood forests. During breeding season, absent from southeastern pine forests, except in the Appalachians. In the West, shares its habitat with Pygmy Nuthatch, but ranges to higher elevations.

Length **4¼in (11cm)**	Wingspan **8½in (22cm)**	Weight **⅜–⁷⁄₁₆oz (10–13g)**
Social **Solitary/Pairs**	Lifespan **Up to 7 years**	Status **Secure**

DATE SEEN	WHERE	NOTES

| Order **Passeriformes** | Family **Sittidae** | Species *Sitta carolinensis* |

White-breasted Nuthatch 🔊

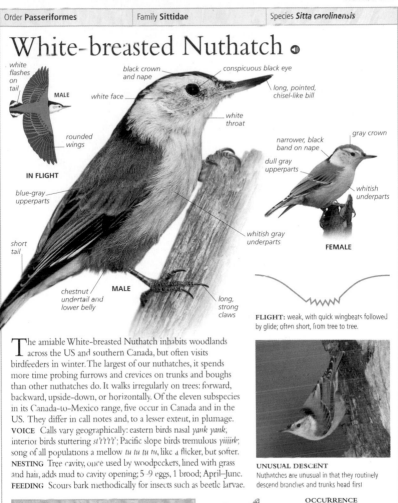

white flashes on tail

MALE

white face

rounded wings

IN FLIGHT

blue-gray upperparts

short tail

chestnut undertail and lower belly

MALE

black crown and nape

conspicuous black eye

long, pointed, chisel-like bill

white throat

narrower, black band on nape

dull gray upperparts

gray crown

whitish underparts

whitish gray underparts

FEMALE

long, strong claws

FLIGHT: weak, with quick wingbeats followed by glide; often short, from tree to tree.

The amiable White-breasted Nuthatch inhabits woodlands across the US and southern Canada, but often visits birdfeeders in winter. The largest of our nuthatches, it spends more time probing furrows and crevices on trunks and boughs than other nuthatches do. It walks irregularly on trees: forward, backward, upside-down, or horizontally. Of the eleven subspecies in its Canada-to-Mexico range, five occur in Canada and in the US. They differ in call notes and, to a lesser extent, in plumage.
VOICE Calls vary geographically: eastern birds nasal *yank yank*; interior birds stuttering *st'r'r'r'r'*; Pacific slope birds tremulous *yiiiirk*; song of all populations a mellow *tu tu tu tu*, like a flicker, but softer.
NESTING Tree cavity, once used by woodpeckers, lined with grass and hair, adds mud to cavity opening; 5–9 eggs, 1 brood; April–June.
FEEDING Scours bark methodically for insects such as beetle larvae.

UNUSUAL DESCENT
Nuthatches are unusual in that they routinely descend branches and trunks head first

OCCURRENCE
More liberal than other nuthatches in use of forest types; overlaps with the smaller species in coniferous forest ranges, but also common in broadleaf deciduous or mixed forests; weakly migratory: little movement in most falls, but moderate departures from breeding grounds in some years.

SIMILAR SPECIES

BROWN-HEADED NUTHATCH
see p.312
brown crown

RED-BREASTED NUTHATCH
see p.310
black eye-stripe

smaller overall

reddish underparts

smaller overall

| Length **5¾in (14.5cm)** | Wingspan **11in (28cm)** | Weight **¹¹⁄₁₆–⅞oz (19–25g)** |
| Social **Solitary/Pairs** | Lifespan **Up to 9 years** | Status **Secure** |

DATE SEEN	WHERE	NOTES

| Order **Passeriformes** | Family **Sittidae** | Species *Sitta pusilla* |

Brown-headed Nuthatch

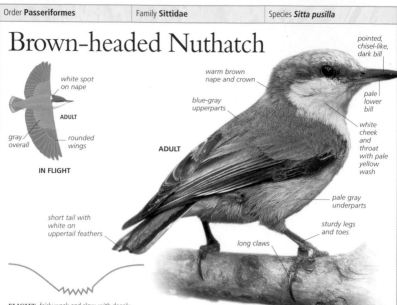

pointed, chisel-like, dark bill

white spot on nape

ADULT

gray overall

rounded wings

IN FLIGHT

warm brown nape and crown

blue-gray upperparts

ADULT

pale lower bill

white cheek and throat with pale yellow wash

pale gray underparts

sturdy legs and toes

short tail with white on uppertail feathers

long claws

FLIGHT: fairly weak and slow, with deeply undulating motion; appears tiny in flight.

This pine-loving species is the southeastern counterpart of the western Pygmy Nuthatch, but separated from it by the Great Plains. In most aspects of their history, these two nuthatch species are very similar and play the same ecological roles in their respective ecosystems. Like the Pygmy, the Brown-headed is a busy bird that travels in noisy packs. In each species, the young are raised by both parents and one or more nonparental relatives, or "helpers."

VOICE Call a short *bek*; foraging flocks *buvee! tutututu*, emphatic first note followed by soft series; chorus of sounds when calling in flocks.

NESTING Excavates cavity in pine tree; nest of plant material lined with fur and feathers; 4–6 eggs; 1–2 broods; March–May.

FEEDING Forages high in pine trees; in summer, gleans beetles, bugs, other insects, and also spiders; in winter, supplements diet with pine seeds.

INTREPID FORAGING
The Brown-headed Nuthatch forages upside down along branches, and head-first down tree trunks.

SIMILAR SPECIES

RED-BREASTED NUTHATCH
see p.310

black eyestripe

rusty underparts

PERCHED ADULT
This bird depends upon forest tracts with standing dead wood and snags for nesting.

OCCURRENCE
Breeds in pine forests and oak pine woods in southeastern US: Delaware, Virginia, and Maryland southward to Florida, westward to Oklahoma and Texas; also in the Bahamas. Prefers old and extensive forest stands with dead trunks for nesting. Resident; small groups wander in fall, but not far from breeding areas.

| Length **4¼in (11cm)** | Wingspan **8in (20cm)** | Weight **⅜oz (10g)** |
| Social **Small flocks** | Lifespan **Up to 2 years** | Status **Declining** |

DATE SEEN	WHERE	NOTES

| Order **Passeriformes** | Family **Certhiidae** | Species **Certhia americana** |

Brown Creeper 🔊

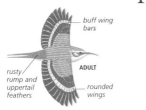

thin, downward-curving bill

whitish streak above eye

white chin, throat, and breast

finely streaked crown

mottled brown above

ADULT

rusty rump and uppertail feathers

rounded wings

IN FLIGHT

pale streaks on brown background

FLIGHT: short, floppy flights from one tree to another; also capable of sustained migration.

ADULT (SUMMER)

rusty tint to belly and undertail

long, forked tail

Although distinctive, widespread, and fairly common, the Brown Creeper is one of the most understated of the forest birds, with its soft vocalizations and cryptic plumage. As it forages, it hops up a tree trunk, then flies down to another tree, starts again from near the ground, hops up, and so on. These birds have adapted to habitat changes in the Northeast and their numbers have increased in regenerating forests. Mid- and southwestern populations, by contrast, have declined because forest cutting has reduced their breeding habitat. The Brown Creeper is a partial migrant—some individuals move south in the fall, and head north in the spring; others remain close to their breeding grounds.
VOICE High-pitched and easily overlooked call a buzzy *zwissss*, flight call an abrupt *tswit*; song a wheezy jumble of thin whistles and short buzzes.
NESTING Unique hammock-shaped nest, behind piece of peeling bark; 5–6 eggs, 1 brood; May–July.
FEEDING Probes bark for insects, especially larvae, eggs, pupae, and aphids.

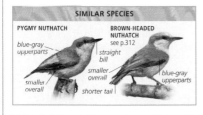

SIMILAR SPECIES

PYGMY NUTHATCH

blue-gray upperparts

smaller overall

BROWN-HEADED NUTHATCH see p.312

straight bill

smaller overall

shorter tail

blue-gray upperparts

STRONG TAIL
The Brown Creeper uses its forked tail to prop it against the trunk of this tree.

OCCURRENCE
The only North American creeper, it breeds in a variety of forests, particularly fairly moist coniferous or mixed hardwood forests, also large stands with snags and standing dead trees. In winter, it is seen in small groves without coniferous trees; also in residential districts or suburbs.

| Length **5¼in (13.5cm)** | Wingspan **8in (20cm)** | Weight **¼–⅜oz (7–10g)** |
| Social **Solitary** | Lifespan **Up to 4 years** | Status **Declining** |

DATE SEEN	WHERE	NOTES

| Order **Passeriformes** | Family **Troglodytidae** | Species *Troglodytes aedon* |

House Wren 🔊

faintly barred wings

ADULT (EASTERN)

IN FLIGHT

thin, indistinct eyebrow

narrow, pale eye-ring

grayish brown back

thin, slightly curved bill

pale gray-brown underparts

narrow, black barring on tail

**ADULT
T. a. parkmanii
(WESTERN)**

browner upperparts

plain brown crown

pale buffy throat

**ADULT
T. a. aedon
(EASTERN)**

FLIGHT: straight, with fast wingbeats; typically over short distances.

Of all the North American wrens, the House Wren is the plainest, yet one of the most familiar and endearing, especially when making its home in a backyard nest box. However, it can be a fairly aggressive species, driving away nearby nesting birds of its own and other species by destroying nests, puncturing eggs, and even killing young. In the 1920s, distraught bird lovers mounted a campaign calling for the eradication of House Wrens, though the campaign did not last long as most people were in favor of letting nature take its course.

VOICE Call a sharp *chep* or *cherr*; song opens with several short notes, followed by bubbly explosion of spluttering notes.

NESTING Cup lined with soft material on stick platform in natural, manmade cavities, such as nest boxes; 5–8 eggs; 2–3 broods; April–July.

FEEDING Forages for insects and spiders in trees and shrubs, gardens, and yards.

SIMILAR SPECIES

WINTER WREN *dark brown*
see p.315 *overall*
shorter tail
heavily barred flanks

NESTING MATERIAL
This small bird has brought an unusually large twig to its nest inside an old woodpecker hole.

OCCURRENCE
Breeds in cities, towns, parks, farms, yards, gardens, and woodland edges. Rarely seen during migration period (late July to early October). Winters south of its breeding range, from southern US to Mexico, in woodlands, shrubby areas, and weedy fields. Nests or is resident as far south as Tierra del Fuego.

| Length **4½in (11.5cm)** | Wingspan **6in (15cm)** | Weight **⅜oz (11g)** |
| Social **Solitary** | Lifespan **Up to 9 years** | Status **Secure** |

DATE SEEN	WHERE	NOTES

Order **Passeriformes**	Family **Troglodytidae**	Species *Troglodytes hiemalis*

Winter Wren 🔊

distinct, tan eyebrow

stubby tail, usually cocked straight up

dark brown, barred back

small, thin bill

ADULT

short, barred tail

ADULT

flanks strongly barred

barred, rounded wings

IN FLIGHT

The Winter Wren has one of the loudest songs of any small North American species. Once considered more widespread, it has recently been split from the Pacific Wren, which occupies much of the western fringe of the continent. It is a bird of low undergrowth and tangled roots, often foraging in the upturned roots and broken branches of fallen trees, appearing mouse-like as it creeps amid the shadows. It frequently appears in full view, gives a few harsh, scolding calls, then dives back out of sight into the low cover. It can survive periods of intense cold and even snow cover by finding insects and spiders, in crevices in bark and soil-encrusted roots. Several Winter Wrens may roost together in small cavities for warmth.
VOICE Call a double *chek-chek* or *chimp-chimp*; song a loud, extremely long, complex series of warbles, trills, and single notes.
NESTING Well-hidden in a cavity near ground with dead wood and crevices; nest a messy mound lined with feathers; 4–7 eggs; 1–2 broods; April–July.
FEEDING Forages for insects in low, dense undergrowth, often in wet areas along streams; sometimes thrusts its head into water to capture prey.

FLIGHT: fast and direct, with rapid beats of its short, broad wings.

VOCAL VIRTUOSO
The Winter Wren is a skulker, but in the breeding season singing males show up on lower perches.

SIMILAR SPECIES

HOUSE WREN
see p.314
pale brown back

long tail

plain, unbarred flanks

NERVOUS REACTION
When alarmed, this wren cocks its tail almost vertically, before escaping into a mossy thicket.

OCCURRENCE
Breeds in northern and mountain forests dominated by evergreen trees with a dense understory, fallen trees, and banks of streams. In the Appalachians, breeds in treeless areas with grass near cliffs. Northernmost birds migrate south to winter in woodlands, brush piles, tangles, and secluded spots.

Length **4in (10cm)**	Wingspan **5½in (14cm)**	Weight **5⁄16oz (9g)**
Social **Solitary/Family groups**	Lifespan **At least 4 years**	Status **Secure**

DATE SEEN	WHERE	NOTES

| Order **Passeriformes** | Family **Troglodytidae** | Species *Cistothorus platensis* |

Sedge Wren

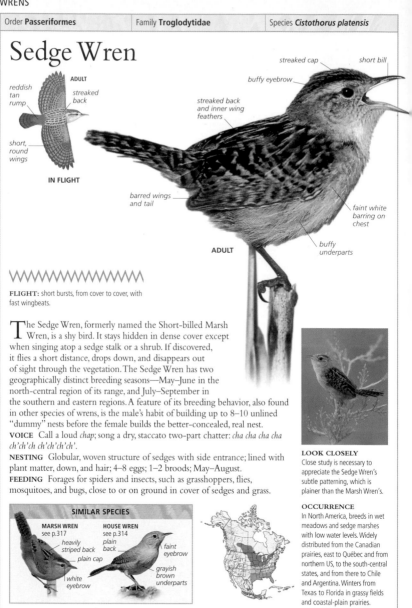

streaked cap

short bill

buffy eyebrow

ADULT

reddish tan rump

streaked back

streaked back and inner wing feathers

short, round wings

IN FLIGHT

barred wings and tail

faint white barring on chest

ADULT

buffy underparts

FLIGHT: short bursts, from cover to cover, with fast wingbeats.

The Sedge Wren, formerly named the Short-billed Marsh Wren, is a shy bird. It stays hidden in dense cover except when singing atop a sedge stalk or a shrub. If discovered, it flies a short distance, drops down, and disappears out of sight through the vegetation. The Sedge Wren has two geographically distinct breeding seasons—May–June in the north-central region of its range, and July–September in the southern and eastern regions. A feature of its breeding behavior, also found in other species of wrens, is the male's habit of building up to 8–10 unlined "dummy" nests before the female builds the better-concealed, real nest.

VOICE Call a loud *chap*; song a dry, staccato two-part chatter: *cha cha cha cha ch'ch'ch ch'ch'ch'ch'*.

NESTING Globular, woven structure of sedges with side entrance; lined with plant matter, down, and hair; 4–8 eggs; 1–2 broods; May–August.

FEEDING Forages for spiders and insects, such as grasshoppers, flies, mosquitoes, and bugs, close to or on ground in cover of sedges and grass.

LOOK CLOSELY
Close study is necessary to appreciate the Sedge Wren's subtle patterning, which is plainer than the Marsh Wren's.

OCCURRENCE
In North America, breeds in wet meadows and sedge marshes with low water levels. Widely distributed from the Canadian prairies, east to Québec and from northern US, to the south-central states, and from there to Chile and Argentina. Winters from Texas to Florida in grassy fields and coastal-plain prairies.

SIMILAR SPECIES

MARSH WREN
see p.317

heavily striped back

plain cap

white eyebrow

HOUSE WREN
see p.314

plain back

faint eyebrow

grayish brown underparts

| Length **4½in (11.5cm)** | Wingspan **5½–6in (14–15.5cm)** | Weight **5⁄16oz (9g)** |
| Social **Loose colonies** | Lifespan **Unknown** | Status **Secure** |

DATE SEEN	WHERE	NOTES

| Order **Passeriformes** | Family **Troglodytidae** | Species *Cistothorus palustris* |

Marsh Wren

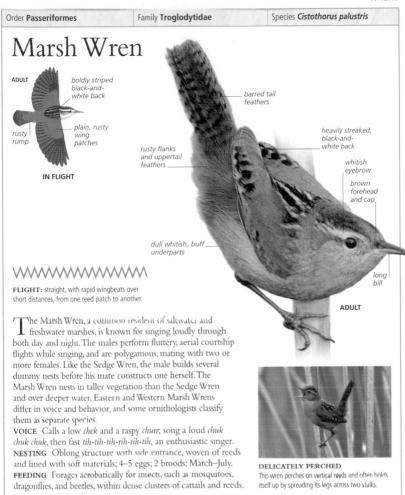

ADULT

boldly striped black-and-white back

barred tail feathers

plain, rusty wing patches

rusty rump

heavily streaked, black-and-white back

rusty flanks and uppertail feathers

whitish eyebrow

brown forehead and cap

IN FLIGHT

dull whitish, buff underparts

long bill

ADULT

FLIGHT: straight, with rapid wingbeats over short distances, from one reed patch to another.

The Marsh Wren, a common resident of saltwater and freshwater marshes, is known for singing loudly through both day and night. The males perform fluttery, aerial courtship flights while singing, and are polygamous, mating with two or more females. Like the Sedge Wren, the male builds several dummy nests before his mate constructs one herself. The Marsh Wren nests in taller vegetation than the Sedge Wren and over deeper water. Eastern and Western Marsh Wrens differ in voice and behavior, and some ornithologists classify them as separate species.

VOICE Calls a low *chek* and a raspy *churr*; song a loud *chuk chuk chuk*, then fast *tih-tih-tih-rih-tih-tih*, an enthusiastic singer.

NESTING Oblong structure with side entrance, woven of reeds and lined with soft materials; 4–5 eggs; 2 broods; March–July.

FEEDING Forages acrobatically for insects, such as mosquitoes, dragonflies, and beetles, within dense clusters of cattails and reeds.

DELICATELY PERCHED
This wren perches on vertical reeds and often holds itself up by spreading its legs across two stalks.

SIMILAR SPECIES

SEDGE WREN see p.316

streaked cap

HOUSE WREN see p.314

plain back

barred wings

buffy underparts

grayish brown underparts

OCCURRENCE
Breeds from Canada down to the mountains of western US as well as the central and northeastern US states. Inhabits freshwater and saltwater marshes with tall vegetation, above water, sometimes more than 3ft (1m) deep. It is irregularly distributed in its range. Winters in grassy marshes.

| Length **5in (13cm)** | Wingspan **6in (15cm)** | Weight **⅜oz (11g)** |
| Social **Loose colonies** | Lifespan **Unknown** | Status **Localized** |

DATE SEEN	WHERE	NOTES

| Order **Passeriformes** | Family **Troglodytidae** | Species *Thryothorus ludovicianus* |

Carolina Wren 🔊

ADULT

thin, black barring on tail

white wing spots

IN FLIGHT

tiny tail

ADULT

large head

duller overall

FLEDGLING

conspicuous white eyebrow bordered by black above

rufous upperparts

powerful-looking, bluish bill

white spots on wing

ADULT

buffy underparts

pinkish legs and toes

The Carolina Wren is a popular and common backyard bird in most of its range. It is rarely still, often flicking its tail and looking around nervously. Extremely harsh winters at the northernmost fringe of the Carolina Wren's range in New England can cause a sudden decline in numbers, as food resources are covered for long periods by ice and heavy snow. At such times, survival may depend on human help for food and shelter.

VOICE Calls variable; often a sharp *chlip* or long, harsh chatter; song a loud, long, fast *whee'dle-dee whee'dle-dee whee'dle-dee*.

NESTING Cup of weeds, twigs, leaves in natural or manmade cavity; 4–8 eggs; 2–3 broods; April–July.

FEEDING Forages for insects in shrubs and on ground; in winter, favorite foods are peanut butter or suet at a feeder.

FLIGHT: fast and straight over short distances, with rapid wingbeats.

DISTINCTIVE BORDER
A unique feature of this wren, not always noticed but visible here, is the black border on the eyebrow.

OCCURRENCE
Breeds in a variety of bushy woodland habitats, such as thickets, parks with shrubby undergrowth, suburban yards with dense, low trees or bushes, and gardens; from northeastern Mexico to the Great Lakes and northeast to New England. Four subspecies occur from Mexico to Nicaragua.

TIRELESS SINGER
Unlike many birds, the male Carolina Wren sings all year long, even on cold winter days.

SIMILAR SPECIES

BEWICK'S WREN
see p.319

dull brown or gray upperparts

longer tail

| Length **5¼ in (13.5cm)** | Wingspan **7½ in (19cm)** | Weight **¹¹⁄₁₆ oz (19g)** |
| Social **Pairs/Family groups** | Lifespan **At least 9 years** | Status **Secure** |

DATE SEEN	WHERE	NOTES

| Order **Passeriformes** | Family **Troglodytidae** | Species *Thryomanes bewickii* |

Bewick's Wren

white eyebrow

brown cheeks

long, slightly curved bill

whitish throat and breast

ADULT
T. b. drymoecus
(PACIFIC COAST)

black-and-white outer tail tips

ADULT

dark brown flight feathers

long, rounded tail

IN FLIGHT

plain gray upperparts

pale gray underparts

ADULT
T. b. eremophilus
(SOUTHWESTERN)

FLIGHT: fast and straight; over short distances.

Like the House Wren, but less common and occupying a smaller range, Bewick's Wren is also familiar around human habitations. It is known to nest in any sort of hole or crevice in barns, houses, abandoned machinery, woodpiles, and even trash heaps in farms and towns. Bewick's Wren has undergone large-scale changes in geographic distribution: in the 19th century its range expanded northward to the eastern and midwestern US, but it gradually disappeared from those regions in the 20th century. It has been suggested that the more aggressive House Wren slowly replaced Bewick's Wren in these areas.

VOICE Loud, complex, and varied mixture of cheeps, buzzes, and clear notes; vocalizations differ according to geographic location; also mimics other birds.
NESTING Cup of sticks lined with leaves, and other soft materials, in natural or manmade cavity, including nest boxes; 5–10 eggs; 2 broods; March–June.
FEEDING Forages for insects in brush, shrubs, crannies of buildings, and leaf litter on ground.

TALENTED MIMIC
Bewick's is sometimes known as the "Mocking Wren," because of its imitations of other species' songs.

OCCURRENCE
Year-round resident in brushy areas, open woodlands, and around human structures; from southern British Columbia southward to Baja California, east to Arkansas, and as far south as Oaxaca in Mexico. May withdraw slightly southward from northernmost portions of its range in winter.

SIMILAR SPECIES

CAROLINA WREN
see p.318
rufous upperparts
buffy underparts

TYPICAL POSTURE
Bewick's Wren may often be spotted with its distinctive tail cocked vertically.

| Length **5in (13cm)** | Wingspan **7in (18cm)** | Weight **⅜oz (11g)** |
| Social **Solitary/Pairs** | Lifespan **At least 8 years** | Status **Secure** |

DATE SEEN	WHERE	NOTES
....	....	....
....	....	....
....	....	....
....	....	....
....	....	....

| Order **Passeriformes** | Family **Polioptilidae** | Species **Polioptila caerulea** |

Blue-gray Gnatcatcher 🔊

MALE

paler
upperparts

FEMALE

lacks black line

black
line above
eye; absent
in winter

blue-gray
nape

pale gray
overall

white
outer tail
feathers

IN FLIGHT

white
eye-ring

blue-gray
upperparts

white
throat

black central
tail feathers

pale patch
on wing

pale gray
underparts

MALE

FLIGHT: short, straight and fluttering; usually
in short bursts from tree-top to tree-top.

If it did not give its continual wheezy call, the Blue-gray
Gnatcatcher might often be missed, as it spends much of
its time foraging high up in tall trees. In winter it becomes
even harder to find as it is generally silent. This species is the
most northern of the North American gnatcatchers and is
also the only one to migrate. It can exhibit aggressive behavior
and is capable of driving off considerably larger birds than
itself. The range of the Blue-gray Gnatcatcher appears to
be expanding and populations are increasing.
VOICE Call soft, irregular *zhee, zhee*, uttered constantly while
foraging; song soft combination of short notes and nasal wheezes.
NESTING Cup of plant fibers, spider webs, mosses; usually high
on branch; lined with soft plant material; 4–5 eggs; 1–2 broods;
April–June.
FEEDING Forages for small insects and spiders by acrobatically
flitting from twig to twig, while twitching long tail.

LISTEN CLOSELY
The rather faint complex song is best heard
when the bird is singing from a low perch.

SIMILAR SPECIES

BLACK-TAILED GNATCATCHER
see p.463

black
cap

tail
white
only at
tip

short
tail

TENNESSEE WARBLER
see p.407

no eye-
ring

greenish
upperparts

white
underparts

OCCURRENCE
In eastern North America,
breeds in deciduous or pine
woodlands; in the West, in
scrubby habitats, often near
water. Winters in brushy
habitats in southern US,
Mexico, and Central America.
Also breeds in Mexico,
Belize, and the Bahamas.

| Length **4¼in (11cm)** | Wingspan **6in (15cm)** | Weight **⁷⁄₃₂oz (6g)** |
| Social **Solitary/Flocks** | Lifespan **At least 4 years** | Status **Secure** |

DATE SEEN	WHERE	NOTES

| Order **Passeriformes** | Family **Regulidae** | Species *Regulus satrapa* |

Golden-crowned Kinglet

orange-and-yellow patch on crown, with black border

whitish wing bars

MALE

IN FLIGHT

yellow crown patch, with black border

FEMALE

broad whitish stripe above eye

olive-green upperparts

short, straight bill

MALE

white wing bar

notched tail

pale buff to whitish underparts

FLIGHT: quick and erratic, but not direct; high in the air; can hover while foraging.

This hardy little bird, barely more than a ball of feathers, breeds in northern and mountainous coniferous forests in North America. Other unconnected populations are resident in high-elevation forests in Mexico and Guatemala. Planting of spruce trees in parts of the US Midwest has allowed this species to increase its range in recent years to Ohio, Indiana, Illinois, and Pennsylvania.

VOICE Call a thin, high-pitched and thread-like *tsee* or *see see*; song a series of high-pitched ascending notes for 2 seconds; complex song *tsee-tsee-tsee-tsee-teet-leetle*, followed by brief trill.

NESTING Deep, cup-shaped nest with rims arching inward, made of moss, lichen, and bark, and lined with finer strips of the same; 8–9 eggs; 1–2 broods; May–August.

FEEDING Gleans flies, beetles, mites, spiders, and their eggs from tips of branches, under bark, tufts of conifer needles; eats seeds, and persimmon fruit.

EXPANDING RANGE
This bird has expanded its range southward following spruce forestation.

SIMILAR SPECIES

RUBY-CROWNED KINGLET
see p.322

white eye-ring

no eye-stripe

olive underparts

HIGHER VOICE
The Golden-crowned has a higher-pitched and less musical song than the Ruby-crowned.

OCCURRENCE
Breeds in remote northern and subalpine spruce or fir forests, mixed coniferous-deciduous forests, single-species stands, and pine plantations; winters in a wide variety of habitats—coniferous and deciduous forests, pine groves, low-lying hardwood forests, swamps, and urban and suburban habitats.

| Length **3¼–4¼in (8–11cm)** | Wingspan **5½–7in (14–18cm)** | Weight **⁵⁄₃₂–⁹⁄₃₂oz (4–8g)** |
| Social **Solitary/Pairs** | Lifespan **Up to 5 years** | Status **Secure** |

DATE SEEN	WHERE	NOTES

| Order **Passeriformes** | Family **Regulidae** | Species *Regulus calendula* |

Ruby-crowned Kinglet

red patch on crown

incomplete white eye-ring

ADULT

white wing bars

patch on crown often concealed

olive-green upperparts

notched tail

IN FLIGHT

no red patch on crown

FEMALE

two white wingbars

MALE

olive underparts

MALE

small upturned bill

brown legs with paler brown legs

The Ruby-crowned Kinglet is perhaps one of the most easily recognizable songbirds in North America because of its very small size, incomplete white eye-ring, two white wing bars, and habit of incessantly flicking its wings while foraging. This bird is renowned for its loud, complex song and for laying up to 12 eggs in a clutch—probably the highest of any North American songbird. Despite local declines resulting from logging and forest fires, the Ruby-crowned Kinglet is common across the continent. It will sometimes be found in mixed-species flocks in winter, together with nuthatches and titmice.

VOICE Call a low, husky *jidit*; song, remarkably loud for such a small bird, begins with 2–3 high, clear notes *tee* or *zee* followed by 5–6 lower *tu* or *turr* notes, and ends with ringing galloping notes *tee-da-leet, tee-da-leet, tee-da-leet*.

NESTING Globular or elongated nest hanging from or on large branch with an enclosed or open cup, made of mosses, feathers, lichens, spider's silk, bark, hair, and fur; 5–12 eggs; 1 brood; May–October.

FEEDING Gleans a wide variety of insects, spiders, and their eggs among the leaves on the outer tips of higher, smaller branches; eats fruit and seeds; often hovers to catch prey.

FLIGHT: short bursts of rapid wingbeats, but overall quick and direct flight.

CONCEALED COLOR
This bird's red patch is often concealed unless the bird is agitated or excited.

OCCURRENCE
Within the northern forest zone, breeds near water in black spruce and tamarack forests, muskegs, forests with mixed conifers and northern hardwoods; in the mountainous West, spruce-fir, lodgepole pine, and douglas fir forests. Winters in a broad range of forests, thickets, and borders.

SIMILAR SPECIES

HUTTON'S VIREO
see p.459

larger head

stouter bill

heavier overall

ALWAYS FLICKING
Ruby-crowned Kinglets are easily identified by their habit of constantly flicking their wings.

| Length **3½–4¼in (9–11cm)** | Wingspan **6–7in (15–18cm)** | Weight **³⁄₁₆–³⁄₈oz (5–10g)** |
| Social **Winter flocks** | Lifespan **Up to 5 years** | Status **Secure** |

DATE SEEN	WHERE	NOTES

THRUSHES AND CHATS

THRUSHES, CHATS (Wheatears and Bluethroats), and their relatives are small- to medium-sized birds. Many are forest species but feed mostly on the ground, while others such as the Mountain Bluebird and Northern Wheatear are birds of open countryside. Many thrushes have a plain, brown upperside and spotted underside, but make up for lack of color with their beautiful, flute-like songs. Some, however, are brightly colored and strongly patterned: the Varied Thrush is one of the most distinctive of all thrushes and the American Robin is one of the most familiar birds. The smaller bluebirds are renowned for their bright blues while the Townsend's Solitaire is a much grayer species.

GROUND BIRDS
Though they perch to sing, thrushes, including this Varied Thrush, spend a lot of their time on or near the ground. Varied Thrushes are rare in the East.

THRASHERS

THE FAMILY NAME for thrashers, mockingbirds, and catbirds, Mimidae, is derived from the Latin for "to imitate," or mimic. Perhaps no other word better describes the dozen or so thrashers of North America. They are well known for their ability to mimic the songs of other species and incorporate phrases into their own complex song sequences. In appearance, they are superficially thrush like but thrashers are more elongated and have long, more or less curved bills, long legs, and long tails. While mockingbirds may be bold, brash, and conspicuous—they are often found on open perches—thrashers are more reclusive, tending to forage deep within thickets or low vegetation, hopping on their strong legs, and digging into the leaf layer to find food with their bills. Only one species of thrasher, the Brown Thrasher, is found in the eastern US.

DISTINCTIVE BILL
Like other thrashers, the Long-billed Thrasher is characterized by its slender, curved bill, long, thin legs, and long, rounded tail.

| Order **Passeriformes** | Family **Turdidae** | Species *Sialia sialis* |

Eastern Bluebird 🔊

MALE

bluish gray underwings

bright blue upperparts

white belly

rufous breast and throat

IN FLIGHT

spotted throat and breast

gray-brown upperparts

JUVENILE

chestnut-brown chin, throat, breast, and flanks

MALE

white belly

white undertail

pale chestnut throat

gray upperparts

blue wings, rump, and tail

FEMALE

The Eastern Bluebird's vibrant blue and chestnut body is a beloved sight in eastern North America, especially after the remarkable comeback of the species in the past 30 years. It is also New York's State Bird. After much of the bird's habitat was eliminated by agriculture in the mid-1900s, nest boxes were designed and constructed for the bluebirds to provide alternatives for their traditional nesting sites in tree cavities. The Eastern Bluebird's mating system involves males seeking (or not minding) multiple partners.

VOICE Main song a melodious series of soft, whistled notes; *churr-wi* or *churr-li*; songs for mating and asserting territoriality.

NESTING Cavity nester, in trees or manmade boxes; nest of grass lined with weeds and twigs; uses old nests of other species; 3–7 eggs; 2 broods; February–September.

FEEDING Feeds on insects, like grasshoppers, and caterpillars in breeding season; in winter, also takes fruit and plants.

FLIGHT: shallow wingbeats; slow and easy.

HOME DELIVERY
A female bluebird delivers food to a nest box.

SIMILAR SPECIES

WESTERN BLUEBIRD ♀

brownish back

grayish throat

MOUNTAIN BLUEBIRD ♀
see p.472

gray-brown head and body

OCCURRENCE
Found in eastern Canada and the eastern US, where it lives in clearings and woodland edges; occupies multiple open habitats in rural, urban, and suburban areas: woodlands, plains, orchards, parks, and spacious lawns. Breeds and winters across the eastern half of the US.

| Length **6–8in (15–20cm)** | Wingspan **10–13in (25–33cm)** | Weight **1¹⁄₁₆ oz (30g)** |
| Social **Flocks** | Lifespan **8–10 years** | Status **Secure** |

DATE SEEN	WHERE	NOTES

Order **Passeriformes**	Family **Turdidae**	Species *Catharus fuscescens*

Veery 🔊

pale, reddish brown upperparts

less distinct spotting on breast

brownish tan upperparts

ADULT

IN FLIGHT

IMMATURE
C. f. fuscescens
(EASTERN)

inconspicuous, pale eye-ring

creamy pink at base of bill

poorly marked brown spots on buff breast and throat

white underparts

ADULT

tan wash on flanks

creamy pink legs and toes

The least spotted of the North American
Catharus thrushes, the Veery is medium-sized,
like the others, but browner overall. It has been
described as "dusky," but there is a geographical variation
in duskiness; four subspecies have been described to
reflect this. The Veery is a long-distance migrant,
spending the northern winter months in central
Brazil, in a variety of tropical habitats.

VOICE A series of descending *da-vee-ur, vee-ur,
veer, veer,* somewhat bitonal, sounding like the
name Veery; call a rather soft *veer.*

NESTING Cup of dead leaves, bark, weed stems,
and moss on or near ground; 4 eggs; 1–2 broods;
May–July.

FEEDING Forages on the ground for insects,
spiders, snails, eats fruit and berries after breeding.

FLIGHT: rapid and straight, with intermittent
hops and glides; makes long hops when on ground.

DAMP DWELLINGS
The Veery breeds in damp habitats
such as moist wooded areas or
in trees near or in swamps.

OCCURRENCE
In summer, mainly found in
damp deciduous forests, but
in some places habitat near
rivers preferred. In winter,
choice of habitat flexible; found
in tropical broadleaf evergreen
forest, on forest edges, in open
woodlands, and in second-
growth areas regenerating
after fires or clearing.

SIMILAR SPECIES

GRAY-CHEEKED THRUSH
see p.326

gray face

bold black-brown breast spots

BICKNELL'S THRUSH
see p.327

bold brown breast spots

grayish brown upperparts

SWAINSON'S THRUSH
see p.328

buffy-colored face

bold brown-black breast spots

Length **7in (18cm)**	Wingspan **11–11½in (28–29cm)**	Weight **1¹⁄₁₆–2oz (28–54g)**
Social **Pairs**	Lifespan **Up to 10 years**	Status **Declining**

DATE·SEEN	WHERE	NOTES

Order **Passeriformes**	Family **Turdidae**	Species *Catharus minimus*

Gray-cheeked Thrush

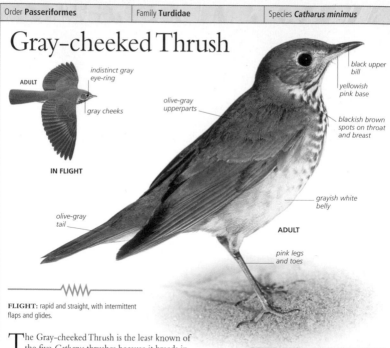

ADULT

indistinct gray eye-ring

gray cheeks

IN FLIGHT

olive-gray tail

olive-gray upperparts

black upper bill

yellowish pink base

blackish brown spots on throat and breast

grayish white belly

ADULT

pink legs and toes

FLIGHT: rapid and straight, with intermittent flaps and glides.

The Gray-cheeked Thrush is the least known of the five *Catharus* thrushes because it breeds in remote areas of Canada and Alaska. In fact, most of the existing information on this species is a result of research on the Bicknell's Thrush, which was considered to be a subspecies of the Gray-cheeked Thrush until 1993. During migration, the Gray-cheeked Thrush is more likely to be heard in flight at night than seen on the ground by birdwatchers.
VOICE Call a thin *kweer*, sometimes two notes; song flute-like, somewhat nasal, several notes ending on a lower pitch.
NESTING Cup of grass, twigs, moss, dead leaves, and mud, placed near ground in shrubbery; 4 eggs; 1 brood; May–July.
FEEDING Forages insects, including beetles, ants, spiders, earthworms; and also fruit.

FEEDING HABITAT
A Gray-cheeked Thrush hops across the forest floor looking for prey.

SIMILAR SPECIES

BICKNELL'S THRUSH see p.327

olive-brown upperparts

brownish spots

TREETOP SINGER
This bird is most likely to be seen in the evening, singing from treetops on its nesting grounds.

OCCURRENCE
On breeding grounds occupies densely vegetated areas with small shrubs; preference for spruce forests in northern Canada and Alaska. During migration, favors wooded areas with dense understory. In winter, prefers forested areas and secondary succession woodlands.

Length **6½–7in (16–18cm)**	Wingspan **11½–13½in (29–34cm)**	Weight **⅞–1¹⁄₁₆ oz (26–30g)**
Social **Mixed flocks**	Lifespan **Up to 7 years**	Status **Secure**

DATE SEEN	WHERE	NOTES

| Order **Passeriformes** | Family **Turdidae** | Species *Catharus bicknelli* |

Bicknell's Thrush

olive-brown upperparts

ADULT

IN FLIGHT

rufous tail

indistinct eye-ring

blackish upper bill

olive-brown head

pale base to bill

brownish olive back

tan spots

brown specks and spots

olive-brown wings

buff breast

whitish to buff belly

grayish buff wash on flanks

whitish to buff undertail feathers

IMMATURE

pink legs

FLIGHT: rapid and straight, with intermittent flaps and glides.

Named for E.P. Bicknell (1859-1925), a founding member of the American Ornithologists' Union, Bicknell's Thrush was considered a subspecies of the Gray-cheeked Thrush. In 1993, it was shown to be a distinct species with slight differences in color, song, habitat, and migration. In the field, it is best distinguished from the Gray-cheeked Thrush by its song, which is less full and lower in pitch. Bicknell's Thrush breeds only in dwarf conifer forests on mountain tops in the northeastern US and adjacent Canada. Habitat loss threatens this species on its wintering grounds in Cuba, Hispaniola, and Puerto Rico. Males and females mate with multiple partners in a single season; because of this, males may care for young in multiple nests.
VOICE Call *pheeuw*, one or two notes; complicated flute-like song of about four parts, ending with rising pitch; males sing, especially during flight.
NESTING Cup of moss and evergreen twigs, near ground; 3–4 eggs; 1 brood; June–August.
FEEDING Feeds mainly on caterpillars and insects; eats fruit during migration and possibly in winter.

MOUNTAIN-TOP BREEDING
This species breeds in high-elevation woodland areas, especially in conifers.

SIMILAR SPECIES

GRAY-CHEEKED THRUSH see p.326
olive-gray brown
grayish face

OCCURRENCE
Restricted to dense spruce or fir forest at or near the treeline, at 4,000ft (1,000m), often in disturbed areas undergoing successional changes. During migration, found in a variety of habitats, such as woodlots and beaches. In winter, strong preference for wet mountain Caribbean forests.

| Length 6½–7in (16–18cm) | Wingspan 12in (30cm) | Weight ⅞–1 1/16 oz (26–30g) |
| Social **Solitary/Small flocks** | Lifespan **Up to 8 years** | Status **Vulnerable** |

DATE SEEN	WHERE	NOTES

| Order **Passeriformes** | Family **Turdidae** | Species *Catharus ustulatus* |

Swainson's Thrush

ADULT

IN FLIGHT

more rufous in upperparts

russet back

smaller, less distinct, sparser spotting

olive-brown rump and tail

ADULT
C. u. ustulatus
(WESTERN)

buffy eye-ring

olive-brown upperparts

buff breast

distinct blackish spots

ADULT
C. u. swainsoni
(EASTERN)

Swainson's Thrush can be distinguished from other spotted thrushes by its buffy face and the rising pitch of its flute-like, melodious song. This species is also distinctive as it feeds higher up in the understory than most of its close relatives. The eastern subspecies of Swainson's Thrush migrates to eastern South America, where it spends the winter.

VOICE Single-note call *whit* or *whooit*; main song delivered by males, several phrases, each one spiraling upward; flute-like song is given during breeding and migration.

NESTING Open cup of twigs, moss, dead leaves, bark, and mud, on branches near trunks of small trees or in shrubs; 3–4 eggs; 1–2 broods; April–July.

FEEDING Forages in the air, using fly-catching methods to capture a wide range of insects during breeding season; berries during migration and in winter.

FLIGHT: rapid and straight, with intermittent flaps and glides.

DISTINCTIVE SONG
This bird's song distinguishes it from other thrushes.

TREE DWELLER
Shy and retiring, Swainson's Thrush feeds higher in trees than other *Catharus* thrushes.

SIMILAR SPECIES

VEERY
see p.325

tawny brown back

lightly spotted breast

HERMIT THRUSH
see p.329

grayish cheeks

streaks on sides of breast

rust-colored tail

OCCURRENCE
Breeds mainly in coniferous forests, especially spruce and fir, except in California, where it prefers deciduous riverside woodlands and damp meadows with shrubbery. During spring and fall migrations, dense understory is preferred. Winter habitat is mainly old-growth forest.

| Length **6½–7½in (16–19cm)** | Wingspan **11½–12in (29–31cm)** | Weight **⅞–1⁹⁄₁₆ oz (25–45g)** |
| Social **Pairs/Flocks** | Lifespan **Up to 11 years** | Status **Declining** |

DATE SEEN	WHERE	NOTES

| Order **Passeriformes** | Family **Turdidae** | Species *Catharus guttatus* |

Hermit Thrush

thin white eye-ring

gray-brown upperparts

ADULT C. g. faxoni (EASTERN)

IN FLIGHT

darker brown upperparts

dark spots on whitish breast

paler gray flanks

brownish back

gray-brown upperparts

more extensive breast spotting

ADULT C. g. guttatus (NORTHWESTERN)

dark spots on buff breast

ADULT C. g. auduboni (ROCKIES)

reddish tail

ADULT C. g. faxoni (EASTERN)

tawny buff flanks

The Hermit Thrush's song is the signature sound of northern forests in the East—fluted, almost bitonal, far-carrying, and ending up with almost a question mark. The Hermit Thrush is Vermont's State Bird. It is so named because of its solitary lifestyle, especially in winter, when birds maintain inter-individual territories. Geographical variation within the vast range of the species has led to the recognition of nine subspecies (three are shown here). It winters in southern US, Mexico, Guatemala, and El Salvador.

VOICE Calls *tchek*, soft, dry; song flute-like, ethereal, falling, repetitive, and varied; several phrases delivered on a different pitch.

NESTING Cup of grasses, mosses, twigs, leaves, mud, hair, on ground or in low tree branches; 4 eggs; 1–2 broods; May–July.

FEEDING Mainly forages on ground for insects, larvae, earthworms, and snails; in winter, also eats fruit.

FLIGHT: rapid and straight, with intermittent flaps and glides.

URBAN VISITOR
This thrush is frequently seen in wooded areas in urban and suburban parks.

SIMILAR SPECIES

VEERY see p.325
tawny brown back
lightly spotted breast

BICKNELL'S THRUSH see p.327
olive-brown back
yellow base of bill

SWAINSON'S THRUSH see p.328
olive-brown upperparts

OCCURRENCE
Occurs in coniferous forests and mixed conifer–deciduous woodlands; prefers to nest along the edges of a forest interior, like a bog. During migration, found in many wooded habitats. Found in forest and other open woodlands during winter in Mexico.

| Length **6–7in (15–18cm)** | Wingspan **10–11in (25–28cm)** | Weight **⅞–1¹⁄₁₆ oz (25–30g)** |
| Social **Solitary** | Lifespan **Up to 9 years** | Status **Secure** |

DATE SEEN	WHERE	NOTES

| Order **Passeriformes** | Family **Turdidae** | Species *Hylocichla mustelina* |

Wood Thrush 🔊

ADULT

rusty orange head and back

reddish brown lower back and rump

roundish, brown wings

IN FLIGHT

short, reddish brown tail

pink legs and toes

white eye-ring

rusty orange head

black bill with pink base

large, black triangular spots on breast, sides, and flanks

ADULT

FLIGHT: straight, direct flight with consistent wingbeats.

The Wood Thrush is perhaps the most striking of the small North American thrushes, because of the triangular black spots that cover its underparts and its rich rufous head and back. In the breeding season, its flute-like song echoes through the Northeastern hardwood forests and suburban wooded areas. Wood Thrush populations have sharply decreased over the past 30 years, as a direct result of forest destruction and fragmentation. Sadly, this decline has been exacerbated by its susceptibility to brood parasitism by the Brown-headed Cowbird.
VOICE Rapid *pip-pippipip* or *rhuu-rhuu*; a three-part flute-like song—first part indistinct, second part loudest, third part trilled; males have variations of all three parts; mainly before sunrise.
NESTING Cup-shaped nest made with dried grass and weeds in trees or shrubs; 3–4 eggs; 1–2 broods; May–July.
FEEDING Forages in leaf litter, mainly for worms, beetles, moths, caterpillars; eats fruit after breeding season.

STUNNING SOLOIST
The Wood Thrush can often be seen singing its melodious songs from a conspicuous perch.

SIMILAR SPECIES

VEERY
see p.325

smaller overall

longer tail

fainter spotting

HERMIT THRUSH
see p.329

reddish tail

spotting only on throat and upper breast

OCCURRENCE
Hardwood forests in the East, from Texas and Florida northward to Minnesota and the Canadian Maritimes. Breeds in interior and at edges of deciduous and mixed forests; needs dense understory, shrubbery, and moist soil. Winters from eastern Mexico south through Central America to Panama; also Cuba.

| Length **7½–8½in (19–21cm)** | Wingspan **12–13½in (30–34cm)** | Weight **1⁷⁄₁₆–1¾oz (40–50g)** |
| Social **Pairs/Flocks** | Lifespan **Up to 9 years** | Status **Declining** |

DATE SEEN	WHERE	NOTES

| Order **Passeriformes** | Family **Turdidae** | Species *Turdus migratorius* |

American Robin 🔊

MALE

dark head

IN FLIGHT

more complete white eye-ring

gray back

orangish red breast

white rump

broken white eye-ring

yellow bill

dark streaks on chin

dark gray back

FEMALE

mottled gray back

spotted breast

JUVENILE

brick-red underparts

MALE

fairly long, dark tail

〜〜〜〜

FLIGHT: strong, swift flights with intermittent flaps and glides.

The American Robin, the largest and most abundant of the North American thrushes, is probably also the most familiar bird across the entire continent. Its presence on suburban lawns is a clear sign of spring. Unlike other species, it has adapted and prospered in human-altered habitats. It breeds in the entire US and Canada, winters across the US, and migrates out of most of Canada in the fall. The decision to migrate is largely governed by changes in the availability of food. As the breeding season approaches, it is the males that sing first, either late in winter or early spring. The bird's brick red breast—more vivid in males than in females—is its most distinguishing feature.

VOICE Calls a high pitch *tjip* and a multi-note, throaty *tjuj-tjuk*; primary song a melodious *cheer up, cheer up, cheer-wee*, one of the first birds to be heard during the dawn chorus, and one of the last to cease singing in the evening.

NESTING Substantial cup of grass, weeds, twigs, strengthened with mud, in tree or shrub, in fork of tree, or on branch on tree; 4 eggs; 2–3 broods; April–July.

FEEDING Forages in leaf litter, mainly for earthworms and small insects; mostly consumes fruit in the winter season.

SEASONAL DIET
Robins are particularly dependent on the availability of fruit during the winter months.

OCCURRENCE
Breeding habitat a mix of forest, woodland, suburban gardens, lawns, municipal parks, and farms. A partial migrant, these robins tend to be found in woodlands where berry-bearing trees are present. Nonmigrating populations' winter habitat is similar to breeding habitat. Winters in Guatemala.

SIMILAR SPECIES

VARIED THRUSH *see p.412*

orange eyebrow

bluish gray upperparts

wide black necklace

| Length **8–11in (20–28cm)** | Wingspan **12–16in (30–41cm)** | Weight **2⅝oz (75g)** |
| Social **Flocks** | Lifespan **Up to 13 years** | Status **Secure** |

DATE SEEN	WHERE		NOTES
....	....		....
....	....		....
....	....		....
....	....		....
....	....		....

Order **Passeriformes**	Family **Mimidae**	Species *Dumetella carolinensis*

Gray Catbird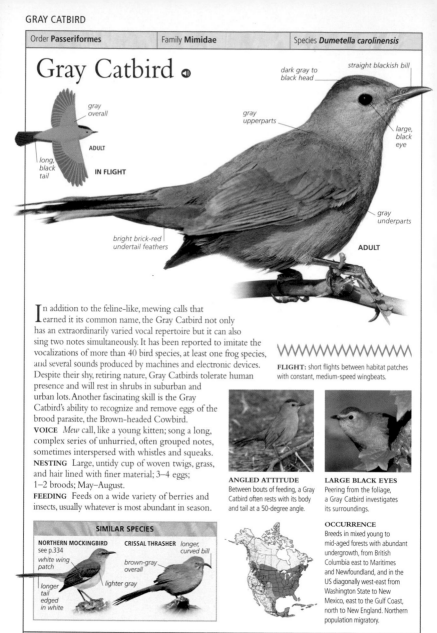

gray overall

ADULT

IN FLIGHT

long, black tail

dark gray to black head

straight blackish bill

gray upperparts

large, black eye

gray underparts

bright brick-red undertail feathers

ADULT

In addition to the feline-like, mewing calls that earned it its common name, the Gray Catbird not only has an extraordinarily varied vocal repertoire but it can also sing two notes simultaneously. It has been reported to imitate the vocalizations of more than 40 bird species, at least one frog species, and several sounds produced by machines and electronic devices. Despite their shy, retiring nature, Gray Catbirds tolerate human presence and will rest in shrubs in suburban and urban lots. Another fascinating skill is the Gray Catbird's ability to recognize and remove eggs of the brood parasite, the Brown-headed Cowbird.

VOICE *Mew* call, like a young kitten; song a long, complex series of unhurried, often grouped notes, sometimes interspersed with whistles and squeaks.

NESTING Large, untidy cup of woven twigs, grass, and hair lined with finer material; 3–4 eggs; 1–2 broods; May–August.

FEEDING Feeds on a wide variety of berries and insects, usually whatever is most abundant in season.

FLIGHT: short flights between habitat patches with constant, medium-speed wingbeats.

ANGLED ATTITUDE Between bouts of feeding, a Gray Catbird often rests with its body and tail at a 50-degree angle.

LARGE BLACK EYES Peering from the foliage, a Gray Catbird investigates its surroundings.

OCCURRENCE
Breeds in mixed young to mid-aged forests with abundant undergrowth, from British Columbia east to Maritimes and Newfoundland, and in the US diagonally west-east from Washington State to New Mexico, east to the Gulf Coast, north to New England. Northern population migratory.

SIMILAR SPECIES

NORTHERN MOCKINGBIRD see p.334
white wing patch
longer tail edged in white

CRISSAL THRASHER *longer, curved bill*
brown-gray overall
lighter gray

Length **8–9½in (20–24cm)**	Wingspan **10–12in (25–30cm)**	Weight **1¼–2⅛oz (35–60g)**
Social **Solitary/Pairs**	Lifespan **Up to 11 years**	Status **Secure**

DATE SEEN	WHERE	NOTES

| Order **Passeriformes** | Family **Mimidae** | Species *Toxostoma rufum* |

Brown Thrasher 🔊

- bright yellow eye
- fairly straight, dark bill
- grayish cheeks
- indistinct "mustache"
- reddish brown upperparts
- dark streaking on pale underparts

ADULT

- rufous wings and upperparts
- long tail with pale outer tips

IN FLIGHT

- two pale wing bars

- long tail, paler than back

ADULT

The Brown Thrasher is usually difficult to view clearly because it keeps to dense underbrush. Like most other thrashers, this species prefers running or hopping to flying. When nesting, it can recognize and remove the eggs of brood parasites like the Brown-headed Cowbird. The current population decline is most likely the result of fragmentation of large, wooded habitats into patches, which lack the forest interior habitat this species needs.

FLIGHT: slow and heavy with deep wingbeats; below treetops, especially in and around ground.

VOICE Calls varied, including rasping sounds; song a long series of musical notes, sometimes imitating other species; repeats phrase twice before moving onto the next one.

NESTING Bulky cup of twigs, close to ground, lined with leaves, grass, bark; 3–5 eggs; 1 brood; April–July.

FEEDING Mainly insects (especially beetles) and worms gathered from leaf litter on the forest floor; will peck at cultivated grains, nuts, berries, and fruit.

STREAKED BREAST
Displaying its heavily streaked underparts, this Brown Thrasher is perched and ready to sing.

OCCURRENCE
Widespread across central and eastern North America, from Canada to Texas and Florida, in a variety of densely wooded habitats, particularly those with thick undergrowth, but will use woodland edges, hedges, and riverside trees. A partial migrant, it winters in the southern part of its range.

SIMILAR SPECIES

LONG-BILLED THRASHER see p.464
- longer, curved bill
- duller brown back
- heavily streaked underparts

CURVE-BILLED THRASHER see p.464
- orange eye
- mouse gray-brown upperparts
- pale brown spots, not streaks

| Length **10–12in (25–30cm)** | Wingspan **11–14in (28–36cm)** | Weight **2⅛–2⅞oz (60–80g)** |
| Social **Solitary/Flocks** | Lifespan **Up to 13 years** | Status **Declining** |

DATE SEEN	WHERE	NOTES

| Order **Passeriformes** | Family **Mimidae** | Species *Mimus polyglottos* |

Northern Mockingbird 🔊

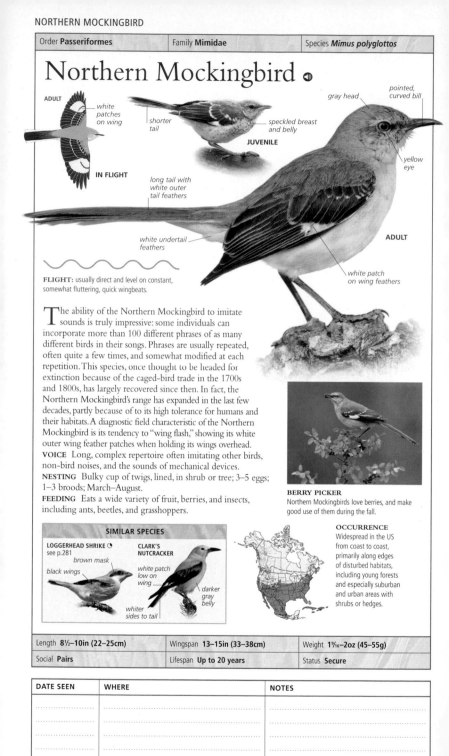

ADULT

white patches on wing

shorter tail

JUVENILE

speckled breast and belly

IN FLIGHT

long tail with white outer tail feathers

white undertail feathers

gray head

pointed, curved bill

yellow eye

ADULT

white patch on wing feathers

FLIGHT: usually direct and level on constant, somewhat fluttering, quick wingbeats.

The ability of the Northern Mockingbird to imitate sounds is truly impressive: some individuals can incorporate more than 100 different phrases of as many different birds in their songs. Phrases are usually repeated, often quite a few times, and somewhat modified at each repetition. This species, once thought to be headed for extinction because of the caged-bird trade in the 1700s and 1800s, has largely recovered since then. In fact, the Northern Mockingbird's range has expanded in the last few decades, partly because of to its high tolerance for humans and their habitats. A diagnostic field characteristic of the Northern Mockingbird is its tendency to "wing flash," showing its white outer wing feather patches when holding its wings overhead.

VOICE Long, complex repertoire often imitating other birds, non-bird noises, and the sounds of mechanical devices.

NESTING Bulky cup of twigs, lined, in shrub or tree; 3–5 eggs; 1–3 broods; March–August.

FEEDING Eats a wide variety of fruit, berries, and insects, including ants, beetles, and grasshoppers.

BERRY PICKER
Northern Mockingbirds love berries, and make good use of them during the fall.

SIMILAR SPECIES

LOGGERHEAD SHRIKE ⊙
see p.281
brown mask
black wings
whiter sides to tail

CLARK'S NUTCRACKER
white patch low on wing
darker gray belly

OCCURRENCE
Widespread in the US from coast to coast, primarily along edges of disturbed habitats, including young forests and especially suburban and urban areas with shrubs or hedges.

| Length **8½–10in (22–25cm)** | Wingspan **13–15in (33–38cm)** | Weight **1⁹⁄₁₆–2oz (45–55g)** |
| Social **Pairs** | Lifespan **Up to 20 years** | Status **Secure** |

DATE SEEN	WHERE	NOTES

| Order **Passeriformes** | Family **Sturnidae** | Species *Acridotheres tristis* |

Common Myna

bold white wing band

dark face

yellow bill and face patch

black, hooded head

pinkish gray body

JUVENILE

IN FLIGHT

crest can be raised

white tail tip

ADULT

ADULT

white undertail

yellow legs

FLIGHT: fast, swooping, with flurries of wingbeats and short glides.

This stocky, noisy bird of the starling family is native to southern Asia but has been introduced, deliberately or accidentally, into many other countries. In the US, it is found in Florida (since 1980s) and in Hawaii, where it was introduced to control pests in 1865. It now competes with more sensitive and specialized native species for food and nest sites. Other species nest in tree holes, but the Common Myna is typically more aggressive and assertive; it frequently preys on small nestlings, causing considerable conservation concern. Almost everywhere it is an adaptable and successful species. The Common Myna is easily recognized by its dark brown body, black head, and yellow eye patch; in flight, the wings flash large white patches.

FIGHTING FOR FOOD
Although usually found in pairs or families, Mynas often gather to squabble noisily over scraps of food.

VOICE Many croaks, chirping and clicking notes, loud, fluty whistles, and a screech in alarm.
NESTING Requires a hole or cavity in a tree or wall for the nest, and often evicts other birds; 4–6 eggs; 1–2 broods; March–August.
FEEDING Very varied, diet includes insects—especially grasshoppers and crickets—mostly picked from the ground, other small invertebrates, reptiles, seeds, and fruit.

OCCURRENCE
Established in Florida, found in grasslands, parks, open woodland, and on bushy slopes, roosting communally in dense trees.

| Length **9in (23cm)** | Wingspan **15in (39cm)** | Weight **3oz (125g)** |
| Social **Small groups, especially at roost** | Lifespan **5 years** | Status **Secure** |

Order **Passeriformes**	Family **Sturnidae**	Species ***Sturnus vulgaris***

European Starling 🔊

short, square tail

pointed, triangular wings

ADULT (BREEDING)

IN FLIGHT

body feathers tipped whitish or buff

wing feathers edged bright orange-buff

large spots on undertail

ADULT (NONBREEDING)

black face with hints of shiny, glossy purple

glossy black body with mostly green sheen

blue-based, sharp, yellow bill; pink-based on female

dark, glossy, blue-black belly

MALE (BREEDING)

long, pinkish brown legs and strong toes

dull brownish head

dark bill

IMMATURE (FALL)

plain brown body

JUVENILE

This distinctive non-native species is perhaps the most successful bird in North America—and probably the most maligned. In the 1890s, 100 European Starlings were released in New York City's Central Park; these were the ancestors of the many millions of birds that now live all across the US. This adaptable and aggressive bird competes with native species for nest sites, and the starling usually wins—even against larger species such as the Northern Flicker.

VOICE Highly varied; gives whooshing *ssssheer*, often in flight; also whistled *wheeeooo*; song an elaborate pulsing series with slurred whistles and clicking notes; imitates other species' vocalizations.

NESTING Natural or artificial cavity of any sort; 4–6 eggs; 1–2 broods; March–July.

FEEDING Omnivorous; picks at anything that might be edible; insects and berries are common food items; also visits birdfeeders and trash cans; often feeds on grubs in lawns.

FLIGHT: individuals fly in direct, buzzy manner; flocks bunch up tightly in flight.

INSECT EATER
Despite its parents' omnivorous diet, the nestlings are fed almost exclusively on insects and larvae.

SIMILAR SPECIES

BRONZED COWBIRD ♂
see p.469

red eye

no spots

BROWN-HEADED COWBIRD
see p.391

no spots

longer tail

OCCURRENCE
In North America from southern Canada to the US–Mexico border; also Puerto Rico and other Caribbean islands. Common to abundant in cities, towns, and farmlands; also occurs in relatively "wild" settings far from human habitation. Forms flocks at all times, huge in winter.

Length **8½ in (21cm)**	Wingspan **16in (41cm)**	Weight **2⅝– 3⅜oz (75–95g)**
Social **Colonies**	Lifespan **Up to 17 years**	Status **Secure**

DATE SEEN	WHERE	NOTES

| Order **Passeriformes** | Family **Bombycillidae** | Species ***Bombycilla garrulus*** |

Bohemian Waxwing

yellow edges to outer flight feathers

ADULT
IN FLIGHT

wispy crest

black throat

gray upperparts

FEMALE

yellow tail band

variable crest

gray-brown upperparts

reduced wing markings

FEMALE (1ST WINTER)

gray underparts

MALE

chestnut undertail feathers

ornate wing markings

FLIGHT: quick wingbeats interspersed with glides; often flies in tightly bunched flocks.

The Bohemian Waxwing is the wilder and rarer of the two waxwing species in North America. It breeds mainly in Alaska and western Canada. The species is migratory, but the extent of its wintertime movement is notoriously variable, depending on the availability of wild fruit. In most winters, relatively few Bohemian Waxwings visit the lower 48 states, but in special "irruption" years, tens of thousands may reach as far south as Colorado.
VOICE Call a dull trill, but effect of hundreds of birds calling at the same time is remarkable and sounds like a high-pitched chorus; flocks vocalize constantly.
NESTING Dishevelled cup of sticks and grasses, placed in tree; 4–6 eggs; number of broods unknown; June–July.
FEEDING Catches insects on the wing in summer; flocks devour berries of native and exotic trees and shrubs throughout the year.

STRIKING TAIL
The Bohemian Waxwing's yellow tail band and chestnut undertail are evident here.

OCCURRENCE
Breeds in subarctic coniferous forest, favoring disturbed areas such as beaver ponds and logging sites. Flocks gather at forest edges, hedges, and residential areas in winter. Hundreds or thousands of birds appear in an area, then disappear once food is depleted.

SIMILAR SPECIES		
CEDAR WAXWING see p.338	**CEDAR WAXWING** ☾ see p.338	
plainer wing markings	warmer tones overall	smaller overall
	unmarked wings	

Length **8½in (21cm)**	Wingspan **14½in (37cm)**	Weight **1⁹⁄₁₆–2½oz (45–70g)**
Social **Flocks**	Lifespan **Up to 12 years**	Status **Localized**

DATE SEEN	WHERE	NOTES

Order **Passeriformes**	Family **Bombycillidae**	Species *Bombycilla cedrorum*

Cedar Waxwing 🔊

short yellow tip to tail

ADULT

brown neck and breast

ADULT

yellow belly

black mask

IN FLIGHT

lacks red on wing

streaks on underparts

JUVENILE

whitish undertail feathers

wispy crest

white lines on face

brownish tan back

black "bandit" mask

ADULT

waxy red tips on inner wing

FLIGHT: straight and direct with alternate glides; usually in small to medium flocks.

Flocks of Cedar Waxwings, a nomadic species, move around North America looking for berries, which are their main source of food. Common in a specific location one year, they may disappear the next and occur elsewhere. Northern breeders tend to be more migratory than southern ones. In winter, their nomadic tendencies can send Cedar Waxwings as far south as South America. They can often be heard and identified by their calls, long before the flock settles to feed.

VOICE Basic vocalization a shrill trill: *shr-r-r-r-r-r* or *tre-e-e-e-e-e*, which appears to serve the function of both call note and song.
NESTING Open cup placed in fork of tree, often lined with grasses, plant fibers; 3–5 eggs; 1–2 broods; June–August.
FEEDING Eats in flocks at trees and shrubs with ripe berries throughout the year; also catches flying insects in summer.

BATHING ADULT
Cedar Waxwings love to take baths, and use birdbaths in suburban gardens.

SIMILAR SPECIES

BOHEMIAN WAXWING ♂
see p.337

larger overall

more ornate wing pattern

rufous undertail

BOHEMIAN WAXWING ♀ ●
see p.337

pale gray breast

OCCURRENCE
Breeds in woodlands across northern US and southern Canada, especially near streams and clearings. Winters anywhere where trees and shrubs have ripe fruits, especially in Mexico and South America. Spends a lot of time in treetops, but sometimes comes down to shrub level.

Length **7½in (19cm)**	Wingspan **12in (30cm)**	Weight **1¹⁄₁₆–1¼oz (30–35g)**
Social **Flocks**	Lifespan **Up to 7 years**	Status **Secure**

DATE SEEN	WHERE	NOTES

OLD WORLD SPARROWS

THESE SMALL, SHORT-LEGGED, short-billed, principally seed-eating birds were introduced to North America from Europe and Asia, and their name has carried over to many unrelated New World species. House and Tree Sparrows are small and finch-like, but always unstreaked below. Male and female House Sparrows differ in appearance, while Tree Sparrows of both sexes are more like the male House Sparrow, with pale cheeks and a black bib. House Sparrows are familiar urban and suburban birds, always associated with buildings, parks, or farmsteads.

MATCHED MARKINGS
Unlike House Sparrows, which have marked sexual dimorphism, both sexes of the Eurasian Tree Sparrow are alike, with brown caps, black bibs, and black cheek spots. This species is rare in the East.

FEEDING FRENZY
House Sparrows feed their chicks on caterpillars, visiting the nest scores of times each day.

WAGTAILS AND PIPITS

THERE ARE FOUR SPECIES of these ground-living birds in North America, although two are rarely seen as they breed in remote parts of Alaska. All are slim and long-tailed, with the wagtails typically bobbing their tails up and down. The pipits are dull, brown birds, although more streaked than wagtails. They inhabit open, treeless country, walking rather than hopping on the ground. They are more likely to be seen in their widespread wintering areas than in their remote breeding range.

COUNTRY-LOVERS
Pipits, such as this American Pipit, live in open country, including beaches, dunes, and tundra.

| Order **Passeriformes** | Family **Passeridae** | Species *Passer domesticus* |

House Sparrow

white wing bar

pale rump

MALE (SUMMER)

IN FLIGHT

buff eyestripe

yellowish bill

black-and-brown streaks on upperparts

drab brown underparts

FEMALE

brown nape

gray crown

black throat

gray breast

white wing bar

MALE (SUMMER)

This is the familiar "sparrow" of towns, cities, suburbs, and farms. The House Sparrow is not one of the American Sparrows—family Passerellidae—more commonly known in North America; rather it is a member of the Eurasian family, Passeridae. It was first introduced in Brooklyn, New York, in 1850. From this modest beginning, and with the help of several other introductions up until the late 1860s, this hardy and aggressive bird eventually spread right through the North American continent. In a little more than 150 years, the House Sparrow has evolved and shows the same sort of geographic variation as some widespread native birds. It is pale in the arid Southwest, and darker in wetter regions.
VOICE Variety of calls, including a *cheery chirp*, a dull *jurv* and a rough *jigga*; song consists of *chirp* notes repeated endlessly.
NESTING Untidy mass of dried vegetable material in either natural or artificial cavities; 3–5 eggs; 2–3 broods; April–August.
FEEDING Mostly seeds; sometimes gleans insects and fruit.

FLIGHT: fast and bouncing, with rapid wingbeats; short wings and tail give it a portly profile.

APTLY NAMED
This sparrow is seen near human structures—roofs, outbuildings, loading docks, curbs, and streetlights.

SIMILAR SPECIES

DICKCISSEL ♀
see p.442

pale bill

pale throat

yellowish highlights

DICKCISSEL ♂ ❉
see p.442

black and tan streaks

pale bill

OCCURRENCE
Flourishes in the downtown sections of cities and around human habitations, including agricultural outbuildings in remote areas of the continent. Also found in Mexico, Central and South America, the West Indies, Eurasia, southern Africa, Australia, and New Zealand.

| Length **6in (15.5cm)** | Wingspan **9½in (24cm)** | Weight **⅝–1¹⁄₁₆oz (18–30g)** |
| Social **Flocks** | Lifespan **Up to 7 years** | Status **Declining** |

DATE SEEN	WHERE	NOTES

| Order **Passeriformes** | Family **Motacillidae** | Species **Anthus rubescens** |

American Pipit

ADULT

faint streaking on gray upperparts

pale eyebrow

"mustache"

gray cheek with buffy eyestripes

whitish with heavier streaking on chest and flanks

ADULT (NONBREEDING)

white outer tail feathers

IN FLIGHT

buffy eyestripe

thin, dark bill

dark "mustache"

no streaking on grayish back

wing bars

pale edges to wing feathers

long tail with white outer tail feathers

ADULT (BREEDING)

light reddish buffy chest and flanks

long hind claw

dark legs and toes

FLIGHT. typically strong with a distinct, undulating, rise and fall pattern.

The American Pipit is divided into four subspecies, three of which breed in North America, and the fourth in Siberia. In nonbreeding plumage, the American Pipit is a drab-looking, brownish gray bird that forages for insects along waterways and lake shores, or in cultivated fields with short stems. In the breeding season, molting transforms it into a beauty—with gray upperparts and reddish underparts. American Pipits are known for pumping their tails up and down. When breeding, males display by rising into the air, then flying down with wings open and singing. Its migration takes the American Pipit as far south as Guatemala.
VOICE Alarm call a *tzeeep*; song repeated *tzwee-tzooo* from the air.
NESTING Cup in shallow depression on ground, outer frame of grass, lined with fine grass and hair; 4–6 eggs; 1 brood; June–July.
FEEDING Picks insects; also eats seeds during migration.

WINTER DRAB
Foraging in short vegetation, this bird is almost the same color as its surroundings.

SIMILAR SPECIES

HORNED LARK ♂
see p.297

less white on tail edge

SPRAGUE'S PIPIT
see p.342

heavy streaking on back

less streaking on throat and chest

pale cheeks and throat

pale legs

OCCURRENCE
Breeds in Arctic tundra in the North, and alpine tundra in the Rockies; also breeds on treeless mountaintops in Maine and New Hampshire. Winters in open coastal areas and harvested agricultural fields across the US. Some North American migrants fly to Asia for the winter.

| Length **6–8in (15–20cm)** | Wingspan **10–11in (25–28cm)** | Weight **¹¹/₁₆oz (20g)** |
| Social **Flocks** | Lifespan **Up to 6 years** | Status **Secure** |

DATE SEEN	WHERE	NOTES

Order **Passeriformes**	Family **Motacillidae**	Species **Anthus spragueii**

Sprague's Pipit

ADULT

broken "collar"

white outer tail feathers

IN FLIGHT

FLIGHT: strong with distinct up and down bobbing; prefers running to escape predators.

eyes appear large

pale cheeks

thin "mustache"

thick, two-tone bill

heavily streaked back

two pale wing bars

buffy wash on flanks

pale whitish belly, unstreaked

ADULT

long, pale pink legs and toes

white outer tail feathers

long, dark hind claw

Sprague's is the only wholly North American pipit. Males perform a very extraordinary fluttering display flight, circling high above the ground while singing an unending series of high-pitched calls, for periods of up to an hour. The current decline in the population of the Sprague's Pipit is quite likely the result of the conversion of tall-grass native prairie to extensive farmland. Interestingly, the Pampas Pipit of Argentina now breeds almost exclusively in wheat fields, offering some hope for this species.
VOICE Call a high *squeeek*; song a high, repetitive series of *szee- szee-szee*, usually given during lengthy aerial displays.
NESTING Small cup of loose woven grass on the ground and level with it, often attached to standing vegetation to form a sort of dome; 4–5 eggs; 1–2 broods; May–August.
FEEDING Feeds almost exclusively on insects when breeding, especially crickets and grasshoppers; eats seeds occasionally.

SONG PERCH
This Sprague's Pipit sings from a perch in its vanishing tall-grass prairie habitat.

SIMILAR SPECIES

HORNED LARK ♂
see p.297
shorter tail, less white

less-streaked on throat and chest

AMERICAN PIPIT
see p.341
unstreaked gray back
thin, dark bill
streaked chest, belly and flanks
dark legs

OCCURRENCE
Sprague's Pipit is truly North American; it breeds along the border of Canada with the US, in dry, open, grassland habitats, especially native prairie systems in the northern part of the Great Plains; most birds migrate to Mexico in winter, where habitat is similar to breeding grounds.

Length **4–6in (10–15cm)**	Wingspan **6–8in (15–20cm)**	Weight **¹¹⁄₁₆–⅞oz (20–25g)**
Social **Solitary**	Lifespan **Unknown**	Status **Vulnerable**

DATE SEEN	WHERE	NOTES

FINCHES

FINCHES IN THE FAMILY Fringillidae comprise a family of seed-eating birds, of which 16 species can be found in North America. They vary in size and shape from the small and fragile-looking redpolls to the robust and chunky Evening Grosbeak. Finch colors range from whitish with some pink (redpolls) to gold (American Goldfinch), bright red (crossbills), and yellow, white, and black (Evening Grosbeak). However, irrespective of body shape, size, and color, all have conical bills with razor-sharp edges. Finches do not crush seeds. Instead, they cut open the hard hull, then seize the seed inside with their tongue and swallow it. The bills of conifer-loving crossbills are crossed at the tip, a unique arrangement that permits them to open tough-hulled pine cones. Roughly 50 percent of crossbills are "left-billed" and 50 percent "right-billed"—lefties are right-footed, and vice versa. Most finches are social. Although they breed in pairs, after nesting finches form flocks, some of which are huge. Most finch populations fluctuate in size, synchronized with seed production and abundance. All finches are vocal, calling constantly while flying, and singing in the spring. Calls are usually sharp, somewhat metallic sounds, although the American Goldfinch's tinkling calls are sweeter. Songs can be quite musical, clear-sounding melodies, like that of the Cassin's Finch. Finches make open cup-shaped nests of grasses and lichens, in trees or shrubs, and are remarkably adept at hiding them.

CROSSBILL
Perched on a pine tree branch, a female Red Crossbill grinds a seed in her bill to break open the hull and reach the fat-rich kernel inside.

NOT REALLY PURPLE
The inaccurately named Purple Finch actually has a lovely wine-red color.

GARDEN GLOW
Even pink flower buds cannot compete with the yellow of a male American Goldfinch.

| Order **Passeriformes** | Family **Fringillidae** | Species ***Coccothraustes vespertinus*** |

Evening Grosbeak

conspicuous yellow eyebrow

black wing tips

very dark gray head and shoulders

yellow rump

MALE

large white wing patches

large white wing patch

IN FLIGHT

black outer wing feathers

short, square tail

huge, yellowish bill

MALE

large grayish bill

mustard yellow underparts

grayish wing patch

FEMALE

There is no mistaking a noisy, boisterous winter flock of husky gold-and-black Evening Grosbeaks when they descend on a birdfeeder. The bird's outsize yellow bill seems to be made as much for threatening would-be rivals as it is designed for efficiently cracking sunflower seeds. In the breeding season, by contrast, the Evening Grosbeak is secretive and seldom detected, neither singing loudly nor displaying ostentatiously and nesting high in a tree. Once a bird of western North America, it has extended its range eastward in the past 200 years, and now breeds as far as Newfoundland. This may be a result of the planting of ornamental box elder, which carries its abundant seeds winter-long, ensuring a ready food supply for the bird.

FLIGHT: undulating, with dips between bouts of wingbeats, may hover briefly.

VOICE Call descending *feeew*; also buzzy notes and beeping chatter.
NESTING Loose, grass-lined twig cup, usually on conifer branch; 3–4 eggs; 1–2 broods; May–July.
FEEDING Eats seeds of pines and other conifers; also maple and box elder seeds; also insects and their larvae, particularly spruce budworms, which are actually tortricid moths.

SIMILAR SPECIES

PINE GROSBEAK ♀
see p.345

stubby bill

wing bars

gray underparts

BALTIMORE ORIOLE ♀
see p.389

slender aspect

pale orange underparts

mottled head

CAPABLE BILL
This bird's extremely robust bill can deal with all kinds of winter fruit and seeds.

OCCURRENCE
Breeds in mixed conifer and spruce forests from the Rocky Mountain region to eastern Canada, and in western mountain ranges south to Mexico. Winters in coniferous or deciduous woodlands, often in suburban locations; may move south from northern range, depending on food supply.

| Length **6½–7in (16–18cm)** | Wingspan **12–14in (30–36cm)** | Weight **2–2½oz (55–70g)** |
| Social **Flocks** | Lifespan **Up to 15 years** | Status **Secure** |

DATE SEEN	WHERE	NOTES

Order **Passeriformes**	Family **Fringillidae**	Species *Pinicola enucleator*

Pine Grosbeak

greenish head

pale patch under eye

two white wing bars

greenish rump

gray belly

MALE

FEMALE

IN FLIGHT

pinkish rump

stubby, curved, blackish bill

pinkish red head

short neck

long, blackish tail

IMMATURE MALE

pinkish red underparts (but regionally variable)

MALE

FLIGHT: undulating, buoyant, calm wingbeats interrupted by glides.

The largest member of the Fringillidae family in North America, and easily distinguished by the male's unmistakable thick, stubby bill, the Pine Grosbeak is a resident of boreal forests across Canada and Alaska and some mountain ranges in the western US. In winter, northern birds occasionally move south into the northern US. Because of extensive color variation of individual plumages, the age and sex of given individuals are not always easily determined.

VOICE Contact calls of eastern birds *tee-tew*, or *tee-tee-tew*, western forms give more complex *tweedle*; warbling song.
NESTING Well-hidden, open cup nest usually in spruce or larch trees; 2–5 eggs, 1 brood; June–July.
FEEDING Eats spruce buds, maple seeds, and mountain ash berries throughout the year; consumes insects in summer.

FRUIT LOVER
This species can often be seen hanging from branches, gorging on ripe fruit.

SIMILAR SPECIES

RED CROSSBILL
see p.349

brownish back

mandibles crossed

WHITE-WINGED CROSSBILL
see p.350

mandibles crossed

white bars on wing

OCCURRENCE
Found in the boreal zone from Alaska to Newfoundland in Canada, and the Rockies in the US. Occurs in open, northerly coniferous forests in summer, usually near freshwater. Winters throughout its breeding range, but may move southward to southern Canada and the northeastern US.

Length **8–10in (20–25cm)**	Wingspan **13in (33cm)**	Weight **2–2½oz (55–70g)**
Social **Flocks**	Lifespan **Up to 10 years**	Status **Secure**

DATE SEEN	WHERE	NOTES

| Order **Passeriformes** | Family **Fringillidae** | Species *Haemorhous mexicanus* |

House Finch 🔊

- red face
- **MALE (BREEDING)**
- **IN FLIGHT**
- brown upperparts
- brown cap
- usually brick-red bib and head
- grayish streaks all over
- **FEMALE**
- pinkish head
- pale brown streaking
- streaked belly
- **MALE (NON-BREEDING)**
- brown streaked undertail feathers
- long tail feathers
- **MALE (BREEDING)**

FLIGHT: bouncy, undulating flight typical of finches; usually flies above treetop level.

Historically, the House Finch was a western bird, and was first reported in the eastern side of the US on Long Island, New York, in 1941. These birds are said to have originated from the illegal bird trade. The population of the eastern birds started expanding in the 1960s, by the late 1990s, their population had expanded westward to link up with the original western population. The male House Finch is distinguished from the Purple and Cassin's Finches by its brown streaked underparts, while the females have plainer faces and generally blurrier streaking.

VOICE Call note *queet*; varied jumble of notes, often starting with husky notes to whistled and burry notes, and ending with a long *wheeerr*.

NESTING Females build nests from grass stems, thin twigs, and thin weeds in trees and on manmade structures; 1–6 eggs; 2–3 broods; March–August.

FEEDING Eats, almost exclusively, vegetable matter, such as buds, fruit, and seeds; readily comes to feeders.

RED IN THE FACE
The breeding male House Finch can be identified by its stunning brick-red plumage.

OCCURRENCE
Found in urban, suburban, and settled areas; in the East almost exclusively in settled areas, including the centers of large cities; in the West also in wilder areas such as savannas, desert grasslands, and chaparral, particularly near people. Resident, some birds move after breeding.

SIMILAR SPECIES

PURPLE FINCH
see p.347
- pinkish neck
- whitish underparts

CASSIN'S FINCH
- reddish head
- white underparts

| Length **5–6in (12.5–15cm)** | Wingspan **8–10in (20–25cm)** | Weight **⁹⁄₁₆–1oz (16–27g)** |
| Social **Flocks** | Lifespan **Up to 12 years** | Status **Secure** |

DATE SEEN	WHERE	NOTES

| Order **Passeriformes** | Family **Fringillidae** | Species *Haemorhous purpureus* |

Purple Finch 🔊

pinkish red body

pale brown overall

lightly streaked overall

MALE

darker, streaked wings

round, brownish wings

IN FLIGHT

brownish, conical bill

FEMALE

brown stripe between eye and bill

raspberry-red crown

pink-and-brown streaked upperparts

pink rump and upper tail

MALE

whitish belly with rosy patches

One of three difficult-to-distinguish members of the genus *Haemorhous* in North America, the Purple Finch is best known as a visitor to winter feeding stations. The western subspecies (*californicus*) is slightly darker and duller than the eastern form (*purpureus*). Only moderately common, the raspberry-red males pose less of an identification challenge than the brown-streaked females. Even on their breeding grounds in open and mixed coniferous forest, Purple Finches are more often heard than seen.

VOICE Flight call single, rough *pikh*; songs rich series of notes, up and down in pitch.
NESTING Cup of sticks and grasses on a conifer branch; 4 eggs; 2 broods; May–July.
FEEDING Eats buds, seeds, flowers of deciduous trees; insects and caterpillars in summer; also seeds and berries.

FLIGHT: rapid wingbeats, alternating with downward glides.

RASPBERRY TINTED
On a lichen-covered branch this male's delicate coloring is quite striking.

SIMILAR SPECIES

HOUSE FINCH ♀
western;
see p.346

thinner streaks

CASSIN'S FINCH ♀

more marked facial patterning

RED-WINGED BLACKBIRD ♀
see p.390

larger overall

heavily streaked

darker overall

OCCURRENCE
Breeds in northern mixed conifer and hardwood forests in the East, where it is partially migratory, moves as far south as the Gulf Coast. Resident from Baja California north along the Pacific Coast and the Cascade Mountains to Washington and a small part of southern British Columbia.

| Length **4¾–6in (12–15cm)** | Wingspan **8½–10in (22–26cm)** | Weight **¹¹⁄₁₆–1¹⁄₁₆oz (20–30g)** |
| Social **Flocks** | Lifespan **Unknown** | Status **Declining** |

DATE SEEN	WHERE	NOTES

| Order **Passeriformes** | Family **Fringillidae** | Species *Acanthis flammea* |

Common Redpoll

ruby-red cap

small, pointed yellow bill

red cap

MALE

wing bars

IN FLIGHT

reddish cap

MALE (BREEDING)

rosy-red breast

streaked underparts

FEMALE

black streaks on rosy-red breast

MALE (NONBREEDING)

notched tail

pale wing bar

pale wing bars

JUVENILE

Every other year, spruce, birch, and other trees in the northern forest zone fail to produce a good crop of seeds, forcing the Common Redpoll to look for food farther south than usual—as far south as the northern US states. The Common Redpoll is oddly tame around people and is easily attracted to winter feeders. The degree of whiteness in its plumage varies greatly among individuals, related to sex and age. The taxonomy of the Common Redpoll includes three subspecies around the world, and there are suggestions that some may be distinct species.

VOICE Flight call dry *zit-zit-zit-zit* and rattling *chirr*; also high *too-ee* call while perched; song series of rapid trills.

NESTING Cup of small twigs in spruces, larches, willows, alders; 4–6 eggs; 1–2 broods; May–June.

FEEDING Feeds on small seeds from conifers, sedge, birch, willow, alder; also insects and spiders.

FLIGHT: deeply undulating, with dips between bouts of wingbeats.

SIMILAR SPECIES

PINE SISKIN see p.351

yellow on tail

two wing bars

HOARY REDPOLL see p.465

brownish upperparts

red cap

pale overall

whitish underparts

FRIENDLY FLOCK
Common Redpolls are only weakly territorial, sometimes even nesting close together.

OCCURRENCE
Mainly in extreme northern North America from Alaska to Québec and Labrador, in low forest, subarctic, and shrubby tundra habitats. More southern winter appearances typically occur every other year, rarely south of northern US, from Dakota east to New York and New England.

Length **4¾–5½in (12–14cm)**	Wingspan **6½–6¾in (16–17cm)**	Weight **⅜–¹¹⁄₁₆oz (11–19g)**
Social **Flocks**	Lifespan **Up to 10 years**	Status **Secure**

DATE SEEN	WHERE		NOTES

| Order **Passeriformes** | Family **Fringillidae** | Species *Loxia curvirostra* |

Red Crossbill

black wings

MALE

red body

IN FLIGHT

black stripe over eye

streaked belly

JUVENILE

dark brown wings

red rump

crown usually brick-red

crossed mandibles

some males greenish red overall

MALE

MALE

greenish breast

dark wings

FEMALE

Crossbills have evolved an efficient mechanism to unlock the seeds of conifers. They push the tips of their slightly open, cross-tipped bills between the scales of a conifer cone to pry it apart and lift out the seeds with their tongues. Red Crossbills occur in many forms, varying in size and bill shape. They have slightly different flight calls and rarely interbreed. One, the Cassia Crossbill, is treated as a separate species, *Loxia sinesciuris*. Other forms are nomadic, but this species remains in a tiny part of Idaho all year, feeding on lodgepole pine. It is nearly impossible to identify the different forms of the Red Crossbill other than by voice or DNA.

VOICE Common call *jit* repeated 2–5 times; song complex, continuous warbling of notes, whistles, and buzzes.

NESTING Cup nest on lateral conifer branch; 3–5 eggs; 2 broods; can breed year-round.

FEEDING Feeds on pine seeds; also insects and larvae, particularly aphids; also other seeds.

FLIGHT: strong and deeply undulating.

PROCESSING SEEDS
The Red Crossbill manipulates seeds with its tongue before swallowing them.

SIMILAR SPECIES		
WHITE-WINGED CROSSBILL see p.350	**SCARLET TANAGER** see p.436	
conspicuous wing bars	vivid red plumage	no black stripe
pinker plumage		

OCCURRENCE
Range covers coniferous or mixed-coniferous and deciduous forests from Newfoundland to British Columbia and southern Alaska; also mountain forests in the Rockies, south to Mexico; irregular movements, depending on the availability of pine cones.

| Length **5–6¾in (13–17cm)** | Wingspan **10–10½in (25–27cm)** | Weight **⅞–1¼oz (25–35g)** |
| Social **Flocks** | Lifespan **Up to 10 years** | Status **Secure** |

DATE SEEN	WHERE	NOTES

| Order **Passeriformes** | Family **Fringillidae** | Species *Loxia leucoptera* |

White-winged Crossbill

two conspicuous white wing bars

brownish green head

variable dark patch on cheek

dark brown wings

red body

MALE

greenish streaked underparts

FEMALE

crossed mandibles

MALE

IN FLIGHT

blackish wings

pinkish red underparts

notched tail

FLIGHT: strong and undulating with quick wingbeats alternating with glides.

Cone debris, needles, and whole cones clatter down from a spruce in the otherwise silent winter forest. Some twittering is heard, and then a chorus of metallic, yanking notes reveals that a flock of a dozen White-winged Crossbills has been causing all the commotion. In an instant, the entire flock erupts into the air, calling loudly in flight, only to disappear completely in the distance. Few other creatures of the northern forests go about their business with such determined energy, and no others accent a winter woodland with hot pink and magenta—the colors of the White-winged Crossbill's head and breast.

VOICE Calls are sharp, chattering *plik*, or deeper *tyoop*, repeated in series of 3–7 notes; song melodious trilling.

NESTING Open cup nest, usually high on end of a spruce branch; eggs 3–5; 2 broods; July, January–February.

FEEDING Eats seeds from small-coned conifers; spruces, firs, larches; feeds on insects when available.

EATING SNOW
The White-winged Crossbill frequently eats snow to provide essential moisture.

SIMILAR SPECIES

PINE GROSBEAK
see p.345

blunt bill

longer tail

RED CROSSBILL
see p.349

no wing bars

redder plumage

OCCURRENCE
Nomadic; most common in the spruce zone of Alaska and Canada but has bred as far south as Colorado in the West; in the East, from Québec and Newfoundland southward to New York and New England.

| Length **5½–6in (14–15cm)** | Wingspan **10–10½in (26–27cm)** | Weight **¹¹⁄₁₆–1¹⁄₁₆oz (20–30g)** |
| Social **Flocks** | Lifespan **Up to 10 years** | Status **Secure** |

DATE SEEN	WHERE	NOTES

| Order **Passeriformes** | Family **Fringillidae** | Species *Spinus pinus* |

Pine Siskin 🔊

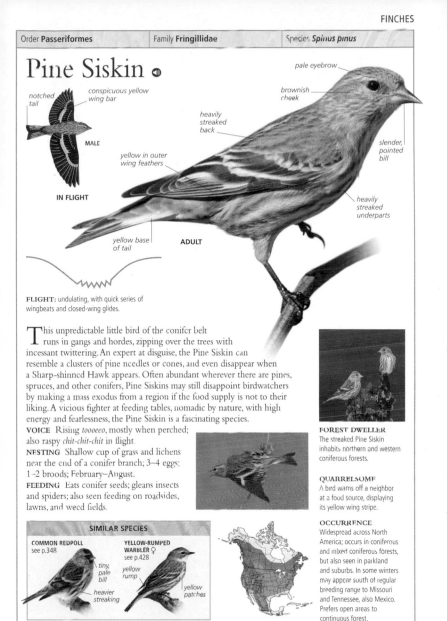

notched tail

conspicuous yellow wing bar

MALE

yellow in outer wing feathers

IN FLIGHT

yellow base of tail

ADULT

heavily streaked back

pale eyebrow

brownish cheek

slender, pointed bill

heavily streaked underparts

FLIGHT: undulating, with quick series of wingbeats and closed-wing glides.

This unpredictable little bird of the conifer belt runs in gangs and hordes, zipping over the trees with incessant twittering. An expert at disguise, the Pine Siskin can resemble a clusters of pine needles or cones, and even disappear when a Sharp-shinned Hawk appears. Often abundant wherever there are pines, spruces, and other conifers, Pine Siskins may still disappoint birdwatchers by making a mass exodus from a region if the food supply is not to their liking. A vicious fighter at feeding tables, nomadic by nature, with high energy and fearlessness, the Pine Siskin is a fascinating species.

VOICE Rising *toooeeo*, mostly when perched; also raspy *chit-chit-chit* in flight.

NESTING Shallow cup of grass and lichens near the end of a conifer branch; 3–4 eggs; 1–2 broods; February–August.

FEEDING Eats conifer seeds; gleans insects and spiders; also seen feeding on roadsides, lawns, and weed fields.

FOREST DWELLER
The streaked Pine Siskin inhabits northern and western coniferous forests.

QUARRELSOME
A bird warns off a neighbor at a food source, displaying its yellow wing stripe.

OCCURRENCE
Widespread across North America; occurs in coniferous and mixed coniferous forests, but also seen in parkland and suburbs. In some winters may appear south of regular breeding range to Missouri and Tennessee, also Mexico. Prefers open areas to continuous forest.

SIMILAR SPECIES

COMMON REDPOLL
see p.348

tiny, pale bill

heavier streaking

YELLOW-RUMPED WARBLER ♀
see p.428

yellow rump

yellow patches

| Length **4¼–5½in (11–14cm)** | Wingspan **7–9in (18–23cm)** | Weight **⁷⁄₁₆–⅝oz (12–18g)** |
| Social **Flocks** | Lifespan **Up to 10 years** | Status **Secure** |

DATE SEEN	WHERE	NOTES

| Order **Passeriformes** | Family **Fringillidae** | Species *Spinus tristis* |

American Goldfinch 🔊

MALE (BREEDING)
bright yellow back

IN FLIGHT

tan back
brownish bill
yellow throat and collar
pale tan underparts
MALE (NONBREEDING)

brownish olive back
pinkish bill
FEMALE (BREEDING)

black forehead and crown
short, conical pinkish bill
bright yellow underparts
pinkish legs and toes
MALE (BREEDING)

black tail
white rump
white wing bar
brownish overall
dull yellow throat
FEMALE (NONBREEDING)

FLIGHT: deeply undulating; wingbeats alternating with closed-wing dips.

The male American Goldfinch is a spectacular summer sight. Goldfinches reveal their presence before they are seen by their tinkling, bell-like calls. If there are weeds in seed around, goldfinches will find them and feed energetically on the manna. This all-American species is the State Bird of Washington State.

VOICE Loud, rising, quizzical pter-yee? by males; 3–5-note tit-tse-tew-tew by both sexes, usually in flight; song complex, warbling, tinkling, and melodious.

NESTING Neat open cup of grass, shaded by leaves, in a tree or tall shrub; 4–5 eggs; 1–2 broods; July–September.

FEEDING Feed mainly on seeds from annuals; also birch and alder; some insects; love sunflower and thistle seed, whether on flower heads or at feeders.

SIMILAR SPECIES

LESSER GOLDFINCH see p.465
greenish back
conspicuous wing bars

LAWRENCE'S GOLDFINCH
yellow wing bars
black face
yellow breast

WILSON'S WARBLER see p.433
black cap
black face
yellow face

OCCURRENCE
In low shrubs, deciduous woodlands, farmlands, orchards, suburbs, and gardens across much of North America, from southern Canada to California and Georgia; in winter south to northern Mexico and Florida; winter habitats similar to those used at other times.

| Length **4¼–5in (11–13cm)** | Wingspan **7–9in (18–23cm)** | Weight **⅜–¹¹/₁₆oz (11–20g)** |
| Social **Small flocks** | Lifespan **Up to 11 years** | Status **Secure** |

DATE SEEN	WHERE	NOTES

LONGSPURS AND SNOW BUNTING

FOUR SPECIES OF longspurs, the Snow Bunting, and McKay's Bunting all generally forage on bare or open ground, from tundra and mountain tops to open prairies, often in flocks. Their short, blackish legs help give longspurs a long, low shape on the ground. Their calls provide useful clues for identification as they fly. Snow Buntings have distinctive white bands on their wings.

CHANGING COLORS
Snow Buntings are well camouflaged against exposed rocks and snow throughout the year. Brown edges on the feathers in winter wear off, so they become pristine black and white in spring.

NEW WORLD SPARROWS

NEW WORLD SPARROWS are more akin to Old World buntings than other sparrows, but, as with robins, familiar names were given to quite different birds by early European settlers and have stayed with us. New World sparrows are rounded but long-tailed, and have small, conical or triangular bills that are adapted to feed on grass seeds. While some birds are distinctive, especially the more brightly patterned males, many are small, "streaky-brown" species that present considerable identification difficulties. Range, habitat, behavior, and voice are all often used together as a suite of characteristics for identification. Not only are the species much alike, but studies conducted in recent years have revealed different relationships between them, with some subspecies being split as separate species and others being grouped together. Nevertheless, their neat, subtle patterns make even the duller species worth studying: the delicateness of a Sagebrush Sparrow or the exquisite streaking of Lincoln's Sparrow, for example, repay close observation.

TYPICAL SPECIES
A White-crowned Sparrow shows the typical stout beak of New World sparrows.

Order **Passeriformes**	Family **Calcariidae**	Species *Calcarius lapponicus*

Lapland Longspur

thin white edge to tail

MALE (BREEDING)

black face

IN FLIGHT

streaked crown

white eye-line

black streak on throat

thick yellowish bill

bright rufous nape

FEMALE (BREEDING)

rich buffy hood

rusty wing panel

ADULT (NONBREEDING)

thick streaking on flanks

white underparts

black flanks

MALE (BREEDING)

FLIGHT: deeply undulating, with birds often calling in troughs as they flap.

The genus name, *Calcarius*, refers to the long hind claw of this bird, hence "longspur" in American usage. The Lapland Longspur is one of the most numerous breeding birds in the Arctic tundra, from Labrador west to Alaska, and across northern Eurasia. In winter, they form huge flocks in open habitats of southern Canada and the US. They are found on gravel roads and barren countryside immediately after heavy snowfalls. The longspurs and the snow bunting were formerly part of the Emberizidae family but are now placed in a distinct family of their own.
VOICE Flight call a dry rattle, *tyew*, unlike other longspurs; song a series of thin tinklings and whistles, melodious often in flight.
NESTING Cup of grass and sedges placed in depression on ground next to a clump of vegetation; 4–6 eggs; 1 brood; May–July.
FEEDING Eats insects during breeding season; seeds in winter.

CONSPICUOUS SPECIES
This longspur is one of the most conspicuous breeding birds of the Arctic tundra.

OCCURRENCE
Breeds in tundra right across the High Arctic of North America and Eurasia. Winters in open grasslands and barren fields, and on beaches across the northern and central US and south-central and northeastern Canada.

SIMILAR SPECIES

SMITH'S LONGSPUR ♀
see p.356
white bars on wing
thin bill

CHESTNUT-COLLARED LONGSPUR ♀ ❊
see p.355
more white in tail
dark cheek patch

Length **6½in (16cm)**	Wingspan **10½–11½in (27–29cm)**	Weight **⅞–1¹⁄₁₆oz (25–30g)**
Social **Large flocks**	Lifespan **Up to 5 years**	Status **Secure**

DATE SEEN	WHERE	NOTES

| Order **Passeriformes** | Family **Calcariidae** | Species *Calcarius ornatus* |

Chestnut-collared Longspur

white patch on wing

MALE (BREEDING)

IN FLIGHT

pale rufous on nape

buff-white underparts

MALE (NONBREEDING)

gray-brown overall

buff eyebrow

FEMALE (NONBREEDING)

streaked upperparts

white eyebrow

chestnut neck

tan cheeks

black underparts

MALE (BREEDING)

white outer tail feathers

The Chestnut-collared Longspur was once much more widespread and numerous than today. This is because it traditionally bred in areas of the western prairies that had been recently disturbed by huge, roaming herds of bison, or by wild fires. After the elimination of the bison, however, and the "taming" of the plains, such areas were hard to find, and so the bird declined. One of the Chestnut-collared Longspur's distinguishing features is the triangular black patch on its tail. The breeding male's black belly is also unique among the North American longspurs.
VOICE Flight call a chortling *KTI-uhl-uh*, often in series; also a soft rattle and short buzz; song a sweet, rich, whistled series, in fluttering, circular flights over the prairies.
NESTING Grassy cup on ground, in grass clump or next to rock; 3–5 eggs, 1–2 broods; May–August.
FEEDING Eats seeds year-round; also feeds on insects when breeding.

FLIGHT: deeply undulating, with birds often calling in troughs as they flap.

OCCURRENCE
Breeds in shortgrass prairie from Alberta east to Minnesota, south to northeastern Colorado and northwestern Nebraska; on migration, grasslands and cultivated fields. Winters in grasslands and other barren areas in the southern Great Plains west to southeastern Arizona and south to Mexico.

NOW AND THEN
The male bird usually sings from the air, but occasionally from a prominent perch.

SIMILAR SPECIES
MCCOWN'S LONGSPUR ♀ see p.472 — shorter, mostly white tail
SMITH'S LONGSPUR ♀♂ see p.356 — larger, thicker bill, less white in tail, rich, buff coloration

| Length 5½–6in (14–15cm) | Wingspan 10–10½in (25–27cm) | Weight ⅜–¹¹⁄₁₆oz (11–20g) |
| Social **Large flocks** | Lifespan **Up to 4 years** | Status **Declining** |

DATE SEEN	WHERE	NOTES

| Order **Passeriformes** | Family **Calcariidae** | Species *Calcarius pictus* |

Smith's Longspur

MALE (BREEDING)

rich, buffy overall

black-and-white "helmet"

fine breast streaks

white cheek patch

white outer tail feathers

wings extend past tail

relatively long wings

FEMALE

small bill

orange collar

IN FLIGHT

white shoulder

rich pumpkin-colored underparts

MALE (BREEDING)

white undertail feathers

With their pumpkin colored breast and black-and-white "helmet," breeding males Smith's Longspurs contrast strongly with their drab winter plumage. Females are pale versions of the males. On both its remote breeding grounds in the Arctic, and its restricted range of shortgrass prairie in winter, this bird hides on the ground at all times, making it hard to spot. Smith's Longspurs migrate through the Great Plains to reach their wintering grounds, but on the return journey they swing east, making their migration path elliptical. This species breeds communally and does not hold territories: males mate with several females who, in turn, mate with other males.

VOICE Flight call a mechanical, dry, sharp rattle; also a nasal *nief* when squabbling; song a series of thin, sweet whistles.

NESTING Concealed cup of sedges, lined with feathers, placed in hummock on ground; 3–5 eggs; 1 brood; June–July.

FEEDING Eats mainly seeds and insects; migrants may rely heavily upon introduced foxtail grass.

FLIGHT: deeply undulating, with birds often calling in troughs as they flap.

LINEBACK LONGSPUR
On his breeding or spring staging grounds, the male sports a striking black-and-white "helmet."

SIMILAR SPECIES

LAPLAND LONGSPUR ♀✳
see p.354
thicker bill
broad, reddish edges to wings

CHESTNUT-COLLARED LONGSPUR ♀✳
see p.355
lacks rich buff color and streaks
more white in tail

OCCURRENCE
Breeds along the tundra-taiga timberline from northern Alaska southeastwards to northern Ontario; also mountainous southeastern Alaska and southwestern Yukon. Migrants are found in shortgrass prairies. Winters in open areas with shortgrass in Kansas, Oklahoma, Texas, and Arkansas.

| Length **6–6½in (15–16cm)** | Wingspan **10–11½in (25–29cm)** | Weight **⅞–1¹⁄₁₆oz (25–30g)** |
| Social **Large flocks** | Lifespan **Up to 5 years** | Status **Secure** |

DATE SEEN	WHERE	NOTES

| Order **Passeriformes** | Family **Calcariidae** | Species *Plectrophenax nivalis* |

Snow Bunting

less white in wings

white outer tail feathers

MALE (NONBREEDING)

white head and underparts

black back

yellow bill

black bill

pale rufous crown

white underparts

dark brown eyes

FEMALE (BREEDING)

rusty-orange cheek patch

black peeks through buffy feather edgings

IN FLIGHT

large white patches on black wings

MALE (BREEDING)

FEMALE (NONBREEDING)

gray body

white eye-ring

MALE (NONBREEDING)

white underparts

rusty-orange breast patch

JUVENILE

The bold white wing patches of the Snow Bunting make it immediately recognizable in a whirling winter flock of dark-winged longspurs and larks. In winter, heavy snowfall forces flocks onto roadsides, where they can be seen more easily. To secure and defend the best territories, some males arrive as early as April in their barren High Arctic breeding grounds; these buntings breed farther north than any other songbirds. The Snow Bunting is very similar in appearance to the rare McKay's Bunting, localized to western Alaska. Although McKay's Bunting generally has less black on the back, in the wings, and on the tail, the two species cannot always be conclusively identified. This is especially true as they sometimes interbreed, producing hybrids.
VOICE Flight call a musical, liquid rattle, also *tyew* notes and short buzz; song a pleasant series of squeaky and whistled notes.
NESTING Bulky cup of grass and moss, lined with feathers, and placed in sheltered rock crevice; 3–6 eggs; 1 brood; June–August.
FEEDING Eats seeds (sedge in Arctic), flies and other insects, and buds on migration.

FLIGHT: deeply undulating; flocks "roll" along as birds at back overtake those in front.

ROCKY GROUND
About the only perches in the Snow Bunting's barren breeding grounds are large boulders.

SIMILAR SPECIES

McKAY'S BUNTING

mostly white tail, back, and wings

OCCURRENCE
Breeds in rocky areas, usually near sparsely vegetated tundra, right across the Arctic in both North America and Eurasia. North American birds winter in open country and along shores across the southern Canada and the northern US, and in southern and western coastal areas of Alaska.

| Length 6½–7in (16–18cm) | Wingspan 12½–14in (32–35cm) | Weight 1¼–2oz (35–55g) |
| Social **Large flocks** | Lifespan **Unknown** | Status **Declining** |

DATE SEEN	WHERE		NOTES

| Order **Passeriformes** | Family **Passerellidae** | Species *Peucaea aestivalis* |

Bachman's Sparrow

ADULT (EASTERN)

rufous eyestripe

brown, lightly streaked upperparts

long, dark, round tail

IN FLIGHT

**ADULT
P. a. illinoensis
(INDIANA, MISSOURI,
LOUISIANA, TEXAS)**

long tail

yellowish tan breast

**ADULT
P. a. aestivalis
(SOUTH CAROLINA,
GEORGIA, FLORIDA)**

gray eyebrow

grayish brown cheek

bold, rufous-and-black streaks on back

streaked crown

long grayish bill

tan-buffy breast

pale gray belly

This rather shy, skulking species is predominantly associated with pine woods in the South, and can be identified by its melodious song. It was first described in 1833 by John James Audubon in honor of his friend, John Bachman, a social reformer and naturalist. This sparrow invaded the open, shrubby habitats along the Ohio River Valley as far north as Chicago in the early 20th century, only to abandon the area by the 1970s. The reddish subspecies from the south-central US was even named *P. a. illinoensis,* which is now ironic, as it has been extirpated from Illinois. Bachman's Sparrow populations have been declining for some time, primarily as a result of habitat loss.
VOICE Call a thin *tseep*; song a melodious, high, thin whistle followed by a loose, musical trill.
NESTING Cup of grasses, sometimes domed, placed on ground, often in thicket; 2–5 eggs; 1–3 broods; May–September.
FEEDING Forages on the ground for insects, such as weevils and beetles; also eats various seeds.

FLIGHT: direct, low, and fairly weak; usually over short distances.

PINE SPARROW
This species was once known by this name, which refers to its preferred habitat.

SIMILAR SPECIES

SWAMP SPARROW
see p.380
gray nape

dark throat stripe

BOTTERI'S SPARROW
much grayer in Texas;
see p.466
long, dark tail

grayish underparts

OCCURRENCE
Found in open, grassy old-growth and pine woods with dense undergrowth of palmettos, and orchards from eastern Texas and southwestern Missouri to southeastern Kentucky, and south around the Appalachians to southeastern Virginia. Northernmost populations winter in the Southeast and Florida.

| Length **6in (15cm)** | Wingspan **7¼in (18.5cm)** | Weight ⅝–¹¹⁄₁₆oz (18–20g) |
| Social **Solitary** | Lifespan **Unknown** | Status **Vulnerable** |

DATE SEEN	WHERE	NOTES

| Order **Passeriformes** | Family **Passerellidae** | Species *Ammodramus savannarum* |

Grasshopper Sparrow

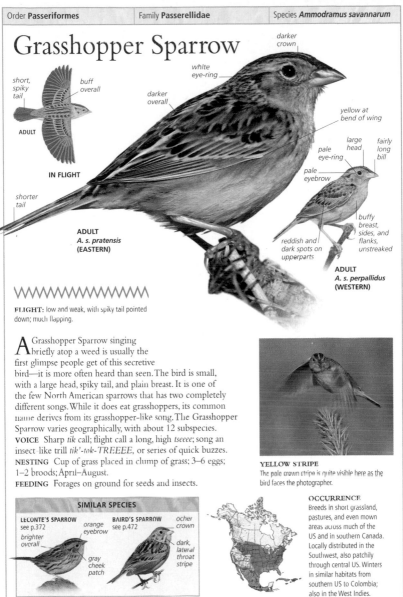

darker crown

white eye-ring

darker overall

short, spiky tail

buff overall

ADULT

IN FLIGHT

shorter tail

ADULT
A. s. pratensis
(EASTERN)

yellow at bend of wing

pale eye-ring

large head

fairly long bill

pale eyebrow

buffy breast, sides, and flanks, unstreaked

reddish and dark spots on upperparts

ADULT
A. s. perpallidus
(WESTERN)

FLIGHT: low and weak, with spiky tail pointed down; much flapping.

A Grasshopper Sparrow singing briefly atop a weed is usually the first glimpse people get of this secretive bird—it is more often heard than seen. The bird is small, with a large head, spiky tail, and plain breast. It is one of the few North American sparrows that has two completely different songs. While it does eat grasshoppers, its common name derives from its grasshopper-like song. The Grasshopper Sparrow varies geographically, with about 12 subspecies.

VOICE Sharp *tik* call; flight call a long, high *tseeee*; song an insect-like trill *tik'-tok-TREEEE*, or series of quick buzzes.

NESTING Cup of grass placed in clump of grass; 3–6 eggs; 1–2 broods; April–August.

FEEDING Forages on ground for seeds and insects.

YELLOW STRIPE
The pale crown stripe is quite visible here as the bird faces the photographer.

SIMILAR SPECIES

LECONTE'S SPARROW
see p.372
brighter overall
orange eyebrow
gray cheek patch

BAIRD'S SPARROW
see p.472
ocher crown
dark, lateral throat stripe

OCCURRENCE
Breeds in short grassland, pastures, and even mown areas across much of the US and in southern Canada. Locally distributed in the Southwest, also patchily through central US. Winters in similar habitats from southern US to Colombia; also in the West Indies.

| Length **5in (13cm)** | Wingspan **8in (20cm)** | Weight **½–¹¹⁄₁₆oz (15–20g)** |
| Social **Solitary/Flocks** | Lifespan **Up to 7 years** | Status **Declining** |

DATE SEEN	WHERE	NOTES

Order **Passeriformes**	Family **Passerellidae**	Species *Chondestes grammacus*

Lark Sparrow

rounded tail with white corners

ADULT

IN FLIGHT

thick gray bill

pale patch at base of outer wing feathers

central breast spot

JUVENILE

unique bold facial pattern

brown upperparts

central breast spot

long tail

ADULT

pale plain rump

FLIGHT: strong flight, in straight lines; often perches when flushed.

The bold harlequin facial pattern, single central breast spot, and long, rounded black tail with white outer corners make the Lark Sparrow one of the most easily identifiable of North American sparrows. Lark Sparrows have declined precipitously in the East, where they are mostly associated with western-like sandy soils. It is likely, that this species' presence in the East has been possible because of forest clearing. In the West, by contrast, Lark Sparrows are common, and often found singing from the top of a fencepost or small tree, and perched on barbed wire fences.

VOICE Thin, up-slurred *tseep* call, flight call sharp *tink*; song series of trills, whistles, and rattles on varying pitches.

NESTING Cup usually placed on ground at base of plant, or off-ground in tree or bush; 3–5 eggs; 1–2 broods; April–August.

FEEDING Eats seeds and insects.

ON THE FENCE
The Lark Sparrow is a common roadside bird, often found perching on barbed wire fences.

OCCURRENCE
Localized breeder in the East, associated with well-drained soils. Breeds east to Ohio. In the West, breeds in a variety of habitats such as sagebrush flats of the Great Basin, and grasslands from British Columbia and Saskatchewan to Baja California and central Mexico. Winters in southern US and Mexico.

Length **6–6¾in (15–17cm)**	Wingspan **11in (28cm)**	Weight **¹¹⁄₁₆–1¹⁄₁₆oz (20–30g)**
Social **Large flocks**	Lifespan **Up to 8 years**	Status **Secure**

DATE SEEN	WHERE	NOTES

| Order **Passeriformes** | Family **Passerellidae** | Species *Calamospiza melanocorys* |

Lark Bunting

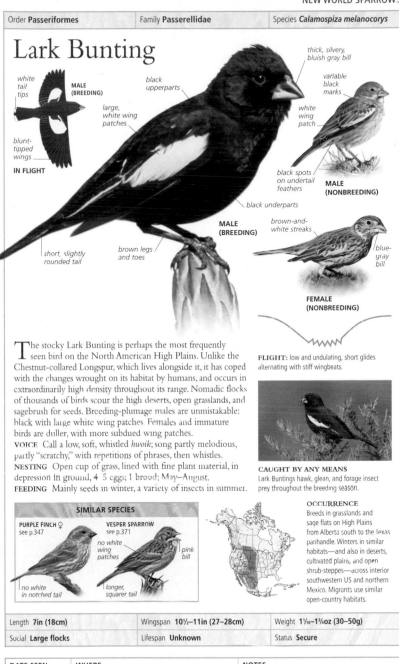

white tail tips

MALE (BREEDING)

black upperparts

thick, silvery, bluish gray bill

variable black marks

white wing patch

large, white wing patches

blunt-tipped wings

IN FLIGHT

black spots on undertail feathers

MALE (NONBREEDING)

black underparts

MALE (BREEDING)

brown-and-white streaks

blue-gray bill

short, slightly rounded tail

brown legs and toes

FEMALE (NONBREEDING)

FLIGHT: low and undulating, short glides alternating with stiff wingbeats.

The stocky Lark Bunting is perhaps the most frequently seen bird on the North American High Plains. Unlike the Chestnut-collared Longspur, which lives alongside it, it has coped with the changes wrought on its habitat by humans, and occurs in extraordinarily high density throughout its range. Nomadic flocks of thousands of birds scour the high deserts, open grasslands, and sagebrush for seeds. Breeding-plumage males are unmistakable: black with large white wing patches. Females and immature birds are duller, with more subdued wing patches.

VOICE Call a low, soft, whistled *hwoik*; song partly melodious, partly "scratchy," with repetitions of phrases, then whistles.

NESTING Open cup of grass, lined with fine plant material, in depression in ground, 4–5 eggs; 1 brood; May–August.

FEEDING Mainly seeds in winter, a variety of insects in summer.

CAUGHT BY ANY MEANS
Lark Buntings hawk, glean, and forage insect prey throughout the breeding season.

SIMILAR SPECIES

PURPLE FINCH ♀
see p.347

no white in notched tail

VESPER SPARROW
see p.371

no white wing patches

pink bill

longer, squarer tail

OCCURRENCE
Breeds in grasslands and sage flats on High Plains from Alberta south to the Texas panhandle. Winters in similar habitats—and also in deserts, cultivated plains, and open shrub-steppes—across interior southwestern US and northern Mexico. Migrants use similar open-country habitats.

| Length **7in (18cm)** | Wingspan **10½–11in (27–28cm)** | Weight **1¹⁄₁₆–1¾oz (30–50g)** |
| Social **Large flocks** | Lifespan **Unknown** | Status **Secure** |

DATE SEEN	WHERE	NOTES

Order **Passeriformes**	Family **Passerellidae**	Species *Spizella passerina*

Chipping Sparrow 🔊

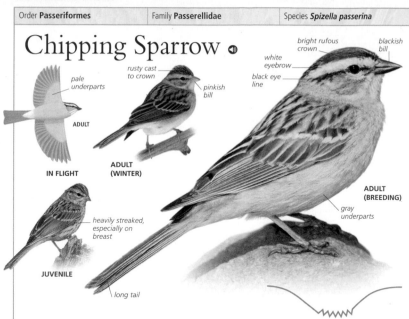

pale underparts

ADULT

IN FLIGHT

rusty cast to crown

pinkish bill

ADULT (WINTER)

bright rufous crown

blackish bill

white eyebrow

black eye line

ADULT (BREEDING)

gray underparts

heavily streaked, especially on breast

JUVENILE

long tail

The Chipping Sparrow is a common and trusting bird, which breeds in backyards across most of North America. While they are easily identifiable in the summer, "Chippers" molt into a drab, nonbreeding plumage during the fall, at which point they are easily confused with the Clay-colored and Brewer's Sparrows they flock with. Most winter reports of this species in the North are actually of the larger American Tree Sparrow. In winter, Chipping Sparrows lack their bright, rusty crown and are restricted to southern states.

VOICE Call a sharp *tsip*; flight call a sharp, thin *tsiiit*; song an insect-like trill of *chip* notes, variable in duration and intensity.

NESTING Neat cup usually placed well off the ground in tree or shrub; 3–5 eggs; 1–2 broods; April–August.

FEEDING Eat seeds of grasses and annuals, plus some fruit; when breeding, also eat insects and other invertebrates.

FLIGHT: lIghtly undulating, often to open perch when flushed.

BACKYARD BIRD
Chipping Sparrows are common in gardens and backyards all across the continent.

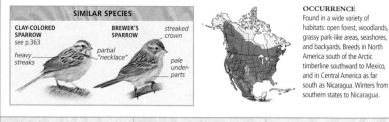

SIMILAR SPECIES

CLAY-COLORED SPARROW see p.363

heavy streaks

BREWER'S SPARROW

partial "necklace"

streaked crown

pale underparts

OCCURRENCE
Found in a wide variety of habitats: open forest, woodlands, grassy park-like areas, seashores, and backyards. Breeds in North America south of the Arctic timberline southward to Mexico, and in Central America as far south as Nicaragua. Winters from southern states to Nicaragua.

Length **5½in (14cm)**	Wingspan **8½in (21cm)**	Weight **⅜–½oz (10–15g)**
Social **Large flocks**	Lifespan **Up to 9 years**	Status **Secure**

DATE SEEN	WHERE	NOTES

| Order **Passeriformes** | Family **Passerellidae** | Species *Spizella pallida* |

Clay-colored Sparrow

IN FLIGHT

long tail

white wing bars

thick, white eyebrow

brown rump

ADULT

bold, dark cheek stripes

white crown stripe

unstreaked gray nape

bold dark brown streaks on upperparts

pale buffy wash across breast

whitish gray underparts

ADULT

long notched tail

FLIGHT: lightly undulating, often flies to open perch when flushed.

The small Clay-colored Sparrow is best known for its mechanical, buzzy song. This bird spends much of its foraging time away from its breeding habitat; consequently, males' territories are very small, allowing for dense breeding populations. Clay-colored Sparrows have shifted their breeding range eastward and northward over the last century, most likely because of changes in land practices. During the nonbreeding season, they form large flocks in open country, associating with other *Spizella* sparrows, especially Chipping and Brewer's.
VOICE Call a sharp *tsip*; flight a call short, rising *sip*; song a series of 2–7 mechanical buzzes on one pitch.
NESTING Cup of grass placed just off the ground in shrub or small tree; 3–5 eggs; 1–2 broods; May–August.
FEEDING Forages on or near the ground for seeds and insects.

CHRISTMAS PRESENT
The Clay-colored Sparrow is fond of low conifers for breeding, so Christmas tree farms form a perfect habitat.

SIMILAR SPECIES

CHIPPING SPARROW ❁
see p.362

grayish rump

dark stripe through eye

grayer breast

BREWER'S SPARROW

streaked nape

lacks bold, crown stripe

OCCURRENCE
Breeds in open habitats: prairies, shrubland, forest edges, and Christmas tree farms along the US/Canadian border and northward to the southern Northwest Territory. Winters in a large variety of brushy and weedy areas from south Texas to Mexico. Migration takes it to the Great Plains.

| Length **5½in (14cm)** | Wingspan **7½in (19cm)** | Weight **⅜–½oz (10–15g)** |
| Social **Large flocks** | Lifespan **Up to 5 years** | Status **Secure** |

DATE SEEN	WHERE	NOTES

| Order **Passeriformes** | Family **Passerellidae** | Species *Spizella pusilla* |

Field Sparrow 🔊

small pink bill

whitish eye-ring

streaking on back

ADULT (REDDISH FORM)

rusty markings on head

light rust cheek and crown

white wing bars

ADULT (GRAYISH FORM)

long, notched tail

IN FLIGHT

tan underparts

duller overall

dusky chest

JUVENILE

distinctive pink legs

long tail

ADULT (REDDISH FORM)

FLIGHT: lightly undulating; female may use moth-like flight to approach the nest.

The distinctive accelerating trill song of the Field Sparrow is a characteristic sound of shrubby fields and scrubby areas in the eastern US. The bird's bright-pink bill, plain "baby face," and whitish eye-ring make this sparrow one of the easiest to identify. The Field Sparrow has a brighter plumage in the eastern part of its range than farther west, a pattern also seen in other sparrows, like the Vesper Sparrow. Although quite dissimilar at first glance, the Black-chinned Sparrow may in fact be the Field Sparrow's closest relative, sharing its pink bill, relatively unpatterned plumage, and song.

VOICE Call a sharp *tsik*; flight call a strongly descending *tsiiiu*; song a series of sweet, down-slurred whistles accelerating to a rapid trill.

NESTING Grass cup placed on or just above ground in grass or bush; 3–5 eggs; 1–3 broods; March–August.

FEEDING Eats seeds; also insects, insect larvae, and spiders in the summer.

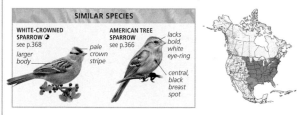

FAMILIAR SONG
Male Field Sparrows sing their familiar song, an accelerated trill, throughout the summer.

OCCURRENCE
Breeds in overgrown fields, woodland edges, roadsides, and other shrubby, overgrown areas; occasionally in orchards and parks in the eastern US, west to the Dakotas, east to New England. Winters in similar habitats in the southern US. Casual in Atlantic Canada and on the Pacific Coast.

SIMILAR SPECIES

WHITE-CROWNED SPARROW 🔊
see p.368

larger body

pale crown stripe

AMERICAN TREE SPARROW
see p.366

lacks bold, white eye-ring

central, black breast spot

| Length **5½in (14cm)** | Wingspan **8in (20cm)** | Weight **⅜–½oz (11–15g)** |
| Social **Solitary/Flocks** | Lifespan **Up to 6 years** | Status **Declining** |

DATE SEEN	WHERE	NOTES

| Order **Passeriformes** | Family **Passerellidae** | Species *Passerella iliaca* |

Fox Sparrow 🔊

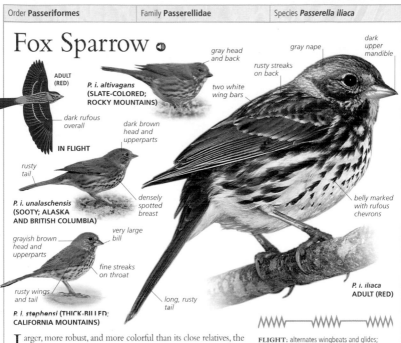

ADULT (RED)

P. i. altivagans
(SLATE-COLORED;
ROCKY MOUNTAINS)

gray head
and back

two white
wing bars

dark rufous
overall

IN FLIGHT

dark brown
head and
upperparts

rusty
tail

densely
spotted
breast

P. i. unalaschensis
(SOOTY; ALASKA
AND BRITISH COLUMBIA)

very large
bill

grayish brown
head and
upperparts

fine streaks
on throat

rusty wings
and tail

long, rusty
tail

P. i. stephensi (THICK-BILLED;
CALIFORNIA MOUNTAINS)

gray nape

rusty streaks
on back

dark
upper
mandible

belly marked
with rufous
chevrons

P. i. iliaca
ADULT (RED)

FLIGHT: alternates wingbeats and glides;
straight and fluttery, from cover to cover.

FOXY RED
The Fox Sparrow gets its name from the rusty
coloration of the eastern "Red" birds.

Larger, more robust, and more colorful than its close relatives, the Fox Sparrow is a beautiful species. When it appears in backyards, its presence can be detected by its foraging habits; it crouches low in leaf litter, and hops back and forth, noisily, to disturb leaves, under which it finds seeds or insects. It varies considerably over its huge range. Eastern birds are the distinctive Red Fox Sparrows in taiga forest from Newfoundland to Alaska. Thick-billed birds are found in the Sierras, sooty ones in the Pacific Northwest, and slate-colored ones in the Rockies.

VOICE Call is sharp, dry *tshak* or *tshuk;* flight call a high-pitched *tzeep!;* song is complex and musical with trills and whistles.

NESTING Dense cup of grasses or moss lined with fine material; usually placed low in shrub; 2–5 eggs; 1 brood; April–July.

FEEDING Forages for insects, seeds, and fruit.

SIMILAR SPECIES

HERMIT THRUSH
see p.329

unstreaked
flanks

SONG SPARROW
see p.378

thinner
bill

different
bill shape

longer
tail

breast
streaking
less
marked

OCCURRENCE
Encompasses the entire boreal forest zone, from Alaska in the West to Québec, Labrador, and Newfoundland in the East. In the East, it occurs in boreal forests. Winters in the Pacific West, south to Baja California; also from Texas to Massachusetts.

| Length **6–7½in (15–19cm)** | Wingspan **10½–11½in (27–29cm)** | Weight **⅞–1⁹⁄₁₆oz (25–45g)** |
| Social **Solitary/Small flocks** | Lifespan **Up to 9 years** | Status **Secure** |

DATE SEEN	WHERE	NOTES

365

Order **Passeriformes**	Family **Passerellidae**	Species *Spizelloides arborea*

American Tree Sparrow

rufous crown

black-and-yellow bill

gray eyebrow and nape

rusty stripe behind eye

rusty tones on shoulder and wings

streaked underparts

ADULT (BREEDING)

JUVENILE

IN FLIGHT

black and rust streaking on back

two wing bars

striped back

rust patch at shoulder

dark central breast spot

tan, unstreaked flanks and underparts

ADULT (BREEDING)

ADULT (NONBREEDING)

long tail

FLIGHT: lightly undulating, often flies to open perch when flushed.

T he first heavy snowfalls of winter often bring flocks of American Tree Sparrows to birdfeeders in the Northeast. This bird is commonly mistaken for the smaller Chipping Sparrow, but the two species look different in winter. The American Tree Sparrow is larger and has a central breast spot and a bicolored bill. American Tree Sparrows are social birds and some winter flocks can number in the hundreds. Poorly named, this species actually breeds in boggy habitats of the far North.

VOICE Call a bell-like *teedle-ee*; flight call a thin, slightly descending *tsiiiu*; song *seee seee di-di-di di-di-di dyew dyew*.
NESTING Neat cup on ground concealed within thicket; 4–6 eggs; 1 brood; June–July.
FEEDING Feeds on seeds, berries, and a variety of insects.

WINTER HABITATS
In winter this species frequents barren habitats, like old fields and roadsides, as well as feeders.

OCCURRENCE
Breeds in scrubby thickets of birch and willows in the area between taiga and tundra across Alaska and northern Canada. Nonbreeders choose open, grassy, brushy habitats. Winters across southern Canada and the northern US. Casual to Pacific Coast and southern US.

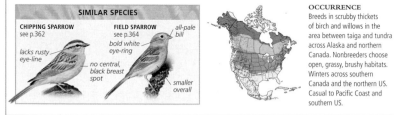

SIMILAR SPECIES

CHIPPING SPARROW
see p.362

lacks rusty eye-line

FIELD SPARROW
see p.364

all-pale bill

bold white eye-ring

no central, black breast spot

smaller overall

Length **6¼in (16cm)**	Wingspan **9½in (24cm)**	Weight **⁷⁄₁₆–⁷⁄₈oz (13–25g)**
Social **Flocks**	Lifespan **Up to 11 years**	Status **Secure**

DATE SEEN	WHERE	NOTES

| Order **Passeriformes** | Family **Passerellidae** | Species *Junco hyemalis* |

Dark-eyed Junco

IN FLIGHT

white outer tail feathers

MALE (SLATE-COLORED)

dull, brownish back

bluish gray hood

pinkish flanks

FEMALE (PINK-SIDED)

dark area between eye and bill

gray body with darker gray back

dark gray head

white belly

MALE
J. h. hyemalis
(SLATE-COLORED; EAST)

reddish brown back

gray rump

black mask

pale gray underparts

MALE (GRAY-HEADED)

rust back

blackish hood

MALE (OREGON)

reddish flanks

The Dark-eyed Junco's arrival at birdfeeders during winter snowstorms has earned it the colloquial name of "snowbird." The name "Dark-eyed Junco" is used to describe a group of birds that vary geographically in such a strikingly diverse way that 16 subspecies have been described. "Slate-colored" populations occur in central Alaska, Canada, and the northeastern US. "White-winged" birds nest in the Black Hills of South Dakota. "Pink-sided" ones breed in Idaho, Montana, and Wyoming, and "Oregon" birds breed in the West, from coastal Alaska to British Columbia and the mountains of the western US in the Sierras south to Mexico. Birds from the Appalachians are ascribed to the subspecies *J. h. carolinensis.*

VOICE Loud, smacking *tick* and soft *dyew* calls; flight call a rapid, twittering, and buzzy *zzeet*; song a simple, liquid, 1-pitch trill.

NESTING Cup placed on ground hidden under vegetation or next to rocks; 3–5 eggs; 1–2 broods; May–August.

FEEDING Eats insects and seeds; also berries.

FLIGHT: low and direct, staying within cover whenever possible.

BRIGHTER MALE
Like other juncos, this male is brighter than females.

OCCURRENCE
Breeds in coniferous and mixed forests across Canada, south to the east Appalachians and Georgia, and in the West, in mountains from Alaska and British Columbia to New Mexico and northern Baja California. Winters from southern Canada to northern Mexico, but not in Florida.

SIMILAR SPECIES

YELLOW-EYED JUNCO

red back

yellow eyes

buff wash to belly

| Length **6–6¾in (15–17cm)** | Wingspan **8–10in (20–26cm)** | Weight **⅝–1¹⁄₁₆oz (18–30g)** |
| Social **Flocks** | Lifespan **Up to 11 years** | Status **Secure** |

DATE SEEN	WHERE		NOTES

Order **Passeriformes**	Family **Passerellidae**	Species *Zonotrichia leucophrys*

White-crowned Sparrow 🔊

gray rump and uppertail

duller overall

white crown with two black stripes

yellowish bill

black line

gray cheek

longish tail

ADULT

two wing bars

IN FLIGHT

brown crown

two wing bars

ADULT
Z. l. nuttalli
(CALIFORNIA-COAST)

gray breast

IMMATURE

unmarked, grayish underparts

ADULT

FLIGHT: low and direct, staying within cover whenever possible.

The White-crowned Sparrow breeds far north in eastern Canada in open boreal forests ranging westward to Alaska. Geographic variation in this species is well-marked, and recognized by five subspecies. Eastern birds belong to *Z. l. leucophrys*. Four western subspecies have been described. Eastern birds migrate south to wintering grounds in a number of states, southward of a line from southern Minnesota to New York to the Gulf Coast (but not Florida).
VOICE Call a sharp *tink*; flight call a thin *seep*; song a buzzy whistle.
NESTING Bulky cup of grass placed on or near the ground in bushes; 4–6 eggs; 1–3 broods; March–August.
FEEDING Forages for seeds, insects, fruit, buds, and grass.

LOOKING RESTED
Perched on a shrub, this sparrow's white eyestreak is highly visible.

SIMILAR SPECIES

WHITE-THROATED SPARROW
see p.370
chunkier overall

yellow patch
gray bill
more reddish

GOLDEN-CROWNED SPARROW 🔊
yellowish forecrown
plain face
gray bill

OCCURRENCE
Widespread across the boreal forest and the taiga-tundra border, from Alaska eastward to Québec and Labrador, and southward from British Columbia to coastal California and the Intermontane West. In the North, breeds in willow thickets, wet forest; in the west, habitats are more varied.

Length 6½–7in (16–18cm)	Wingspan 9½–10in (24–26cm)	Weight 1¹⁄₁₆–1¼oz (20–35g)
Social **Flocks**	Lifespan **Up to 13 years**	Status **Secure**

DATE SEEN	WHERE	NOTES

| Order **Passeriformes** | Family **Passerellidae** | Species *Zonotrichia querula* |

Harris's Sparrow

ADULT
(NONBREEDING)

two wing bars

pinkish bill

gray cheeks

black crown

pinkish or yellow bill

indistinct facial markings

ADULT (NONBREEDING)

black cheek patch

black chin and throat

IN FLIGHT

gray rump and undertail feathers

tan cheek

white chin

concentration of streaks on chest

JUVENILE

ADULT (BREEDING)

An unmistakable black-faced, pink-billed bird, Harris's Sparrow is the only breeding bird endemic to Canada. It can be seen in the US during migration or in winter on the Great Plains. This species is occasionally found in large flocks of White-throated and White-crowned Sparrows. Harris's Sparrow is the largest sparrow in North America, approaching the Northern Cardinal in size. Its scientific name, *querula*, comes from the plaintive quality of its whistled song. The first Harris's Sparrow nest was found in 1907 in the Northwest Territories.
VOICE Call a sharp *weeek*; song a melancholy series of 2–4 whistles on the same pitch.
NESTING Bulky cup placed on ground among vegetation or near ground in brush; 3–5 eggs; 1 brood, June–August.
FEEDING Eats seeds, insects, buds, and even young conifer needles in summer.

FLIGHT: low and direct, staying within cover whenever possible.

NORTHERN ACROBAT
This nonbreeding Harris's Sparrow grips two different weeds, one in each foot.

SIMILAR SPECIES

HOUSE SPARROW
see p.340

much smaller

WHITE-THROATED SPARROW ♂
see p.370

lacks bright pink bill

smaller and shorter-tailed

no black necklace

OCCURRENCE
Breeds in scrub-tundra along the Canadian taiga-tundra timberline from northern Northwest Territories to northern Ontario. Winters in US Great Plains from South Dakota and Iowa south to northern Texas. Nonbreeders found in thickets, hedges. Casual in the East, and rare in the West.

| Length 6¾–7½in (17–19cm) | Wingspan 10½–11in (27–28cm) | Weight 1¹⁄₁₆–1⁷⁄₁₆oz (30–40g) |
| Social **Flocks** | Lifespan **Up to 12 years** | Status **Secure** |

DATE SEEN	WHERE	NOTES

| Order **Passeriformes** | Family **Passerellidae** | Species *Zonotrichia albicollis* |

White-throated Sparrow 🔊

yellow patch

two white wing bars

ADULT
IN FLIGHT

tan stripe

browner face

bold white stripe

bright rufous back and tail

white throat

**ADULT
(TAN-STRIPED FORM)**

gray bill

streaking on breast

**IMMATURE
(TAN-STRIPED)**

fairly long tail

gray underparts

**ADULT
(WHITE-STRIPED FORM)**

Common almost everywhere in eastern North America, White-throated Sparrows sing all year round. Their distinctive, whistled, rhythmic song can be remembered with the popular mnemonics *Oh sweet Canada Canada Canada*, or the less accurate *Old Sam Peabody*. This species has two different color forms, one with a white stripe above its eye, and the other with a tan stripe. In the nonbreeding season, large flocks roam the leaf litter of woodlands in search of food. Often the only indication of their presence is the occasional moving leaf or thin, lisping flight call.
VOICE Call loud, sharp *jink*; flight call lisping *tsssssst!*; song clear whistle comprising 1–2 higher notes, then three triplets.
NESTING Cup placed on or near ground in dense shrubbery; 2–6 eggs; 1 brood; May–August.
FEEDING Mainly forages on the ground for seeds, fruit, insects, buds, and various grasses.

FLIGHT: low and direct, staying within cover whenever possible.

DIFFERENT COLOR FORMS
The presence of white or tan stripes on White-throated Sparrows is not related to their sex.

SIMILAR SPECIES

WHITE-CROWNED SPARROW
slimmer overall; see p.368

no yellow patch

GOLDEN-CROWNED SPARROW ♀
yellowish forecrown

orange or pink bill

plain, grayish breast

OCCURRENCE
Breeds in forests from eastern Yukon to Newfoundland, south to the Great Lakes region and northern Appalachians. Nonbreeders prefer wooded thickets and hedges. Winters across the eastern US and extreme south of the Southwest. Rare but regular along the Pacific Coast.

| Length **6½–7½in (16–17.5cm)** | Wingspan **9–10in (23–26cm)** | Weight **¹¹⁄₁₆–1¼oz (20–35g)** |
| Social **Flocks** | Lifespan **Up to 10 years** | Status **Secure** |

DATE SEEN	WHERE	NOTES

| Order **Passeriformes** | Family **Passerellidae** | Species **Pooecetes gramineus** |

Vesper Sparrow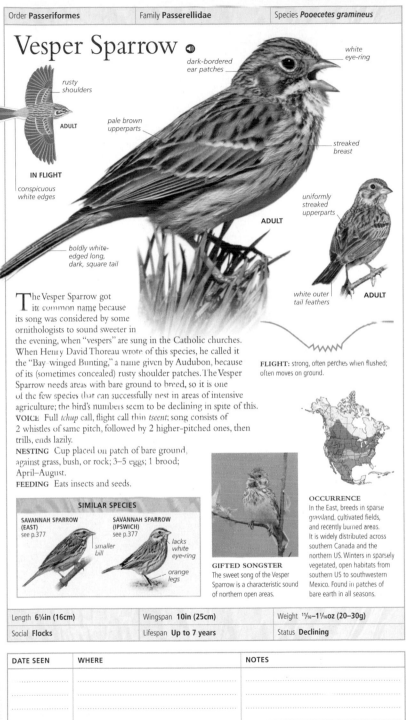

dark-bordered ear patches

white eye-ring

rusty shoulders

ADULT

pale brown upperparts

streaked breast

IN FLIGHT

conspicuous white edges

uniformly streaked upperparts

ADULT

boldly white-edged long, dark, square tail

white outer tail feathers

ADULT

The Vesper Sparrow got its common name because its song was considered by some ornithologists to sound sweeter in the evening, when "vespers" are sung in the Catholic churches. When Henry David Thoreau wrote of this species, he called it the "Bay-winged Bunting," a name given by Audubon, because of its (sometimes concealed) rusty shoulder patches. The Vesper Sparrow needs areas with bare ground to breed, so it is one of the few species that can successfully nest in areas of intensive agriculture; the bird's numbers seem to be declining in spite of this.

VOICE Full *tchup* call, flight call thin *tseent*; song consists of 2 whistles of same pitch, followed by 2 higher-pitched ones, then trills, ends lazily.

NESTING Cup placed on patch of bare ground, against grass, bush, or rock; 3–5 eggs; 1 brood; April–August.

FEEDING Eats insects and seeds.

FLIGHT: strong, often perches when flushed; often moves on ground.

SIMILAR SPECIES

| SAVANNAH SPARROW (EAST) see p.377 | SAVANNAH SPARROW (IPSWICH) see p.377 |

smaller bill

lacks white eye-ring

orange legs

GIFTED SONGSTER
The sweet song of the Vesper Sparrow is a characteristic sound of northern open areas.

OCCURRENCE
In the East, breeds in sparse grassland, cultivated fields, and recently burned areas. It is widely distributed across southern Canada and the northern US. Winters in sparsely vegetated, open habitats from southern US to southwestern Mexico. Found in patches of bare earth in all seasons.

| Length **6¼in (16cm)** | Wingspan **10in (25cm)** | Weight **¹¹⁄₁₆–1¹⁄₁₆oz (20–30g)** |
| Social **Flocks** | Lifespan **Up to 7 years** | Status **Declining** |

DATE SEEN	WHERE	NOTES

Order **Passeriformes**	Family **Passerellidae**	Species *Ammospiza leconteii*

LeConte's Sparrow

spiky tail

ADULT

boldly striped back

pale, tawny rump

IN FLIGHT

white-edged wing feathers

white median crown stripe

purplish and gray streaks on nape

rich orange eyebrow

small bill

orange throat

grayish brown cheeks

buffy breast and flanks with bold streaks

ADULT

FLIGHT: low and weak, with spiky tail pointed down; much fast flapping.

Intricately patterned in browns and buffs, LeConte's Sparrow is usually very difficult to see. Not only is it tiny—one of the smallest of all North American sparrows—but in its grassland and marsh habitats of interior North America, it darts for cover, hiding under grasses instead of flushing when disturbed. The flight call and song of this elusive little bird are remarkably insect-like. Many people who hear it believe that the unseen caller is a grasshopper. Its nest is even harder to find, making this bird a real challenge to study as well as observe.

VOICE Call long, down-slurred *zheeep*; flight call similar to grasshopper; song insect-like, buzzy *tik'-uht-tizz-ZHEEEEEE-k*.

NESTING Concealed little cup placed on or near ground; 3–5 eggs; 1 brood; June–August.

FEEDING Forages on the ground and in grasses for insects, insect larvae, spiders, and seeds.

HIDEAWAY BIRD
LeConte's Sparrow is usually found skulking in medium-to-tall grass.

OCCURRENCE
Breeds in marshes, wet meadows, and bogs from the southwestern Yukon east to Lake Superior and western Québec. Migrants and wintering birds are found in tall grass and marshes from southwestern Kansas to southern Indiana, and from central Texas to the Carolinas.

SIMILAR SPECIES

NELSON'S SPARROW
see p.374

gray nape

less streaked

GRASSHOPPER SPARROW
see p.359

duller overall

larger bill

Length 4½–5in (11.5–13cm)	Wingspan 6½–7in (16–18cm)	Weight ⁷⁄₁₆–⁹⁄₁₆oz (12–16g)
Social **Solitary/Loose flocks**	Lifespan **Unknown**	Status **Secure**

DATE SEEN	WHERE	NOTES

| Order **Passeriformes** | Family **Passerellidae** | Species **Ammospiza maritima** |

Seaside Sparrow

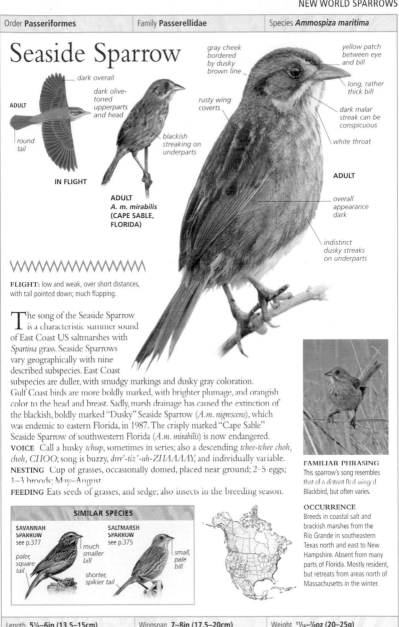

ADULT

IN FLIGHT

round tail

dark overall

dark olive-toned upperparts and head

ADULT
A. m. mirabilis
(CAPE SABLE, FLORIDA)

blackish streaking on underparts

rusty wing coverts

gray cheek bordered by dusky brown line

yellow patch between eye and bill

long, rather thick bill

dark malar streak can be conspicuous

white throat

ADULT

overall appearance dark

indistinct dusky streaks on underparts

FLIGHT: low and weak, over short distances, with tail pointed down; much flapping.

The song of the Seaside Sparrow is a characteristic summer sound of East Coast US saltmarshes with *Spartina* grass. Seaside Sparrows vary geographically with nine described subspecies. East Coast subspecies are duller, with smudgy markings and dusky gray coloration. Gulf Coast birds are more boldly marked, with brighter plumage, and orangish color to the head and breast. Sadly, marsh drainage has caused the extinction of the blackish, boldly marked "Dusky" Seaside Sparrow (*A.m. nigrescens*), which was endemic to eastern Florida, in 1987. The crisply marked "Cape Sable" Seaside Sparrow of southwestern Florida (*A.m. mirabilis*) is now endangered.
VOICE Call a husky *tchup*, sometimes in series; also a descending *tchee-tchee choh, choh, CHOO*; song is buzzy, *drrr'-tiz'-uh-ZHAAAAY,* and individually variable.
NESTING Cup of grasses, occasionally domed, placed near ground; 2–5 eggs; 1–3 broods; May–August.
FEEDING Eats seeds of grasses, and sedge; also insects in the breeding season.

FAMILIAR PHRASING
This sparrow's song resembles that of a distant Red-winged Blackbird, but often varies.

OCCURRENCE
Breeds in coastal salt and brackish marshes from the Rio Grande in southeastern Texas north and east to New Hampshire. Absent from many parts of Florida. Mostly resident, but retreats from areas north of Massachusetts in the winter.

SIMILAR SPECIES

SAVANNAH SPARROW
see p.377

paler, square tail

much smaller bill

SALTMARSH SPARROW
see p.375

small, pale bill

shorter, spikier tail

| Length **5¼–6in (13.5–15cm)** | Wingspan **7–8in (17.5–20cm)** | Weight **¹¹⁄₁₆–⁷⁄₈oz (20–25g)** |
| Social **Solitary** | Lifespan **Up to 8 years** | Status **Vulnerable** |

DATE SEEN	WHERE	NOTES

Order **Passeriformes**	Family **Passerellidae**	Species **Ammospiza nelsoni**

Nelson's Sparrow

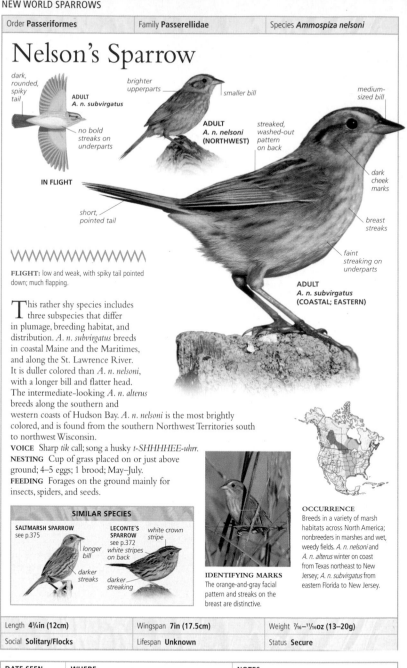

dark, rounded, spiky tail

ADULT
A. n. subvirgatus

no bold streaks on underparts

IN FLIGHT

short, pointed tail

brighter upperparts

smaller bill

ADULT
A. n. nelsoni
(NORTHWEST)

streaked, washed-out pattern on back

medium-sized bill

dark cheek marks

breast streaks

faint streaking on underparts

ADULT
A. n. subvirgatus
(COASTAL; EASTERN)

FLIGHT: low and weak, with spiky tail pointed down; much flapping.

This rather shy species includes three subspecies that differ in plumage, breeding habitat, and distribution. *A. n. subvirgatus* breeds in coastal Maine and the Maritimes, and along the St. Lawrence River. It is duller colored than *A. n. nelsoni*, with a longer bill and flatter head. The intermediate-looking *A. n. alterus* breeds along the southern and western coasts of Hudson Bay. *A. n. nelsoni* is the most brightly colored, and is found from the southern Northwest Territories south to northwest Wisconsin.

VOICE Sharp *tik* call; song a husky *t-SHHHHEE-uhrr.*
NESTING Cup of grass placed on or just above ground; 4–5 eggs; 1 brood; May–July.
FEEDING Forages on the ground mainly for insects, spiders, and seeds.

SIMILAR SPECIES

SALTMARSH SPARROW
see p.375

longer bill

darker streaks

LECONTE'S SPARROW
see p.372

white crown stripe

white stripes on back

darker streaking

IDENTIFYING MARKS
The orange-and-gray facial pattern and streaks on the breast are distinctive.

OCCURRENCE
Breeds in a variety of marsh habitats across North America; nonbreeders in marshes and wet, weedy fields. *A. n. nelsoni* and *A. n. alterus* winter on coast from Texas northeast to New Jersey; *A. n. subvirgatus* from eastern Florida to New Jersey.

Length **4¾in (12cm)**	Wingspan **7in (17.5cm)**	Weight **⁷⁄₁₆–¹¹⁄₁₆oz (13–20g)**
Social **Solitary/Flocks**	Lifespan **Unknown**	Status **Secure**

DATE SEEN	WHERE	NOTES

| Order **Passeriformes** | Family **Passerellidae** | Species *Ammospiza caudacuta* |

Saltmarsh Sparrow

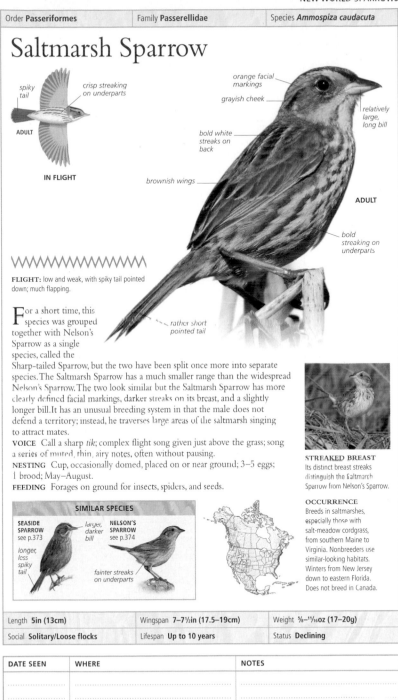

spiky tail

crisp streaking on underparts

ADULT

IN FLIGHT

orange facial markings

grayish cheek

relatively large, long bill

bold white streaks on back

brownish wings

ADULT

bold streaking on underparts

FLIGHT: low and weak, with spiky tail pointed down; much flapping.

rather short pointed tail

For a short time, this species was grouped together with Nelson's Sparrow as a single species, called the Sharp-tailed Sparrow, but the two have been split once more into separate species. The Saltmarsh Sparrow has a much smaller range than the widespread Nelson's Sparrow. The two look similar but the Saltmarsh Sparrow has more clearly defined facial markings, darker streaks on its breast, and a slightly longer bill. It has an unusual breeding system in that the male does not defend a territory; instead, he traverses large areas of the saltmarsh singing to attract mates.

VOICE Call a sharp *tik*; complex flight song given just above the grass; song a series of muted, thin, airy notes, often without pausing.

NESTING Cup, occasionally domed, placed on or near ground; 3–5 eggs; 1 brood; May–August.

FEEDING Forages on ground for insects, spiders, and seeds.

STREAKED BREAST
Its distinct breast streaks distinguish the Saltmarsh Sparrow from Nelson's Sparrow.

OCCURRENCE
Breeds in saltmarshes, especially those with salt-meadow cordgrass, from southern Maine to Virginia. Nonbreeders use similar-looking habitats. Winters from New Jersey down to eastern Florida. Does not breed in Canada.

SIMILAR SPECIES

SEASIDE SPARROW see p.373

longer, less spiky tail

larger, darker bill

NELSON'S SPARROW see p.374

fainter streaks on underparts

| Length **5in (13cm)** | Wingspan **7–7½in (17.5–19cm)** | Weight **⅝–¹¹⁄₁₆oz (17–20g)** |
| Social **Solitary/Loose flocks** | Lifespan **Up to 10 years** | Status **Declining** |

DATE SEEN	WHERE	NOTES

| Order **Passeriformes** | Family **Passerellidae** | Species **Centronyx henslowii** |

Henslow's Sparrow

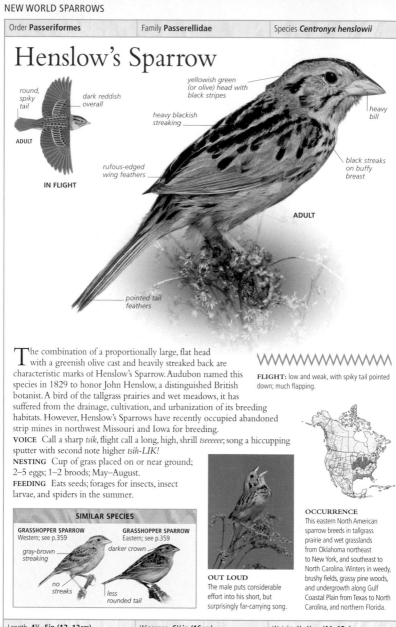

round, spiky tail

dark reddish overall

ADULT

IN FLIGHT

rufous-edged wing feathers

yellowish green (or olive) head with black stripes

heavy blackish streaking

heavy bill

black streaks on buffy breast

ADULT

pointed tail feathers

The combination of a proportionally large, flat head with a greenish olive cast and heavily streaked back are characteristic marks of Henslow's Sparrow. Audubon named this species in 1829 to honor John Henslow, a distinguished British botanist. A bird of the tallgrass prairies and wet meadows, it has suffered from the drainage, cultivation, and urbanization of its breeding habitats. However, Henslow's Sparrows have recently occupied abandoned strip mines in northwest Missouri and Iowa for breeding.

VOICE Call a sharp *tsik*, flight call a long, high, shrill *tseeeeee*; song a hiccupping sputter with second note higher *tsih-LIK!*

NESTING Cup of grass placed on or near ground; 2–5 eggs; 1–2 broods; May–August.

FEEDING Eats seeds; forages for insects, insect larvae, and spiders in the summer.

FLIGHT: low and weak, with spiky tail pointed down; much flapping.

OCCURRENCE
This eastern North American sparrow breeds in tallgrass prairie and wet grasslands from Oklahoma northeast to New York, and southeast to North Carolina. Winters in weedy, brushy fields, grassy pine woods, and undergrowth along Gulf Coastal Plain from Texas to North Carolina, and northern Florida.

OUT LOUD
The male puts considerable effort into his short, but surprisingly far-carrying song.

SIMILAR SPECIES

| GRASSHOPPER SPARROW Western; see p.359 | GRASSHOPPER SPARROW Eastern; see p.359 |

gray-brown streaking

darker crown

no streaks

less rounded tail

| Length **4¾–5in (12–13cm)** | Wingspan **6½in (16cm)** | Weight **⅜–½oz (11–15g)** |
| Social **Solitary/Loose flocks** | Lifespan **Unknown** | Status **Declining** |

DATE SEEN	WHERE	NOTES

| Order **Passeriformes** | Family **Passerellidae** | Species *Passerculus sandwichensis* |

Savannah Sparrow

brown overall

ADULT

IN FLIGHT

tail short with whitish edges

yellow patch between eye and bill

small bill

white belly

pale yellow eyebrow

crisp black streaking on underparts

ADULT (WESTERN)

pale sandy overall

reddish streaks on underparts

ADULT P. s. princeps (IPSWICH SPARROW)

FLIGHT: square-tailed with an often undulating or "stair step" flight pattern.

short, notched tail, edged with white

pinkish legs and toes

ADULT (EASTERN)

The Savannah Sparrow shows tremendous geographic variation—21 subspecies—across its vast range, but it is always brown, with dark streaks above and white with dark streaks below. The pale "Ipswich Sparrow" (*P. s. princeps*), originally described as a species, breeds on the very isolated Sable Island, Nova Scotia, and winters along the East Coast. Eastern Savannah Sparrows breed in eastern Canada and the northwestern US, and winter in the southern half of the US, Mexico, and the West Indies.
VOICE Call a sharp, but full *stip*; flight call a thin, weak, down-slurred *tseew*; song a *sit sit sit sit suh-EEEEE say*, from perch or in display flight with legs dangling.
NESTING Concealed cup of grass placed in depression on ground, protected by overhanging grass or sedges; 2–6 eggs; 1–2 broods; June–August.
FEEDING Forages on the ground, mostly for insects; in summer also eats seeds; in winter berries and fruit when available; also small snails and crustaceans.

SAVANNAH SPARROW
This bird's yellow eyebrow matches the color of its surroundings.

OCCURRENCE
Breeds in meadows, grasslands, pastures, bushy tundra, and some cultivated land across northern North America. Also along the Pacific Coast and in Mexican interior. Nonbreeders use varied open habitats. Eastern birds winter across southern US to Honduras, also Cuba.

SIMILAR SPECIES

SONG SPARROW
see p.378

larger overall

longer, rounded tail

VESPER SPARROW
see p.371

rusty shoulder

dark tail

| Length **5½–6in (14–15cm)** | Wingspan **6¾in (17cm)** | Weight **½–1¹⁄₁₆oz (15–30g)** |
| Social **Solitary/Loose flocks** | Lifespan **Unknown** | Status **Secure** |

DATE SEEN	WHERE	NOTES

Order **Passeriformes**	Family **Passerellidae**	Species *Melospiza melodia*

Song Sparrow 🔊

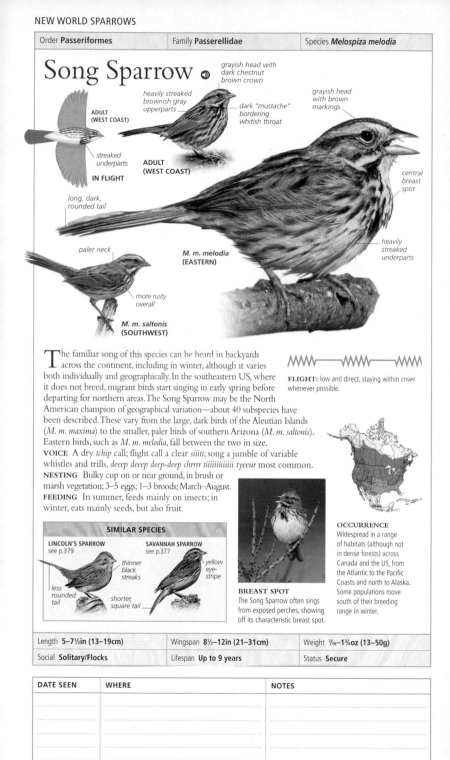

grayish head with
dark chestnut
brown crown

**ADULT
(WEST COAST)
IN FLIGHT**

heavily streaked
brownish gray
upperparts

dark "mustache"
bordering
whitish throat

**ADULT
(WEST COAST)**

streaked
underparts

long, dark,
rounded tail

grayish head
with brown
markings

central
breast
spot

heavily
streaked
underparts

paler neck

M. m. melodia
(EASTERN)

more rusty
overall

M. m. saltonis
(SOUTHWEST)

The familiar song of this species can be heard in backyards across the continent, including in winter, although it varies both individually and geographically. In the southeastern US, where it does not breed, migrant birds start singing in early spring before departing for northern areas. The Song Sparrow may be the North American champion of geographical variation—about 40 subspecies have been described. These vary from the large, dark birds of the Aleutian Islands (*M. m. maxima*) to the smaller, paler birds of southern Arizona (*M. m. saltonis*). Eastern birds, such as *M. m. melodia*, fall between the two in size.

VOICE A dry *tchip* call; flight call a clear *siiiti*; song a jumble of variable whistles and trills, *deeep deeep deep-deep chrrrr tiiiiiiiiiiiii tyeeur* most common.

NESTING Bulky cup on or near ground, in brush or marsh vegetation; 3–5 eggs; 1–3 broods; March–August.

FEEDING In summer, feeds mainly on insects; in winter, eats mainly seeds, but also fruit.

FLIGHT: low and direct, staying within cover whenever possible.

SIMILAR SPECIES

LINCOLN'S SPARROW
see p.379

SAVANNAH SPARROW
see p.377

thinner
black
streaks

less
rounded
tail

shorter,
square tail

yellow
eye-
stripe

BREAST SPOT
The Song Sparrow often sings from exposed perches, showing off its characteristic breast spot.

OCCURRENCE
Widespread in a range of habitats (although not in dense forests) across Canada and the US, from the Atlantic to the Pacific Coasts and north to Alaska. Some populations move south of their breeding range in winter.

Length **5–7½in (13–19cm)**	Wingspan **8½–12in (21–31cm)**	Weight **⁷⁄₁₆–1¾oz (13–50g)**
Social **Solitary/Flocks**	Lifespan **Up to 9 years**	Status **Secure**

DATE SEEN	WHERE	NOTES
. . . .	. . . .	. . . .
. . . .	. . . .	. . . .
. . . .	. . . .	. . . .
. . . .	. . . .	. . . .
. . . .	. . . .	. . . .

| Order **Passeriformes** | Family **Passerellidae** | Species *Melospiza lincolnii* |

Lincoln's Sparrow

crested or peaked, rufous crown

broad gray eyebrow

bold eye-ring

small, thin bill

dark brown streak under cheek

streaks on throat

pencil-thin streaking on buffy breast

rounded tail

ADULT

rufous-edged wing feathers

ADULT

IN FLIGHT

A t first glance, Lincoln's Sparrow appears plain, but close inspection reveals its subtly varying, but crisply outlined, markings. In the breeding season, it seeks out moist willow scrub at the tundra–taiga timberline; outside the breeding season, Lincoln's Sparrow occurs in scrubby habitats right across North America. It will occasionally visit backyard feeders in winter, but it is generally secretive and stays within fairly dense cover. Lincoln's Sparrow's rich, musical song is unmistakable, and it varies remarkably little from region to region. Audubon named this species in 1834 in honor of his collector Thomas Lincoln.

VOICE Call a variable, loud *tchip*, flight call a rolling *ziiiit*; song series of rich, musical trills, *ju-ju-ju dodododo didididididi whrrrrr*.

NESTING Grass cup, lined with fine grass, and hidden in depression in ground under overhanging sedges or grasses; 3–5 eggs;1 brood; June–August.

FEEDING Mainly seeds in winter; in summer, mostly insects, such as beetles, mosquitoes, and moths.

FLIGHT: low and direct, staying within cover whenever possible.

RAISE THE ALARM
When disturbed, Lincoln's Sparrow often raises its central crown feathers, which form a crest.

SIMILAR SPECIES

SONG SPARROW
see p.378
larger overall

SAVANNAH SPARROW
see p.377

yellow stripe above eye

short, square, notched tail

more coarse streaking

OCCURRENCE
Breeds in muskeg and wet thickets across northern North America, also south into the western ranges of California and Arizona. Migrants and wintering birds use a variety of scrubby habitats. Winters in southern US (and farther south), and on Pacific Coast north to British Columbia.

| Length **5¼–6in (13.5–15cm)** | Wingspan **7½–8½in (19–22cm)** | Weight **½–⅞oz (15–25g)** |
| Social **Solitary/Small flocks** | Lifespan **Up to 7 years** | Status **Secure** |

DATE SEEN	WHERE	NOTES

| Order **Passeriformes** | Family **Passerellidae** | Species **Melospiza georgiana** |

Swamp Sparrow 🔊

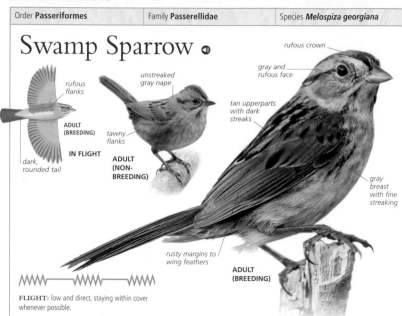

rufous crown

gray and rufous face

tan upperparts with dark streaks

gray breast with fine streaking

rufous flanks

ADULT (BREEDING)

IN FLIGHT

dark, rounded tail

unstreaked gray nape

tawny flanks

ADULT (NON-BREEDING)

rusty margins to wing feathers

ADULT (BREEDING)

FLIGHT: low and direct, staying within cover whenever possible.

The Swamp Sparrow is a common breeder in wet habitats across eastern North America and Canada west to the southern Yukon and eastern British Columbia. It is abundant in its preferred habitat of tall reed and cattail marshes. A somewhat skittish bird, the Swamp Sparrow is often seen darting rapidly into cover, but usually repays the patient observer with a reappearance, giving its characteristic *chimp* call. Though often confused with both the Song Sparrow and Lincoln's Sparrow, the Swamp Sparrow never shows more than a very faint, blurry streaking on its gray breast, and sports conspicuous rusty-edged wing feathers. Its song is also quite different.

VOICE Call a slightly nasal, forceful *chimp*, flight call a high, buzzy *ziiiiii*; song a slow, monotonous, loose trill of chirps.

NESTING Bulky cup of dry plants placed 1–4ft (30–120cm) above water in marsh vegetation; 3–5 eggs; 1–2 broods; May–July.

FEEDING Mostly insects in the breeding season, especially grasshoppers; seeds in winter; occasionally fruit.

HIGH PERCH
This male Swamp Sparrow is checking his territory from atop a seeding cattail flower.

SIMILAR SPECIES

SONG SPARROW see p.378
brown tail
brown wings
streaked breast

LINCOLN'S SPARROW see p.379
less red overall
fine breast streaks

OCCURRENCE
Breeds in marshes, cedar bogs, damp meadows, and wet hayfields, from the Yukon east to Newfoundland and south to Nebraska and the Delmarva Peninsula; winters in marshes in eastern US and south through Mexico; rare but regular along Pacific Coast.

| Length **5–6in (12.5–15cm)** | Wingspan **7–7½in (18–19cm)** | Weight **½–⅞oz (15–25g)** |
| Social **Solitary/Small flocks** | Lifespan **Up to 6 years** | Status **Secure** |

DATE SEEN	WHERE	NOTES

Order **Passeriformes**	Family **Passerellidae**	Species *Piplio erythrophthalmus*

Eastern Towhee

single white patch in each wing

white corners to tail

ADULT

IN FLIGHT

black hood and upperparts

red eye

MALE

white belly

rusty-red flanks

white wing patches

long tail

brown hood and upperparts

small white markings on wings

rusty flanks

FEMALE

The Eastern Towhee gets its name from the up-slurred *chew-eee* (or *to-whee*) call it makes. Eastern Towhees are famous for their vocalizations and have one of the best-known mnemonics for their song: "drink your tea." The Eastern Towhee was once lumped with the western Spotted Towhee under the name "Rufous-sided Towhee," because they interbreed in the Great Plains. In the southeastern US, Eastern Towhees have paler eyes the farther south they are located; individuals with nearly white eyes are found in Florida. Like all towhees, the Eastern Towhee feeds noisily by jumping backward with both feet at once to move leaves and reveal the insects and seeds that may be hidden underneath.

VOICE Call a nasal, up-slurred *chew-eee*; flight call *zeeeooooweeet*; song sounds like *dweee, dyooo di i i i-i-i-i-i-i-i-i-i.*

NESTING Large cup in depression on ground under cover, also low in thicket; 3–5 eggs; 1–2 broods; May–August.

FEEDING Eats seeds, fruit, insects, and buds.

FLIGHT: low and direct with much gliding, usually within cover.

TERRESTRIAL LIFE
Eastern Towhees stay near the ground, and are usually found not more than a few feet above it.

SIMILAR SPECIES

SPOTTED TOWHEE ♂
see p.472

two white wing bars

SPOTTED TOWHEE ♀
see p.472

two white wing bars

white spots on shoulder

OCCURRENCE
Found in dense thickets, woodlands, shrubbery, forest edges, and disturbed forests from southeastern Saskatchewan, eastern Nebraska, western Louisiana, east to southern Québec, southern Maine, and southern Florida. Retreats from the northern parts of its range to winter in the southeastern US.

Length **7½–8in (19–20cm)**	Wingspan **10½in (27cm)**	Weight **1¹⁄₁₆–1¾oz (30–50g)**
Social **Solitary/Small flocks**	Lifespan **Up to 12 years**	Status **Secure**

DATE SEEN	WHERE	NOTES

ORIOLES AND BLACKBIRDS

THE ICTERIDS EXEMPLIFY the wonderful diversity that exists among birds. Most members are common and widespread, occurring from coast to coast. They are present in nearly every habitat in North America, from the arid Southwest and Florida to the boreal forest zone in the North but do not live in the tundra. The species reveal a tremendous variety in color, nesting, and social behavior—from solitary orioles to vast colonies of blackbirds. One group of icterids, the cowbirds, are obligatory brood parasites, and make no nest, but lay their eggs in the nests of other species, mostly small songbirds.

ORIOLES

Orioles are generally recognized by their contrasting black and orange plumage, although some species tend more toward yellow or chestnut shades. They are common tropical to subtropical seasonal migrants to North America, and their intricate hanging nests are an impressive combination of engineering and weaving. Most oriole species have a loud and melodious song and show tolerance of humans, a combination that makes them popular throughout their range. The Orchard Oriole and the Baltimore Oriole are widespread in the East, but the other North American species live either in the West, the Southwest, or in southern Texas. The Eastern North American orioles spend the winter in tropical America.

COWBIRDS

These strictly parasitic birds have been known to lay eggs in the nests of nearly 300 different bird species in North and South America. The males of all three North American species are readily identified by their thick bills and dark,

SUBTLE BRILLIANCE Although its plumage is dark, the Common Grackle displays a beautiful iridescence.

iridescent plumage. The females and immatures, however, are drab, brownish, or blackish birds. The eastern species, the Brown-headed Cowbird, has dramatically increased in recent years.

BLACKBIRDS & GRACKLES

This group of birds is largely covered with dark feathers, and has a streamlined appearance because of long, pointed bills and tails. Not as brilliantly colored as some of the other icterids, these are among the most numerous birds on the continent. After the breeding season they gather in huge flocks and form an impressive sight.

BIG VOICE A Meadowlark's melodious voice is a defining feature in many rural landscapes.

MEADOWLARKS

Meadowlarks occur in both North and South America. The North American species have yellow breasts; the South American species have bright red ones. Only one species breeds in the East. It can be distinguished from its western counterpart by its song.

NECTAR LOVER
The magnificently colored Baltimore Oriole inserts its bill into the base of a flower, taking the nectar but playing no part in pollination.

| Order **Passeriformes** | Family **Icteriidae** | Species *Icteria virens* |

Yellow-breasted Chat

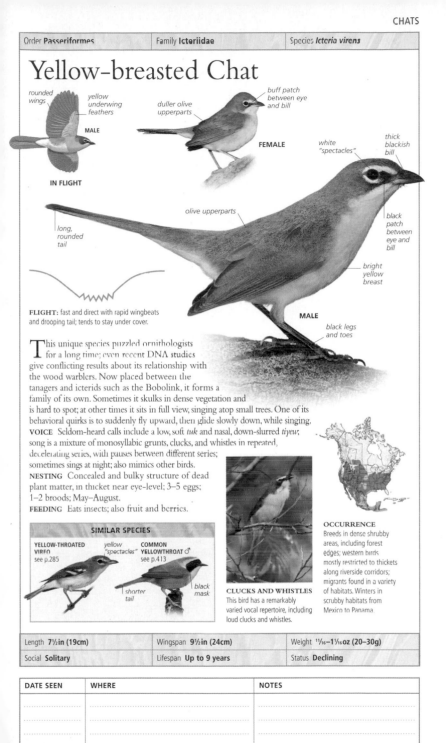

rounded wings

yellow underwing feathers

MALE

IN FLIGHT

duller olive upperparts

buff patch between eye and bill

FEMALE

white "spectacles"

thick blackish bill

black patch between eye and bill

olive upperparts

long, rounded tail

bright yellow breast

FLIGHT: fast and direct with rapid wingbeats and drooping tail; tends to stay under cover.

MALE

black legs and toes

This unique species puzzled ornithologists for a long time; even recent DNA studies give conflicting results about its relationship with the wood warblers. Now placed between the tanagers and icterids such as the Bobolink, it forms a family of its own. Sometimes it skulks in dense vegetation and is hard to spot; at other times it sits in full view, singing atop small trees. One of its behavioral quirks is to suddenly fly upward, then glide slowly down, while singing.

VOICE Seldom-heard calls include a low, soft *tuk* and nasal, down-slurred *tiyeu*; song is a mixture of monosyllabic grunts, clucks, and whistles in repeated, decelerating series, with pauses between different series; sometimes sings at night; also mimics other birds.

NESTING Concealed and bulky structure of dead plant matter, in thicket near eye-level; 3–5 eggs; 1–2 broods; May–August.

FEEDING Eats insects; also fruit and berries.

CLUCKS AND WHISTLES
This bird has a remarkably varied vocal repertoire, including loud clucks and whistles.

OCCURRENCE
Breeds in dense shrubby areas, including forest edges; western birds mostly restricted to thickets along riverside corridors; migrants found in a variety of habitats. Winters in scrubby habitats from Mexico to Panama.

SIMILAR SPECIES

| YELLOW-THROATED VIREO see p.285 | yellow "spectacles" | COMMON YELLOWTHROAT ♂ see p.413 |

shorter tail

black mask

| Length **7½in (19cm)** | Wingspan **9½in (24cm)** | Weight **¹¹⁄₁₆–1¹⁄₁₆oz (20–30g)** |
| Social **Solitary** | Lifespan **Up to 9 years** | Status **Declining** |

DATE SEEN	WHERE	NOTES

Order **Passeriformes**	Family **Icteridae**	Species *Xanthocephalus xanthocephalus*

Yellow-headed Blackbird 🔊

MALE

yellow head

conspicuous white wing patches

IN FLIGHT

black, conical bill

black mask and crown on yellow head

JUVENILE MALE

bright yellow head and chest

brownish overall

yellowish throat and facial patch

black overall

white wing patch

MALE

FEMALE

FLIGHT: direct with shallow rise and fall pattern; flaps and glides.

long tail

The male Yellow-headed Blackbird is unmistakable, with its conspicuous bright yellow head. Females, however, are more drab. Populations of this species fluctuate widely in numbers, but locally, depending on rainfall, which controls the availability and quality of its breeding marshland habitat. In some wetlands, the Yellow-headed Blackbird can be extremely abundant, and is easily noticed because of its amazing song, which, once heard, can never be forgotten.
VOICE Call a nasal *whaah*; song a series of harsh, cackling noises, followed by a brief pause, and a high, long, wailing trill.
NESTING Cup of plant strips woven into standing aquatic vegetation; 3–4 eggs; 1 brood; May–June.
FEEDING Eats insects while breeding; agricultural grains and grass seeds in winter.

SIMILAR SPECIES	
TRICOLORED BLACKBIRD ♀	**RUSTY BLACKBIRD ♂ ♀** see p.392
lacks yellow throat	pale eye
	lacks yellow throat
larger	

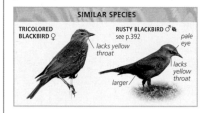

YELLOW GARLAND Five evenly spaced Yellow-headed males watch over their wetland habitat from a twig.

OCCURRENCE Widely distributed in western Canada and the central and western US, this species breeds in marshes with cattail and bullrush vegetation, and also, locally, in wetlands within wooded areas. Winters in Mexico; resident in Baja California.

Length **8½–10½in (21–27cm)**	Wingspan **15in (38cm)**	Weight **2⅛–3½oz (60–100g)**
Social **Flocks/Colonies**	Lifespan **Up to 9 years**	Status **Localized**

DATE SEEN	WHERE	NOTES

Order **Passeriformes**	Family **Icteridae**	Species *Dolichonyx oryzivorus*

Bobolink

black wings

buff-colored hind neck

MALE (BREEDING)

IN FLIGHT

blackish brown crown

gold-buff overall

pinkish bill

central crown stripe

FEMALE (BREEDING)

sparrow-like markings

buffy throat

black face and crown

white shoulder feathers

ADULT (FALL)

pointed tail feathers

white rump

black underparts

MALE (BREEDING)

black tail with pointed feathers

FLIGHT: typically direct flight; series of rapid wingbeats; glides of varying length.

The Bobolink is a common summer resident of open fallow fields through much of the northern US and southern Canada. In spring, the males perform a conspicuous circling or "helicoptering" display, which includes singing, to establish territory and to attract females. Bobolink populations have declined on its breeding grounds and in wintering areas because of habitat loss and changing agricultural practices.

VOICE Calls like the end of its name *link*; song a long, complex babbling series of musical notes varying in length and pitch.

NESTING Woven cup of grass close to or on the ground, well hidden in tall grass; 3–7 eggs; 1 brood; May–July.

FEEDING Feeds mostly on insects, spiders, grubs in breeding season, but seasonally variable; also cereal grains and grass seeds.

TAKING A BREAK
This male has fled the sun of the open fields to seek shelter in the shade of a tree.

SIMILAR SPECIES

RED-WINGED BLACKBIRD
see p.390
red shoulder patches

lacks buff-colored hind neck

larger overall

LARK BUNTING
see p.361
lacks buff-colored hind neck

larger

white wing patches

OCCURRENCE
Breeds in open fields with a mixture of tall grasses and other herbaceous vegetation, especially old hayfields. In Canada from British Columbia to the Atlantic Coast; in the US from Idaho to New England. Migrates through the southern US and the Caribbean; winters in northern South America.

Length **6–8in (15–20cm)**	Wingspan **10–12in (25–30cm)**	Weight **1¹⁄₁₆–2oz (30–55g)**
Social **Winter flocks**	Lifespan **Up to 10 years**	Status **Declining**

DATE SEEN	WHERE	NOTES

| Order **Passeriformes** | Family **Icteridae** | Species ***Sturnella magna*** |

Eastern Meadowlark 🔊

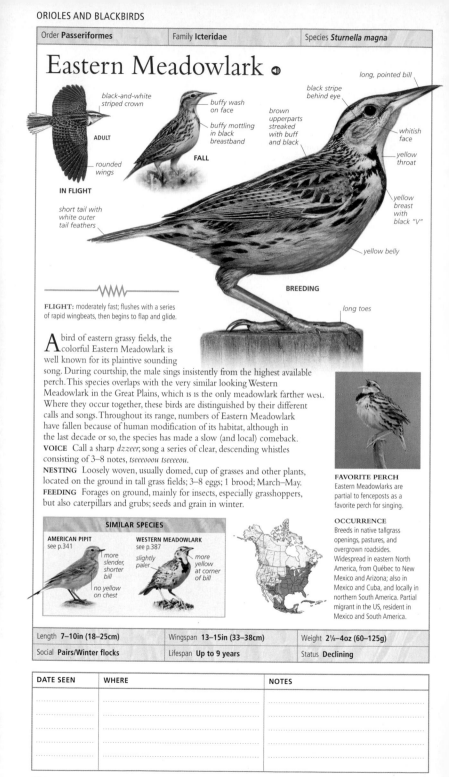

black-and-white striped crown

ADULT

rounded wings

IN FLIGHT

short tail with white outer tail feathers

buffy wash on face

buffy mottling in black breastband

FALL

long, pointed bill

black stripe behind eye

brown upperparts streaked with buff and black

whitish face

yellow throat

yellow breast with black "V"

yellow belly

BREEDING

long toes

FLIGHT: moderately fast; flushes with a series of rapid wingbeats, then begins to flap and glide.

A bird of eastern grassy fields, the colorful Eastern Meadowlark is well known for its plaintive sounding song. During courtship, the male sings insistently from the highest available perch. This species overlaps with the very similar looking Western Meadowlark in the Great Plains, which is is the only meadowlark farther west. Where they occur together, these birds are distinguished by their different calls and songs. Throughout its range, numbers of Eastern Meadowlark have fallen because of human modification of its habitat, although in the last decade or so, the species has made a slow (and local) comeback.
VOICE Call a sharp *dzzeer*; song a series of clear, descending whistles consisting of 3–8 notes, *tseeeooou tseeeeou*.
NESTING Loosely woven, usually domed, cup of grasses and other plants, located on the ground in tall grass fields; 3–8 eggs; 1 brood; March–May.
FEEDING Forages on ground, mainly for insects, especially grasshoppers, but also caterpillars and grubs; seeds and grain in winter.

FAVORITE PERCH
Eastern Meadowlarks are partial to fenceposts as a favorite perch for singing.

OCCURRENCE
Breeds in native tallgrass openings, pastures, and overgrown roadsides. Widespread in eastern North America, from Québec to New Mexico and Arizona; also in Mexico and Cuba, and locally in northern South America. Partial migrant in the US, resident in Mexico and South America.

SIMILAR SPECIES

AMERICAN PIPIT
see p.341

more slender, shorter bill

no yellow on chest

WESTERN MEADOWLARK
see p.387

slightly paler

more yellow at corner of bill

| Length **7–10in (18–25cm)** | Wingspan **13–15in (33–38cm)** | Weight **2⅛–4oz (60–125g)** |
| Social **Pairs/Winter flocks** | Lifespan **Up to 9 years** | Status **Declining** |

DATE SEEN	WHERE	NOTES

| Order **Passeriformes** | Family **Icteridae** | Species *Sturnella neglecta* |

Western Meadowlark 🔊

ADULT

short wings

yellow throat

IN FLIGHT

white outer tail feathers

duller pattern than breeding bird

ADULT (NONBREEDING)

yellow patch between bill and eye

long, pointed bill

blackish brown stripe behind eye

chunky body

black "V" on yellow chest

black spots and streaks on sides and flanks

yellow underparts

ADULT (BREEDING)

short, wide tail

long toes

FLIGHT: several rapid wingbeats followed by a short glide.

The Western Meadowlark is one of the most abundant and widespread grassland birds in North America. It inhabits open country in the western Great Plains, the Great Basin, and the Central Valley of California It is frequently encountered along roadsides, singing its melodious song from atop a fencepost or utility pole. Although the range of the Western Meadowlark overlaps widely with that of its Eastern counterpart, hybrids between the two species are very rare and usually sterile.

VOICE Series of complex, bubbling, whistled notes descending in pitch.

NESTING Domed grass cup, well hidden in tall grasses; 3–7 eggs; 1 brood; March–August.

FEEDING Feeds mostly on insects, including beetles, grubs, and grasshoppers; also grains and grass seeds.

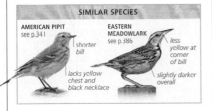

SIMILAR SPECIES

AMERICAN PIPIT
see p.341

shorter bill

lacks yellow chest and black necklace

EASTERN MEADOWLARK
see p.386

less yellow at corner of bill

slightly darker overall

A SHRUB WILL DO
In spring and summer male Western Meadowlarks can be seen perching on shrubs to sing.

OCCURRENCE
Common in western North America, across much of southern Canada and the western US, south to Mexico. Breeds primarily in open grassy plains, but also uses agricultural fields with overgrown edges and hayfields. Partial migrant in US, winters south to Mexico.

| Length **7–10in (18–26cm)** | Wingspan **13–15in (33–38cm)** | Weight **2⅞–4oz (80–125g)** |
| Social **Pairs/Winter flocks** | Lifespan **Up to 10 years** | Status **Secure** |

DATE SEEN	WHERE	NOTES

| Order **Passeriformes** | Family **Icteridae** | Species ***Icterus spurius*** |

Orchard Oriole 🔊

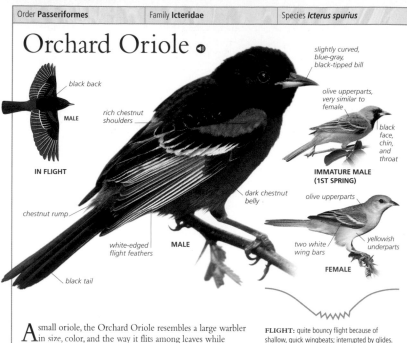

IN FLIGHT

black back

MALE

rich chestnut shoulders

slightly curved, blue-gray, black-tipped bill

olive upperparts, very similar to female

black face, chin, and throat

IMMATURE MALE (1ST SPRING)

chestnut rump

white-edged flight feathers

dark chestnut belly

MALE

black tail

olive upperparts

two white wing bars

yellowish underparts

FEMALE

A small oriole, the Orchard Oriole resembles a large warbler in size, color, and the way it flits among leaves while foraging for insects. It flutters its tail, unlike other orioles. It spends less time on the breeding grounds than other migrant orioles, often arriving there as late as mid-May and leaving as early as late-July. The Orchard Oriole tolerates humans and can be found breeding in suburban parks and gardens. In recent years, its numbers have increased in the eastern part of its range.
VOICE Fast, not very melodious, series of high warbling notes mixed with occasional shorter notes ending in slurred *shheere*.
NESTING Woven nest of grass suspended in fork between branches; 4–5 eggs; 1 brood; April–July.
FEEDING Mainly eats insects during breeding season, but will also feed on seeds, fruit, and occasionally, nectar; in winter, mostly fruit and nectar, and some insects.

FLIGHT: quite bouncy flight because of shallow, quick wingbeats; interrupted by glides.

CHESTNUT SPLASH
The male Orchard Oriole has distinctive black upperparts and rich chestnut underparts.

SIMILAR SPECIES

SCOTT'S ORIOLE
see p.468

yellow shoulder

bright yellow underparts

BALTIMORE ORIOLE
see p.389

black breast

orange underparts

larger overall

OCCURRENCE
Breeds in the eastern US, in open forest and woodland edges with a mixture of evergreen and deciduous trees, especially along river bottoms and in shelter belts surrounding agricultural land. Winters in Mexico, Central America, and South America.

| Length **7–8in (18–20cm)** | Wingspan **9in (23cm)** | Weight **¹¹⁄₁₆oz (20g)** |
| Social **Pairs** | Lifespan **Up to 9 years** | Status **Secure** |

DATE SEEN	WHERE	NOTES

Order **Passeriformes**	Family **Icteridae**	Species *Icterus galbula*

Baltimore Oriole 🔊

black and orange tail

white-edged black wings

orange-yellow shoulder patch

MALE

IN FLIGHT

orange-yellow head

black back

MALE (1ST FALL)

black head

straight blue-gray bill

black upper breast

orange underparts

MALE

orange rump

black tail with orange outer tail feathers

yellow-olive rump

olive upperparts

pale orange underparts

two wing bars

FEMALE

The Baltimore Oriole's brilliant colors are familiar to many persons in the East because this bird is tolerant of human presence. This species originally favored the American elm for nesting, but Dutch elm disease decimated these trees. The oriole has since adapted to using sycamores, cottonwoods, and other tall trees for its nesting sites. Its ability to use suburban gardens and parks has helped expand its range to areas densely occupied by humans. The Baltimore Oriole is Maryland's State Bird, somewhat ironically.
VOICE Loud, clear, melodious song comprising one or two, or several short notes in series, often of varying lengths.
NESTING Round-bottomed basket usually woven of grass, hung toward the end of branches; 4–5 eggs, 1 brood; May–July.
FEEDING Hops or flits among leaves and branches picking insects and spiders; fond of caterpillars; also eats fruit and sips nectar.

FLIGHT: strong with rapid wingbeats; full downstrokes during flight provide great power.

PERFECT FOR FORAGING
The Baltimore Oriole forages alone in dense foliage of trees and bushes or on the ground.

SIMILAR SPECIES

ORCHARD ORIOLE see p.388
darker overall
chestnut-colored belly

BULLOCK'S ORIOLE see p.468
incomplete black hood
black eyeline
orange cheeks
huge white patch

OCCURRENCE
Forest edges and tall, open mixed hardwoods, especially close to rivers; regularly uses forested parks, suburban and urban areas with abundant tall trees. Small numbers winter in southeastern US and Florida, but most birds move to Central and South America.

Length **8–10in (20–26cm)**	Wingspan **10–12in (26–30cm)**	Weight **1¹⁄₁₆–1¼oz (30–35g)**
Social **Solitary/Pairs**	Lifespan **Up to 11 years**	Status **Secure**

DATE SEEN	WHERE	NOTES

Order **Passeriformes**	Family **Icteridae**	Species *Agelaius phoeniceus*

Red-winged Blackbird 🔊

MALE

red and yellow "flags"

dark, grayish brown body

no clear yellow edging on red shoulder patches

dull reddish or yellowish shoulder patches

pale throat

buff to brown edging on feathers

JUVENILE (BICOLORED)

ADULT (FRESH PLUMAGE)

black outer wings

IN FLIGHT

light brown eyebrow

MALE (BICOLORED)

black eye

all-black back and tail

black eye

pointed bill

off-white underparts with dark streaks

bright red shoulder patches ("epaulettes") with yellow edge

FEMALE

MALE

FLIGHT: swift wingbeats interrupted by brief bobbing, flapping, and gliding sequences.

One of the most abundant native bird species in North America, the Red-winged Blackbird is also one of the most conspicuous in wetland habitats. The sight and sound of males singing from the tops of cattails is a sure sign that spring is near. This adaptable species migrates and roosts in flocks that may number in the millions. There are 22 subspecies, one of the most distinctive being the "Bicolored" Blackbird (*A. p. gubernator*) from Mexico.

VOICE Various brusk *chek*, *chit*, or *chet* calls; male song a *kronk-a-rhee* with a characteristic nasal, rolling and metallic "undulating" ending.

NESTING Cup of grasses and mud woven into dense standing reeds or cattails; 3–4 eggs; 1–2 broods; March–June.

FEEDING Forages for seeds and grains; largely insects when breeding.

DENSE FLOCKS
The huge flocks of Red-winged Blackbirds seen in the fall and during migration are an amazing sight.

SIMILAR SPECIES

TRICOLORED BLACKBIRD ♂

all-black body

white-edged red shoulder patches

RUSTY BLACKBIRD
see p.392

pale eye

longer tail

OCCURRENCE
Widespread across Canada and the US from Alaska to the Maritimes, and south to Mexico, Central America, and the Bahamas. Lives in wetlands, especially freshwater marshes with cattails, and also saltwater; wet meadows with tall grass and open woodlands with reeds. Migrates south in winter.

Length **7–10in (18–25cm)**	Wingspan **11–14in (28–35cm)**	Weight **1⁹⁄₁₆–2½oz (45–70g)**
Social **Flocks**	Lifespan **At least 14 years**	Status **Secure**

DATE SEEN	WHERE	NOTES

Order **Passeriformes**	Family **Icteridae**	Species **Molothrus ater**

Brown-headed Cowbird 🔊

rounded, black wings

MALE

IN FLIGHT

dull, unmarked brownish plumage

faintly streaked underparts

FEMALE

thick short bill

dull sepia-brown head

glossy greenish black back and wings

brown throat and upper breast

MALE

black toes

fairly long black tail

FLIGHT: somewhat undulating, with rapid wingbeats.

North America's most common brood parasite, the Brown-headed Cowbird was once a bird of the Great Plains, following the vast herds of bison to feed on insects kicked up by their hooves. Now, most likely as a result of forest clearance and suburban development, it is found continent-wide and north to the Yukon and Canada. It has become a serious threat to the breeding success of North American songbirds. It lays its eggs in the nests of more than 220 different species, and its young are raised to fledglings by more than 140 species, including the highly endangered Kirtland's Warbler.
VOICE High-pitched, squeaky whistles and bubbling notes, *dub-dub-come-tzeee*; also various clucks and *cheks*.
NESTING No nest, lays eggs in nests of other species; a female may lay an astounding 25–55 (or more) eggs per season; April–August.
FEEDING Primarily eats grass seeds and cereal grains, but also insects when available, especially grasshoppers and beetles.

AT A FEEDER
A female Brown-headed Cowbird enjoys a snack of seeds at a suburban feeder.

SIMILAR SPECIES

BRONZED COWBIRD ♂
see p.469

red eye

glossy blue-black wings and tail

longer, thicker bill

SHINY COWBIRD ♂
see p.469

glossy purplish-black

thinner, more pointed bill

OCCURRENCE
Favors habitats modified by human activity, such as open wooded patches, low grass fields, orchards, agricultural pastures with livestock, and suburban residential areas. Widespread across North America in both Canada and the US. Eastern birds spend the winter locally, and south to central Mexico.

Length **6–8in (15–20cm)**	Wingspan **11–13in (28–33cm)**	Weight **1⁷⁄₁₆–1³⁄₄oz (40–50g)**
Social **Large flocks**	Lifespan **Up to 16 years**	Status **Secure**

DATE SEEN	WHERE	NOTES

| Order **Passeriformes** | Family **Icteridae** | Species **Euphagus carolinus** |

Rusty Blackbird 🔊

MALE (BREEDING)
long tail
short, narrow bill

yellowish eyes
gray-brown eyebrow
pale gray to rusty brown underparts

FEMALE (FALL)
rusty brown crown

purplish sheen on head
pale whitish or yellow eye

IN FLIGHT
pale eyebrow
rusty brown edging to feathers

yellowish eyes
black "mask" between eye and bill

black overall, with blue-green to greenish sheen

MALE (FALL)

MALE (BREEDING)

FLIGHT: strong, direct, with slight undulations between flapping and brief gliding.

The Rusty Blackbird is perhaps the least known of all North American blackbirds. This is mainly because it breeds in remote, inaccessible swampy areas, and is much less of a pest to agricultural operations than some of the other members of its family. Unlike most other blackbirds, the plumage on the male Rusty Blackbird changes to a dull, reddish brown during the fall—giving the species its common name. It is also during the fall migrations that this species is most easily observed, moving south in long flocks that often take several minutes to pass overhead.

VOICE Both sexes use *chuk* call during migration flights; male song a musical *too-ta-lee*.

NESTING Small bowl of branches and sticks, lined with wet plants and dry grass, usually near water; 3–5 eggs; 1 brood; May–July.

FEEDING Eats seasonally available insects, spiders, grains, seeds of trees, and fleshy fruit or berries.

WIDE OPEN
Seldom seen, the male's courtship display includes gaping and tail-spreading.

OCCURRENCE
Breeds in moist to wet forests up to the timberline in the far north from Alaska to NE Canada; but barely in the continental US (farther north than any other species of North American blackbird); winters in eastern US, in several kinds of swampy forests.

SIMILAR SPECIES

BREWER'S BLACKBIRD see p.393
purplish sheen on head
longer tail

COMMON GRACKLE see p.394
bill thicker at base
large tail

bluish sheen on head
glossy bronze body

| Length **8–10in (20–25cm)** | Wingspan **12–15in (30–38cm)** | Weight **1⁹⁄₁₆–2⁷⁄₈oz (45–80g)** |
| Social **Pairs/Winter flocks** | Lifespan **At least 9 years** | Status **Declining** |

DATE SEEN	WHERE	NOTES

Order **Passeriformes**	Family **Icteridae**	Species *Euphagus cyanocephalus*

Brewer's Blackbird 🔊

purplish sheen on head

yellow eyes

black body with greenish blue sheen

MALE

brown eyes

gray brown overall

FEMALE

stout bill

MALE

long, dark tail

IN FLIGHT

black legs and toes

FLIGHT: several wingbeats followed by short glides with shallow rise and fall pattern.

The Brewer's Blackbird, unlike the swamp loving Rusty Blackbird, seems to prefer areas disturbed by humans to natural ones throughout much of its range. It is likely that the relatively recent eastward range expansion of Brewer's Blackbird has been aided by changes in land practices. Interestingly, when the Brewer's Blackbird range overlaps with that of the Common Grackle, it wins out in rural areas, but loses out in urban areas. This species can be found feasting on waste grains left behind after the harvest.

VOICE Buzzy *tshrrep* song ascending in tone.

NESTING Bulky cup of dry grass, stem and twig framework lined with soft grasses and animal hair; 3–6 eggs; 1–2 broods; April–July.

FEEDING Forages on the ground for many species of insects during breeding season, also snails; seeds, grain, and occasional fruit in fall and winter.

BROWN-EYED BIRD
Brown eyes distinguish the female Brewer's from the yellow-eyed, female Rusty Blackbird.

SIMILAR SPECIES

RUSTY BLACKBIRD see p.392

shorter tail

COMMON GRACKLE see p.394

bill thinner at base

glossy bronze body

long, wedge-shaped tail

OCCURRENCE
Breeds and winters in open areas, readily adapting to, and preferring, disturbed areas and human developments such as parks, gardens, clear-felled forests, and fallow fields edged with dense trees or shrubs.

Length **10–12in (25–30cm)**	Wingspan **13–16in (33–41cm)**	Weight **1¾–2½oz (50–70g)**
Social **Flocks/Colonies**	Lifespan **Up to 13 years**	Status **Secure**

DATE SEEN	WHERE	NOTES

| Order **Passeriformes** | Family **Icteridae** | Species *Quiscalus quiscula* |

Common Grackle 🔊

ADULT

dark wings

IN FLIGHT

iridescent brownish bronze back

iridescent bluish purple head

pale yellow eye

long, thick bill

long V-shaped tail

MALE (BRONZED FORM)

bluish to purplish head

iridescent purplish to greenish or bluish back

MALE (PURPLE FORM)

pale eye

dull purplish bronze overall

FEMALE

This adaptable species has expanded its range rapidly in the recent past, thanks to human land clearing practices. The Common Grackle is so well suited to urban and suburban habitats that it successfully excludes other species from them. During migration and winter, Common Grackles form immense flocks, some of which may be made up of more than one million individuals. This tendency, combined with its preference for cultivated areas, has made this species an agricultural pest in some regions.

VOICE Call a low, harsh *chek*; loud song series of odd squeaks and whistles.

NESTING Small bowl in trees, with a frame of sticks filled with mud and grasses; 4–6 eggs; 1–2 broods; April–July.

FEEDING Eats beetles, flies, spiders, and worms, as well as small vertebrates; also seeds and grain, especially in nonbreeding season; an omnivore.

FLIGHT: straight, level, and direct without the up and down undulation of blackbird species.

OCCURRENCE
The Common Grackle lives in a wide variety of open woodlands, suburban woodlots, city parks, gardens, and hedgerows. It is absent west of the Great Plains. Wintering range extends south to the Gulf Coast.

HIGHLY ADAPTABLE
This grackle is comfortable near human developments, resulting in the expansion of its range.

SIMILAR SPECIES

GREAT-TAILED GRACKLE
larger; see p.396

very long, deeply wedged tail

BOAT-TAILED GRACKLE
see p.395

purplish gloss to feathers

longer tail

bluish gloss on black feathers

| Length **11–13½in (28–34cm)** | Wingspan **15–18in (38–46cm)** | Weight **3⅛–4oz (90–125g)** |
| Social **Flocks** | Lifespan **Up to 20 years** | Status **Secure** |

DATE SEEN	WHERE	NOTES

| Order **Passeriformes** | Family **Icteridae** | Species *Quiscalus major* |

Boat-tailed Grackle

round head

brown or yellow eyes

glossy blue-black overall

ADULT

long, black bill

tawny cinnamon eyebrow

dark brown upperparts

long, spread out, wedge-shaped tail

much smaller overall

FEMALE

IN FLIGHT

black wings

MALE

black legs and toes

very long tail, often spread out

FLIGHT: swift wingbeats with occasional glides, maintaining same level; no undulating pattern.

So similar to each other are the Boat-tailed Grackle and the Great-tailed Grackle that they were once thought to belong to the same species. The Boat-tailed Grackle lives in coastal marshes, but readily scavenges in nearby human settlements. In spring, females form large nesting colonies. These attract many males, but only the most dominant males succeed in mating. Their preferred breeding habitat is saltmarshes.

VOICE Long, loud, three-part series of high pitched notes, *chreeet chreeet*, followed by low growl, and finally by *shreet shreet*.

NESTING Rough cups of grass and mud, woven into standing marsh vegetation like cattails or branches of shrubs or trees; 2–5 eggs; 1–2 broods; March–June.

FEEDING Highly varied diet includes insects, crayfish, clams, seeds, fruit, fish, frogs, lizards, nestling birds; also human refuse.

PLAIN BROWN
Unlike the glossy blue-black males, females are brown, with darker wings and tail.

SIMILAR SPECIES

| **COMMON GRACKLE** see p.394 | | **GREAT-TAILED GRACKLE** see p.396 | |

paler eye

smaller overall

shorter tail

longer tail

larger overall

OCCURRENCE
Breeds along the Gulf and Atlantic Coasts of the US, and in Florida along interior waterways; resident in tidal areas of coastal marshes and their neighboring upland components; also urban and suburban, human-altered habitats. Roosts colonially in same areas in winter.

| Length **13–18in (33–46cm)** | Wingspan **16–24in (41–61cm)** | Weight **3½–8½oz (100–240g)** |
| Social **Loose colonies/Winter flocks** | Lifespan **Up to 12 years** | Status **Localized** |

DATE SEEN	WHERE	NOTES

| Order **Passeriformes** | Family **Icteridae** | Species *Quiscalus mexicanus* |

Great-tailed Grackle 🔊

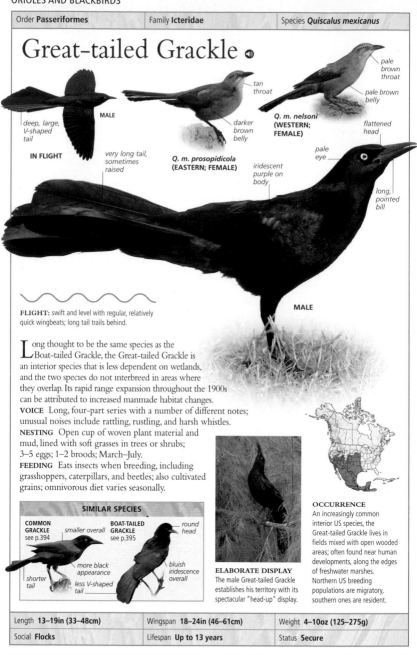

deep, large, V-shaped tail

MALE

IN FLIGHT

very long tail, sometimes raised

tan throat

darker brown belly

Q. m. prosopidicola (EASTERN; FEMALE)

pale brown throat

pale brown belly

Q. m. nelsoni (WESTERN; FEMALE)

flattened head

pale eye

iridescent purple on body

long, pointed bill

MALE

FLIGHT: swift and level with regular, relatively quick wingbeats; long tail trails behind.

Long thought to be the same species as the Boat-tailed Grackle, the Great-tailed Grackle is an interior species that is less dependent on wetlands, and the two species do not interbreed in areas where they overlap. Its rapid range expansion throughout the 1900s can be attributed to increased manmade habitat changes.
VOICE Long, four-part series with a number of different notes; unusual noises include rattling, rustling, and harsh whistles.
NESTING Open cup of woven plant material and mud, lined with soft grasses in trees or shrubs; 3–5 eggs; 1–2 broods; March–July.
FEEDING Eats insects when breeding, including grasshoppers, caterpillars, and beetles; also cultivated grains; omnivorous diet varies seasonally.

SIMILAR SPECIES

COMMON GRACKLE see p.394
smaller overall
BOAT-TAILED GRACKLE see p.395
round head
more black appearance
shorter tail
less V-shaped tail
bluish iridescence overall

ELABORATE DISPLAY
The male Great-tailed Grackle establishes his territory with its spectacular "head-up" display.

OCCURRENCE
An increasingly common interior US species, the Great-tailed Grackle lives in fields mixed with open wooded areas; often found near human developments, along the edges of freshwater marshes. Northern US breeding populations are migratory, southern ones are resident.

| Length **13–19in (33–48cm)** | Wingspan **18–24in (46–61cm)** | Weight **4–10oz (125–275g)** |
| Social **Flocks** | Lifespan **Up to 13 years** | Status **Secure** |

DATE SEEN	WHERE	NOTES

WOOD WARBLERS

THE FAMILY PARULIDAE is restricted to the Americas, and is remarkable for its diversity in plumage, song, feeding, breeding biology, and sexual dimorphism. In general, however, wood warblers share similar shapes: all are smallish, slender birds with longish, thin bills (unlike thick vireo bills) used mostly for snapping up insects. Their varied colors and patterns make the lively, busy mixed groups seen on migration especially appealing and fascinating to watch. Ground-dwelling warblers tend to be larger and clad in olives, browns, and yellows, whereas many arboreal species are smaller and sport bright oranges, cool blues, and even ruby reds. The location and presence or absence of wingbars and tail spots is often a good identification aid. Warblers are especially diverse in the East,

PLASTIC PLUMAGE
Some male *Setophaga* warblers (like this Blackburnian) are only brightly colored when breeding.

where more than 30 species may be seen in a single morning of spring birding, which may be the highlight of the year for some birdwatchers. Eastern species have three different migration routes to deal with the obstacle of the Gulf of Mexico when going to or coming from their Neotropical wintering grounds. Circum-Gulf migrants fly along the eastern shore of Mexico; Caribbean migrants travel through Florida then island-hop through the West Indies; and trans-Gulf migrants fly directly across the Gulf of Mexico, from the Yucatán Peninsula to the US Gulf Coast. Birds flying this third route are subjected to weather changes that sometimes result in spectacular fallouts at locations such as High Island, Texas.

FEEDING STRATEGIES
Some warblers, such as this Black-and-White, probe the cracks in tree trunks for food.

STATIC PLUMAGE
In other warbler species, such as this Golden-winged, males keep their stunning plumage year-round.

| Order **Passeriformes** | Family **Parulidae** | Species *Seiurus aurocapilla* |

Ovenbird 🔊

plain olive overall

ADULT

IN FLIGHT

orange-and-black striped crown

bold white eye-ring

olive upperparts

white throat

black streaked underparts

ADULT

FLIGHT: fast, slightly undulating, and direct with rapid wingbeats.

Like members of the unrelated, tropical ovenbird family (Furnariidae), this little bird is so-called for the domed, oven-like nests it builds on the ground; unique structures for a North American bird. The Ovenbird is also noted for its singing. Males flit about boisterously, often at night, incorporating portions of their main song into a jumble of spluttering notes. In the forest, one male singing loudly to declare his territory can set off a whole chain of responses from his neighbors, until the whole forest rings.

VOICE Call variably pitched, sharp *chik* in series; flight call high, rising *siiii*; song loud, ringing crescendo of paired notes *chur-tee' chur-tee' chur-tee' chur-tee' chur-TEE chur-TEE chur-TEE*.

NESTING Domed structure of leaves and grass on ground with side entrance; 3–6 eggs; 1 brood; May–July.

FEEDING Forages mainly on the forest floor for insects and other invertebrates.

STRUTTING ITS STUFF
The Ovenbird is noted for the way it struts across the forest floor, a little like a tiny chicken.

SIMILAR SPECIES

NORTHERN WATERTHRUSH much slimmer; see p.401
dark brown upperparts
no eye-ring

LOUISIANA WATERTHRUSH see p.400
white eyebrow
dark brown upperparts

OCCURRENCE
Breeds from parts of Yukon and British Columbia to the eastern US in closed-canopy mixed and deciduous forests with suitable amount of fallen plant material for nest building and foraging; migrants and wintering birds use similar habitats. Winters in Florida, Central America, and the West Indies.

| Length **6in (15cm)** | Wingspan **9½in (24cm)** | Weight **⁹⁄₁₆–⁷⁄₈oz (16–25g)** |
| Social **Solitary/Flocks** | Lifespan **Up to 7 years** | Status **Declining** |

DATE SEEN	WHERE	NOTES

| Order **Passeriformes** | Family **Parulidae** | Species *Helmitheros vermivorum* |

Worm-eating Warbler

short tail

ADULT

IN FLIGHT

dull olive overall

boldly striped buff-and-black crown

blurry pattern on undertail feathers

ADULT

large pinkish bill

tawny wash on breast

FLIGHT: fast, slightly undulating, and direct with rapid wingbeats.

Contrary to its name, the Worm-eating Warbler does not eat real worms such as earthworms. Rather, it consumes inchworms and other caterpillars. It can often be found hanging upside down, quietly prying into a mass of suspended dead leaves in search of unsuspecting prey. It specializes in probing the curled leaves that have been adopted by caterpillars as safe havens for feeding or resting, examining them carefully for potential occupants and then levering the curl open with its bill to claim its prize. Although this bird nests on the ground and tends to forage fairly low, singing males may perch quite high in trees. It is the only member of the genus *Helmitheros* and is unlike any other North American warbler, except perhaps the elusive Swainson's Warbler.

VOICE Thick *chip* call; flight call an up-slurred, thin, rolling *ziiit*, often given in series of two to three notes; song a thin, dry trill.

NESTING Well-concealed cup of leaf litter at base of sapling or shrub often on a steep hillside; 3–6 eggs; 1 brood; May–July.

FEEDING Forages in low shrubs, mainly for caterpillars, but also insects and spiders.

CAMOUFLAGED WARBLER
Worm eaters are patterned to blend in with the leaf litter of rich deciduous forests.

SIMILAR SPECIES

SWAINSON'S WARBLER see p.406

paler head

paler underparts

OCCURRENCE
Breeds locally in large expanses of hilly, rich, mature, deciduous forests with abundant leaf litter and dense undergrowth; migrants prefer similar forested habitats. Winters in Central America and the Caribbean, in varied forested habitats, but prefers dense undergrowth.

| Length **5in (13cm)** | Wingspan **8½in (21cm)** | Weight **7/16–5/8oz (12–17g)** |
| Social **Solitary/Flocks** | Lifespan **Up to 7 years** | Status **Secure** |

DATE SEEN	WHERE	NOTES

| Order **Passeriformes** | Family **Parulidae** | Species *Parkesia motacilla* |

Louisiana Waterthrush

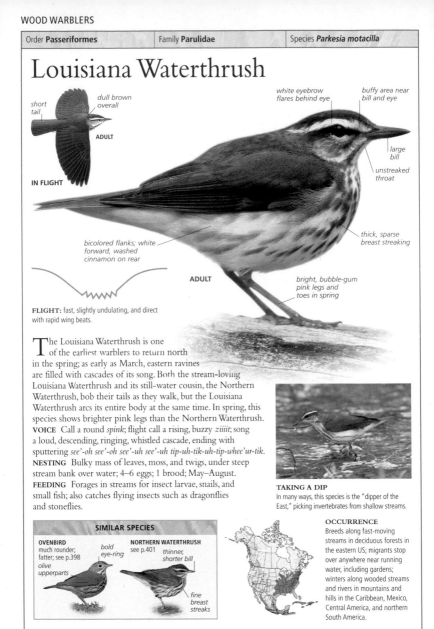

short tail

dull brown overall

ADULT

IN FLIGHT

white eyebrow flares behind eye

buffy area near bill and eye

large bill

unstreaked throat

thick, sparse breast streaking

bicolored flanks; white forward, washed cinnamon on rear

ADULT

bright, bubble-gum pink legs and toes in spring

FLIGHT: fast, slightly undulating, and direct with rapid wing beats.

The Louisiana Waterthrush is one of the earliest warblers to return north in the spring; as early as March, eastern ravines are filled with cascades of its song. Both the stream-loving Louisiana Waterthrush and its still-water cousin, the Northern Waterthrush, bob their tails as they walk, but the Louisiana Waterthrush arcs its entire body at the same time. In spring, this species shows brighter pink legs than the Northern Waterthrush.
VOICE Call a round *spink*; flight call a rising, buzzy *ziiiit*; song a loud, descending, ringing, whistled cascade, ending with sputtering *see'-oh see'-oh see'-uh see'-uh tip-uh-tik-uh-tip-whee'ur-tik*.
NESTING Bulky mass of leaves, moss, and twigs, under steep stream bank over water; 4–6 eggs; 1 brood; May–August.
FEEDING Forages in streams for insect larvae, snails, and small fish; also catches flying insects such as dragonflies and stoneflies.

TAKING A DIP
In many ways, this species is the "dipper of the East," picking invertebrates from shallow streams.

SIMILAR SPECIES

OVENBIRD
much rounder; fatter; see p.398 olive upperparts

bold eye-ring

NORTHERN WATERTHRUSH
see p.401 thinner, shorter bill

fine breast streaks

OCCURRENCE
Breeds along fast-moving streams in deciduous forests in the eastern US; migrants stop over anywhere near running water, including gardens; winters along wooded streams and rivers in mountains and hills in the Caribbean, Mexico, Central America, and northern South America.

| Length **6in (15cm)** | Wingspan **10in (25cm)** | Weight ⅝–⅞oz (18–25g) |
| Social **Solitary** | Lifespan **Up to 8 years** | Status **Secure** |

DATE SEEN	WHERE	NOTES

| Order **Passeriformes** | Family **Parulidae** | Species *Parkesia noveboracensis* |

Northern Waterthrush 🔊

pale eyebrow
narrows behind eye

dull brown
upperparts

short tail

small,
short
bill

ADULT

pale
eyebrow

fine, dense
breast
streaking

streaking
on white or
yellowish
flanks

IN FLIGHT

ADULT

dull, fleshy-colored
legs and toes

FLIGHT: fast, slightly undulating, and direct
with rapid wingbeats.

The tail-bobbing Northern Waterthrush is often
heard giving a *spink!* call as it swiftly flees from
observers. Although this species may be mistaken for the closely
related Louisiana Waterthrush, there are clues that are helpful in
its identification. While the Northern Waterthrush prefers still
water, its relative greatly prefers running water; in addition, its
song is quite unlike that of the Louisiana Waterthrush.
VOICE Call a sharp, rising, ringing *spink!*; flight call a rising,
buzzy *zuut*; song a loud series of rich, accelerating, staccato notes,
usually decreasing in pitch *teet, teet, toh-toh toh-toh tyew-tyew!*.
NESTING Hair-lined, mossy cup placed on or near ground,
hidden in roots of fallen or standing tree or in riverbank;
4–5 eggs; 1 brood; May–August.
FEEDING Mostly eats insects such as ants, mosquitoes, moths,
and beetles, both larvae and adult, plus slugs, and snails; when
migrating, also eats small crustaceans, and even tiny fish.

YELLOW FORM
Many Northern Waterthrushes have yellow
underparts, like this one, while others have white.

SIMILAR SPECIES

OVENBIRD
much rounder;
fatter; see p.398
olive
upperparts

bold
eye-ring

**LOUISIANA
WATERTHRUSH**
see p.400

eyebrow
widens behind
eye

thicker,
longer
bill

orange
wash to
flanks

OCCURRENCE
Breeds right across northern
North America in dark,
still-water swamps and bogs;
also in the still edges of rivers
and lakes; migrant birds use
wet habitats, winters in
shrubby marshes, mangroves,
and occasionally in crops, such
as rice fields and citrus groves.
Rare in Baja California in winter.

| Length **6in (15cm)** | Wingspan **9½in (24cm)** | Weight **½–⅞oz (14–23g)** |
| Social **Solitary** | Lifespan **Up to 9 years** | Status **Secure** |

DATE SEEN	WHERE	NOTES

Order **Passeriformes**	Family **Parulidae**	Species ***Vermivora chrysoptera***

Golden-winged Warbler

gray back

bright yellow wing panel

MALE

white outer tail feathers

IN FLIGHT

black "mask"

gray back suffused with yellow

unstreaked wings

bright yellow crown

black throat

yellow wing panel

white undertail

gray "mask"

FEMALE

greenish yellow crown

MALE

One of the continent's most beautiful warblers, this species is unfortunately being genetically swamped by the more southerly Blue-winged Warbler. This situation is worsening as more habitat is cleared and climate changes take place. The Golden-winged interbreeds with the Blue-winged, resulting in two more frequently seen hybrid forms: Brewster's Warbler, which resembles the Blue-winged Warbler, and Lawrence's Warbler, which looks like a Blue-winged Warbler with the mask and black throat of a Golden-winged.

VOICE Call a sharp *tsip*; flight call high, slightly buzzy *ziiih*; song buzzy *zee zuu zuu zuu*, first note higher; birds that deviate from this song pattern may be hybrids.

NESTING Shallow bulky cup, on or just above ground; 4–6 eggs; 1 brood; May–July.

FEEDING Hangs upside down at clusters of curled-up dead leaves; feeds on moth larvae, other winged insects, and spiders.

FLIGHT: typical warbler flight: fast, slightly undulating, and direct with rapid wingbeats.

SMALL TREES REQUIRED
Golden-winged Warblers breed in shrubby habitats created by clearance and re-growth.

SIMILAR SPECIES

CAROLINA CHICKADEE
see p.305
yellowish wash on underparts

black cap

BLACK-CAPPED CHICKADEE
see p.306

black cap

white cheek

buffy underparts

OCCURRENCE
Breeds in the northeastern US and southern Canada in secondary growth habitat with dense patches of deciduous shrubs or tangles, or in marshes with a forest edge; uses any wooded habitat on migration; winters in Central America from Guatemala to northern Colombia; mostly along the Caribbean.

Length **4¾in (12cm)**	Wingspan **7½in (19cm)**	Weight **⁹⁄₃₂–³⁄₈oz (8–11g)**
Social **Migrant/Winter flocks**	Lifespan **Unknown**	Status **Declining**

DATE SEEN	WHERE	NOTES

| Order **Passeriformes** | Family **Parulidae** | Species *Vermivora cyanoptera* |

Blue-winged Warbler 🔊

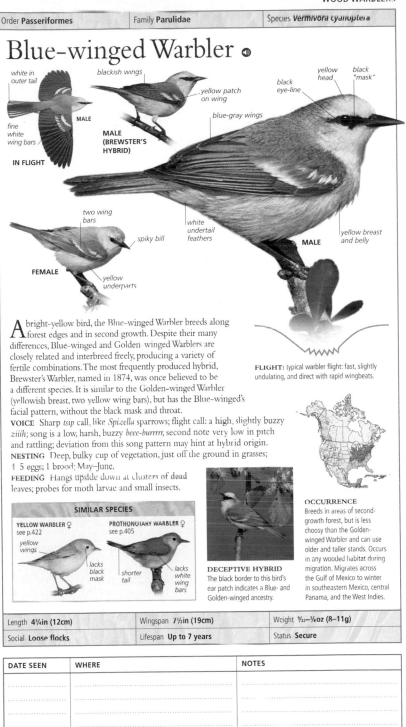

white in outer tail

blackish wings

MALE

yellow patch on wing

blue-gray wings

yellow head

black "mask"

black eye-line

fine white wing bars

MALE (BREWSTER'S HYBRID)

IN FLIGHT

two wing bars

spiky bill

white undertail feathers

MALE

yellow breast and belly

FEMALE

yellow underparts

A bright-yellow bird, the Blue-winged Warbler breeds along forest edges and in second growth. Despite their many differences, Blue-winged and Golden-winged Warblers are closely related and interbreed freely, producing a variety of fertile combinations. The most frequently produced hybrid, Brewster's Warbler, named in 1874, was once believed to be a different species. It is similar to the Golden-winged Warbler (yellowish breast, two yellow wing bars), but has the Blue-winged's facial pattern, without the black mask and throat.

VOICE Sharp *tsip* call, like *Spizella* sparrows; flight call: a high, slightly buzzy *ziiih*; song is a low, harsh, buzzy *beee-burrrrr*, second note very low in pitch and rattling; deviation from this song pattern may hint at hybrid origin.

NESTING Deep, bulky cup of vegetation, just off the ground in grasses; 4–5 eggs; 1 brood; May–June.

FEEDING Hangs upside down at clusters of dead leaves; probes for moth larvae and small insects.

FLIGHT: typical warbler flight: fast, slightly undulating, and direct with rapid wingbeats.

SIMILAR SPECIES

YELLOW WARBLER ♀ see p.422

yellow wings

lacks black mask

PROTHONOTARY WARBLER ♀ see p.405

shorter tail

lacks white wing bars

DECEPTIVE HYBRID The black border to this bird's ear patch indicates a Blue- and Golden-winged ancestry.

OCCURRENCE Breeds in areas of second-growth forest, but is less choosy than the Golden-winged Warbler and can use older and taller stands. Occurs in any wooded habitat during migration. Migrates across the Gulf of Mexico to winter in southeastern Mexico, central Panama, and the West Indies.

| Length **4¾in (12cm)** | Wingspan **7½in (19cm)** | Weight **⁹⁄₃₂–³⁄₈oz (8–11g)** |
| Social **Loose flocks** | Lifespan **Up to 7 years** | Status **Secure** |

DATE SEEN	WHERE	NOTES

| Order **Passeriformes** | Family **Parulidae** | Species *Mniotilta varia* |

Black-and-white Warbler 🔊

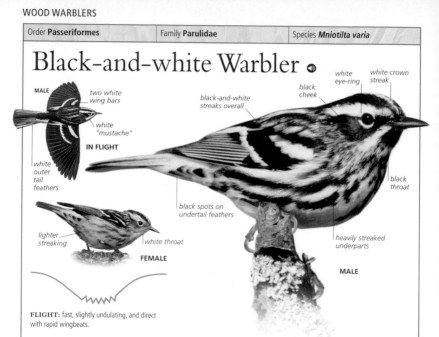

MALE

two white wing bars

white "mustache"

IN FLIGHT

white outer tail feathers

black-and-white streaks overall

white eye-ring

black cheek

white crown streak

black throat

black spots on undertail feathers

heavily streaked underparts

MALE

lighter streaking

white throat

FEMALE

FLIGHT: fast, slightly undulating, and direct with rapid wingbeats.

The Black-and-white Warbler is best known for its creeper-like habit of feeding in vertical and upside-down positions as it pries into bark crevices, where its relatively long, curved bill allows it to reach into tiny nooks and crannies. These habits, combined with a streaked plumage, make this bird one of the most distinctive warblers in North America. It is a long-distance migrant, with some birds wintering in parts of northern South America.

VOICE Sharp *stik* call; flight call a very high, thin *ssiit*, often doubled; song a thin, high-pitched, wheezy series *wheesy wheesy wheesy wheesy wheesy wheesy*.

NESTING Cup on ground against stump, fallen logs, or roots; 4–6 eggs; 1 brood; April–August.

FEEDING Creeps along branches and trunks, probing into bark for insects and insect larvae.

SQUEAKY WHEEL
The high-pitched, wheezy song of this warbler is said to be reminiscent of a squeaky wheel.

UPSIDE DOWN
Black-and-white Warblers often creep head-first along trunks and branches of trees.

OCCURRENCE
Breeds in deciduous and mixed mature and second-growth woodlands; migrants occur on a greater variety of habitats; winters in a wide range of wooded habitats in southern US, Mexico and into Central and South America. Rare along West Coast in winter.

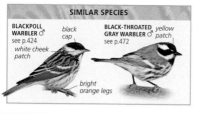

SIMILAR SPECIES

BLACKPOLL WARBLER ♂
see p.424

black cap

white cheek patch

BLACK-THROATED GRAY WARBLER ♂
see p.472

yellow patch

bright orange legs

| Length **5in (13cm)** | Wingspan **8in (20cm)** | Weight **⁵⁄₁₆–¹⁄₂oz (9–14g)** |
| Social **Migrant/Winter flocks** | Lifespan **Up to 11 years** | Status **Secure** |

DATE SEEN	WHERE	NOTES

| Order **Passeriformes** | Family **Parulidae** | Species *Protonotaria citrea* |

Prothonotary Warbler

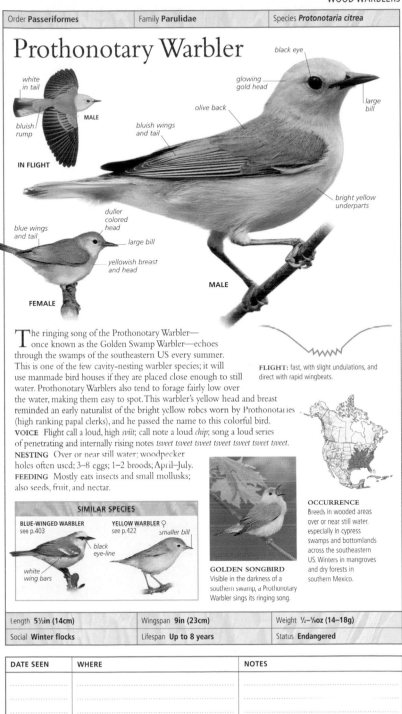

IN FLIGHT

white in tail

bluish rump

MALE

black eye

glowing gold head

olive back

bluish wings and tail

large bill

bright yellow underparts

MALE

FEMALE

duller colored head

blue wings and tail

large bill

yellowish breast and head

The ringing song of the Prothonotary Warbler—once known as the Golden Swamp Warbler—echoes through the swamps of the southeastern US every summer. This is one of the few cavity-nesting warbler species; it will use manmade bird houses if they are placed close enough to still water. Prothonotary Warblers also tend to forage fairly low over the water, making them easy to spot. This warbler's yellow head and breast reminded an early naturalist of the bright yellow robes worn by Prothonotaries (high ranking papal clerks), and he passed the name to this colorful bird.

VOICE Flight call a loud, high *sviit*; call note a loud *chip*; song a loud series of penetrating and internally rising notes *tsveet tsveet tsveet tsveet tsveet tsveet tsveet*.

NESTING Over or near still water; woodpecker holes often used; 3–8 eggs; 1–2 broods; April–July.

FEEDING Mostly eats insects and small mollusks; also seeds, fruit, and nectar.

FLIGHT: fast, with slight undulations, and direct with rapid wingbeats.

GOLDEN SONGBIRD
Visible in the darkness of a southern swamp, a Prothonotary Warbler sings its ringing song.

OCCURRENCE
Breeds in wooded areas over or near still water, especially in cypress swamps and bottomlands across the southeastern US. Winters in mangroves and dry forests in southern Mexico.

SIMILAR SPECIES

BLUE-WINGED WARBLER
see p.403

black eye-line

white wing bars

YELLOW WARBLER ♀
see p.422

smaller bill

| Length **5⅓in (14cm)** | Wingspan **9in (23cm)** | Weight **½–⅝oz (14–18g)** |
| Social **Winter flocks** | Lifespan **Up to 8 years** | Status **Endangered** |

DATE SEEN	WHERE	NOTES

Order **Passeriformes**	Family **Parulidae**	Species *Limnothlypis swainsonii*

Swainson's Warbler

short tail

ADULT

IN FLIGHT

rusty-brown crown

pale eyebrow

plain brown upperparts

long bill

dusky wash on underparts

ADULT

FLIGHT: fast, slightly undulating, and direct with rapid wingbeats.

Few people ever get to see Swainson's Warbler—not even those enthusiasts who regularly go looking for it. The species' remarkable song makes it relatively easy to track, but its reclusive nature, drab plumage, and liking for dense thickets make it one of the most difficult birds in North America to actually spot. The species is also quite unusual in that it has two seemingly identical populations that breed in distinct habitats—one in dense, giant canebreaks in swampy lowlands, and the other in Appalachian rhododendron or mountain laurel thickets.
VOICE Flight call high *siiii*, often doubled; song loud series of down-slurred whistles ending emphatically and purposefully *su see-a see-oh WEE-chuh WEE-oh*.
NESTING Bulky mass of vegetation placed low in dense understory thicket; 2–5 eggs; 1 brood; May–July.
FEEDING Forages slowly and methodically on the forest floor for insects, insect larvae, and spiders.

PROUD SURVEYOR
A male Swainson's Warbler surveys his breeding territory from the vantage of a perch.

SIMILAR SPECIES

WORM-EATING WARBLER see p.399

black head stripe

buff underparts

black eyebrow

LOUISIANA WATERTHRUSH see p.400

dark gray crown

bold streaks below

OCCURRENCE
Breeds in floodplains, often in areas of dense undergrowth, and in mountain forests with suitable undergrowth; during migration and in winter found in forests with dense understory and abundant leaf litter. Winters in Central America and the West Indies.

Length **5½in (14cm)**	Wingspan **9in (23cm)**	Weight **⁷⁄₁₆–¹¹⁄₁₆oz (12–20g)**
Social **Solitary/Winter flocks**	Lifespan **Up to 7 years**	Status **Declining**

DATE SEEN	WHERE	NOTES

Order **Passeriformes**	Family **Parulidae**	Species *Leiothlypis peregrina*

Tennessee Warbler

gray head
white eyestripe

MALE (BREEDING)

IN FLIGHT

olive-green upperparts

olive-gray head

whitish belly

FEMALE

blue-gray crown

spiky bill

olive back and wings

grayish white underparts

MALE (BREEDING)

olive-gray back

yellowish throat and breast

white undertail feathers

MALE (FALL)

The Tennessee Warbler was named on the basis of a specimen found in that state on migration, as this species breeds almost entirely in Canada and winters in Central America. These warblers inhabit fairly remote areas and their nests are difficult to find. It is one of a number of species that takes advantage of outbreaks of spruce budworms (actually tortricid moths); their populations tend to increase in years when budworms themselves increase.

VOICE Call a sharp *tzit*; flight call a thin slightly rolling *seet*; song usually three-part staccato series, *chip-chip-chip*, each series increasing in pitch and usually in tempo.

NESTING Nest woven of fine plant matter, in ground depression, concealed from above by shrubbery; 4–7 eggs; 1 brood; June.

FEEDING Searches outer branches of trees for caterpillars, bees, wasps, beetles, and spiders; also eats fruit in winter and drinks nectar by piercing base of flowers.

FLIGHT: fast, slightly undulating, and direct with rapid wingbeats.

UNIQUE UNDERPARTS
The breeding male is the only North American wood warbler with unmarked grayish white underparts.

SIMILAR SPECIES

PHILADELPHIA VIREO
see p.287

white eyebrow

yellowish underparts

ORANGE-CROWNED WARBLER
see p.408

shorter wings

greenish yellow rump

muted markings

OCCURRENCE
Breeds in a variety of habitats, especially woodlands with dense understory and thickets of willows and alders. Very common in suburban parks and gardens during migration, particularly in the Midwest. Winters from southern Mexico to northern Ecuador and northern Venezuela; also Cuba.

Length **4¾in (12cm)**	Wingspan **7¾in (19.5cm)**	Weight **⁹⁄₃₂–⁵⁄₈oz (8–17g)**
Social **Flocks**	Lifespan **Up to 6 years**	Status **Secure**

DATE SEEN	WHERE	NOTES

Order **Passeriformes**	Family **Parulidae**	Species *Leiothlypis celata*

Orange-crowned Warbler

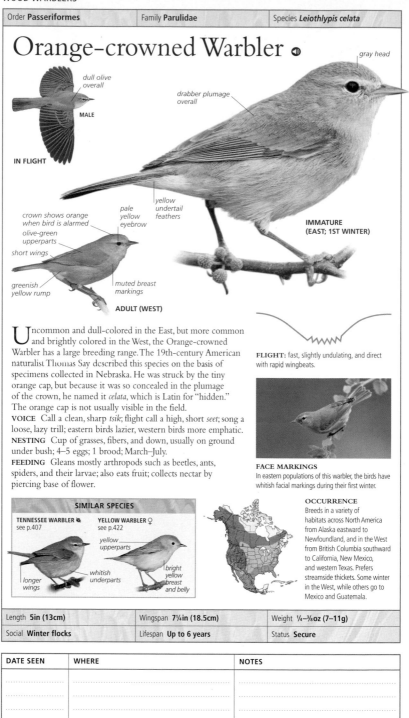

gray head

dull olive overall

MALE

IN FLIGHT

drabber plumage overall

IMMATURE (EAST; 1ST WINTER)

yellow undertail feathers

pale yellow eyebrow

crown shows orange when bird is alarmed

olive-green upperparts

short wings

greenish yellow rump

muted breast markings

ADULT (WEST)

Uncommon and dull-colored in the East, but more common and brightly colored in the West, the Orange-crowned Warbler has a large breeding range. The 19th-century American naturalist Thomas Say described this species on the basis of specimens collected in Nebraska. He was struck by the tiny orange cap, but because it was so concealed in the plumage of the crown, he named it *celata*, which is Latin for "hidden." The orange cap is not usually visible in the field.

VOICE Call a clean, sharp *tsik*; flight call a high, short *seet*; song a loose, lazy trill; eastern birds lazier, western birds more emphatic.
NESTING Cup of grasses, fibers, and down, usually on ground under bush; 4–5 eggs; 1 brood; March–July.
FEEDING Gleans mostly arthropods such as beetles, ants, spiders, and their larvae; also eats fruit; collects nectar by piercing base of flower.

FLIGHT: fast, slightly undulating, and direct with rapid wingbeats.

FACE MARKINGS
In eastern populations of this warbler, the birds have whitish facial markings during their first winter.

SIMILAR SPECIES		
TENNESSEE WARBLER see p.407	**YELLOW WARBLER** ♀ see p.422	

yellow upperparts

longer wings

whitish underparts

bright yellow breast and belly

OCCURRENCE
Breeds in a variety of habitats across North America from Alaska eastward to Newfoundland, and in the West from British Columbia southward to California, New Mexico, and western Texas. Prefers streamside thickets. Some winter in the West, while others go to Mexico and Guatemala.

Length **5in (13cm)**	Wingspan **7¼in (18.5cm)**	Weight **¼–⅜oz (7–11g)**
Social **Winter flocks**	Lifespan **Up to 6 years**	Status **Secure**

DATE SEEN	WHERE	NOTES

| Order **Passeriformes** | Family **Parulidae** | Species *Leiothlypis ruficapilla* |

Nashville Warbler 🔊

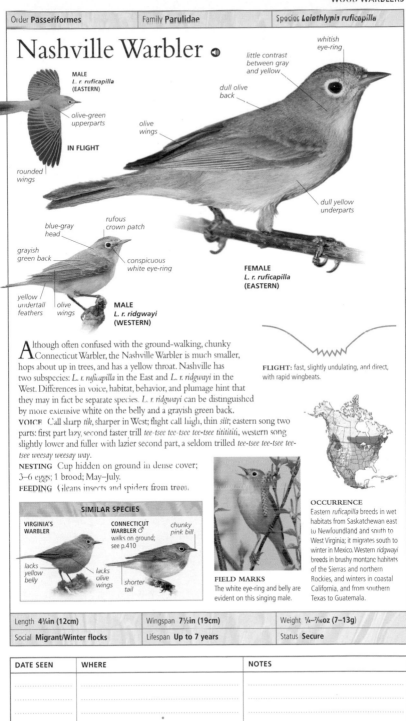

MALE
L. r. ruficapilla
(EASTERN)

olive-green
upperparts

IN FLIGHT

rounded
wings

whitish
eye-ring

little contrast
between gray
and yellow

dull olive
back

olive
wings

dull yellow
underparts

blue-gray
head

rufous
crown patch

grayish
green back

conspicuous
white eye-ring

yellow
undertail
feathers

olive
wings

MALE
L. r. ridgwayi
(WESTERN)

FEMALE
L. r. ruficapilla
(EASTERN)

Although often confused with the ground-walking, chunky Connecticut Warbler, the Nashville Warbler is much smaller, hops about up in trees, and has a yellow throat. Nashville has two subspecies: *L. r. ruficapilla* in the East and *L. r. ridgwayi* in the West. Differences in voice, habitat, behavior, and plumage hint that they may in fact be separate species. *L. r. ridgwayi* can be distinguished by more extensive white on the belly and a grayish green back.

VOICE Call sharp *tik*, sharper in West; flight call high, thin *siit*; eastern song two parts: first part lazy, second faster trill *tee-tsee tee-tsee tee-tsee titititiii*, western song slightly lower and fuller with lazier second part, a seldom trilled *tee-tsee tee-tsee tee-tsee weesay weesay way*.
NESTING Cup hidden on ground in dense cover; 3–6 eggs; 1 brood; May–July.
FEEDING Gleans insects and spiders from trees.

FLIGHT: fast, slightly undulating, and direct, with rapid wingbeats.

OCCURRENCE
Eastern *ruficapilla* breeds in wet habitats from Saskatchewan east to Newfoundland and south to West Virginia; it migrates south to winter in Mexico. Western *ridgwayi* breeds in brushy montane habitats of the Sierras and northern Rockies, and winters in coastal California, and from southern Texas to Guatemala.

SIMILAR SPECIES

VIRGINIA'S WARBLER

CONNECTICUT WARBLER ♂
walks on ground;
see p.410

chunky
pink bill

lacks
yellow
belly

lacks
olive
wings

shorter
tail

FIELD MARKS
The white eye-ring and belly are evident on this singing male.

| Length **4¾in (12cm)** | Wingspan **7½in (19cm)** | Weight **¼–⁷⁄₁₆oz (7–13g)** |
| Social **Migrant/Winter flocks** | Lifespan **Up to 7 years** | Status **Secure** |

DATE SEEN	WHERE	NOTES

Order **Passeriformes**	Family **Parulidae**	Species *Oporornis agilis*

Connecticut Warbler

olive upperparts

grayish green hood

FEMALE

olive flanks

MALE

IN FLIGHT

very long, yellow undertail feathers

gray hood

conspicuous white eye-ring

olive upperparts

short tail

MALE

dark gray bib

pale sunshine-yellow underparts

pink legs and toes

FLIGHT: fast, slightly undulating, and direct with rapid wingbeats.

The shy Connecticut Warbler, which incidentally does not breed in Connecticut—it breeds in remote, boggy habitats in Canada and is hard to spot during its spring and fall migrations. It arrives in the US in late May and leaves its breeding grounds in August. It is the only warbler that walks along the ground in a bouncy manner, with its tail bobbing up and down.

VOICE Seldom-heard call a nasal *champ*, flight call a buzzy *ziiiit*; song a loud "whippy," accelerating series, often ending with upward inflection *tweet, chuh WHIP-uh chee-uh-WHIP-uh chee-uh-WAY*.

NESTING Concealed cup of grass or leaves, lined with fine plant matter and hair; placed near or on ground in damp moss or grass clump; 3–5 eggs; 1 brood; June–July.

FEEDING Gleans a variety of adult insects, insect larvae, and spiders from under leaves; also eats small fruit.

EXCEPTIONAL UNDERTAIL
The yellow undertail feathers nearly reach the tip of the Connecticut Warbler's tail.

SIMILAR SPECIES

NASHVILLE WARBLER ♀
see p.409

MOURNING WARBLER ♂
see p.411

darker breast patch

pale gray back

yellowish throat

OCCURRENCE
Breeds across Canada from British Columbia to Québec and in the US in Minnesota and the Great Lakes region, in bogs and pine forests. Winters in forest habitats of Amazonian Peru and Brazil.

Length **6in (15cm)**	Wingspan **9in (23cm)**	Weight **⁷⁄₁₆–¹¹⁄₁₆oz (13–20g)**
Social **Solitary**	Lifespan **Up to 4 years**	Status **Secure (p)**

DATE SEEN	WHERE	NOTES

Order **Passeriformes**	Family **Parulidae**	Species *Geothlypis philadelphia*

Mourning Warbler

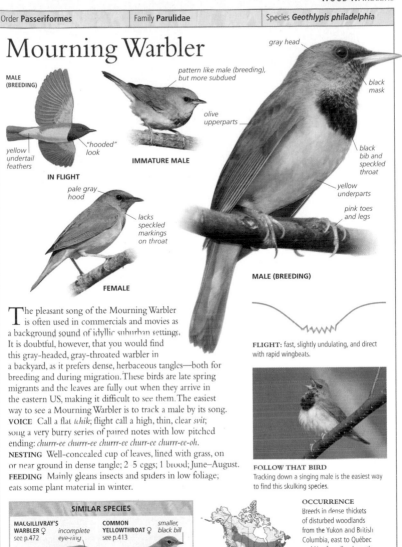

MALE (BREEDING)

gray head

black mask

black bib and speckled throat

yellow underparts

pink toes and legs

MALE (BREEDING)

pattern like male (breeding), but more subdued

olive upperparts

IMMATURE MALE

yellow undertail feathers

"hooded" look

IN FLIGHT

pale gray hood

lacks speckled markings on throat

FEMALE

The pleasant song of the Mourning Warbler is often used in commercials and movies as a background sound of idyllic suburban settings. It is doubtful, however, that you would find this gray-headed, gray-throated warbler in a backyard, as it prefers dense, herbaceous tangles—both for breeding and during migration. These birds are late spring migrants and the leaves are fully out when they arrive in the eastern US, making it difficult to see them. The easiest way to see a Mourning Warbler is to track a male by its song.
VOICE Call a flat *whik*; flight call a high, thin, clear *svit*; song a very bury series of paired notes with low pitched ending: *churrr-ee churrr-ee churrr-ee churr-ee churrr-ee-oh*.
NESTING Well-concealed cup of leaves, lined with grass, on or near ground in dense tangle; 2–5 eggs; 1 brood; June–August.
FEEDING Mainly gleans insects and spiders in low foliage; eats some plant material in winter.

FLIGHT: fast, slightly undulating, and direct with rapid wingbeats.

FOLLOW THAT BIRD
Tracking down a singing male is the easiest way to find this skulking species.

SIMILAR SPECIES

MACGILLIVRAY'S WARBLER ♀ see p.472 — incomplete eye-ring — longer tail

COMMON YELLOWTHROAT ♀ see p.413 — smaller, black bill — longer tail

OCCURRENCE
Breeds in dense thickets of disturbed woodlands from the Yukon and British Columbia, east to Québec and Newfoundland, south to the Great Lakes, New England, New York, and the Appalachians. Winters in dense thickets in Central and South America.

Length **5in (13cm)**	Wingspan **7.5in (19cm)**	Weight **⅜–⁷⁄₁₆oz (10–13g)**
Social **Solitary**	Lifespan **Up to 8 years**	Status **Secure**

DATE SEEN	WHERE	NOTES

Order **Passeriformes**	Family **Parulidae**	Species *Geothlypis formosa*

Kentucky Warbler

black crown
with gray spots

black-and-yellow facial pattern

yellow streak above eyes

black cheek

dark olive upperparts

ADULT

short tail

IN FLIGHT

yellow chin and throat

ADULT

bright yellow underparts

pale pinkish legs and toes

pale olive upperparts

less black on face

FEMALE

FLIGHT: fast, slightly undulating, and direct with rapid wingbeats.

The loud and cheery song of the Kentucky Warbler is one of the characteristic sounds of dense, moist eastern US forests. Unlike the Connecticut Warbler, it is appropriately named, because it actually breeds in its namesake state, Kentucky. This is a rather secretive species. It forages close to or on the ground, looking for insects that live on the forest floor.

VOICE Call a low, hollow *chup*, flight call a buzzy *dziiip*; song a loud rolling series of paired notes *chur-ee' chur-ee' chur-ee' chur-ee' chur-ee'*, with little variation.

NESTING Concealed bulky cup of leaves and grass on or just above ground in shrub; 4–5 eggs; 1–2 broods; May–August.

FEEDING Gleans beetles, spiders, and other arthropods, mainly in low vegetation.

LUCKY SHOT
This bird is mostly seen in the forest understory, not out in the open like this migrant.

SIMILAR SPECIES

COMMON YELLOWTHROAT ♂
smaller; see p.413

longer tail

black-and-gray face

HOODED WARBLER ♀
see p.414

longer tail

greenish crown

plain, yellow face

OCCURRENCE
Breeds in eastern US moist, deciduous forests with dense understory. Migrants prefer woodlands and thickets. Winters from Mexico to Panama and northern South America.

Length **5in (13cm)**	Wingspan **8½in (21cm)**	Weight **7/16–11/16oz (12–19g)**
Social **Solitary/Flocks**	Lifespan **Up to 7 years**	Status **Declining**

DATE SEEN	WHERE	NOTES

Order **Passeriformes**	Family **Parulidae**	Species *Geothlypis trichas*

Common Yellowthroat 🔊

plain, olive-green overall

olive upperparts

pale eye-ring

pale stripe over "mask," varies from gray to white or yellowish

black "mask" including forehead

black mask

yellow throat

olive-green upperparts

MALE

FEMALE

IN FLIGHT

olive-green tail

yellow throat

greenish gray underparts

MALE

FLIGHT: fast, slightly undulating, and direct with rapid wingbeats.

This common and easy-to-see warbler is noticeable partly because of its loud, simple song. This species varies in voice and plumage across its range and 14 subspecies have been described. In the western US, the birds have yellower underparts, brighter white head stripes, and louder, simpler songs than eastern birds. The male often flies upward rapidly, delivering a more complex version of its otherwise simple song.
VOICE Call a harsh, buzzy *tchak*, repeated into chatter when agitated; flight call a low, flat, buzzy *dzzzit*; song a variable but distinctive series of rich (often 3-note) phrases: *WITCH-uh-tee WITCH-uh-tee WITCH-uh-tee WHICH*; more complex flight song.
NESTING Concealed, bulky cup of grasses just above ground or water; 3–5 eggs; 1 brood; May–August.
FEEDING Eats insects and spiders in low vegetation; also seeds.

UNFORGETTABLE CALL
The song of the male Common Yellowthroat is an extremely helpful aid in its identification.

SIMILAR SPECIES

KENTUCKY WARBLER ♂ much larger; see p.412

yellow eyebrow

bright yellow belly

shorter tail

MOURNING WARBLER ♀ see p.411

gray head

pink-based bill

bright yellow on belly

OCCURRENCE
Found south of the tundra, from Alaska and the Yukon to Québec and Newfoundland, and south to California, Texas, and to southeastern US. Inhabits dense herbaceous understory, from marshes and grasslands to pine forest and hedgerows. Winters from Mexico to Panama and the Antilles.

Length **5in (13cm)**	Wingspan **6¾in (17cm)**	Weight **29oz (825g)**
Social **Migrant/Winter flocks**	Lifespan **Up to 11 years**	Status **Secure**

DATE SEEN	WHERE	NOTES

| Order **Passeriformes** | Family **Parulidae** | Species *Setophaga citrina* |

Hooded Warbler

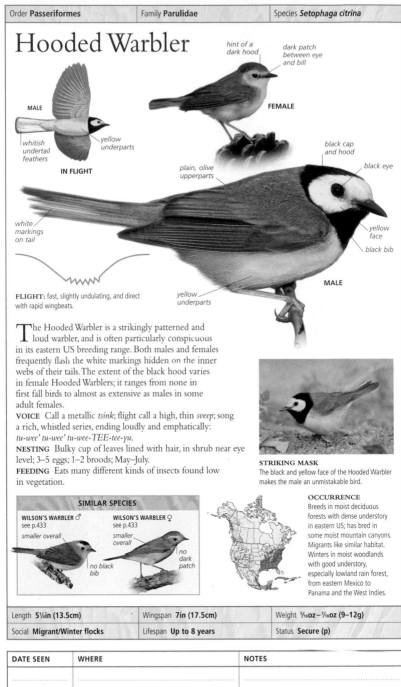

hint of a dark hood

dark patch between eye and bill

FEMALE

MALE

whitish undertail feathers

yellow underparts

IN FLIGHT

plain, olive upperparts

white markings on tail

black cap and hood

black eye

yellow face

black bib

MALE

FLIGHT: fast, slightly undulating, and direct with rapid wingbeats.

yellow underparts

The Hooded Warbler is a strikingly patterned and loud warbler, and is often particularly conspicuous in its eastern US breeding range. Both males and females frequently flash the white markings hidden on the inner webs of their tails. The extent of the black hood varies in female Hooded Warblers; it ranges from none in first fall birds to almost as extensive as males in some adult females.

VOICE Call a metallic *tsink*; flight call a high, thin *sweep*; song a rich, whistled series, ending loudly and emphatically: *tu-wee' tu-wee' tu-wee-TEE-tee-yu.*

NESTING Bulky cup of leaves lined with hair, in shrub near eye level; 3–5 eggs; 1–2 broods; May–July.

FEEDING Eats many different kinds of insects found low in vegetation.

STRIKING MASK
The black and yellow face of the Hooded Warbler makes the male an unmistakable bird.

SIMILAR SPECIES

WILSON'S WARBLER ♂
see p.433
smaller overall

WILSON'S WARBLER ♀
see p.433
smaller overall

no black bib

no dark patch

OCCURRENCE
Breeds in moist deciduous forests with dense understory in eastern US; has bred in some moist mountain canyons. Migrants like similar habitat. Winters in moist woodlands with good understory, especially lowland rain forest, from eastern Mexico to Panama and the West Indies.

| Length **5¼in (13.5cm)** | Wingspan **7in (17.5cm)** | Weight **⁵⁄₁₆oz–⁷⁄₁₆oz (9–12g)** |
| Social **Migrant/Winter flocks** | Lifespan **Up to 8 years** | Status **Secure (p)** |

DATE SEEN	WHERE	NOTES

| Order **Passeriformes** | Family **Parulidae** | Species *Setophaga ruticilla* |

American Redstart 🔊

MALE
- conspicuous orange wing bar

grayish head

olive back

IN FLIGHT

yellow tail base
yellowish flanks

whitish underparts

FEMALE

black inverted "T" on tail

long, black tail with orange on sides

black head and back

yellow tail base

blackish smudge on undertail

orange flank patch with black border

yellow flanks

irregular, dark patches

white belly

IMMATURE MALE

MALE

The American Redstart is a vividly colored, energetic and acrobatic warbler with a reasonably broad range across North America. One of its behavioral quirks is to fan its tail and wings while foraging, supposedly using the flashes of bold color to scare insects into moving, making them easy prey. It possesses well-developed rictal bristles, hair-like feathers extending from the corners of the mouth, which help it to detect insects.

VOICE Harsh *tsiip* call; flight call a high, thin *sweep*; song a confusingly variable, high, thin, yet penetrating series of notes; one version burry, emphatic, and down-slurred *see-a see-a see-a see a ZEE-urrrr*.

NESTING Cup of grasses and rootlets, lined with feathers; placed low in deciduous tree; 2–5 eggs; 1–2 broods; May–July.

FEEDING Gleans insects and spiders from leaves at mid-levels in trees; also catches moths, flies in flight; will also eat fruit.

FLIGHT: fast, slightly undulating, and direct with rapid wingbeats.

COMMON SONG
This bird's short, ringing song is a common sound in the moist deciduous woods of the East and North.

MALE CAREGIVER
As with most warblers, male Redstarts help raise the young, though they may be polygamous.

OCCURRENCE
Breeds in moist deciduous and mixed woodlands across North America; migrants and wintering birds use a wide range of habitats. Winters from Baja California and south Florida through Middle America and the Caribbean to northern South America.

Length **5in (13cm)**	Wingspan **8in (20cm)**	Weight ⁷⁄₃₂–³⁄₈oz (6–11g)
Social **Flocks**	Lifespan **Up to 10 years**	Status **Secure**

DATE SEEN	WHERE	NOTES

| Order **Passeriformes** | Family **Parulidae** | Species *Setophaga tigrina* |

Cape May Warbler

MALE

IN FLIGHT

white patches
on wings

gray back

pale yellow
nape

FEMALE

white patches
on flanks and
breast

white marks
on outer tail
feathers

thin,
pointed
bill

black
cap

yellow
nape

rufous
cheeks

yellow
underparts,
heavily
streaked
with black

MALE

FLIGHT: fast, slightly undulating, and direct
with rapid wingbeats.

The Cape May Warbler is a spruce budworm specialist, and its
populations increase during outbreaks of this pest (which is a
moth actually, not a worm). Cape May Warblers chase other birds
aggressively from flowering trees, where they use their semitubular
tongue to suck the nectar from blossoms. In its summer spruce
forest habitat, the Cape May Warbler plucks insects from clumps of
needles. The "Cape May" Warbler was named this way because the
first specimen was collected there—it doesn't breed at Cape May!
VOICE Song a high, even-pitched series of whistles *see see see see.*
NESTING Cup placed near trunk, high in spruce or fir near
top; 4–9 eggs; 1 brood; June–July.
FEEDING Gleans arthropods, especially spruce budworms, and
also flies, adult moths, and beetles from mid-high levels in
canopy; also fruit and nectar during the nonbreeding season.

SPRING FLASH
Magnificently colored, a male shows its chestnut
cheek, yellow necklace, and yellow rump.

SIMILAR SPECIES

**YELLOW-RUMPED WARBLER
(MYRTLE) ♀**
see p.428

yellow
rump

thicker,
heavier
bill

yellow flank
patches

**PALM WARBLER
(WESTERN)**
see p.426

browner
overall

yellow
undertail feathers

OCCURRENCE
Breeds from the Yukon and
British Columbia to the Great
Lakes, the Maritimes, and
New England in mature
spruce-fir forests. Migrants
occur in a variety of habitats.
Winters in varied habitats
in Central America, as far
south as Honduras.

| Length **5in (13cm)** | Wingspan **8in (20cm)** | Weight **⁵⁄₁₆–⁷⁄₁₆oz (9–13g)** |
| Social **Migrant flocks** | Lifespan **Up to 4 years** | Status **Secure** |

DATE SEEN	WHERE	NOTES

| Order **Passeriformes** | Family **Parulidae** | Species *Setophaga cerulea* |

Cerulean Warbler

short tail with white band

MALE

two white wing bars

IN FLIGHT

bright blue crown

black breastband

MALE

whitish eyebrow

sea-green upperparts

pale blue crown

yellowish underparts

FEMALE

blue upperparts

indistinct eyestripe

white chin and throat

white undertail feathers

MALE

black streaks on flanks

white belly

FLIGHT: fast, slightly undulating, and direct with rapid wingbeats.

This unusually colored species is difficult to spot, as it spends its time foraging high in the canopy of tall deciduous forests. It was once common across the Midwest and the Ohio River Valley, but its habitat is being cleared for agriculture and fragmented by development. In winter, this bird lives high in the canopy of forests in the Andean foothills, but this habitat is threatened by coffee cultivation.

VOICE Call a slurred *chip*; flight call a buzzy *zeet*; three-part, buzzy song consisting of a short series of low paired notes followed by a mid-range trill and up-slurred high-pitched *zhree*.

NESTING Compact cup high on fork in deciduous tree, far from trunk; 2–5 eggs; 1 brood; May–July.

FEEDING Gleans insects high in canopy, especially from leaf bases.

UNIQUE COLOR
Female Cerulean Warblers have a unique pale blue color on their crown and back.

OCCURRENCE
Breeds mostly in mature deciduous forests across the northeastern US; tends to prefer dense woodlands during migration. Winters in evergreen forests along the foothills of the Andes, from Colombia to Peru.

SIMILAR SPECIES

BLACKBURNIAN WARBLER ♀
see p.421

pale streaking on back

yellow throat

BLACK-AND-WHITE WARBLER ♀
see p.404

white streaks on upperparts

white eyebrow

black undertail markings

| Length **4¾in (12cm)** | Wingspan **7¾in (19.5cm)** | Weight **⁹⁄₃₂–³⁄₈oz (8–10g)** |
| Social **Migrant/Winter flocks** | Lifespan **Up to 6 years** | Status **Vulnerable** |

DATE SEEN	WHERE	NOTES

| Order **Passeriformes** | Family **Parulidae** | Species **Setophaga americana** |

Northern Parula

MALE

two white
wing bars

IN FLIGHT

dark patch
between eye
and bill

interrupted white
eye-ring

yellow
throat

blue-gray neck
and head

chestnut
streaks
on chest

yellow chest,
lacks chestnut
streaks

olive
back

FEMALE

gray rump and
uppertail

delicate,
pale gray
belly

FLIGHT: fast, slightly undulating, and direct
with rapid wingbeats.

MALE

dark
legs

pinkish
yellow
toes

white patches on
outer tail feathers

The Northern Parula is a small wood warbler that somewhat resembles a chickadee in its active foraging behavior. This bird depends on specific nesting materials—*Usnea* lichens, or "Old Man's Beard," in the North, and *Tillandsia*, or Spanish Moss, in the South. The Northern Parula's song is one of the early signs that May has arrived. The Northern Parula interbreeds with the Tropical Parula in southern Texas where their ranges overlap, producing hybrids.

VOICE Call a very sharp *tsip*; flight call a thin, weak, descending *tsiif*; song a variable, most common buzzy up-slurred trill, variably continuous or in steps, ending very high, but then dropping off in an emphatic *zip*.

NESTING Hanging pouch in clump of lichens; 4–5 eggs; 1 brood; May–July (south) or April–August (north).

FEEDING Gleans for caterpillars, flies, moths, beetles, wasps, ants, spiders; also eats berries, nectar, some seeds.

THE AMERICAN FINCH-CREEPER
Carl Linnaeus described this bird on the basis of a plate in Catesby's *Natural History of Carolina*, called Finch-creeper.

SIMILAR SPECIES

TROPICAL
PARULA
see p.469

dark
face

more
yellow

OCCURRENCE
Nests in almost any kind of wooded area if *Tillandsia* or *Usnea* are available. Migrants (some of which cross the Gulf of Mexico) occur in almost any habitat; winters in varied habitats from southern Texas and Florida across Caribbean and Mexico south to Panama.

| Length **4¼in (11cm)** | Wingspan **7in (18cm)** | Weight **¼–⅜oz (7–10g)** |
| Social **Winter flocks** | Lifespan **Up to 7 years** | Status **Secure** |

DATE SEEN	WHERE	NOTES

Order **Passeriformes**	Family **Parulidae**	Species *Setophaga magnolia*

Magnolia Warbler 🔊

yellow rump

gray crown

MALE (BREEDING)

broken white tail band

IN FLIGHT

greenish back

white undertail feathers

IMMATURE (FALL)

plain face with pale eye-ring

black face

white eyebrow

incomplete eye-ring

large white patch on wing

greenish back with black stripes

black streaking on breast and flanks not as heavy

FEMALE (BREEDING)

MALE (BREEDING)

yellow underparts with black streaks

FLIGHT: fast, slightly undulating, and direct with rapid wingbeats.

The bold, flashy, and common Magnolia Warbler is hard to miss as it flits around at eye level, fanning its uniquely marked tail. This species nests in young forests and winters in almost any habitat, so its numbers have not suffered in recent decades, unlike some of its relatives. Although it really has no preference for its namesake plant, the 19th century ornithologist Alexander Wilson discovered a Magnolia Warbler feeding in a magnolia tree during migration, which is how it got its name.

VOICE Call a tinny *jeinf*, not particularly warbler-like; also short, simple whistled series *wee'-sa wee'-sa WEET-a-chew*, short, distinctive, flight call a high, trilled *zeep*.

NESTING Flimsy cup of black rootlets placed low in dense conifer against trunk; 3–5 eggs; 1 brood; June–August.

FEEDING Gleans mostly caterpillars, beetles, and spiders.

SPRUCE WARBLER
The conspicuous male Magnolia Warbler can be found singing its distinctive, loud song, often throughout the day, in a spruce tree.

SIMILAR SPECIES

PRAIRIE WARBLER ♀
yellowish undertail; see p.430

greenish yellow upperparts

thinner streaks

CANADA WARBLER ♀
see p.432

yellow patch between eye and bill

dark gray wings

OCCURRENCE
Breeds in dense, young mixed and coniferous forests from Yukon east to Newfoundland and south into Appalachians of Tennessee; migrates across the Gulf and Caribbean; winters in varied habitats in Caribbean and from southeast Mexico to Panama; rare vagrant in the West.

Length **5in (13cm)**	Wingspan **7½in (19cm)**	Weight **7/32–7/16oz (6–12g)**
Social **Migrant/Winter flocks**	Lifespan **Up to 6 years**	Status **Secure**

DATE SEEN	WHERE	NOTES

Order **Passeriformes**	Family **Parulidae**	Species **Setophaga castanea**

Bay-breasted Warbler

olive crown and back

two wing bars

greenish cheeks

IMMATURE FEMALE (FALL)

unstreaked breast

MALE (BREEDING)

two white wing bars

white tips on outer tail feathers

bold buffy neck patch

IN FLIGHT

FEMALE (BREEDING)

chestnut crown, streaked black

buffy wash on flanks and under tail

dusky ear patch

gray upperparts with black streaks

chestnut brown crown

black face

two white wing bars

chestnut brown chin and flanks

buff undertail

yellowish buff belly

MALE (BREEDING)

FLIGHT: fast, slightly undulating, and direct, with rapid wingbeats.

Splashed with deep chestnut, crisp white, warm buff, and jet black, a male Bay-breasted Warbler in breeding plumage is a particularly striking bird, but fall females are very different with their dull, greenish plumage. Like the Tennessee Warbler, this species depends largely on outbreaks of spruce budworms (a major food source), so its numbers rise and fall according to those outbreaks. Overall, the Bay-breasted Warbler population has decreased because of the increased use of pesticide sprays.

VOICE Call a somewhat up-slurred *tsip*; flight call a high, buzzy, short, and sharp *tzzzt*; song of very high, thin notes, often ending on lower pitch: *wee-si wee-si wee-si wee*.

NESTING Fragile-looking cup of grass and lichens on horizontal branch at mid-level in forest; 4–5 eggs; 1 brood; May–July.

FEEDING Mostly eats moths, smaller insects, worms, spiders, and caterpillars during migration and on breeding grounds; eats mainly fruit in winter.

SINGING IN THE FOREST
A brilliantly colored breeding male sings its high-pitched song on a spruce branch.

SIMILAR SPECIES

BLACKPOLL WARBLER ♂
see p.424

streaked breast

PINE WARBLER ♀
see p.427

yellow around eye

white sides to tail

OCCURRENCE
Breeds in mature spruce-fir-balsam forest across the boreal forest belt from Yukon to the Maritimes, and south to the Great Lakes area and northern New England. Migrants occur in varied habitat, but especially woodland edges. Winters in wet forest in Central America.

Length **5½in (14cm)**	Wingspan **9in (23cm)**	Weight **⅜–½oz (11–15g)**
Social **Migratory/Winter flocks**	Lifespan **Up to 4 years**	Status **Vulnerable**

DATE SEEN	WHERE	NOTES

| Order **Passeriformes** | Family **Parulidae** | Species *Setophaga fusca* |

Blackburnian Warbler

pale orange line in center of crown

white edges to outer tail feathers

bold white wing patches

complex black-and-orange face pattern

white streaks on black back

white patch on wing

MALE

IN FLIGHT

white belly

brilliant orange throat

black streaks on breast and belly

MALE

more subdued facial pattern

white wing bars

orange throat and breast

black streaks on flanks

FEMALE

This fiery beacon of the treetops is considered one of the most beautiful members of its family; its orange throat is unique among the North American warblers. The Blackburnian Warbler coexists with many other *Setophaga* warblers in the coniferous and mixed woods of the North and East, but is able to do so by exploiting a slightly different niche for foraging—in this case the treetops. It also seeks the highest trees for nesting.

VOICE Call a slightly husky *chik*; flight-call a high, thin *zzee*; song variable, but always high-pitched; swirling series of lisps, spiraling upward to end in an almost inaudible *trill*.

NESTING Fine cup in conifer on horizontal branch away from trunk, usually high in tree; 4–5 eggs; 1 brood; May–July.

FEEDING Gleans arthropods, such as spiders, worms, and beetles; also fruit.

FLIGHT: fast, slightly undulating, and direct with rapid wingbeats.

DISTINGUISHING FEATURES
The female is like a dull adult male, but with two wing bars and no black on the face.

AVIAN FIREFLY
This male in breeding plumage glows when seen against a dark forest background.

SIMILAR SPECIES

BAY-BREASTED WARBLER (FALL) ♀ ♂
see p.420
greenish back

unstreaked underparts

CERULEAN WARBLER ♀
see p.417
sea-green back

shorter tail

white corners to tail

OCCURRENCE
Breeds in coniferous and mixed forests from Alberta east through the northern Great Lakes area to Newfoundland and south into the Appalachians of Georgia; migrants found in wooded, shrubby, or forest edge habitats. Winters in wet forests in Costa Rica and Panama, and southward as far as Peru.

Length **5in (13cm)**	Wingspan **8½in (21cm)**	Weight **⁵⁄₁₆–⁷⁄₁₆oz (9–12g)**
Social **Winter flocks**	Lifespan **Up to 8 years**	Status **Vulnerable**

DATE SEEN	WHERE	NOTES

| Order **Passeriformes** | Family **Parulidae** | Species *Setophaga petechia* |

Yellow Warbler 🔊

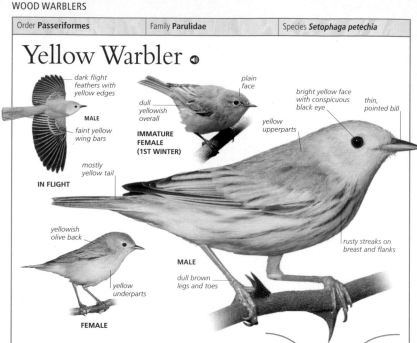

MALE
- dark flight feathers with yellow edges
- faint yellow wing bars

IN FLIGHT
- mostly yellow tail

IMMATURE FEMALE (1ST WINTER)
- dull yellowish overall
- plain face

- bright yellow face with conspicuous black eye
- thin, pointed bill
- yellow upperparts

MALE
- dull brown legs and toes
- rusty streaks on breast and flanks

FEMALE
- yellowish olive back
- yellow underparts

By May, the song of the Yellow Warbler can be heard across North America as the birds arrive for the summer. This warbler is treated as a single species with about 35 subspecies, mostly in its tropical range (West Indies and South America). The Yellow Warbler is known to build another nest on top of an old one when cowbird eggs appear in it, which can result in up to six different tiers. The Yellow Warbler does not walk, but rather hops from branch to branch.

VOICE Call a variable *chip*, sometimes given in series; flight call buzzy *zeep*; song variable series of fast, sweet notes; western birds often add an emphatic ending.

NESTING Deep cup of plant material, grasses in vertical fork of deciduous tree or shrub; 4–5 eggs; 1 brood; May–July.

FEEDING Eats mostly insects and insect larvae, plus some fruit.

FLIGHT: fast, slightly undulating, and direct, with rapid wingbeats.

ONE OF A KIND
This species has more yellow in its plumage than any other North American wood warbler.

SIMILAR SPECIES

ORANGE-CROWNED WARBLER see p.408
- olive-green overall

WILSON'S WARBLER ♀ see p.433
- dark crown
- longer tail

OCCURRENCE
Widespread in most shrubby and second-growth habitats of North America. Migrates to southern US and southward to Mexico, Central America, and South America. Resident populations live in Florida and the West Indies.

| Length **5in (13cm)** | Wingspan **8in (20cm)** | Weight **⁹⁄₃₂–½oz (8–14g)** |
| Social **Flocks** | Lifespan **Up to 9 years** | Status **Secure** |

DATE SEEN	WHERE	NOTES

Order **Passeriformes**	Family **Parulidae**	Species *Setophaga pensylvanica*

Chestnut-sided Warbler 🔊

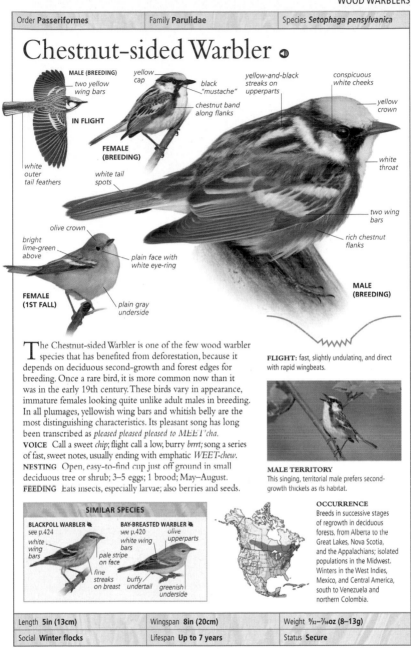

MALE (BREEDING)
- two yellow wing bars

IN FLIGHT

yellow cap

black "mustache"

chestnut band along flanks

FEMALE (BREEDING)

yellow-and-black streaks on upperparts

conspicuous white cheeks

yellow crown

white throat

white outer tail feathers

white tail spots

two wing bars

olive crown

bright lime-green above

plain face with white eye-ring

rich chestnut flanks

FEMALE (1ST FALL)

plain gray underside

MALE (BREEDING)

The Chestnut-sided Warbler is one of the few wood warbler species that has benefited from deforestation, because it depends on deciduous second-growth and forest edges for breeding. Once a rare bird, it is more common now than it was in the early 19th century. These birds vary in appearance, immature females looking quite unlike adult males in breeding. In all plumages, yellowish wing bars and whitish belly are the most distinguishing characteristics. Its pleasant song has long been transcribed as *pleased pleased pleased to MEET'cha*.

VOICE Call a sweet *chip*; flight call a low, burry *brrrt*; song a series of fast, sweet notes, usually ending with emphatic *WEET-chew*.
NESTING Open, easy-to-find cup just off ground in small deciduous tree or shrub; 3–5 eggs; 1 brood; May–August.
FEEDING Eats insects, especially larvae; also berries and seeds.

FLIGHT: fast, slightly undulating, and direct with rapid wingbeats.

MALE TERRITORY
This singing, territorial male prefers second-growth thickets as its habitat.

SIMILAR SPECIES

BLACKPOLL WARBLER see p.424
- white wing bars
- fine streaks on breast

BAY-BREASTED WARBLER see p.420
- olive upperparts
- white wing bars
- pale stripe on face
- buffy undertail
- greenish underside

OCCURRENCE
Breeds in successive stages of regrowth in deciduous forests, from Alberta to the Great Lakes, Nova Scotia, and the Appalachians; isolated populations in the Midwest. Winters in the West Indies, Mexico, and Central America, south to Venezuela and northern Colombia.

Length **5in (13cm)**	Wingspan **8in (20cm)**	Weight **⁹/₃₂–⁷/₁₆oz (8–13g)**
Social **Winter flocks**	Lifespan **Up to 7 years**	Status **Secure**

DATE SEEN	WHERE	NOTES
....	....	....
....	....	....
....	....	....
....	....	....
....	....	....

| Order **Passeriformes** | Family **Parulidae** | Species **Setophaga striata** |

Blackpoll Warbler 🔊

white tail spots

MALE

two white wing bars

IN FLIGHT

greenish upperparts with fine black streaks

faint, fine streaking on underparts

FEMALE (BREEDING)

black cap

white cheek

greenish overall

streaking on breast

MALE (FALL)

pale toes contrasting with darker legs

bold black streaks on gray back

white undertail feathers

orange legs

MALE (BREEDING)

streaked underparts

The Blackpoll Warbler is well known for undergoing a remarkable fall migration that takes it over the Atlantic Ocean from the northeastern US to northern Venezuela. Before departing, it almost doubles its body weight with fat to serve as fuel for the nonstop journey. With the return of spring, most of these birds travel the shorter Caribbean route back north.

VOICE Call piercing *chip*; flight call high, buzzy yet sharp *tzzzt*; common song crescendo of fast, extremely high-pitched ticks, ending with a decrescendo *tsst tsst TSST TSST TSST tsst tsst*; less commonly, ticks run into even faster trill.

NESTING Well-hidden cup placed low against conifer trunk; 3–5 eggs; 1–2 broods; May–July.

FEEDING Gleans arthropods, such as worms and beetles, but will take small fruit in fall and winter.

FLIGHT: fast, slightly undulating, and direct, with rapid wingbeats.

REACHING THE HIGH NOTES
The song of the male Blackpoll is so high-pitched that it is inaudible to many people.

SIMILAR SPECIES

BAY-BREASTED WARBLER ♀
see p.420

greenish sides to neck

warm wash to flanks

BLACK-AND-WHITE WARBLER ♂
see p.404

black cheek

distinct black-and-white stripes

OCCURRENCE
Breeds in spruce-fir forests across the northern boreal forest zone from Alaska eastward to Newfoundland, southward to coastal coniferous forests in the Maritimes and northern New England. Migrants fly over the Atlantic Ocean to a landfall in the Caribbean and northern South America.

| Length **5½in (14cm)** | Wingspan **9in (23cm)** | Weight **⅜–⅝oz (10–18g)** |
| Social **Flocks** | Lifespan **Up to 8 years** | Status **Secure** |

DATE SEEN	WHERE	NOTES

| Order **Passeriformes** | Family **Parulidae** | Species *Setophaga caerulescens* |

Black-throated Blue Warbler 🔊

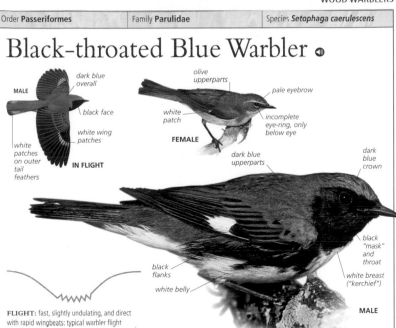

MALE
- dark blue overall
- black face
- white wing patches
- white patches on outer tail feathers

IN FLIGHT

- olive upperparts
- pale eyebrow
- white patch
- incomplete eye-ring, only below eye

FEMALE

- dark blue upperparts
- dark blue crown
- black "mask" and throat
- white breast ("kerchief")
- black flanks
- white belly

MALE

FLIGHT: fast, slightly undulating, and direct with rapid wingbeats: typical warbler flight

Male and female Black-throated Blue Warblers look so different that early ornithologists thought they belonged to different species. Many of the females have a blue wash to their wings and tail, and almost all have a subdued version of the male's white "kerchief," so identification is not difficult. This beautiful eastern North American species migrates northward in spring, along the eastern flank of the Appalachians, but a small number of birds fly, along an imaginary line, northwestward to the Great Lakes. This "line" is so clearly defined that this bird is common in Chicago but extremely rare in St. Louis.

VOICE Call a husky junco-like *tchunk*; flight call a distinctive, drawn-out, metallic *ssiiink*, reminiscent of some Northern Cardinal calls; song a relatively low-pitched series of up-slurred buzzes *zu zu zo zhray zhree*, or slower *zhray zhray zhreee*.

NESTING Bulky cup of plant material a meter off ground in dense forest; 3–5 eggs; 1–2 broods; May–August.

FEEDING Gleans arthropods, mainly caterpillars, from mid-low level in forest; takes small fruit and nectar.

BLACK, WHITE, AND BLUE
Males are gorgeous year-round, especially when viewed against contrastingly colored fall foliage.

SIMILAR SPECIES

YELLOW-RUMPED WARBLER (MYRTLE) ♀ see p.428
- yellow rump
- two wing bars

OCCURRENCE
Breeds in relatively undisturbed deciduous and mixed hardwood forests from southern Ontario and northern Minnesota to Nova Scotia and into the Appalachians of Georgia. Fall migration through wooded habitats; a Caribbean migrant. Winters almost exclusively in the Antilles.

| Length **5in (13cm)** | Wingspan **7½in (19cm)** | Weight **⁹⁄₃₂–⁷⁄₁₆oz (8–12g)** |
| Social **Migrant flocks** | Lifespan **Up to 10 years** | Status **Secure** |

DATE SEEN	WHERE	NOTES

| Order **Passeriformes** | Family **Parulidae** | Species ***Setophaga palmarum*** |

Palm Warbler

ADULT (EASTERN)
chestnut crown
dark upperparts
white-edged tail
IN FLIGHT

grayish green "mustache"
ring below eye
yellow throat
dusky streaks on breast and belly
dark gray upperparts
ADULT
***S. p. palmarum* (WESTERN MALE; BREEDING)**
yellowish rump

yellow eyestripe

dull gray upperparts

chestnut streaks on breast

dull grayish brown overall
yellow undertail coverts
whitish below with brown streaks
ADULT
***S. p. palmarum* (WESTERN; NONBREEDING)**
yellow undertail coverts

rich yellow underparts
ADULT
***S. p. hypochrysea* (EASTERN; BREEDING)**

The Palm Warbler is one of North America's most abundant warblers. Its tail-pumping habit makes it easy to identify in any plumage. It was named *palmarum* (meaning "palm") in 1789 because it was first recorded among palm thickets on the Caribbean island of Hispaniola. The eastern subspecies (*S. p. hypochrysea*) has a yellow face, and breeds in southwestern Canada and northeastern US. The western subspecies (*S. p. palmarum*) breeds in western and central Canada. It is grayish brown above and lacks the chestnut streaks of the eastern subspecies.

VOICE Call a husky *chik* or *tsip*; flight call a light *ziint*; slow, loose, buzzy trill: *zwi zwi zwi zwi zwi zwi zwi zwi*.

NESTING Cup of grasses on or near ground in open area of conifers at forest edge of a bog; 4–5 eggs; 1 brood; May–July.

FEEDING Eats insects, sometimes caught in flight; also takes seeds and berries.

FLIGHT: fast, slightly undulating, and direct with rapid wingbeats.

OCCURRENCE
In North America, breeds in spruce bogs within the northern forest zone, across Canada from the Yukon to the Maritimes and Labrador, and in the US from Minnesota to Maine. Often migrates through central portions of eastern US; winters in southeastern US, Florida, and Central America.

SIMILAR SPECIES

CAPE MAY WARBLER ♀
see p.416
olive gray back
thin patch of yellow on throat and neck

YELLOW-RUMPED WARBLER (MYRTLE) ♀
see p.428
streaking on back
white throat

FAR FROM THE PALMS
This male Palm Warbler is far north of the coastal palms where its kin spend the winter.

| Length **5½in (14cm)** | Wingspan **8in (20cm)** | Weight **¼–⁷⁄₁₆oz (7–13g)** |
| Social **Flocks** | Lifespan **Up to 6 years** | Status **Secure** |

DATE SEEN	WHERE	NOTES

| Order **Passeriformes** | Family **Parulidae** | Species *Setophaga pinus* |

Pine Warbler

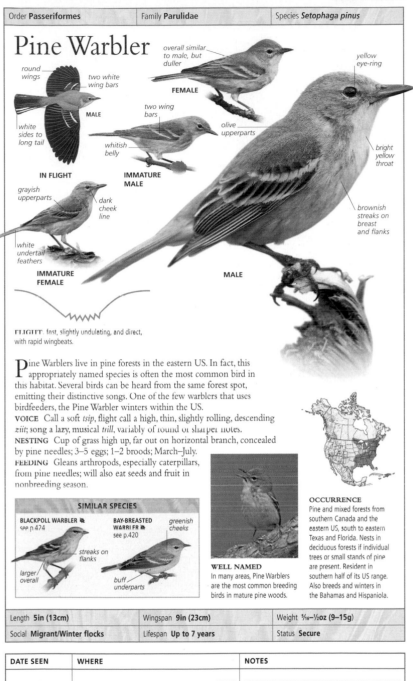

round wings

two white wing bars

MALE

white sides to long tail

IN FLIGHT

overall similar to male, but duller

FEMALE

yellow eye-ring

two wing bars

whitish belly

olive upperparts

IMMATURE MALE

bright yellow throat

brownish streaks on breast and flanks

grayish upperparts

dark cheek line

white undertail feathers

IMMATURE FEMALE

MALE

FLIGHT: fast, slightly undulating, and direct, with rapid wingbeats.

Pine Warblers live in pine forests in the eastern US. In fact, this appropriately named species is often the most common bird in this habitat. Several birds can be heard from the same forest spot, emitting their distinctive songs. One of the few warblers that uses birdfeeders, the Pine Warbler winters within the US.

VOICE Call a soft *tsip*, flight call a high, thin, slightly rolling, descending *ziit*; song a lazy, musical *trill*, variably of round or sharper notes.

NESTING Cup of grass high up, far out on horizontal branch, concealed by pine needles; 3–5 eggs; 1–2 broods; March–July.

FEEDING Gleans arthropods, especially caterpillars, from pine needles; will also eat seeds and fruit in nonbreeding season.

SIMILAR SPECIES

BLACKPOLL WARBLER see p.474

streaks on flanks

larger overall

BAY-BREASTED WARBLER see p.420

greenish cheeks

buff underparts

WELL NAMED
In many areas, Pine Warblers are the most common breeding birds in mature pine woods.

OCCURRENCE
Pine and mixed forests from southern Canada and the eastern US, south to eastern Texas and Florida. Nests in deciduous forests if individual trees or small stands of pine are present. Resident in southern half of its US range. Also breeds and winters in the Bahamas and Hispaniola.

| Length **5in (13cm)** | Wingspan **9in (23cm)** | Weight **⁵⁄₁₆–½oz (9–15g)** |
| Social **Migrant/Winter flocks** | Lifespan **Up to 7 years** | Status **Secure** |

DATE SEEN	WHERE	NOTES

| Order **Passeriformes** | Family **Parulidae** | Species *Setophaga coronata* |

Yellow-rumped Warbler

MALE (MYRTLE; EAST)
- white wing bars
- dark cheeks
- black streaks on gray back
- white throat

IN FLIGHT
- bright yellow rump
- white corners on outer tail feathers

same pattern as male, but duller

- whitish eyebrow
- whitish throat
- yellow flanks

FEMALE
S. c. coronata
(MYRTLE; EAST)

lacks white eyebrow

MALE
S. c. coronata
(MYRTLE; EAST)
- black streaks across breast

large, white wing patch

- solid black breast

unmarked undertail

FEMALE
S. c. auduboni
(AUDUBON'S)

- yellowish throat
- grayish overall

MALE
S. c. auduboni
(AUDUBON'S)

The abundant and widespread Yellow-rumped Warbler is not choosy about its wintering habitats. It was often considered to consist of two species, "Myrtle" (*S. c. coronata*) in the North, and "Audubon's" (*S. c. auduboni*) in the West. Because they interbreed freely in a narrow zone of contact in British Columbia and Alberta, the American Ornithologists Union merged them. The two forms differ in plumage and voice, and their hybrid zone appears stable.
VOICE Myrtle's call a flat, husky *tchik*; Audubon's a higher-pitched, relatively musical, rising *jip*; flight call of both a clear, up-slurred *sviiit*; song loose, warbled trill with an inflected ending; Myrtle's song higher and faster, Audubon's lower and slower.
NESTING Bulky cup of plant matter in conifer; 4–5 eggs; 1 brood; March–August.
FEEDING Feeds mostly on flies, beetles, wasps, and spiders during breeding; takes fruit and berries at other times of the year, often sallies to catch prey.

FLIGHT: fast, slightly undulating, and direct with rapid wingbeats.

WIDESPREAD WARBLER
Yellow-rumped Warblers are widespread and are likely to be spotted often.

SIMILAR SPECIES

MAGNOLIA WARBLER ♂
see p.419

CAPE MAY WARBLER ♀
see p.416

- more white in tail
- yellow throat and breast
- dark eye-line
- thin, curved bill

OCCURRENCE
Both northern and western populations are widespread across the continent from Alaska eastward to Québec and Newfoundland, and westward in the mountains south to Arizona, New Mexico, and Northern Mexico. Prefers coniferous and mixed hardwood coniferous forests.

| Length **5in (13cm)** | Wingspan **9in (23cm)** | Weight **⅜–⅝oz (10–17g)** |
| Social **Flocks** | Lifespan **Up to 7 years** | Status **Secure** |

DATE SEEN	WHERE	NOTES

| Order **Passeriformes** | Family **Parulidae** | Species *Setophaga dominica* |

Yellow-throated Warbler

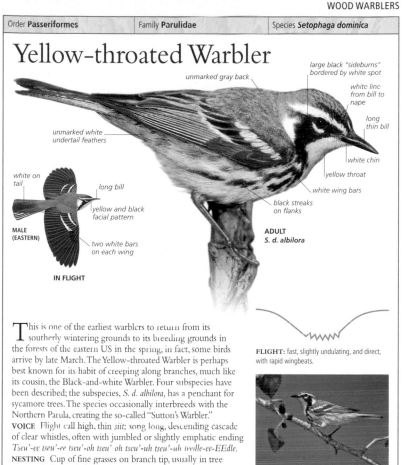

unmarked gray back

large black "sideburns" bordered by white spot

white line from bill to nape

long thin bill

unmarked white undertail feathers

white chin

yellow throat

white wing bars

black streaks on flanks

ADULT
S. d. albilora

white on tail

long bill

yellow and black facial pattern

MALE (EASTERN)

two white bars on each wing

IN FLIGHT

This is one of the earliest warblers to return from its southerly wintering grounds to its breeding grounds in the forests of the eastern US in the spring, in fact, some birds arrive by late March. The Yellow-throated Warbler is perhaps best known for its habit of creeping along branches, much like its cousin, the Black-and-white Warbler. Four subspecies have been described; the subspecies, *S. d. albilora*, has a penchant for sycamore trees. The species occasionally interbreeds with the Northern Parula, creating the so-called "Sutton's Warbler."
VOICE Flight call high, thin *siit*; song long, descending cascade of clear whistles, often with jumbled or slightly emphatic ending *Tseu'-ee tseu'-ee tseu'-oh tseu' oh tseu'-uh tseu'-uh tredle-ee-EEdle.*
NESTING Cup of fine grasses on branch tip, usually in tree canopy; 3–5 eggs; 1–2 broods; April–July.
FEEDING Gleans spiders, insects, and insect larvae, especially caterpillars, from foliage and bark.

FLIGHT: fast, slightly undulating, and direct, with rapid wingbeats.

SOUTHERNER
The Yellow-throated Warbler is a species of southern woodlands, such as cypress swamps.

SIMILAR SPECIES

GRACE'S WARBLER	BLACK-AND-WHITE WARBLER see p.404
yellow around eye	shorter bill
	black and white markings
	black streaks

OCCURRENCE
Breeds in the eastern half of the US, but not in southern Florida, in woods with cypress, sycamore, or live oak; wintering birds may prefer tall palms and park-like settings. Range has extended northward in recent years. Southern US population is non-migratory.

Length **5in (13cm)**	Wingspan **8in (20cm)**	Weight **⁹/₃₂–³/₈oz (8–11g)**
Social **Winter flocks**	Lifespan **Up to 5 years**	Status **Secure**

DATE SEEN	WHERE	NOTES

| Order **Passeriformes** | Family **Parulidae** | Species **Setophaga discolor** |

Prairie Warbler

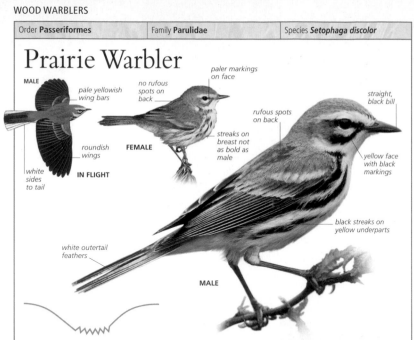

MALE

pale yellowish wing bars

no rufous spots on back

paler markings on face

straight, black bill

rufous spots on back

roundish wings

FEMALE

streaks on breast not as bold as male

yellow face with black markings

white sides to tail

IN FLIGHT

white outertail feathers

black streaks on yellow underparts

MALE

FLIGHT: fast, slightly undulating, and direct, with rapid wingbeats.

Contrary to its common name, the Prairie Warbler does not live on the "prairie." Its distinctive song is a quintessential sound of scrubby areas across the eastern US. Although its populations increased in the 19th century as a result of the widespread cutting of forests, the later maturation of this habitat, along with human development, is having a negative impact on local populations.

VOICE Call a thick *tsik* or *tchip*, flight call a high, thin *sssip*; song variable in tempo, but always series of husky, buzzy notes that increase in pitch: *zzu zzu zzu zzo zzo zzo zzee zzee.*

NESTING Cup of plant material in fork of sapling or low trees, often within human reach; 3–5 eggs; 1 brood; May–July.

FEEDING Eats various insects, such as flies and crickets; also berries.

HIGH AND LOUD
Males sing from preferred elevated perches, producing their characteristic buzzy song that increases in pitch and tempo.

SIMILAR SPECIES

MAGNOLIA WARBLER ♀
see p.419

white eye-ring

less prominent streaking

PINE WARBLER ♂
see p.427
thin, dark line through eye

white wing bars

larger overall

OCCURRENCE
Breeds in shrubby, open-canopied, second-growth habitats, and mangroves; migrant and wintering birds prefer similar-looking brushy habitats. Florida birds are partially resident. Winters in the Bahamas, Greater and Lesser Antilles, and along the coast from southern Mexico to El Salvador.

| Length **4¾in (12cm)** | Wingspan **9in (23cm)** | Weight **⁷⁄₃₂–⁵⁄₁₆oz (6–9g)** |
| Social **Solitary/Winter flocks** | Lifespan **Up to 10 years** | Status **Declining** |

DATE SEEN	WHERE	NOTES

Order **Passeriformes**	Family **Parulidae**	Species *Setophaga virens*

Black-throated Green Warbler

olive-green back

MALE

two white wing bars

IN FLIGHT

same as male, but duller

greenish flanks

FEMALE

greenish cap

yellow face

white outer tail feathers

yellowish flanks

black bib and chin

heavily streaked underparts

MALE

FLIGHT: fast, slightly undulating, and direct with rapid wingbeats; typical warbler flight.

This species is easy to distinguish as its bright yellow face is unique among birds inhabiting northeastern North America. It is a member of the *virens* "superspecies," a group of nonoverlapping species that are similar in plumage and vocalizations—the Black-throated Green, Golden-cheeked, Townsend's, and Hermit Warblers. Sadly, this species is vulnerable to habitat loss in parts of its wintering range.

VOICE Flat *tchip* call; flight call a rising *siii*; two high-pitched, buzzy songs, fast *zee zee zee zee zoo zee*; and lower, slower *zu zee zu-zu zee*.

NESTING Cup of twigs and grasses around 10–65ft (3–20m) on horizontal branch near trunk in the North, away from trunk in the South; 3–5 eggs; 1 brood; May–July.

FEEDING Gleans arthropods, especially caterpillars; also takes small fruit, including poison ivy berries, in nonbreeding season.

YELLOW-AND-BLACK GEM
From a high perch in a spruce tree, a male advertises his territory with persistent singing

SIMILAR SPECIES

GOLDEN-CHEEKED WARBLER ♂ see p.470

black crown

thin, black eye-line

GOLDEN-CHEEKED WARBLER ♀ see p.470

darker crown

darker upper breast

OCCURRENCE
Breeds in many forest types, especially a mix of conifers and hardwood, from British Columbia east to Newfoundland and the southeastern US along the Appalachians. Migrants and wintering birds use a variety of habitats. Winters from southern Texas into Venezuela; small numbers in Caribbean.

Length **5in (13cm)**	Wingspan **8in (20cm)**	Weight **⁹⁄₃₂–³⁄₈oz (8–11g)**
Social **Migrant/Winter flocks**	Lifespan **Up to 6 years**	Status **Secure**

DATE SEEN	WHERE	NOTES

| Order **Passeriformes** | Family **Parulidae** | Species *Cardellina canadensis* |

Canada Warbler

paler crown
bicolored eye-ring
faint necklace
FEMALE
conspicuous yellow eye-ring

plain gray tail
MALE
white undertail feathers
IN FLIGHT

plain gray upperparts
MALE

yellow patch between eye and bill
dark crown
yellow throat
black "necklace" across breast
yellow belly

O ne of the last species of wood warblers to arrive in the US and Canada in the spring, and among the first to leave in the fall, the Canada Warbler is sometimes called the "Necklaced Warbler," for the conspicuous black markings on its chest. This uncommon bird is sadly declining, probably because of the maturation and draining of its preferred breeding habitat, consisting of old mixed hardwood forests with moist undergrowth.

VOICE Call a thick *tchip;* flight call a variable, clear *plip;* song a haphazard jumble of sweet notes, often beginning with or interspersed with *tchip,* followed by a pause.

NESTING Concealed cup of leaves, in moss or grass, on or near ground; 4–5 eggs; 1 brood; May–June.

FEEDING Gleans at mid-levels for many species of insects; also flycatches and forages on ground.

FLIGHT: fast, slightly undulating, and direct with rapid wingbeats.

TAKING FLIGHT
This species often waits for prey to fly by, before launching into flight to pursue it.

FAMILIAR MEAL
Flying insects, including crane flies, make up the bulk of the Canada Warbler's diet.

SIMILAR SPECIES

MAGNOLIA WARBLER ♀
see p.419
white eyebrow
streaked flanks

KIRTLAND'S WARBLER ♂
see p.469
streaked mantle and flanks

OCCURRENCE
Breeds in moist deciduous, mixed, and coniferous forests with well-developed understory, especially swampy woods; migrants use well-vegetated habitats; winters in dense, wet thickets and a variety of tropical woodlands in South America.

| Length **5in (13cm)** | Wingspan **8in (20cm)** | Weight **⁹⁄₃₂–¹⁄₂oz (8–15g)** |
| Social **Flocks** | Lifespan **Up to 8 years** | Status **Declining** |

DATE SEEN	WHERE	NOTES

Order **Passeriformes**	Family **Parulidae**	Species *Cardellina pusilla*

Wilson's Warbler

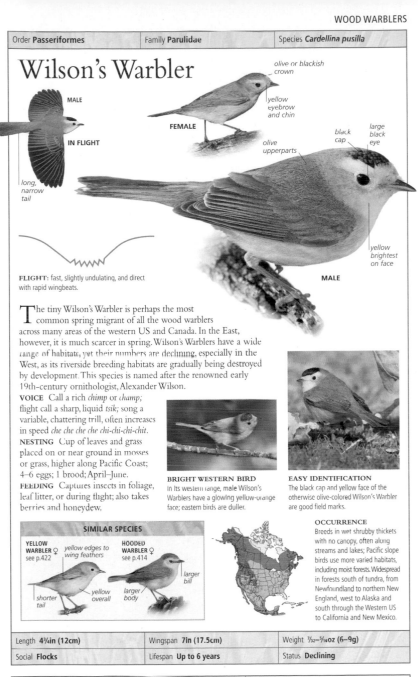

olive or blackish crown

MALE

yellow eyebrow and chin

FEMALE

olive upperparts

black cap

large black eye

IN FLIGHT

long, narrow tail

yellow brightest on face

MALE

FLIGHT: fast, slightly undulating, and direct with rapid wingbeats.

The tiny Wilson's Warbler is perhaps the most common spring migrant of all the wood warblers across many areas of the western US and Canada. In the East, however, it is much scarcer in spring. Wilson's Warblers have a wide range of habitats, yet their numbers are declining, especially in the West, as its riverside breeding habitats are gradually being destroyed by development. This species is named after the renowned early 19th-century ornithologist, Alexander Wilson.

VOICE Call a rich *chimp* or *champ;* flight call a sharp, liquid *tsik;* song a variable, chattering trill, often increases in speed *che che che che chi-chi-chi-chit.*

NESTING Cup of leaves and grass placed on or near ground in mosses or grass, higher along Pacific Coast; 4–6 eggs; 1 brood; April–June.

FEEDING Captures insects in foliage, leaf litter, or during flight; also takes berries and honeydew.

BRIGHT WESTERN BIRD
In its western range, male Wilson's Warblers have a glowing yellow-orange face; eastern birds are duller.

EASY IDENTIFICATION
The black cap and yellow face of the otherwise olive-colored Wilson's Warbler are good field marks.

OCCURRENCE
Breeds in wet shrubby thickets with no canopy, often along streams and lakes; Pacific slope birds use more varied habitats, including moist forests. Widespread in forests south of tundra, from Newfoundland to northern New England, west to Alaska and south through the Western US to California and New Mexico.

SIMILAR SPECIES

YELLOW WARBLER ♀ see p.422
yellow edges to wing feathers
shorter tail
yellow overall

HOODED WARBLER ♀ see p.414
larger bill
larger body

Length **4¾in (12cm)**	Wingspan **7in (17.5cm)**	Weight **⁷⁄₃₂–⁵⁄₁₆oz (6–9g)**
Social **Flocks**	Lifespan **Up to 6 years**	Status **Declining**

DATE SEEN	WHERE	NOTES

CARDINALS AND RELATIVES

Birds belonging to the cardinalidae family are visually stunning, noisy birds. Some tanagers (those in the genus *Piranga*) and grosbeaks and buntings (those in the genus *Passerina*) are grouped together with the Northern Cardinal and Pyrrhuloxia in this family. Tanagers are slender-bodied, cone-billed, finch-like birds that feed on insects, such as wasps and bees, and fruit in high foliage. Males are brightly colored, while the females are duller and greener. They have similar songs but more distinctive calls.

CARDINALS

Cardinals are striking birds: the Northern Cardinal is almost entirely red, while the Pyrrhuloxia of the southwestern states is gray with vivid red patches. Both species have pointed, upstanding crests. Females are grayer, but still have the crest. Their bills are stout but short, adapted to feed on tough fruits, berries, and seeds.

GROSBEAKS AND BUNTINGS

Grosbeaks in the genus *Pheucticus* are stocky, heavily built, sluggish species, with characteristically heavy, deeply triangular bills for splitting and peeling seeds. Again, males are bright and boldly colored, while females are duller but distinctively patterned. The colorful buntings in this family (with a preponderance of blues in their plumage) are similar to the grosbeaks, but more lightly built and with more delicate, triangular bills.

WINTER RED
Male Northern Cardinals are the only bright red bird in the United States all year round. They are very aggressive and often fiercely defend their territories.

| Order **Passeriformes** | Family **Cardinalidae** | Species *Piranga rubra* |

Summer Tanager 🔊

tail appears short in flight

MALE (BREEDING)

IN FLIGHT

dark eye

bright red upperparts

thick, long, yellowish bill

variable red-and-yellow patchwork

red head and breast

IMMATURE (1ST SPRING)

lacks grayish cheek patches

red wash overall

crested head

olive-yellow upperparts

FEMALE P. r. rubra (EASTERN)

brownish legs and toes

MALE (BREEDING)

FEMALE P. r. cooperi (SOUTHWESTERN)

FLIGHT: strong and direct with quick wingbeats; occasionally glides.

The stunning male Summer Tanager is the only North American bird that is entirely bright red. Immature males in their first spring plumage are almost equally as striking, with their patchwork of bright yellow-and-red plumage. The two subspecies of Summer Tanager are quite similar—*P. r. rubra* breeds in the East while *P. r. cooperi* breeds in the West. The latter is, on average, paler, larger, and longer-billed.

VOICE Call an explosive *PIT-tuck!* or *PIT-a TUK*; flight call a muffled, airy *vreee*; song similar to American Robin, but more muffled and with longer pauses.

NESTING Loosely built cup of grasses usually placed high up in tree; 3–4 eggs; 1 brood; May–August.

FEEDING Eats bees, wasps, and other insects; also consumes fruit.

MAD FOR MULBERRIES
All *Piranga* tanagers are frugivores in season, and mulberries are one of their favorites.

SIMILAR SPECIES

HEPATIC TANAGER ♀
yellowish upperparts
reddish brown wings

SCARLET TANAGER ♀
see p.436
greenish overall
smaller, grayish bill
darker wings and tail

OCCURRENCE
P. r. rubra breeds in deciduous and mixed woodlands from New Jersey and Nebraska south to Texas; *P. r. cooperi* in cottonwood-willow habitats near streams and rivers from California and Utah to Texas and Mexico. Both winter from southern Texas and Mexico to Bolivia and Brazil, and the West Indies.

| Length **8in (20cm)** | Wingspan **12in (31cm)** | Weight **⅞–1⁷⁄₁₆oz (25–40g)** |
| Social **Solitary** | Lifespan **Unknown** | Status **Secure** |

DATE SEEN	WHERE	NOTES

Order **Passeriformes**	Family **Cardinalidae**	Species *Piranga olivacea*

Scarlet Tanager 🔊

black wings

red body

vibrant scarlet head and body

dark brown eyes

yellow patches in red plumage

grayish yellow bill

MALE (MOLTING)

tail appears short in flight

MALE (BREEDING)

IN FLIGHT

black wings

black tail

greenish rump and upper tail

overall greenish upperparts

FEMALE

dark gray toes and legs

yellow-green body, head, and rump

MALE (BREEDING)

MALE (NONBREEDING)

FLIGHT: strong and direct; rapid wingbeats.

In breeding plumage, the male Scarlet Tanager is one of the brightest and most easily identified North American birds. Its secretive nature and preference for the canopies of well shaded oak woodlands, however, make it difficult to spot. Males are most easily located by their distinctive and easily recognizable song. Male Scarlet Tanagers vary in appearance—some are orange, not scarlet, and others have a faint reddish wing bar.
VOICE Call a hoarse, drawn out *CHIK-breeer*, often shortened to *CHIK*; flight call an up-slurred, whistled *pwee*; song a burry, slurred *querit-queer-query-querit-queer*.
NESTING Loosely woven cup of grass, lined with fine material, high up in tree; 3–5 eggs; 1 brood; May–July.
FEEDING Gleans insects, larvae, fruit, buds, and berries.

STUNNING MALE
Taking a bath away from the treetops, a male Scarlet Tanager can be seen in all its glory.

SIMILAR SPECIES

VERMILION FLYCATCHER ♂
see p.459
brown wings and tail

SUMMER TANAGER ♀
see p.435
larger bill
olive-yellow upperparts
thinner bill
yellowish underparts

OCCURRENCE
Breeds in mature deciduous and mixed forests (especially with large oaks) from southern Manitoba and eastern Oklahoma east to the Maritime Provinces and the Carolinas. Trans-Gulf migrant. Winters in a variety of habitats along the eastern slope of the Andes from eastern Panama to Bolivia.

Length **7in (18cm)**	Wingspan **11½in (29cm)**	Weight **¹¹⁄₁₆–1¼oz (20–35g)**
Social **Solitary/Small flocks**	Lifespan **At least 10 years**	Status **Secure**

DATE SEEN	WHERE	NOTES

| Order **Passeriformes** | Family **Cardinalidae** | Species *Cardinalis cardinalis* |

Northern Cardinal 🔊

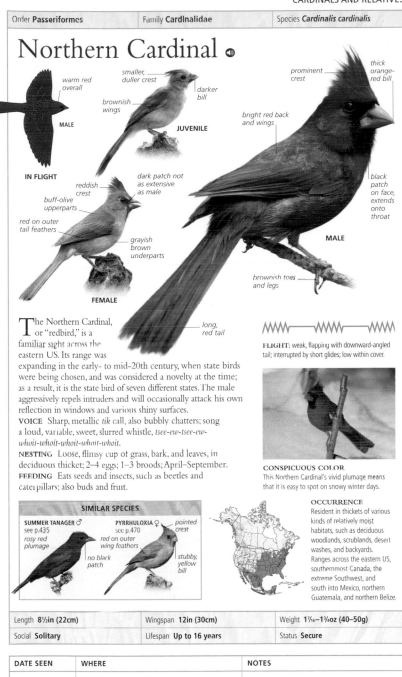

MALE

warm red overall

IN FLIGHT

smaller, duller crest

brownish wings

darker bill

JUVENILE

reddish crest

buff-olive upperparts

red on outer tail feathers

dark patch not as extensive as male

grayish brown underparts

FEMALE

long, red tail

prominent crest

thick orange-red bill

bright red back and wings

black patch on face, extends onto throat

MALE

brownish toes and legs

The Northern Cardinal, or "redbird," is a familiar sight across the eastern US. Its range was expanding in the early- to mid-20th century, when state birds were being chosen, and was considered a novelty at the time; as a result, it is the state bird of seven different states. The male aggressively repels intruders and will occasionally attack his own reflection in windows and various shiny surfaces.

VOICE Sharp, metallic *tik* call, also bubbly chatters; song a loud, variable, sweet, slurred whistle, *tsee-ew-tsee-ew-whoit-whoit-whoit-whoit-whoit.*

NESTING Loose, flimsy cup of grass, bark, and leaves, in deciduous thicket; 2–4 eggs; 1–3 broods; April–September.

FEEDING Eats seeds and insects, such as beetles and caterpillars; also buds and fruit.

FLIGHT: weak, flapping with downward-angled tail; interrupted by short glides; low within cover.

CONSPICUOUS COLOR
This Northern Cardinal's vivid plumage means that it is easy to spot on snowy winter days.

SIMILAR SPECIES

SUMMER TANAGER ♂
see p.435
rosy red plumage
no black patch

PYRRHULOXIA ♀
see p.470
red on outer wing feathers
pointed crest
stubby, yellow bill

OCCURRENCE
Resident in thickets of various kinds of relatively moist habitats, such as deciduous woodlands, scrublands, desert washes, and backyards. Ranges across the eastern US, southernmost Canada, the extreme Southwest, and south into Mexico, northern Guatemala, and northern Belize.

Length 8½in (22cm)	Wingspan 12in (30cm)	Weight 1⁷⁄₁₆–1¾oz (40–50g)
Social **Solitary**	Lifespan **Up to 16 years**	Status **Secure**

DATE SEEN	WHERE	NOTES

| Order **Passeriformes** | Family **Cardinalidae** | Species *Pheucticus ludovicianus* |

Rose-breasted Grosbeak 🔊

black head
and back

white
rump

**MALE
(BREEDING)**

bold, white
wing patches

rosy or
orange
breast

**IMMATURE
MALE
(1ST FALL)**

IN FLIGHT

short
tail
with
white
corners

white
marks
on head

white
wing bars

large,
pinkish bill

rose-red
breast

thick streaks
on underparts

FEMALE

white belly

brown patches
on back

streaked
underparts

**MALE
(BREEDING)**

**MALE
(NONBREEDING)**

The massive bill of this species earned it the name "grosbeak."
For many birdwatchers in the East, the appearance of a flock
of dazzling male Rose-breasted Grosbeaks in early May signals the
peak of spring songbird migration. Adult males in their tuxedo
attire, with rose-red ties, are unmistakable, but females and immature
males are more somber. In the fall, immature male Rose-breasted Grosbeaks
often have orange breasts, and are commonly mistaken for female Black-
headed Grosbeaks. The difference is in the pink wing lining usually visible
on perched birds, pink bill, and streaking across the center of the breast.
VOICE Call a high, sharp, explosive *sink* or *eeuk*, flight call an airy *vreee*; song a
liquid, flute-like warble, rather slow in delivery, almost relaxed.
NESTING Loose, open cup or platform, usually in deciduous saplings, mid
to high level; 2–5 eggs; 1–2 broods; May–July.
FEEDING Eats arthropods, fruit, seeds, and buds.

FLIGHT: undulating but powerful flight with
bursts of wingbeats.

SIMILAR SPECIES

PURPLE FINCH ♀
see p.347

much
smaller

smaller,
dark bill

thick, lateral
throat stripe

**BLACK-HEADED
GROSBEAK** ♀
see p.472

tawny
breast

pencil-thin
streaks on
underparts

STUNNING MALE
A striking male Rose-breasted
Grosbeak in springtime is quite
unmistakable on a tree.

OCCURRENCE
Breeds in deciduous and mixed
woods, parks, and orchards
across the northeastern
quarter of the US, and across
Canada westward from
Newfoundland through
Ontario to southeast Yukon.
Winters from Mexico and the
Caribbean, south to Guyana
and Peru. Rare in the West.

| Length **8in (20cm)** | Wingspan **12½in (32cm)** | Weight **1¼–2oz (35–55g)** |
| Social **Solitary/Small flocks** | Lifespan **Up to 13 years** | Status **Secure** |

DATE SEEN	WHERE	NOTES

Order **Passeriformes**	Family **Cardinalidae**	Species *Passerina caerulea*

Blue Grosbeak 🔊

MALE

rufous wing bars

blue upperparts

IN FLIGHT

upperparts like adult male, but with brown patches

IMMATURE MALE (1ST SUMMER)

uniform dark indigo head

black patch between eye and bill

black streaks on shoulder feathers

rufous shoulder

MALE

tawny wing bars

huge bill

pale tan overall

FEMALE

FLIGHT: lightly undulating, fast, and direct.

Blue Grosbeaks, formerly seen only in the South, have expanded their range northward and westward in recent years, especially in the Great Plains. Nevertheless, they are not abundant anywhere and spotting one is a treat. In the East, dull-plumaged male Indigo Buntings with brown wing bars can be misidentified as Blue Grosbeaks in the spring. Features that help identification are the Blue Grosbeak's huge bill, uniformly dark plumage, black face, and reddish shoulder, which the buntings lack.

VOICE Call a loud, sharp, metallic *tchink*; similar to Indigo Bunting, but lower-pitched, louder, and burrier; song rambling, husky.
NESTING Compact cup placed low in deciduous tangle; 3–5 eggs; 1–2 broods; April–July.
FEEDING Eats seeds in winter, insects such as beetles, caterpillars, and grasshoppers in summer, and fruit.

SIMILAR SPECIES

INDIGO BUNTING ♂ 1ST ⚥ see p.440	LAZULI BUNTING ♀ see p.472
pale blue markings overall	*pale brown upperparts* — *much smaller bill*

TRUE INDIGO
The Blue Grosbeak is actually indigo in color, with rufous shoulders and wing bars.

OCCURRENCE
Breeds in dense undergrowth of disturbed habitats: old fields, hedgerows, and desert scrub across the southern US from California to New Jersey, and southward to northwestern Costa Rica; breeders are trans-Gulf migrants; winters from Mexico to Panama and West Indies.

Length **6¾in (17cm)**	Wingspan **11in (28cm)**	Weight **⅞–1¹⁄₁₆oz (25–30g)**
Social **Large flocks**	Lifespan **Up to 6 years**	Status **Secure**

DATE SEEN	WHERE	NOTES

| Order **Passeriformes** | Family **Cardinalidae** | Species *Passerina cyanea* |

Indigo Bunting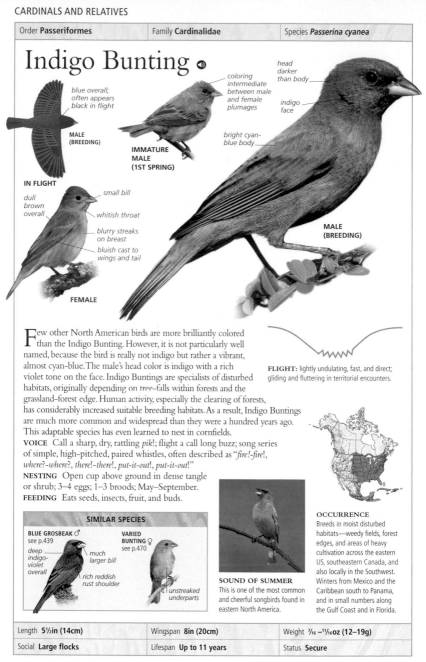

MALE (BREEDING)
blue overall; often appears black in flight

IN FLIGHT

IMMATURE MALE (1ST SPRING)
coloring intermediate between male and female plumages

head darker than body

indigo face

bright cyan-blue body

MALE (BREEDING)

FEMALE
dull brown overall
small bill
whitish throat
blurry streaks on breast
bluish cast to wings and tail

Few other North American birds are more brilliantly colored than the Indigo Bunting. However, it is not particularly well named, because the bird is really not indigo but rather a vibrant, almost cyan-blue. The male's head color is indigo with a rich violet tone on the face. Indigo Buntings are specialists of disturbed habitats, originally depending on tree-falls within forests and the grassland-forest edge. Human activity, especially the clearing of forests, has considerably increased suitable breeding habitats. As a result, Indigo Buntings are much more common and widespread than they were a hundred years ago. This adaptable species has even learned to nest in cornfields.

VOICE Call a sharp, dry, rattling *pik*!; flight a call long buzz; song series of simple, high-pitched, paired whistles, often described as "*fire!-fire!*, *where?-where?*, *there!-there!*, *put-it-out!*, *put-it-out!*"

NESTING Open cup above ground in dense tangle or shrub; 3–4 eggs; 1–3 broods; May–September.

FEEDING Eats seeds, insects, fruit, and buds.

FLIGHT: lightly undulating, fast, and direct; gliding and fluttering in territorial encounters.

SIMILAR SPECIES

BLUE GROSBEAK ♂
see p.439
deep indigo-violet overall
much larger bill
rich reddish rust shoulder

VARIED BUNTING ♀
see p.470
unstreaked underparts

SOUND OF SUMMER
This is one of the most common and cheerful songbirds found in eastern North America.

OCCURRENCE
Breeds in moist disturbed habitats—weedy fields, forest edges, and areas of heavy cultivation across the eastern US, southeastern Canada, and also locally in the Southwest. Winters from Mexico and the Caribbean south to Panama, and in small numbers along the Gulf Coast and in Florida.

| Length **5½in (14cm)** | Wingspan **8in (20cm)** | Weight **⁷/₁₆ –1¹/₁₆oz (12–19g)** |
| Social **Large flocks** | Lifespan **Up to 11 years** | Status **Secure** |

DATE SEEN	WHERE	NOTES

| Order **Passeriformes** | Family **Cardinalidae** | Species *Passerina ciris* |

Painted Bunting 🔊

IN FLIGHT

blue head

irregular bluish patches on head

irregular reddish patches on wings and underparts

MALE (BREEDING)

lime-green color above

yellowish underparts

FEMALE

glowing lime-green back

red-and-green wings

MALE (1ST SPRING)

violet-blue hood

red rump

red underparts

MALE

FLIGHT: lightly undulating, fast, and direct hovering "butterfly flight" when males meet.

With its violet-blue head, red underparts, and vibrant lime-green back, the adult male Painted Bunting is the most brightly colored North American bunting. Although duller, the female is distinctive as one of the few truly green songbirds of the region. Young males take on a variety of appearances and can resemble an adult male, a female, or something in between. There are two populations, differing in molt pattern. The more western birds molt after leaving the breeding grounds, whereas the more eastern molt before they depart south for the winter.

VOICE Call a soft, ringing, upward slurred *pwip!;* flight call slurred, softer, and flatter than Indigo Bunting; song a sweet, rambling, relatively clear warble.

NESTING Deep cup in dense tangle or shrub, just above ground; 3–4 eggs; 1–3 broods; May–August.

FEEDING Eats seeds, fruit, and insects.

SIMILAR SPECIES

INDIGO BUNTING ♀ see p.440

lacks green upperparts

bluish wash to tail

VARIED BUNTING ♀ see p.470

streaked breast

tan overall

lacks green upperparts

stubbier bill

tan overall

"NONPAREIL"
In Louisiana, the French word for "unparalleled" is fittingly used to describe this gorgeous species.

OCCURRENCE
Breeds in thickets and disturbed areas, across the south-central US and northern Mexico, and along the East Coast from Florida to North Carolina. Nonbreeders use similar habitats. Western birds (New Mexico, Texas) winter from tropical Mexico to western Panama; eastern birds winter in southern Florida and Cuba.

| Length **5½in (14cm)** | Wingspan **8½in (22cm)** | Weight **7/16–11/16oz (12–21g)** |
| Social **Solitary/Flocks** | Lifespan **Up to 12 years** | Status **Declining** |

DATE SEEN	WHERE	NOTES

Order **Passeriformes**	Family **Cardinalidae**	Species *Spiza americana*

Dickcissel

streaked back

MALE (BREEDING)

IN FLIGHT

yellow eyebrow

gray nape

rufous shoulder

large pointed bill

yellow-tinged eyebrow

bold braces on back

black "V" on yellow breast

FEMALE

finely streaked underparts

paler gray on face

no rufous shoulder

MALE (BREEDING)

MALE (NONBREEDING)

The Dickcissel is a tallgrass prairie specialist and seldom breeds outside the range of this habitat. Known for its spectacular seasonal movements, the Dickcissel winters in Venezuela, with flocks in the tens of thousands ravaging rice fields and damaging seed crops. Immature birds, without yellow and rusty plumage, are very similar to female House Sparrows—vagrant and wintering Dickcissels in North America are often mistaken for sparrows.
VOICE Call a flat *chik*; flight call a distinctive, low, electric buzz *frrrrrrrt*; song a short series of sharp, insect-like stutters followed by few longer chirps or trill *dick-dick-dick-SISS-SISS-suhl*.
NESTING Bulky cup placed near ground in dense vegetation; 3–6 eggs; 1–2 broods; May–August.
FEEDING Forages on ground for insects, spiders, and seeds.

FLIGHT: strong, direct, and slightly undulating; flocks in tight balls.

UNIQUE SONG
The Dickcissel's onomatopoetic song is the characteristic sound of a healthy tallgrass prairie.

SIMILAR SPECIES

HOUSE SPARROW ♀ see p.340
shorter bill

EASTERN MEADOWLARK see p.386
longer bill
shorter tail
no streaking on underparts
bright yellow underparts

OCCURRENCE
Breeds in tallgrass prairie, grasslands, hayfields, unmown roadsides, and untilled cropfields across the eastern and central US. Barely reaches southernmost Canada and northeastern Mexico. Winters in huge flocks in Venezuela, in open areas with tall grass-like vegetation, including rice fields.

Length **6½in (16cm)**	Wingspan **9½in (24cm)**	Weight **⅞–1¼oz (25–35g)**
Social **Large flocks**	Lifespan **Up to 5 years**	Status **Secure**

DATE SEEN	WHERE	NOTES

RARE SPECIES

Family **Anatidae**	Species ***Dendrocygna autumnalis***

Black-bellied Whistling-Duck

With its distinctive red bill and long, pink legs, this Whistling-Duck is spectacular and unmistakable. Unlike most other waterfowl, it has long legs and an upright posture when standing. Whistling-ducks used to be known as "tree-ducks" because they perch on trees when they roost and nest.

OCCURRENCE Prefers shallow, freshwater wetlands; rice fields are a common foraging habitat; also occurs along shorelines and mud bars.

Casual west to southeastern California and occasionally east as far as Florida.

VOICE Soft wheezy series of 5–6 notes *pit pit weee do dew*; flight calls include a *chit-chit-chit*.

black belly

ADULT

long pink legs

Length **18½–20in (47–51cm)**	Wingspan **34–36in (86–91cm)**

Family **Anatidae**	Species ***Cygnus buccinator***

Trumpeter Swan

North America's quintessential swan and heaviest waterfowl, the magnificent Trumpeter Swan has made a remarkable comeback after numbers were severely reduced by hunting; by the mid-1930s, fewer than a hundred birds were known to exist. Active reintroduction efforts were made in the upper Midwest and Ontario to reestablish the species to its former breeding range. Its typical far-reaching call is usually the best way to identify it.

OCCURRENCE Alaskan and northern Canadian breeders go south to winter; others remain year round at local places such as Yellowstone National Park. Found on freshwater lakes and marshes with plenty of vegetation. Occurs in estuaries in winter.

VOICE Call nasal, resonant *oh-OH* reminiscent of a French horn, is usually the best way to identify it.

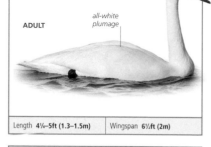

all-white plumage

ADULT

Length **4¼–5ft (1.3–1.5m)**	Wingspan **6½ft (2m)**

Family **Anatidae**	Species ***Nomonyx dominicus***

Masked Duck

A small, widespread, Neotropical species, the Masked Duck is rarely seen because of its secretive behavior. Masked Ducks stay hidden in dense vegetation. Like grebes, it sinks below the surface to avoid detection, and drags its tail under the water. In flight, its white wing patch is characteristic. Females have two dark bars across their face, and a mottled brown body. They are related to the Ruddy Duck, both of which are called stiff-tailed ducks.

OCCURRENCE Resident of southern Texas, with scattered records elsewhere. Found in heavily vegetated freshwater marshes and ponds. Resident from Mexico to Argentina, and in the Caribbean.

VOICE Male gives a throaty *coo-coo-coo*, or *kir-roo-kirroo-kiroo* call during courtship; female a short, repeated hiss.

blue bill with black tip

deep chestnut with black mottling

MALE

Length **13–15in (33–38cm)**	Wingspan **17in (43cm)**

Family **Cracidae**	Species ***Ortalis vetula***

Plain Chachalaca

A large, dull-brown to olive-green bird, the Plain Chachalaca deftly moves through trees and shrubs when foraging, running along branches and hopping from tree to tree. Males develop a distinct reddish to pink, naked-skin facial patch and throat during the breeding season.

OCCURRENCE Occurs only along the lower Rio Grande River valley of Texas, in shrubby and wooded areas, and edges of brushy thickets along river bottoms.

VOICE Boisterous, three-syllable *cha-ca-lak*; especially loud when pairs or groups call in chorus.

ADULT

long, fanned-out, white-tipped tail

Length **20–23in (51–58cm)**	Wingspan **24–27in (61–68cm)**

Family *Odontophoridae*	Species *Callipepla squamata*

Scaled Quail

Named for the scale-like appearance of its chest, neck, and belly feathers, this quail is also called the "Blue Quail," because of its bluish sheen in some lights, or "Cottontop," because of the fluffy white tip to its crest. Its populations periodically go through "boom and bust" cycles that may be tied to rainfall and its impact on their food supply, but are also influenced by grazing practices.

OCCURRENCE Common in arid rangeland and semidesert of western Texas, New Mexico, and eastern Arizona, preferring less dense vegetation than other quails.

VOICE Flushed or separated covey (flock) uses 2-syllable *CHE-kar* call to reunite.

short tail

MALE

Length **10–12in (25–30cm)**	Wingspan **13–15in (33–38cm)**

Family **Podicipedidae**	Species *Tachybaptus dominicus*

Least Grebe

This tiny, tropical and subtropical species is the most easily overlooked of the North American grebes. This is primarily because it breeds only in fresh or brackish water in southern Texas. It is a good diver, capable of remaining submerged for more than 25 seconds. While adults are not seen on land, swimming chicks can clamber ashore when they are threatened.

OCCURRENCE Temporary or permanent bodies of fresh and brackish water, such as mangrove swamps, marsh openings, small ponds, ditches, lakes, and slow-moving rivers, often with very little or no emergent vegetation.

VOICE Metallic, sputtering trill, accelerating at the start, then slowing down then accelerating again; alarm call a single *beep*.

yellowish orange eye

ADULT (SUMMER)

Length **9–10½in (23–27cm)**	Wingspan **19–21in (48–53cm)**

Family **Podicepedidae**	Species *Aechmophorus occidentalis*

Western Grebe

A strictly North American species, the Western Grebe shares much of its breeding habitat and elaborate mating rituals with Clark's Grebe. Until 1985, they were considered to be different color forms of a single species. Females are smaller than males and have smaller, thinner, slightly upturned bills. This species dives more frequently than Clark's, and remains submerged for about 30 seconds.

OCCURRENCE Western North America, breeds in freshwater lakes and marshes with open water and emergent vegetation; also manmade marshes and artificial habitats. Winters along the Pacific Coast.

VOICE At least nine different calls, each with a specific information content, such as alarm, begging, and mating calls; advertising call is a harsh, rolling 2-noted *krrrikk-krrreek*.

black behind eye

ADULT

Length **21½–30in (55–75cm)**	Wingspan **30–39in (76–100cm)**

Family **Podicipedidae**	Species *Aechmophorus clarkii*

Clark's Grebe

Clark's and Western Grebes are closely related and very difficult to distinguish from each other except by call, bill, or facial pattern. They rarely fly except when migrating at night. As their legs and toes are set far back making their movement awkward, they seldom come on land. However, they have been reported to run upright rapidly. Their flight muscles are quite reduced after they arrive on their breeding grounds.

OCCURRENCE Breeds in freshwater lakes and marshes bordered by emergent vegetation; has been nesting in manmade Lake Havasu marshes since 1960s. Winters along the Pacific Coast.

VOICE Variety of calls, including a harsh, grating, 2-syllable, single, rising *kree-eekt* advertising call.

ADULT

white around eye

Length **21½–30in (55–75cm)**	Wingspan **32in (82cm)**

Family **Columbidae**	Species *Patagioenas flavirostris*

Red-billed Pigeon

The only North American area where this Mexican and Central American pigeon occurs is riverside woodlands of southern Texas. Wine-red below, bluish gray above, with yellow eyes and a red eye-ring, it is unmistakable. It is similar in size and posture to a Rock Pigeon but it has a longer tail and a more slender body. In comparison to a Band-tailed Pigeon, it appears heavier.

OCCURRENCE Prefers to perch in tall trees above brushy understory in wooded bottomlands of Texas's Rio Grande Valley.

VOICE Long, high-pitched, hoarse *coooo* followed by 2–5 *up*, *cup-a-coos*.

bill
red
at base

ADULT

Length **14½in (37cm)**	Wingspan **24in (62cm)**

Family **Columbidae**	Species *Patagioenas leucocephala*

White-crowned Pigeon

Similar in size and shape to the Rock Pigeon, the White-crowned Pigeon has a distinctive white crown, slate-gray back, and slightly longer tail. In addition, it is only found in the Florida Keys and the southern tip of Florida. It occasionally feeds around hotels and in suburban backyards. This strict frugivore is uncommon in the United States.

OCCURRENCE Nests in both red and black mangrove islands. Winters in seasonal deciduous forests of the Florida Keys and Everglades National Park. May travel some distance each day to visit feeding sites.

white
crown

VOICE Loud, deep *coo-curra-coo*, repeated 5–8 times; also low, purring growl.

ADULT

Length **13–14in (33–35cm)**	Wingspan **23in (59cm)**

Family **Columbidae**	Species *Leptotila verreauxi*

White-tipped Dove

The North American range of the White-tipped Dove is restricted to southern Texas, but it is actually a widespread species, occurring from Mexico through Central and South America to Argentina. A rather shy bird, the White-tipped Dove keeps out of sight, foraging on the floor of mesquite and other woodlands, but its distinctive, two- or three-syllable mournful whistle is often heard.

OCCURRENCE Occurs in the US only in southeastern Texas, where it breeds and winters in dense woodlands of mesquite, Texas ebony, and cedar elm near rivers and oxbow lakes.

VOICE Long, quavering *wh'whoo'oo*, which sounds like someone blowing into an empty bottle.

ADULT

short
tail

Length **10–12in (25–30cm)**	Wingspan **18in (46cm)**

Family **Cuculidae**	Species *Crotophaga ani*

Smooth-billed Ani

The Smooth-billed Ani colonized southern Florida in the early 1930s, then steadily declined in the 1980s. It is a communal breeder. Several females lay eggs in the same nest. Their large bills distinguish Smooth-billed Anis from other all-black birds like grackles or crows. They feed on or near the ground on insects, small vertebrates, and fruit.

upper mandible
lacks grooves

OCCURRENCE Prefers shrubby areas, agricultural lands, and hedges in southern Florida. Common in the West Indies, Central, and South America.

VOICE Main call is a whiny, ascending *yaahnee.*

ADULT

Length **14½in (37cm)**	Wingspan **18½in (46cm)**

Family **Cuculidae**	Species *Crotophaga sulcirostris*

Groove-billed Ani

Anis, members of the cuckoo family, have black plumage, long tails, and high, narrow, blackish bills. They always appear dishevelled—as if their feathers were about to fall off. Two of their toes point forward and two backward. These social birds have an unusual communal nesting behavior for cuckoos: several females lay eggs in the same nest, and both males and females share incubation duties.

OCCURRENCE Breeds from southern Texas and Mexico to Central and South America.

VOICE Call a liquid *Tee-ho*, accented on first syllable, given in flight and when perched, chorus like when many birds call together.

high blackish bill

long tail

Length **13½in (34cm)**	Wingspan **17in (43cm)**

Family **Cuculidae**	Species *Cocczyus minor*

Mangrove Cuckoo

The Mangrove Cuckoo's solitary and secretive behavior, as well as its preference for dense, nearly inaccessible mangrove habitats, make it difficult to study. This, combined with the continued human development of mangroves in Florida make the future of this cuckoo uncertain in the US. Widespread in the Caribbean, and from Mexico to Colombia.

OCCURRENCE Found in Florida, in coastal areas from Tampa Bay southward and in the Florida Keys, in mangrove swamps, and also locally in other woodland habitats.

VOICE Series of up to 2 dozen harsh, frog-like notes, *aarhm aarhm aarrhmmm*; also fast *coo coo coo*.

black mask

large, white spots on underside of tail

ADULT

Length **11–12½in (28–32cm)**	Wingspan **16in (41cm)**

Family **Caprimulgidae**	Species *Chordeiles acutipennis*

Lesser Nighthawk

Well camouflaged when it rests on the ground during daytime, the Lesser Nighthawk is an aerial forager that is most active at dusk and dawn. It swoops low over water, bush, and desert in pursuit of insect prey, which it tracks with agile and abrupt changes in direction. This species was formerly known as the Trilling Nighthawk because of its distinctive call, which distinguishes it from the similar-looking Common Nighthawk, which has a *peent* call.

OCCURRENCE Breeds in desert, open scrub, and along watercourses. Occurs from the southern US to Central and South America.

VOICE Low, trilled whistle which lasts up to 12 seconds and resembles the calls of some species of toads.

white band across wing tips

MALE

Length **8–9in (20–23cm)**	Wingspan **21–23in (53–58cm)**

Family **Caprimulgidae**	Species *Nyctidromus albicollis*

Common Pauraque

The Common Pauraque is found only in South Texas, where it is a nonmigratory resident. It is possible to get quite close to pauraques during the day, as they rely on their camouflage for protection. Common Pauraques feed at night. They perch in open locations and ambush passing insects with sudden bursts of flight.

OCCURRENCE Found in open scrub, sparsely wooded areas, and hedgerows; feeds over open fields, forest clearings, and roads. Breeds from southern Texas to Central and South America.

VOICE Strange, slurred, or buzzed *p'wheeerr* whistle; also various harsh-sounding calls.

dark spots on back

ADULT

Length **10–11in (25–28cm)**	Wingspan **21–23in (53–58cm)**

Family **Caprimulgidae**	Species *Phalaenoptilus nuttallii*

Common Poorwill

This nocturnal bird is the smallest North American nightjar, with much shorter wings than its relatives, a stubbier tail, but a comparatively larger head. It can go into a state of torpor, somewhat similar to mammalian hibernation and hummingbird torpor, remaining in this state for several days, perhaps even weeks, during cold weather or when food is unavailable. The male has whitish corners to its tail, while the female is buffy.

OCCURRENCE Breeds in arid habitats from the western US southward to Mexico. Winters in northern Mexico.

VOICE Call low, whistled, *purr-WHEEOO* or *pooor-WEELLUP*.

delicately mottled brownish gray to pale gray plumage

ADULT

Length **7½–8½in (19–21cm)**	Wingspan **15½–19in (40–48cm)**

Family **Trochilidae**	Species *Archilochus alexandri*

Black-chinned Hummingbird

The Black-chinned Hummingbird is widespread in the western US, where it occurs in a variety of habitats. It readily accepts sugar water at birdfeeders. During courtship, the males perform a distinctive dive display comprising several broad arcs in addition to a short, back-and-forth shuttle flight. The latter is accompanied by a droning sound produced by the bird's wings.

OCCURRENCE Widespread in scrub and woodlands close to rivers and streams, irrigated urban areas, and semiarid scrub; also found in drier habitats; forages away from breeding habitats where nectar sources are found. Winters along the Pacific Coast of Mexico

VOICE Call a soft, thick *chic*; fast, buzzy *tsi-tsi-tsi-tsi-tsi-tsi-tsi-tsi* is used to chase off other birds; song soft, warbling, very rarely heard.

MALE

blackish gorget

Length **3½in (9cm)**	Wingspan **4¾in (12cm)**

Family **Trochilidae**	Species *Amazilia yucatanensis*

Buff-bellied Hummingbird

A resident of the southeastern coast of Texas, the Buff-bellied Hummingbird can be identified by its large size, iridescent emerald body, and tawny belly. It is locally common in gardens, where it is dominant over other species of hummingbirds. Planted flowers and feeders have helped this species expand its range. It now winters from its breeding range eastward to gardens along the Gulf Coast to Florida.

OCCURRENCE In the US, found in a variety of lowland habitats with brushy vegetation, including gardens, mesquite woodland edges; partial migrant.

VOICE Call hard, sharp *tik*, often doubled or rolled into series; chase call buzzier and in fast series; no well-defined song, usually mix of slurred chip notes.

tawny belly

MALE

Length **4in (10cm)**	Wingspan **5½in (14cm)**

Family **Gruidae**	Species *Grus americana*

Whooping Crane

The majestic Whooping Crane is one of the most compelling success stories of the US Endangered Species Act. The species has rebounded from just a few dozen birds in the mid-20th century to hundreds of individuals in the early 21st. However, it still remains in a critical state because it reproduces slowly in a restricted range. More intervention measures are required to help this fragile species continue its recovery.

OCCURRENCE Breeds in marshy country with scattered ponds and prairies in a restricted region of Canada; winters in coastal estuaries in Texas; uses marshland and agricultural fields during migration.

VOICE Piercing and trumpeting, *kerloo!* and *kerleeyew*; bugling calls during courtship dances.

white overall

ADULT

Length **4–4½ft (1.2–1.4m)**	Wingspan **7¼ft (2.2m)**

Family **Charadriidae**	Species *Charadrius montanus*

Mountain Plover

Unlike many other North American shorebirds, this rather plain-looking plover is rarely found near water. Unusually wary, the Mountain Plover often faces away from danger and squats motionless on the ground, "disappearing" into the landscape and earning it the nickname of "Prairie Ghost." It is declining, and endangered because of habitat loss from overgrazing and pesticides.

OCCURRENCE Patchily distributed in west–central North America. Breeds in dry, flat, short grass prairies, semidesert areas with sparse vegetation; winters south to Mexico.

VOICE Generally silent; flight call grating *kirrp*; wintering birds in flight give short *kip* call; courtship song rolling, drawled, whistled *wee-wee*.

tan-colored overall

ADULT (BREEDING)

Length 8½–9½ in (21–24cm)	Wingspan 21½–23½in (54–60cm)

Family **Scolopacidae**	Species *Numenius americanus*

Long-billed Curlew

This large curlew has the southernmost breeding and northernmost wintering ranges of the four North American curlews. It is also one of nine bird species that are endemic to the grasslands of the Great Plains. It is remarkably tame on its wintering grounds.

OCCURRENCE Breeds in prairies, short grass and mixed-grass habitats of the Great Basin and Great Plains. Some stragglers occur in Florida, most birds winter in California, Texas, and Mexico.

VOICE Flight call a 2-note *cur-LUoo*, often accompanied by rapid *qui-pi-pi-pi-pi*; flight song haunting whistles, trills *werr-EEEer*.

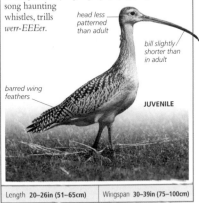

head less patterned than adult

bill slightly shorter than in adult

barred wing feathers

JUVENILE

Length 20–26in (51–65cm)	Wingspan 30–39in (75–100cm)

Family **Scolopacidae**	Species *Calidris ferruginea*

Curlew Sandpiper

The Curlew Sandpiper, a medium-sized Eurasian sandpiper, breeds in northern Siberia. It can be confused with the Dunlin and Stilt Sandpiper in nonbreeding plumage. It is slimmer than the Dunlin, with longer wings, neck, legs, and bill, and differs from the Stilt Sandpiper by its shorter legs and faint white eyebrow.

OCCURRENCE Rare, but regular migrant along the Atlantic Coast; accidental elsewhere. Found in a variety of habitats, including beaches, coastal mudflats, impoundments, and lake margins.

VOICE Flight call a characteristic, musical, trilled, or rolled *chrreep*, dropping in the middle.

JUVENILE

long, decurved bill

black legs

Length 7¼–7½in (18–19cm)	Wingspan 16¾–18½in (42–46cm)

Family **Stercorariidae**	Species *Stercorarius skua*

Great Skua

The Great Skua can be distinguished from the South Polar Skua by its heavier streaking and usually more reddish tones to its brown body. The Great Skua is closely related to several species of Southern Hemisphere skuas including the South Polar Skua. The Great Skua is aggressive, and is often seen harassing other birds, like Herring Gulls, to make them disgorge their food.

OCCURRENCE Rare visitor, mostly in fall through spring, to pelagic waters off the Atlantic Coast of North America.

VOICE Rough, cackling *rah-rah-rah* at colonies. Usually silent at sea.

strong, hooked bill

dark nape

mottled gray to warm brown plumage

ADULT

Length 19½–23in (50–58cm)	Wingspan 4–4½ft (1.2–1.4m)

Family **Stercorariidae**	Species *Stercorarius maccormicki*

South Polar Skua

Probably a regular visitor to US waters, the South Polar Skua is a large, aggressive relative of the jaegers. It pursues other seabirds to make them disgorge their food, or battles for scraps behind fishing boats. It is a severe threat to penguins on its breeding grounds, roaming around their colonies and waiting to take an egg or snatch a chick. The South Polar Skua takes several years to mature, and stays at sea for long periods until it reaches adulthood.

OCCURRENCE Spends southern winters offshore in the North Atlantic and Pacific; breeds in the South Shetland Islands and along the coast and islands of the Antarctic Peninsula.

VOICE Deep gull-like burbling; generally silent at sea.

ADULT

hooked bill

generally unstreaked parts

Length 21in (53cm)	Wingspan 4¼ft (1.3m)

Family **Laridae**	Species *Rhodostethia rosea*

Ross's Gull

Named for the great British Polar explorer, James Clark Ross, this species is unmistakable in its adult breeding plumage. Dove-gray upperparts, pale-pink underparts, red legs, small black bill, and black collar, make it an elegant and beautiful bird. In winter it lacks the distinctive black neck ring and the delicate pink blush on the underside may be more muted.

OCCURRENCE Siberian breeder found along the north coast of Alaska in fall; breeds along Hudson Bay in Canada; winter strays found across Canada and in northeastern and northwestern US.

VOICE Rarely heard in winter; a tern-like *kik-kik-kik* on the breeding grounds.

black "necklace"

ADULT
(BREEDING)

red legs

rosy underparts

Length 11½–12in (29–31cm)	Wingspan 35–39in (90–100cm)

Family **Laridae**	Species *Anous minutus*

Black Noddy

This species is the rarest and has the most restricted occurrence of any tern that regularly occurs in North America. Since 1962 small numbers of nonbreeding Black Noddies have been seen nearly annually in the Brown Noddy colony of the Dry Tortugas, off the Florida Keys. The Black Noddy is slightly smaller than the Brown Noddy, and has a thinner bill, black upperparts and a white forehead.

OCCURRENCE Subtropical and tropical seas; pelagic away from breeding colonies; regular at Dry Tortugas, but does not breed; accidental along Texas Coast.

VOICE High-pitched *caw* or *kark* calls when breeding; otherwise silent.

white forehead

ADULT

black upperparts

Length 14–15½in (35–40cm)	Wingspan 26–28in (65–72cm)

Family **Laridae**	Species *Anous stolidus*

Brown Noddy

The Brown Noddy resembles a typical tern species but with the colors reversed, its pale gray forehead and crown contrasting with its dark body. Noddies nest on rocks and islands in tropical waters around the world. Its only breeding ground in North America is a few miles off the Florida Keys. It is very tame and shows little fear of humans, hence its scientific name, *Anous stolidus*, which is Latin for "foolish" and "slow-witted."

OCCURRENCE Only nesting site in the US is at Dry Tortugas, off the Florida Keys; during summer occurs offshore in Gulf of Mexico, as far north as the Outer Banks, North Carolina.

VOICE Variety of crow-like *caw* or *kark* calls given around nesting colonies; otherwise silent.

very dark brown upperparts

ADULT

Length 15½–17½in (40–45cm)	Wingspan 30–33in (77–85cm)

Family **Laridae**	Species *Onychoprion fuscatus*

Sooty Tern

Except when nesting, the Sooty Tern spends most of its life flying over the tropical and subtropical oceans of the world. After fledging, the young do not return to land for six to eight years. The Sooty Tern's plumage is not particularly waterproof so the bird rarely settles on the water. It sometimes perches on floating debris or even on sea turtles.

OCCURRENCE A large colony breeds at the Dry Tortugas, off the Florida Keys. Small numbers breed along the coast of Texas and near the mouth of the Mississippi River. In summer, found in the Gulf Stream north to Virginia.

VOICE Distinctive nasal call: *wide-a-wake*, *wide-a-wake* has given it the vernacular name of "Wideawake Tern." Vocal throughout year, particularly when breeding.

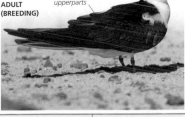

black
upperparts

**ADULT
(BREEDING)**

Length **14–17½in (36–45cm)**	Wingspan **32–37in (82–94cm)**

Family **Laridae**	Species *Onychoprion anaethetus*

Bridled Tern

Compared with other terns, the Bridled Tern has darker, browner upperparts, and in strong subtropical light its underparts appear shaded, giving the bird an overall dark look. When perched, breast and shoulders stand out pure white. Note the long white line, or bridle, tapering above each eye, and the black legs and bill, with no hint of red. It first bred in the Florida Keys in 1987, and has nested there occasionally since then. It spends most of its life at sea.

OCCURRENCE Nests in the West Indies and Bahamas, irregularly in Florida. Regular, but mostly far offshore in the Gulf of Mexico.

VOICE Rising, whistled *wheeep* call; also barking *wup, wup*; vocal at colonies.

white
supercilium

forked
tail

**ADULT
(BREEDING)**

Length **12–12½in (30–32cm)**	Wingspan **30–32in (77–81cm)**

Family **Hydrobatidae**	Species *Hydrobates castro*

Band-rumped Storm-Petrel

This uncommon summer visitor forages 25–35 miles (40–56km) in warm offshore waters of the Gulf Stream and the Gulf of Mexico. Its origin is unclear, but it probably comes from colonies in the eastern Atlantic. They appear brawny, long-winged, and square-tailed with the white at the base of their tail extending along the flanks to the belly.

OCCURRENCE A warm-water petrel of the Gulf Stream and Gulf of Mexico. Breeds on islands in the tropical and subtropical Pacific (*H. c. bangsi*) and Atlantic Oceans (*H. c. castro*). Most birds seen in North America probably breed in the eastern Atlantic Ocean.

VOICE Silent at sea; squeaking and purring sounds at nest.

white
extends
to sides

feet do not
extend beyond
tail in flight

ADULT

Length **7½–8½in (19–21cm)**	Wingspan **17–18½ in (43–47cm)**

Family **Procellariidae**	Species *Pterodroma hasitata*

Black-capped Petrel

Until recently, the Black-capped Petrel was almost unknown in North America because of its offshore feeding grounds. After breeding in the West Indies, they move northwestward to feed in the warm Gulf Stream during the summer, where they are seen fairly commonly during deep-water birdwatching trips. Their flight is characteristic of *Pterodroma* species: they rocket up above the ocean and then drop back down while moving forward swiftly, using lift from the air currents above the water.

OCCURRENCE When not breeding, forage at sea over the deep, warm water of the Gulf Stream off the southeastern US.

VOICE Silent at sea but vocal on breeding grounds.

white
forehead

long,
pointed
wings

ADULT

Length **13in (33cm)**	Wingspan **35in (88cm)**

Family **Procellariidae**	Species **Puffinus lherminieri**

Audubon's Shearwater

Audubon's Shearwater is smaller and more slender than all the other regularly occurring shearwaters in North American waters. It has especially short wings that, when combined with its small size, make its flight similar to that of members of the family Alcidae (auks, murres, and puffins).
OCCURRENCE Breeds on Caribbean islands; widespread in tropical waters; spends warmer months feeding in the Gulf of Mexico and along the East Coast of the US.
VOICE Occasional thin, high-pitched call; twittering and mewing calls at colonies, but silent at sea.

dark undertail feathers

white underparts

ADULT

Length **12in (31cm)**	Wingspan **27in (69cm)**

Family **Sulidae**	Species **Sula leucogaster**

Brown Booby

The Brown Booby, which is actually bicolor, sooty brown and white, overlaps with the Masked and Red-footed Boobies and often nests in mixed colonies with them.
OCCURRENCE Breeds on tropical islands of the Atlantic, Pacific, and Indian Oceans, and on Caribbean islands. Rare along Atlantic and Pacific Coasts. Occurs closer to shore than Masked Booby.
VOICE Silent, but can make loud or subdued quacking, honking, or braying noises, especially when nesting.

wings black and white underneath

long, yellowish bill

ADULT

Length **30in (76cm)**	Wingspan **4½ft (1.4m)**

Family **Phalacrocoracidae**	Species **Phalacrocorax brasilianus**

Neotropic Cormorant

The slender Neotropic Cormorant ranges widely in the Western Hemisphere. In the US, it breeds and winters along the Gulf Coast and in the lower Rio Grande Valley. Unlike other cormorant species, it tolerates human activities. In the 1960s, their numbers declined as a result of coastal development and pesticide use, but they have recovered in recent years. The nest is a platform of sticks lined with leaves, grass, and seaweed, cemented with guano.
OCCURRENCE Breeds in coastal marshes, swamps, and inland reservoirs from southeastern Texas and western Louisiana to Tierra del Fuego in South America; found in a wide variety of wetlands in fresh, brackish, or saltwater. Winters close inshore in protected bays, inlets, estuaries, and lagoons.
VOICE Series of low, pig-like grunts; croaks in alarm.

dull orange base to bill

ADULT

Length **24in (61cm)**	Wingspan **3¼ft (1m)**

Family **Accipitridae**	Species **Rostrhamus sociabilis**

Snail Kite

Formerly known as the Everglade Kite, this bird is found only in peninsular Florida, where it was discovered in 1844. They are nomadic, following the apple snail and breeding in colonies when the snails are abundant. The males may breed with several females in one season, but sequentially, rather than all at one time.
OCCURRENCE In Florida, found locally, year-round, in inland freshwater marshes and along shallow lakes. Also found in Mexico, Central and South America, and the Caribbean.
VOICE Grating cackle given by both sexes: *ka-ka-ka-ka-ka-ka* or a harsh *krrrr*, variations of nasal, sheep-like bleating *k-a-a-a-a-a-a*, while being harassed or when begging for food.

long pointed bill

bright orange feet

MALE

Length **14–16in (36–41cm)**	Wingspan **3½ft (1.1m)**

Family **Accipitridae**	Species *Chondrohierax uncinatus*

Hook-billed Kite

This kite occurs in tropical America from Mexico all the way south to Argentina, but in the US it is found only in the Rio Grande Valley of southeastern Texas, where fewer than 60 pairs have nested since the late 1960s. The Hook-billed Kite is long tailed, and broad at its wing tips. It is mostly seen flying in the morning and is rarely spotted later in the day.

OCCURRENCE Breeds and winters only in the Rio Grande Valley of extreme southern Texas; breeds in riverside scrub and woodlands.
VOICE Rapid rattle; *kekekekekekekeke* highest in the middle.

wings broad at tip

FEMALE

barred underparts

Length **18in (46cm)**	Wingspan **36in (92cm)**

Family **Accipitridae**	Species *Parabuteo unicinctus*

Harris's Hawk

Named by the renowned ornithologist John James Audubon in honor of his friend and patron, Edward Harris, Harris's Hawks nest in social units, unlike other American birds of prey. These groups engage in cooperative hunting: members take turns leading the chase to wear down their prey and share in the kill. This bird is popular with falconers.
OCCURRENCE Forages and breeds year-round in semiopen desert scrub, savanna, grassland, and wetland containing scattered large trees and cacti. Occasionally appears in suburban areas. Essentially a Central and South American species with a restricted range north of the Rio Grande.
VOICE Main territorial alarm call a prolonged, harsh growl lasting about 3 seconds; also chirps, croaks, and screams.

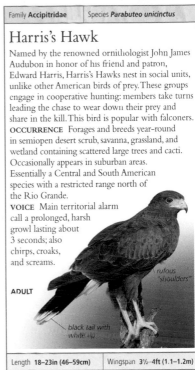

rufous "shoulders"

ADULT

black tail with white tip

Length **18–23in (46–59cm)**	Wingspan **3½–4ft (1.1–1.2m)**

Family **Accipitridae**	Species *Geranoaetus albicaudatus*

White-tailed Hawk

The White-tailed Hawk's distribution in the US is limited to southeastern Texas. An easily identifiable hawk, it is gray above, has a striking white breast, reddish shoulder patches, and black-banded white tail. Unlike other hawks, the adult's outer flight feathers extend noticeably beyond the tail when perched. It is a versatile forager, capturing prey by soaring, hovering, or by still-hunting from a perch. It likes to hunt at the edges of river basins.
OCCURRENCE Found in Texas in savanna, prairie, grasslands, lightly grazed pastures, open woodlands, and woody understory with yucca, mesquite, and thorny shrubs. Widespread in South America.
VOICE Series of scream-like calls *raa kad-ik kad-ik kad-ik kad-ik*.

dark gray facial pattern

broad black tail band

ADULT

wing broad at base and pointed at tip

Length **18–23in (46–58cm)**	Wingspan **4¼ft (1.3m)**

Family **Accipitridae**	Species *Buteo plagiatus*

Gray Hawk

The elegant Gray Hawk is found from Mexico south to Argentina, but in North America is only seen in southwestern Texas and southeastern Arizona. The Gray Hawk's breeding system can include trios, one female and two males, all of whom cooperate with chick rearing. About 100 pairs exist in the US, but their numbers are stable and possibly even increasing. Cottonwood and mesquite woodlands are key to their survival.
OCCURRENCE Breeds in riverside woodlands of mesquite and cottonwoods, especially along streams in the Gila River (Arizona) and Rio Grande (Texas) drainages. Little information exists about its winter habitats.
VOICE High-pitched whistled alarm, *creee*, rising and descending.

yellow legs and toes

ADULT

Length **16–17in (41–43cm)**	Wingspan **35in (89cm)**

Family **Accipitridae**	Species *Buteo brachyurus*

Short-tailed Hawk

In North America this species is found only in peninsular Florida, where it numbers only about 500 individuals. Like some other hawks, it has light and dark forms, the latter the more common one. This hawk is not easy to spot, as it seldom perches in the open and soars quite high. Its habitat is dwindling, and population studies are needed to learn more about its status and its future.

OCCURRENCE Found in woodlands, flooded upland habitats, savanna, prairies, and open country. Nests in cypress or bay swamps with closed canopy; winters where mangrove forest meets tidal sawgrass marsh, in wet prairies, also in suburban areas with forest tracts.

VOICE High-pitched cat-like *keeea* call; also a variety of *keee* calls.

dark brown head and white chin

ADULT (LIGHT FORM)

Length **15½–17½in (39–44cm)**	Wingspan **33–39in (83–100cm)**

Family **Accipitridae**	Species *Buteo albonotatus*

Zone-tailed Hawk

Widely distributed in Mexico, Central, and South America, the Zone-tailed Hawk's range barely reaches the Southwest. In Arizona, it shares the same riparian woodlands as the Common Black Hawk, but their behavior is quite different. Zone-tailed Hawks join kettles of high-flying Turkey Vultures, which they resemble to the point of mimicry. Using the vultures as a sort of decoy, the hawks spot live prey, then dive to catch it.

OCCURRENCE Nests in lowland riverside woodlands in Arizona, in pine and mixed woodlands at higher elevations in Texas and New Mexico. A migrant in the US, but largely resident from Central America south to Paraguay.

VOICE Harsh scream, 1-syllable *kreeee*, or 2-syllable *kreeee-arr*.

barred flight feathers

long wings

ADULT

Length **17½–22in (45–56cm)**	Wingspan **4–4½ft (1.2–1.4m)**

Family **Accipitridae**	Species *Buteo regalis*

Ferruginous Hawk

An inhabitant of open country, the Ferruginous Hawk is the largest North American hawk. It is a versatile nester, building its nest on cliffs, nearly level ground, trees, or manmade structures. Its numbers are threatened by its preference for prairie dog habitat, which is declining because of human encroachment, shooting, and pesticide use.

OCCURRENCE Breeds in low-elevation grasslands interrupted by cliffs or isolated trees in western North America; winters in the southwestern US and Mexico.

VOICE Screaming *Kree-aa* or *kaah, kaah* during courtship; quieter, lower-pitched, longer alarm call.

relatively long pointed wings

white undertail

ADULT (LIGHT FORM)

Length **22–27in (56–69cm)**	Wingspan **4¼–4½ft (1.3–1.4m)**

Family **Strigidae**	Species *Micrathene whitneyi*

Elf Owl

The diminutive Elf Owl is perhaps the most common bird of prey in the upland deserts of the southwestern US. Being strictly nocturnal it is more often heard than seen. Once heard, its distinctive voice is easy to recognize. Elf Owls defend their nests aggressively, and several birds can get together to mob an intruder.

OCCURRENCE Breeds in southern Nevada, Arizona, California, New Mexico, and Texas; also thorn scrub, woodlands along rivers, and suburban areas.

VOICE Call is a loud chatter of 5–6 notes; also trills and barks.

no "ear" tufts

thin white eyebrow

ADULT

Length **4¾–5½in (12–14cm)**	Wingspan **15in (38cm)**

| Family **Alcedinidae** | Species *Megaceryle torquata* |

Ringed Kingfisher

The largest of the three North American kingfishers, the Ringed Kingfisher is also easily identified by its color. It perches on trees and branches over water. Because of its shy nature this bird is difficult to spot despite its bright colors. It flies off at the least intrusion, but its loud rattle calls signal its presence. Like other kingfishers it nests in a burrow, which it digs in a muddy or sandy riverbank.

OCCURRENCE Found from the Rio Grande Valley in southern Texas to southern South America. Resident throughout range.

VOICE Loud rattle; also loud, double-syllabled *ktok-ktok* in flight.

white chest band between blue breast and chestnut belly

FEMALE

| Length **16in (41cm)** | Wingspan **25in (63cm)** |

| Family **Alcedinidae** | Species *Chloroceryle americana* |

Green Kingfisher

The smallest of the three species of North American kingfishers, the Green Kingfisher can also be distinguished by its proportionately longer bill and conspicuous white collar. Females lack the rufous breast of the male, and instead, have a broken greenish breastband. Like other kingfishers, the Green Kingfisher dives from perches over water to catch aquatic prey.

OCCURRENCE Breeds and winters near wooded shorelines of lakes, ponds, and streams. Found in South Texas, Arizona, and from Mexico all the way to southern South America.

VOICE Staccato "ticking" call; also a harsh, buzzy scold; quieter than other two North American kingfishers.

white collar

bronze-green upperparts

long, black bill

MALE

| Length **8½in (22cm)** | Wingspan **11in (28cm)** |

| Family **Picidae** | Species *Melanerpes aurifrons* |

Golden-fronted Woodpecker

Although the bright orange color of the nape is more visible than the yellow forehead, this is what gives this woodpecker its name. Males also have a red crown patch; females do not This species occasionally interbreeds with the closely related Red-bellied Woodpecker.

OCCURRENCE Southern Oklahoma and Texas, Mexico and Central America, south to Nicaragua.

VOICE A noisy, "rolled" *churr*, closely resembling the calls of other woodpeckers, especially the Red-bellied Woodpecker, but harsher; drumming rather short.

yellow forehead

MALE

| Length **10–12in (25–30cm)** | Wingspan **17in (43cm)** |

| Family **Picidae** | Species *Dryobates scalaris* |

Ladder-backed Woodpecker

A bird of the Southwest, the Ladder-backed Woodpecker has conspicuous black-and-white barring on the back and black-and-white facial pattern. Like many other North American woodpeckers, males have a red crown. This resident species uses cacti and trees both for breeding and to forage for insects.

OCCURRENCE Breeds in semidesert scrub, wooded canyons, and pine oak woodlands from California eastward to Texas, and from Mexico to Nicaragua.

VOICE Two main calls: a short, sharp *peek!*, and a whinny-like rattle with many notes that descend in pitch at the end.

conspicuous black-and-white facial pattern

MALE

| Length **7¼in (18.5cm)** | Wingspan **11–12in (28–30cm)** |

| Family **Falconidae** | Species *Caracara cheriway* |

Crested Caracara

In North America, the large, hawk-like Crested Caracara is only found locally in Texas, southern Arizona, and central Florida. The Crested Caracara is monogamous and territorial. Known locally as the "Mexican Buzzard," the Crested Caracara is a member of the family Falconidae (falcons) not Accipitridae (hawks).

OCCURRENCE Common in Central and South America. Breeds and winters in open areas ranging from desert to grassland with scattered tall trees; around agricultural land; dumps and slaughterhouses.
VOICE Adults disturbed at the nest emit cackles, hollow rattles, and high-pitched screams; nestlings utter high-pitched screams and raspy *swee-swee* calls.

dark bars on white breast and nape

ADULT

| Length **19–23in (48–58cm)** | Wingspan **4ft (1.2m)** |

| Family **Psittacidae** | Species *Psittacara holochlorus* |

Green Parakeet

A native of Mexico, Central America, and northern South America, this parakeet appeared in southern Texas in the 1980s. Since then, numbers have greatly increased, and are thought to have reached 2,000. Some birds have scattered yellow, orange, or red feathers on the head and breast.
OCCURRENCE Breeds and winters in urban and suburban areas in southern Texas and Florida; prefers exotic trees and shrubs. In Mexico and Central America, occurs in evergreen and deciduous forests up to 6,500 ft (2,000m).
VOICE High-pitched screeches; also shrill chattering when in flocks.

all green plumage

| Length **13in (33cm)** | Wingspan **21in (53cm)** |

| Family **Psittacidae** | Species *Amazona viridigenalis* |

Red-crowned Parrot

Red-crowned Parrots are becoming increasingly rare in their native range in northeastern Mexico because of habitat destruction and capture for the pet trade. Ironically, the naturalized population in California may now exceed in size that of the native Mexican one. These parrots forage and roost in flocks and often breed in loose nesting colonies.
OCCURRENCE Nonmigratory species, locally common in southern California and uncommon in southern Florida, southern Texas, and Puerto Rico. Lives in deciduous tropical rainforests in its native range.
VOICE Variety of loud squawks or shrieks; can mimic human speech and other sounds.

blue hind crown

red patch on wings

ADULT

| Length **12in (30cm)** | Wingspan **25in (63cm)** |

| Family **Tyrannidae** | Species *Camptostoma imberbe* |

Northern Beardless-Tyrannulet

This tiny flycatcher is usually first detected by its whistled calls. Once seen, it has a distinctive tail-flipping motion, crested look, and vireo-like foraging behavior. Unlike other flycatchers, it lacks bristles at the base of its bill, hence the name "beardless." "Tyrannulet" refers to its diminutive size.
OCCURRENCE Riparian woodlands with mesquite in southeastern Arizona and the lower Rio Grande Valley in Texas. Resident from Mexico to Costa Rica.
VOICE Calls are clear, piping, whistled *peeeuuu* or *peeut di-i-i-i*; song is a descending series of whistles *pee-pee-pee-pee*.

short, stubby bill, pale at base

grayish back

ADULT

| Length **4½–5½in (11.5–14cm)** | Wingspan **7in (18cm)** |

Family **Tyrannidae**	Species ***Myiarchus cinerascens***

Ash-throated Flycatcher

Of the three western species of *Myiarchus* flycatchers found in the US, this is the palest and also the most widespread and ecologically versatile. Desert scrub, mesquite woodland, riparian habitats with cottonwoods, juniper shrublands, and saguaro cactus are all places it chooses for breeding. Ash-throated Flycatchers, which are cavity-nesters, can adapt to manmade structures including pipes, the eaves of houses, and nest boxes.

OCCURRENCE Breeds in a variety of habitats at low to medium elevations. Migrates south to Mexico and Central America. Resident populations from Mexico to Costa Rica.

VOICE Call a rolled whistle, *wheer*, or exclamatory *huit*. Dawn song a repetitious *ha-wheer* or *ka-brick*.

relatively smooth crest

pale yellow belly

ADULT

Length **7–8in (18–20cm)**	Wingspan **12–13in (30–33cm)**

Family **Tyrannidae**	Species ***Myiarchus tyrannulus***

Brown-crested Flycatcher

The Brown-crested Flycatcher is the largest of the three western *Myiarchus* species. It is slender-looking, with a thick black bill, and a ragged, tan or brown crest. In flight, the rufous outer tail feathers are usually conspicuous. Although mostly insectivorous, it will sometimes catch a hummingbird. This late-spring migrant competes aggressively with other birds, such as woodpeckers, for nest holes.

OCCURRENCE Occurs from Nevada to Texas; breeds in riparian woodlands. Migrates south to Mexico and Guatemala. Resident populations from Honduras to South America.

VOICE Call a loud *huit*, often with a question mark at the end. Song a repetition of either *come-here* or *whit-will-do* heard only at dawn.

tan, bushy crest

ADULT

Length **8½in (22cm)**	Wingspan **13in (33cm)**

Family **Tyrannidae**	Species ***Pitangus sulphuratus***

Great Kiskadee

The Great Kiskadee is named after its loud song, which, together with its black mask, yellow belly, large size, and habit of perching in the open, make it quite a conspicuous bird. In Spanish it is called the Benteveo, which means "I see you well." Aggressive in defense of its roundish nest, the Great Kiskadee attacks birds of prey and snakes.

OCCURRENCE Local in Texas, in riverside woodlands, shady plantations, thorn scrub, and woodland edges. Resident.

VOICE Calls include loud exclamatory *reee* or *weeer*, *Chik-reee*, and harsh *Reep*, or *ick*; distinctive 3-syllable song *KIK-Chi-wee*, or *Kiss-ka-dee*, is most common during breeding season; highly vocal year-round.

conspicuous yellow belly

JUVENILE

Length **8½–10in (21–26 cm)**	Wingspan **15in (38cm)**

Family **Tyrannidae**	Species ***Tyrannus melancholicus***

Tropical Kingbird

Often found in residential areas, the Tropical Kingbird occurs in southeastern Arizona (where it is a migrant) and extreme southern Texas (where it is resident). After the breeding season, young Tropical Kingbirds disperse northward along the West Coast to British Columbia. This species is widespread from Mexico southward to Central and South America.

OCCURRENCE Breeds in open habitats of Arizona and Texas. In its tropical range, occurs in a wide variety of habitats, including pastureland, forest edges, suburban areas, urban parks, and riparian corridors.

VOICE Typical kingbird-like, loud, high-pitched twittering calls, given all year and throughout the day; song is a longer and more tremulous version of the call.

ADULT

pale grayish olive upperparts

thick bill

Length **7–9in (18–23cm)**	Wingspan **14½in (37cm)**

Family **Tyrannidae**	Species *Tyrannus couchii*

Couch's Kingbird

Spencer Fullerton Baird described this bird in 1860 as *Tyrannus melancholicus couchii*, to honor the famous ornithologist Elliott Coues. It is so similar to the Tropical Kingbird that it was not until the 1980's that W. John Smith realized they were two separate species that can easily be distinguished by their different voices, especially the dawn song.

OCCURRENCE Range restricted to southern Texas and eastern Mexico. Most Texas birds move south to Mexico in winter; occasional in Florida.

VOICE Does not have twittering calls of Tropical flycatcher; instead they are dry *peep* followed by rather jumbled series of notes, increasing in tempo, *tuwit, tuwit, tuwit, tuwitcheer.*

brownish gray wings

ADULT

Length **8–9in (20–23cm)**	Wingspan **15½in (39cm)**

Family **Tyrannidae**	Species *Tyrannus dominicensis*

Gray Kingbird

At first sight the Gray Kingbird appears similar to the widespread and familiar Eastern Kingbird, but careful observation quickly shows its larger size, distinctly longer bill, and paler, less contrasted plumage color (largely grayish above, paler below). Vocalizations are also somewhat different. A species of West Indian, Central and South American distribution, it occurs in the Southeast, especially in Florida.

OCCURRENCE Winters as far south as Colombia; disperses north to New England and west to Texas after nesting. Usually found near water, especially mangroves, but also adapts to suburban areas in the Florida Keys. Often occurs where Mangrove Cuckoos are found.

VOICE A loud *pe-cheeerrr*, rolled and descending in pitch at the end. A strong vocalist.

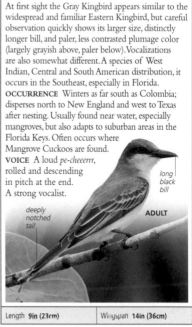

long black bill

deeply notched tail

ADULT

Length **9in (23cm)**	Wingspan **14in (36cm)**

Family **Tyrannidae**	Species *Sayornis nigricans*

Black Phoebe

North America's only black-and-white flycatcher, this species is resident from California to Texas. South of the US, the bird's range extends to Argentina. It commonly forages close to water. Black Phoebes wag their tails like other phoebes, and their calls are also phoebe-like whistles.

OCCURRENCE Breeds and winters in areas close to water such as coastal cliffs, river banks, streams, lakes, and ponds. Also fountains and cattle troughs.

VOICE A whistled *phee-bee*; also a simple *tsip* call; *tweedle-deedle-eek* during courting or when chasing rivals; song a *tee-hee, tee-hoo* or *sisee, sitsew.*

ADULT

black legs and toes

Length **6in (15.5cm)**	Wingspan **11in (28cm)**

Family **Tyrannidae**	Species *Sayornis saya*

Say's Phoebe

Say's Phoebe breeds farther north than any other New World flycatcher in North America, reaching the Yukon and Alaska. It is a common sight on ranches and farms from early spring to late fall. Its contrasting dark cap is conspicuous even at a distance as it perches on bushes, boulders, or power lines, wagging its tail.

OCCURRENCE Breeds in dry, open, or semi-open country, such as agricultural areas, desert canyons, and sagebrush; also breeds in tundra in Alaska; breeds south of the US in Mexico.

VOICE Call a *pee-ee* or *pee-ur*; also a whistled *churr-eep* that may be integrated with a chatter; primary song *pit-see-eur* and *pit-eet.*

ADULT

rufous undertail and lower belly

Length **7in (17.5cm)**	Wingspan **13in (33cm)**

Family **Tyrannidae**	Species **Pyrocephalus rubinus**

Vermilion Flycatcher

The most colorful North American flycatcher, this species is a resident through most of its vast range, which includes Mexico, Central America, and South America south to Argentina. Only the male is a vibrant red; the female is rather drab by comparison. Breeding territories are defended during spectacular flight displays accompanied with stuttering vocalizations; intruders are chased and if one fails to depart, a fight may ensue.
OCCURRENCE Breeds in riparian woodlands with cottonwoods, willows, and sycamores.
VOICE Contact call *peeent*; male song an excited *p-p-pik-zee*, *pit-a-zee*, or *ching-tink-a-link*.

fiery red head and underparts

MALE

Length **5–6in (13–15cm)**	Wingspan **10in (25cm)**

Family **Vireonidae**	Species **Vireo atricapilla**

Black-capped Vireo

The only vireo to show a sexually dimorphic (different) plumage, the Black-capped Vireo is restricted to the central southern US and Mexico. Despite its broad white "spectacles" and red eye, it is not easy to spot as it forages in dense shrubby vegetation. It sings persistently from near the top of bushes, often long into the day. Habitat changes and Brown-headed Cowbird parasitism have caused declines in the bird's population.
OCCURRENCE Breeds only in the Hill Country of central southern Texas and adjacent Mexico, casually in Oklahoma. Winters on the foothill country of western Mexico.
VOICE Calls are variable scolds; song an extensive repertoire of trills, whistles, chips, and squeaks, with individual variations.

red eye

broad white "spectacles"

MALE

Length **4½in (11.5cm)**	Wingspan **7½in (19cm)**

Family **Vireonidae**	Species **Vireo vicinior**

Gray Vireo

A drab, inconspicuous vireo of the hot and arid southwestern US, the Gray Vireo is reminiscent of a miniature shrike in terms of posture and shape. Found mainly in dense, shrubby vegetation such as piñon and juniper, it is most often detected by its distinctive voice. In its restricted habitat, it can be confused with other small gray birds such as gnatcatchers, titmice, and the Bushtit.
OCCURRENCE Breeds in the hot and arid shrubby scrublands of the southwestern US; short-distance migrant. Winters mostly in Mexico, in similarly arid areas.
VOICE Varied calls, include trills and chatters; song given by male, harsh three- to four-note phrase.

hooked bill

lead-gray body

ADULT

Length **5½in (14cm)**	Wingspan **8in (20cm)**

Family **Vireonidae**	Species **Vireo huttoni**

Hutton's Vireo

This unobtrusive bird is geographically variable and has about a dozen subspecies. One of them comprises coastal populations from British Columbia to Baja California; the second subspecies is found from the Southwest to Central America. These two isolated populations, widely separated by desert, may actually represent different species. Very similar in appearance to the Ruby-crowned Kinglet with which it flocks in winter, Hutton's Vireo is distinguishable by its larger size and thicker bill.
OCCURRENCE Year-round resident in mixed evergreen forests; prefers live oak woods. Breeds in mixed oak pine woodlands along the Pacific Coast.
VOICE Varied calls include harsh *mewing* and nasal, raspy *spit*; male's song a repetition of a simple phrase.

white wing bars

pale eye-ring

ADULT

Length **5in (13cm)**	Wingspan **8in (20cm)**

Family **Vireonidae**	Species *Vireo altiloquus*

Black-whiskered Vireo

This Caribbean breeder is restricted to mangrove and hardwood forests along both coasts of southern Florida. During migration (October–November) it can also be found along the Gulf and Atlantic Coasts. Its restricted range and habitat and secretive habits make this vireo difficult to spot. Its song, however, is distinctive, with phrases ending on alternate ascending and descending notes.

OCCURRENCE In the US, found in coastal Florida, along the Atlantic Coast south to the Keys, and along the southern Gulf Coast. Winters south to South America; breeds in the West Indies.

VOICE Nasal *mewing* call; male song a series of loud, clear one to four note phrases with distinct pauses between them.

Length **6½in (16cm)**	Wingspan **10in (26cm)**

Family **Corvidae**	Species *Cyanocorax yncas*

Green Jay

Known in southern Texas as the "Rio Grande Jay," this brightly colored species is common and conspicuous. It will readily get food at birdfeeders, but away from them it is rather secretive. Its varied vocalizations, however, allow it to be located easily. The Green Jay is a nonmigratory bird.

OCCURRENCE Lives in woodlands and thickets. Occurs southward through Mexico, Central America, and South America to Bolivia.

VOICE Sounds much like the Blue Jay; repeated *chah-chah-chah* calls; also clicks and buzzes, and mewing notes.

Length **10–11½in (25–29cm)**	Wingspan **13½in (34cm)**

Family **Corvidae**	Species *Psilorhinus morio*

Brown Jay

Both the very large Brown Jay and the colorful Green Jay are hard to miss. Groups of three to six Brown Jays can be heard calling long before they are seen. In the US, they are found very locally along the Rio Grande, in riparian woodlands. Juveniles have bright yellow bare parts, which fade as they become adults.

OCCURRENCE This bird is a resident of dense woodlands from Texas (rare in the Upper Rio Grande Valley) to Panama.

VOICE Makes loud, raucous screams, *keee-uh!* or *kaaah!*, which are often repeated. Begins with percussive popping sound at close range.

Length **16½in (42cm)**	Wingspan **26in (66cm)**

Family **Corvidae**	Species *Aphelocoma coerulescens*

Florida Scrub-Jay

Threatened by increasing habitat loss because of development, the endemic and tame Florida Scrub-Jay has been intensely studied by ornithologists. Young birds stay with their parents after fledging and help them raise their next brood, a social system called cooperative breeding. The Florida, California, Woodhouse's, and Island Scrub-Jays used to be considered to comprise one species, the Scrub-Jay.

OCCURRENCE Habitat restricted to chaparral-like evergreen oak scrub, growing on sandy soil and regularly kept open by fire. A highly sedentary bird.

VOICE Harsh and raspy call notes, *krrrahh*, as well as a number of other vocalizations.

Length **10–11½in (25–29cm)**	Wingspan **13½in (34cm)**

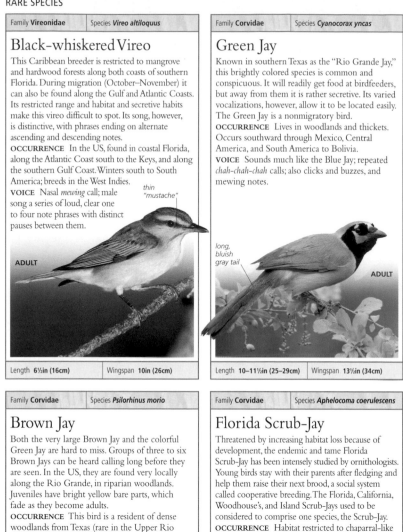
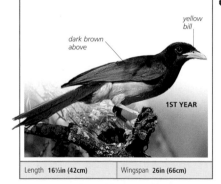

Family **Corvidae**	Species *Aphelocoma californica*

California Scrub-Jay

Western Scrub-Jays have recently been separated into two distinct species. The California Scrub-Jay is a brighter blue, with a more distinct buff-gray back and dark breastband, than the Woodhouse's Scrub-Jay. These birds are active and vocal, moving in jerky hops and jumps, often in groups of up to 30 birds, most of which are immatures. Established pairs defend their territories year-round. California Scrub-Jays are easily attracted to suburban backyards with feeders.

OCCURRENCE From British Columbia to southern California, typically in dry, open woodland, especially oak, scrubby chaparral, orchards, and backyards.

VOICE Short, harsh, rising shriek and quicker, repeated *chirr chirr chirr chirr chirr.*

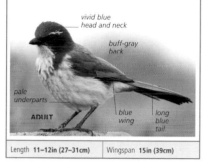

vivid blue
head and neck

buff-gray
back

pale
underparts

ADULT

blue
wing

long
blue
tail

Length **11–12in (27–31cm)**	Wingspan **15in (39cm)**

Family **Corvidae**	Species *Aphelocoma woodhouseii*

Woodhouse's Scrub-Jay

Western Scrub-Jays were a single species until 2016, but the duller, less strongly patterned Woodhouse's Scrub-Jay is now considered a separate species. Slightly duller and "dustier" than its California cousin, it has a straighter bill, which is adapted to pick seeds from between the open scales of pine cones. This bird is plainer gray beneath, and lacks the crest of a Blue Jay or Steller's Jay.

OCCURRENCE From Oregon and Idaho to Mexico, in oak or piñon woodland; sometimes found in mahogany, cactus, or oak scrub.

VOICE A nasal, buzzy *chairp* and soft *weep*; quiet, bubbly song and other notes; bill-rattling sounds.

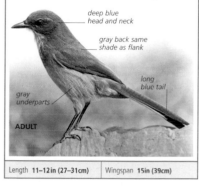

deep blue
head and neck

gray back same
shade as flank

long
blue tail

gray
underparts

ADULT

Length **11–12in (27–31cm)**	Wingspan **15in (39cm)**

Family **Corvidae**	Species *Corvus imparatus*

Tamaulipas Crow

Barely larger than the Fish Crow and restricted to southeastern Texas and northeastern Mexico, this bird is easy to identify because it is the only species of crow in this range. The Chihuahuan Raven, occurring near Brownsville in Texas, is huge by comparison. Tamaulipas Crows have low voices, long wings and tails, and glossy plumage.

OCCURRENCE Lowlands of northeastern Mexico; winters (rarely) near Brownsville, Texas, especially around the dump and the harbor.

VOICE Call a very low, nasal, frog-like croak, sometimes doubled. Also a low-pitched *whaah.*

rather
thin bill

very glossy
plumage

long tail

ADULT

Length **14½in (37cm)**	Wingspan **3ft 3in (1m)**

Family **Corvidae**	Species *Corvus cryptoleucus*

Chihuahuan Raven

Smaller than the Common Raven but bigger than the American Crow, the Chihuahuan Raven was previously called the White-necked Raven. This former name refers to the concealed white feathers of its neck, which are sometimes visible in the bird's windswept environment. A highly gregarious and vocal raven, it is often seen wheeling about in flocks that may contain thousands of individuals.

OCCURRENCE Breeds in the southwestern US and northern Mexico in grasslands, scrublands, and deserts. Northerly populations winter in Mexico.

VOICE High-pitched croak; little variety in vocal repertoire compared to the Common Raven.

concealed white base
of neck feathers

ADULT

Length **17½–20in (44–51cm)**	Wingspan **3½ft (1.1m)**

Family **Paridae**	Species *Baeolophus atricristatus*

Black-crested Titmouse

Found only in Texas and Oklahoma in the US, the Black-crested Titmouse is like a Tufted Titmouse with a taller, and black, crest. Black-crested and Tufted Titmice have largely non-overlapping ranges, yet in a small area of Texas they occur together and produce hybrids, a situation that suggests to some ornithologists that they belong to one species. Others disagree. The Black-crested Titmouse is a bird of woodlands, including evergreen oaks.

OCCURRENCE Scrubby oak woodlands; frequents feeders in winter. Sometimes reported as high as 6,000ft (2,000m) in mountain forests of Mexico in the southern part of its range.

VOICE Call a *pew-pew-pew* (or *peter-peter-peter*) like that of the Tufted Titmouse; other calls a rasping, scolding *jhree, jhree, jhree*.

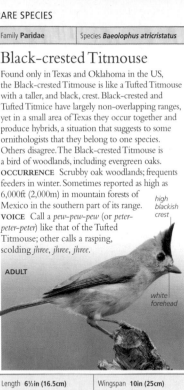

high blackish crest

ADULT

white forehead

Length **6½in (16.5cm)**	Wingspan **10in (25cm)**

Family **Remizidae**	Species *Auriparus flaviceps*

Verdin

Common in the Southwest from California east to Texas, this yellow-headed, gray-bodied little bird moves constantly from shrub to shrub, inspecting flowers and cobwebs in search of insects. Verdins resemble chickadees and bushtits in behavior and habitat preferences. Interestingly, however, the Verdin is the only American species of a family that is otherwise exclusively Eurasian and African in distribution, the Remizidae (or Penduline Tits): a fascinating evolutionary puzzle!

OCCURRENCE Thorn shrubs, mesquite woodlands, and tamarisk groves in dry creek beds, desert oases, and riverside corridors. Found in northern Mexico besides the southern US.

VOICE Call a bright, simple *beef*, emitted frequently as the bird forages, all day long and throughout the year.

yellow head

ADULT

Length **4½in (11.5cm)**	Wingspan **6½in (16cm)**

Family **Aegithalidae**	Species *Psaltriparus minimus*

Bushtit

The Bushtit is most often found roaming the foothills and valleys of the western US in flocks that usually number just a few birds, but may occasionally include hundreds. It is always on the move, foraging for insects in the foliage of shrubs and small trees. Even during the breeding season, when most other perching birds become territorial, Bushtits retain something of their social nature—raising the young communally, with both siblings and single adults helping in the rearing.

OCCURRENCE Common in open woodlands and shrublands, mainly on hillsides in summer; some birds move down to lower elevations in the fall. Also in cities and gardens.

VOICE Basic call a 2–3-part soft lisp, *ps psss pit*, interspersed with hard *spit* and *spick* notes, like little sparks.

mouse-gray upperparts

tiny bill

MALE

Length **4½in (11.5cm)**	Wingspan **6in (15.5cm)**

Family **Troglodytidae**	Species *Salpinctes obsoletus*

Rock Wren

The Rock Wren's varied voice, echoing through canyon walls, will usually reveal its owner's presence. Very active, hopping around rock faces, probing crevices for insects, Rock Wrens have the habit of bobbing and swaying when humans approach. A fascinating behavior of Rock Wrens is to "pave" the area in front of their nest entrance with a walkway of pebbles, the purpose of which is unknown.

OCCURRENCE Widespread in the West (and from Mexico to Costa Rica), in arid and rocky country with cliffs and canyons; also quarries and rock piles. Found from lowlands up to mountaintops at 10,000ft (3,000m).

VOICE Call a sharp *ch'keer*, varied series of warbles, trills, chatters, and repeated *chuwee chuwee, teedee teedee*.

pale yellowish or buffy

ADULT

Length **6in (15cm)**	Wingspan **9in (23cm)**

Family **Troglodytidae** | Species *Catherpes mexicanus*

Canyon Wren

Loud, musical, clear, the marvelous whistled song of the Canyon Wren signals this shy bird's presence and often astonishes listeners by its tonal purity. The singer, however, remains usually out of sight, and it takes work to locate it. But the reward is great: Canyon Wrens can walk up, down, or sideways on rock walls, as they search tiny crevices for insect prey.

OCCURRENCE Maintains year-round territory on rocky hillsides, outcroppings, and vertical rock-walled canyons. Sometimes nests in holes in manmade structures.

VOICE Remarkable, musical series of 10–15 loud, ringing whistles, descending in pitch, gradually slowing down, and ending with several buzzes.

ADULT

white throat

Length **5¾in (14.5cm)** | Wingspan **7½in (19cm)**

Family **Troglodytidae** | Species *Campylorhynchus brunneicapillus*

Cactus Wren

The largest and among the most colorful species of North American wren, the Cactus Wren is common and conspicuous in the arid Southwest from California east to Texas. As its name suggests, it prefers areas with cactus, especially perhaps cholla, although it also occurs in other dry habitats. Unlike some other wrens, the Cactus Wren is easy to observe, as it often perches in full view.

OCCURRENCE Lives in deserts and arid hillsides with cacti, yucca, thorn shrubs, and mesquite woodlands; also in suburban areas.

VOICE Call a loud *chack*; song a grating *kchar kchar kchar kchar*, with a cluck-like quality; sings repeatedly from top of cactus or shrub, especially in the morning.

conspicuous white eyebrow

long tail, barred black-and-white

ADULT

Length **8½in (22cm)** | Wingspan **11in (28cm)**

Family **Polioptilidae** | Species *Polioptila melanura*

Black-tailed Gnatcatcher

Few birds favor the hot, low-elevation deserts of the Southwest. Yet this is the Black-tailed Gnatcatcher's preferred habitat. This tiny bird spends most of its time flitting about in the foliage of shrubs, constantly flicking its long tail from side to side. A monogamous bird, pairs defend their territory aggressively throughout the year.

OCCURRENCE Thorn scrub, acacias, mesquite, saguaro cactus, creosote bush, and dry riverbeds; also bushy groves along waterways. Resident in the southwestern US and northern Mexico.

VOICE Various scolding notes *zhee-zhee-zhee*, *chih-chih-chih*, and *chee-chee-chee*; song, rarely heard, soft *tse-dee-dee-dee*.

black cap

long tail

MALE

Length **4½in (11.5cm)** | Wingspan **5½in (14cm)**

Family **Turdidae** | Species *Ixoreus naevius*

Varied Thrush

The most beautiful of North American thrushes, the Varied Thrush has a song so haunting and ethereal that to hear it can give the listener goosebumps. To see the bird is another matter, as it is often rather shy, except when bringing food to its nestlings. The Varied Thrush's orange and black head, deep bluish black back, and its two rusty wing bars are an unmistakable combination of markings.

OCCURRENCE Breeds from Alaska south to Montana; prefers moist coniferous forests throughout breeding range. Winters south of its breeding range; habitat varies between ravines and thickets to suburban lawns.

VOICE Song is a single note that rises or falls; repeats its song after about 10 seconds; sings for a long time from one perch, then moves to another to start anew.

orange eyebrow

black cheeks

MALE

rusty orange breast, faintly spotted on flanks

Length **7–10in (18–25cm)** | Wingspan **13–15in (33–38cm)**

| Family **Mimidae** | Species *Toxostoma curvirostre* |

Curve-billed Thrasher

The arid-country-loving Curve-billed Thrasher is somewhat unkempt-looking, with a thick bill and powerful legs. Less of a mimic than other thrashers, it is nevertheless quite vocal, and its two-note *twit-twit* call is a characteristic sound of the southwestern semideserts.

OCCURRENCE In the US, the Curve-billed Thrasher inhabits open, scrubby, arid to semiarid areas, where it is often found along edges between brush and clearings. Its Mexican range extends south to Veracruz and Oaxaca. It is largely resident throughout its US and Mexican range.

VOICE Two-note *qwit-qweet*; song a series of clear, warbled whistles broken into distinct phrases; some mimicry of other species' calls.

strong bill

ADULT

| Length **10–13in (25–33cm)** | Wingspan **12–15in (30–38cm)** |

| Family **Mimidae** | Species *Toxostoma longirostre* |

Long-billed Thrasher

In the US, this largely Mexican species is found only in southern Texas, where the semiarid thickets and riverside habitats it favors have been largely destroyed by land-clearing. If this habitat loss is offset by an increase in invasive scrubland, and if the thrasher moves into this new habitat, then it will meet the range of the Brown Thrasher, creating an interesting biological problem: will they interbreed?

OCCURRENCE Lives in thick, scrubby vegetation on mountain slopes up to around 3,300ft (1,100m), and in lowlands along the Gulf of Mexico, commonly found in woodland by streams. Sedentary.

VOICE Call a harsh *tchek*; song a loud, harsh series of notes, usually repeated 2–4 times in succession.

ADULT

heavily streaked underparts

| Length **10–11in (25–28cm)** | Wingspan **12–13in (30–33cm)** |

| Family **Mimidae** | Species *Oreoscoptes montanus* |

Sage Thrasher

This plain-colored bird is the smallest of the North American thrashers. Like several other species of thrashers, it removes the eggs of the parasitic Brown-headed Cowbird. The English name for this bird, "Sage Thrasher," correctly describes its habitat in the West.

OCCURRENCE Prefers sagebrush habitat in low-elevation, semiarid valleys of the western US. Winters from southwestern US to Mexico.

VOICE Song varies in duration: low, repeated, very musical notes or phrases that may blend together in a melodious song.

thin "mustache"

dusky, brownish gray upperparts

ADULT

| Length **8–9in (20–23cm)** | Wingspan **10–13in (25–33cm)** |

| Family **Pycnonotidae** | Species *Pycnonotus jocosus* |

Red-whiskered Bulbul

With its black head, large crest, and red-and-white cheeks, the Red-whiskered Bulbul is a striking bird. The dark back contrasts with the white underparts and reddish undertail feathers. This shy species is often found in small groups, and is more often heard than seen. The primary breeding population in the US is restricted to the area around and south of Miami.

OCCURRENCE Wooded parks, gardens, and suburbs in Florida. Introduced from tropical and subtropical Asia.

VOICE Call *kinka-choo*; song a choppy, musical whistle.

tall crest

dark back

ADULT

red-and-white cheek

white underparts

| Length **6–8in (15–20cm)** | Wingspan **10–12in (25–30cm)** |

| Family **Muscicapidae** | Species *Oenanthe oenanthe* |

Northern Wheatear

Widely distributed in Eurasia, the Northern Wheatear visits North America only during its brief breeding season—the subspecies *O. o. leucorhoa* breeds in the Northeast and *O. o. oenanthe* breeds in the Northwest. Both North American populations winter in sub-Saharan Africa—*oenanthe* flies across Asia, whereas *leucorhoa* crosses the Atlantic Ocean.

OCCURRENCE In North America, breeds in rocky tundra at high latitudes; habitats are more varied in Eurasia.

VOICE Multiple calls, a sharp *tuc* or *tek* common; three types of songs—territorial, conversational, and perched—mixtures of sweet and harsh notes; imitates other species.

tan throat and breast

FEMALE (BREEDING)

| Length 5½–6in (14–15cm) | Wingspan 10¾in (27cm) |

| Family **Passeridae** | Species *Passer montanus* |

Eurasian Tree Sparrow

Introduced to the US in 1870, this sparrow has not spread widely, unlike the House Sparrow. It occurs locally in parts of Illinois and Missouri, generally in parks, agricultural areas, and woodland edges, and also occasionally near human dwellings. Unlike the House Sparrow, both sexes of the Eurasian Tree Sparrow look alike.

OCCURRENCE In North America, only found locally in Missouri, Iowa, and Illinois. Favors parks, farmyards, and residential neighborhoods.

VOICE Call notes tend to be dry and metallic: *chirp, chep*; song consists of series of dry notes interspersed with few more liquid ones.

rufous-brown cap

white "necklace"

ADULT

| Length 6in (15cm) | Wingspan 9in (23cm) |

| Family **Fringillidae** | Species *Acanthis hornemanni* |

Hoary Redpoll

Distinctly white, fluffy-looking and with a stubby bill, male Hoary Redpolls are much paler than females. Where the smaller Common Redpoll occurs in the same location as the Hoary Redpoll the two species coexist but do not interbreed. The Hoary Redpoll is a true Arctic bird.

OCCURRENCE Breeds in the High Arctic, including the Canadian Arctic Archipelago; prefers low trees of the open tundra; winters within the boreal forest belt.

VOICE Flight calls dry *zit-zit zit-zit* and rattling *chirr*; also high *too-ee* call while perched; song series of rapid trills.

small pinkish red patch on forehead

lightly streaked breast

white rump

FEMALE

whitish belly

| Length 5–5½in (12.5–14cm) | Wingspan 8½–9¼in (21–23.5cm) |

| Family **Fringillidae** | Species *Spinus psaltria* |

Lesser Goldfinch

A highly vocal bird, the Lesser Goldfinch is common in gardens, suburbs, and farmlands, as well as in its natural habitats of open fields and scrub. The male has a brighter yellow breast and belly than the female, as well as a black cap, which she lacks. Nape and back color varies from black in Texas and Mexico to green along the Pacific Coast.

OCCURRENCE Breeds from California to Texas; occurs south to Mexico in winter.

VOICE Call descending *peeyee* and 2-note *tee-eee*, with second note higher; also rapid *dididit*; song warbles and trills.

white wing bar

MALE (PACIFIC COAST)

| Length 3½–4¼in (9–11cm) | Wingspan 6–6¾in (15–17cm) |

| Family **Passerellidae** | Species *Peucaea botterii* |

Botteri's Sparrow

Of the nine or ten subspecies of Botteri's Sparrow, a species of the Mexican grasslands, two occur in the US: *P. b. texana* is found in coastal southern Texas, and *P. b. arizonae* in the Southwest. Botteri's Sparrow is usually difficult to spot, as its flees stealthily from disturbance, and quickly hides itself out of sight.

OCCURRENCE Breeds in grasslands of southeastern Arizona and southwestern New Mexico, and in coastal prairies of southern Texas. Winters in Mexico.

VOICE Call a *chip* or double *tsip*; song starts with stuttering, mechanical *chips* and ends in an accelerating trill.

dark brown, rusty, and gray streaks on upperparts

ADULT

| Length **18–20in (46–51cm)** | Wingspan **27–38in (68–96cm)** |

| Family **Passerellidae** | Species *Peucaea cassinii* |

Cassin's Sparrow

Cassin's Sparrow, named for the famous Philadelphia ornithologist John Cassin, is drab-looking, even for an American sparrow. Its plain appearance is made up for by its rather spectacular flight displays, during which it emits a whistled song. This sparrow is found in grasslands interspersed with shrubs, and shows variations in numbers in different years and localities.

OCCURRENCE Grasslands with shrubs, like mesquite and cactus, from western Nebraska to central Mexico; US populations mostly winter in Mexico.

VOICE Calls high seeps and chips, often in series; song *see-eee sii-ii-i-i-i-i-i-i-i zee-zooo' zee-ZWAAAY*, ending on a questioning note.

scalloped upperparts

ADULT

| Length **6in (15cm)** | Wingspan **9in (23cm)** |

| Family **Passerellidae** | Species *Arremonops rufivirgatus* |

Olive Sparrow

The rather drab, shy Olive Sparrow spends most of its time hopping around in the undergrowth of dense woodlands and thorn scrub. This resident of the Lower Rio Grande Valley can be heard more than it is seen, although some individuals appear at birdfeeders.

OCCURRENCE From southern Texas and northwestern Mexico south locally to northwestern Costa Rica, mostly in thorn scrub.

VOICE Dry *chip* call, also a drawn-out *sreeeeee*; song a series of accelerating chips.

distinctive head pattern

ADULT

dull olive upperparts

| Length **6½in (16cm)** | Wingspan **8in (20cm)** |

| Family **Passerellidae** | Species *Amphispiza bilineata* |

Black-throated Sparrow

Because of a certain resemblance in their songs, the Black-throated Sparrow has been called the "Song Sparrow of the desert." This bird is easy to identify as it possesses a bold white "eyebrow" in all plumages. The Black-throated Sparrow is common within its western range, in a variety of arid habitats containing cactus and mesquite.

OCCURRENCE Found in desert scrub of the Great Basin east to Texas, south to Baja California and central Mexico. Breeds locally in eastern Washington state. Casual visitor to the Pacific Coast and the East.

VOICE Weak *tink* call; song consists of few short, clear notes, followed by higher trill: *tink tink-tink treeeeee*, also *ti-ti-tink churrrrrrrrrr*.

bold white eyebrow

ADULT

| Length **5½in (14cm)** | Wingspan **7¾in (19.5cm)** |

Family **Passerellidae**	Species ***Melozone fusca***

Canyon Towhee

Once included with the California Towhee as a single species, the Canyon Towhee is a bird of the arid Southwest, where it occurs in a wide variety of bushy habitats. Its pale, sandy coloration helps it to blend in with the grayish, dusty ground on which it forages. The Canyon Towhee can be distinguished from similarly colored birds in its range by its stubby, conical bill. Its rusty undertail feathers are not always easy to see.

OCCURRENCE Lives in rocky hillside scrub, desert grasslands, and suburban areas of the southwestern US and central Mexico. Largely resident, but some birds undertake local movements.

VOICE Call a nasal *cheemp*; also various clicking and lisping notes; song a variable slow trill.

ADULT

rusty undertail feathers

Length **8½in (21cm)**	Wingspan **11½in (29cm)**

Family **Passerellidae**	Species ***Aimophila ruficeps***

Rufous-crowned Sparrow

The Rufous-crowned Sparrow is a resident of dry canyons and sparsely wooded hillsides across the Southwest, locally up to 5,000ft (1,500m). It tends to run and hide at the first sign of danger. For this reason, it is often first detected by its unique *deeer* call note, which it sometimes gives in a laughter-like series. Visually it is similar to the rarer Rufous-winged Sparrow, but has very different calls and lives in separate habitats.

OCCURRENCE Breeds in arid scrub and low trees on hillsides and in canyons in California, Colorado, Utah, Arizona, New Mexico, Oklahoma, Texas, and Arkansas; also in Mexico.

VOICE Call a low, nasal *deeer*; song a jumble of chattering notes.

rufous crown

ADULT

Length **6in (15cm)**	Wingspan **7½in (19cm)**

Family **Passerellidae**	Species ***Pipilo chlorurus***

Green-tailed Towhee

This is North America's most distinctive towhee, with a rusty crown and green plumage, but it is seldom seen. It tends to stay hidden on the ground in dense cover, both in the breeding season and on its wintering grounds. In winter it sometimes emerges to feed on seeds on deserted, dusty roads, but this bird is more likely to be heard scratching about in the undergrowth than seen.

OCCURRENCE Breeds in a variety of brushy and semi-open habitats of the western US and northern Baja California. Winters along the US–Mexican border southward to central Mexico.

VOICE Call a nasal mewing, rapid chips in excitement; flight call a high *tzhreeee*; song a slurred whistle followed by 1–2 trills.

ADULT

bright, yellow-green tail and wing edgings

Length **7¼in (18.5cm)**	Wingspan **9½in (24cm)**

Family **Icteridae**	Species ***Icterus cucullatus***

Hooded Oriole

Tall palm trees of suburban and urban landscapes, especially in California, have become favored nesting sites for the Hooded Oriole. The increasing number of palm trees and offerings of nectar intended for hummingbirds have led to the expansion of its range in California and the southwestern US. By contrast, its numbers in Texas have been shrinking, in part because of its susceptibility to brood parasitism by Brown-headed and Bronzed Cowbirds.

OCCURRENCE Breeds in open woodlands along water courses, especially those with palm trees, in Mexico, Belize, California, and the southwestern US, and also in southern Texas. Winters in Mexico.

VOICE A harsh *weeek* call; song a weakly whined and rapid series of whistles where notes often run together; imitates other birds.

long, curved bill

bright orange

MALE (BREEDING)

Length **7–8in (18–20cm)**	Wingspan **9–11in (23–28cm)**

Family **Icteridae**	Species *Icterus bullockii*

Bullock's Oriole

This oriole is the western counterpart of the Baltimore in both behavior and habitat. The two were considered to belong to a single species, the Northern Oriole (*L. galbula*), because they interbreed where they overlap in the Great Plains, but recent studies suggest that they are actually separate species. The Bullock's is more resistant to brood parasites than other orioles, and either punctures or removes cowbird eggs from its nest.
OCCURRENCE Prefers riverside woodlands with willows and cottonwoods; also mixed hardwood forests, mesquite woodland, and groves of fruit trees.
VOICE Varied string of one- and two-part notes often mumbled or slurred at the end.

black back and wings

MALE

Length **6½–7½in (16–19cm)**	Wingspan **10–12in (25–30cm)**

Family **Icteridae**	Species *Icterus gularis*

Altamira Oriole

The Altamira Oriole, a Central American species, is now common in a restricted area of the Lower Rio Grande Valley. This Texas population has increased since its discovery in 1939. The largest oriole in the US, it can occasionally be seen at birdfeeders. The large size of its hanging nest makes it a target for brood parasites such as cowbirds, but whether the parasites are cared for and fledged successfully remains unknown.

bright orange head

OCCURRENCE Limited to riverside woodlands along the Rio Grande. In Mexico and Central America, occurs in a variety of dry to moist tropical woodlands.
VOICE Call harsh, nasal *drrike*; song loud but musical series of whistles *thoo-thoo-thoo-theeoo*.

ADULT

Length **8–10in (20–25cm)**	Wingspan **13–15in (33–38cm)**

Family **Icteridae**	Species *Icterus graduacauda*

Audubon's Oriole

Because it is secretive and lives in dense vegetation, Audubon's Oriole remains little studied, and estimates of its population in the US are few. It was once thought to be declining, because of its restricted habitat (mostly riverside thickets) along the lower Rio Grande Valley in Texas, and because of the negative impact of brood parasitism by the Bronzed Cowbird. However, this oriole has recently adapted to suburban areas and uses birdfeeders, developments that may help its numbers increase.
OCCURRENCE Woodlands, mesquite thickets, and pine oak woodlands of southeastern Texas, also parks and gardens; more common in Mexico.
VOICE Low, slow whistle with slurred, broken notes: *heoo-heeooo-heeeww*.

ADULT

yellowish back

Length **9–10in (23–26cm)**	Wingspan **11–13in (28–33cm)**

Family **Icteridae**	Species *Icterus parisorum*

Scott's Oriole

This oriole's lemon-yellow plumage is unusual among North American orioles, as most other species are rather orange-colored. Scott's Oriole lives in semiarid and rocky slopes, a habitat preference that earned it the names of "Desert Oriole" and "Mountain Oriole." Its loud, clear song signals its presence from afar.
OCCURRENCE Breeds at mid-elevations in semiarid scrub on level ground or along slopes with oak and pinion. Winters in pine oak woodlands of Mexico. Individuals can wander widely: the species has even been reported from New York City.
VOICE Call a sharp *chek*; song a musical series of whistles *tew-tew-treew*, loud and ringing.

MALE

black hood and back

black-tipped tail

lemon-yellow underparts

Length **8–9in (20–23cm)**	Wingspan **11–13in (28–33cm)**

Family **Icteridae**	Species *Molothrus bonariensis*

Shiny Cowbird

The Shiny Cowbird is native to South America, where it ranges south to Chile and Argentina. It has only recently expanded its distribution to Florida, presumably from the West Indies. Over its vast range, the species is known to lay its eggs in the nests of about 200 other bird species, 80 of which raise the cowbird's young as their own.
OCCURRENCE Found in open areas with a mixture of woodlands; agricultural fields, and rural and suburban parks, gardens, and backyards.
VOICE Low pitched, rambling series of soft *purr-purr-purr*, interspersed with *tee-tsss-tseeee* running higher to slurred finish.

MALE
(BREEDING)

long tail

Length **7in (18cm)**	Wingspan **10–12in (25–30cm)**

Family **Icteridae**	Species *Molothrus aeneus*

Bronzed Cowbird

The range of the Bronzed Cowbird has been expanding in the US since it was first recorded in the early 1900s. This could be the result of human clearing of its native habitats, which are then replaced with agricultural crops. A brood parasite, it has been recorded as laying eggs in the nests of about 80 bird species, with its young fledging from about 30 of these. Females may work cooperatively to identify and parasitize the nests of other birds.
OCCURRENCE Inhabits open fields, pastures, scattered scrub, and suburban parks. Ranges from Mexico to Panama and northern Colombia, in the US occurs along the Mexico border from California to Texas.
VOICE High and metallic with short notes, can be described as *gug-gub-bub-tzee-pss-tzee.*

bright red eye

MALE

Length **8in (20cm)**	Wingspan **13–14in (33–36cm)**

Family **Parulidae**	Species *Setophaga pitiayumi*

Tropical Parula

The Tropical Parula is widespread in tropical America, but in the US is found only in southern Texas. There, it occasionally interbreeds with the Northern Parula, which is very close to it in appearance. Their offspring are difficult to identify, so that in southern Texas some parula warblers cannot be identified to species.
OCCURRENCE Breeds from the southern edge of the Hill Country to coastal Kleberg County (Texas) southward to central Argentina. Much local movement in the winter months.
VOICE Songs and calls very similar to those of the Northern Parula.

white wing patch   dark mask

MALE

yellow underparts

Length **4½in (11cm)**	Wingspan **6¼in (16cm)**

Family **Parulidae**	Species *Setophaga kirtlandii*

Kirtland's Warbler

Named for a physician from Ohio, Kirtland's Warbler is one of the rarest North American songbirds. The suppression of fires and spread of the parasitic Brown-headed Cowbird decreased this warbler's population to a low of 167 males in 1987, but successful conservation allowed the population to climb back to more than 3,500 mature individuals.
OCCURRENCE In northern Michigan, in dense, low, 6- to 20-year-old jack pine stands on sandy soil, regrowing after fires.
VOICE A strong *chip*; flight call a high *zit*; song a loud, low-pitched series of staccato *chips*, rising in pitch and intensity and ending with whistled phrase: *tup-CHUP-chup tup CHEEP-cheep.*

interrupted, white eye-ring

MALE

Length **6in (15cm)**	Wingspan **9in (23cm)**

Family **Parulidae**	Species *Setophaga chrysoparia*

Golden-cheeked Warbler

Males of this strikingly beautiful warbler species often sing throughout the day, from conspicuous perches in oak-juniper woodlands. The Golden-cheeked Warbler breeds only in a restricted area of Texas, on and near the Edwards Plateau. Habitat loss has made this already scarce species even less common, and it has been listed as an Endangered Species since 1990.

OCCURRENCE Breeds in extensive oak-juniper forests mixed with hardwood trees like maple and ash. Winters in high-elevation pine oak woodlands.

VOICE Dry *tsk* call; song a variable series of relatively low, buzzy notes, often ending on a high, clear note *zo zu zu zo zu zhray ZHEE*; another version ends at a lower pitch *ZOH zu ZO-ZOH zhray*.

striking yellow-
and-black face

MALE

Length **5in (13cm)**	Wingspan **8in (20cm)**

Family **Thraupidae**	Species *Sporophila morelleti*

Morelet's Seedeater

As many as 40 species of *Sporophila* seedeaters breed in tropical America, but Morelet's Seedeater is the only species to breed as far north as the US. These tiny birds feed on grass seeds. They remain hidden in vegetation, and it is important to know their calls in order to locate them. While females are drab and tan colored, males have a distinctive black-and-white plumage.

OCCURRENCE Weedy fields and marshy grasslands, from southeastern Texas southward to Panama. In Texas, restricted to the Rio Grande Valley between Laredo and Zapata.

VOICE Calls a nasal *wink!* and *wheer!*; song a sweet, goldfinch-like series of whistles and trills.

brown
upperparts

tan or buffy
underparts

**FEMALE
(BREEDING)**

Length **4½in (11cm)**	Wingspan **6¼in (16cm)**

Family **Cardinalidae**	Species *Cardinalis sinuatus*

Pyrrhuloxia

The "Pyro" is the Southwest's equivalent of the Northern Cardinal, and was once known as the "Arizona Cardinal." The ranges of the two species do overlap and, although the two birds share very similar habits and vocalizations, they tolerate each other's presence.

OCCURRENCE Desert scrub of southwestern US and Mexico. Prefers drier, more upland habitats than the Northern Cardinal, at elevations up to 6,500ft (2,000m).

VOICE Call a distinctive, dry, low *chik*, often accelerating into chatter; song generally higher, thinner, and less musical than the Northern Cardinal's.

MALE

long,
conspicuous
crest

red belly

Length **8½in (22cm)**	Wingspan **12in (30cm)**

Family **Cardinalidae**	Species *Passerina versicolor*

Varied Bunting

The Varied Bunting is the only purple-and-red songbird in North America. When seen in bright light, males are a rich plum color with ruby-red napes and sparkling, sapphire-blue foreheads and rumps. The female, however, is the dullest member of the family Cardinalidae. A largely Mexican species, the Varied Bunting is localized and hard to find.

OCCURRENCE Breeds in desert scrub in canyons and washes, and in thorn woodlands of the southwestern US. In winter, most migrate to the coastal slopes of Mexico.

VOICE Call a sharp, dry, rattling *pik!*; song a pleasant, rambling, and burry warble.

red nape

MALE

blue
rump

Length **5½in (14cm)**	Wingspan **7½–8in (19–20cm)**

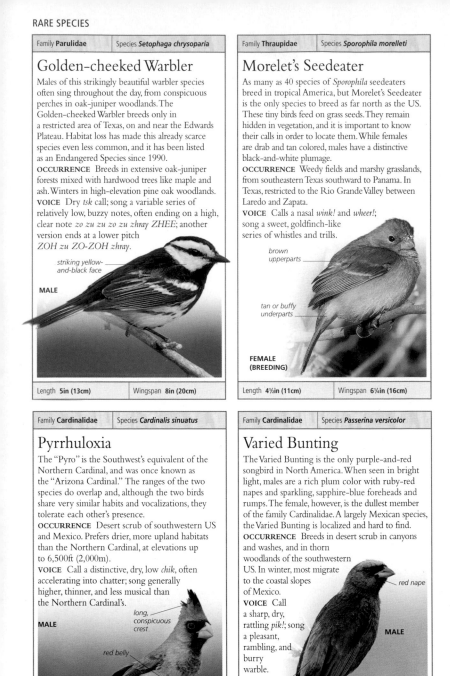

VAGRANTS AND ACCIDENTALS

THE LIST THAT FOLLOWS includes species that occur rarely in eastern North America (defined in this book as Canada and the continental United States *east* of the 100th Meridian). These species can reach North America from Eurasia, Central or South America, Africa, and even Oceania and Antarctica. The US and Canada can receive birds that drift off course, during migration, from eastern Asia across the Pacific Ocean, or from Europe across the Atlantic.

The occurrence of these "vagrant" species is classified by the American Birding Association, depending on their relative frequency, and this terminology is followed in the "status" column for each species. **Rare** species are reported every year in small numbers. **Casual** visitors have been recorded at least a dozen times. **Accidental** species have been recorded no more than five times.

Because of biological, climatological, or other factors, the status of "vagrant" species is constantly changing. The ever greater number of competent birdwatchers also permits the regular, even annual, detection of species that were once considered rare or accidental.

COMMON NAME	SCIENTIFIC NAME	FAMILY NAME	STATUS
Ducks, Geese, and Swans			
Pink-footed Goose	Anser brachyrhynchus	Anatidae	Accidental from Greenland, Iceland, or Europe to eastern Canada
Lesser White-fronted Goose	Anser erythropus	Anatidae	Accidental from Eurasia to Alaska
Muscovy Duck	Cairina moschata	Anatidae	Rare visitor from Mexico in southern Texas (also escapees)
Garganey	Spatula querquedula	Anatidae	Casual visitor from Eurasia to eastern North America
Cinnamon Teal	Spatula cyanoptera	Anatidae	Casual visitor from West to eastern US
Eurasian Wigeon	Mareca penelope	Anatidae	Rare visitor from Eurasia along East Coast of US
Tufted Duck	Aythya fuligula	Anatidae	Rare visitor from Eurasia to eastern Canada; casual in eastern US
Smew	Mergellus albellus	Anatidae	Accidental from Eurasia to eastern US
Pigeons and Doves			
Ruddy Ground Dove	Columbina talpacoti	Columbidae	Casual visitor from Mexico to southern Texas
Nightjars			
Antillean Nighthawk	Chordeiles gundlachii	Caprimulgidae	Rare visitor from Bahamas and West Indies to Florida Keys (breeds) and accidental along mainland coast from Florida to North Carolina
Hummingbirds			
Calliope Hummingbird	Selasphorus calliope	Trochilidae	Rare to casual visitor from the West to the East, north to New England
Shorebirds, Gulls, Auks, and Relatives			
Pacific Golden-Plover	Pluvialis fulva	Charadriidae	Casual visitor from Alaska in the Northeast
Common Ringed Plover	Charadrius hiaticula	Charadriidae	Casual visitor from high Canadian Arctic to East Coast
Lesser Sand-Plover	Charadrius mongolus	Charadriidae	Rare visitor from Asia to West Alaska, Pacific Coast, and the East
Bar-tailed Godwit	Limosa lapponica	Scolopacidae	Casual visitor from Alaska and Eurasia to East Coast
Black-tailed Godwit	Limosa limosa	Scolopacidae	Casual visitor from Eurasia along Atlantic Coast
Sharp-tailed Sandpiper	Calidris acuminata	Scolopacidae	Casual visitor from eastern Russia to the East
Ruff	Calidris pugnax	Scolopacidae	Rare visitor from Eurasia to East Coast
Red-necked Stint	Calidris ruficolis	Scolopacidae	Rare visitor from Siberia to both coasts in summer and fall
Wood Sandpiper	Tringa glareola	Scolopacidae	Accidental from Eurasia to East Coast
Mew Gull	Larus canus	Laridae	Rare visitor from either Alaska or Europe to East Coast of Canada and US
California Gull	Larus californicus	Laridae	Casual visitor from the West to East Coast
Slaty-backed Gull	Larus schistisagus	Laridae	Casual visitor from eastern Eurasia to the East
Ivory Gull	Pagophila eburnea	Laridae	Casual visitor from the Arctic to the East Coast; also inland

VAGRANTS AND ACCIDENTALS

COMMON NAME	SCIENTIFIC NAME	FAMILY NAME	STATUS
Loons			
Pacific Loon	*Gavia pacifica*	Gaviidae	Casual visitor from Arctic to East Coast
Yellow-billed Loon	*Gavia adamsii*	Gaviidae	Casual visitor from Arctic to East Coast and Interior US
Tubenoses			
Fea's Petrel	*Pterodroma feae*	Procellariidae	Rare visitor from eastern Atlantic to East Coast; accidental to Nova Scotia
Storks			
Jabiru	*Jabiru mycteria*	Ciconiidae	Casual visitor to southern Texas from Central America
Flamingos			
Greater Flamingo	*Phoenicopterus ruber*	Phoenoicpteridae	Rare or casual visitor from West Indies to Florida and Texas
Pelicans and Relatives			
Masked Booby	*Sula dactylatra*	Sulidae	Breeds in Dry Tortugas; rare at sea, Gulf Coast, Atlantic Coast, Florida to North Carolina
White-tailed Tropicbird	*Phaethon lepturus*	Phaethontidae	Rare visitor from tropical waters off Atlantic Coast north to North Carolina
Owls			
Ferruginous Pygmy-Owl	*Glaucidium brasilianum*	Strigidae	Uncommon breeder from Mexico in southern Texas
Woodpeckers			
Lewis's Woodpecker	*Melanerpes lewis*	Picidae	Casual visitor from the West to the East
New World Flycatchers			
Western Wood-Pewee	*Contopus sordidulus*	Tyrannidae	Rare to casual visitor from the West to the East
Vireos			
Yellow-green Vireo	*Vireo flavoviridis*	Vireonidae	Casual visitor from Mexico to Gulf Coast and central Texas
Thrushes			
Mountain Bluebird	*Sialia currucoides*	Turdidae	Casual visitor from the West to the eastern states
Townsend's Solitaire	*Myadestes townsendi*	Turdidae	Casual visitor from the West to eastern US
Longspurs, New World Sparrows			
McCown's Longspur	*Rhynchophanes mccownii*	Calcariidae	Accidental from central Canada and US to East Coast
Baird's Sparrow	*Centronyx bairdii*	Passerellidae	Accidental from central Canada and US to the East
Spotted Towhee	*Pipilo maculatus*	Passerellidae	Rare to casual visitor from the West to the East
Orioles			
Spot-breasted Oriole	*Icterus pectoralis*	Icteridae	Uncommon in S Florida; introduced from Central America
Wood Warblers			
MacGillivray's Warbler	*Geothlypis tolmiei*	Parulidae	Casual visitor from the West to eastern US
Black-throated Gray Warbler	*Setophaga nigrescens*	Parulidae	Casual visitor from the West to eastern US
Townsend's Warbler	*Setophaga townsendi*	Parulidae	Casual visitor from the Northwest to eastern US
Hermit Warbler	*Setophaga occidentalis*	Parulidae	Casual visitor from the West to eastern US
Cardinals and Relatives			
Western Tanager	*Piranga ludoviciana*	Cardinalidae	Rare to casual visitor from the West to the East
Black-headed Grosbeak	*Pheucticus melanocephalus*	Cardinalidae	Rare visitor from the West to the East
Lazuli Bunting	*Passerina amoena*	Cardinalidae	Casual visitor from the West to the East

GLOSSARY

Many terms defined here are illustrated in the general introduction (pp.10–21).

adult A fully-developed, sexually mature bird. It is in its final plumage, which no longer changes pattern with age and remains the same after yearly molt, although it may change with season. *See also* **immature, juvenile.**
aerie The nest of birds of prey, like eagles or peregrine falcons, usually on a cliff, and often used by the same pair of adult birds in successive years.
alarm call A call made by a bird to signal danger. Alarm calls are often short and urgent in tone, and a few species use different calls to signify the precise nature of the threat. *See also* **call.**
allopreening Mutual preening between two birds, the main purpose of which is to reduce the instinctive aggression when birds come into close contact. In the breeding season, allopreening helps to strengthen the pair bond between the male and female. *See also* **preening.**
altitudinal migrant *see* **vertical migrant**
alula A small group of two to six feathers projecting from a bird's "thumb," at the bend of its wing that reduces turbulence when raised.
Audubon, John James (1785–1851) American naturalist and wildlife illustrator, whose best known work was his remarkable collection of prints, *Birds of North America.*
axillary A term describing feathers at the base of the underwing. Axillary feathers often form small patches, with coloration differing from the rest of the underwing.
barred With marks crossing the body, wing, or tail; the opposite of streaked. *See also* **streaks.**
bastard wing *see* **alula**
beak *see* **bill**
bill A bird's jaws. A bill is made of bone, with a hornlike outer covering of keratin.
bird of prey Any of the predatory birds in the orders Accipitriformes (eagles, hawks, kites, and ospreys), Falconiformes (falcons), and Strigiformes (owls). They are characterized by their acute eyesight, powerful legs, strongly hooked bill, and sharp talons. Also known as raptors. *See also* **talon, raptor.**
body feather *see* **contour feather**
booming A sound produced by bitterns and some species of grouse. The booming of male bitterns is a deep, resonant, hollow sound that can carry for several miles. The booming of male grouse is produced by wind from air pouches in the sides of the bird's neck.
brackish Containing a mixture of saltwater and freshwater.
breeding plumage A general term for the plumage worn by adult birds when they display and form breeding pairs. It is usually (but not always) worn in the spring and summer. *See also* **nonbreeding plumage.**
brood (noun) The young birds produced from a single clutch of eggs and incubated together. *See also* **clutch. (verb)** In birds, to sit on nestlings to keep them warm. Brooding is usually carried out by the adult female. *See also* **incubate.**
brood parasite A bird that lays its eggs in the nest of other birds. Some brood parasites always breed this way, while others do so only occasionally.
brood patch An area of bare skin on the belly of a parent bird, usually the female, that is richly supplied with blood vessels and thus helps keep the eggs warm during incubation. This area loses its feathers in readiness for the breeding season and is fully feathered at other times.
caged-bird A species of bird commonly kept in captivity.
call A sound produced by the vocal apparatus of a bird to communicate a variety of messages to other birds. Calls are often highly characteristic of individual species and can help to locate and identify birds in the field. Most bird calls are shorter and simpler than songs. *See also* **alarm call, booming, contact call, song.**
casque A bony extension on a bird's head.
cere A leathery patch of skin that covers the base of a bird's bill. It is found only in a few groups, including birds of prey, pigeons, and parrots.
claw In birds, the nail that prolongs their toes.
cloaca An opening toward the rear of a bird's belly. It is present in both sexes and is used in reproduction and excretion.
clutch The group of eggs in a single nest, usually laid by one female and incubated together.
cock A term sometimes used to describe the adult male in galliforms and songbirds. *See also* **hen.**
collar The area around a bird's neck, which in some species is a prominent feature of its plumage pattern and can be used for identification.
color form One of two or more clearly defined plumage variations found in the same species. Also known as a color morph or phase, a color form may be restricted to part of a species's range or occur side by side with other color forms over the entire range. Adults of different color forms are able to interbreed, and these mixed pairings can produce young of either form.
comb A fleshy growth of bare skin usually above the eyes.
contact call A call made by a bird to give its location as a means of staying in touch with others of the same species. Contact calls are used by birds in flocks and by breeding pairs. Contact calls are crucial for nocturnal migrants. *See also* **call.**
contour feather A general term for any feather that covers the outer surface of a bird, including its wings and tail. Contour feathers are also known as body feathers, and help streamline the bird.
cooperative breeding A breeding system in which a pair of parent birds are helped in raising their young by several other birds, which are often related to them and may be young birds from previous broods.
courtship display Ritualized, showy behavior used in courtship by the male, and sometimes by the female, involving plumage, sound (vocal and non-vocal), and movements.
covert A small feather covering the base of a bird's flight feather. Together, coverts form a well-defined feather tract on the wing or at the base of the tail. *See also* **feather tract.**
creche A group of young birds of about the same age, produced by different parents but tightly packed together. One or more adults guard the entire creche.
crepuscular Relating to the period just before dawn, when many birds are active, especially during courtship. When used in connection with birds, the term is often used to refer to both dawn and twilight.
crest A group of elongated feathers on top of a bird's head, which may be raised during courtship or to indicate alarm.
crown The area on top of a bird's head. It is often a prominent plumage feature, with a different color from the feathers on the rest of the head.
dabble To feed in shallow water by sieving water and obtains food through comb-like filters in the bill, used mostly for ducks (dabbling ducks or dabblers).
decurved A term describing a bird's bill that curves downward from the forehead toward the tip.
dimorphism *see* **sexual dimorphism**
display *see* **courtship display, distraction display, threat display**
distraction display A display in which a bird deliberately attempts to attract a predator's attention in order to lure it away from its nest or nestlings.
diurnal Active during the day.
down feather A soft, fluffy feather, lacking the system of barbs of contour or flight feathers, that provides good insulation. Young birds are covered by down feathers until they molt into their first juvenile plumage. Adult birds have a layer of down feathers under their contour feathers. *See also* **contour feather, juvenile.**
drake An adult male duck. The adult female is known as the duck.
drift The diversion of migrating birds from their normal migration route by strong winds.
dynamic soaring *see* **soaring**
ear tuft A distinct tuft of feathers on each side of a bird's forehead, with no connection to the true ears, which can be raised as a visual signal. Many owls have ear tufts.
echolocation A method of sensing nearby objects using pulses of high-frequency sound. Echoes bounce back from obstacles, enabling the sender to build up a "picture" of its surroundings.
eclipse plumage A female-like plumage worn in some birds, especially waterfowl, by adult males for a short period after the breeding season is over. The eclipse plumage helps camouflage them during their molt, when they are flightless.
elevational migrant *see* **vertical migrant**
endemic A species (or subspecies) native to a particular geographic area—such as an island, a forest patch, a mountain, or state, or country—and found nowhere else.
escape An individual bird that has escaped from a zoo or other collection to live in the wild. *See also* **exotic**
eye-ring A ring of color, usually narrow and well defined, around the eye of a bird.
eyestripe A stripe of color running as a line through the eye of a bird.
eyrie *see* **aerie**
exotic A bird found in a region from which it is not native. Some of these are escapees, or were originally, but now live as wild birds.
feather tract A well-defined area on a bird's skin where feathers grow, leaving patches of bare skin inbetween.
fledge In young birds, to leave the nest or acquire the first complete set of flight feathers. Known as fledglings, these birds may still remain dependent on their parents for some time. *See also* **flight feather.**
fledging period The average time taken by the young of a species to fledge, timed from the moment they hatch. Fledging periods in birds range from 11 days in some small songbirds to as long as 280 days in the Wandering Albatross.
fledgling *see* **fledge**
flight feather A collective term for a bird's wing and tail feathers, used in flight. More specifically, it refers to the largest feathers on the outer part of the wing, the primaries and secondaries.
forewing The front section of a bird's wing, including the primary coverts and secondary coverts. *See also* **hindwing.**
gamebird Generally, any bird that is legally hunted, including some doves and waterfowl. This name is generally used for members of the order Galliforms.
gular sac Also known as a gular pouch, it is a large, fleshy, extendable sac just below the bill of some birds, especially fish-eaters such as pelicans. It forms part of the throat.
habitat The geographical and ecological area where a particular organism usually lives.
hen A term sometimes used to describe the adult female in galliforms, especially grouse and songbirds. *See also* **cock.**
hindwing The rear section of a bird's spread wing, including the secondary feathers, especially when it has a distinctive color or pattern. *See also* **forewing.**
hybrid The offspring produced when two species, sometimes from different genera, interbreed. Hybrids are usually rare in the wild. Among birds, they are most frequent in galliforms and waterfowl, especially ducks. Hybrid progeny may or may not be fertile.
immature In birds, an individual that is not yet sexually mature or able to breed. Some birds pass through a series of immature plumages over several years before adopting their first adult plumage and sexual maturity. *See also* **adult, juvenile.**
incubate In birds, to sit on eggs to keep them warm, allowing the embryo inside to grow. Incubation is often carried out by the female. *See also* **brood.**
incubation period In birds, the period when a parent incubates its eggs. It may not start until the clutch is completed.
injury feigning *see* **distraction display.**
inner wing The inner part of the wing, comprising the secondaries and rows of coverts (typically marginal, lesser, median, and greater coverts).
introduced species A species that humans have accidentally or deliberately brought into an area where it does not normally occur.
iridescent plumage Plumage that shows brilliant, luminous colors, which seems to sparkle and change color when seen from different angles.
irruption A sporadic mass movement of animals outside their normal range. Irruptions are usually short-lived and occur in response to food shortage. Also called irruptive migration.
juvenile A term referring to the plumage worn by a young bird at the time it makes its first flight and until it begins its first molt. *See also* **adult, immature.**

keratin A tough but lightweight protein. In birds, keratin is found in the claws, feathers, and outer part of the bill.
kleptoparasite A bird that gets much of its food by stealing it from other birds, usually by following them in flight and forcing them to disgorge their food.
lamellae Delicate, comb-like structures on the sides of the bill of some birds used for filtering tiny food particles out of water.
leap-frog migration A pattern of migration in which some populations of a species travel much further than the other populations, by "leap-frogging" over the area where these sedentary (nonmigratory) birds are found. *See also* **migration**.
lek An area, often small, used by males as a communal display arena, where they show off special plumage features accompanied by vocal and non-vocal sounds, to attract females. Females wait along the lek and select the male or males that they will mate with.
lobed feet Feet with loose, fleshy lobes on the toes, adapted for swimming.
lore A small area between a bird's eye and the base of its upper bill.
mandible The upper or lower part of a bird's bill, known as the upper or lower mandible respectively.
mantle The loose term used to define the back of a bird, between its neck and rump.
migrant A species that regularly moves between geographical areas. Most migrants move on an annual basis between a breeding area and a wintering area. *See also* **partial migrant, sedentary.**
migration A journey to a different region, following a well-defined route. *See also* **leap-frog migration, partial migrant, reverse migration, sedentary, vertical migrant.**
mobbing A type of defensive behavior in which a group of birds gang up to harass a predator, such as a bird of prey or an owl, swooping repeatedly to drive it away.
molt In birds, to shed old feathers so that they can be replaced. Molting enables birds to keep their plumage in good condition, change their level of insulation, and change their coloration or markings so that they are ready to breed or display.
monogamous Mating with a single partner, either in a single breeding season or for life. *See also* **polygamous**.
morph *see* **color form**
nape The back of the neck.
nestling A young bird still in the nest.
New World The Americas, from Alaska to Cape Horn, including the Caribbean and offshore islands in the Pacific and Atlantic Oceans. *See also* **Old World**.
nictitating membrane A transparent or semiopaque "third eyelid," which moves sideways across the eye. Waterbirds often use the membrane as an aid to vision when swimming underwater.
nocturnal Active at night.
nomadic Being almost constantly on the move. Birds of deserts, grasslands, and the coniferous forests of the far north are commonly nomadic.
nonbreeding plumage The plumage worn by adult birds outside the breeding season. In many species, particularly in temperate regions, it is also known as winter plumage. *See also* **breeding plumage**.
nonmigrant *see* **sedentary**
nonpasserine Any bird that is not a member of the order Passeriformes (or passerines). *See also* **passerine**.
oil gland Also called the preen gland, a gland at the base of a bird's tail that secretes oils that are spread over the feathers for waterproofing them during preening.
Old World Europe, Asia, Africa, and Australasia. *See also* **New World.**
orbital ring A thin, bare, fleshy ring around the eye, sometimes with a distinctive color. *See also* **eye-ring.**
outer wing The outer half of the wing, comprising the primaries, their coverts, and the alula (the "thumb").
partial migrant A species in which some populations migrate while others are sedentary. This situation is common in broadly distributed species that experience a wide range of climatic conditions. *See also* **migration, sedentary**.
passerine A bird belonging to the vast order Passeriformes (the passerines). This group contains more species than all other orders of birds combined. Passerines are also called songbirds or perching birds. *See also* **nonpasserine.**
pelagic Relating to the open ocean. Pelagic birds spend most of their life at sea and only come to land to nest.
phase *see* **color form**
polygamous Mating with two or more partners during the course of a single breeding season. *See also* **monogamous**.
population A group of individual birds of the same species living in a geographically and ecologically circumscribed area.
preening Routine behavior by which birds keep their feathers in good condition. A bird grasps a feather at its base and then "nibbles" upward toward the tip, and repeats the process with different feathers. This helps smooth and clean the plumage. Birds often also smear oil from their preen gland onto their feathers at the same time. *See also* **allopreening**.
primary feather One of the large outer wing feathers, growing from the digits of a bird's "hand." *See also* **secondary feather.**
race *see* **subspecies**
range A term to indicate the geographical distribution of a species or population.
raptor A general name for birds belonging to the orders Falconiformes and Accipitriformes, often used interchangeably with bird of prey. *See also* **bird of prey**.
ratite A member of an ancient group of flightless birds that includes the ostrich, cassowaries, emus, rheas, and kiwis. In the past, the group was larger and more diverse.
resident *see* **sedentary**
reverse migration A phenomenon that occurs when birds from a migratory species mistakenly travel in the opposite direction from normal, causing birds to turn up in places far outside their normal range. *See also* **migration**.
roost A place where birds sleep, either at night or by day.
rump The area between a bird's back and the base of its upper tail coverts. In many species, the rump is a different color from the rest of the plumage and can be a useful diagnostic character for identification.
sally A feeding technique (sallying), used especially by tyrant flycatchers, in which a bird makes a short flight from a perch to catch an insect, often in midair, followed by a return to a perch, often the same one.
salt gland A gland located in a depression of the skull, just above the eye of some birds, particularly seabirds. This enables them to extract the fluids they need from saltwater and then expel the excess salts through the nostrils.
scapular Any one of a group of feathers on the "shoulder," forming a more or less oval patch on each side of the back, at the base of the wing.
scrape A simple nest that consists of a shallow depression in the ground, which may be unlined or lined with material such as feathers, bits of grass, or pebbles.
secondary feather One of the row of long, stiff feathers along the rear edge of a bird's wing, between the body and the primary feathers at the wingtip. *See also* **primary feather.**
sedentary Having a settled lifestyle that involves little or no geographic movement. Sedentary birds are also said to be resident or nonmigratory. *See also* **migration**.
semipalmated The condition in which two or more of the toes are partially joined by an incomplete membrane at their base.
sexual dimorphism The occurrence of physical differences between males and females. In birds, the most common differences are in size and plumage.
shorebird Also known as a wader, any member of several families in the order Charadriiformes, including plovers, sandpipers, godwits, snipe, avocets, stilts, oystercatchers, and curlews. Not all species actually wade in water and some live in dry habitats.
soaring In birds, flight without flapping of the wings. A soaring bird stays at the same height or gains height. Updraft soaring is a type of soaring in which a bird benefits from rising currents that form at cliffs or along mountain ridges. Seabirds are experts at dynamic soaring, repeatedly diving into the troughs between waves and then using the rising air deflected off the waves to wheel back up into the air.
song A vocal performance by a bird, usually the adult male, to attract and impress a potential mate, advertise ownership of a territory, or drive away rival birds. Songs are often highly characteristic of individual species and can be a major aid in locating and identifying birds in the field. *See also* **call**.
songbird A general term used to describe a member of the suborder Passeri (or oscines), a subdivision of the largest order of birds, the Passeriformes (passerines).
species A group of similar organisms that are capable of breeding among themselves in the wild and producing fertile offspring that resemble themselves, but that do not interbreed in the wild with individuals of another similar group, are called a species. *See also* **subspecies, superspecies.**
speculum A colorful patch on the wing of a duck, formed by the secondary feathers. *See also* **secondary feather**.
spur A sharply pointed, claw-like structure at the back of the leg of some birds, like the Wild Turkey.
staging ground A stopover area where migrant birds regularly pause while on migration, to rest and feed.
stoop A near-vertical and often very fast dive made by falcons and some other birds of prey when chasing prey in the air or on the ground.
streaks Marks that run lengthwise on feathers; opposite of bars.
subspecies When species show geographical variation in color, voice, or other characters, these differentiated populations are recognized by ornithologists as subspecies (formerly also called races). *See also* **species**.
superspecies Closely related species that have different geographical ranges. *See also* **species**.
syrinx A modified section of a bird's trachea (windpipe), equivalent to the voicebox in humans, that enables birds to call and sing.
talon One of the sharp, hooked claws of a bird of prey.
territory An area that is defended by an animal, or a group of animals, against other members of the same species. Territories often include useful resources, such as good breeding sites or feeding areas, which help a male attract a mate.
tertial Any one of a small group of feathers, sometimes long and obvious, at the base of the wing adjacent to the inner secondaries.
thermal A rising bubble or column of warm air over land that soaring birds can use to gain height with little effort. *See also* **soaring**.
threat display A form of defense in which a bird adopts certain postures, sometimes accompanied by loud calls, to drive away a rival or a potential predator.
trachea The breathing tube in animals, also known as the windpipe.
tubenose A general term used to describe members of the order Procellariiformes, including albatrosses, petrels, and shearwaters; their nostrils form two tubes on the upper mandible.
underwing The underside of a bird's wing, usually visible only in flight or when a bird is preening, displaying, or swimming.
upperwing The upper surface of a bird's wing clearly exposed in flight but often mostly hidden when the bird is perched.
vagrant A bird that has strayed far from its normal range. Usually, vagrants are long-distance migrants that have been blown off course by storms, have overshot their intended destination because of strong winds, or have become disoriented.
vent Also called the crissum, the undertail feathers between the lower belly feathers and tail feathers, which in some species are differently colored from either belly or tail feathers. Can be helpful in identification.
vertical migrant A species that migrates up and down mountains, usually in response to changes in the weather or food supply. *See also* **migration.**
wader *see* **shorebird.**
waterfowl A collective term for members of the family Anatidae, including ducks, geese, and swans.
wattle A bare, fleshy growth that hangs loosely below the bill in some birds. It is often brightly colored, and may play a part in courtship.
wildfowl *see* **waterfowl**
Wilson, Alexander (1766–1813) A contemporary of J.J. Audubon, Wilson's seminal *American Ornithology* marks the start of scientific ornithology in the US.
wingbar A line or bar of color across the upper surface of a bird's wing. Wingbars can often be seen when a bird is on the ground or perched and its wings are in the closed position, but they are normally much more obvious in flight. Wingbars may be single or in groups of two or more.
wingspan The distance across a bird's outstretched wings and back, from one wingtip to the other.

INDEX